third edition

# SALES MANAGEMENT

## Decisions, Policies, and Cases

RICHARD R. STILL
*University of Georgia*

EDWARD W. CUNDIFF
*University of Texas*

NORMAN A. P. GOVONI
*Babson College*

PRENTICE-HALL, INC., *Englewood Cliffs, New Jersey*

*Library of Congress Cataloging in Publication Data*

Still, Richard Ralph (date)
  Sales management.

  Includes bibliographical references.
  1. Sales management. I. Cundiff, Edward W.,
joint author. II. Govoni, Norman A. P., joint author. III. Title.
HF5438.4.S84 1976          658.8          75-34049
ISBN   0-13-788042-1

Printed in the United States of America

10   9   8   7   6   5

PRENTICE-HALL INTERNATIONAL, INC., *London*
PRENTICE-HALL OF AUSTRALIA PTY. LIMITED, *Sydney*
PRENTICE-HALL OF CANADA, LTD., *Toronto*
PRENTICE-HALL OF INDIA PRIVATE LIMITED, *New Delhi*
PRENTICE-HALL OF JAPAN, INC., *Tokyo*
PRENTICE-HALL OF SOUTH-EAST ASIA PRIVATE LIMITED, *Singapore*

TO
KATY, PEGGY, AND TERRY

# Contents

# List of Cases

## CASES FOR PART III

## CASES FOR PART IV

# Preface

In the nearly twenty years since the first edition of this book appeared, both business executives and educators have been giving increasing emphasis to the philosophy that a company needs a marketing orientation to improve its chances of surviving and growing in today's dynamic and highly competitive environment. Business plans—and the systems, policies, and procedures used to implement them—should be geared not only toward satisfying customers' needs and desires but toward securing profitable sales volume. With this spreading recognition of the importance of "the marketing concept," many excellent books on marketing management, sales management, and "promotion" have been published—all underscoring the important roles played by sales executives in managing successful marketing programs. Increasingly, top executives and educators alike have focused on the key importance of personal selling in marketing strategy. We have attempted to reflect this importance throughout this book.

In this third edition of *Sales Management: Decisions, Policies, and Cases* we seek to analyze the field of marketing management from the standpoint of sales executives. Such executives in most companies have as their major responsibility either the management of company sales personnel or the maintenance of relationships with independent middlemen or both. Usually they are responsible not only for planning and administering their company's personal selling operations but also are major participants in planning other aspects of marketing strategy. Thus, they participate in, and sometimes are primarily or jointly responsible for, formulating strategies on the product line, on pricing, on physical distribution, on marketing channels, and on other forms of promotion (such as advertising.)

In this edition, as in previous editions, we have attempted to apply the management approach to an analysis of the sales executive's job, his or her duties and responsibilities, and the various roles played in making marketing decisions. In Part I the focus is on the interrelationships of personal selling and marketing strategy, including the setting of personal selling objectives, the determination of sales policies, and the formulation of personal selling strategy. In Part II the focus shifts to problems of organizing the selling effort both within the company and relative to the distributive network. In Part III the emphasis is on the primary responsibility of most sales executives—sales force management. Finally, in Part IV the analysis concentrates on techniques of controlling the sales effort, including the sales budget, quota determination, and sales and marketing cost analysis.

Those familiar with earlier editions will recognize the considerable changes that have been made. Nearly all of Part I—Personal Selling and Marketing Strategy—is new and reflects the sales executive's growing stature in the councils of top management. Increased attention has been given in Part III—Sales-Force Management—to such topics as job analysis, compliance with laws relative to discrimination in employment, training sales personnel in salesmanship, motivating salespeople as individuals and in groups, assignment of salespeople to territories, and evaluation of job performance. Parts II and IV—Organizing the Sales Effort and Controlling the Sales Effort—represent considerable reorganization of materials from the second edition. Finally, more than half of the cases are new.

As indicated by its title, *Sales Management: Decisions, Policies, and Cases,* this book is directed toward accomplishing three main objectives:

1. to delineate the chief areas in which the sales executive has responsibilities for or plays a role in making decisions;
2. to set forth the principal strategic alternatives available in making decisions in these areas; and
3. to provide case histories which, we hope, will help the reader sharpen his or her managerial skills.

For successful completion of this book, we owe a great deal to a great many people. Such pioneer professors of marketing as James R. Hawkinson of Northwestern University and David E. Faville of Stanford University stimulated our early interest in the field of sales management. Our present and former colleagues at the University of Georgia, The University of Texas at Austin, Babson College, and Syracuse University have given generously of their time and have been ever willing to share the benefits of their teaching and business experience. Numerous businessmen provided materials for case histories, and our graduate students cheerfully and competently assisted in collecting these case histories.

Professor Sumner M. White of Massachusetts Bay Community College read the entire manuscript for this edition with discernment and made numerous sound and helpful suggestions. Similar contributions to the two earlier editions were made by: Jon G. Udell, University of Wisconsin; John M. Rathmell, Cornell University; Allan D. Shocker, University of Pittsburgh; Richard M. Clewett, Northwestern University; Jack Holland, California State University at San Jose; and Walter Horvath, marketing consultant. Among those at Prentice-Hall, Inc., who gave us tireless help, encouragement, and advice were: Wilbur F. Eastman, Jr., John F. Pritchard, Donald A. Schaefer, Garret White, Burton Gabriel, and Judith L. Rothman—each of whom was responsible, at one time or another, for seeing to it that this or previous editions were completed. Mary C. Still, Margaret Cundiff, and Terry Govoni, our wives, were good critics and continual sources of encouragement. For all this assistance, we express our sincere thanks.

*Richard R. Still*
*Edward W. Cundiff*
*Norman A. P. Govoni*

# Part I

# PERSONAL SELLING
# AND
# MARKETING STRATEGY

# 1

# Introduction

Sales executives have important responsibilities both to their employers and to those who buy and use their firms' products. Top management holds sales executives responsible for (1) obtaining sufficient sales volume, (2) providing ample contributions to profits, and (3) continuing business growth. Society looks to them to assure the delivery of goods and services that final buyers want at prices that final buyers are willing to pay, and—of increasing importance—to work toward the development and marketing of products whose potentials for damaging the environment are minimal. If the goods and services made and sold are needed and accepted by the buying public, and if these products are "socially responsible" in terms of damaging the environment as little as possible, then it is likely that management's objectives will have been achieved. Ultimately, the earnings that accrue to a business depend upon how well, or how poorly, the interests of the firm, the final buyers, and society are blended. To the extent that these interests are in harmony, the firm experiences sales volume, net profits, and business growth.

Modern sales executives are professionals. They know how to plan, how to build and maintain an effective and efficient organization, and how to design and utilize appropriate control procedures. The professional approach to sales management requires careful analysis of market situations, intelligent setting of personal-selling objectives, the choice of appropriate sales policies, and the formulation of personal-selling strategy. The professional approach also calls for skillful application of the principles of organization to the conduct of sales operations. Similarly, the professional approach is characterized by an ability to install, operate, and use control procedures appropriate to the firm's situation and its objectives. Executives capable of applying the professional approach to sales management are very much in demand today.

## EVOLUTION OF THE SALES DEPARTMENT

Prior to the Industrial Revolution, when small-scale enterprises dominated the economic scene, the selling task was relatively simple. The chief problem was to produce enough goods for nearby consumers, and selling was no problem. Orders generally were obtained with minimum effort, and they were usually on hand before goods were produced. It was common for one individual to supervise all phases of the business operation, including both manufacturing and selling. Major attention was devoted to manufacturing problems. Selling and other marketing problems could be handled strictly on a part-time basis.

With the Industrial Revolution, which began about 1760 in England and shortly after the American Revolution in the United States, it became increasingly necessary to find and sell new and untapped markets. Newly built factories were turning out huge quantities of goods of every description. Their continued operation demanded great expansions in the area of sales coverage, since adjacent markets were not able to absorb the increased quantities being manufactured. But even under these circumstances other business problems took precedence over selling. These were mainly the problems associated with hiring large numbers of workers, and acquiring land, buildings, and machinery. To solve them, large amounts of capital had to be raised. The result was that more and more businesses adopted the corporate form of organization, and the day of large-scale manufacturing enterprises had arrived. Firsthand administration of all phases of the operation of such concerns being beyond the capabilities of most individuals, authority was increasingly delegated to others. Separate functional departments were established, but sales departments were usually set up only after the activation of manufacturing and financial departments.

Although the appearance of specialized sales departments helped to solve the organizational problems of market expansion, another problem remained—that of communicating with customers. Little by little, manufacturers shifted parts of the marketing function forward to middlemen. At the start, goods were sold to retailers, who resold them directly to consumers. Eventually, though, some of the larger retailers began to make purchases for resale to other retailers and, as time passed, many of these evolved into full-fledged wholesale institutions. At the same time other wholesalers had developed out of the import-export business. The manufacturer's sales department was becoming more remote from consumers, and it was increasingly difficult to maintain contact with final buyers and users of the product and to control the conditions under which wholesalers and retailers made their sales. Thus, in some respects, the addition of middlemen to the channel of distribution served to complicate the problem of market expansion.

Meanwhile, marketing activities conducted by the manufacturer's sales department continued to grow in importance. Many tasks, such as advertising and sales promotion, became increasingly complex. A common solution to this problem was to split the marketing function, a trend that is still continuing. New departments were and are being organized for the performance of specialized marketing tasks. Today marketing activities are carried on not only by the sales department, but by such departments as advertising, marketing research, export, sales promotion, merchandising, traffic and shipping, and credits and collections. In spite of this growing fragmentation of marketing operations, the sales department still occupies a strategically important position. The underlying responsibility for the making of sales has not shifted elsewhere, and most businesses continue to rely primarily upon their sales departments for the inward flow of income. It has been aptly said that the sales department is the income-producing division of business.

## SALES MANAGEMENT

The meaning of "sales management" has changed gradually over the years. Originally, businessmen used the term to refer solely to the direction of sales force personnel.

Later, the term took on broader significance—in addition to the management of personal selling, well into the twentieth century, "sales management" also included management of all marketing activities, including advertising, sales promotion, marketing research, physical distribution, pricing, and product merchandising. But, in time, business—adopting academic practice—came to use the term "marketing management" rather than "sales management" to describe the broader concept. In 1948 the Definitions Committee of the American Marketing Association agreed that sales management means "the planning, direction, and control of personal selling, including recruiting, selecting, equipping, assigning, routing, supervising, paying, and motivating as these tasks apply to the personal salesforce."[1]

Although the American Marketing Association's definition makes sales management essentially synonymous with management of the sales force, modern sales managers continue to have considerably broader responsibilities. It is true that "sales managers" today are the administrators in charge of personal-selling activity, and, of course, their primary assignment involves management of the personal sales force. However, since personnel-related tasks do not comprise their total responsibility, we prefer to refer to their personnel-related responsibilities as "sales-force management." Another important part of the job of sales managers relates to organizing the sales effort, both within and outside the organization. Within the organization, they must build formal and informal organizational structures that ensure effective communication not only inside the sales department itself but also in the department's relations with other organizational units. They also serve as one of their companys' most important points of contact with customers and other external publics, and it is their responsibility to build and maintain an effective distributive network.

Today's sales managers have still other responsibilities. They are responsible not only for using but for participating in the preparation of information critical to the making of key marketing decisions, such as those involving budgeting, quotas, and territories. They also participate—to an extent that varies with the company—in making marketing decisions on products, marketing channels and distribution policies, advertising and other forms of promotion, and pricing. Thus, the modern sales manager is both an administrator in charge of personal-selling activity and a member of the executive group that makes marketing decisions of all types.

Many kinds of firms have sales-management problems. The wide range of problems in sales management encountered by manufacturing and wholesale enterprises often makes it appear that they are the only firms with such problems. Retail institutions, however, also have sales-management problems, even though the differences are so great that retailing problems (at least in the academic world) are ordinarily considered separately. Nevertheless, some retailers have sales problems more closely akin to those of manufacturers and wholesalers than to those of other retailers—the automobile dealer, the direct-to-consumer marketer, and the real-estate broker all are in this category. Firms selling intangibles, such as the insurance company, the investment house, the stockbroker, and the airline, also have and must solve problems of sales management. Although the primary orientation in this text is on problems in sales management faced by manufacturers and wholesalers, frequent references are made to similar problems confronting other kinds of enterprises.

[1]"Report of the Definitions Committee of the American Marketing Association," *Journal of Marketing*, Vol. 13, No. 2 (October 1948), p. 202; and Committee on Definitions, American Marketing Association, *Marketing Definitions* (Chicago: American Marketing Association, 1960), p. 20.

## OBJECTIVES OF SALES MANAGEMENT

As stated earlier, from the company viewpoint there are three general and underlying objectives of sales management: achieving sufficient sales volume, providing ample contribution to profits, and experiencing continuing growth. Sales and other marketing executives do not carry the full burden in the effort to reach these general objectives, but they do make major contributions. Top management bears the final responsibility, because it is accountable for the success or failure of the enterprise as a whole. Furthermore, top management is ultimately accountable for supplying an ever-increasing volume of "socially responsible" products that final buyers want at satisfactory prices. In the fulfillment of this obligation, top management coordinates the operations of all departments, including the sales department, so that progress is made toward both commercial and social goals.

Top management delegates to marketing management, which then delegates to sales management, part of the authority needed for achieving these three general objectives. But, to be useful for planning and operating purposes, these objectives must be translated into more specific terms. Therefore, they are broken down and restated as definite goals that the company has a reasonable chance of reaching. For planning purposes, marketing management, with some assistance from sales and other marketing executives and from other divisions, is expected to contribute informed estimates on market potentials, the capabilities of the sales force and the middlemen, and the like. Once definite goals are established, it is up to sales executives to guide and lead those who are charged with implementing the plans of action.

Sales management, then, plays an influential role in charting the course of future operations. It provides higher executives with many of the facts needed for making high-level marketing decisions and for setting realistic sales and profit goals. On the basis of its appraisal of market opportunities, targets for sales volume, gross margin, and net profit are established in units of product and in dollars, with benchmarks of growth projected for sales and profits for specific future dates. Whether or not the expectations of top management are realized depends mainly upon the performance of sales and other marketing personnel. The most excellent planning is of little value if marketing executives are unskilled in carrying forward sales operations.

For both planning and operating purposes, sales and marketing management are well advised to keep in mind two basic accounting formulas:

$$\text{sales} - \text{cost of sales} = \text{gross margin}$$
$$\text{gross margin} - \text{expenses} = \text{net profit}$$

Periodically, these formulas become the company operating statement, and they are used by the board of directors, and by stockholders, in appraising the performance of top management. Moreover, top management invariably uses them in judging the effectiveness of sales and marketing management. The cost of sales factor cannot be affected directly by sales management, but it can be affected indirectly. Indeed, it is vitally important that sales volume be of sufficient magnitude to permit the maintaining of low unit costs of production and distribution. Sales volume, gross margin, and expenses are directly affected by the caliber and performance of sales and marketing management, and these are the major determinants of net profit. The company maximizes its net profits only if an optimum relationship among the three factors is obtained. All three must be given due consideration, both in the planning and operating phases.

Sometimes, sales executives stress sales volume while neglecting gross margin and expenses. In such instances, even though sales volume increases, gross margin declines, expenses increase proportionately, and net profits are reduced. If these conditions prevail for long, profits disappear entirely and losses are incurred. Often the best managerial treatment for this situation is to shrink sales volume and expenses. Even with a somewhat lower sales volume, skilled sales management can reduce expenses and raise gross margin sufficiently to convert a loss into a profit.

It is also possible to err in the opposite direction. High gross margins and low expenses are overemphasized usually because of management's preoccupation with percentage relationships. While percentages of gross margin and expense are important, sales management should be more concerned with dollar relationships. The most important net profit is dollar net profit, not the percentage of net profit. It is small consolation to have satisfactory gross margin and expense percentages if total sales volume and dollar profit are inadequate. In such cases sales management should reorient its thinking, worrying more about securing sales and profit dollars and less about maintaining rigid percentage relationships.

## SALES EXECUTIVE AS COORDINATOR

Optimum marketing performance in terms of sales volume, net profits, and long-term growth requires effective coordination, and sales executives play significant roles in various coordinating activities. Sales executives look upon their responsibilities for coordination as involving: the organization, planning, the other elements in the marketing program, the distributive network, and the implementation of overall marketing strategy. While higher-ranking sales executives are those most concerned with obtaining effective coordination, all sales executives at all organizational levels have some degree of responsibility for coordinating activity.

### Organization and Coordination

Coordination of diverse order-getting methods (personal selling, advertising, and so forth) in the modern organization is achieved through a single responsible, top-ranking executive. Generally, this executive has the title of marketing vice-president, director of marketing, or marketing manager. Basically, this executive is responsible for minimizing the possibility that the different order-getting departments will work at cross-purposes or that they will try to accomplish the sale goals with little or no knowledge of what other departments are doing.

Similarly, within the sales department itself, from the chief sales executive down, all sales executives are responsible for coordinating that part of the organization under their control. Democratic administration, where decisions are made at all management levels and in every organizational segment from the chief sales executive down to the sales staff, needs emphasizing to obtain an organization that functions in the smoothest possible manner. If all subordinates affected by a decision are consulted in advance and allowed to participate in making it, there is less tendency to resist the directives issued by superiors, and little friction is likely to occur. Not only is there less chance of misunderstanding, but subordinates as well as superiors are enabled to visualize the circumstances that gave rise to the decision.

### Planning and Coordination

The chief sales executive, with a unique knowledge of the market and of the capabilities of the sales force, necessarily is involved in achieving coordination in marketing planning. The marketing planners must know what the marketing objectives are and draft plans that achieve desired results at optimum cost. They must decide the various marketing elements (personal selling, advertising, and so forth) that should make up the marketing program, apportioning the relative amounts of each so as—at least theoretically—to equate its marginal effectiveness with that of other elements. Coordination among the marketing planners, then, is essential if they are to lay out specific programs of marketing action for achieving predetermined sales, profit, and growth objectives. The chief sales executive, as a key member of the planning group, is vitally concerned that the marketing program finally decided upon is both appropriate for market conditions and reflects accurately the probable contribution of the sales force.

### Coordination with Other Elements in the Marketing Program

Many responsibilities of chief sales executives relate to coordinating the personal-selling effort with the other order-getting methods. The personal-selling effort must be coordinated effectively with advertising, display, and other promotional efforts if the total marketing effort is to achieve the expected results. Just as they must be concerned in "building coordination into" the marketing plan, chief sales executives must be concerned with achieving coordination during the time the plan is being implemented.

Synchronizing personal selling with advertising is particularly important. Advertising may prove uneconomic unless the activities of the sales force are directed to capitalize upon the interest aroused. Personal-selling effort is wasted in explaining many details that might well be explained by advertising; but when the sales personnel use the same appeals that are used in the advertising—if both tell the same story—the force of promotional impact is often magnified. Furthermore, the timing and sequence with which different phases of the personal-selling and advertising efforts are executed directly affect the chances for marketing success. Therefore, coordinating the personal-selling and advertising efforts is much more involved than merely selling the benefits of the advertising program to the sales force. An advertising effort should be implemented within the context of being part of a larger marketing effort, and the same is true of the personal-selling effort.

Sales executives are also involved in coordinating other promotional efforts with the personal-selling effort. Point-of-purchase displays, for example, must be set up in retail stores where customers will see them at the precise time that tie-in advertisements appear in national and local media. It is the job of the sales force to achieve this careful timing and coordination. In a similar manner, the sales personnel must alert dealers to special couponing or sampling efforts so that they can reap maximum advantage from heightened consumer interest.

### Coordinating with the Distributive Network

Chief sales executives and their subordinates are concerned with coordinating the personal-selling effort with the marketing efforts of the middlemen. Among the most important aspects of this coordinating activity are those involved in gaining product distribution, obtaining dealer identification, reconciling business goals, and sharing promotional risks.

**Gaining Product Distribution.** Whenever a new product is introduced, chief sales executives are responsible for obtaining its distribution. Except in cases where the product is sold directly to final users, the sales department must persuade middlemen to associate themselves with the new product's distribution. Gaining such distribution is no easy task. Middlemen very frequently refuse to stock a new product unless the manufacturer's sales staff present convincing arguments of its salability to the middlemen's customers. Although some manufacturers succeed in "pulling" their products through the distribution channel by means of heavy advertising to final buyers, such instances of "forced distribution" are rare.

Regardless of the distribution channels used, the manufacturer of a new product, as often as not, faces distributor lethargy and dealer indifference and must resort to missionary selling effort. But, as often happens in marketing a new consumer product, even missionary selling may be handicapped, because corporate chains and other integrated retailers commonly do not permit decentralized calls on their individual outlets. Thus, the manufacturer of a new product frequently is in the position of having to build a demand for the product in as many outlets as are initially willing to handle it, and then of proving the existence of an established market demand to the remaining "desired outlets" before adequate distribution is finally secured. Consequently, it is important for the chief sales executive to assure that the manufacturer's initial promotional efforts are tied in closely with those of the middlemen who first stock the product. As distribution in more outlets is secured, the chief sales executive sees to it that progressively larger shares of the promotional burden are shifted to the middlemen. Thus, coordinating the promotional efforts of the manufacturer and its middlemen grows increasingly important as the product is made available in more outlets, and chief sales executives must adjust their coordinating efforts accordingly.

**Obtaining Dealer Identification.** In furthering the chances that the personal-selling effort will succeed, the chief sales executive often must take steps to assure that final buyers know which local outlets stock the product. Even if the manufacturer's advertising is sufficiently powerful to presell the product, no sales will result if final buyers are unable to find the outlets that stock it. The dealer should be as interested in this problem as the manufacturer, for inadequate dealer identification results in clogged distribution channels —all the way from the dealer's stockroom to the factory. In some instances, dealers take the initiative in publicizing the availability of the product in their outlets. But, in most cases, sales executives must direct their sales personnel to promote dealer identification through such means as providing store signs, furnishing preprints and reprints of advertisements, supplying advertising mats for local insertion, and assisting in building merchandise displays. In other cases, sales executives arrange for the placing of local advertising over the dealers' names.

The sales force plays a somewhat related role in the marketing of many consumer products, particularly those distributed through self-service retailers. It is often important to make certain that consumers, once in the right retail stores, are able to locate the product with minimum difficulty. Display at the point of purchase is a practical way to bridge the gap that so often exists between advertising impact and the retail sale. Whenever merchandising aids such as interior display pieces or shelf markers are used by a marketer, sales executives must take care in teaching salespeople how to obtain the retailers' permission to erect displays or affix shelf markers. Frequently, timing is important in securing such permissions—at the start of a special promotional campaign, for example, retailers generally are more willing to allow the erection of displays (particularly if they have ample supplies of the product on hand) than they are during traditionally slow selling seasons.

**Reconciling Business Goals.**   Skillful coordinating effort by sales executives and the sales force is needed to minimize the natural friction that develops because of conflicts, imaginary or real, between the business goals of the manufacturer and his middlemen. The less the manufacturer and the middlemen work at cross-purposes, the greater the return should be to both parties. One way to eliminate some natural friction is for the manufacturer to share business information with the middlemen. Certain information can be imparted through trade advertising, but salespeople must still be relied upon to personalize many data to make them meaningful for individual middlemen. When the results of marketing research studies, for example, have significance for individual middlemen, sales executives should see that special reports are prepared for personal presentation and explanation by the sales force.

Similarly, it is important for the manufacturer to receive information pertaining to the operating situation and problems of the middlemen. Here again, the sales personnel, through their regular and special reports, can and should serve as the vehicles of communication. Sales executives recognize that only if timely information is available on the needs and attitudes of middlemen is it possible to provide them with effective promotional and other assistance. The chief sales executive, as well as other marketing policymakers, should make periodic appraisals of existing marketing policies in the light of information provided by salespeople in the field, thus assuring that those already in effect, as well as those newly formulated, are appropriate in view of the total marketing situation.

Sales executives must also take care to assure that sales personnel are fair and impartial in all their dealings with middlemen. No outlet should be favored at the expense of another; all should receive equitable treatment. Salespeople generally need continual training to keep them abreast of current operating policies, practices, and procedures; they require effective supervision to make certain that they are applying them fairly as well as properly. Providing this type of training and supervision usually is the responsibility of lower-level sales executives, such as branch and district sales managers.

**Sharing Promotional Risks.**   The marketing program often calls for the manufacturer and the middlemen to share promotional risks such as those which occur when cooperative advertising is used. In these cases, sales executives are responsible for taking steps to assure that the sales personnel make effective presentations designed to convince dealers to participate in the cooperative program. Manufacturers utilizing selective or exclusive agency distribution stand to gain the most from sharing promotional risk with middlemen; in such situations, sales executives and the sales force play important roles in both the initial selection of middlemen as well as in obtaining their consent to share certain promotional risks. Manufacturers using mass distribution generally do not find it feasible to delegate much promotional authority to their middlemen. However, regardless of the company's distribution policy, any steps that the sales executive takes to make the job of the middleman more interesting, more profitable, and more challenging facilitate the task of coordination.

### Coordination and Implementation of Overall Marketing Strategy

When the overall marketing strategy is being put into effect, problems in coordination occur in timing and securing the best sequence of execution of the plan's various phases. For example, if a new product is to be introduced at a trade show or exhibition, the chief sales executive needs to coordinate with advertising executives to make certain that the proper interval will elapse before advertisements appear or salespeople make calls on dealers in the product's behalf. Similar coordinating action is needed to assure proper spacing of the advertising in relation to the call schedules of salespeople. Furthermore, chief sales executives must see to it that their subordinates in the field integrate every phase and segment of the manufacturer's marketing program with corresponding phases and segments of the promotional programs of distributors and dealers.

Successful market introduction of a new brand is a severe test of the mettle and the level of competence possessed by all members of the marketing management team, including sales executives. Introduction of a new brand requires the formulation of policies, the drafting of strategies, and the making of detailed plans, all of which have to be appropriate to the marketing situation faced by the particular company. Proper timing of the several stages in the introduction plan is highly important, because launching a brand at the wrong time, or faulty timing at any stage of introduction, may kill or seriously reduce the chances for success. All the promotional efforts in behalf of the new brand require expert coordination: advertising with the personal selling, and the manufacturer's total promotional effort with different activities of the middlemen.

It is not enough for sales executives merely to know the techniques and problems of new-brand introduction. They must be capable of putting the plans into action, to implement them, effectively. They must execute the program of market introduction with the highest degree of skill. Figure 1.1 illustrates one sales department's planned coordinating action and emphasizes the importance of timing of coordination effort in the introduction of a new product. Notice, for instance, that publicity releases are planned to break at about the same time that the product becomes available. Notice, too, that salespeople are alerted ahead of time, but not too far in advance for them to lose their enthusiasm for the product.

## SALES MANAGEMENT AND CONTROL

All sales executives are responsible for controlling the personal-selling effort of the organizational units they head. The general purpose of control from sales management's standpoint is to assure that sales-department objectives are reached with as little wasted effort as possible. Control is part of the larger process of management, as are planning, organizing, and coordinating. The several phases of control are presented in the following discussion in their normal chronological sequence, but in the "real world" several phases might occur simultaneously or overlap in time in some other manner. The purpose of this discussion is to provide—from the viewpoint of chief sales executives—a clear-cut picture of sales control as a process.

**Sizing Up the Situation.** Chief sales executives start by reviewing the personal-selling objectives of the firm. They analyze these objectives with respect to the present, the past, and the future, in an attempt to answer four questions: (1) Where are we now? (2) How did we get here? (3) Where are we going? (4) How do we get there? After satisfying themselves that the company's personal-selling objectives, long range and short range, are reconcilable, chief sales executives appraise them relative to the plans, policies, and procedures that have been used, are being used, or are intended for use in the effort to reach specific personal-selling objectives. In the course of sizing up the situation, chief sales executives pay particular attention to finding and correcting weaknesses or imperfections in the sales plans and the policies and procedures used in their implementation.

**Setting Quantitative Performance Standards.** After chief sales executives iron out

FIGURE 1.1

Coordination and Timing by the Sales Department in the Introduction of a New Product

| | First Month | Second Month | Third Month | Fourth Month | Fifth Month | Sixth Month | | | |
|---|---|---|---|---|---|---|---|---|---|
| | | | | | | 1st Week | 2nd Week | 3rd Week | 4th Week |
| *General Sales Management* | | Supervision of Sales and Advertising Plans | | | Coordinating Final Sales Activities | | | | Concentrated |
| *Sales Branch Inventory Control* | | | Setting Up Standard Stocks for Branches | | Notifying Branches of Stock | | | | Sales |
| *Sales Branch Sales* | Study of Problems by Branch Management | Recommendations to Management | Revising Territories and Personnel | Training New Sales Personnel re New Product | | Preliminary Sales Approach to Major Customers | | Active Selling to Everyone | Effort ... by Entire |
| *Sales Training* | | Prepare Training Bulletins | | Distribute Bulletins and Other Sales Information to Sales Personnel | | Distribute Information for Jobber Sales Meeting | | | Sales |
| *Sales Operation* | | | Prepare Price Sheets and Other Price Information | | | Distribute Price Information | | | Organization |
| *Coordination with Outside Departments* | | | | | | | | | |
| *Publicity* | Inform Them of New Product | | Prepare Publicity Material | Distribute "Stories" to Media | | Break Publicity in Business Media | Break Publicity in Consumer Media | | Continue Publicity |
| *Sales Promotion* | Work on Preliminary Planning | Approve Plans for Catalogs, Brochures, Sales Kits | Preliminary Layout and Copy | Final Proofs | Promotional Material Approved for Distribution | First Mailing to Users | | Second Mailing to Users | Continuing Promotion |
| *Advertising* | | Consult Ad Agency on Plans | Preliminary Layouts and Copy | Final Proofs | Reprints of Ads Sent to Sales Personnel | | First Ads | Balance of First Month Ads | Continuing Ads |

any "planning weaknesses" that they have detected, they set quantitative standards against which to measure performance. Standard setting requires continual experimentation, and most standards used by sales executives are far from precise. The ultimate test of a particular standard's appropriateness should result from the sales executive's judgment as to whether it will contribute more to personal-selling efficiency than it will cost.

Intelligent standard setting requires sales management to determine the specific individuals who are responsible for the activity or group of activities being put under control. No two salespersons or executives perform exactly alike, even though they may operate in circumstances that are identical in every other respect. Thus, it is appropriate to express standards as ranges of acceptable performance. Although it is convenient to think of a standard as a fixed value, there should be an upper and lower limit within which human variation may reasonably be expected to take place. When the performance of an organizational unit passes either of these control limits, the danger flag is up, signaling that the situation may be out of control.

**Gathering and Processing Data on Actual Performance.**   The type and amount of information needed for controlling sales depends, of course, upon the specific performance standards selected by sales management. But, regardless of the exact nature of this information, it should not be in excess of sales management's real needs, nor should its cost of collection and processing be more than its worth to management. Consequently, management should determine—at regular intervals—whether the information being reported is sufficiently important and being used often enough to justify its costs. Chief sales executives must also keep in mind that changes in executives, basic policies, or other matters may alter the usefulness of information currently being collected. Occasionally, too, they should look for cases where the same or similar information is being obtained from more than one source, representing opportunities for possible savings through eliminating duplications in reporting. Sometimes, also, savings can be realized through reducing or lengthening the intervals at which information is gathered and processed.

For standards to be of maximum value for sales-control purposes, sales executives must have information on actual performances soon enough to permit them to take timely corrective action. Timeliness is important inasmuch as an efficient system of sales control not only furnishes information necessary to managerial evaluation of performance but also promptly relays this information, together with suggestions for action, to the appropriate organizational unit. But information on actual sales performance is often slow in arriving on the sales executive's desk, considerably delaying evaluations of performance. For example, many companies, perhaps even most, require sales personnel to make weekly sales reports; in such cases, a week or more may pass before the sales executive can act on the report. Fortunately, however, progress is being made in improving the timeliness of sales control information. Utilization of electronic data-processing systems for handling sales control data is speeding up the evaluation and feedback of such information.

**Evaluating Performance.** Evaluation of performance basically consists of comparing actual results with standards. Because of differences in territorial and other conditions it is usually difficult to compare performances of members of the sales force. However, it is possible, at least most of the time, to explain each individual salesperson's variations from standard. Departures from standard should be classified and divided into uncontrollable and controllable variations. Variations outside the control of the person whose performance is being appraised include those caused by rapid and unexpected changes in economic conditions, changes in governmental activities, wars, strikes, floods, droughts, and other natural disasters. Variations over which the person held responsible has some control include such items as: failing to obtain proper sales coverage, neglecting to follow up leads, not selling a balanced line, not securing adequate credit information, and the like. The principle is that subordinates—sales executives or salespersons—should not be held responsible for conditions outside their control. Therefore, in appraising performance, it is important to exclude from consideration all such uncontrollable variations.

**Action to Correct Controllable Variation.** Management should take action to correct that part of the variation explained by factors within the control of the person whose performance is being evaluated. Management, in other words, needs to take steps to move the individual's performance in the direction of the standards. The specific actions taken, of course, differ with the nature of the variation. But almost always management's actions assume one or more of three forms: (1) direction, or pointing out more effective ways to perform certain tasks; (2) guidance, or providing additional instructions or training; and (3) restraint, or the installation of procedures and practices aimed at keeping results within desired bounds.

**Adjusting for Uncontrollable Variation.** The amount of uncontrollable variation in the comparison indicates the relative need for making adjustments in sales plans and policies. In fact, if uncontrollable variation is sufficient to suggest that present sales objectives are unrealistic or not in line with current expectations, basic revisions in the objectives may have to be made. Thus, if a comparison of results with standards reveals substantial uncontrollable variation, adjustments of standards to attainable performance levels is in order.

### Sales Control—Informal and Formal

**Informal Control.** Circumstances exist in which awareness of the changing situation, and the ability to analyze it, are adequate control devices. Good sales executives constantly have their "fingers on the pulse of the business"—they have an almost uncanny ability to detect situations that require managerial attention and action. But the larger a company is, and the higher up in the administrative hierarchy the sales executive is, the harder it becomes to use "fingertip" control. As the business grows and the structure of the sales organization becomes more complex, the more pressing the need is for formal control mechanisms. For effective management, a growing business needs dependable machinery to provide the facts for making workable decisions and for formulating appropriate policies.

**Formal Control and Written Sales Policies.** One of the first evidences of the introduction of formal sales controls is the appearance of sales policies in writing. No enterprise, however small, can survive for long without policies, but smaller firms often operate satisfactorily even though they do not put their policies in written form. As the sales organization grows larger, the limits within which action is to take place in given problem situations should be spelled out in specific language. A large organization is not only likely to have more problems and more complex problems than a small organization, there is much less probability that everyone in it will know what to do in every set of circumstances. Thus, the large organization needs written sales and marketing policies to ensure substantial uniformity of action in dealing with problems of similar nature. Uniformity is essential both among different persons handling similar problems and among the same persons handling similar problems at different times. Written policies also conserve executive time, a matter of great importance to chief sales executives. Because policies are written, they can devote more time to planning and to making decisions on problems not covered by existing policies. They reserve time for handling "policy exceptions," and if they encounter enough exceptions of similar nature, a new policy is formulated and is put in writing.

**Policy Formulation and Review.** The process of policy formulation and review illustrates the dynamics of executive control. Skilled administrators agree that a good policy should evolve from thorough study and evaluation of tangible information. However, many sales policies necessarily deal with subjects on which quantitative data are lacking, especially when management is experimenting with new ideas. When objectives are not set clearly because of lack of information on the problem situation, actual results vary from the established standard because of factors ("uncontrollable variations") beyond the control of the individual whose performance is evaluated. Thus, coincident to the scaling down of objectives, sales management must necessarily review the plans originally made in the effort to achieve the objectives and the policies used in their implementation. Eventually, then, through successive revisions, policies initially based on inadequate data often become appropriate and "good."

**Formal Control over Sales Volume.** One device of formal sales control, which is introduced early in the history of a firm, is that over sales volume. Estimating how much of a product can be sold in a specified future period is prerequisite both for planning and control. The sales-volume performance of the company is best appraised by comparing it with the potential sales volume present during the period studied. The "sales or market forecast," therefore, serves as a standard against which to evaluate sales performance. However, the periodic forecast of sales is not enough for effective control over sales volume. During the intervals between forecasts, sales management must watch such factors as industry sales trends, activities of competitors, and share-of-the-market percentages. Significant changes in these factors may call for changes in sales objectives, plans, policies, and procedures.

**Budgetary Control.** Ultimately, formal control over sales operations requires the installation of sales budgetary controls and the setting up of sales territories. Budgetary control represents an extension of control over sales volume to control over margins and expenses, and hence over profits. When control reaches this stage of development, it is possible for sales management to project individual profit-and-loss statements for such units as sales territories, products, marketing channels, and classes of customers. Through use of such estimating devices as standard costs of distribution, sales management sets standards for controlling individual expense items and various components of the gross margin. Through use of marketing cost analysis, it can appraise sales performance against predetermined standards. In this way, the soft points, the areas where sales performance is below par, are called to management's attention. The net result is to reduce the time between a significant drop in the performance of a selling unit and the initiation of appropriate corrective action.

### Sales Control and Organization

Control should pervade the entire structure of the sales organization. The implications of the "centralized" sales organization are often such as to preclude timeliness in detection of variations from objectives, plans, programs, budgets, and quotas. Therefore, paradoxically the points in the organizational structure at which effective control is exercised depend primarily upon the degree to which management adheres to the philosophy expressed in the word "decentralization." In the decentralized sales organization, a relatively larger amount of control is exercised by executives lower in the hierarchy than is true in the centralized organization. For purposes of effective sales control, the higher up executives are in the organization, the more they should deal with "policy" or "control" exceptions rather than with the control mechanism itself. At all organizational levels other than the top, situations that fall outside the control limits should be handed up in the organization to the executive who has authority to deal with the exceptional circumstances or to formulate policy on the matter. For speed in the initiation of corrective action, it is desirable that the power to make decisions be delegated as far down in the organizational structure as is consistent with the caliber and experience of executives.

## CONCLUSION

Sales management is a challenging profession. Top management holds sales executives responsible for obtaining sales volume, handling the selling operation so as to make contributions to profits, and for seeing to it that the business continues to grow. Society looks to them to assure the delivery of products that final buyers want and can pay for and to use their influence to see to it that the company's products are "socially responsible."

Sales managers have broad responsibilities. Their primary responsibility is to recruit, select, and train sales personnel; provide them with reasonable assignments and goals; and motivate them to optimum effort. They have responsibilities for coordinating the personal selling operation with other order-getting methods (such as advertising), with marketing activities of the distributive network, and with the implementation of the company's over-all marketing strategy. They are also responsible for controlling the personal-selling effort of the organizational units they lead, assuring that sales-department objectives are reached with as little wasted effort as possible. Thus, modern sales executives are professionals in every sense of the word—they recognize that their main assignment is to build and maintain an effective sales organization, but they also know that they must be skilled in planning, coordinating, and controlling to make certain that personal selling activities make their optimum contribution to the company's marketing effort.

# 2

# Setting
# Personal-Selling Objectives

Personal selling is a form of promotion, and it is marketing management's responsibility to determine the role of personal selling in the promotional mix. Figure 2.1 shows how personal selling fits into the promotional program. While an occasional marketer shifts the entire personal-selling activity to middlemen, most must concern themselves with setting personal-selling objectives, determining sales policies, formulating personal-selling strategies, and determining sales budgets, as well as with managing their own sales forces. As Figure 2.1 indicates, these interrelated tasks collectively make up the personal-selling portion of the promotional program.

## TYPES OF PERSONAL-SELLING OBJECTIVES

There are both qualitative and quantitative personal-selling objectives. The qualitative objectives generally are long-term objectives and mainly concern the contributions management expects personal selling to make in achieving overall long-term company objectives. Such objectives change very little over time and essentially are carried over from one period's promotional program to the next. Depending upon the overall long-term company objectives and the nature of the promotional mix, personal selling may be assigned such qualitative objectives as:

1. To do the entire selling job (as when there are no other elements in the promotional mix).
2. To "service" existing accounts (that is, to maintain contacts with present customers, take orders, etc.).
3. To search out and obtain new customers.
4. To secure and maintain customers' cooperation in stocking and promoting the product line.
5. To keep customers informed on changes in the product line and other aspects of marketing strategy.
6. To assist customers in selling the product line (as through "missionary selling").
7. To provide technical advice and assistance to customers (as with complicated products and where products are especially designed to fit buyers' specifications).
8. To assist with (or handle) the training of middlemen's sales personnel.

17

FIGURE 2.1
Personal Selling as Part of the Promotional Program

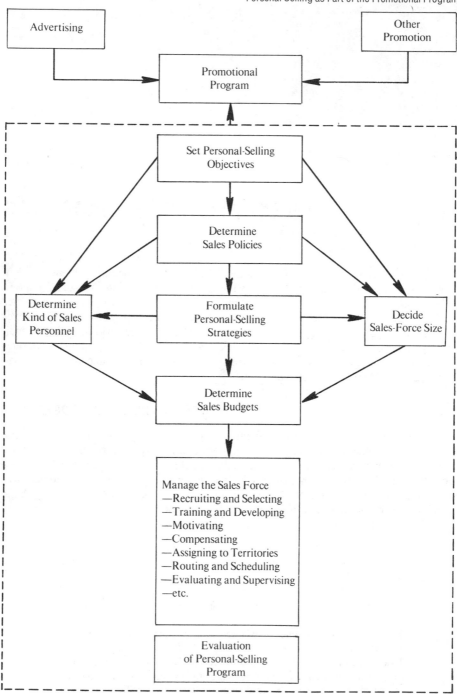

9. To provide advice and assistance to middlemen on various management problems.
10. To collect and report market information of interest and use to company management.

The quantitative objectives assigned to personal selling are short-term and adjusted from one promotional period to the next. By far the most critical is the sales-volume objective, that is, the dollar or unit sales volume management seeks to obtain during a particular time interval. Most of this chapter is concerned with the planning and analysis that precedes the derivation of sales-volume objectives. However, other types of quantitative personal-selling objectives exist, among them the following:

1. To obtain sales volume in ways that contribute to profit objectives (for example, by selling the "proper" mix of products).
2. To keep personal-selling expenses within certain limits.
3. To secure and retain a certain share of the market.
4. To obtain some number of new accounts of given types.
5. To secure a given percentage of certain accounts' business.

## SOME IMPORTANT TERMS

Before we examine the planning and analytical work that lies behind the setting of sales-volume objectives, it is necessary to define three important terms: market potential, sales potential, and sales forecast. Up until recently, it was common for executives to use these terms synonomously. However, as the following discussion indicates, there are good reasons to distinguish among them.

### Market Potential

A market potential is a quantitative estimate of the maximum possible sales opportunities present in a particular market segment and open to all sellers of a good or service during a stated future period. Thus, an estimate of the maximum number of low-priced pocket cameras that might be sold in San Mateo County, California, during the calendar year 1976 by all sellers competing for this market would represent the 1976 San Mateo County market potential for low-priced pocket cameras. A market potential indicates how much of a particular product can be sold to a particular market segment over some future period, assuming the application of appropriate marketing methods.

### Sales Potential

A sales potential is a quantitative estimate of the maximum possible sales opportunities present in a particular market segment open to a specified company selling a good or service during a stated future period. To illustrate, an estimate of the number of low-priced pocket cameras that might be sold in San Mateo County, California, during the calendar year 1976 by the Eastman Kodak Company would be the 1976 San Mateo County sales potential for Eastman Kodak low-priced pocket cameras. Note carefully that a sales potential represents sales opportunities available to a particular manufacturer, such as to Eastman Kodak Company, while a market potential indicates sales opportunities available to an entire industry.

### Sales Forecast

A sales forecast is an estimate of sales, in dollars or physical units, for a specified future period under a proposed marketing plan or program and under an assumed set of economic and other forces outside the unit for which the forecast is made.[1] A sales forecast may be for a single product, or for the entire product line. Similarly, a sales forecast may be for a manufacturer's entire marketing area, or for any subdivision of it. More precisely, such forecasts are known as short-term, or operating, sales forecasts to distinguish them from long-range sales forecasts, which are used mainly for planning changes in production capacity and for assisting in long-run financial planning. Predictions of the probable sales experience of the firm in the comparatively distant future, although naturally of interest, are normally so tentative that sales planners give them only passing attention. It is the short-term, or operating, sales forecast with which the sales executive is mainly concerned. Keep in mind, then, that the basic purpose of an operating sales forecast is to predict how much of a company's particular product (or product line) can be sold during a specified future period in certain markets under a given marketing plan or program and under an assumed set of economic and other outside forces.

## DETERMINING MARKET POTENTIAL

### Market Identification

An essential step in determining a product's market potential is to identify its market. Market identification requires finding answers to one or more of these questions:

1. Who buys the product?
2. Who uses it?
3. Who are the prospective buyers and/or users?

Occasionally these questions are at least partially answered through analyzing internal company records; but in most companies, especially those that use long marketing channels, more complete answers are obtained only through field research. In consumer-goods marketing, buyers, users, and prospects are identified and classified according to such characteristics as age, sex, education, income, and social class. In industrial-goods marketing, buyers, users, and prospects are identified and classified by such characteristics as size of firm, geographical location, and type of industry.

Market identification studies reveal the characteristics that distinguish the vrious market segments making up the product's total market potential. Frequently they uncover unexploited market segments whose patronage might be obtained by, for example, redirecting personal-selling effort or changing promotionl strategy. Sometimes, market identification studies provide, as a side result, customer data on such factors as purchase frequency, searching time expended, unit of purchase, and seasonal buying habits. When these data are assembled and analyzed, they are helpful in estimating market potential.

### Market Motivation

A second important step in determining a product's market potential relates to the determination of buying reasons. Market motivation studies are aimed at answering twin

---

[1]Committee on Definitions, *Marketing Definitions* (Chicago: American Marketing Association, 1960), p. 20.

questions: Why do people buy? Why don't people buy? Answers to these questions provide information that is helpful not only in estimating a product's market potential but is of immense value to the sales executive seeking to improve promotional programs and to increase their effectiveness.

Motivation research techniques vary, but all derive from psychological theory. Probably the most widely used are the projective techniques, in which respondents project themselves, their feelings, and desires, into interpretations of special materials presented by the researcher. Motivation researchers use such information-gathering devices as sentence-completion tests, thematic-apperception tests, and word-association tests. Most motivation research studies make no use, or minimal use, of formal questionnaires; and interviews are usually of the "depth" type, the interviewer's main role being that of keeping the respondent talking, sometimes for several hours. Later analysis of interview results by trained specialists seeks to lay bare what actually goes on in buyers' minds, including, importantly, the real reasons for buying or not buying the product under study. Most motivation studies have been directed toward explaining the buying behavior of ultimate consumers rather than that of industrial users. Information derived from motivation studies is helpful not only in estimating a product's market potential but assists in deciding:

1.  How to present the product in sales talks.
2.  The relative effectiveness of different selling appeals.
3.  The relative appropriateness of various promotional methods and advertising media.

### Measuring Market Potential

Market identification and market motivation data provide important insights on a product, but they do not indicate the size of its potential market. Having identified the types of potential buyers and with information available about their buying behavior, it is necessary next to measure the market potential. Generally it is not possible to measure market potential directly, so the analyst approaches the measurement task by using market factors (a market factor is a feature or characteristic of a market that is related to the demand of the product). For instance, the number of males reaching shaving age each year is a market factor influencing the demand for mens' electric shavers. However, not every male reaching shaving age in a given year is a prospective buyer of an electric shaver—some will be late in starting to shave, others will adopt other shaving methods, many will either not have the money to buy a shaver or will prefer to use the money for something else, and still others will use borrowed shavers or, perhaps, simply not shave at all. This demonstrates, then, that using marketing factors for measuring a product's market potential is a two-step process:

1.  Select the market factor(s) most closely associated with the product's demand.
2.  Eliminate those market segments that for one reason or another are not prospective buyers of the product.

Measurements of market potential usually are expressed in relative terms, such as in percentages or index form, rather than in absolute numbers of units or dollar value. One reason for this has already been implied—only rarely is it possible to find market factors directly related to a product's demand; most market factors relate indirectly to the demand of specific products. Another important reason for expressing market-potential measurements in relative terms is that estimates of absolute market size are obtained through sales forecasting (described later in this chapter).

Manufacturers of consumer products are fortunate in that several market-potential indexes are readily available. The most widely used indexes are population as a percentage of U.S. total, effective buying income as a percentage of U.S. total, and retail sales as a percentage of U.S. total. Many companies refine these indexes further by breaking them down into greater detail; for example, the population index may be divided into subindexes covering various age groups and the income index into subindexes for different income groups.

The well-known *Sales Management Buying Power Index* combines effective buying income, retail sales, and population into a single index using weighting of factors of five for income, three for retail sales, and two for population. This particular combination and weighting of market factors serves as a satisfactory measure of market potential for many consumer-products manufacturers; but many others construct their own indexes, including different or additional market factors and using different weighting systems. One manufacturer of lighting fixtures, for instance, includes data on new housing starts as a factor, and a maker of automobile seat covers includes motor vehicle registrations. Other market factors frequently used in constructing consumer-goods indexes of market potential are: registrations of new automobiles, home ownership, marriage licenses issued, births, and deaths. Manufacturers of industrial products construct their indexes of market potentials using such market factors as value added by manufacture, number of employees engaged in certain types of manufacturing, number of manufacturing establishments, man-hours worked, total value of shipments of various items, and capital expenditures for new plant and equipment.

## SALES POTENTIAL AND SALES FORECASTING

Sales potentials, as defined earlier, are quantitative estimates of the *maximum* possible sales opportunities present in particular market segments open to a specified company selling a good or service during a stated future period. They are generally derived from market potentials after analyses of historical market-share relationships and through the making of adjustments for recent or impending changes in company and competitors' selling strategies and practices. However, a firm's sales potential and its sales forecast are not usually identical—in most instances, the sales potential will be greater than the sales forecast. There are several possible reasons for this: Some companies do not have sufficient production capacity to capitalize on the full sales potential; other firms have not yet developed their distributive networks to the point where they are capable of reaching every potential customer; others do not attempt to realize their total sales potentials because of limited financial resources; and others, being more profit-oriented than sales-oriented, seek to maximize profitable sales and not possible sales. The estimate for sales potential indicates how much a company could sell *if* it had all the necessary resources and desired to use them for this purpose. The sales forecast is a related but different estimate—it indicates how much a company with a given amount of resources can sell if it implements a particular marketing program. Thus, the sales-potential estimate is a much more speculative figure than is the sales forecast.

# SALES-FORECASTING METHODS

There are two main classes of forecasting methods: unsophisticated and sophisticated. The unsophisticated methods rely primarily on judgment to produce sales forecasts; the basic reasoning underlying these methods is easily understood. The sophisticated methods, in contrast, involve applying statistical techniques of varying degrees of difficulty. In the following sections we consider six methods at some length: the jury of executive opinion and the poll of sales force opinion (both unsophisticated methods); projection of past sales and survey of customers' buying plans (both of which may be either unsophisticated or sophisticated, depending upon how they are applied); and regression analysis and econometric model building and simulation (both sophisticated methods).

## Jury of Executive Opinion

There are two steps in this forecasting method: (1) a small number of high-ranking executives register their individual opinions concerning the probable future level of sales, and (2) the forecast is derived from a rough averaging of these opinions. The executives whose opinions are solicited should be ones who are well informed about the industry outlook and the company's relative market position and capabilities. All participating executives should support their estimates with factual material to the maximum extent possible and be prepared to supply the rationale behind their estimates.

Companies using the jury-of-executive-opinion method generally do so for one or more of four reasons:

1. This is a relatively easy way to turn out a forecast in a short time.
2. This is a way to pool the experience and judgment of people who "are in a position to know."
3. This may be the only feasible approach to forecasting if the company is so young that it has not yet accumulated the experience necessary to use other methods.
4. This method may have to be used when adequate sales and market statistics are missing, or when these figures have not yet been put into the form required for more sophisticated forecasting methods.

The jury-of-executive-opinion approach to sales forecasting has some obvious weaknesses. As the name indicates, its findings are based primarily on opinion, and factual evidence to support the forecast is often sketchy. Using this approach adds to the workload of key executives, requiring them to spend time that they would otherwise devote to their areas of primary responsibility. And a forecast made by this method is difficult to break down into estimates of probable sales by products, by time intervals, by markets, by customers, and so on; if the sales forecast is to be of maximum value for operating purposes breakdowns of this sort are needed.

## Poll of Sales-Force Opinion

Under the poll-of-sales-force-opinion method, often tagged "the grass-roots approach," individual sales personnel forecast sales for their respective territories; then these individual forecasts are combined and modified, as management thinks necessary, to form the company sales forecast. The logic underlying this approach is that forecasting responsibility is assigned to those who must later produce the results. Furthermore, this method has the merit of utilizing the specialized knowledge of those company personnel who are in closest touch with market conditions. In addition, because the salespeople have helped to develop the forecast, it seems reasonable that they should have greater confidence in any quotas based upon it that are later assigned to them. Still another attractive feature is that forecasts developed by this method are easy to break down according to products, territories, customers, middlemen, and sales force.

But the poll-of-sales-force-opinion approach to sales forecasting has basic weaknesses. Not generally trained to do forecasting, and heavily influenced by current business conditions in their territories, salespersons tend to be overoptimistic or overpessimistic about their prospects for making future sales. They are entirely too near the trees to see the forest—they often are unaware of broad changes taking place in the economy and of trends in business conditions outside their own territories. Furthermore, if the "forecasts" of the sales staff are used in setting quotas, some sales personnel deliberately underestimate so that they can reach their quotas more easily. To some extent these weaknesses can be overcome through training the sales force in forecasting techniques, by orienting them on factors influencing company sales, and by adjusting for consistent biases in individual salespersons' forecasts detected through analysis of their forecasting records. For most companies, however, implementing such corrective actions is an almost endless task, because turnover among sales personnel is constantly going on and new staff members (whose biases are unknown at the start) submit their forecasts along with the forecasts of long-experienced sales personnel with known forecasting biases. In short, this method is based to such a large extent on judgment that it is an unreliable approach for most companies to use as their only forecasting method. The poll of sales-force opinion, where used, usually serves as a method of getting an alternative estimate of sales for use as a check on a sales forecast obtained through some other approach.

### Projection of Past Sales

The projection-of-past-sales method of sales forecasting takes a variety of forms. In its simplest form, the sales forecast for the coming year may be set at the same figure as the current year's actual sales. Alternatively, the forecast may be made merely by adding a set percentage to last year's sales or to a moving average of the sales figures for several past years. For instance, if it is assumed that there will be the same percentage sales increase next year as this year, the forecaster might utilize a naive-model projection such as:

$$\text{next year's sales} = \text{this year's sales} \times \frac{\text{this year's sales}}{\text{last year's sales}}$$

This year's sales are inevitably related to last year's. Similarly, next year's sales are related to this year's and to those of all preceding years. Projecting present sales levels is a simple and inexpensive forecasting method and it may be appropriate for companies in more or less stable or "mature" industries—it is rare in such industries for a company's sales to vary more than 15 percent plus or minus from the preceding year's experience.

**Time-Series Analysis.**   Not greatly different in principle from the simple projection of past sales is time-series analysis, a statistical procedure for studying historical sales data. This procedure involves isolating and measuring four chief types of sales variations: long-term trends, cyclical changes, seasonal variations, and irregular fluctuations. Then a mathematical model describing the past behavior of the series is selected, assumed values for each type of sales variation are inserted, and the sales forecast is "cranked out."[2]

For companies in most industries, time-series analysis finds practical application mainly in the making of long-range forecasts. The results obtained may be reliable for a period of several years ahead; but the chances are great that predictions on a year-to-year basis, such as are necessary for an operating sales forecast, will not be reliable. Only where sales patterns are clearly defined and relatively stable from year to year is time-series analysis used successfully for making short-term operating sales forecasts.

Another drawback of time-series analysis is that it is extremely difficult to "call the turns." Trend and cycle analysis often makes it possible to do a good job in explaining why a trend, once it is under way, continues in a certain direction; but it is predicting the turns that is important. On their correct prognostication depends to a large extent the maximization of sales opportunities when the trend is favorable, and the minimization of losses when the trend reverses itself.

**Exponential Smoothing.** A statistical technique for short-range sales forecasting, which has received increasing acceptance in recent years, is called "exponential smoothing." Exponential smoothing is a type of moving average which represents a weighted sum of all past numbers in a time series, with the heaviest weight placed on the most recent data.[3] To illustrate, consider this relatively simple but widely used form of exponential smoothing—a weighted average of this year's sales is combined with the forecast of this year's sales to arrive at the forecast for next year's sales. The forecasting equation, in other words, is:

$$\text{next year's sales} = a \text{ (this year's sales)} + (1 - a) \text{ (this year's forecast)}$$

The $a$ in the equation is called the *smoothing constant* and is set at a value between 0.0 and 1.0. If, for example, actual sales for this year came to 320 units of product, the sales forecast for this year was 350 units, and the smoothing constant was 0.3, the forecast for next year's sales is:

$$(0.3)(320) + (0.7)(350) = 341 \text{ units of product}$$

Determining the value of $a$ is the main problem in using exponential smoothing. If the series of sales data changes slowly, $a$ should be small to retain the effect of earlier observations. If the series changes rapidly, $a$ should be large so that the forecasts respond to these changes. In practice, $a$ is esimated by trying several values and making retrospective tests of the associated forecast error. The $a$ value leading to the smallest forecast error is then chosen for future smoothing.[4]

**Evaluation of Past-Sales Projection Methods.** The main limitation of all forecasting methods involving projections of past sales is that past sales history is assumed to be the only factor influencing future sales. No allowance is made for sharp and rapid upswings or downturns in business activity, nor is it usual to make corrections for poor

---

[2]For a good discussion of this technique, see F. E. Croxton and D. J. Cowden, *Applied General Statistics*, 3rd ed. (Englewood Cliffs, N.J.: Prentice-Hall, Inc., 1967).

[3]P. E. Green and D. S. Tull, *Research for Marketing Decisions*, 2nd ed. (Englewood Cliffs, N.J.: Prentice-Hall, Inc., 1970), pp. 552-553.

[4]*Ibid.*, p. 554.

sales performance extending over previous periods. Another difficulty encountered in using past-sales projection methods is that the accuracy of the forecast may depend largely upon how close the company is to the market-saturation point. If the market is entirely saturated, it sometimes is defensible to predict sales by applying, for instance, a certain percentage figure which is equivalent to the annual replacement demand. More often, however, the firm whose product has achieved full market saturation is likely to find, since most companies of this type market durables or semidurables, that its prospective customers can postpone or accelerate their purchases to a considerable degree. However, because numerous computer programs are available for using such statistical techniques as time-series analysis and exponential smoothing, many companies rely, to some extent at least, on past-sales projections for making their sales forecasts.

### Survey of Customers' Buying Plans

What could seem more like a sensible sales forecasting approach than that of asking customers about their future buying plans? Industrial marketers use this approach more than consumer-goods marketers, probably because it is best adapted for use in situations where the potential market consists of small numbers of customers and prospects, substantial sales are made to individual customers, the manufacturer sells direct to users, and customers are concentrated in a few geographical areas. In such instances, it is relatively easy and inexpensive to survey a sample of customers and prospects to obtain their estimated requirements for the product during the next operating period, and to project the sample results in order to obtain a sales forecast. The results of such surveys, however, need to be tempered by management's specialized knowledge, and few companies are willing to base their forecasts exclusively on a survey of customers' buying plans. The main reason lies in the assumptions inherent in this forecasting method—that customers know what they are going to do and, in addition, that buyers' plans, once made, will not change. At least part of the time, either or both assumptions are likely to be unwarranted.

Even though the survey of customers' buying plans is generally classified as an unsophisticated forecasting method, it *can* be rather sophisticated—that is, if it is a true survey (in the marketing research sense) and if the selection of respondents is made by probability sampling techniques. However, since it gathers opinions rather than measuring actions, substantial amounts of nonsampling error are likely to be present in the results. Respondents do not always have well-formulated buying plans and, even if they do, they are not always willing to relate them to an interviewer. In actual practice, most companies using this approach appear to pay little attention to the composition of the sample and devote minimum effort to measuring sampling and nonsampling errors.

### Regression Analysis

Regression analysis is a statistical process and, as used in sales forecasting, determines and measures the association between company sales and other variables. Briefly stated, the method involves the fitting of an equation to explain the fluctuations in sales in terms of related and presumably causal variables, substituting for these variables values considered likely during the period to be forecasted, and solving for the value of sales. In other words, there are three major steps in forecasting sales by use of regression analysis:

1. Identify variables causally related to company sales.
2. Determine or estimate the values of these variables related to sales.
3. Derive the sales forecast from these estimates.

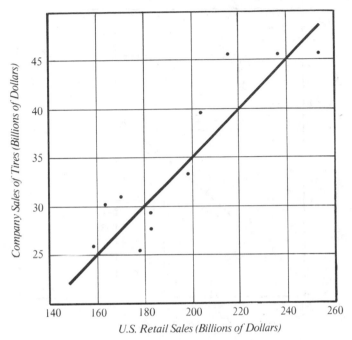

Computers and improved computer programs have made it relatively easy to use regression analysis for sales forecasting. One tire manufacturer, for instance, used simple regression analysis to determine the association between various economic variables and its own sales. This company quickly discovered that a positive correlation existed between gross national product and its own sales, but the correlation coefficient was too low to use in forecasting company sales. The same was found to be true of personal disposable income and retail sales; their correlation coefficients with company sales were too low to use in forecasting company sales. Figure 2.2 is a scatter diagram illustrating the relation between total U.S. retail sales and the tire manufacturer's sales. The straight line is the result of the mathematical computation of the correlation between the two series of data. If the correlation had been perfect, all the dots would have fallen on the line. The tire manufacturer also measured the relationship between its own sales and the sales of new automobiles and found a much higher degree of correlation (see Figure 2.3); notice that the dots on this scatter diagram cluster closely around the line.

In forecasting situations where sales are influenced by two or more independent variables acting together, multiple-regression-analysis techniques are applied (generally through use of a computer). To illustrate, consider the following situation. An appliance manufacturer was considering adding an automatic dishwasher to its line and, in the course of studying the feasibility of adding this product, decided to develop a forecasting equation for use in predicting industry sales of dishwashers. From published sources, such as the *Statistical Abstract of the United States,* data were collected on manufacturers'

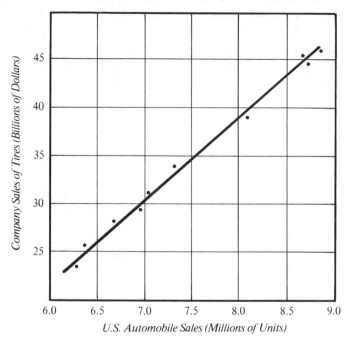

*U.S. Automobile Sales (Millions of Units)*

sales of dishwashers for a period of twenty years (the dependent variable). Also collected from similar sources were data on four possible independent variables:

1.  The Consumer Price Index for durables.
2.  Disposable personal income deflated by the Consumer Price Index in terms of 1957-59 dollars.
3.  The change in the total number of households.
4.  New nonfarm housing starts.

Then, the analysts decided to use a stepwise multiple-linear-regression technique to esti-mate the relationship among the variables.[5] Figure 2.4 shows the computer printout used in developing the forecasting equation. The following is a step-by-step explanation of the program output:

1.  Means and standard deviations for all variables:
    X(1)  is Consumer Price Index for durables (CPI)
    X(2)  is disposable personal income deflated by the Consumer Price Index (DPI/CPI)
    X(3)  is the change in the total number of households (DNH)
    X(4)  is new nonfarm housing starts (NFHS)
    X(5)  is sales (the dependent variable)
2.  Simple pairwise correlation coefficients (note that sales volume is highly correlated with DPI/CPI and CPI).

[5]Computer program developed for Conversational Programming System (for remote terminal) by A. R. Grimes, Jr., and C. B. Kavan, University of Georgia, Athens, Georgia, 1971.

3.  Program enters independent variables in order of highest explained variation of the dependent variable:

    3.1  Program states distribution of dependent variable (sales) before the first independent variable is added.

    3.2  Variable X(2): DPI/CPI enters the model first. The standard error of Y is reduced to 147.209. The coefficient of determination is 0.96234; that is, X(2) explains approximately 96 percent of the variation in Y.

    3.3  Variable X(1): CPI enters the model next. [This means that X(1) explains the greatest portion of the variation in Y left over after the entry of X(2) in the model.] The standard error of Y is now reduced to 105.65553. The coefficient of multiple determination is increased to 0.98162.

    3.4  After the addition of variables X(2) and X(1), less than 2 percent of the variation in Y is left to be explained.

    3.5  The results of the additions of X(3) DNH and of X(4) NFHS indicate that these variables are not statistically significant; this is shown by the low $F$ values as well as by the low $t$ values:

$$t = \frac{\text{coefficient}}{\text{standard error of coefficient}}$$

Therefore, the effect of adding these two variables to the model is not to reduce the standard error of Y, but, in fact, in this case it is increased slightly.

These results indicated, then, that the forecasting equation was as follows:

$$\text{Manufacturers' sales of dishwashers (in thousands)} = -4{,}404.97 + 28.85\text{CPI} + 6.36\text{DPI/CPI}$$

So if the manufacturer had estimates for the coming year that CPI would be 125 and DPI/CPI would be 550, its forecast of industry sales of dishwashers (in thousands) would be:

$$\text{sales} = -4{,}404.97 + (28.85)(125) + (6.36)(550)$$
$$= 2{,}699.28 \quad \text{(or approximately 2,700,000 dishwashers)}$$

**Evaluation of Regression Analysis for Sales Forecasting.**   If high coefficients of correlation exist between company sales and certain independent variables, the forecasting problem may be simplified, especially if the related variables "lead" company sales. The probable course of sales may then be charted on an apparently reliable basis, and the forecaster's attention can be concentrated on factors that might cause deviations from the indicated movement. But it is still necessary for the forecaster to examine other circumstances that might upset past relationships upon which the correlations are based. A forecast made through regression-analysis techniques is founded on the assumption that relations which the variables have borne to each other in the past will also hold for the future. To have a "lead-lag" association in which deviations regularly occur in the related independent variable(s) prior to a change in company sales is a near-ideal situation; unfortunately it rarely holds except over short periods. Although lead-lag relationships are fairly common, associations between the lead variables and sales in which the intervening time intervals remain relatively stable are uncommon. These periods not only contract or expand without warning; they also exhibit great variations during different phases of the business cycle.

FIGURE 2.4
Computer Printout Used in Developing an Equation for Forecasting Industry
Sales of Automatic Dishwashers

MULTIPLE REGRESSION ANALYSIS FOR: GRIMES
PROJECT TITLE: SALES     F(CPI, DPI/CPI, DNH, NFHS)

| | | Mean | Standard Deviation |
|---|---|---|---|
| Step 1 | X(1) | 103.0000 | 6.5012 |
| | X(2) | 373.2286 | 89.4190 |
| | X(3) | 1.0299 | 0.3833 |
| | X(4) | 1428.8571 | 188.1014 |
| | X(5) | 938.9524 | 739.3600 |

Step 2     CORRELATION COEFFICIENTS

r(1,2)     0.836915
r(1,3)     0.415448
r(1,4)     0.486596
r(1,5)     0.897006

r(2,3)     0.443997
r(2,4)     0.229535
r(2,5)     0.980989

r(3,4)     0.240009
r(3,5)     0.469477

r(4,5)     0.316022

Step 3.1   THE STANDARD ERROR OF Y WILL NOW BE   739.35996

| | Coefficient | Standard Error of Coefficient |
|---|---|---|
| b(0) | 938.95238 | |

Coefficient of Determination is 0.00000

Step 3.2   THE VARIABLE X(2) IS NOW BEING ENTERED INTO THE
MODEL WITH AN F  =  485.51400
THE STANDARD ERROR OF Y WILL NOW BE   147.20898

| | Coefficient | Standard Error of Coefficient |
|---|---|---|
| b(2) | 8.11130 | 0.36812 |
| b(0) | −2088.41491 | |

Coefficient of Determination is 0.96234

Step 3.3   THE VARIABLE X(1) IS NOW BEING ENTERED INTO THE
MODEL WITH AN F  =  18.88398
THE STANDARD ERROR OF Y WILL NOW BE   105.65553

| | Coefficient | Standard Error of Coefficient |
|---|---|---|
| b(1) | 28.85239 | 6.63949 |
| b(2) | 6.35570 | 0.48272 |
| b(0) | −4404.97376 | |

Coefficient of Determination is 0.98162

Step 3.4   THE VARIABLE X(3) IS NOW BEING ENTERED INTO THE
MODEL WITH AN F  =  0.62558
THE STANDARD ERROR OF Y WILL NOW BE   106.77186

FIGURE 2.4 (cont.)

|        | Coefficient | Standard Error of Coefficient |
|--------|-------------|-------------------------------|
| b(1)   | 28.37586    | 6.73664                       |
| b(2)   | 6.27963     | 0.49721                       |
| b(3)   | 55.19663    | 69.78644                      |
| b(0)   | —4384.34552 |                               |

Coefficient of Determination is 0.98227

Step 3.5   THE VARIABLE X(4) IS NOW BEING ENTERED INTO THE
MODEL WITH AN F = 0.25544
THE STANDARD ERROR OF Y WILL NOW BE   109.18975

|        | Coefficient | Standard Error of Coefficient |
|--------|-------------|-------------------------------|
| b(1)   | 26.09639    | 8.23421                       |
| b(2)   | 6.38803     | 0.55185                       |
| b(3)   | 50.42226    | 71.98926                      |
| b(4)   | 0.08159     | 0.16143                       |
| b(0)   | —4301.67933 |                               |

Coefficient of Determination is 0.98255

If forecasters discover close associations between company sales and a reliable baro-meter, their estimates will be improved by the predictions of probable changes in the barometer made by expert analysts. However, one great danger in using regression analy-sis for forecasting is that forecasters may put too much faith in the statistical output; that is, they may be tempted to abandon independent appraisals of future events in favor of a forecast developed entirely by computer. It may be only natural to place blind faith in a method that seems infallible; but it is wise to check unaccountably good results with forecasts arrived at through other methods.

### Econometric Model Building and Simulation

Econometric model building and simulation holds considerable promise as a sales forecasting method for companies marketing durable goods (consumer or industrial). This approach uses a mathematical model in the form of an equation or system of equations to represent a set of relationships among different demand-determining independent variables and sales. Then, by "plugging in" values (or estimates) for each independent variable (that is, by "simulating" the total situation), a sales forecast is produced. Forecasting equations derived through regression-analysis techniques resemble, but, strictly speaking, are not regarded as, econometric models. An econometric model (unlike a regression model) is based upon an *underlying theory* about the relationships that exist among a set of vari-ables and parameters are estimated by statistical analysis of past data.[6] Thus, an econo-metric sales forecasting model is an abstraction of a real-world situation, expressed in equation form and used to predict sales. For example, the sales equation for a durable good can be written:

$$S = R + N$$

where

$S$ = total sales

[6] Green and Tull, *op. cit.,* p. 550.

$R=$ replacement demand (i.e., purchases made to replace units of the good going out of use, as measured by the scrappage of old units).

$N=$ new-owner demand (i.e., purchases made not to replace existing units of the product, but to add to the total stock of the product in users' possession).

Total sales of a durable good, in other words, consist of purchases made to replace units that have been scrapped and purchases by new owners. Thus, a family buys its first new automatic washing machine and becomes a part of the new-owner demand for that machine; another family, which has a five-year-old machine, trades it to a dealer for a new machine and becomes part of the replacement demand (although only effectively so when the five-year-old machine, perhaps passing through several families' hands in the process,- finally comes to be owned by a family that goes ahead and consigns its even-older machine to the scrap heap).

Replacement demand, then, is normally measured by the scrappage of old units of products, that is, by the percentage of the total stock of the product in users' hands that is actually taken out of service either through consignment to the trash pile, by sale to a junk dealer, or merely by being stowed away and never used again. So replacement demand in any one year does not necessarily include demand originating from the family that had a five-year-old machine which it traded to a dealer for a new machine, with the dealer reselling the old machine to another family who buys it second-hand. Only when the particular washing machine involved goes *completely out of service* is it considered as having been scrapped and, at that time (through a chain of purchases and trade-ins), some family becomes a part of the replacement demand. Econometricians estimate replacement demand by using life expectancy tables or survival tables, which are similar to the life (or mortality) tables used by life insurance actuaries. An example of such a survival table is shown in Figure 2.5.

If some durable good has a maximum service life of 11 years and 10,000 units of the good enter service in some year, the table indicates that five years later 8,621 will probably still be in service and ten years later, 54. For this batch of 10,000 product units, scrappage would amount to 1,035 in the fifth year (that is, 1,379 — 344, the difference

FIGURE 2.5

Durable-Goods Survival Coefficients (Maximum Service Life: 11 years; Average Service Life: 6.5 years)

| Year | Survival Coefficient |
|------|----------------------|
| 1 | 1.0000 |
| 2 | 0.9995 |
| 3 | 0.9946 |
| 4 | 0.9656 |
| 5 | 0.8621 |
| 6 | 0.6406 |
| 7 | 0.3594 |
| 8 | 0.1379 |
| 9 | 0.0344 |
| 10 | 0.0054 |
| 11 | 0.0000 |

Source: M. Spencer, C. Clark, and P. Hoguet, *Business and Economic Forecasting* (Homewood, Ill.: Richard D. Irwin, Inc., 1961), p. 256.

between the accumulated total scrappage at the close of the fifth and fourth years, respectively). In the fifth year, then, 1,035 replacement sales would trace back to the batch of 10,000 product units that entered service five years before.

In this model, new-owner demand is defined as the net addition to users' stocks of the product which occurs during a given period. For instance, if 2,000,000 units of some appliance were in service at the start of a period and 2,500,000 at the end, new-owner demand would have been 500,000 during the period. Forecasting the number of sales to new owners is a matter of treating the stock of a durable good in the hands of users as a "population" exhibiting "birth" and "death" characteristics, that is, thinking of this stock as behaving in ways analogous to a human population.

Constructing an econometric model of the replacement demand + new-owner demand type involves going through a three-step procedure. First, the various independent variables affecting each demand category (replacement and new-owner) are studied and those that bear some logical relationship to sales (the dependent variable) are chosen for correlation analysis. Second, the forecaster detects (through correlation analysis) that combination of independent variables which correlates best with sales, sometimes including a time trend in this combination to represent other variables, which cannot be measured directly. Third, a suitable mathematical expression is chosen to show the quantitative relationships among the various independent variables and sales, the dependent variable.[7] This expression becomes, then, the econometric model that is used for sales forecasting.

The general procedure for building econometric models seems simple enough, but such models, when actually constructed, can take on rather formidable appearances. Consider, for example, the following econometric model for forecasting the sales of washing machines.[8]

$$S_{tc} = Y_t - y_t + Y_t \left\{ H_t \left[ 0.03 - 0.0157 \times \left( \frac{(I_t + 3C_t)/P_t}{10^{0.01818t} - 33.1143} \right) \right] - 0.0000283 Y_t \right\}$$

where

$S_{tc}$ = calculated value for forecasted sales of washing machines during some time period.
$Y_t$ = level of consumers' stock of washing machines in any period (as of January 1)
$y_t$ = level of consumers' stock that would occur in the following period (as of January 1) if no washing machines were sold and scrappage rates remained the same
$H_t$ = number of wired (i.e., electrified) dwelling units, in millions
$I_t$ = disposable personal income
$C_t$ = net credit extended (excluding credit extended for automobiles)
$P_t$ = price index for house furnishings
$10^{0.01818t} - 33.1143$ = trend of real purchasing power over time
$I_t + 3C_t/P_t$ real purchasing power

Thus, new-owner demand in this model is represented by $Y_t - y_t$, both members of the expression being determined through application of appropriate survival coefficients to previous years' sales of washing machines, and through estimation of consumers' total stocks of washing machines in each year. Replacement demand is represented by other symbols in the remaining part of the expression, which takes into account the number of

[7]M. H. Spencer and T. Mattheis, "Forecasting Sales of Consumers' Durable Goods," *California Management Review*, Vol. 4, No. 3 (Spring 1962), p. 79.
[8]*Ibid.*, p. 98.

wired dwelling units (washing machines are not likely to be sold to people who live in homes with no electricity), real purchasing power (disposable personal income plus credit availability divided by a price index), and real purchasing power adjusted for the historical trend of real purchasing power over time. Correlation-analysis techniques were used to derive the various numerical values in this model.

The econometric model-building approach seems a nearly ideal way to forecast sales. Not only does it take into account the interaction of independent variables that bear logical and measurable relationships to sales; it also uses correlation-analysis techniques to quantify these relationships. Such models, however, are used far more to forecast industry sales than they are to forecast the sales of individual companies. This is because the independent variables affecting an individual company's sales are more numerous and more difficult to measure than those determining the sales of an entire industry. Many companies use an econometric model to forecast industry sales, and then apply an estimate of the company's share-of-the-market percentage to the industry forecast to arrive at the company's sales forecast.

## CONVERSION OF INDUSTRY FORECAST INTO COMPANY SALES FORECAST

The sequence of forecasting procedure usually provides, first, for making an industry sales forecast and, second, for breaking down this forecast into a company sales forecast. Previous discussion reflects this usual sequence. We examined six main forecasting approaches, and only in two of them—the poll of sales force opinion (the most unsophisticated approach), and in some rather unsophisticated forms of past sales projections—is the industry sales forecast skipped and a company sales forecast arrived at directly. The other approaches—jury of executive opinion, survey of buying plans, regression analysis, and econometric model building—usually result in industry sales forecasts.

Converting an industry sales forecast into a company sales forecast requires that company strengths and weaknesses relative to those of competitors be appraised and a quantitative estimate of the company's share-of-the-market be arrived at, which then can be used to derive a company sales forecast. The poll-of-sales-force-opinion approach leaves this appraisal largely up to the sales personnel—they focus on estimating how much the company can sell, not on how much the industry can sell. The unsophisticated forms of the past-sales-projection approach carry the implicit assumption that no changes will occur in the company's strengths and weaknesses relative to those of its competitors. In the other four approaches, management makes this appraisal at the time it determines the company's probable share-of-the market percentage and, although some companies check such estimates with their sales personnel, the main appraisal of competitive position is made by executives who should be better informed on the overall sales outlook than any salesperson is likely to be.

Forecasting a company's market share varies greatly in complexity from one industry to another. In an industry such as steel, where the number of competitors is small and market share is fairly stable, determining a given company's market share is a relatively simple task—mostly a matter of projecting past trends and adjusting for anticipated changes in the company's relative strengths and weaknesses. But in an industry such as women's clothing, where the number of competitors is large and the market share fluctuates widely, determination of market share is difficult: The ability to evaluate a style's salability is a key element in forecasting, and this requires both thorough knowledge of market trends and keen judgment. Most companies, however, operate in industries that lie somewhere between these two extremes, with market shares neither as stable as in steel nor as volatile as in women's apparel. Forecasters in most companies therefore need information on competitors' plans to launch new and improved products, advertising and selling plans, pricing strategies, and so on. When forecasters evaluate such information in relation to their own company's proposed marketing and selling plans, they are in a position to exercise, informed judgment in predicting the company's probable market share. If, for example, a forecaster knows that a major competitor plans a substantial price cut on a product that many buyers buy mainly on the basis of price, it will be necessary to lower the estimate of the company's market share accordingly unless management is willing to match the price cut. Forecasting a particular company's market share is a matter both of examining past trends and of appraising significant changes in competitive relationships which may alter these past trends.

## DERIVATION OF A SALES-VOLUME OBJECTIVE

A sales-volume objective for the coming operating period is the hoped-for outcome of a company's short-range sales-forecasting procedure. In order to understand the relationship of the sales-volume objective and the sales forecast, recall the two main parts of the definition of a sales forecast: (1) it contains an estimate of sales tied to a proposed marketing plan or program, and (2) it assumes a particular set of economic and other forces outside the unit for which the forecast is made. Thus, the sales-forecast estimate does not necessarily and automatically become the company's sales-volume objective, but it does provide an orientation point for management's thinking. Further adjustments in the sales-forecast estimate are usually necessary, perhaps because management decides to alter its marketing plan or program or because changes appear to be occurring in competitor's marketing strategies.

The sales-volume objective finally established should be consistent with management's profit aspirations and the company's marketing capabilities. In other words, it must be attainable at costs low enough to permit the company to reach its net-profit objective, and for the company's marketing forces (that is, its sales force, the advertising program, the dealer organization, and so on) to be capable of reaching the objective set. All three of these items—the sales-volume objective, management's profit objective, and the company's marketing capabilities—are interrelated. Using the sales estimate in the sales forecast as a point of departure, management juggles these three items until it satisfies itself that the relationship between them is the best that can be obtained. Only then does the sales forecast result in the setting of a sales-volume objective. And at that time, the chief sales executive (along with other marketing executives) accepts a major share of the responsibility for making the forecast "come true." Sales policies and selling strategies, formulated by the chief sales executive and subordinate sales executives, must be put into effect in the grand effort to reach the sales volume, profit, and other objectives derived from the sales forecast.

## EVALUATION OF FORECASTS

Before submitting forecasts to higher management, sales executives should evaluate them carefully, regardless of the extent of their personal involvement in the preparation. Since every forecast necessarily pertains to the future, all contain some element of uncertainty; consequently, all forecasts are based on assumptions. So a good first step in evaluating a sales forecast is to examine the assumptions (including any hidden ones) on which it is based. Sales executives should view each assumption critically and note particularly any that seem unwarranted, testing each by asking: If this assumption were removed, or changed, what would be the effect on the forecast? They should also evaluate the forecasting methods as objectively as possible, and then ask themselves such questions as: Are there any variations here from what past experience would seem to indicate? Has sufficient account been taken of trends in the competitive situation and of changes in competitors' marketing and selling strategies? Has account been taken of any new competitive products that might affect the industry's and company's sales? Have inventory movements at all distribution levels (including those at wholesale and retail levels) been considered? Sales executives should also continue evaluating the accuracy and economic value of the forecast as the forecast period advances. Forecasts should be checked against actual results, differences explained, and indicated adjustments made for the remainder of the period. When the period's sales results are all recorded, all variations should be explained and stored for possible future use in improving forecasting accuracy.

## CONCLUSION

Considerable planning and analysis precedes the setting of a company's sales-volume objective: that is, the dollar or unit sales volume which management seeks to obtain during a particular future time interval. Determining the market potential—the maximum possible sales opportunities present in a market and open to all industry members—requires identification of the market, the determination of buying reasons, and quantification of market size. Sales potentials, representing the maximum possible sales opportunities present in given markets and open to a particular company, are generally derived from market potentials after analyses of past market-share relationships and through making adjustments for recent or anticipated changes in company and competitors' marketing and selling programs. Estimates of sales potentials, however, differ from estimates contained in sales forecasts. An estimate for sales potential indicates how much a company could sell *if* it had all the necessary resources and desired to use them for this purpose, whereas a sales-forecast estimate indicates how much a company with a given amount of resources can sell if it implements a particular marketing program.

The basic purpose of an operating sales forecast is to predict how much of a product a company can sell during a specified future period under a given marketing plan. There are many different methods of sales forecasting, some unsophisticated and some sophisticated, and in this chapter we have considered six methods in some detail. Most methods look both forward and backward, each has its own merits and limitations, and all call for judgment on someone's part. The guiding rule in sales forecasting should be to select methods that stand the best chance of achieving the desired degree of accuracy at the most reasonable costs in terms of time and money. Most forecasting procedures provide, first, for making an industry sales forecast and, second, for breaking down this forecast into a company sales forecast; converting an industry sales forecast into a company sales forecast requires assessment of company strengths and weaknesses vis-à-vis those of competitors and quantitative estimates of market shares.

The sales-forecast estimate does not necessarily and automatically become the company's sales-volume objective. Adjustments in the sales-forecast estimate are usually needed to take account of changes in marketing plans or in competition. The sales-volume objective finally established must be attainable at costs low enough to permit the company to reach its net-profit objective; at the same time, it must be in line with the company's marketing capabilities.

# 3

# Determining
# Sales Policies

Sales policies are the guidelines set up by management within which the company is to seek to reach its personal selling objectives. There are three major types: (1) product policies (what to sell), (2) distribution policies (who to sell to), and (3) pricing policies. Sales executives' roles in the determination of sales policies vary considerably from company to company. At one extreme, in some companies, this role is not to determine, but to administer, sales policies laid down by top management. At the opposite extreme, in other companies, the sales executive alone is responsible for determining sales policies, subject, of course, to top management's approval. In most companies, however, the sales executive participates as a member of an executive group charged with the responsibility for determination of sales policies. In all cases, the nature of the sales policies in effect directly influences the jobs of sales executives. They provide them with a sense of direction as they plan how the organization will reach its personal selling objectives, as they organize the sales effort, as they manage the sales force, and as they control the sales effort.

## PRODUCT POLICIES—WHAT TO SELL

The basic nature of a company is determined by the product it has to sell. A company comes into existence because its organizers visualize an opportunity to make and/or market some product(s). As the company grows, management must make many key decisions on products—whether to drop old products, whether to add new products, whether to expand the current product line or add new product lines—and on product design and product quality as well as on such product-related matters as product guarantees and product service.

### Relation to Product Objectives

Product policies are the general rules set up by management to guide itself in making important product decisions. They should derive from, and be wholly consistent with, product objectives. If a product objective, for example, states that "this company desires to make and market products requiring only a minimum of service after their purchase by consumers," then a product policy (or policies) is needed to spell out how this objective will be attained. Or, as another example, if a product objective states that "this company desires to make and market only products that are superior to those of competitors in ways of great importance to users," then product policies are needed to define the nature of superiority from the standpoint of product users. Often these policies take the form of a series of short definitions or of questions arranged as a checklist.

### Product-Line Policy

Policies relating to the width of a product line are classified as either short-line or full-line. The company following a short-line policy handles only a portion of a line, while the company with a full-line policy handles all or most of the items making up a line. For example, a manufacturer concentrating exclusively on a cornflakes product has a short-line policy, whereas a company offering a complete, or almost complete, line of breakfast cereals has a full-line policy. Companies often use short-line policies for some product groupings and full-line policies for others. Management must decide for each group of products whether the basis of competition should be specialization (short-line) or wide selection (full-line).

The extent to which a company should pursue a short-line policy is governed chiefly by the amount of risk that management is willing to assume—the narrower the line, the greater the risk. If a firm can afford to concentrate on a single product, the rewards may be great. Product specialization may enable the manufacturing division to achieve extremely low unit costs. In turn, this may mean that the company becomes almost invulnerable to price competition, even though the product that it markets is of the highest quality. But the penalty for failure is also great. If the product is displaced in the market by substitutes introduced by competitors, the company finds itself "locked out" of the market entirely.

The extent to which a full-line policy should be followed is determined by such factors as: the number of items the sales force can sell effectively, the need for service in connection with the sale of the products involved, the desires of middlemen and product users, the expenses of promotion, and the effect on production costs. The wider the product line, the more the risk is spread. Thus, in sharp contrast to the short-line policy, business risk is diversified over many products. But, while there is less penalty attached to failure of any one item in the line, there also is less reward for the success of any single item in the line.

**Changes in Product Offerings.**    All items in a product line should be subject to continuing evaluation, and reappraisals should occur at regular intervals. Such reappraisals serve two main purposes: (1) to determine whether each item is still in tune with market demand, and (2) to identify items that should be dropped from, or added to, the line. Unless each item in a product line is reappraised fairly regularly, market demand may shift, and more alert competitors may succeed in capturing larger market shares. Regardless of which executive or group in a company is responsible for determining product policies, sales executives should participate in product-line appraisals. Compared with other company executives, they have the closest contact with and most intimate contact with the markets. They should make certain that effective procedures exist for receiving communications on customer product acceptance from the field sales force, and should make this information available regularly to those responsible for determining product policies.

**Appraising the Product Line and Line Simplification.**    Each item in the product line should be compared with similar and competing items in the lines of other manufacturers. The focus should be upon identifying relative strengths and weaknesses, especially with regard to which features of each item consumers consider to be desirable or undesirable. During the appraisal process, too, special attention should be paid to significant trends in usage. Management should seek the answers to several questions: How much of the item is used? What is it used for? When is it used? Where is it used? The answers to these questions may have supplemental benefits of importance to sales executives; they may provide insights useful in the construction of sales presentations and in the motivation of the sales force and dealer organization.

By all odds, however, the most critical factor in analyzing the individual items in a product line is profitability. Generally, an item should not be retained in the line unless it meets management's standards for profitability, or shows promise of meeting those standards. Nevertheless, before an item is dropped because of its poor profitability showing, other factors need considering. Will modifications in price policy or in promotion cause the item to improve in profitability? Even if the item would continue with a poor profit showing regardless of changes in price or promotion, do other factors dictate its retention? Some companies cater to customers and dealers who, logically or not, expect a full-line offering. If distribution is through exclusive agencies, for instance, dealers often insist that the manufacturer provide them with a complete line. Also, certain items, such as repair and replacement parts, are by nature unprofitable for many manufacturers; but, because of the need for providing service on major products, most manufacturers find they must retain such items in their product offerings. Furthermore, since markets are not characteristically homogeneous but are made up of various segments with unique tastes and preferences, many companies find that some unprofitable products must be retained in order to help sell profitable products. This happens, for instance, when customers combine individual products into "product systems," as in the case of sprayer fixtures used with insecticides. Subject to exceptions such as those mentioned, however, unprofitable products should be eliminated from the line.[1]

Under certain conditions, it is appropriate even to drop some profitable products. A product should be dropped if the resources involved in marketing it could be used to better advantage in behalf of a product which has a brighter future or in which the company has a greater investment. An item should also be dropped if it causes sales personnel to divert their efforts from more profitable items. Products with slow turnover rates should be discontinued if dealers might then place more emphasis on the better-selling products in the line. Finally, any item that does not fit logically into the basic line is always a likely candidate for elimination.

**Appraising the Product Line and Line Diversification.**   Management also needs to make periodic appraisals of the product line relative to the company's growth objectives. These objectives are necessarily restricted as an established product line approaches the point of market saturation. Such objectives are restricted, too, when the industry is slowly dying, or when competitors have succeeded in making permanent inroads in a company's "natural" market. In fact, if action in the product policy area is long delayed in such situations, the survival of the firm itself is at stake. In most cases of this kind, the indicated action is to diversify by adding new products or even entirely new product lines.

Although some firms diversify to survive, others diversify to expand or to reduce costs. For example, a decision to shorten marketing channels almost always causes

---

[1]C. Fulop, "Why Products Fail," *Statist* (February 3, 1967), p. 167.

parallel consideration to be given to widening the line. If sales personnel are to write orders large enough to justify the higher costs of direct selling, addition of new products may be necessary. On occasion, too, top management assigns the sales organization a substantially larger task than previously. When sales volume must be expanded greatly, one solution is to add new products. Sometimes, too, new products are added to stimulate the sales force or dealer organization. An addition to the line not only has news value, it may help salespeople earn larger commissions, and assist dealers in increasing sales and profits.

Furthermore, circumstances elsewhere in the company may result in adding new products. The production department may initiate the search for new products if there are unused plant facilities or if seasonal sales fluctuations cause manufacturing irregularities. The treasurer may advocate diversification if idle funds cause financial criticism of the company or if there is an opportunity for profitable acquisition of a firm manufacturing related products. The purchasing department sometimes suggests the addition of new products, particularly when difficulty is experienced in procuring adequate supplies of materials for the fabrication of existing products. Pressure for line diversification may originate in the scientific research division, which may discover or perfect a new product, or in the marketing research department, which may uncover natural additions to the line as an additional result of other studies. Occasionally, too, either through research or by chance, uses for industrial waste materials are found which result in net additions to the product line.

The sales department is often the division that pushes hardest for line diversification. Its intimate contact with the market enables it to keep close watch on the degree of market acceptance enjoyed by new products of other manufacturers. Therefore, with the objective of holding or improving an established market position, sales executives exert strong pressure for the addition of new products. Consequently, any significant shift in customers' buying patterns may be a signal for line diversification.

**Ideas for New Products.**   Once management decides to add new products or new product lines, it faces the problem of finding candidates for addition. Progressively managed companies seek to tap both internal and external sources of new-product ideas. Ideas for products that come from within the company generally are related to the company's regular operations. The sales department, for instance, may identify unsatisfied market needs in its day-to-day contacts with customers and prospects. Or the production department may develop improvements in existing products, and the research and development department may turn up ideas for new products as a routine part of its activities.

Because they represent thinking undulled by close association with the established product line, ideas from outside the company are often unique. Here are a few examples: A pottery company got its idea for a new vase from a museum exhibit. One plastics manufacturer secured an idea for a film-viewing device from an unsolicited outside suggestion, and another plastics manufacturer got an idea for a similar device from a list of needed inventions published by a bank. A chemical company picked up an idea for an insecticide from a list of government-owned patents available for licensing. Thus, product ideas from external sources often result in the addition of items that otherwise might never have been considered.

**Appraisal of Proposed New Products.**   What criteria should be used for appraising products or product lines proposed as candidates for addition? As in the evaluation of established product offerings, the key question is: Will this item (line) add to the profitability of the company? The next factors to be considered include the nature and size of likely markets, competition, price policy, sales programs, and legal implications.

The marketing and production characteristics of a proposed product should be compared with those of items in the existing line. Ideally, any addition should be in alignment on both the marketing and production sides. Such products are natural additions; they round out the line and make marketing and production efforts more efficient and more profitable. From the marketing standpoint, the same sales force can sell the product, and distribution can be through existing channels. Also, the ideal product reaps the benefits of good will previously built up for other items in the line; its seasonal sales dovetail with the present sales patterns; and it broadens the market base (diversifies the compamy's business by adding new classes of customers).

**Product Design Policy.**   Manufacturers have two main policy decisions to make with respect to product design: (1) the frequency with which designs will be changed, and (2) the extent to which product designs should be protected from the copying of competitors.

Frequent introduction and promotion of design changes and design improvements has become an important marketing factor in many industries, such as in clothing, automobiles, home appliances, and office machines. Through design changes that make the product more attractive, for example, users are persuaded to replace old models, which in many instances are still usable, with new models. In addition to weakening the sales resistance of buyers, changes in design reduce the emphasis on price, assist in the stimulation of salespeople and dealers, and provide new inspiration for the advertising department.[2] However, this design change policy is not appropriate for all companies or for all types of products, since the successful promotion of a design change (especially if it involves only the product's external appearance) requires not only a high degree of skill in design but exceptional skill in the planning and execution of promotional programs.

A company's policy with respect to design protection is closely related to its policy on frequency of design change. In certain industries in which designs change very rapidly, such as in the women's apparel field, it is usually impractical to attempt to protect a new design. In fact, the rapid rate of fashion change in most areas of the apparel industry makes legal protection impractical. Indeed, success in high-fashion fields partially depends upon the extent to which designs are adopted by competing firms so that the style becomes fashionable. In other industries, where design changes occur less frequently, design protection is practical and desirable. This is true, for instance, in the home appliance, furniture, and jewelry industries. Legal protection is effected through design patents granted by the United States Patent Office for terms of up to fourteen years. While they are in force, these patents protect a company against use of the design by others.

**Product Quality and Service Policy.**   For consumer durables, and most industrial goods, product quality and the amount of service rendered in connection with the sale are closely related. Generally speaking, in other words, high-quality products tend to require less service and low-quality products, more service. Since buyers ordinarily expect the performance of different products to vary with their quality, manufacturers marketing high-quality products usually have the more liberal service policies. Often, too, product quality

---

[2]O. W. Karger, "Product Design, Marketing, and Manufacturing Innovation," *California Management Review,* Vol. 9, No. 2 (Winter 1966), p. 32.

is largely a matter of those characteristics built into a product that the buyer is unable to judge until after he has made the purchase and begun to use the product. Since such technical features are apt to be deeply hidden, a liberal service policy helps reduce customers' reluctance to buy items whose quality cannot be judged in advance of actual purchase. The maintenance and, if feasible, the improvement of product quality are also important matters for the sales department—if quality deteriorates, for example, the sales department bears the brunt of customer and middleman dissatisfaction.

Manufacturers' service policies take a variety of forms. The simplest merely provides for education of the buyer in the use and care of the product. Other service policies— particularly for industrial products and such consumer lines as air-conditioning and heating equipment—provide for installation, inspection, and repair of the product. When a company adopts a formal service policy, sales management should make it an integral part of the promotional program. An appropriate service policy not only facilitates the making of initial sales but also helps in keeping products sold, stimulating repeat sales, and building customer goodwill. There is no legitimate place in a promotional program for a service policy that fails to accomplish these aims. Success or failure of service policies depends on sales management, since the chief sales executive is responsible for their administration.

Many manufacturers, at least for a specified period after sale of the product, do not charge for service. This "free" service may be provided either under the terms of a written guarantee or as a matter of policy. When the buyer requests service a considerable time after the date of purchase, most manufacturers charge for it. Firms maintaining centralized service facilities, or operating their own service stations, generally make the charge a nominal one. Such a charge pays part of the costs of service and handling and eliminates many unreasonable demands by buyers. Companies that depend upon dealers or distributors to provide service have less control over the size of the charge. It may be a nominal amount, with the manufacturer absorbing part and the user the remainder; or it may be larger, and borne entirely by the user. Unless the manufacturer pays some portion of the cost, middlemen hesitate to assume responsibility for service.

**Guarantee Policy.** *Guarantees,* or *warranties* as they are sometimes called, serve as sales promotional devices and as a protection to limit liability and guard against abuses of the service policy. If the product does not perform as represented, the guarantor may promise to replace it, to refund the purchase price or a multiple of that price, to furnish the purchaser with a competitive product at no expense, or to remedy defects free of charge or for a small fee. When a guarantee is used for promotional purposes, its terms are likely to be extremely liberal. When used as protection, its terms are not only less generous but are hedged with various conditions and restrictions. It is unusual for a guarantee to serve both purposes satisfactorily. The guarantee is weakened as a tool for sales promotion when clauses are inserted to protect the manufacturer; and the absence of such clauses makes it less effective as a protective device. However, this does not mean that a promotional guarantee should be without some protective provisions. Nor does it mean that a protective guarantee should be absolutely useless for promotional purposes. But the guarantee must emphasize one purpose, not both.

## DISTRIBUTION POLICIES—WHO TO SELL

The distribution policies of a company are important determinants of the functions of its sales department. The decision to utilize a particular marketing channel, or channels, sets the pattern for sales-force operations, both geographically and from the standpoint of the kinds and classes of customers from whom sales personnel solicit orders. The decision with respect to the number of outlets that are to handle the product at each distribution level affects the size and nature of the manufacturer's sales organization and the scope of its activities. Related decisions concerning the cooperation that is extended to and expected from the various middlemen also strongly influence both the nature of the sales department's operations and the salespersons' jobs.

### Policies on Marketing Channels

One of the most basic of all marketing decisions is that of choosing the most appropriate marketing channel(s). Figure 3.1 shows the principal choices normally available, although this diagram, of course, omits many channel variations that see less common use. Detailed descriptions of these channels would be superfluous here, since the conditions under which each is an appropriate choice, the problems met and the advantages gained through using each, and descriptions of the service rendered by different middlemen are exhaustively covered in most basic marketing texts.[3] As shown in Figure 3.1, manufacturers selling goods to the consumer market have a choice of five main channels, and those selling to the industrial market have four main options. Few manufacturers use only one marketing channel; most use combinations of two or more. Firms that sell to both the consumer and industrial market are in this classification, as are the many manufacturers who sell through both chain and independent outlets. Recognize, of course, that the actual situation is commonly more complex than that depicted in the diagram. The typical manufacturer of toothpaste, for instance, sells through both chain and independent outlets in the drug, grocery, variety, and department store fields.

Decisions concerning the selection of marketing channels are required more often than is commonly supposed. The obvious occasions are those following the initial organization of a manufacturing enterprise, and when additions to the product line are made. At such times, the relative desirability and appropriateness of the various channel options are discussed, and the selection is made (or should be) only after all factors influencing it are evaluated. However, at other times—even though the product line remains unchanged—continuous review and reappraisal of the channel system are advisable. Frequent shifts occur in the nature and comparative importance of the factors that governed the original selection. New market institutions appear, marketing innovations develop, the characteristics of markets change, and so on. Marketing is highly dynamic, and the relative effectiveness of various marketing channels is always changing. Consequently, one of the chief sales executive's responsibilities is not only to keep higher management fully apprised of changes in the factors affecting the marketing channels (both those currently used and those available), but also to call attention to the need for policy decisions.

The initial selection, or subsequent reevaluation, of marketing channels is essentially a problem in determining which channel, or channels, affords the opportunity for returning the greatest net profit to the enterprise. Channels, in other words, should be so chosen as to obtain the optimum combination of profit factors. This is no simple task. Neither maximum sales volume, nor minimum cost, should be considered alone; the most profitable combination of both must be sought. Furthermore, the time dimension also must be

[3]See, for example, E. W. Cundiff and R. R. Still, *Basic Marketing,* 2nd ed. (Englewood Cliffs, N.J.: Prentice-Hall, Inc., 1971); E. J. McCarthy, *Basic Marketing,* 4th ed. (Homewood, Ill.: Richard D. Irwin, Inc., 1971); and W. J. Stanton, *Fundamentals of Marketing.* 3rd ed. (New York: McGraw-Hill Book Company, 1971).

FIGURE 3.1

Marketing Channels Commonly Used in Industrial and Consumer Markets

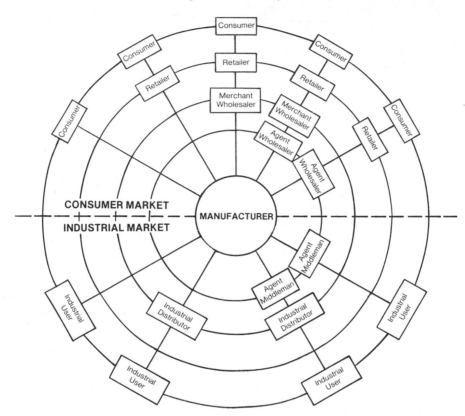

considered—management must look to the probable long-run effect as well as to the short-term impact upon net profits. The policymakers, then, should keep in mind all three profit factors—sales volume, costs, and resultant net profits—and they should consider the effect of different channel options and combinations on each factor over both short and long periods.

**Sales-Volume Potential.**   For each channel option, the basic question is: Can enough potential buyers be reached to absorb the desired quantity of product? The answers to such questions are found through market analysis. The raw data are secured from the company's own records, external sources of market statistics, and field investigations. When these data are analyzed, and after allowances have been made of the strengths of competitors, the potential sales volume of each channel option can be estimated. Among the most important factors influencing any channel's sales potential are the ability of the company's sales management, the excellence of its planning, and the skill with which it implements sales programs and campaigns. In appraising the sales potentials of alternative channels, therefore, one must assume that, regardless of the channel chosen, the sales-management functions will be performed with the same degree of managerial competence. In the absence of this assumption, comparisons of alternative channels have little meaning. It makes little sense, for instance, to compare a well-designed and skillfully executed plan for selling through wholesalers with a poorly designed and awkwardly executed plan for selling direct to retailers.

**Comparative Distribution Costs.** Most distribution-cost studies have shown that the costliest channels are the shortest ones. For instance, when a manufacturer decides to sell directly to the consumer, it assumes responsibility for the additional performance of marketing functions. It incurs larger expenses as it steps up its performance of such functions as selling, transportation, storage, financing, and risk bearing. If the manufacturer chooses to use the door-to-door direct-selling method, it faces, in addition, problems related to the selection, training, supervision, and general management of this class of sales personnel. If the manufacturer decides instead to open its own retail outlets, it has such added problems as selecting store locations and buildings, negotiating for leases, designing store fronts, obtaining equipment, arranging interior store layouts, managing retail personnel, conducting retail advertising, and procuring executives who are retail-minded. The manufacturer using short distribution channels has a higher gross margin to compensate for additional selling costs; but its net profits are often lower, because it may perform these functions less efficiently than the middleman. Most middlemen carry a broader line of merchandise, and their fixed costs are spread over more products. However, direct distribution has important nonfinancial advantages resulting from more intimate contacts with consumers and closer control over the conditions under which the product is sold. Nevertheless, before a manufacturer decides in favor of direct-to-the-consumer selling in any form, it should recognize that it will face a broader range of problems and incur additional distribution expenses. Furthermore, the shorter the channel, the more the manufacturer's selling costs will tend to be of fixed rather than of variable nature. This is important, especially in times of fluctuating sales volumes, because the break-even point is almost always higher when short marketing channels are used.

Direct sale is more common in the industrial field than in the consumer field. But the costs of selling directly, even to large buyers, are still high. In the industrial market, for example, many direct-to-user sales personnel need to possess considerable technical education; their training is long and expensive; and necessarily their compensation is high when compared to that of less qualified persons. Nevertheless, selling directly to industrial users enables the manufacturer to provide special attention to each customer's needs. In many cases, this advantage more than offsets the additional expenses involved.

The longer marketing channels result in lower selling costs for the manufacturer. When middlemen are used, they perform some functions that would otherwise be performed by the manufacturer. It is necessary to compensate the middlemen for performance of these functions and to provide them with the opportunity for net profit. Consequently, when a manufacturer switches from short to longer channels, its own gross margins are reduced. However, this usually is accompanied by a reduction in selling expense more than offsetting the loss in gross margin. Thus, the result of using indirect distribution is often higher profit per unit of product sold. In addition, the manufacturer shifts a wide range of problems to the middlemen and, in most situations, operates with a lower break-even point. However, the disadvantages of indirect distribution are (1) greater remoteness from final consumers, and (2) less control over the conditions under which the product is sold to them, which may produce lower sales volume.

**Net-Profit Possibilities.** Sales-volume potentials for various channels are meaningful only when considered in relation to the respective distribution costs. A channel with high sales potential might conceivably involve distribution costs so high that net profit is extremely low. A second channel might not produce a worthwhile sales volume, even though it involves extremely low distribution costs. For each alternative, total costs of distribution should be deducted from the estimated sales potential to determine the net-profit possibility present.

Those formulating policy on marketing channels must keep in mind the relation among gross margin, expenses, and net profit. High gross margins, such as those obtained by manufacturers using short channels, do not always mean higher net profits. Expenses of distribution, in the final analysis, are incurred for the performance of marketing activities. Choosing marketing channels, in essence, is a matter of determining the extent to which the manufacturer should perform these activities and the extent to which their performance should be delegated to middlemen. The rule should be: Determine which agency—the manufacturer or the middleman—can perform this particular activity most efficiently. If this rule is followed, the manufacturer's total costs of moving the product to final buyers should be lower, and its net profits are almost certain to be higher.

### Policies on Distribution Intensity

The manufacturer's choice of marketing channels affects, and is affected by, its policy on distribution intensity. At each level of distribution making up the channel, decisions must be made concerning the number of outlets to be utilized. Ordinarily it is advisable to decide first upon the policy to be followed at the distribution level nearest the final buyer, because that decision generally requires application of the same policy at other distribution levels. Once the policy on distribution intensity has been set, the chief sales executive's responsibility is to interpret and implement it. The chief sales executive, subordinate sales executives, and often even the sales personnel in the field must make decisions to use or not to use particular distributive outlets.

**Mass Distribution.**    The company following a policy of mass distribution obtains maximum sales exposure by securing distribution through all those outlets from which final buyers might expect to purchase the product. This is the policy used in distributing many consumer convenience items. Cigarettes, candy, and chewing gum, for instance, can be bought by consumers in food stores, drugstores, cigar stores, candy shops, variety stores, restaurants, theater and hotel lobbies, at newstands, and from vending machines in numerous other types of locations. Often, the manufacturer using this policy needs not one but several marketing channels. But even though the manufacturer may maintain a sizable sales organization, its sales personnel cannot possibly sell directly to all retail outlets. Consequently, the manufacturer must determine how large each account must be before it is sold directly. In areas where retail outlets are concentrated, the manufacturer may find that it can sell directly to all accounts, large and small; but, in other markets, such manufacturers generally find it necessary to secure distribution through wholesalers.

**Selective Distribution.**    Selective distribution involves selecting only those outlets that can best serve the manufacturer's interests. In a firm following a selective distribution policy, the chief sales executive sees to it that criteria are set up to provide guidance to subordinate sales executives and the company's sales personnel in their selection of accounts. These criteria relate to such matters as sizes of orders, volume of purchases, profitability, type of operation, and geographical location. In practice, the policy of selective distribution almost always represents, directly or indirectly, an attempt to make every account a contributor to net profit.

The basic procedure in applying a policy of selective distribution, then, is to set up criteria for the selection of accounts. An account analysis helps to identify the characteristics that differentiate profitable from unprofitable accounts. It may reveal that a fairly small percentage of the customers contribute a relatively large proportion of the total net sales and profits. It is not unusual for 20 percent of the accounts to be responsible for 80 percent of the net sales, and an even higher percentage of the net profits. But there are exceptions to the general rule that only profitable accounts should be retained or solicited. Some losing accounts may be retained because of long-standing relationships, and others because of their future promise. Furthermore, unprofitable accounts, if they contribute to the payment of overhead expenses, may add enough to sales volume to enable the firm to realize certain economies in manufacturing. Usually, however, it is possible to make savings through the elimination of most unprofitable accounts. One manufacurer of industrial tools, for example, found that it was losing money on almost one third of its dealers. By discontinuing sales to these dealers, it was possible to reduce the number of salespeople by almost one half. Through more effective use of the remaining sales staff and the surviving dealers, this manufacturer reduced selling costs from 32 percent of sales to 18 percent.

**Exclusive Agency Distribution.**   Exclusive agency distribution is an extreme form of selective distribution. To implement a policy of exclusive agency distribution the manufacturer makes an agreement, either written or oral, with a middleman in each market area stipulating that the distribution of the manufacturer's product or products within that area is to be confined solely to that middleman. Exclusive agencies are common in marketing such lines as automobiles, musical instruments, household appliances, machine tools, high-quality men's and women's shoes, and branded men's clothing and furnishings. In return for the exclusive right to sell the product line, the middleman is expected to provide more aggressive selling (and sometimes product service, as in the case of appliances) than under milder forms of selective distribution or under mass distribution.

For many years, most such agreements were mutually exclusive; that is, they required the exclusive dealer to refrain from selling competitive lines. Section Three of the Clayton Antitrust Act prohibits exclusive dealing when the effect is "to substantially lessen competition or tend to create a monopoly in any line of commerce."[4] Until 1949, court interpretation of Section Three was that exclusive dealing was not illegal unless the actual or probable monopolistic consequences of the agreements could be shown in court. However, in the Standard Oil Company of California case, the court made it clear that exclusive dealing contracts employed by the larger firms in an industry could result in a "substantial lessening of competition" and would likely constitute a violation of the antitrust laws.[5] The result has been to weaken the status of exclusive distribution, particularly of mutually exclusive contracts.

Implementing a policy of exclusive agency distribution presents a number of problems for the sales executive. In some markets the most desirable dealers may be under agreement with another supplier, and the company may have to select a second- or third-rate dealer or open up its own outlet. Furthermore, some middlemen want no part of an

[4]38 Stat. 731, 15 U.S.C. Sec. 14.
[5]*Standard Oil Company of California and Standard Stations, Inc.* v. *United States,* U.S. 793, 69 S.Ct. 1051 (1949), p. 1062.

exclusive agency contract, perhaps because of the history of exclusive agencies in the food field.[6] If exclusive distribution is used at the wholesale level, the wholesaler may not reach certain highly desirable outlets on the dealer level. In addition, it is sometimes difficult to sever relations with a middleman whose performance is unsatisfactory, and some middlemen accept an exclusive agency merely to deprive a competitor of it.

A policy of using exclusive agency distributors does, however, have a number of attractive features from the sales executive's standpoint. It should be fairly easy to develop distributor enthusiasm for the product and stimulate them to sell it aggressively. The manufacturer should be able to persuade the exclusive outlets to stock a more complete line and to service the product or handle repair and replacement parts. Relations between company sales personnel and the middlemen are likely to be of long duration and, after the agreements have been reached, salespeople can focus more on "servicing" and less on "selling." The sales force should, therefore, be able to spend more time assisting dealers in planning local promotions of the product. Not to be overlooked either is the fact that with exclusive distribution, the sales force can be smaller and subject to more effective supervision and control.

## PRICING POLICIES

Although the chief sales executive's role in formulating pricing policies generally is solely an advisory one, in almost all companies they bear the primary responsibility for implementation of pricing policies. The sales personnel in the field are, after all, the company employees whose jobs consist most directly of persuading buyers to accept the company's products at the prices asked by the company.

We shall discuss next the main types of pricing policies of direct interest to the sales department.

### Policy on Pricing Relative to the Competition

Every company has a policy regarding the level at which its products are priced relative to the competition. If competition is principally price-based, a company generally sells its products at the same price as its competitors. If there is nonprice competition, each company chooses from among one of three alternative policies, discussed next.

**Meeting the Competition.**   Meeting the competition is the most widely used policy. Companies competing on a nonprice basis simply meet competitors' prices, hoping thereby to minimize the use of price as a competitive weapon. A meeting-competition price policy does not mean meeting every competitor's prices, only the prices of important competitors—"important" in the sense that what such competitors do in their pricing may lure customers away.

**Pricing above the Competition.** Pricing above the competition is a less common policy but is appropriate in certain situations. Sometimes higher-than-average prices convey an impression of above-average product quality or prestige. Many buyers relate a product's quality to its price, especially when it is difficult to judge quality before actually buying. Almost always, the policy of pricing above the competition needs the support of

---

[6]It was formerly the practice of most manufacturers in the food field to grant exclusive agencies to grocery wholesalers. With the rise of corporate chains, most of these agreements were revoked and manufacturers either opened their own sales branches or made their lines available to all wholesalers in each market area.

strong promotion (both advertising and personal selling) by both the manufacturer and the middlemen.

One way in which the manufactuer using this policy obtains the strong promotional support of its dealers is by setting relatively high list prices on its products. These prices, the prices which the manufacturer suggests the dealers use in reselling the products, are set at levels that include above-average markups. Middlemen pass the higher markups on to final buyers in the form of higher prices, but increased support by the dealers of the manufacturer's product often more than offsets the sales-depressing tendency of the higher prices and may even increase total unit sales. For a product to compete successfully at a price above the competition, it must generally either be so strongly differentiated that buyers believe it to be superior to competitors' offerings, or middlemen must enthusiastically and heavily promote it. The manufacturer's sales personnel play key roles, of course, in securing this kind of promotion from the middlemen.

**Pricing under the Competition.** Not many manufacturers, at least those with sales forces, willingly follow a policy of pricing under the competition. However, some manufacturers, such as a number in the clothing industry, price under their competitors and appear to have demonstrated, at least to their own satisfaction, that aggressive pricing increases market demand appreciably and helps to keep new competitors from entering the field. Sales executives, quite generally, dislike this type of pricing policy and contend that it tends to cause sales personnel to sell price more than the product.

### Policy on Pricing Relative to Costs

Every company has a policy regarding the relationships between its products' prices and the underlying costs. Long-run sales revenues must cover all long-run costs, but short-run prices do not necessarily have to cover short-run costs. There are two main policy alternatives.

**Full-Cost Pricing.** Under a full-cost pricing policy, no sale is made at a price lower than that covering total costs, including both variable costs and an allocated share of fixed costs. The reasoning is that if prices cover short-run costs, they will also cover long-run costs. Nevertheless, rigid adherence to this policy is not only difficult but often ridiculously stupid: the price buyers are willing to pay may bear little or no relationship to the seller's costs, and there are complex problems involved in determining "real" costs. Furthermore, prices on items already in the inventory often must be cut below full cost in order to sell at all. Although most companies should seek to keep prices above short-run costs in *most* situations, they should also permit below-cost prices under certain conditions.

**Contribution Pricing.** A company with a contribution-pricing policy uses full-cost pricing whenever possible but will price, under certain conditions, at any level above the relevant incremental costs.[7] Suppose, for instance, that a seller is offered a special contract to supply a large buyer, who will not pay the going price. The buyer may argue that the price differential is justified because of savings to the seller in selling time, credit costs, handling expenses, and the like. Still, the demanded price concession may exceed the likely savings, so that total sales dollars from the proposed transaction is not enough to

---

[7]Incremental costs are those incurred in changing the level or nature of an activity—for example, making and/or selling a larger quantity of a product. Incremental costs may be either variable or a combination of variable and fixed costs.

cover total costs. In most such situations, the seller should accept the order *if* the resulting sales dollars are sufficient not only to cover all incremental costs but to make a contribution to fixed costs and/or profits. After all, current sales at the going price may already be large enough to cover the fixed costs, and the proposed sale at a special price will not raise fixed costs (assuming the incremental costs are all variable ones), so this sale need not bear an allocated share of fixed costs to yield net profit. In other words, as long as the proposed price more than covers the out-of-pocket costs of the transaction, the excess over these costs is profit. However, two important conditions should both be present for such offers to be accepted: (1) the company has the capacity and can put it to no more profitable use, and (2) the portion of the output sold below full cost is destined for a different market segment. Both conditions are important, but the second is critical to the continuance of prices at full cost or above for the bulk of the output.

### Policy on Uniformity of Prices to Different Buyers

Concerning the prices charged to different buyers, companies make a choice between following (1) a one-price policy, under which an item is offered for sale to all similar buyers at the same price, or (2) a variable-price policy, under which the price to each buyer is determined by individual bargaining. In the United States, most marketers of consumer goods adhere to a one-price policy, even though many do vary their prices among different classes of customers and from one geographic region to the next. The variable-price policy, however, is in common use wherever individual sales transactions involve large sums, as characteristically happens in marketing many industrial goods. The bargaining power of individual buyers varies with the size of the transaction and, as in the industrial market, a large buyer generally represents a greater potential for future business than a small buyer, so a seller may make price concessions to gain or retain the large buyer's patronage.

There are two main reasons why sales executives consider the one-price policy attractive: (1) since prices are not negotiated with individual customers, sales personnel need to spend only a minimum amount of time in discussing price and can devote nearly all their time to "creative selling"; and (2) there is less risk of alienating customers because of preferential prices given others. Furthermore, the existence of laws prohibiting price discrimination, such as the Robinson-Patman Act, make it safer legally for a marketer to apply a one-price policy than a variable-price policy.

### Policy on Resale Price Maintenance

A marketer distributing its products through middlemen follows a policy of (1) not attempting to suggest or maintain standardized resale prices on its products, or (2) seeking to control the prices at which middlemen resell its products. Such "resale price maintenance" may be either informal or formal. Informal resale price maintenance takes the form of suggesting resale prices to middlemen—perhaps by printing the price on the package or through suggestions made by the manufacturer's sales personnel. Formal resale price maintenance is effected by using the provisions of various states' "fair-trade" laws.[8] Informal price maintenance is easiest to implement when the marketer utilizes some form of selective distribution, inasmuch as the difficulties of enforcement of suggested

---

[8] In mid-1975, it appeared all but certain that the U.S. Congress would repeal the federal legislation that made "fair trade" legally permissible.

prices tend to multiply with increases in the number of middlemen handling the product. Marketers following policies of mass distribution, if they desire to maintain resale prices at all, generally find that they must take formal advantage of the resale-price-maintenance (fair-trade) laws of the various states.

## Policy on Use of Discounts

**Trade Discounts.**   A manufacturer selling to more than one class of middleman, such as both to wholesalers and retailers, may quote different prices, that is, offer different "trade discounts," to each class of customer. Under the federal laws prohibiting price discrimination, discounts, to be legal, must be made available on proportionately equal terms to all similar customers. Wholesalers and retailers are not similar customers; each group performs a different distributive function. For this reason, the law permits a manufacturer to charge a higher price to retailers than to wholesalers, even though some buyers in each class may buy in the same quantities. A company's policy on trade discounts depends on the importance (to the manufacturer) of each class of buyer and on the relative bargaining power of each class of buyer as a whole.

**Quantity Discounts.**   Quantity discounts are price reductions granted for purchases in a stated quantity or quantities, and are normally aimed to increase the quantities customers buy. Through such price reductions, sellers try to increase sales by passing on to buyers part of the savings that can result from large purchases. These savings can be considerable, for it may take little, if any, more of a salesperson's time to sell a very large order than to sell a small one. The same holds for order processing, order filling, billing, and transportation costs.

The firm using a quantity discount policy must keep two legal restrictions in mind: (1) the discounts must reflect actual savings—the price reduction can be no greater than the actual savings resulting from the larger quantity ordered; and (2) the discounts must be available on proportionately equal terms to all similar purchasers.

## Geographical Pricing Policies

One type of pricing policy of particular interest to sales executives is that regarding "who should pay the freight for delivering the product to buyers." The company's answer to this question is important to the sales executive, because it directly affects price quotations given to buyers in different geographical areas. In general, the farther away the customer is from the factory, the greater are the freight charges for a given size of order. No matter what policy the company adopts on this matter, freight differentials are reflected one way or another in price quotations. Likewise, regardless of the company's policy on payment of shipping charges, its administration is the sales executive's responsibility. There are three policy alternatives: (1) F.O.B., or "free on board" pricing, under which the customer pays the freight; (2) delivered pricing, under which the seller pays the freight; and (3) freight absorption, a compromise between F.O.B. and delivered pricing used in certain competitive situations but not described here in detail.

**F.O.B. Pricing.**   The marketer using this policy quotes its selling prices at the factory (or other point from which it makes sales), and buyers pay all the freight charges. Each buyer, in other words, adds the appropriate freight charges to the quoted F.O.B. factory price and thus determines the total delivered cost. Thus, F.O.B. pricing results in variations in the resale price that middlemen put on the product in different geographical areas. In consumer-goods marketing, F.O.B. pricing is widely used for items that are heavy or bulky relative to their value—for example, canned foods and fresh vegetables. In marketing such industrial goods as raw materials and heavy machinery, F.O.B. pricing is also in widespread use.

**Delivered Pricing.**   The marketer using a delivered pricing policy pays all freight charges and includes them in its price quotations to buyers. In other words, the price is really an "F.O.B destination" price, and the net return to the seller varies with the buyer's location. Delivered pricing generally is most appropriate when freight charges account for only a small part of the product's price. It is also usually a necessary policy when a marketer attempts to suggest or maintain resale prices. Standardized resale prices are most likely to be obtained if middlemen are assured of uniform markups, regardless of their location.

The simplest form of delivered pricing policy provides a uniform nationwide delivered price—sometimes called a "postage stamp" price. Makers of chewing gum,- candy bars, and many drug items, particularly patent medicines, use postage stamp pricing. Because under this policy all middlemen pay the same price to the manufacturer, the resale price should be roughly the same figure throughout the entire market.

A variation of delivered pricing is zone pricing, under which the market is divided into zones and different prices quoted to buyers in each zone, depending upon the zone's distance from the factory. The manufacturer still builds the freight charges into its quoted price (as in any delivered pricing policy), but it quotes different prices to buyers situated in different geographical zones.

### Policy on Price Leadership

All marketers should decide whether, as a matter of policy, they will initiate or follow price changes. In some industries there are well-established patterns of price leadership and following. In selling basic industrial materials, such as steel and cement, one company is the price leader and is usually the first to raise or cut prices; other industry members simply follow—or, sometimes, fail to follow, as sometimes happens in the case of a price increase, thus causing the leader to reconsider and perhaps to cancel the announced increase. Similar patterns exist in marketing such consumer products as gasoline and bakery goods, where, usually market by market, one company serves as the price leader and others follow. Generally, price leaders have rather large market shares and price followers, small market shares.

Even when final buyers (for example, ultimate consumers) are not particularly price conscious, most producers know that the middlemen handling their products are extremely sensitive to price changes. In response to even very small price changes, up or down, they will consider switching suppliers. Thus, even the marketer of a consumer product competing on a nonprice basis must be alert to impending price changes; the important policy question is whether to initiate or simply to follow price changes. The answer depends upon the marketer's relative market position and the image of leadership that it desires to build and maintain.

### Product-Line Pricing Policy

Pricing the individual members of a product line calls for certain policy decisions. The different items in a product line tend to "compete" with each other; that is, a buyer buying one member of the line usually does so to the exclusion of others. One policy decision relates to the amount of "price space" that should exist between the prices of individual members of the line. Having the right amount of price space is critical; too little may confuse buyers, and too much may leave "gaps" into which competitors can move and make sales. Sales executives contribute major inputs to this decision through their knowledge of the market, of buyers' motivations, and of competitors' offerings and prices.

Other important policy decisions concern the pricing of the "top" (highest-priced item) and the "bottom" (lowest-priced item) in the line. Generally, companies try to price the "in-between" members of the line so that they account for the greatest sales volume, using the bottom of the line as a traffic builder and the top of the line as a prestige builder. As the traffic builder, the lowest-priced item ordinarily affects the line's total sales far more than the price of any other item in the line. Price changes on it tend to directly affect the sales of other line members. A price increase on the traffic builder tends to cause higher sales on other line members. The same is true for the prestige builder: a change in the price of the top of the line also tends to strongly influence sales of other line members.

### Competitive-Bidding Policy

In purchasing certain products, industrial and governmental buyers customarily solicit competitive bids from several potential suppliers and award the business to the bidder offering the best proposal. A proposal may be selected as best for a number of reasons (for example, price, delivery dates, reputation for quality), depending on which is most important to the buyer. In some industries, competitive bidding is the general rule, and individual manufacturers have virtually no choice but to participate. But in other industries, only a part of the volume is sold on this basis, and each manufacturer must decide whether it is to its advantage to participate. For example, a typewriter manufacturer who sells to industry on a uniform price basis must participate in competitive bidding if it wants orders from governmental agencies (since government purchasing agents at all levels of government are ordinarily required to request competitive bids on most of their purchases). However, many manufacturers believe that competitive bidding reduces competition to almost entirely a price basis; consequently, they prefer to avoid this kind of business, unless the share of the total market involved is too large to ignore.

In companies that do participate in competitive bidding, the sales executive and the sales personnel play particularly important roles. Their close contact with the market puts them in a good position to estimate just how low a particular price must be to obtain the order. Furthermore, the long-term relationships developed between salespersons and their customers are very important in giving the company a chance to make a "second bid" in those cases where industrial buyers give favored suppliers the chance to meet lower bids submitted by competitors. This chance does not exist in competitive bidding for government business, where closed bids are usually specified (that is, all bids are opened at the same time and there is no chance for high bidders to adjust their quotes downward). But an effective salesperson can often remove competition from closed government bids by persuading the purchasing agent of the value of a differentiating characteristic of the product so that the purchasing agent will include this characteristic in the written specification supplied to potential bidders.

## CONCLUSION

A company's sales policies directly and importantly influence the sales executive's job and effectiveness. They provide the sales executive with guidance in drafting plans for achieving the organization's personal-selling objectives, in organizing the sales effort, in managing the sales force, and in controlling the sales effort. Sales executives in various companies play different roles in deciding sales policies, but in all companies they bear the main responsibility for implementing such policies. Deciding what to sell (product policies) and who to sell to (distribution policies) shapes the basic nature of a company and sets the pattern for its sales-force operations. Pricing policies are important to sales executives because their subordinates, the sales staff in the field, are expected to persuade target buyers not only to accept the company's products but at the prices asked. Sales executives, then, play a highly critical role in implementing sales policies in the field—of making them work in ways that facilitate achievement of personal-selling objectives.

# 4

# Formulating
# Personal-Selling Strategy

A company's competitive posture in the marketplace is determined both by its overall marketing strategy and by the effectiveness with which this strategy is implemented. Management shapes various features of the company's competitive posture as it makes key marketing decisions on products (what to sell), distribution (who to sell to), pricing, and promotion (how to sell). Marketing management's task is to unify the company's product, distribution, pricing, and promotion policies and strategies into an appropriate overall marketing strategy—that is, into a deliberately planned competitive posture. Sales management's task is to plan and implement the personal-selling aspects of promotional strategy.

Sales management seeks to achieve the company's personal-selling objectives both through its sales policies and through its personal-selling strategy. Sales policies provide the general guidelines for making decisions on the personal-selling effort, while personal-selling strategies are adaptations of sales policies, individualized tailorings of personal-selling decisions to fit particular marketing situations. Formulating personal-selling strategy requires management to make key decisions on (1) the kind of sales personnel needed, and (2) the size of the sales force. Ultimately, however, it is the salespeople in the field who adjust and adapt personal-selling strategy to fit individual customers; and the composite performance of the entire sales force determines the extent to which the company achieves its overall personal-selling objectives.

## COMPETITIVE SETTINGS AND
## PERSONAL- SELLING STRATEGY

Different industries provide different types of competitive settings within which individual companies must operate. From industry to industry there are important differences with respect to whether the industry is new or old and whether the number of competitors is small or large. Economists identify four basic kinds of competitive settings: (1) no direct competition, (2) pure competition, (3) monopolistic competition, and (4) oligopolistic competition. The various components of overall marketing strategy assume different levels of importance in each of these competitive settings. In the discussion that follows, note particularly how the personal-selling component of overall marketing strategy varies in importance with each kind of competitive setting.

### No Direct Competition

Neither the monopolist nor the company marketing a radically new and different product in its market-pioneering life-cycle stage has direct competitors. But both the monopolist and the innovating marketer have indirect competitors; both must vie with sellers in other industries for the same prospects' interest and buying decisions, the monopolist on a long-term basis and the innovating marketer for the limited period it has free from direct competition. Both the monopolist and the innovating marketer must initiate and stimulate primary demand—that is, demand for the product category—through promotional (personal selling and advertising) strategies aimed to influence final buyers and middlemen. Both need distribution strategies providing for marketing channels, middlemen's cooperation, and the product's physical distribution; and the putting into effect of these distribution strategies requires the effective implementation of personal-selling strategy in terms of both kind and number of sales personnel. Both require a pricing strategy; the monopolist (at least in theory) being free to maximize profits through "charging what the traffic will bear"; the innovating marketer choosing between either a price-skimming or a penetration-pricing strategy, depending mainly upon how soon it expects direct competitors to enter the market. Here, too, putting into effect the chosen pricing strategy calls for the effective implementation of personal-selling strategy by sales executives and sales personnel alike. Further, both the monopolist and the innovating marketer seek to integrate their individual product, distribution, promotion (including personal selling and advertising), and pricing strategies into overall marketing strategies (that is, competitive postures) consistent with their long-term goals. Such consistency is obtained only when all elements of overall strategy are "in balance."

### Pure Competition

Economists define pure competition as a market setting with large numbers of buyers and sellers, none of whom is powerful enough to control or to influence the prevailing market price. In this definition, the economist assumes, among other things, that (1) no single buyer or seller is so large relative to the market that it can appreciably affect the product's total demand or supply; (2) all sellers' products are identical in every respect, so buyers are indifferent as to which sellers they buy from; (3) no artificial restraints on prices of any kind exist (there is no governmental price fixing or administering of prices by individual companies, trade associations, labor unions, or others); and (4) all buyers are always informed about all sellers' prices.

If these assumptions held true in the real world, there would be no need for a company to concern itself with marketing strategies of any kind. Each seller would be too small to gain business through price cutting at the expense of its competitors, and if it did cut the price, they would immediately match the cut. No seller could compete by offering a "better" product, because product differentiation is ruled out. It would be futile for a seller to push its product through personal selling or stimulate its sale through advertising or other promotion, inasmuch as all potential buyers are already fully informed and buy only on the basis of price. Because the economist also implicitly assumes that sellers and buyers are in direct contact, no seller would need to worry about marketing channels or physical distribution. Under the type of competitive setting visualized in the economist's definition of pure competition, there would be no need for marketing strategies of any kind. In this competitive setting, then, there also would be no need for personal-selling strategy or for sales personnel. The real world contains no known instances of industries operating under conditions of pure competition, and we need not concern ourselves further here with this kind of competitive setting.

### Monopolistic Competition

Most modern marketers in most situations operate in competitive settings under conditions that approximate monopolistic competition, which means that some or all of the assumptions of pure competition do no hold. More precisely, monopolistic competition exists when there is a large number of sellers of a generic kind of product but each seller's brand is in some way differentiated from every other seller's brand. Furthermore, under monopolistic competition, it is comparatively easy for additional competitors to enter the market, such as for retailers to enter as private-label competitors. This competitive setting describes that of many products during late phases of their market growth and during much of their market-maturity life-cycle stages.

Nearly every seller's brand of product, whether it be nailpolish remover or pet food, can be differentiated (at least in final buyers' minds) from competing brands. Most ultimate consumers appear convinced that different brands of even such "identical" products as aspirin, table salt, and flour are not exactly alike, providing individual marketers with opportunities to build brand preferences among buyers and hence to control a share of the market. Furthermore, most ultimate consumers (and even many industrial users) are not really fully informed—frequently not even adequately informed—about the offerings of competing sellers. Sellers of such products seek to differentiate their "market offerings" through individualizing one or several components of overall marketing strategy. Unique packaging may serve to differentiate the product (for example, table or picnic-sized shakers of salt); an unusual distribution method, such as house-to-house selling of cosmetics, may serve to differentiate the product's distribution; various pricing gimmicks, such as "cents-off" pricing and fair-trade pricing, may differentiate the product's pricing; but usually the main way in which sellers of products that are in the market-growth and market-maturity stages differentiate them is through promotional strategy. Advertising is used to differentiate the brand in the minds of final buyers and to stimulate selective demand, while personal selling sees to it that the desired distribution intensity is secured and maintained and that middlemen provide the needed "push" in the product's behalf.

Competitive settings characterized by monopolistic competition provide not only marketing opportunities but clearly require skill in planning and implementing overall marketing strategy. Whereas the key element in the overall marketing strategy for such products is the ability to differentiate the product, even if ever so slightly, in some way(s), appropriate promotional strategy (usually some blend of advertising and personal selling) is the critical element in implementing such an overall marketing strategy. In this type of competitive setting, advertising's role appears most often to be that of relating market messages to final buyers, while personal selling's role is that of servicing the distribution network and stimulating promotional efforts by the middlemen.

### Oligopolistic Competition

Increasing numbers of marketers operate under conditions approximating oligopolistic competition, a competitive setting within which the number of competitors is small enough that they are individually identified and known to each other and it is difficult for new competitors to enter the market. Each competitor is a large-enough organization and has a large-enough market share that changes in its overall marketing strategy have direct repercussions on the others. Each marketer in an oligopolistic industry must weigh the possible reactions of each of its competitors in formulating and implementing its own overall marketing strategy. Oligopolistic competition tends to develop in the marketing of many products either during a late phase of their market growth or an early phase of their market maturity.

In the United States oligopolies exist in such industries as automobiles, appliances, soap and detergents, and shoes in the consumer-goods field, and in steel, aluminum, textile machinery, and machine tools in the industrial-goods field. There is a strong trend for the more successful firms to keep on growing, and for the less successful to fail or disappear (through merger). The soap and auto industries provide dramatic examples, both having been reduced from numerous competitors to a very small group in fairly recent times. Although governmental authorities try continually to discourage the merger movement as a threat to "free competition," the drift toward oligopoly continues but through the slower process of expansion by the successful, and failure or withdrawal by the others.

Oligopoly produces the most aggressive kind of competition. When a few large companies dominate an industry, the competitive moves of any one can significantly affect the entire market. When, for instance, one competitor introduces a new variation of a basic product (such as a new scent in hand soap), the other competitors risk a rapid loss in market share if they do not respond appropriately and almost at once. For this reason, competitors' actions are watched closely, and marketing changes by one firm are almost certain to be matched or otherwise countered by its competitors. Changes in one competitor's product, in its distribution, in its promotion—if they hold some promise of increasing its market share—are imitated, improved upon, or otherwise countered by its competitors as rapidly as they can launch their counteroffensives. Price changes by individual industry members can be and often are matched by others almost immediately. Industry-wide price adjustments are often made so quickly that they appear to result from collusion, when, in fact, there has been none whatever. Personal selling strategy under oligopolistic competition plays important roles in building and maintaining dealer cooperation, in servicing the distribution network, and in gathering information on competitors' activities. Again, as happens under monopolistic competition, promotional strategy generally features both advertising and personal selling, with both playing highly critical roles, particularly with respect to the successful implementation of overall marketing strategy.

## PERSONAL-SELLING OBJECTIVES AND PERSONAL-SELLING STRATEGY

Personal-selling objectives, as brought out in Chapter 2, are of two broad types, qualitative and quantitative. The qualitative objectives vary importantly and directly with the kind of competitive setting and mainly concern the nature of the contribution management expects personal selling to make in achieving overall long-term company objectives. Qualitative personal-selling objectives influence both the nature of the sales job (that is, the kind of sales personnel needed) and the size of the sales force. For instance, a company that expects its salespeople to do the entire selling job (as when it has no other elements in its promotional mix) needs a different kind of sales staff, and a larger staff, than a company which expects its salespeople only to "service" already existing accounts and backs them up with heavy advertising. Qualitative objectives usually are long-term objectives and are carried over from one promotional period to the next. But when a qualitative objective is changed, it involves changing the nature of the sales job and usually the size of the sales force as well.

In contrast to the qualitative personal-selling objectives, the quantitative objectives assigned to personal selling are short-term and are adjusted from promotional period to promotional period. The sales-volume objective—the dollar or unit sales volume that management expects the company to obtain during a particular promotional period—is by far the most critical quantitative personal-selling objective. Regardless of the competitive setting within which a company operates, if it has a quantitative personal-selling objective at all, it will be one relating to the sales volume desired for the period. Most companies, too, benefit from assigning other types of quantitative objectives to personal selling, as, for instance, one directing that sales volume be obtained in ways that contribute to profit objectives (for example, by selling the "proper" mix of products). In monopolistic and oligopolistic competitive settings, most companies assign still other types of quantitative objectives, including ones specifying the securing and/or retaining of a certain market share. Quantitative personal-selling objectives have direct implications both for the nature of the sales job and the number of sales personnel needed. For instance, a company that increases its sales-volume objective significantly must also expect its sales force to do a more effective selling job (that is, to change the nature of their job) or expect to increase the number of salespeople or, perhaps, expect to do both.

## SALES POLICIES AND PERSONAL-SELLING STRATEGY

Sales policies are the guidelines set up by management within which the company is to seek to reach both its qualitative and quantitative personal-selling objectives. They provide general guidance with respect to what to sell (product policies), who to sell to (distribution policies), and the terms of sales (pricing policies). Decisions on what to sell and who to sell to not only shape the fundamental nature of a company but are important determinants both of the kind of sales personnel needed and their total number (the two components of personal-selling strategy). Pricing policies, too, have an important impact, especially on the kind of sales staff needed—salespeople in the field are the ones who have to persuade target buyers not only to accept the company's products but at the prices asked. The exact nature of sales policies, like personal-selling objectives, vary somewhat with the competitive setting of the industry, but it is of critical importance that they be apropriate to a company's particular situation under conditions of monopolistic or oligopolistic competition.

## DETERMINING THE KIND OF SALES PERSONNEL NEEDED

Management makes one of its two key decisions on personal selling strategy when it decides the kind of sales force that the company should employ. A clear determination of the kind of salesperson required is an important prerequisite to recruitment and selection. There is a great diversity among selling jobs, ranging from truck-driver route selling to selling complex industrial installations such as lathes and presses. Different selling jobs require different levels of selling ability, training, and technical knowledge, and unique marketing factors (such as the nature of the products, buying practices and motivations of customers and prospects, and strengths and weaknesses of competitors) cause each company in each industry to have individualized requirements as to the kind of salesperson best fitted to serve its needs.

In determining the kind of sales staff best fitted to serve a company's marketing needs, we must thoroughly understand what its salespeople will be expected to accomplish —the objectives of their jobs and the tasks necessary to achieve them. Knowing the salesperson's job means knowing the particular job for the particular salesperson, knowledge that enables management to avoid "putting square pegs into round holes." It helps management, in other words, in fitting the job to the person and the person to the job.

### Product-Market Analysis

No one person is capable of selling all kinds of products to all kinds of customers. In one situation, an individual may be trained to sell one or a few products to many kinds of customers. In a second situation, the same individual may be trained to sell a wide line of products to one or a few kinds of customers. It is possible to hire, or to hire and train, salespeople either as product specialists or as market specialists. An advisable step in analyzing the sales job, then, is to delineate the precise nature of product-market interactions. One way is to construct a "product-market grid," as illustrated in Figure 4.1. In actual use, of course, such grids are constructed showing much finer details of product-

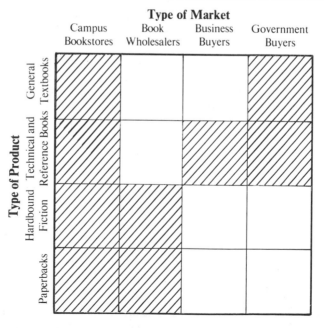

FIGURE 4.1
Product-Market Grid for a Book Publishing Company

market interactions; this demands thorough analysis and classification both of markets and products. Note that the various product-market "boxes" on the grid indicate the different customers who might be sold the different products. As management decides which customers should be sold which products, some boxes are blacked in, others left empty. The result helps answer the question: Should our sales personnel be product specialists, market specialists, or a combination? Product specialization usually is indicated when the product is highly technical, requiring salespeople to advise on uses and applications. Market specialization generally is called for when the product is nontechnical but different kinds of customers have unique buying problems, require special sales approaches, or need special service. In many cases detailed study of product-market grids reveals that sales personnel need not only considerable knowledge of the product line and its applications but skill in dealing with various kinds of customers.

In addition to product-market interactions, other elements in a company's marketing situation may affect the caliber of salesperson required. If most customers are large, for instance, salespeople may need different talents than if most customers are small. Sometimes, too, the geographical location of a territory has a bearing on the best type of salesperson for it, particularly where local prejudice exists in favor of "natives," as opposed to "outsiders." If management considers these or similar elements important, it may be advisable to construct appropriate grids to assist in the analysis.

### Analysis of Salesperson's Role in Securing Orders

The nature of the role that a company expects its sales personnel to play in securing orders influences the kind of sales staff it should have. Even though all salespeople must seek orders aggressively in some situations while in others they need only take orders coming their way, the relative emphasis on order taking and order getting varies in different kinds of selling environments. The driver-salesperson for a soft drink bottling company is primarily an order taker, because the product has been strongly presold to consumers and retailers reorder automatically. The encyclopedia salesperson calling on householders most often functions as an order getter, since getting the order is this salesperson's main goal. If the promotional strategy of a manufacturer is to rely heavily upon advertising to attract business and build demand, marketing channels are likely to include several layers of middlemen, and the role of the manufacturer's salesperson is likely to be that of order taker primarily and order getter only incidentally. The opposite situation obtains when advertising is used mainly to back up personal selling—marketing channels contain a minimum number of layers of middlemen, and the salesperson's role is chiefly one of order getting. Depending on whether promotional strategy places major reliance on personal selling or advertising, salespeople may be either active or passive forces in securing orders.

There are cases both in consumer-goods and industrial-goods marketing in which the salesperson plays only a minor and indirect role in securing orders, the salesperson's major role being concerned with other matters. In consumer-goods marketing, the missionary salesperson's major role is to assist middlemen in their efforts to make sales to their customers. Orders from customers, then, result indirectly, rather than directly, from the missionary salesperson's efforts. In industrial-goods marketing, the "sales engineer" plays two major roles: (1) advisor to middlemen and customers on technical-product features and applications, and (2) design consultant to middlemen and industrial users on installations or processes incorporating the manufacturer's products. Sales engineers, then, also secure orders indirectly, rather than directly, and as the result of playing their major roles as advisors and design consultants.

### Choice of Basic Selling Style

Differences in many marketing factors cause each company to have rather individual-ized requirements as to the kind of salesperson that is best for it to have in its employ. These differences cause each company to expect its own sales staff to play somewhat unique roles (at least in some respects) even relative to "similar" companies employing "similar" kinds of sales personnel. Nevertheless, it is revealing to group sales job roles into a limited number of categories. Specifically, sales roles can be grouped into four basic styles of selling that cut, to a large degree, across industry and company boundaries: trade selling, missionary selling, technical selling, and new-business selling.[1]

**Trade Selling.**   The trade saleperson develops long-term relations with a relatively stable group of customers. For the most part, this style of selling is low key with little or no pressure, and the job tends to be rather dull and routine. This selling style, which pre-dominates in marketing food and apparel and in wholesaling, applies primarily to products that have well-established markets. In such cases, advertising and other forms of promo-tion are often more important components of overall marketing strategy than is personal selling. One important responsibility of the trade salesperson is to help customers build up their volume through giving them promotional assistance. For example, the salesperson for a line of breakfast cereals devotes much time to promotional work with retailers and wholesalers—taking inventory, refilling shelves, suggesting reorders, setting up displays, and the like.

**Missionary Selling.**   The missionary salesperson's responsibility is to increase the company's sales volume by assisting customers with their selling efforts. The missionary salesperson is concerned only incidentally with securing orders, since the orders obtained result from the missionary's primary public relations and promotional efforts with customers of the customers (indirect customers). The missionary salesperson's job is to persuade indirect customers to buy from the company's direct customers. For example, the salesperson for a pharmaceutical manufacturer calls on retail druggists to acquaint them with a new product and to urge them to stock it. Thus, the missionary seeks to persuade them to buy from drug wholesalers, who are the company's direct customers. In some situations, missionary sales staff members call on individuals and institutions who do not buy the product themselves but who influence its purchase by others. The medical "detail man" who calls on doctors and hospitals to acquaint them with new drugs is an example. Missionary selling, like trade selling, is low key and generally does not require high-level technical training or ability.

**Technical Selling.**   The technical salesperson deals primarily with the company's established accounts, and the main job objective is to increase their volume of purchase by providing technical advice and assistance. The technical salesperson performs advisory functions similar to those of the missionary salesperson but, in addition, this type of sales-person normally sells direct to industrial users and other buyers. The technical salesperson devotes considerable time to acquainting industrial users with technical characteristics of products and with product applications and to helping them design installations or

[1]D. A. Newton, "Get the Most Out of Your Sales Force," *Harvard Business Review*, Vol. 47, No. 5 (September-October 1969), pp. 131-141.

processes that incorporate the company's products. In this style of selling, the ability to identify, analyze, and solve customers' problems is important. Technical salespeople often specialize, either by products or markets. In selling heavy made-to-order installations, such as steam turbines and electric generators, different technical salespersons work with different items in the product line. Other technical salespeople specialize in servicing either industrial accounts or government procurement agencies.

**New-Business Selling.** The new-business salesperson's main responsibility is to find new customers—that is, to convert prospects into customers. The salesperson specializing in new-business selling needs to be unusually creative and ingenious and possesses a high degree of resourcefulness. Few companies, however, have sales personnel who do nothing but new-business selling; most firms expect their regular sales staff, who primarily do trade selling, to do new-business selling also. However, since it is rare for the same individual to possess both needed sets of talents and because there is a common tendency for salespeople to neglect new-business selling in favor of servicing established accounts, some experts advocate the specialization of sales personnel into two separate groups, one to concentrate on retaining existing accounts, and the other to focus on converting prospects into customers.[2]

## DETERMINING THE SIZE OF THE SALES FORCE

Management makes the second of its two key decisions on personal selling strategy when it decides the size of the sales force that the company should have. Having determined the kind of salesperson that should best fit the company's needs, management must now determine how many such salespersons should be employed to meet the company's sales volume and profit objectives. If the company employs too few salespersons, opportunities for sales and profits go unexploited, and if it employs too many, excessive expenditures for personal selling (even though they may bring in additional sales dollars) reduce net profits. In practice, it is extremely difficult, perhaps impossible, to determine the exact number of salespersons that a particular company should have; however, there are three basic approaches used in approximating this number: (1) the work-load method, (2) the sales-potential method, and (3) the incremental method. Each approach provides needed insights on the "right size" of sales force, although none produces a definitive answer to the "how-many-salespersons" question.

### Work-Load Method

In the work-load method of determining sales-force size, the basic assumption is that all sales personnel should shoulder equal work loads. Management first estimates the total work load involved in covering the company's entire market, then divides by the work load that an individual salesperson should be able to handle, thus determining the total number of salespeople required. Companies applying this approach generally assume that the interactions of three major factors—customer size, sales-volume potential, and travel load—determine the total work load involved in covering the entire market.[3] There are six steps involved in applying the work-load approach, as shown in the following example:

[2]G. N. Kahn and A. Shuckman, "Specialize Your Salesmen!" *Harvard Business Review,* Vol. 39 No. 1 (January-February 1961), pp. 94-95.

[3]See W. J. Talley, Jr., "How to Design Sales Territories," *Journal of Marketing,* Vol. 25, No. 3 (January 1961), p. 7.

1. *Classify customers, both present and prospective, into sales-volume-potential categories.* (Classification criteria, other than sales volume or sales-volume potential, can be used as long as it is possible to distinguish the differences in selling effort required for each class.) For purposes of this example, assume that there are 880 present and prospective customers, classified by sales-volume potential as follows:

| | |
|---|---|
| Class A—large | 150 accounts |
| Class B—medium | 220 |
| Class C—small | 510 |

2. *Decide on the length of time per sales call and desired call frequencies on each class.* (Several inputs are used in making these two decisions—for example, personal judgment, the opinions of sales personnel, and actual time studies). For purposes of this example, assume that both present and prospective customers require the same amounts of time per sales call and the same frequencies per year as follows:

Class A:  60 minutes/call x 48 calls/year  = 48 hours/year
Class B:  30 minutes/call x 24 calls/year  = 12 hours/year
Class C:  15 minutes/call x 12 calls/year  =  3 hours/year

3. *Calculate the total work load involved in covering the entire market.* In our example, this calculation is:

Class A:  150 accounts x 48 hours/year  = 7,200 hours
Class B:  220 accounts x 12 hours/year  = 2,640 hours
Class C:  510 accounts x  3 hours/year  = 1,530 hours
                                      Total        11,370 hours

4. *Determine the total work time available per salesperson.* Suppose that management decides that salespeople should work 40 hours per week, 48 weeks per year (allowing 4 weeks for vacations, holidays, sickness, etc.), then each salesperson has available

40 hours/week x 48 weeks  =  1,920 hours/year

5. *Divide the total work time available per salesperson by task.* Assume that management specifies that sales personnel should apportion their time as follows:

| | | |
|---|---|---|
| Selling tasks | 45% | 864 hours |
| Nonselling tasks | 30 | 576 |
| Traveling | 25 | 480 |
| | 100% | 1,920 hours |

6. *Calculate the total number of salespeople needed.* This is a matter of dividing the total market work load by the total selling time available per salesperson:

$$\frac{11,370 \text{ hours}}{864 \text{ hours}} = 13 + \text{ salespeople needed}$$

The work-load approach to determining the size of the sales force is attractive to practicing sales executives. Perhaps, the main reasons are that it is easy to understand

and easy to apply to practical situations. Such large firms as Celanese, IBM, and AT&T all have been reported to use this approach.[4]

However, there is an inherent flaw in the work-load approach. As usually applied, this approach disregards profit as an explicit consideration; but, of course, it is possible for management to take profit criteria into account in determining lengths and frequencies of sales calls. In appraising this approach, P. Kotler concludes that:

> The optimality of the overall solution depends upon management's accuracy in estimating appropriate call frequencies for different-size accounts. Actually, desirable call frequencies depend on aspects other than account size, such as the probable response of the account to additional effort, the costs of servicing, and the gross margin on the product mix purchased by the account.[5]

Still another shortcoming inherent in this approach lies in the assumption that not only all sales personnel should have the same work load but that they all can and will utilize their time with equal efficiency. Although a relation exists between the amount of time spent on calling on an account and the size of the order received, some salespeople are able to accomplish more in a shorter time than others can. In other words, as experienced sales executives assert, the "quality of time invested in a sales call" is at least as important as the "quantity of time spent on a sales call."

### Sales-Potential Method

The sales-potential method of determining the size of the sales force is based on the assumption that performance of the set of activities contained in the salesperson's job description represents one sales-personnel unit, not necessarily that of any particular salesperson. A particular salesperson may represent either more or less than one sales-personnel unit. If the individual's performance is excellent, that individual may do the job of more than one unit; if the individual's performance is below par, he or she may do less. However, if management expects all company sales personnel to perform as specified in the job description, then the number of salespersons required equals the number of units of sales personnel required. Generally, it must be noted, sales job descriptions are constructed on management's assumption that they describe what the average salesperson with average performance will accomplish. With that assumption, then, one can estimate the number of dollars of sales volume that each salesperson (that is, each sales-personnel unit) should produce. Dividing this amount into forecasted sales volume—the company's sales-volume objective—and allowing for sales-force turnover results in an estimate of the number of salespeople needed. These relationships are summarized in the equation

$$N = \frac{S}{P} + T(S/P)$$

This reduces to

$$N = \frac{S}{P}(1 + T)$$

---

[4]M. A. Brice, "Art of Dividing Sales Territories," *Dun's Review* (May 1967), p. 93; R. F. Vizza, *Measuring the Value of the Field Sales Force* (New York: Sales Executives Club of New York, Inc., 1963), pp. 23-24.

[5]P. Kotler, *Marketing Management: Analysis, Planning, and Control,* 2nd ed. (Englewood Cliffs, N.J.: Prentice-Hall, Inc., 1972), p. 710.

where

$N =$ number of sales-personnel units
$S =$ forecasted sales volume
$P =$ estimated sales productivity of one sales-personnel unit
$T =$ allowance for rate of sales-force turnover

Consider, for example, a firm with forecasted sales of $1 million, estimated sales productivity per sales-personnel unit of $100,000, and an estimated annual rate of sales-force turnover of 10 percent. Inserting these figures in the equation, we have

$$N = \frac{\$1,000,000}{\$100,000} \times 1.10$$

$$N = 11 \text{ sales-personnel units}$$

This is a highly simplified model for determining the size of a sales force. It does not, for instance, include the lead times required for seeking out, hiring, and training salespeople up to the desired level of sales productivity. Actual planning models have built-in lead and lag relations to allow for such requirements. If two months of full-time training are required to bring a new salesperson up to the desired productivity, recruiting must lead actual need for the new salesperson by two months. Another assumption implicit in this simple model is that sales potentials are identical in all territories, which is similar to the assumption that the number of sales-personnel units required is the same as the number of salespersons needed; where this assumption does not hold, the model should be adjusted accordingly.

Difficulties in making estimates for this model vary both with the factor being estimated ($N$, $S$, $P$, or $T$) and with the company. The crucial estimate for the sales productivity of one unit of sales manpower relies heavily on the accuracy and completeness of the sales job description; it depends also on management's appraisal of what reasonably may be expected of those who fill the position. Estimating the sales-force-turnover rate is mainly a matter of reviewing previous experience and anticipating such changes as retirements and promotions. Both the estimates for unit sales productivity and the sales-force-turnover rate require management to have some means of evaluating the efficiency of individual salespersons, and of determining the probabilities that individuals will remain with or leave the sales force during the planning period.

The estimate for forecasted sales volume deserves special comment. In many situations, the magnitude of the sales forecast is itself influenced by the planned size of the sales force. Indeed, since it takes time to add significant numbers to the sales force, a realistic sales forecast must take into account the number of salespersons (or sales-personnel units) likely to be at management's disposal during the planning period. In a new and rapidly growing company, potential sales volume often depends chiefly on the number and ability of its sales staff. Then management actually may derive its sales forecast by multiplying the estimated sales productivity of its average salesperson by the number it has, can expect to keep, and can recruit and train during the planning period. By contrast, as a company expands distribution geographically and its growth rate slows down, the procedure reverses itself. Under these circumstances, the number of sales-personnel units required is determined by making the sales forecast first, and dividing this by the expected sales productivity of an individual salesperson, making adjustments in the process for anticipated sales-force turnover, lead times for recruiting and training, and other relevant factors.

## Incremental Method

The incremental method represents the most conceptually correct approach to the problem of determining the size of the sales force. It is based on one main proposition: net profits will increase when additional sales personnel are added *if* the incremental sales revenues exceed the incremental costs incurred. Thus, to apply this method, one needs two important items of information, incremental revenue and incremental costs.

To illustrate the application of the incremental method, assume this situation. A certain company has found that its total sales volume varies directly and significantly with the number of salespeople it has in the field. Its costs of goods sold do not vary significantly with increases in sales, but hold steady at 65 percent of sales. All company sales personnel receive a straight salary ($10,000 annually per person) and in addition are paid commissions of 5 percent on the sales volume they generate. In addition, each salesperson receives a travel and expense allowance of $6,000 per year, that is, $500 per month. The company now has 15 people on its sales force and wants to determine whether it should add additional staff. Its sales executives have estimated that the following increases in sales volume, costs of good sold, and gross margin would result from the addition of the sixteenth, seventeenth, eighteenth, and nineteenth salespersons:

| With the Addition of Salesperson No.: | There Will Be Additional | | |
|---|---|---|---|
| | Sales Volume of: | − Cost of Goods Sold of: | = Gross Margin of: |
| 16 | $200,000 | − $130,000 | = $70,000 |
| 17 | 150,000 | − 97,500 | = 52,500 |
| 18 | 100,000 | − 65,000 | = 35,000 |
| 19 | 50,000 | − 32,500 | = 17,500 |

The next step is to calculate the *net profit contribution* resulting from the addition of each salesperson, as summarized in the following table:

| With the Addition of Salesperson No.: | There Will Be Additional | | | | |
|---|---|---|---|---|---|
| | Gross Margin of: | − Sales Salaries of: | + Commissions of: | + Travel and Expense Allowances of: | = Net-Profit Contribution of: |
| 16 | $70,000 | − ($10,000 | + $10,000 | + $6,000) | = $44,000 |
| 17 | 52,500 | − ( 10,000 | + 7,500 | + 6,000) | = 29,000 |
| 18 | 35,000 | − ( 10,000 | + 5,000 | + 6,000) | = 14,000 |
| 19 | 17,500 | − (10,000 | + 2,500 | + 6,000) | = −1,000 |

Adding the eighteenth salesperson results in an additional net profit contribution of $14,000, but adding the nineteenth salesperson produces a negative net profit contribution of $1,000. Thus, in this illustration the optimal size of sales force is 18 people.

Although this method is the most conceptually correct, it is also the most difficult to apply in the real world. It requires, first, that the company develop a sales-response function which can be used to approximate (in terms of sales volume) the market's behavior in relation to alternative levels of personal-selling effort. A sales-response function is a quantitative expression which describes the relationship between the amount of personal-selling effort and the resulting sales volume. For the response function to be a useful tool in setting the size of the sales force, sales volume must be sensitive to changes in the number of sales personnel.[6] Not many companies yet have the degree of research sophistication required for the development of sales-response functions, but there is some evidence that companies are beginning to apply the basic concept.[7] Furthermore, doubt exists that the incremental method is applicable in situations where personal selling is not the primary means of making sales—that is, in cases where other forms of promotion, such as advertising, have stronger influences on sales volume than does personal-selling effort. Two additional problems in applying this approach are noted by T. R. Wotruba: "It fails to account for possible competitive reactions as well as for the long-term 'investment' effect of personal selling effort."[8]

## INDIVIDUALIZING SELLING STRATEGIES
## FOR EACH CUSTOMER

Ultimately, the acid test of the basic appropriateness of personal-selling strategy comes when particular salespeople interact with particular customers. From the composite of all such interactions evolves the company's achievement of its personal-selling objectives. Management makes one critical decision on personal-selling strategy when it determines the kind of salesperson best fitted to serve the company's marketing needs. It makes another critical decision when it determines the number of salespeople that should make up the company sales force. But after these two key decisions are implemented—after the desired number of the desired kind of sales personnel have been recruited, trained, and assigned to the field—each salesperson must individualize his or her own dealings with each customer. The job, when boiled down to its essentials, is to influence customer behavior in ways that both benefit the customer and contribute to the achievement of the company's personal-selling objectives.

Regardless of whether the salesperson's major role is that of order getter or order taker and regardless of the "basic selling style," the extent of the salesperson's success (in performing the job) still depends on the outcome of interactions with the customers. Each time the salesperson comes into contact with a customer, the salesperson says certain things, does certain things, and behaves and reacts in certain ways to what the customer says and does. What the salesperson says and does and how the salesperson behaves and reacts to the customers' behavior should, and generally does, vary from one

---

[6] On this point and for an interesting report on a research study utilizing this approach, see Z. V. Lambert, *Setting the Size for the Sales Force* (University Park, Pa.: The Pennsylvania State University, 1968), especially pp. 4-7.

[7] See, for example, C. D. Fogg and J. W. Rokos, "A Quantitative Method for Structuring a Profitable Sales Force," *Journal of Marketing,* Vol. 37, No. 3 (July 1973), pp. 8-17.

[8] T.R. Wotruba, *Sales Management* (New York: Holt, Rinehart and Winston, Inc., 1971), p. 171.

sales call to the next. The nature of the variation in the salesperson's approach to each customer, of course, is a matter of selling skill. This skill is a function of both how good the salesperson's preplanning of each sales call has been and performance on the call itself. In doing the preplanning, the highly skilled salesperson analyzes a great deal of information about the customer and the nature of its business. What are its key objectives and problems? Who in the customer's organization makes and influences buying decisions, and what are their aspirations, needs, motives, fears, anxieties, drives, and the like? What rival sales personnel from what companies compete for the account's orders, and what are they like? After analyzing these and similar items of information, the skilled salesperson sets definite goals to accomplish on each call made to each customer. Next, the skilled salesperson plots the selling strategy to use on each successive call in an effort to achieve these definite goals—that is, what the salesperson plans to do and when. Then the salesperson makes the scheduled sales calls. If all goes according to plan, the salesperson achieves the goals set for each call, and thus the salesperson contributes to the achievement of the company's overall personal-selling objectives.

While the individual members of the sales force ultimately determine the success or failure of the company's overall personal-selling strategy, sales management has the important responsibility for helping them develop and improve their selling skills. How effectively salespeople perform their assigned tasks, in other words, is closely related to sales management's effectiveness in providing them with instruction on sales techniques. (Chapter 12 is devoted entirely to this important topic.)

## CONCLUSION

Personal-selling strategy involves the implementation of sales policies to achieve personal-selling objectives. Formulating personal-selling strategy requires analysis of a company's competitive posture to determine the kind of salesperson needed and the size of the sales force. Personal-selling strategy ultimately must be individualized for each customer and prospect; each salesperson, in the final analysis, determines how and when to do what in the contacts with each assigned customer. Although management makes the key decisions on personal-selling strategy, each salesperson determines (through the quality of the job performance) the effectiveness of that strategy in achieving the company's overall personal-selling objectives.

# Cases for Part I

## I-1.  SCRIPTO, INC. (A):
## Manufacturer of Writing Instruments—
## Relationship Between Sales and Marketing

Scripto, Inc.'s "19¢er" fiber-tip pen, released in 1972, figured prominently in the company's marketing plan. The 19¢er was introduced to reestablish Scripto's reputation within the writing-instrument industry and to help improve the company's financial situation. Scripto's major objective for the 19¢er was to achieve a 15 percent share of the market in dollar sales by the end of 1973, nearly two years after the pen's introduction.

### WRITING-INSTRUMENT INDUSTRY

Although writing instruments were used in early Egyptian times, the most rapid developments took place in the twentieth century. During the first half of the century, the fountain pen was extremely popular. It was with the invention of the ballpoint pen in 1945, however, that the writing-instrument industry began its rise to the multimillion dollar level ($281 million in 1971), with ballpoint-pen sales alone totaling $160 million (1.3 billion units) in 1971. In late 1963, when the Japanese entered the American writing market with the 49-cent Pentel fiber-tip pen, American firms set out quickly to produce an equivalent product before the Japanese could secure a major share of the market. Despite a shorter writing life than the ballpoint pen, porous-tip pens rapidly achieved consumer acceptance. From 1965 to 1971, porous-tip-pen sales soared from $15 million to $60.7 million and were expected to increase 20 percent per year for several years thereafter. Exhibit 1 shows dollar sales of the various types of writing instruments from 1951 to 1971, and Exhibit 2 shows the average price by product for the same period.

### SOFT-TIP PEN MARKET

The number of soft-tip-pen manufacturers had increased each year after 1963 until, by 1972, there were nearly forty such manufacturers. Gillette's Papermate Division domi-

EXHIBIT 1
Manufacturers' Sales of Writing Instruments
by Product for the Period 1951-1971

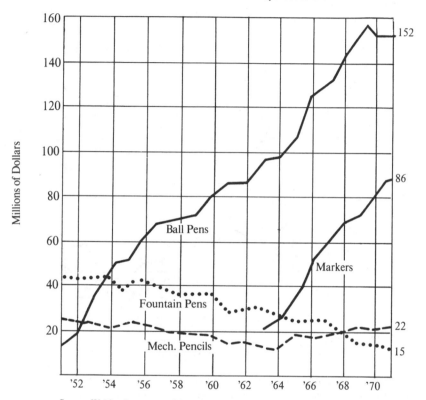

Source: Writing Instruments Manufacturers Association.

nated the market with its Flair pen through 1971, achieving 49 percent of the market sales. In early 1972, Scripto introduced its 19¢er fiber-tip pen, in July, BIC introduced its Banana, and also in July, Papermate followed with its Write Brothers pen. Thus began the largest marketing and advertising war the porous-tip-pen industry had yet experienced. Whereas the entire industry had spent only $2.7 million for advertising in 1971 (Flair accounted for $2 million of that total), Scripto spent nearly $750,000, BIC $3 million, and Papermate more than $1 million for Write Brothers during the first ten months of 1972 to promote the entry of low-priced porous-tip pens into the market.

All soft-tip pens were of similar appearance. The shaft and the cap of the pen were plastic and of the same color as the ink inside the pen (except for the BIC Banana, which had a yellow shaft). Scripto and Flair had twelve colors, while BIC and Write Brothers offered ten. Scripto's 19¢er was 30 cents cheaper than Flair's 49-cent retail price and 10 cents less than the BIC Banana and the Write Brothers markers.

The fiber-tip pen market consisted of two principal segments: students and in various business usages. Advertising, which mainly appeared on network and spot television and also in newspapers and magazines, focused on these groups by emphasizing themes of individuality, distinction, and a pleasant experience from writing with porous-tip pens.

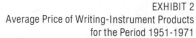

EXHIBIT 2
Average Price of Writing-Instrument Products
for the Period 1951-1971

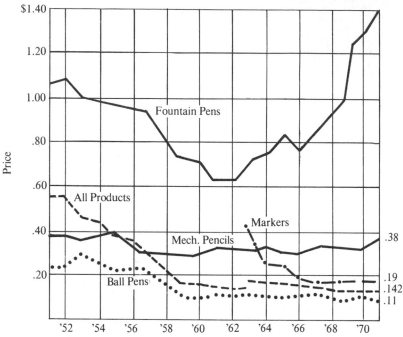

*All product lines adjusted in 1963 to include calculation for markers.
Source: Writing Instruments Manufacturers Association.

Approximately 22 percent of annual writing-instrument sales occurred between mid-August and the end of September, or during the back-to-school rush.

## SCRIPTO, INC.

Scripto was initially incorporated as the Atlantic Manufacturing Company in 1923 and adopted the Scripto name in 1946. The company originally produced only mechanical pencils but gradually expanded its product line to include, besides mechanical pencils, ballpoint pens, fiber-tip pens, ink, components for its pens (one of the few writing-instrument manufacturers to offer this), lighters, and even wide-angle camera lenses. In 1969, Scripto acquired the Butane Match Corporation of America. Notwithstanding foreign subsidiaries in Mexico, Canada, England, and Ireland, Scripto's Atlanta Division was its largest, most important operation, as well as being the company's headquarters. Scripto was the world's largest combined manufacturer of pens and lighters.

Until the late 1950s, Scripto was successful and profitable in the writing-instrument industry. However, owing to managerial shortcomings and ill-advised decisions on capital expenditures and new products at a time when heavy competition made such decisions crucial, the company began to slide downward. By 1964, Scripto's share of the writing-instrument market had declined to 10 percent from a high of 16 percent a few years earlier. At the same time, Scripto dropped from second to fifth place in sales volume.

After 1964, under new management, Scripto spent heavily to improve production facilities, diversified its investments, reorganized management personnel and positions, and gave new emphasis to the marketing program. The result was a reversal of Scripto's slide, with sales increasing by 40 percent in two years, 1964 to 1966. However, the revival was short-lived, because, from 1968 through 1970, the company operated at an average annual loss of more than $800,000, with the losses of each of the last two years at well over $1 million. In 1971, Scripto again was profitable, earning just over $20,000 net income. Indication that the company's financial crisis was over came in 1972, when Scripto had a net income of $239,467 on net sales of $28,378,819. Exhibit 1 shows the net-sales and net-income figures for Scripto, Inc., for the 11-year period 1962-1972.

EXHIBIT 1
Net Sales and Net Income for Period 1962-1972

| Year | Net Sales | Net Income |
|------|-----------|------------|
| 1972 | $28,378,819 | $ 239,467 |
| 1971 | 30,979,108 | 20,012 |
| 1970 | 31,928,975 | (d) 1,074,558 |
| 1969 | 31,229,204 | (d) 1,183,335 |
| 1968 | 30,914,857 | (d) 173,145 |
| 1967 | 30,462,424 | 715,777 |
| 1966 | 33,494,076 | 1,149,324 |
| 1965 | 28,714,981 | 1,546,138 |
| 1964 | 25,237,265 | 801,748 |
| 1963 | 26,344,306 | 1,536,181 |
| 1962 | 25,750,279 | 1,705,889 |

Source: *Moody's Industrials,* 1973.

### Scripto's Fiber-Tip Pens and Sales Strategy

Scripto first entered the fiber-tip market with the 49-cent Graffiti pen, which essentially was a "me-too" product. Other than the connotation of the name itself, the Graffiti had no single distinguishing feature. The trade was somewhat reluctant to accept it, because it meant carrying a product that lacked the seling power of the heavily advertised Flair. Graffiti's annual advertising budget was approximately $250,000. Scripto then began to search its resources for a porous-tip pen that would have greater appeal to the ultimate consumer, bolster the company's sagging writing-instrument business, and be profitable.

Consequently, in early 1971, Scripto started development of a fine-line marker that would equal Flair in quality, yet retail for considerably less. Within one year Scripto determined that it could produce large quantities of the new marker, sell it for 19 cents at retail, and still allow the standard margins for middlemen (10 percent for the wholesalers and 50 percent for the retailers), money to promote the product, and profit for the company. Scripto decided to adopt the same price and distribution strategy in marketing its new fiber-tip pen as Marcel L. Bich had so successfully applied when he introduced the BIC 19-cent stickpen in the late 1950s. Bich's successful application of this strategy had revolutionized the writing-instrument industry and transformed the ballpoint pen from a luxury item (the average retail price in the late 1940s and early 1950s exceeded $1.00) to a utility item. His success was indisputable; in 1971, sales of BIC pens accounted for 65 percent of all retail pen sales and amounted to $39.5 million.

Scripto's philosophy behind the pricing strategy was to sell a quality pen for considerably less than the competitors. It was believed that the low price would entice consumers to buy the pen if only to try it, and then the high quality of the pen would serve to secure repeat purchases from initial buyers. The rationale was that, after trying the 19¢er and realizing that it was a marker of quality equal to the higher-priced fiber-tips, yet at a much lower price, consumers would readily switch to the Scripto product. Therefore, by switching from a more expensive to a less costly pen, the consumer would lose nothing and save the difference between the purchase prices. Although the lower retail price meant less revenue per sale for the merchant and the manufacturer, the key to maintaining or increasing profits was to increase sales volume commensurately.

Distribution strategy was to introduce the product regionally rather than nationally, ensuring that orders, deliveries, advertising, and sales were well timed and coordinated and functioning smoothly in one region before moving to the next. By selling to general-line wholesalers who dealt with numerous retailers, the company could achieve extensive distribution throughout the region. As the product became established in the target regions and sales increased, the company could expand its advertising budget to foster greater product awareness among consumers and improve its production facilities to attain greater economies of scale. Management believed that, ultimately, these investments would stimulate sales even more.

### Test Marketing the 19¢er

Scripto enjoyed a particularly good relationship and reputation with the writing-instrument trade in the Dallas-Fort Worth area and its products had always sold well there. Consequently, Scripto selected that area to test market the new fiber-tip and gauge the applicability of the BIC-type strategy to the porous-tip-pen market. The test began with two weeks of intensive personal selling. This was followed by four weeks of spot television advertising. Scripto also began and ended the four-week period with a full-page newspaper advertisement.

The test was much more successful than the company had anticipated. Scripto was surprised and encouraged to discover from several retailers that customers were not saving the difference between purchase prices of the 19¢er and Flair, as had been expected In fact, in the test market, consumers spent as much as or more money than they had previously because of the lower price. Instead of buying one Flair pen for 49 cents, they bought three or four 19¢ers. The retailers also reported that the consumers were buying the unconventional colors, including green, yellow, olive, gray, orange, pink, brown, purple, and turquoise, in greater quantities than anticipated. When the first several retail displays containing the nine unorthodox colors proved insufficient to accommodate consumer demand, Scripto doubled the proportion of these colors and reduced the number of reds, blacks, and blues accordingly.

The favorable results in the Dallas-Fort Worth test market prompted the company to select thirty-two other markets for introducing the 19¢er. Scripto chose these thirty-two markets by synthesizing (1) the company's ranking of the cities in which Scripto products had sold best in the past with (2) the report of a marketing research firm, W. R. Simmons and Associates Research, Inc., detailing the demographics of fiber-tip users, as based upon actual surveys. The result was a list of markets in which Scripto felt the chances of successfully introducing the 19¢er were the greatest.

## Scripto's Sales Force

Scripto, Inc., had fifty salaried salespeople based in the major metropolitan areas throughout the country. There were two types of salespeople: (1) detail salespeople, who visited and sold to local buyers, checked displays, and the like, and (2) district salespeople, who contacted and sold to regional and national buyers. Most Scripto salespeople were between 25 and 35 years of age or 45 and above, with few in between these age groups. Generally, the older salespeople obtained the majority of their purchase orders from established accounts, whereas the younger staff tended to establish accounts with new clients. The sales force dealt directly with several chain-store buyers, but the majority of accounts were sundry merchandise jobbers who resold to varied classes of retailers. All sales personnel handled the entire Scripto line of writing instruments and lighters. In 1972, the company decided to supplement its detail sales force with part-time, salaried salespeople working 30 hours per week.

## Relationship Between Sales and Marketing

In the past, Scripto had placed greatest emphasis on sales. This often resulted in the overall marketing plan being formed around the sales plan, with marketing relegated to a position of less significance than sales. For example, although budgetary restraints also were an important consideration, the company eliminated marketing research. From 1968 through 1970, the advertising program was greatly curtailed. In addition, there was no system of monthly sales forecasts to assist marketing planning and production scheduling efforts. To the extent that marketing plans were formulated, they were verbal, short-range, and largely intuitive.

Since there was somewhat of a preoccupation with sales at the expense of marketing, there was no marketing-orientation, or systems-concept, thinking uniting the various elements of the marketing mix into a coordinated program. Scripto management was determined to implement a conceptually sounder marketing program for the 19¢er and therefore was deeply concerned about the most effective relationship between sales and marketing.

*In your judgment, with reference to the Scripto 19¢er, what should have been the relationship between sales and marketing? Propose a plan in detail.*

## I-2.   SALES AND MARKETING EXECUTIVES
## OF GREATER BOSTON, INC.:
## Sales and Marketing Management Association—
## Proposed Salesman-for-a-Day Program

The Executive Committee of Sales and Marketing Executives of Greater Boston, Inc., was considering a proposal under which students from several area colleges would each spend a day with SME-member company sales personnel to gain better insight into the world of selling. SME of Greater Boston was a local chapter of SME-International, a worldwide association with about 30,000 members. SME of Greater Boston had over 200 members, representing 190 companies.

Stuart Freeman, president of the Boston chapter, received the proposal for a "Salesman-for-a-Day" program from Tom Alden, a member of the marketing faculty at a local college. Several months previously Freeman and Alden had discussed together some of the problems in getting more college students interested in selling careers.

Alden mentioned that the majority of his students had no appreciation or feeling for selling simply because they had never done any. Also, it was his opinion that, among many college students, selling was considered a low-prestige job. As a result, he reasoned, many qualified graduates never even consider a career in selling. Alden then set about to develop a program through which college students could at least become familiar with the life of a personal salesman and gain some understanding of what selling is about. The result was his proposal, entitled "Salesman-for-a-Day," which he submitted to Freeman in the hope that the Boston SME chapter would consider it.

Under Alden's plan, sales executives of the various Boston SME-member companies would be contacted by mail, using SME-letterhead stationery, and asked to participate by identifying one or more salespeople who would agree to have a college student accompany them on their calls for a day. The salespeople then would be mailed a form on which they were to indicate the date, time, and place of meeting with the student. A student would be selected and his or her name forwarded to the participating salesman (which also served as confirmation that the plan was still on). Every effort would be made to assign a student to a salesman who sold a product or service of interest to the student. Finally, the student would meet the salesman and accompany him for the entire day. It was envisioned that the whole procedure, from contacting the sales executive to notifying the salesman of the name of the student and confirming the date, time, and place of meeting, would take no more than two weeks. If done at the beginning of the semester, ample time was guaranteed to arrange a time convenient to both the salespeople and the students.

While the initial program was to be strictly voluntary, Alden felt that each student should complete a questionnaire indicating the value of the salesman-for-a-day program to determine whether the program should be continued. Alden also foresaw the day when the salesman-for-a-day program would be made into a requirement for the selling and sales management courses that he taught. Further, he also had the idea that he could run a parallel sales executive-for-a-day program, if the proposed program met with success.

Alden was enthusiastic as to the possibilities of his salesman-for-a-day plan. Freeman shared that enthusiasm, especially since he had been searching for innovative programs to be pursued by the Education Committee. He believed this was a "natural" for that committee, and he agreed to present the proposal, with one amendment, to the Executive Committee for possible adoption. The amendment was that three of the participating people, a sales manager, a salesperson, and a student, would be invited to one of the regular monthly SME dinner meetings to discuss the results of the salesman-for-a-day program with the membership.

*Should the Boston SME chapter have adopted the proposal? Why or why not?*

## I-3.   COFFREY TOOL COMPANY:
## Manufacturer of Small Tools—
## Sales-Forecasting Procedure

The Coffrey Tool Company manufactured a wide line of quality electric power tools that were sold both for construction use and to the "do-it-yourself" market. Through merger and by carrying forward a program of product diversification, the product line was expanded to include not only portable electric tools but various models of saws, sanders, drills, and planes, and, most recently, electric lawn mowers. In addition, contracts and subcontracts were occasionally accepted for the production of items ordered by agencies of the federal government, including the Department of Defense. In the middle of the year, the manager of marketing research was reviewing company experience with various forecasting procedures, the relation between the sales forecast and the setting of territorial sales quotas for sales personnel, and other aspects of sales-forecasting practice within the company.

The sales force of eighty-five people was assigned to eight selling districts throughout the United States, with each individual responsible for sales within a specific territory composed of a group of contiguous counties. These territories were so arranged that the market potential for each was of approximately the same size; but, partly because of geographical variations in competitive position, some territories accounted for significantly larger sales volumes than others. Sales personnel were paid a base salary, which was adjusted according to length of service and individual bargaining power, plus a 2 percent commission on sales.

The sales-forecasting procedures were essentially of the breakdown type, but the method used for linking the overall sales forecast with territorial sales quotas had varied. For many years, sales quotas were established simply by adding 15 percent to the sales forecast for each territory. The result was that many salespeople experienced considerable difficulty in meeting their quotas; indeed, the sales-force turnover rate had shown a tendency to rise with each succeeding year. One executive had pointed out that it was theoretically impossible under this system for all salespeople to make their quotas, inasmuch as the company could not expect to ship 15 percent more output than had been scheduled for production.

Subsequently, a new policy was adopted: Sales personnel were assigned quotas equal to the sales forecasts for their territories. The overall company sales forecast was broken down into territorial sales forecasts according to the percentage share of total company sales achieved in each territory over a period of several past years. Salespeople who were consistently below their quotas for several years were dismissed unless there were extenuating circumstances of sufficient magnitude to account for the variation from the desired level of performance. Under the new system of quota determination, it became imperative to achieve the highest possible degree of forecasting accuracy.

The sales force sold the product line directly to retail dealers. The marketing research department had performed a number of distribution cost studies and had verified the wisdom of this distribution policy. The total cost of maintaining the sales force, including salaries and commissions, amounted to 8.5 percent of sales; whereas, if wholesalers had been used, an additional 20 percent discount off list price would have been necessary. Executives were of the opinion that, besides the apparent cost saving, direct selling provided better control and resulted in more aggressive retail promotion of the product line.

In preparing the tentative company sales forecast, the manager of marketing research placed some emphasis on the general economic outlook. In making this forecast, he considered such factors as size of population, gross national product, number of families, Federal Research Board index of industrial production, disposable income, housing and utility expenditures, home starts, steel production, and volume of construction activity. He was well acquainted with and made extensive use of generally available statistical data and other information contained in publications of different governmental agencies and in various trade papers and business magazines. In addition, to obtain expert opinions on general economic and trade conditions, he held frequent discussions with economic consultants employed by trade publications. The manager of marketing research believed that the forecast should reflect the overall economic situation, as well as the outlook for the industry.

The manager of marketing research had recently initiated a system under which the ultimate purchasers of Coffrey products filled out and returned warranty cards. These cards were designed in such a way that the company was able to learn a good deal about the characteristics of ultimate buyers. Analysis of the cards indicated that, on the average, 75 percent of all Coffrey products were sold to persons connected with the home construction industry. Thereafter, the manager of marketing research was convinced that the amount of home-building activity was an essential factor to consider in making the sales forecast.

The manager of marketing research had prepared correlation tables comparing Coffrey's total sales with home starts, automobile production, and gross national product (see Exhibit 1). Simple and multiple correlations by product line and total sales failed to reveal other significant correlations. It was concluded, therefore, that activity by the company and its competitors was more important than minor fluctuations in these economic series. Nevertheless, trends in these series were considered by executives in adjusting the final sales forecast.

In developing the yearly operating forecast, the marketing research department started by analyzing product trends. Sales trends for each major product were projected, after consideration had been given to new and replacement products of the company and its competitors. On the average, the sales life of an individual product or model was five years. However, difficulty was experienced in predicting the point at which sales of a

EXHIBIT 1
Correlation of Coffrey Sales with Economic Factors

A. *Coffrey Sales vs. Gross National Product (past 8 years)*

| Year | Sales | Percent Change | GNP (in billions of $) | Percent Change |
|---|---|---|---|---|
| 1 | $ 6,858,000 |  | 258 |  |
| 2 | 10,520,000 | plus 53 | 285 | plus 10 |
| 3 | 11,083,000 | plus 5 | 329 | plus 15 |
| 4 | 10,294,000 | minus 7 | 347 | plus 5.4 |
| 5 | 12,365,000 | plus 20 | 367 | plus 5.7 |
| 6 | 11,935,000 | minus 3.4 | 376 | plus 2.4 |
| 7 | 14,780,000 | plus 24 | 383* | plus 1.8 |
| 8 | 17,145,000 | plus 16 | 388* | plus 1.2 |

*Estimated figure.
Summary, eight years: gross national product, plus 50%; Coffrey sales, plus 150%.

B. *Coffrey Sales vs. Auto Production*

| Year | Sales | Percent Change | Auto Production | Percent Change |
|---|---|---|---|---|
| 1 | $ 6,858,000 |  | 5,119,000 |  |
| 2 | 10,520,000 | plus 53 | 6,665,000 | plus 30 |
| 3 | 11,083,000 | plus 5 | 5,338,000 | minus 20 |
| 4 | 10,294,000 | minus 7 | 4,320,794 | minus 19 |
| 5 | 12,365,000 | plus 20 | 6,121,787 | plus 41 |
| 6 | 11,935,000 | minus 3.4 |  |  |
| 7 | 14,780,000 | plus 24 | 8,700,000 |  |
| 8 | 17,145,000 | plus 16 |  |  |

C. *Coffrey Sales vs. Home Starts*

| Year | Sales | Percent Change | Home Starts | Percent Change |
|---|---|---|---|---|
| 1 | $ 6,858,000 |  | 1,025,000 |  |
| 2 | 10,520,000 | plus 53 | 1,396,000 | plus 36 |
| 3 | 11,083,000 | plus 5 | 1,091,300 | minus 21 |
| 4 | 10,294,000 | minus 7 | 1,127,000 | plus 3.3 |
| 5 | 12,365,000 | plus 20 | 1,103,000 | minus 2.1 |
| 6 | 11,935,000 | minus 3.4 | 1,220,000 | plus 10 |
| 7 | 14,780,000 | plus 24 | 1,200,000* | minus 1.6 |
| 8 | 17,145,000 | plus 16 | 1,200,000 | 0.0 |

*Estimated figure.

product or model would start to decline. The appearance of new products or models often shortened the life of some old product, but the exact effect of such changes could not be predicted accurately. When the sales forecasts for the individual products were totaled, the result was the tentative overall sales-forecast figure for the company.

EXHIBIT 2
Illustrative Sales Forecasts—Coffrey Tool Company

| Product | This Year* | Tentative Forecast (Marketing Research Dept.) | Revised Forecast (Marketing Research Dept.) | Forecast (Sales Manager) | Forecast (General Manager) |
|---|---|---|---|---|---|
| A | 4,127,425 | 4,572,000 | 4,572,000 | 4,191,000 | 4,572,000 |
| B | 3,021,525 | 3,111,500 | 2,984,450 | 2,984,500 | 2,979,420 |
| C | 2,659,634 | 2,832,100 | 2,609,850 | 2,209,800 | 2,703,830 |
| D | 818,549 | 914,400 | 914,400 | 914,400 | 914,400 |
| E | 693,737 | 1,018,000 | 952,500 | 952,500 | 977,900 |
| F | 114,178 | 101,600 | 101,600 | 101,600 | 164,485 |
| G | 210,976 | 222,250 | 222,250 | 222,250 | 272,415 |
| H |  | 889,000 | 622,300 | 622,300 | 889,000 |
| Total | 11,646,024 | 13,658,850 | 12,979,350 | 12,198,350 | 13,473,430 |

*Periods 1-7 actual plus present forecast of periods 8-13.

As soon as the marketing research department finished the tentative sales forecast, it was forwarded together with supporting documents to the sales manager, the general manager, and the president. Based upon summary information, the tentative sales forecast, and their own knowledge and understanding of market conditions, each of these executives made an individual sales forecast for the coming year. Normally, the president accepted the forecast made by the general manager, but sometimes he made slight adjustments on the basis of his special knowledge. Exhibit 2 illustrates the product and total sales forecasts made by the marketing research department, the sales manager, and the general manager. Changes suggested by top management were usually based upon differences of opinion about the general economic outlook.

The forecasts made by the sales manager, general manager, and president were then returned to the marketing research department, where the final revised forecasts were put together. In revising the overall sales forecast and individual product forecasts, the manager of market research referred to an industry forecast based on data supplied by the Electric Tool Institute. These data included sales by units and dollars for all major electric tool products by sizes; but these figures, of course, were not identified. By applying estimated share-of-the-market percentages to the industry forecast, it was possible to derive cross-check forecasts for the company's total sales and its sales by individual product. After the forecast had been put in final form, it was returned to the general manager, who customarily approved it without further change.

The operating sales forecast finally agreed upon was broken down for the thirteen four-week "operating periods" in the year, and dispatched to the production department as a production order. The production department added a 50 percent overload to the figures for the start of the year but made later compensations for orders received and shipments as the year progressed. In Exhibit 3, the year's quota figures are compared with actual orders received for last year and this year. Forecasts for total company sales had usually been within 10 percent of actual sales, but forecasts for sales of individual products during individual four-week periods had been as far off as 30 to 40 percent. Exhibit 4 shows a comparison of orders received by products and sales quotas for operating period 6 and for the first six months of the current year.

Because of problems in production scheduling, revisions in the forecast were made four operating periods (sixteen weeks) ahead of the time of actual manufacture. Because of the lead time required for ordering and receiving materials purchased from outside sources, changes in the production schedule could not be effected in any shorter period. Changes in the production schedule were made only during the first ten operating periods of the year, after which time the schedule was considered firm. Any changes requested after the close of the tenth operating period were taken into account in making the sales forecast for the succeeding year. Exhibit 5 illustrates how changes were made in the production schedule for various products and models; Exhibits 6 and 7 show part of the revisions made in product sales forecasts. Revisions of the operating forecast were made every four weeks.

To aid in making adjustments in the operating forecast, a panel of representative

EXHIBIT 3
Orders Received, Compared with Quota for This
Year and Orders Received Last Year

**Hundreds of Thousands of Dollars**

LEGEND

Orders received this year

Quota this year

Orders received last year

**Operating Periods (four weeks each)**

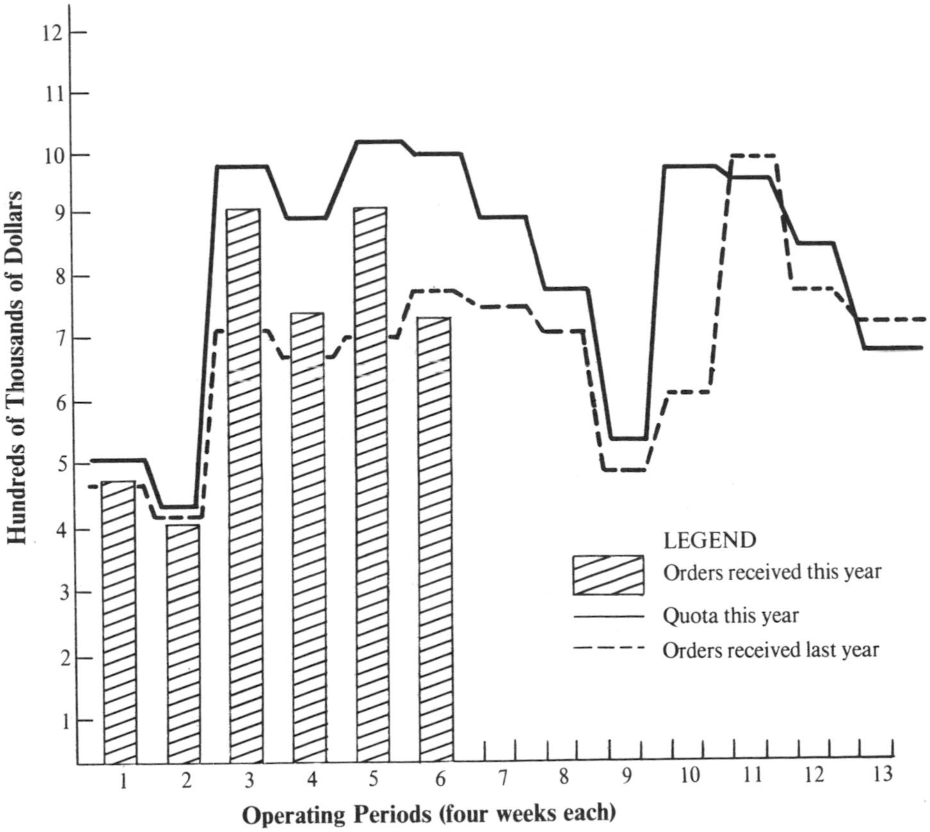

EXHIBIT 4
Operating Period 6, This Year

| Product | Sales Quota | Orders Received | Difference | Percent |
|---|---|---|---|---|
| A | $ 623,453 | $382,249 | $241,204 | 61 |
| B | 228,258 | 169,898 | 58,360 | 74 |
| C | 161,532 | 111,922 | 49,610 | 69 |
| D | 71,419 | 41,638 | 29,781 | 58 |
| E | 66,230 | 59,960 | 6,270 | 91 |
| F | 35,598 | 23,541 | 12,057 | 66 |
| G | 55,485 | 91,500 | 36,015 | 165 |
| H | 11,826 | 13,779 | 1,953 | 117 |
| Total | $1,253,801* | $894,487 | $359,314 | 71 |
| Private brand | 14,884 | 3,105 | 11,779 | 21 |

*$104,375 orders from branches included in above figure.

Cumulative 1 Through 6 Months

| Product | Sales Quota | Orders Received | Difference | Percent |
|---|---|---|---|---|
| A | $2,205,475 | $1,780,503 | $ 424,972 | 81 |
| B | 1,251,412 | 1,044,418 | 206,994 | 83 |
| C | 945,470 | 710,293 | 235,177 | 75 |
| D | 340,639 | 281,917 | 58,722 | 83 |
| E | 529,170 | 386,024 | 143,146 | 73 |
| F | 200,036 | 164,797 | 35,239 | 82 |
| G | 543,507 | 612,862 | 69,355 | 113 |
| H | 90,159 | 88,092 | 2,067 | 98 |
| Total | $6,105,868* | $5,068,906 | $1,036,962 | 83 |
| Private brand | 77,609 | 40,349 | 37,260 | 52 |

*$545,664 from branches included in above figure.

dealers had recently been organized. The dealers who composed this panel were considered key accounts and were responsible for approximately 10 percent of Coffrey's total sales. Dealers sent in monthly inventory figures on the entire Coffrey line, and this provided executives with an indication of the trend of events at the retail level. It was contemplated that eventually the information received from this panel would be more useful in making adjustments in the production schedule than the present statistics on orders received. Sales personnel were also being encouraged to send in additional information relating to general trade conditions in their individual territories. Both the marketing research director and his assistant spent considerable time visiting dealers, company sales personnel, and representatives of different segments of the industry.

The manager of marketing research stated that in addition to the problem of finding a means of relating company sales to general economic conditions or specific market indi-

EXHIBIT 5
Changes in Production Schedule

| Model | | *Operating Period* | | | *Total* |
|---|---|---|---|---|---|
| | | *11* | *12* | *13* | |
| 705 | Was | 130 | 130 | 100 | 2,200 |
| | To | 100 | 100 | 75 | 2,115 |
| 801 | Was | 400 | 400 | 350 | 5,280 |
| | To | 300 | 300 | 250 | 4,980 |
| 305 | Was | 250 | 250 | 250 | 3,360 |
| | To | 200 | 200 | 200 | 3,210 |
| 721 | Was | 300 | 300 | 250 | 3,660 |
| | To | 250 | 250 | 250 | 3,560 |
| 621 | Was | 150 | 120 | 120 | 2,530 |
| | To | 100 | 100 | 100 | 2,440 |
| 901 | Was | 245 | 245 | 235 | 2,900 |
| | To | 200 | 200 | 200 | 2,775 |
| 551 | Was | 320 | 320 | 320 | 3,550 |
| | To | 250 | 250 | 250 | 3,340 |
| 451 | Was | 150 | 150 | 150 | 1,200 |
| | To | 400 | 150 | 150 | 1,450 |
| 841 | Was | 500 | 500 | 400 | 9,400 |
| | To | 600 | 600 | 600 | 9,800 |
| B-4 | Was | 525 | 480 | 430 | 5,780 |
| | To | 400 | 400 | 400 | 5,545 |
| 825 | Was | 400 | 350 | 300 | 5,350 |
| | To | 300 | 300 | 300 | 5,200 |
| 521 | Was | 650 | 600 | 400 | 7,350 |
| | To | 550 | 500 | 400 | 7,150 |
| 610 | Was | 1,500 | 1,000 | 800 | 5,350 |
| | To | 1,350 | 1,000 | 800 | 5,150 |
| 601 | Was | 550 | 600 | 550 | 6,250 |
| | To | 500 | 500 | 500 | 6,050 |
| 541 | Was | 150 | 700 | 400 | 5,850 |
| | To | 150 | 300 | 300 | 5,350 |
| 2,200 | Was | 800 | 800 | 900 | 11,200 |
| | To | 700 | 700 | 800 | 10,900 |
| 2,202 | Was | 900 | 1,000 | 900 | 11,200 |
| | To | 800 | 900 | 800 | 10,900 |
| 8,005 | Was | 500 | 300 | 100 | 3,540 |
| | To | 300 | 300 | 100 | 3,340 |
| 410 | Was | 4,300 | 2,400 | 1,200 | 16,500 |
| | To | 3,300 | 2,400 | 1,200 | 15,500 |
| 1,205 | Was | 310 | 320 | 255 | 5,855 |
| | To | 370 | 380 | 375 | 6,095 |

cators, two other major problems were (1) shortening the lead time required for making changes in production schedules, and (2) finding a better way to predict changes in the direction of product sales. The restriction of only being able to revise forecasts four

EXHIBIT 6

## Sales Forecast—Revision 8

|  |  |  |  |  | Operating Period |  |  |  |  | FIRM |  | Operating Period |  |  |  |
|---|---|---|---|---|---|---|---|---|---|---|---|---|---|---|---|
| Model | 1 | 2 | 3 | 4 | 5 | 6 | 7 | 8 | 9 | 10 | 11 | 12 | 13 | Total | 1 |
| **A** |  |  |  |  |  |  |  |  |  |  |  |  |  |  |  |
| 705 | 100 | 150 | 180 | 160 | 240 | 260 | 230 | 220 | 160 | 140 | 100 | 100 | 75 | 2115 |  |
| 805 | 250 | 300 | 340 | 400 | 400 | 200 | 150 |  |  |  |  |  |  | 2040 |  |
| 825 |  |  |  |  | 800 | 1400 | 900 | 450 | 400 | 350 | 300 | 300 | 300 | 5200 |  |
| 810 | 25 | 25 | 25 | 30 | 40 | 40 | 45 | 35 | 35 | 40 | 40 | 40 | 30 | 450 |  |
| 812 | 5 | 5 | 5 | 8 | 9 | 9 | 8 | 7 | 7 | 7 | 7 | 7 | 7 | 91 |  |
| B-7 | 60 | 70 | 70 | 80 | 100 | 90 | 80 | 80 | 30 | 50 | 50 | 50 | 50 | 860 |  |
| B-8 | 340 | 340 | 490 | 530 |  |  |  |  |  |  |  |  |  | 1700 |  |
| B-9 | 60 | 60 | 70 | 70 |  |  |  |  |  |  |  |  |  | 260 |  |
| 641 | 290 | 300 | 390 | 500 | 3000 | 2500 | 1500 | 800 | 600 | 800 | 1200 | 1200 | 1000 | 13100 |  |
| 801 | 580 | 330 | 630 | 500 | 500 | 500 | 550 | 400 | 300 | 400 | 300 | 300 | 250 | 4980 |  |
| 511 | 700 | 700 | 1100 | 1150 | 1150 | 1150 | 1150 | 1100 | 700 | 700 | 700 | 700 | 600 | 11600 |  |
| 521 |  |  |  | 630 | 630 | 650 | 600 | 600 | 350 | 700 | 550 | 500 | 400 | 7150 |  |
| 610 |  |  |  |  | 1200 | 800 | 800 | 300 | 150 | 2000 | 1350 | 1000 | 800 | 5150 |  |
| 751 |  |  |  |  |  |  |  |  |  | 400 | 400 | 400 | 400 | 4850 | 300 |
| 105 | 70 | 60 | 60 | 70 | 70 | 70 | 60 | 60 | 60 | 60 | 60 | 60 | 60 | 820 | 500 |

| | | | | | | | | | | | | | | |
|---|---|---|---|---|---|---|---|---|---|---|---|---|---|---|
| **B** | | | | | | | | | | | | | | |
| 631 | 700 | 400 | 1000 | 800 | 750 | 800 | 750 | 650 | 600 | 600 | 800 | 800 | 800 | 9450 |
| C-3 | 120 | 140 | 170 | 180 | 180 | 190 | 170 | 120 | 100 | 120 | 120 | 100 | 100 | 1810 |
| C-4 | 260 | 270 | 430 | 440 | 500 | 510 | 540 | 450 | 420 | 525 | 400 | 400 | 400 | 5545 |
| 105 | 30 | 30 | 40 | 40 | 50 | 50 | 60 | 40 | 40 | 45 | 50 | 50 | 40 | 565 |
| 305 | 170 | 210 | 290 | 290 | 290 | 320 | 340 | 300 | 180 | 220 | 200 | 200 | 200 | 3210 |
| 7105 | 25 | 25 | 25 | 25 | 25 | 25 | 25 | 25 | 25 | 25 | 25 | 25 | 25 | 325 |
| 541 | 1800 | 400 | 600 | 600 | 300 | 300 | 150 | 150 | 150 | 150 | 150 | 300 | 300 | 5350 |
| 905 | 75 | 75 | 130 | 130 | 130 | 150 | 120 | 90 | 90 | 140 | 120 | 120 | 120 | 1490 |
| 601 | 350 | 350 | 450 | 450 | 500 | 500 | 500 | 400 | 500 | 550 | 500 | 500 | 500 | 6050 |
| 721 | 260 | 190 | 270 | 330 | 330 | 330 | 340 | 260 | 200 | 300 | 250 | 250 | 250 | 3560 |
| X-1 | 7 | 7 | 7 | 7 | 7 | 7 | 7 | 7 | 7 | 7 | 7 | 7 | 6 | 90 |
| **C** | | | | | | | | | | | | | | |
| 4055 | 150 | 150 | 230 | 240 | 260 | 240 | 240 | 200 | 120 | 130 | 150 | 150 | 150 | 2410 |
| 5055 | 140 | 140 | 210 | 215 | 235 | 210 | 210 | 180 | 100 | 150 | 150 | 150 | 130 | 2220 |
| 6155 | 15 | 15 | 20 | 25 | 20 | 30 | 25 | 25 | 20 | 20 | 20 | 20 | 20 | 275 |
| 7155 | 25 | 25 | 25 | 25 | 25 | 35 | 25 | 25 | 20 | 25 | 25 | 25 | 20 | 325 |
| 1155 | 20 | 25 | 40 | 50 | 55 | 55 | 60 | 55 | 30 | 45 | 55 | 45 | 40 | 575 |
| 2155 | 20 | 25 | 40 | 50 | 55 | 55 | 60 | 55 | 30 | 45 | 55 | 45 | 40 | 575 |
| X-3 | 7 | 7 | 8 | 10 | 10 | 11 | 10 | 10 | 7 | 11 | 10 | 10 | 9 | 120 |

EXHIBIT 7
Sales Forecast in Dollars—Revision 8

| Product | 1-6 | 7 | 8 | 9 | |
|---------|-----|-----|-----|-----|---|
| A | $2,186,490 | $ 492,164 | $312,296 | $221,875 | |
| B | 1,233,885 | 727,076 | 185,407 | 163,862 | |
| C | 1,231,999 | 162,543 | 150,378 | 97,246 | |
| D | 336,124 | 62,598 | 60,393 | 46,842 | |
| E | 522,193 | 95,242 | 151,270 | 74,601 | |
| F | 47,332 | 11,430 | 10,568 | 5,905 | |
| G | 536,356 | 55,472 | 55,472 | 36,981 | |
| H | 88,696 | 11,826 | 11,826 | 11,826 | |
| Private brand | 77,609 | 14,884 | 12,045 | 9,207 | |
| Total | $6,260,684 | $1,633,235 | $949,655 | $668,345 | |

| Product | 10 | 11 | 12 | 13 | Total |
|---------|-----|-----|-----|-----|-------|
| A | $ 373,805 | $ 342,046 | $322,381 | $278,778 | $ 4,529,835 |
| B | 194,075 | 184,303 | 187,763 | 185,976 | 3,062,347 |
| C | 356,047 | 320,683 | 254,678 | 176,335 | 2,749,909 |
| D | 142,054 | 119,307 | 93,270 | 70,845 | 931,433 |
| E | 71,098 | 78,981 | 44,063 | 41,986 | 1,079,434 |
| F | 8,119 | 11,137 | 11,137 | 9,403 | 115,031 |
| G | 55,472 | 55,504 | 55,516 | 55,535 | 906,308 |
| H | 11,826 | 11,826 | 11,826 | 11,826 | 171,478 |
| Private brand | 11,436 | 8,826 | 9,753 | 10,769 | 154,529 |
| Total | $1,223,932 | $1,132,613 | $990,387 | $841,453 | $13,700,304 |

months ahead of time had often meant overproduction and excessive inventories. Even though Coffrey had a shorter lead time than most of its competitors, the manager of marketing research was certain that improved control in this area was possible.

*What is your evaluation of the forecasting techniques used by the Coffrey Tool Company?*

# I-4. PHILLIPS COMPANY:
## Manufacturer of Steam Power Plants—
## Changing a Company Image

Sam McDonald, vice-president for sales of the Phillips Company, was faced with the problem of improving the images of his company and product. The Phillips Company, one of the leading manufacturers of steam power plants in the United States, was located in Philadelphia. The company was started by Aaron Phillips, who began manufacturing small steam engines in Philadelphia in 1846. By 1971, Phillips had annual sales of $190 million and sold power plants to industrial users throughout the world. McDonald was concerned because public utilities, important users of steam power equipment, only accounted for 12 to 15 percent of Phillips' sales. Some utilities were good customers, but many other major utilities never bought from the company at all. At McDonald's suggestion, top management decided to explore the buying attitudes and motivation of electric utility companies as completely as possible. To remove the risk of personal bias, an outside research agency was called in to conduct the survey.

The research agency set out to find out what customers and potential customers really thought of the Phillips Company. Depth interviews were carried out with influential buying personnel in a selected sample of all electric utilities. The results that were presented to the executive committee in September 1971 were not too pleasant to hear. In general, Phillips' engineering skills were rated highly; product quality and workmanship were considered good. However, a number of respondents thought of Phillips as a completely static company. They were completely unaware of Phillips' excellent research organization and many new product developments.

The research organization pointed out other useful information about the Phillips Company and its market. Sales were normally personnel-related; that is, personal relationships and personalities were important in the buying decision. The buying responsibility was widely dispersed for products sold by Phillips. As many as forty people, ranging from the president down, might be involved in a purchase. Many Phillips salespeople were not too well informed about the details of new-product developments and would probably need additional training to be able to answer technical questions.

It was obvious to McDonald that Phillips' communication methods had failed completely to keep potential utility customers aware of changes taking place in the company and in its products. Some method had to be devised to break down the communications barrier and sell Phillips products. Representatives from the sales and advertising departments conferred and finally came up with four possible approaches to improvement in communication with the utilities. First, they might advertise in mass media to get across the Phillips story. Second, they could launch an intensive publicity campaign, blanketing all new media and particularly utilities trade media with information and press releases. Third, the sales staff could make presentations directly to prospects in the field. Flipcharts and visual aids could be used where appropriate. Fourth, the company could try to schedule educational meetings for key electric utility personnel. This would require a traveling symposium, staffed by top personnel and equipped with audiovisual aids, that could spend several hours with groups of employees in selected utilities across the country.

*What action should McDonald have recommended to change the Phillips image in the public utility field?*

# I-5.   PLASTICS INDUSTRIES, INC.:
## Manufacturer of Plastic Pipe—
## Promotion of an Industrial Product

Management of Plastics Industries, Incorporated, was faced with the problem of promoting a new product to the market. The company had been organized in Beaumont, Texas, to manufacture pipe. It was founded by a group of wealthy individuals from the community, and total capitalization had been set with the expectation of four years of operation at a loss. By the second half of the third year of operation, the company had made a profit, and the room for future growth looked very promising. Nevertheless, management believed that sales were not increasing as rapidly as might be expected in light of the clear strengths of the product.

Plastics Industries manufactured plastic pipe by the extrusion process. Its manufacturing plant was located on the outskirts of Beaumont. The major capital investment consisted of an extruder, designed and specially built for the company in Germany at a cost of $250,000. The extruder was almost completely automated, so that only minimal training was needed to operate it. A staff of two engineers was maintained to service the machine. Polypropylene, available from major chemical companies, was used as the raw material, and it was available in a pellet form ready for manufacture. The finished pipe was called Plylene pipe.

The number of manufacturers of plastic pipe in the United States was small but growing. Several major companies, such as Dupont, Shell, and Hercules, were manufacturing or had manufactured plastic pipe. Dupont, a major supplier of the raw materials, had produced a plastic pipe under the Delrin brand name but recently had ceased manufacture of pipe and was buying Plylene pipe from Plastics Industries. The use of plastic pipe as a replacement for other types of pipe was a relatively new development. A first major product was polyethylene pipe, which was first introduced on the market as a nonpressure pipe suitable for mine-drainage operations. The chemical resistance of polyethylene made it a natural for this application; lack of resistance to acid mine waters had caused major corrosion problems with the steel pipe formerly used. Since that successful first, the polyethylene and, subsequently, polypropylene pipe industry had grown at a rapid rate. Some of the major oil companies began manufacturing plastic pipe for use in their fields. However, Plastics Industries quickly became a major supplier in this industry and soon was supplying twelve major oil companies.

Mr. Galloway, president of Plastics Industries, Inc., believed that the greatest single problem for the company, as well as for other makers of plastic pipe, was the setting of standards of quality. A number of laboratories were available for product performance testing. Galloway had made use of the services of the Battelle Memorial Institute in Columbus, Ohio, a leading researcher in the field of thermal polymers, to test samples of its product. But, until specific performance standards were established, no industry enforcement of quality levels was possible. Certain grades of Plastics Industries' pipe had been tested and accepted by the Food and Drug Administration and the Department of Commerce.

Plastics Industries maintained a sales force of three sales engineers, plus one factory representative to sell to major industrial users. These personnel were located in Odessa, Texas; Houston, Texas; and Tulsa, Oklahoma—all major oil-producing centers; they had concentrated their efforts almost exclusively on the oil industry. All orders were shipped directly from the factory, but the very high shipping costs indicated the need for distribution and warehousing points in the near future.

In the opinion of Galloway, the really big market for plastic pipe was in the home-construction industry. He believed that this market was potentially at least five times as large as the present market, but so far neither the users nor middlemen were interested in the product. The image of plastic pipe was of a product that would easily break and, therefore, would not last as long as conventional pipe. The lack of quality standards in the industry had done nothing to improve the image. In addition, the building codes in most cities would have to be completely rewritten to permit the use of plastic pipe as a substitute for metal or other materials. Furthermore, middlemen and users required instruction in installation of plastic pipe. It was not a difficult process—sections were welded together with heat but the methods of cutting and welding needed to be explained to prospective users and distributors.

Galloway felt that a possible solution to the problem of selling the home-construction market lay in advertising to the general public and to builders. He realized that Plastics Industries was too small to advertise in many major media, but to some extent they could benefit from the advertising of their major suppliers of raw material in trade magazines. He planned to reach the general public and builders through cooperative advertising on a shared-cost basis by suppliers.

*What should be the role of advertising for a product such as this? What kind or kinds of promotions would probably have been most productive for Plastics Industries?*

## I-6.   SHWAYDER BROS., INC. (SAMSONITE CORP.):
### Luggage Manufacturer—
### Pricing a Durable Consumer Good

In 1964, Shwayder Bros., Inc., manufacturer of Samsonite luggage, was reconsidering its long-standing policy of offering luggage only in the medium-priced field. Shwayder, a privately held, family-operated business (until 1965, when it adopted the name Samsonite Corp.), was the largest luggage manufacturer in the United States. Sales in 1964 were $56 million, accounting for almost one third of all luggage sales in the country. In an industry of small manufacturers, Shwayder was the only giant. It sold as much luggage as the next ten competitors combined.

Shwayder Bros., which started in business in 1910, built its reputation as a manufacturer of medium-priced luggage. Samsonite luggage had developed a strong image of strength without excessive weight. These characteristics had made it particularly popular for air travel. The basic familiar Samsonite bag consisted of a molded plastic skin over a lightweight magnesium frame. It combined strength (company executives claimed that you could jump on a bag without damaging it) with attractive modern styling that had had a strong influence on styling in the entire industry. Shwayder had also been a consistent innovator, regularly introducing new features and improvements.

Shwayder Bros. achieved its growth by concentrating its efforts in the medium-priced field. Low-priced luggage was made of inexpensive paperboard covered with plastic or fabric. It had the advantage of being light and hence easier to carry and cheaper to send by air, but it was not durable and was quickly damaged and marred by the mass-handling characteristic of major air terminals. High-priced luggage was traditionally made of leather. It was strong and attractive, but on the heavy side, and was subject to marring with excessive handling. The expensive luggage accounted for only about 5 percent of total industry volume, but like the medium-priced-luggage, it was moving increasingly into plastics and away from leather. Shwayder management had felt for many years that the medium-priced market was the most promising. They believed that most people were unwilling to be seen with cheap luggage, even though the infrequency of its use might make this kind of luggage a much more sensible buy for many individuals.

For a number of years Samsonite luggage had been produced in a lower-medium and upper-medium-priced line. The upper-medium-priced Silhouette line, the more popular of the two, was made on magnesium frames. The lower-medium-priced Streamlite line was made on wooden frames. Between these two price lines, Shwayder had been able to satisfy most of the medium-price-range market. But, with the increasing affluence of the American market in the 1960s, a smaller portion of consumers was interested in the Streamlite line. Yet, the price jump to the Silhouette line was too great. For this reason, a new middle line, priced between Streamlite and Silhouette and called Contoura, was test-marketed in 1965. Another new line was also being tested in the higher price range. This line, which was called Fashionaire, was produced in the soft-side design that was particularly popular in expensive luggage.

Shwayder Bros. supported a strong policy of price maintenance among its very large 17,000-store distributive organization. Management believed that protection of retail margins was the main reason that the company had the largest number of dealers in the industry. They believed that department stores and luggage stores would drop their line if they failed to protect dealer profits through price maintenance. The president of the company, King Shwayder, explained that effective price protection was a matter of education. There was no really effective way to enforce or police price maintenance, but it was good business for the stores to maintain prices. Luggage was a staple item, and the 40 to 45 percent margin was excellent. Shwayder informed its dealers that no one gained and everyone lost when price cutting took place. The company also screened new dealers and attempted to eliminate price cutters.

Recognizing the important new role of the discount house in the American market, Shwayder Bros. introduced a special line in 1959—Royal Traveler, to be sold only in discount houses. The Royal Traveler brand was not identified with Samsonite, and it was usually sold at a price 25 to 30 percent below that of the Silhouette line. Shwayder management admitted that this line had probably cut into the sales of the regular Samsonite lines, but since the discount houses were inevitably going to sell luggage, Shwayder might as well provide them with the luggage.

*What kind of success would you have predicted for the two new higher-priced lines? Had Samsonite been missing a bet by restricting its sales to the medium-priced market?*

*Evaluate Shwayder management's stand on the matter of price maintenance.*

# I-7.   THE BANNER COMPANY:

## Integrated Food Products Company—
## Solicitation of New Accounts

The Banner Company, which had annual sales in excess of $800 million, processed and distributed lines of dairy products, foodstuffs, and such specialties as glues and animal-food supplements. These lines were marketed throughout the United States and Canada by five separate sales organizations departmentalized by products. Each of these sales organizations was further divided geographically by districts and branches. The Spokane branch of the Northwest District of the Ice Cream and Fluid Milk Division manufactured and distributed bulk and packaged ice cream, ice cream novelties, and fruit sherbets. Because sales depended to a large extent upon the number of outlets selling Banner ice cream, Mr. Shaw, sales manager of the Spokane branch, was considering ways to aid sales representatives in the solicitation of new accounts.

Banner ice cream was sold to three types of accounts. More than 60 percent of all ice cream sales were made to retail dealers, including soda fountains, drugstores, variety stores, independent grocers, chain supermarkets, and ice cream drive-ins. In the Spokane branch's territory, approximately 500 dealers handled all or part of the Banner line. Depending on the size of the account, deliveries to retailers were made once or twice a week. Approximately 20 percent of the sales of ice cream were made to restaurants, which were serviced two or three times per week. The remaining 20 percent were sold to industrial and institutional accounts, including manufacturing plants and schools, which used the ice cream in connection with the operation of cafeterias. Deliveries to industrial and institutional accounts were usually at the rate of four times per week.

In the Spokane branch there were two sales representatives and four route salespeople, all of whom worked under Shaw's direction. The job of the sales representatives consisted of the solicitation of all types of new accounts, the performance of "missionary" duties, and the changing of point-of-sale displays in retail stores. Each week, sales representatives devoted the first three days to calling on prospective accounts. Normally, a sales representative could make six to twelve calls during the three days allotted for this purpose. On Thursdays and Fridays, the sales representatives visited established accounts and changed displays. Each established account was visited at least once every four to six weeks, but some that demanded special attention were contacted weekly. All point-of-sale displays were changed six times a year. Sales representatives were required to submit daily written reports of their activities and to discuss their plans with Shaw each morning prior to making their first call.

The four route salespersons were primarily deliverymen. Since dealers ordered ice cream directly from the trucks, the route salespeople had to be skilled in the anticipation of dealer wants when they filled out their truckload orders. Although route salespeople did not solicit new accounts, frequently they turned over the names of prospects to sales representatives.

With the objective of obtaining an even pattern of retail distribution, each sales representative regularly made an informal survey of the assigned district. These surveys were conducted monthly during the summer and fall seasons, and bimonthly during the winter and spring. For these surveys, in areas with little or no distribution, the sales representative listed all stores selling ice cream. Each store was then rated as to location, cleanliness, and the like, with the purpose of detecting desirable new distributors for Banner ice cream.

The next step was for the sales representative to attempt the conversion of the best store in the area to a Banner dealership; sometimes, however, the company was satisfied to secure the second- or third-best store as its area outlet. After a sales representative had made the initial call, the new prospect was entered on a rating chart. After subsequent calls, sales representatives entered percentages on the chart, indicating the extent to which it was estimated that the prospects were now sold on the Banner line. All percentage estimates of this type were arrived at solely on the basis of each sales representative's experience in the solicitation of new accounts. For example, when a prospect expressed a real interest in such matters as pricing and terms of sales, the prospect was rated about 75 percent. But when a prospect allowed the sales representative only a few minutes of his time, the prospect was rated approximately 25 percent.

Although chart percentages were used mainly to answer the questions of route salespersons who had turned in the names of prospects, they also served as a general guide for the determination of the frequency of calls by sales representatives. Sales representatives made their second calls on prospects approximately thirty days after the first contacts. Thereafter, the following schedule was used:

| Prospect Rating (%) | Indicated Call Frequency (or Action) |
|---|---|
| 0-4 | Drop the prospect |
| 5-24 | One call every two months |
| 25-59 | One call each month |
| 60-79 | One call every two weeks |
| 80-100 | Weekly calls |

The conversion of a prospect into a Banner account took from one month to a year. The experience had been the same whether the outlet was selling a competitive brand or was not yet selling ice cream at all.

The Spokane branch distributed ice cream north to the Canadian border, east to the Montana-Idaho border, west to Wenatchee, and south to Clarkson, Washington, and Lewiston, Idaho. One sales representative was responsible for the northern and eastern segments of the branch's territory; the other worked the southern and western parts. Sales representatives were paid on a salary-plus-commission plan. Sales quotas were established on the basis of the previous year's sales, plus 10 percent. The arbitrary 10 percent annual increase in quotas was justified by the company on the basis that population in the Spokane branch territory was growing rapidly. Shaw was of the opinion that the size of the Spokane market area and its expanding population would soon mean that the addition of a third sales representative would be desirable and feasible.

Because sales representatives were burdened with a large amount of missionary and sales work, and because their operating territories were very large, they were unable to spend sufficient time in the effective solicitation of new accounts. Some means of making additional time available for this purpose needed to be found. However, Shaw was undecided about a specific approach to this problem.

*In what ways could the distribution of Banner ice cream have been improved in the Spokane sales territory?*

# I-8.   KING DISCOUNT, INC.:
## Discount Store—
## Decision on Becoming a Wholesaler

James L. Jackson, president of King Discount, Inc., had been approached recently by the manager of a local neighborhood convenience store called Burt's. The manager of Burt's wanted to determine if King Discount would consider serving as a wholesaler for Burt's, in the line of health and beauty aids. Burt's manager was very concerned about profitability and felt that if King Discount were to act as his wholesaler for health and beauty aids, Burt's could realize substantial economies, which would help make for a more efficient operation.

King Discount, Inc., was founded seven years ago for the purpose of specializing in health and beauty aids. The store carried a very wide and deep assortment of health and beauty aids, with emphasis on low prices, high volume, and one-stop shopping for such products.

Within seven years, King Discount had expanded to a chain of eight stores (with two more planned) in Alabama, Florida, and Georgia cities ranging in size from 3,000 to 73,000. Two other stores, one in Georgia and one in North Carolina, had been opened but failed after a short time because they were in poor locations. In addition, King Discount had entered into franchise agreements with four stores in Alabama and Georgia. However, the franchise arrangements proved unsatisfactory, and each store was eventually sold or closed. Management at King Discount attributed the failure of the franchises to a lack of managerial talent.

Two additional stores were planned by King Discount and were to feature two major improvements over the existing stores. First, increased selling space would permit an even greater assortment of goods. Second, the new stores would include pharmacies. Jackson believed that the pharmacy would attract a sizable segment of the market in each area and would allow King Discount to become a one-stop center for drug needs as well as for health and beauty needs.

Until recently, King Discount had very limited warehouse facilities. As operations expanded, a building was purchased, and this gave King Discount 3,000 square feet of storage space. However, all available warehouse space was being utilized. With a clear need for additional warehouse space to serve the expanding company, Jackson saw two alternatives: (1) build an addition to the existing warehouse, or (2) lease a building on property adjoining King Discount property. There was such an existing building, now being used by an outdoor advertising firm, but Jackson had learned that the advertising firm would soon be moving to a new facility and the building would then be available for lease. No cost projections had yet been made on the expenses involved in adding to the existing warehouse or in converting the adjoining building to a warehouse facility.

The branch stores in the King Discount chain were widely separated from the main warehouse and, as a result, a tightly controlled distribution system had to be developed. Each store manger carefully monitored the stock situation to determine when stock-out conditions on various items would occur. The individual stores than submitted their needs to King Discount in advance of the stock-out date. The orders from the individual stores were consolidated at the warehouse and a firm delivery schedule was established. One of King Discount's two delivery trucks took orders to each store every two weeks.

After considerable thought, Jackson entered into an agreement with Burt's, whereby King Discount would act as a wholesaler for the health and beauty aids line. Compensation was fixed at cost plus 10 percent. Based on Jackson's personal experience in both the wholesale and retail trades, it was estimated that Burt's would realize approximately a four to five percent savings by using King Discount as its wholesaler rather than other wholesalers serving the area.

As a result of the successful negotiations with Burt's, Jackson was considering the possibility of having King Discount aggressively pursue a wholesaling role for other retail stores in situations similar to Burt's. He felt that the comprehensive line of health and beauty aids carried by King Discount, coupled with its marketing experience, would make it a "natural" for the wholesaling business. Jackson believed there was a need for a specialty wholesaler for many of the small independent stores such as Burt's which could not compete with discount stores on a price basis but which felt they had to carry such goods to round out their lines.

Jackson developed a plan for a pricing structure similar to that used for servicing Burt's. King Discount's price to the retailer was to be based upon King Discount's actual cost of the goods plus 10 percent, which would result in savings up to 5 percent when compared with alternative wholesaling arrangements. Jackson felt that a big problem would be in convincing the retailer of the potential savings, since it was his experience that many retailers did not understand the wholesale cost-markup structure.

In addition, if there were an affirmative decision to pursue wholesaling actively, a decision was required on the type of wholesale operation that would best support Jackson's plan. Despite some unused delivery capability in the present operation, Jackson favored a limited-function wholesaling operation, specifically a cash-and-carry wholesale unit.

A decision on the wholesale proposal had to be made soon so that full consideration could be given to the possibility of leasing warehouse space in the building adjoining King Discount's present warehouse.

*Should King Discount have gone into wholesaling? State the reasons for your answer.*

# I-9.   BENSON'S, INC.—OLD HOME KITCHENS DIVISION:
## Manufacturer of Fruit Cakes—
## Need for Marketing Research

The Five-Year Plan for changing the marketing program of Old Home Kitchens Division of Benson's, Inc., was completing its fourth year of implementation. The plan was introduced in an attempt to counteract recent declining profit margins on sales of Old Home Kitchens products, the largest volume of which was accounted for by the Old Home Fruit Cake. Basic to this marketing plan was a reevaluation of the company's distribution policy and redefining of the actual "business" that Old Home Kitchens was in. Management had decided that distribution would be effected exclusively through clubs and nonprofit organizations; in turn, this decision led to redefining the business, not as the fruit cake business, but as the fund-raising business. Together, these two reevaluations called for a third, an accurate description of the market. This task proved to be quite extensive in implications and formidable in approach.

About fifty years ago, W. Howard Benson and his father opened the first Benson's Bakery in Athens, Georgia, with a product line consisting of bread, rolls, and cakes. The enterprise grew and expanded to include several regional bakeries in towns approximately the same size as Athens. From the very beginning, the Benson name was associated with high quality and personal attention of the owners. Never was Benson's far from the people it served. During the rationing days of World War II, Howard Benson gave away thousands of loaves of bread to hungry people. This generosity had always been evident in many aspects of the company, as recently exemplified by the student program at Old Home Kitchens, where students were allowed college credit for working as telephone salespeople.

Practically everything else about Benson's had changed, however. No longer a small regional bakery, the company had diversified into three main divisions: the Holsum Bakery, which baked and distributed Holsum Bread and related products; Motel Enterprises, which owned and operated a Holiday Inn in Athens; and the Old Home Kitchens. The entire business was owned by the Benson family, with H. E. Benson, the son of Howard Benson, as the president.

### OLD HOME FRUIT CAKE

Twenty years ago, Benson's introduced its Old Home Fruit Cake to civic clubs. The cake was loaf-shaped, had the added distinction of being "pre-sliced," and carried the *Good Housekeeping* Seal of Approval. The fruit cake was also sold through supermarkets, but fund-raising proved more profitable. The product line currently included three sizes of Old Home Fruit Cake, each consisting of 75 percent choice fruits and nuts and 25 percent pound cake batter; and a new Pecan Buttercake. It also included other taste tempters, such as candies, cookies, pound cake, and pecans. Still the Old Home Fruit Cake had continually been the overwhelming best-seller.

## OLD HOME KITCHENS ORGANIZATION

J. B. Smith, Executive Vice-President of Benson's, Inc., was also General Manager of the Old Home Kitchens Division. B. J. Stoll was Marketing Manager, and there were two sales managers. Old Home Kitchens was further divided into four areas—Production (facilities located in Bogart, Georgia), Distribution, Commercial, and Fund-Raising. The commercial division packaged fruit cake under private brands for such independent distributors as Stuckey's, Pet Milk, and Charles Chips. The philosophy regarding private brands was that if Old Home Fruit Cake was to continue selling as well as it had, the image of "fruit cake" must be kept high. However, fund-raising accounted for 90 percent of the previous year's sales of somewhat over $5 million.

## THE CLUB PLAN

Any nonprofit organization with a need to raise money could order the desired number of case lots (no individual cakes were sold). The cakes were then shipped prepaid and final payment was not due until December 31 of that year. (Benson's busiest season was just prior to Thanksgiving.) The company sold direct to the organization and charged a flat rate so that when the products were sold at the suggested retail price, the organization could make a specified profit. An attractive brochure was available fully explaining the club plan to organizations making inquiries.

## COMPETITION

Fund-raising competition, like the fund-raising market, was difficult to pinpoint. The other large fruit cake producer was Claxton Fruit Cake Company of Claxton, Georgia, which sold its fruit cake exclusively through the Civitan Clubs. Benson felt that it had certain distinct advantages over Claxton: a better product, the added convenience of "pre-slicing," and a more aggressive sales strategy. Three years ago, Benson's surpassed Claxton in sales and became the number one producer of fruit cake. Other competition came from such projects as the sale of candy, cookies, light bulbs, and brooms. Stoll estimated that Benson's had 10,000 customers, 5,000 "dropouts" (those who had previously bought from Benson but for some reason had not continued to do so), and 40,000 inquiries (those writing for information about the club plan).

## ADVERTISING AND PROMOTION

Tucker-Wayne Advertising Agency of New York had recently contracted with Benson's to promote the Old Home products. Previously, the account had been handled by the Lowe-Stevens Agency for several years and Stoll felt that it was time for a change. Coupon ads appeared in the September editions of a number of major publications, such as *U.S. News & World Report, TV Guide,* and *Better Homes and Gardens,* and most club magazines, such as the *Lion* and *Kiwanian.* Experience had shown that television was ineffective as an advertising medium, and no use was made of that medium. However, direct mail was an important part of the promotion campaign—over 750,000 pieces of mail were sent out in August to elicit inquiries from organizations (*not* individuals). Other promotions included printed materials, brochures, display posters, sales kits, advertising mats, and sample slices. Sample slices were mailed to each inquirer (over 40,000) and were included with orders. Also included with orders of more than sixteen cases of fruit cake were "Bonus Cakes," free Mainsellers that the club could sell to help pay freight charges. The yearly budget for advertising and promotion was $100,000.

## REEVALUATION OF MARKETING STRATEGY

Until five years ago, Benson's marketed Old Home products through a sales force of about sixty college students employed during summer vacations. After a week's training, the students were assigned territories with coverage in the forty-eight contiguous states. Each student had the use of a company car and had an allowance for expenses. They contacted old accounts and new prospects, took orders, and made weekly call reports. Contacts were followed up by direct mail. Sales personnel were paid a salary and year-end bonuses.

Stoll, who came to Benson's as sales manager for Old Home Kitchens, had some previous experience in telephone selling and considerable experience in direct sales and the use of a part-time sales force. He implemented a research program that led to the adoption of an innovative plan called Phone Power. This plan consisted primarily of the installation of six WATS lines at the headquarters to be used for two months each. To gain complete coverage of the continental United States the lines were chosen as follows: one Georgia line, two for Area Three, two for Area Four, and one for Area Six. Browning Adair, Sales Manager in charge of Phone Power, installed by special legal permit a "monitor" by which he could listen in on the interviews, the purpose of which was to protect the customer as well as the interviewer and Benson's, and also to regulate and improve the content of the interview. A special line was run from Athens to Bogart so that touch-tone phones could be used, as it was known that they are 25 percent more efficient than regular dialing.

Phone Power required twelve part-time sales employees who worked in two shifts so that customers could be contacted at their own convenience and according to their respective time zones. These part-time salespeople were given a three-day sales training program and assigned territories. They were rated on a standard of performance, with interview completions averaging three per hour.

Obvious advantages of Phone Power over former sales methods were better-regulated interviews and less time wasted in traveling and making second calls. Some orders were smaller than those generated by sales representatives, and certain types of calls were more difficult to conduct (such as "cold calls"), but the phones made it easier to contact customers to "feel out" inquiries, and interviewers were not forced to make immediate decisions concerning company policy about which they were not totally familiar. A special arrangement was worked out with the University of Georgia whereby students could receive five hours of college credit for telephone selling.

Along with Phone Power, the independent-agent program was introduced. The number of sales managers was reduced from five to two, one of whom was sent out on a Five-Year Plan to recruit agents, both full-time and part-time, to represent Old Home products in selected metropolitan areas. In its fourth year this plan was right on target, with forty-five agents throughout the United States. Phone Power supplemented the areas where there were no assigned agents. The agent program was motivated by the philosophy that local people were more successful in such an emotional selling atmosphere as club selling. They knew personally the people and organizations with whom they were dealing (Benson's actually leaned toward retired and semiretired personnel, to take full advantage of this acquaintance), and thus would be more likely to sway opinion toward a given project. Concentration of agents was according to population; for example, there were three agents in Los Angeles and its surrounding area but only one for the state of Virginia. The agents worked on a given percentage commission up to their quotas, then 10 percent on the next 10 percent of the basic quota amount and 20 percent above that. They were also given their samples and selling tools. Grading was according to a standard of performance—that is, they made a certain number of contacts and reports to the company—but otherwise they were independent of Benson's, Inc.

Both of these projects had proved profitable in recent years; and profits had increased along with sales, and the unfavorable growth trends had been corrected.

## PROBLEM OF IDENTIFYING THE TARGET MARKET

The management at Old Home Kitchens was interested in knowing whether these trends were as promising as they seemed. So far, their clientele had conveniently been classified on the basis of "nonprofit" organizations. Surveys showed that 80 percent of families in the United States purchased fruit cake sometime during the year and that 75 percent of these did so before Thanksgiving. However, management did not have access to reliable data concerning the fund-raising market. There were many differences among the nonprofit organizations: degree of organization, whether structured or loosely bound; reasons for wanting to raise money; whether a one-time project or a continuous need; duration or stability of membership; life and purpose of the organization. Stoll wanted, among other things, some sort of demographic profile of the type of person who would most likely be a member of such a group so that he could predict future sales, determine the division's share of the market, and measure its competition. In other words, was the division's present level of 10,000 customers a high market penetration, or was the division at a low penetration with a potential of considerably more customers?

Tucker-Wayne Agency had talked at some length with Stoll about providing a research program to gather the needed information. Benson's had the alternative, of course, of trying its own hand at the effort. Previous company research, conducted primarily from a product-oriented viewpoint, had been of the survey type, with mail questionnaires. Stoll had tried various types and found that mail was just as effective for his purposes and much cheaper; therefore, Old Home Kitchens used it exclusively. There were also many national research centers which maintained indexes of consumer behavior and which were highly reputable in the field of market research. However, Stoll felt that the nature of the needed information warranted extensive personal attention. He believed that the advertising agency would serve best in this respect. The scope of the needed research was so great that the agency would have to contract out certain aspects. Actual plans had not been formulated, but the initial efforts would probably be carried out by means of a seminar-type question-and-answer program with participants consisting of a random sampling of the population—both club members and nonclub members. Stoll knew that the future of the division's business depended upon the information that he would receive from this research, and therefore he was willing to spend a considerable sum for it. He intended to implement the program within the next year.

*Should the Old Home Kitchens Division of Benson's, Inc., have undertaken a marketing research program? If so, who should have done the research? What role should the sales personnel have played in the research?*

*Develop an outline for the marketing research. If you feel that there is no need for marketing research, state your reasons.*

# I-10. SCIENTIFIC-ATLANTA, INC.:
## Manufacturer of Electronic Equipment—
## Decision on Adding a New Product by Acquisition

Top management of Scientific-Atlanta, Inc., was faced with a decision concerning whether or not to purchase from Spencer Kennedy Laboratories the design of a new two-way amplifier used in the Community Antenna Television (CATV) industry. Spencer Kennedy wanted to sell its amplifiers because of a lack of business caused by a Federal Communications Commission (FCC) freeze on new cable system construction. Scientific-Atlanta, Inc.'s management felt that purchasing the amplifiers would promise an expanded role in the CATV industry as well as help make up for lost business resulting from a decrease in the military market, upon which the company was heavily dependent.

Scientific-Atlanta, Inc., was started in the 1950s by a group of engineers from Georgia Tech's research facility. Through diversification and innovative research and development, the firm grew to be a world leader in its branch of electronics, enjoying an outstanding reputation for its products and services. The company began by developing and producing high-frequency antennas for military applications, such as rapid-scanning radar antennas. Eventually, Scientific-Atlanta developed products such as an electronic instrument capable of automatically measuring and recording signal patterns transmitted from high-frequency antennas, earth terminals, surveillance receivers, and manual and "slaved" satellite and missile-tracking systems.

For the CATV industry, Scientific-Atlanta, Inc., manufactured a microwave relay system and a full line of "head-end" equipment, which consisted of high-technology items such as a log-periodic antenna, a VHF preamplifier, a superheterodyne signal processor, and a solid-state demodulator. Head-end equipment was critical to the entire cable network, since it was here that the signal quality was either improved or degraded by preamplifiers, amplifiers, and other electronic devices filtering and preparing signals for the cable network. The head-end equipment cleaned up the signal by processing it, translated the frequency of the signal, and amplified the signal to a predetermined level going out of the head end. Scientific-Atlanta had about 30 percent of the head-end market.

The FCC freeze on new cable system construction prohibited further expansion in the top 100 television markets. Cable television systems were initiated in local areas where television reception was either poor or nonexistent. As long as CATV was limited to areas that could not otherwise get a good television signal, the broadcasters and the FCC were happy. However, with the proliferation of cable systems came greater pressure to expand into the cities, where 87 percent of the television sets were located. To enlist subscribers in areas where television reception was good, cable operators had to provide something new to differentiate the service. For example, differentiating features took the form of news and weather reports, the stock-market ticker tape, and time and temperature reports. Another extra provided was a channel from a distant metropolitan area; but when this feature was offered, the broadcasters and the FCC expressed concern. Ultimately, the FCC decided that the CATV industry required regulation, and the agency adopted rules which essentially prohibited any further expansion in the top 100 television markets, but which left the remote areas open for continued development.

During the freeze, considerable thought and study went into the future potential of cable communications. For example, the Stanford Research Institute studied the economics of cable systems and developed projections on return-on-investment. The Sloan Commission investigated the impact of cable systems on American life. It was generally felt by industry experts that if the FCC permitted cable into the cities, the cable system would have to have capability for two-way communications, which required new technology. For example, the line amplifiers had to amplify in both directions, which meant additional electronics in the home. These technical problems were being solved. Scientific-Atlanta was in the process of developing a digital control center for a two-way system and planned to have it ready for the next National Cable Television Association trade show. The new amplifier offered for sale by Spencer Kennedy Labs was a two-way design. During the freeze, many of the applications for future systems were based on the capability for two-way communications, such as that required for pay television, polling, interactive educational programs, and burglar and fire alarms.

All in all, the horizons for CATV seemed promising. Scientific-Atlanta's management believed that to have a greater role in the CATV industry it was necessary to become a full-line supplier, which would be possible with the purchase of the Spencer Kennedy design. Although there were already over 5 million subscribers to cable television in more than 4,000 communities served by about 2,800 cable operators, it was estimated that there was considerable untapped potential. Becoming a full-line equipment supplier would throw Scientific-Atlanta, Inc., into direct competition with full-line suppliers such as Jerrold (which had 50 percent of the market), Theta-Com (20 percent), Anaconda, Sylvania, AEL, C-Cor, and Tocom.

The management of Scientific-Atlanta reasoned that a decision to purchase the new design would affect the company in three major ways: (1) the company would become a full-line supplier; (2) it would mean competing with companies that were formerly customers; and (3) being a full-line supplier would mean orders in the millions instead of orders in the thousands, thus tending to restrict the potential customers to cable system operators.

Management further believed that the financial aspects of the purchase would not be overly burdensome. In order to determine an appropriate price for the Spencer Kennedy design, a study was made to determine the cost of developing an amplifier from scratch.

It was felt that the purchase of the new design would buy about one year's development time.

*Should Scientific-Atlanta, Inc., have purchased the new two-way amplifier from Spencer Kennedy Laboratories? Justify your position.*

## I-11.   REBEL MILLS:
## Textiles Manufacturer—
## Determining Reasons for a Sales Slump

The management of Bulldog Mills was concerned about a three-year sales decline of one of the products of one of its divisions. Bulldog Mills was a medium-sized manufacturer of textiles, with annual sales of over $98 million and with headquarters in Vicksburg, Mississippi. A Bulldog division, Rebel Mills, showed kitchen towel sales of $6 million for the previous year; however, it was the third consecutive year that Rebel's sales had declined. In addition, costs had increased to a level of $5.8 million, leaving a profit margin of $200,000, the company's lowest in twelve years.

Rebel Mills, located in Yazoo City, Mississippi, manufactured textile products for both household and industrial uses, with the latter accounting for a large majority of total sales and profits. The company produced a complete line of industrial textile products but only a very limited line of household textile products. For the household textiles market, Rebel Mills produced only kitchen textiles, with other divisions of Bulldog Mills producing bathroom and bedroom textiles. And, within the kitchen-textiles product line, which consisted of kitchen towels, dishcloths, and tablecloths, Rebel Mills made only kitchen towels. Also, no other division made the other two products in the kitchen textiles line.

Rebel Mills' kitchen towels were distributed nationwide by a sales organization of nineteen sales representatives through a network of wholesalers and retailers. There were eight company salespeople, seven of whom operated out of New York City and who had responsibility for the Northeastern United States, as well as all major department-store-chain accounts regardless of the location of the chain's home office. The other company salesperson specialized in selling to grocery chains, in addition to monitoring the performance of four food brokers who also sold the Rebel Mills line. All company sales personnel received a salary plus a commission based upon a quota.

The four food brokers representing Rebel Mills sold to regional grocery chains located in different geographical areas of the United States. They received a 3 percent commission on all sales.

Besides the company sales staff and food brokers, Rebel Mills used seven manufacturers' agents who handled noncompeting lines of textile products. They received a 3 percent commission on all sales of Rebel Mills products.

For the past five years, Rebel Mills had manufactured private-label kitchen towels for four large department store chains, including the Harmony House brand for Sears, Roebuck and Co. Each of the private labels was manufactured to the buyer's specifications. The result was that the five different weaves, including its own Rebel Mills brand, required varying amounts of yarn and machine time, thereby making it very difficult for efficient scheduling of machinery. Rebel Mills' cost of producing private labels was greater than had been anticipated and, coupled with heavy price competition for the business, was partly responsible for the steadily declining profit margin. At the same time, management was reluctant to abandon the private-label business, since it permitted the use of excess plant capacity and accounted for nearly 40 percent of Rebel's total kitchen towel output.

Rebel Mills did a modest amount of advertising for its own brand. The company typically spent less than 2 percent of sales on advertising, with the previous year's expenditure amounting to $60,000. The entire amount was allocated to *Good Housekeeping* magazine for the sole reason of obtaining that publication's Seal of Approval. It was believed that displaying the Seal of Approval with Rebel Mills kitchen towels provided good point-of-purchase promotion.

Recent developments concerning its own brand of kitchen towels caused great alarm for Rebel Mills' management. During the past two years, a large number of accounts had been lost, and it was becoming increasingly difficult to obtain new accounts. Furthermore, there was growing customer dissatisfaction with Rebel Mills products. The sales staff strongly believed that these difficulties stemmed from the fact that Rebel Mills sold only kitchen towels and most customers, especially the volume buyers, preferred to purchase at least a complete line of kitchen textiles and, even more desirably, a complete line of household textiles, from a single manufacturer.

As a result, the sales force recommended that Rebel Mills begin as soon as possible to manufacture a complete line of kitchen textiles, to include kitchen towels, dishcloths, and tablecloths. The sales force further recommended that when it became financially feasible, Rebel Mills should also produce a complete line of bathroom and bedroom textiles to round out its household textiles offering. However, Rebel Mills' management believed that, because of a heavier commitment to its industrial textiles line, it would be impossible to produce a full line of kitchen textiles, let alone a full line of household textiles.

Added to these difficulties, three other interrelated factors contributed to Rebel Mills' competitive disadvantage: (1) of the three main groups of household textiles, kitchen textiles provided the lowest profit margin, with kitchen towels allowing the smallest margin in its category; (2) the greater sales volume of the larger manufacturers enabled them to realize economies of scale; and (3) the combination of the first two factors led the larger manufacturers to lower the price of the kitchen-textiles product line to induce volume buyers to purchase the higher-margin bathroom and bedroom textiles. Cannon Mills, the industry leader, for example, followed this strategy.

It was in this setting that the management of Rebel Mills decided to evaluate fully the prospects of its kitchen-towel product line. It was generally agreed that some action had to be taken soon.

*What alternatives were available to Rebel Mills' management with respect to its kitchen-towel product line? Evaluate each alternative, suggesting and defending that which you believe represented the best course of action for Rebel Mills.*

# I-12.   UNITED AIRFLOW, INC.:
## Manufacturer of Household Appliances—
## Salesperson's Job

United Airflow, Inc., was a manufacturer of air conditioners, dehumidifiers, humidifiers, vaporizers, and a variety of other small household appliances. The United sales force consisted of 200 people, accounting for about $125 million net sales volume annually. Thomas Rogers had been a salesperson for United Airflow for eight years, calling on department stores, discount houses, appliance stores, and hardware stores. His territory consisted of the western half of Ohio and southern Michigan. Rogers had been one of the leading salespeople for United Airflow over the past three years, ranking tenth among the entire sales force in sales volume. However, despite favorable business conditions in his territory, Rogers' performance had fallen off, with a current ranking of thirtieth in the sales force.

The branch sales manager in Toledo, the office from which Rogers worked, had a conference with Rogers to try to uncover the reasons for the sales decline. The sales manager believed that a first step should be to compare Rogers' daily call reports with the job description of a United Airflow salesperson.

Following is the "Specific Duties and Responsibilities" section of the job description for a United Airflow salesperson:

A.   Present and potential customers
   1.   Achieve sales volume goals as determined in cooperation with sales manager.
   2.   Improve dealers' merchandising methods.
   3.   Call on dealers regularly.
   4.   Introduce new products by discussing with dealers the new products' selling features, new policies, and new campaigns as they apply to the new products.
   5.   Explain United's advertising and promotion plans and assist dealers in carrying out local advertising programs, and make sure that all dealers are aware of current United Airflow advertising.
   6.   Provide assistance in inventory control.
   7.   Assist dealers in training salespeople, setting up point-of-purchase displays, solving retail management problems, and provide any other assistance deemed essential for the maintenance of a long-term relationship with customers.
   8.   Provide feedback of information relating to market trends, demand preferences, dealer suggestions, competitive strategies, and all other information thought to be valuable for the preservation of the United sales operation.
   9.   Handle dealer complaints with an absolute minimum of delay and make sure there is a fair settlement.
   10.  Secure new dealers by making a market analysis as suggested on the Potential New Dealer form, including selection of towns in which there is no dealer for United products, observation of competition, selection of most desirable dealer prospect, and presentation of the United Airflow sales program.
B.   Contact architects, appliance dealers and installers, contractors, and subcontractors and sell them United products, or sell them on specifying United equipment for installation in new buildings and new homes. Keep these persons informed of new developments in the United Airflow line.

C. Keep abreast of competitive practices and dealers handling competing products by checking resale practices, sales plans, advertising, and new products.

D. Prepare all reports and correspondence promptly so as to maintain their timeliness.

E. Make effective utilization of time, being sure to take advantage of every opportunity which will help to sharpen sales skills and develop better all-around selling ability.

Following are Rogers' daily call reports for a typical week during the past several months:

### Monday

Call 1. Nicholson Department Store. United customer. Took order for five Model 78G9 small vaporizers.

Call 2. Drummond's Discount Variety. First call on prospective dealer. Interested in carrying toasters and radios. Call back later.

Call 3. Patton and Swain, Architects. Second call. Tried to interest them in United products. Not interested.

Call 4. Hicks Hardware. First call. Tried to interest in our complete line. Possible interest in smallest air-conditioning unit. Call back later.

Call 5. Klein and Sons. Department store. Buyer unavailable.

Call 6. Poindexter Construction Co. Home builder. Completely unapproachable the moment I mentioned United Airflow. Could not get reason.

Call 7. Tufts Hardware. First call. Happy with present line of small appliances and does not want to take on an additional line.

Call 8. Ames and Wade. Discount store. Sales poor in United dehumidifiers and humidifiers, but okay in air conditioning. Thinking of dropping the poor sellers and concentrating on better-selling competitors. Will let me know next trip.

### Tuesday

Call 1. Sawyer Construction Co. Developers. Tried to interest in air conditioners for apartment-building complex. Appeared interested, but said to contact the architect.

Call 2. Hennessy Appliance Outlet. Regular customer. Needed help with a new point-of-purchase display. Couldn't oblige because of delay in getting the materials from the Promotion Department. Upset, but placed normal monthly order.

Call 3. Feinberg's, Inc. Department store. Regular customer. Business slow, but expect it to get better.

Call 4. Herb's Hardware. Regular customer. Sales call interrupted when a long-lost pal of Herb's appeared on the scene.

Call 5. Skinner's Discount. Regular customer. Overstocked at present.

Call 6. Glick and Sons. Department store. Regular customer. Took big order. Sales good. Complained about lack of advertising support by United.

Call 7. Cambridge Appliances. First call. Buyer too busy. Call back later.

Call 8. Franklin Hardware. First call. Has nothing in this product line, but is expanding store and seems interested in carrying these products. Has been contacted by two competitors. Will call back.

Call 9. Horwitz, Inc. Regular customer. Buyer out all week.

Call 10. Drucker and Hayes. Regular customer. Small order for vaporizers.

### Wednesday

Call 1. Bosco and Baron. Large department store. Regular customer. Carries most complete offering of anyone in territory. Reviewed advantages of United Airflow products.

Call 2. Page's Bargainland. First call. Is in process of eliminating slow movers and not interested in taking on any new brands.

Call 3. Alberts and Machen. Architects for Sawyer Construction Co. Already placed order with competitor for 300 air-conditioning units for Sawyer's new apartments. Expressed little interest for future orders.

Call 4. Callahan's. First call. New discount store in Northeast Mall. Will consider. Call back later.

Call 5. Kirshner Associates. Shopping center developer. Has plans for new center. Call back later.

Call 6. Frost Brothers Appliances. Store closed. Reason unknown.

Call 7. Gridiron State University. First call. Done business with competitor for years and happy.

*Thursday*

Call 1. Thompson's Hardware. Regular customer. Not opened yet.

Call 2. Glenn and Driscoll. Regular customer. Buyer out.

Call 3. Frank's Greasy Spoon. First call. Will consider an air conditioner. Business slow. Call back later.

Call 4. Callahan Excavating. Building five homes now. Would like to install United air-conditioning units but complained about price.

Call 5. Snell, Bascom, and Birch. Real-estate developers. Used to be good customers but switched purchases to competitor for unstated reason. Happy with present supplier.

Call 6. Davis Stores. Department store. Regular customer. Worked with three salespeople on selling techniques.

Call 7. Hardiman's. Discount store. Occasional customer. Business booming. No order as don't want to change anything while business is good.

Call 8. Hoffman's House of Appliances. Regular customer. Complained about lack of good salespeople. No order.

*Friday*

Spent morning in weekly sales meeting at branch sales office. Made first call at 2:00 P.M.

Call 1. Upham's Appliance Store. Regular customer. Took small order.

Call 2. Gaudette's Appliances. Regular customer. Complained about competitive dealers' pricing tactics. Wondered if he could get United air conditioners, dehumidifiers, humidifiers, and vaporizers at lower prices.

Call 3. Roper and Sons. Appliance store. Regular customer. Buyer out.

Call 4. Kostick's. Department store. First call. Buyer out.

Call 5. Jeter and Jones. Hardware store. Regular customer. No order.

Call 6. Hoffman's House of Appliances. Regular customer. Owner-buyer out.

*Compare the daily call reports of Thomas Rogers with the job description of a United Airflow salesperson. What strengths and weaknesses are apparent from the comparison?*

# I-13.   STANAMER CORPORATION:
# Plumbing and Heating Company—
# Sales-Force Expansion

The Plumbing and Heating Division of Stanamer Corporation made and sold plumbing fixtures and fittings, hydronic heating and cooling equipment, food-waste disposals, water softeners, and invalid bath lifts. The largest of seven corporate divisions, it operated fourteen plants from coast to coast. Toward the end of the year the general sales manager, J. B. Samson, was analyzing a problem concerning an increase in the size of the sales force. (See Exhibit 1 for Selling Section organization.) The budget for the next year provided funds for adding fifteen salespeople, and Samson compared two alternatives: (1) hiring sales personnel with previous sales experience in the field, and (2) following the company traditional practice of hiring and training inexperienced persons.

Stanamer led the plumbing and heating industry in sales; its sales of $100 million were double those of the nearest competitor. Well known and respected, the company's market share was estimated at 50 percent. Although its position was enviable, company management recognized the dangers of complacency, particularly as competition stiffened and the market share showed signs of declining.

Activity in the home-building industry, the largest market for plumbing and heating supplies, had fallen off. There were predictions that new housing starts in the first half of the current year would be below the previous year's level; however, an upturn was expected. When new housing starts dropped, total demand for plumbing and heating products also declined; consequently, competition for available business increased. Most firms moved to hire additional sales personnel to provide more intensive market coverage. Samson's decision to hire fifteen additional salespeople was made for the short-term objective of reducing excess inventory. If housing starts recovered, top management might question the value of having fifteen extra persons, since in such circumstances Stanamer normally received sufficient business to support its full productive capacity.

EXHIBIT 1
Selling Section, Marketing Department

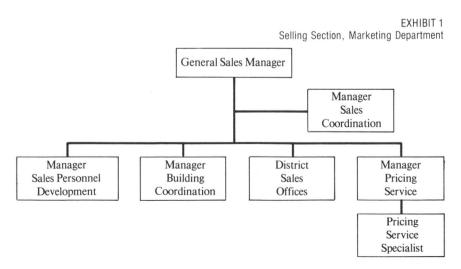

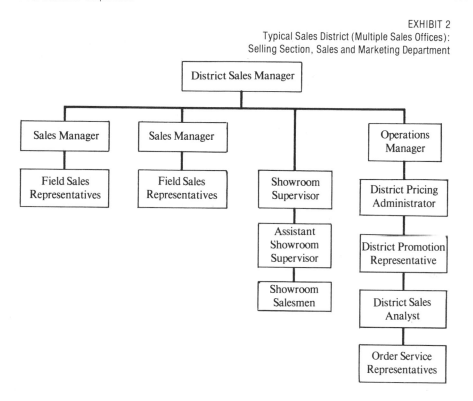

The company's products were of high quality and as such commanded prices about 10 percent above those of competitors. All promotion emphasized the superior product quality. Company sales-training sessions, focusing on product information and selling techniques, also emphasized the price-quality relationship.

Stanamer's sales force sold exclusively through wholesale plumbing and heating distributors. The 250-person force called upon 1,400 wholesalers, who, in turn, sold through 50,000 contractors and plumbers. Sales personnel worked out of twenty-three sales offices located in some but not all of thirteen sales districts. (See Exhibits 2, 3, and 4 for the organizations of the various types of typical sales districts.)

District sales managers performed administrative duties and reported directly to the general sales manager. Their responsibilities included recruiting and training of the sales staff. However, the general sales manager determined the number and the qualifications of those hired.

The average salesperson wrote orders totaling from $400,000 to $800,000 annually. Each received a straight salary of $10,000 to $12,000 per year. Sales personnel maintained contact with distributors and assisted them in inventory control, in the training of their sales staff, and in the use of company promotional plans, programs, and materials. Sales personnel also promoted the use of Stanamer products through their contacts with home-builder and contractor trade associations. In addition, they promoted the use of the division's products in talks with key personnel in hospital and school administrations, public utilities, and governmental agencies. They also inspected consumer products and made service calls.

```
                    ┌─────────────────────────┐
                    │  District Sales Manager │
                    └─────────────────────────┘
          ┌──────────────────┴──────────────────────────┐
  ┌─────────────────┐                          ┌──────────────────┐
  │  Sales Manager  │                          │ Operations Manager│
  └─────────────────┘                          └──────────────────┘
  ┌─────────────────┐   ┌──────────────────┐        ┌──────────────────┐
  │  Field Sales    │   │ District Pricing │        │  Order Service   │
  │ Representatives │   │  Administrator   │        │ Representatives  │
  └─────────────────┘   └──────────────────┘        └──────────────────┘
                        ┌──────────────────┐
                        │District Promotion│
                        │ Representative   │
                        └──────────────────┘
```

Traditionally, Stanamer hired inexperienced people and put them through a six-month program. Sales recruits spent the first three months becoming acquainted with the company's products and policies. They then attended a formal three-month program emphasizing advanced product knowledge and sales techniques. Training costs amounted to approximately $2,000 per person. Once out of training, new salespersons generally became fully operational and productive in from three to six months. (See Exhibit 5.)

To lure salespeople with field experience away from competitors required starting salaries averaging $10,000 annually. Also, considerable recruiting time and effort were involved, and there was the danger that competition might reciprocate. People with previous field experience usually became fully operational Stanamer sales personnel in about one month.

```
                    ┌─────────────────────────┐
                    │  District Sales Manager │
                    └─────────────────────────┘
          ┌──────────────────┴──────────────────────────┐
  ┌─────────────────┐                          ┌──────────────────┐
  │  Field Sales    │                          │ Operations Manager│
  │ Representatives │                          └──────────────────┘
  └─────────────────┘   ┌──────────────────┐        ┌──────────────────┐
                        │ District Pricing │        │  Order Service   │
                        │  Administrator   │        │ Representatives  │
                        └──────────────────┘        └──────────────────┘
                        ┌──────────────────┐
                        │District Promotion│
                        │ Representative   │
                        └──────────────────┘
```

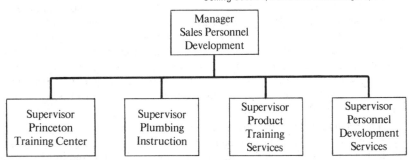

EXHIBIT 5
Sales Personnel Development Unit:
Selling Section, Sales and Marketing Department

Samson wanted to hire the fifteen additional people, but he was not certain whether he should concentrate on those with or without previous selling experience in the industry.

*How should Samson have gone about implementing the decision to add fifteen new sales-persons?*

*In alleviating the excess inventory situation, what other alternatives should have been explored?*

*Evaluate the appropriateness of Stanamer's various policies and practices relating to sales-force management.*

## I-14. THE KRAMER COMPANY:
## Manufacturer of Men's Toiletries—
## Seeking Greater Sales and Profitability

Sales executives of The Kramer Company, manufacturer of a limited line of high-priced men's toiletries, were concerned that the current level of sales volume for Forest Dew, the company's major product, was insufficient to support the present sales organization of the company. Sales for Forest Dew had increased gradually during the past three years; however, the rate of increase was substantially below forecasted figures. At the same time, actual profits for Forest Dew were well below those projected, even for the existing level of sales volume. As a result, Kramer sales executives sought to conduct an overall analysis of the entire sales strategy underlying its primary product, with the two-fold aim of achieving greater sales volume along with increased profitability to bring both figures closer to their desired levels.

The Kramer Company was a division of Mitchell Company, one of the leaders in the men's-grooming-aids industry. The Kramer Company was set up by Mitchell Company as a means of entering the "prestige-price" market for men's personal products and to establish working relationships with department stores and specialty shops. Since its inception, Mitchell had catered to the mass market for men's grooming aids, with an extensive line of successful products. It was hoped that Kramer would permit Mitchell to achieve successful entry into the high-priced market for men's toiletries. Selling unique, high-quality products to a limited market through restricted distribution policy, Kramer also was to be an industry leader in new products and new packaging concepts.

Kramer's first marketing effort was Forest Dew, a shaving cologne. It was packaged in a colorful, uniquely designed bottle and sold in an attractive styrofoam case. Forest Dew was priced at $1.25 per ounce, as Kramer management felt that this price would enhance the prestige of the product. The shaving-cologne segment of the men's-toiletries market was highly competitive; the bulk of Forest Dew's competition came from such brands as Aramis, Braggi, Kanon, English Leather, and Brut.

The product was test marketed for the Christmas season in New York City and Los Angeles before being introduced on a national scale. In New York City, Forest Dew was sold in such stores as Lord and Taylor's, Gimbel's, and Macy's, and in Los Angeles it was sold in such stores as I. Magnin, May's, and The Broadway. With very favorable results in the test markets, Forest Dew was introduced nationally in time for the Father's Day and graduation gift seasons. On the basis of the test markets, Kramer estimated that department stores would account for 60 percent of total sales, men's stores for 30 percent, and independent drug stores for 10 percent.

Kramer employed a sales force of thirty persons, all of whom were selected from the Mitchell Company and included some of Mitchell's best salespersons. There were three sales regions—New York, Chicago, and Los Angeles. The sales regions were further broken down into districts, with district offices in Atlanta, Detroit, St. Louis, Dallas, and San Francisco.

The national sales effort was under the direction of the General Sales Manager, who was headquartered in Philadelphia. The three regional sales managers reported directly to the General Sales Manager. Their major responsibilities were related to directing the sales effort in their respective regions. The district sales managers' duties included the directing, hiring, and training of field sales personnel. District managers also had limited account responsibility, usually calling only on key accounts in their districts. Field sales personnel were required to handle all Kramer business within their respective territories. Salespeople were also responsible for selecting the outlets in their respective areas.

The Kramer Company utilized a policy of exclusive distribution for Forest Dew. The management felt this was necessary if Forest Dew was to be a prestige item. No wholesalers were used in the distribution channel, as Kramer preferred to deal directly with its exclusive retailers. Executives believed that the absence of wholesalers would enable the firm to more closely control the distribution of its product and therefore maintain the prestigious image the company desired for Forest Dew. Kramer also realized that it could exercise more control over the selling price of its product if retailers were given exclusive rights to a territory and did not have to be concerned with price-cutting competition. It was generally recognized by Kramer's sales executives that elimination of wholesalers probably increased the total cost of marketing Forest Dew, since Kramer had to perform the wholesaling functions itself, but this was considered acceptable in light of the heightened image of the product.

Kramer advertising was designed to familiarize the public with the Kramer name and, specifically, the Forest Dew brand of shaving cologne. It was felt that effective advertising that presold the consumer would virtually eliminate the need for personal selling at the retail level. Advertising expenditures were divided among network and local spot television, magazines, and cooperative advertising. To promote a prestige image, Kramer advertised Forest Dew in such magazines as *New Yorker, Esquire, Sports Illustrated, and Playboy*. Its television spots were similarly carefully selected with the Forest Dew image in mind. Kramer engaged in cooperative advertising with some of its larger accounts on a fifty-fifty basis. Kramer's Forest Dew account was handled by the advertising agency of Doyle Dane Bernbach. The heaviest promotions of the year came at Father's Day and Christmas, the seasons that Kramer estimated to account for 75 percent of its sales.

While Forest Dew was in its early stages of market development, Kramer introduced an entirely new line of men's cosmetics. The product was a popularly priced line of aftershave lotion and cologne called Male Image. The new product was intended for the mass men's market, and therefore a policy of intensive distribution was followed. The advertising for Male Image, done by Ogilvy and Mather, used a variety of appeals and concentrated on a relatively hard-hitting approach.

Many retailers that carried Forest Dew would not accept Male Image because of its popular price and because it was being sold in outlets such as K-Mart, Woolco, and a variety of discount department stores and drugstores. The Kramer philosophy in bringing out Male Image was that the company had excluded itself from a segment of the men's-toiletries market and Male Image was introduced to fill that void.

It was much too early to estimate the success of Male Image; however, it was abundantly clear that Forest Dew was experiencing very disappointing sales and profitability. The sales picture of Forest Dew indicated to Kramer's management that present sales volume could not support the company's present sales organization. As a result, Kramer was considering the possibility of introducing the Forest Dew line into more retail outlets, such as Penney's, Ward's, Sears, and various drug chains. Management also believed that such a change in its distribution policy and sales strategy would make it easier to gain dealer acceptance of its new Male Image line.

*What alternatives did the Kramer Company have open to achieve greater profitability for the Forest Dew brand of men's shaving cologne? Analyze each alternative.*

# I-15.   MARTIN PACKAGING COMPANY, INC.:
## Manufacturer of Packaging Products and Systems—
## Evaluation of Sales Strategy

Thomas Steeves, Manager of the Marketing Research and Analysis Department of the Martin Packaging Company, Inc., was faced with the task of evaluating the marketing and sales strategy implications of the new "plasti-shield" bottle being tested by the soft drink industry. The plasti-shield bottle was a new type of soft drink bottle that had a plastic coating around the lower half of the bottle.

Martin Packaging Company was founded about 130 years ago. The company originally produced only paper products; however, in the last 30 years, Martin had purchased a majority stock interest in 24 companies and a minority interest in several others.

As a result, Martin had a diversified product line. One of the 24 companies which Martin controlled was the Dixon Paper Company, a family-held firm.

Dixon was established in 1936 and produced corrugated boxes, folding boxes, dry-cleaning bags, and other types of plastic bags. During World War II, under a government contract, Dixon developed "V-Board" packaging, which consisted of solid fiberboard. V-Board was water-resistant and highly durable packaging that could withstand even the harshest handling abuse. It was used to ship goods across the ocean during the war.

After World War II, it was recognized that V-Board had considerable potential for use as secondary packaging for soft drinks. Therefore, when Dixon developed the V-Board Coca-Cola carton, Dixon Paper Company grew so rapidly that it became the leader in paperboard packaging.

Martin Packaging Company also was involved with paperboard packaging; however, this part of its packaging line was not very profitable. Consequently, when Martin was looking for further vertical integration through a merger, it was evident that Dixon Paper Company offered substantial promise, and Martin began to acquire Dixon stock. After the merger, Martin developed many new packaging methods for the soft drink and beer industries. Martin also advanced into automated systems packaging. Net sales were approximately $1.1 billion.

Martin was organized into two divisions for producing and marketing paper and related products. The Martin Container Division produced folding boxes for frozen foods, dry goods, and hardware. It also produced plastic Cluster-Paks for margarine and other dairy products. The Martin Packaging Division manufactured and marketed secondary packaging for soft drinks, beer, and wine.

The Packaging Division, for which Steeves' research and analysis was conducted, had a direct sales force of forty people operating from the same location. Martin management felt that the secondary packaging industry was changing from one in which the sales force simply took orders to one in which the sales personnel had to provide "technical assistance" to the customer, as this was critical to success in the packaging industry. It was strongly felt that Martin's sales force needed an excellent working knowledge of the packaging industry, plus considerable knowledge of each customer's business.

Martin had maintained a forty-person sales force for several years. It was divided along both geographic and product lines. Martin believed it should deliver a total packaging system to its customers, and that, to do this, ten salespeople must call only on soft drink bottlers in major cities to explain the automatic packaging system Martin had to offer. The remaining thirty salespersons in the Martin Packaging Division were assigned geographic areas within the Southeast. These salespeople handled all breweries as well as soft drink bottlers in their respective areas.

Sales personnel were compensated by salary, with no bonus system in effect, except "across-the-board" bonuses, the size of which was determined by overall company performance.

On the whole, Martin management was pleased with the performance of the sales force and it was regarded as a vital factor in the company's success. However, recently a question had been raised concerning the information-feedback function of the salespeople. A few instances were cited in which communications had been either nonexistent or had broken down somewhat between the sales personnel and the management.

The Packaging Division of Martin was continually being evaluated because secondary packaging, especially for the soft drink industry, was highly competitive. The industry leaders that provided major competition for Martin were International Paper Company, Olin-Mathieson, and Federal Paperboard. Secondary packaging in the soft drink industry consisted of packaging, such as soft drink cartons and wrap-around plastic cartons, which Martin produced. This was in contrast to soft drink primary packaging, which referred to the bottles or cans that contained the soft drink.

Soft drink bottlers traditionally operated small-scale bottling plants in almost every U.S. city of any size. For years they manufactured only returnable bottles. Martin was among the leading producers, in sales volume and profit, of the traditional cardboard carton for returnable bottles.

With the innovation of the canned soft drink, the investment capital necessary to bottle (can) soft drinks increased substantially. Bottlers began consolidating into large-scale operations to gain economies of scale. As the primary packaging changed, the secondary packaging changed also. The revolutionary "wraparound" carton was developed. However, Martin did not adopt this new method for several months after its introduction by a competitor, and thus Martin lost its position as the leader in the secondary packaging of soft drinks.

When the nonreturnable bottle was introduced in the soft drink industry, Martin welcomed this innovation. The canned soft drink had reduced the requirements of secondary packaging, because the cans themselves performed much of the advertising, promotion, and protection functions. The nonreturnable bottle again called for secondary packaging for promotion purposes as well as for product protection and convenience in handling. Martin was among the leaders in developing necessary cartons for the nonreturnable bottles. As sales of the nonreturnable bottles grew, Martin again became the industry leader in secondary packaging in the soft drink industry.

But later, as sales of nonreturnable bottles began to slump, Martin speculated that people simply were becoming less willing to spend the extra money that nonreturnable bottles cost for convenience. To combat this slump, soft drink bottlers began to work on the possibility of a new type of bottle which would have a plastic coating around the lower 50 percent of the bottle. This research product was called the "plasti-shield" bottle. As the industry began research on additional primary packaging, Martin began research on additional secondary packaging.

The plasti-shield bottle was born from interdivision rivalry at Owens-Illinois. Owens-Illinois invested over $40,000,000 in the project. The method of production used could produce up to 580 bottles per minute, with a future anticipated speed of 700 bottles per minute. Based on a forecasted market demand, Owens-Illinois planned to establish between eight and ten production facilities in Boston, New York, Chicago, Los Angeles, and St. Louis for the manufacture of 10- to 16-ounce sizes of primary glass containers.

The plasti-shield bottle weighed about 3.5 ounces less than the lightest nonreturnable bottle of any capacity. The plasti-shield rolls of polystyrene were decorated by printing with up to four colors available, but factory production was to be limited by the number of bottles that could be plastic-wrapped in an "off-line" operation. Initially, machine lines applied the plasti-shield jackets at a rate of only 200 bottles per minute (B.P.M.).

Plasti-shield bottles were to be available in colors of flint, green, and amber glass and were to be produced in five sizes—10, 12, 16, 28, and 32 ounces. The plasti-shield container would have three convenience closures: the wide mouth, the aluminum ring-pull, and the narrow neck.

Owens-Illinois had begun work on plasti-shield several years ago, to combat the efficiencies of the 12-ounce can, with essential emphasis on a secondary packaging system to be developed that would handle at least 1,500 B.P.M. and having a packaging materials cost of less than $200 per thousand.

The current secondary packaging of the wide-mouth plasti-shield bottle used the "top-hold" principle in which paperboard cartons were used. Olin-Mathieson, Martin's leading competitor, had arranged for a 60-day delivery on a lease-only basis of a machine designed to run at about 250 B.P.M. This machine was being used in the test setup at Owens-Illinois. The Olin-Mathieson "top-hold" carton was priced at $19 per thousand for 2 by 4 blanks, and $16 per thousand for 2 by 3 blanks.

Owens-Illinois expected the plasti-shield bottles, plus the secondary packaging "top-hold" principle, to develop into a major part of the soft drink container market. Owens-Illinois was going after the can market by offering high-speed filling lines and lower packaging costs. Olin-Mathieson had the competitive advantage in secondary packaging with its new system, and Owens-Illinois' market success with plasti-shield could bring Olin-Mathieson into some of Martin's volume accounts.

Steeves believed that it would be necessary to react fairly soon to the plasti-shield bottle and to the competitive threat posed by Olin-Mathieson. He also believed that any delay would seriously threaten Martin Packaging Company's position as industry leader. He further believed that development of a sales and marketing strategy was essential to success with the plasti-shield bottle.

*Develop a set of recommendations for the sales and marketing strategy that you believe to be necessary to successfully respond to the plasti-shield bottle and to the competitive threat faced by Martin Packaging Company. Specifically, what role do you see for the Martin sales force in this strategy?*

# I-16.  FIFTY FLAMES CANDLE COMPANY:
## Manufacturer of Candles—
## Determination of Sales Strategy

Edwin Dye, Jr., and Marshall Bartlett, partners in the Fifty Flames Candle Company, had just received the financial report of the company's first eight months of operations. It showed a net loss of $3,514. Among other things, the unanticipated early loss shown by Fifty Flames led Dye and Bartlett to question their overall sales strategy.

Dye began manufacturing candles in his home and developed a new process for making "sand candles" which was relatively simple and which required minimal working space. (A sand candle is a wax candle, usually with an irregular shape, with a coating of sand around its outer edges.) Dye was able to personally sell his entire output of candles to small retailers located within a 100-mile radius. Less than a year after he began producing the candles in his home, Dye opened a retail store in which he sold his candles as well as many handcrafted items, such as jewelry and pottery. The retail store was successful from the beginning, with candles being one of the faster-moving items in his inventory. In fact, in ten months, the demand for the sand candles reached a point where Dye decided to establish a separate company to manufacture them. Consequently, Dye joined into a partnership with Bartlett, and they obtained a business license to manufacture and sell candles. Production of the candles continued in Dye's home for another four months after receiving the license, at which time the company rented a building suitable for the candle-manufacturing operation.

Bartlett managed factory operations and, along with one employee, represented the only personnel working in the factory. Sales were at a level where the two were able to produce the candles and pack them for shipment without additional help. When the work load did become too heavy, Dye, president of Fifty Flames and its source of capital, assisted with operations, or temporary help was hired.

The Fifty Flames Candle Company manufactured five types of sand candles as well as pottery candles and floating candles (see Exhibit 1). The sand candles were considered more attractive than conventional sand candles because of a unique processing step developed by the company. Fifty Flames also had perfected a process to use multicolors in a manner that no other candle manufacturer had yet been able to duplicate. The sand candles were sold as conventional candles and as hanging candles. In addition, the company had developed a completely new type of candle; however, until certain production problems could be solved, it was impossible to economically produce this new item.

The company's price structure was such that the contribution margin on all candles was 50 percent. This price structure originally was based upon estimated sales of $20,000 the first year, which, with fixed costs of $716 per month (rent, $90; electricity, $66; and salaries, $560), would have generated a profit.

The Fifty Flames Candle Company's prices were approximately 25 percent below industry averages, because of the firm's low fixed costs (see Exhibit 1). While quantity

EXHIBIT 1
Wholesale Price, Units Sold, and Gross Sales by
Product Type During Company's First Eight Months

| Product | Code | Description | Wholesale Price | Units Sold | Gross Sales |
|---------|------|-------------|-----------------|------------|-------------|
| Sand candle | R-1 | Small, round, single wick | $0.75 | 675 | $ 506.25 |
| Sand candle | R-2 | Small, free form, single wick | 1.25 | 800 | 1,000.00 |
| Sand candle | R-3 | Large, round, double wick | 1.75 | 775 | 1,356.25 |
| Sand candle | R-4 | Large, free form, double wick | 2.25 | 650 | 1,462.50 |
| Sand candle | S-T | Double (joined) | 1.50 | 425 | 637.50 |
| Special candle | H-C | Pottery | 2.50 | 450 | 1,125.00 |
| Special candle | F-C | Small, floating | 0.25 | 1,200 | 300.00 |
| | | | | | $6,387.50 |

discounts were not given in the candle industry, it was general practice for candle manufacturers to pay 50 percent of the freight on very large orders. Fifty Flames did not adhere to this practice, however, because of its lower-than-average prices.

Exhibit 1 shows the wholesale price, units sold, and gross sales by product for the company's first eight months of operation. It was determined that production had been 25 percent of actual plant capacity during the period and that fixed costs would remain the same at the maximum production level. Also, it was estimated that, for a capital investment of $400, Fifty Flames could double its maximum production level.

Fifty Flames did not use formal advertising. It was felt that the combination of product distinctiveness and low prices was sufficient to sell the candles once candle retailers became aware of the company and its products. Since the company used F.O.B. pricing, the policy had been to concentrate sales in the Southeastern region, which was the location of Fifty Flames. Four small agent wholesalers, each with four or five salespersons, represented Fifty Flames in the region. The agents received a commission of 15 percent on all sales.

The aggregate demand for candles had been growing steadily in the past few years, and this was the reason Dye and Bartlett seriously questioned their sales strategy. More so than ever before, a large segment of the population was purchasing candles with the purpose of burning them, rather than for decorative purposes as in the past. As a result, more candles were being used on a regular basis. Of the people who bought candles for actual use rather than decoration, the majority of sales were made to persons in the age bracket 18 to 39. And, more candles were sold in urban areas than in rural areas.

At a meeting between Dye and Bartlett to discuss possible ways of achieving profitability, it was concluded that the agent wholesalers were not doing an adequate job representing the Fifty Flames Candle Company. It was felt that the agent wholesalers were not devoting enough time or effort to their products. Two suggested solutions resulted from this meeting: (1) wholesale prices could be increased and a larger sales commission could be offered; and (2) the number of agent wholesalers representing Fifty Flames could be increaed. Neither Dye nor Bartlett was sure which, if either, of the two approaches would be the best for the Fifty Flames Candle Company.

*What course of action should have been taken by the Fifty Flames Candle Company to increase sales of its candles? Justify your choice.*

Part **II**

# ORGANIZING
# THE SALES EFFORT

# 5

# The Sales Executive's Job

Basically, the sales executive's job, like the jobs of other line executives, involves making decisions and then seeing to it that others carry out these decisions. What qualifications must sales executives have in order to make decisions? They need a considerable base of experiential and other knowledge, much of which may not be very explicit; however, this knowledge base provides them with a "feel" for problems and their possible solutions. They need keen awareness of both company and sales department goals— they must recognize the key features distinguishing the sort of company that top management is trying to build; and they must visualize the nature and type of contributions that the sales department can and should make toward realizing that future "company image." They need the ability to conceptualize problem situations clearly in areas where they have the main decision-making responsibility, and in those where they help make decisions that have implications in other marketing areas and/or in other parts of the business (such as in production or finance).

In other words, the decisions that the sales executive is involved in may affect only the sales department, or they may have significant repercussions for executives elsewhere in the business. Therefore, in performing the job, sales executives must know how to analyze information, how to combine its significance with their own experiential knowledge and judgment (and their willingness to accept a certain degree of risk), how to apply imagination in searching for alternative solutions to problems, how to predict the likely outcomes of different alternatives, and, finally, how to choose that alternative with the best payoff in terms of company and departmental goals.

## NATURE OF SALES-MANAGEMENT POSITIONS

The requirements of the sales executive's job vary from company to company and from position to position within companies. However, certain responsibilities are pretty typically assigned to the same types of executives in different companies. It is possible, therefore, to generalize to a considerable degree about the activities and responsibilities of sales managers, district sales managers, product managers, and other sales or marketing executives. Some companies have formulated concise statements of the duties associated with various positions, known as position descriptions or position guides. Typical position guides for the jobs of sales manager and district sales manager follow.

### Position Guide—Sales Manager

The sales manager is responsible for securing maximum volume of dollar sales through the effective development and execution of sales programs and sales policies for all products sold by his division. In addition to planning and administrative duties, the sales manager is expected to develop working relations with other department heads and the sales executives of other divisions of the company. The sales manager reports to the marketing manager or vice-president for marketing.

In carrying out the job's responsibilities, this sales executive is expected to be concerned with:

**1. Sales Program.** The sales manager should take the initiative in the establishment of long-range sales objectives of the division, in collaboration with other department heads and the marketing manager, to assure achieving overall marketing objectives.

The sales manager should arrange for the development of detailed sales programs designed to improve competitive positions, reduce distribution costs, and reach established sales goals.

The sales manager should review and approve sales policies, sales strategies, and pricing policies (to the extent of the job's responsibility) for all products to ensure that short-term operations are in accord with long-term profitablility and do not jeopardize other phases of the company's operations.

**2. Organization.** The sales manager should establish an effective plan of organization, and methods of controlling the activities of members of the sales organization, that will provide sufficient time for carrying out the full line of departmental responsibilities.

The sales manager should provide leadership to all levels of the sales organization in establishing a sound basis for each individual's self-development, and in making certain that compensation is in line with responsibilities and performance.

**3. Management of Sales-Department Personnel.** The sales manager should identify promising sources for the recruitment of new sales personnel and set standards for selection of the most promising new personnel from among recruits.

The sales manager should provide for the training of new personnel so as to achieve high-level performance in the shortest possible time. At the same time the sales manager should train sales personnel, so as to have an adequate supply of sales executive talent for replacements up through and including the sales manager's own position. The development of human resources is the sales manager's most important responsibility.[1]

The sales manager should ensure that sales personnel are properly motivated, so as to achieve optimum sales performance.

The sales manager should establish a system of sales supervision that will reduce waste and inefficiency and point sales efforts into the most profitable channels.

**4. Internal and External Relations.** The sales manager should develop effective working relations with other department heads and the marketing manager so that every significant sales development can be translated into an appropriate course of action.

---

[1]L. M. Dawson, "Toward a New Concept of Sales Management," *Journal of Marketing,* Vol. 34, No. 2 (April 1970), p. 36.

The sales manager should develop relationships with key customers that will provide maximum long-term participation in their available business.

**5. Communications.**   The sales manager should keep the general manager and the marketing manager fully informed on sales results and future plans of operation.

The sales manager should also establish a system of communication with other sales management and supervisory personnel that will keep them informed of overall divisional sales objectives, results, and problems and keep him informed of their needs and problems.

**6. Control.**   The sales manager should consult with the production manager so that production rates and inventories can be geared as closely as possible to actual sales needs.

The sales manager should review and approve sales and expense budgets and evaluate periodically the performance of all sales activities in relation to budgets and sales goals and take such corrective actions as are required.

The sales manager should delegate authority and develop control records and performance standards to permit a proper balance of his own time spent on various activities in the position guide.

### Position Guide—District Sales Manager

The district sales manager is responsible for the effective deployment of selling efforts and the maintenance of good trade relations in the assigned district. The district sales manager is expected to secure maximum dollar sales of the division's products in accordance with established sales policies and sales programs, within the limits of the sales budget. The district sales manager is responsible to the sales manager for the overall district performance.

In carrying out the job responsibilities, the district sales manager is expected to be concerned with:

**1. Supervision of Sales Personnel.**   The district sales manager should accurately evaluate the sales opportunities in the district and assign territories that have equitable workloads and that permit minimum travel costs, so as to secure maximum dollar sales at minimum cost.

The district sales manager should direct, assist, and supervise the sales personnel in maintaining and improving the division's competitive position and in handling special sales or competitive problems.

The district sales manager should rate salespeople in the performance of all their duties, and at least annually discuss these ratings with them to direct their attention toward areas where improvement is needed.

The district sales manager should advise the sales manager on important personnel problems.

The district sales manager should evaluate the salespeople's strategies for key accounts, helping each to plan strategy for all accounts assigned to him and to develop new accounts.

**2. Control.**   The district sales manager should forecast short-term sales of the district and work with sales personnel in estimating future sales in their territories so that accurate sales budgets and sales quotas can be developed.

The district sales manager should also prepare a periodic progress report on industry conditions, forward plans, and the progress made toward sales objectives.

The district sales manager should report immediately on significant sales or competitive developments that may affect the company's future.

**3. Administration.** The district sales manager should assume responsibility for the efficient administration of the district office operations and warehouse and stock facilities in accord with established policies and procedures.

The district sales manager should develop effective working relations with technical personnel, other district managers, and home-office personnel, so as to take full advantage of their help to achieve sales goals, reduce costs, and effectively carry out sales programs.

**4. Communication.** The district sales manager should study and analyze the plans, programs, and policies originating in the home office and interpret them to the sales staff so that these plans, programs, and policies can be effectively coordinated in the district's activities.

The district sales manager should communicate to the sales manager and top administration any information about customers and markets or about personnel that should be of interest to them.

The district sales manager should maintain membership in professional organizations whose activities are of interest and concern to the division so as to promote better customer relations and develop intelligence sources.

## TIME APPORTIONMENT BY THE TYPICAL SALES EXECUTIVE

To gain a realistic appreciation of the sales executive's job, one should consider not only the kinds of activities performed but also the amount of time allocated to each activity. One of the most comprehensive analyses of time apportionment among sales executives was conducted by the Metropolitan Life Insurance Company. Although this study is now somewhat old, many of its findings are still valid. Figure 5.1 shows how sixty chief sales executives divided their time among eight major sales functions. The table emphasizes the composite average amount of time devoted to each function; it shows, however, average time allocations for sales managers (1) of different types of products, (2) in companies of various sizes, and (3) by types of supervisory organizations, that is, with direct or indirect supervision of the field force by the chief sales executive. As might have been expected, most sales managers devoted more time to sales direction than to any other activity, the average being 28 percent.

This study also revealed that the significance attached to the different duties varied with the class of product marketed. Consumer-goods sales managers tended to spend more time than industrial sales managers on sales planning and research, advertising and sales promotion, product merchandising, and trade relations. In contrast, industrial sales managers placed relatively heavier emphasis on directing the sales force, making calls with salespeople, and selling personal accounts. Consumer-goods sales managers, in general, spent more time on planning and less on operating than did their counterparts in the industrial field. Commercial-goods sales managers spent far more time on planning and less on operating than did sales managers in either of the other fields.

The amount of executive time devoted to each activity was greatly influenced by the size of the organization. Sales executives in small companies spent relatively less time on planning and more on miscellaneous, unclassified, activities. As the size of the company increased, more time was devoted to such planning functions as advertising and sales planning, and research.

FIGURE 5.1

How Sixty Chief Sales Executives Apportion Their Time Among Eight Major Sales Activities

| Company Classifications | Number of Companies | Operating Functions (%) | | | | | Planning Functions (%) | | | | | Other (%) |
|---|---|---|---|---|---|---|---|---|---|---|---|---|
| | | Directing Sales Organization | Making Calls with Field Personnel | Trade Relations | Selling Personal Accounts | Total Operating | Sales Planning and Research | Advertising and Sales Promotion | Product Merchandising | Sales Training | Total Planning | |
| All companies | 60 | 28 | 14 | 8 | 4 | 54 | 13 | 10 | 9 | 8 | 40 | 6 |
| By type of product: | | | | | | | | | | | | |
| Consumer goods | 27 | 26 | 13 | 10 | 4 | 53 | 15 | 13 | 9 | 7 | 44 | 3 |
| Industrial goods | 28 | 31 | 16 | 7 | 6 | 60 | 9 | 7 | 7 | 8 | 31 | 9 |
| Commercial goods* | 5 | 26 | 3 | 6 | 1 | 36 | 23 | 15 | 16 | 7 | 61 | 3 |
| By size of company: | | | | | | | | | | | | |
| Large (100 to 10,000 salespeople) | 18 | 28 | 13 | 7 | 4 | 52 | 15 | 11 | 10 | 7 | 43 | 5 |
| Medium (26 to 86 salespeople) | 22 | 29 | 14 | 8 | 5 | 56 | 13 | 12 | 9 | 7 | 41 | 3 |
| Small (4 to 25 salespeople) | 20 | 27 | 15 | 10 | 5 | 57 | 11 | 8 | 7 | 8 | 34 | 9 |
| By type of organization: | | | | | | | | | | | | |
| Direct supervision of the field force | 24 | 36 | 13 | 9 | 4 | 62 | 10 | 9 | 6 | 5 | 30 | 8 |
| Supervision through subordinates | 24 | 21 | 13 | 9 | 4 | 47 | 17 | 11 | 11 | 10 | 49 | 4 |
| Number of executives reporting each function | 60 | 60 | 58 | 43 | 32 | — | 55 | 56 | 53 | 51 | — | — |

*Includes products sold principally to offices and stores.

Source: *Function of the Sales Executive*, Metropolitan Life Insurance Company, New York. p. 26. Reprinted by permission.

The type of supervisory organization, the number and caliber of subordinate executives, and the manner of delegating authority also had important influences on the way chief sales executives distributed their time and effort. When sales executives supervised the field force directly, the additional time required for sales direction resulted in their spending 62 percent of their total time on operating functions. But when supervision of the field force was exercised through subordinates, the planning functions were more important, and sales executives were less involved with actual operations.

## COMPENSATION PATTERNS FOR SALES EXECUTIVES

Because selling is normally more important to the success of the enterprise than either production or finance, marketing and sales executives often command substantially higher compensation payments. Chief marketing executives in large companies are likely to earn, on the average, $75,000 or more annually, and some have total compensation running into hundreds of thousands of dollars. Chief sales executives average 70 percent as much as the top marketing man.[2] Top marketing and sales executives usually rank among the highest-paid men in the company. The main reason for this is that as much as one third of their compensation is made up of bonuses for reaching predetermined sales goals. Financial rewards in smaller companies are less spectacular, but even here the top sales executive, along with the chief marketing executive, generally ranks among the highest-paid four or five men in the company.

Naturally, sales executives at lower levels in the organizational hierarchy are paid less than their chiefs. Higher-ranking subordinates, such as regional and district sales managers, have median earnings approximating 90 to 95 percent of those of the chief sales executive. Field sales managers, those on the first step of the ladder in the sales-force executive hierarchy, receive median earnings roughly two thirds of those of the top sales executive, while salespeople earn about half as much as the top sales executive.[3]

Most sales executives receive a portion of their pay in the form of bonuses, commissions, or other "incentive" payments. These incentive payments generally are based upon relative profit performances at higher levels in the sales organizational hierarchy and upon sales volumes achieved (relative to sales potentials) at lower sales executive levels. The prevalence of incentive payments in the compensation packages of sales executives causes their earnings to fluctuate considerably from year to year.

Figure 5.2 shows how top sales executives in fifteen large companies were compensated in a recent year. Notice that eleven of these fifteen top sales executives had stock options (which generally gives them the right to purchase company stock on advantageous terms) and ten received some of their compensation in forms other than salaries—incentive bonuses, profit-sharing plans, stock-purchase plans, and deferred-compensation plans. These and other fringe benefits (such as retirement funds, company-paid insurance policies, and annuities) tend to be effective in reducing executive turnover: Most executives are reluctant to leave companies where they have accumulated sizable fringe benefits.

---

[2]*Compensating Salesmen and Sales Executives,* Conference Board Report No. 579 (New York: The Conference Board, Inc., 1972), p. 4.

[3]*Ibid.*

FIGURE 5.2
Compensation of Top Sales Executives in Selected Large Companies in 1971

| Company | Product Field(s) | 1971 Sales Vol. (in 000s) | Top Sales Executive's Compensation | | |
|---|---|---|---|---|---|
| | | | Total | Stock Options? | Other Nonsalary Compensation from: |
| Simplicity Pattern Co., Inc. | Apparel patterns | $ 90,447 | $ 64,583 | Yes | |
| Jos. Schlitz Brewing Co. | Beer | 522,094 | 133,100 | Yes | |
| Abbott Laboratories | Pharmaceuticals and drugs | 124,117 | 73,859 | Yes | Incentive bonus |
| Chicago Bridge & Iron Co. | Fabricated metals | 394,000 | 76,520 | Yes | Profit sharing |
| Snap-On Tools Corp. | Industrial equipment | 88,399 | 110,389 | Yes | |
| Chicago Pneumatic Tool Co. | Machinery | 394,000 | 57,000 | No | Deferred compensation |
| Cowles Communications, Inc. | Publishing | 171,000 | 39,154 | No | Profit sharing |
| Inland Steel Co. | Steel and iron | 1,253,610 | 119,836 | Yes | Incentive bonus |
| Graniteville Co. | Textiles | 135,204 | 95,975 | Yes | |
| American Brands, Inc. | Tobacco and diversified | 2,827,771 | 87,414 | Yes | Profit sharing |
| Briggs & Stratton Corp. | Industrial parts | 186,225 | 126,166 | No | |
| Beeline Fashions, Inc. | Apparel | 51,506 | 59,300 | Yes | Profit sharing |
| Reichhold Chemicals, Inc. | Chemicals | 194,228 | 37,500 | No | Profit sharing, stock purchase |
| Stokely-Van Camp, Inc. | Food | 280,836 | 60,000 | Yes | Profit sharing |
| Clorox Co. | Household products | 145,000 | 52,050 | Yes | Profit sharing |

Source: Extracted from "What Top Sales and Marketing Executives Earn," *Sales Management* (October 2, 1972), pp. 26-30.

## QUALITIES OF GOOD SALES EXECUTIVES

What qualities should top-flight sales executives possess that will enable them to perform effectively, both as managers and as important members of the marketing executive team? In a complex and variable field such as sales management, it is difficult to list "success" qualifications applicable in all situations and all companies. Sales executives' jobs cover a wide gamut of products, markets, and marketing channels, and there would seem to be few, if any, qualifications in common. Nevertheless, several qualities (or abilities) common to most successful sales executives, whatever their fields, can be identified:

1. *Ability to define clearly the position's exact functions and duties in relation to the goals the company should expect to attain.* Too often, sales executives neglect to calculate what is entailed in their responsibilities. Whether or not the company provides them with a position description, sales executives should draw up their own descriptions consistent with the responsibilities assigned by higher management. Revisions are necessary whenever changes occur in the assigned responsibilities or in company goals.

2. *Ability to select and train capable subordinates, and willingness to delegate sufficient authority to enable them to carry out assigned tasks with minimum supervision.* Inability to delegate authority is a common weakness. Sometimes inexperienced executives select high-caliber subordinates but fail to provide them with authority to make decisions on any except the most routine matters. Such practice destroys the morale of subordinates, and it results in an unnecessarily heavy work load for the superior. Within existing policy limits, decisions should be made by subordinates; when an exception falling outside these limits occurs, the superior should decide. The more capable the subordinates, the wider policy limits can be and the more the superior's time is freed for planning.

3. *Ability to utilize time efficiently.* The time of sales executives is valuable, and they should budget it and use it as carefully as they would money. They should allocate their working time to tasks yielding the greatest return to the company. They must, for instance, arrive at an optimum division between office work and field supervision. To the sales executive, even the use of off-duty hours is important. Excessive work time and too little leisure reduces executive efficiency. Successful sales executives consider the likely values both to themselves and to the company, then balances such leisure-time activities as community service and professional meetings against personal social activities, recreation, and self-improvement.

4. *Ability to allocate sufficient time for thinking and planning.* Able administrators make their major contributions through thinking and planning. They know how and are willing to think. They recognize that reviewing past performances is a prerequisite to planning. They strive continuously to gain new insight that will help bring problems into better focus. Too often, sales executives are so involved in daily administrative tasks that little time remains for thinking and planning. Furthermore, it is easier to procrastinate than to think. Effective sales executives find ways to shield themselves from routine tasks and interruptions. Failing this, they retreat to Shangri-Las where surroundings are more conducive to thinking and planning.

5. *Ability to exercise skilled leadership.* Competent sales executives develop and improve their skills in dealing with people. Although they necessarily rely to a certain extent on an intuitive grasp of leadership skills, they depend far more on careful study of motivational factors, and shrewd analysis of the ever-changing patterns of unsatisfied needs among those with whom they work. They recognize that skilled leadership is important in dealing with subordinates and with everyone else with whom they come into contact.

## RELATIONS WITH TOP MANAGEMENT

The most effective and successful executives are well above average in initiative and personal drive, and sales executives should not be exceptions. Realizing their potentials, however, depends largely upon their relations with top management. Sales executives should want to get ahead, for personal goals are as vital to them as the objectives they set for the sales department, but if they are to achieve these goals, not only must they know where they are going, but top management must be kept abreast of their progress.

Sales executives must plan and implement their own self-development programs, and setting definite career goals is an essential part of such programs. Sales executives must, however, strive to harmonize their own goals with those of the organization, this being an important condition for maximum progress of individual and company alike. Whenever the sales executive and the company cease to move toward mutually compatible goals, the resulting friction causes both to fall short of expected achievement levels. When this happens, either the two sets of goals must be reconciled, or the executive should leave the firm. Sometimes, sales executives unilaterally reconcile such goals conflicts (usually by adjusting their personal goals to fit those of the organization). More often, they reconcile them through interaction with company top management.

In their relations with top management, sales executives should readily accept responsibility for all activities related to their positions, but they should avoid becoming indispensable. Indispensability is undesirable for both the executive and the company. For the sales executive, it means the blocking of opportunities for promotion; for the company, it means that too much is being staked on one individual. Probably the best way for sales executives to avoid becoming indispensable is to practice and advocate delegation of authority; and they should, concurrently, place high priority on training their own replacements. At the same time, junior sales executives climbing the management ladder are well advised to learn and master the duties and responsibilities of the positions immediately above theirs. Promotions come most readily to those prepared for them, and preparation largely consists of setting definite goals and adhering to a program of continuing self-development.

Top management expects sales executives, as important members of management, to be highly qualified as problem solvers and decision makers. Consequently, sales executives should guard against taking too many of their problems to top management. Asking for help in deciding problems on which they clearly possess decision-making authority is tantamount to asking for closer supervision (and less authority). Competent sales executives do not require a close watch over their activities, and those who have the confidence of top management enjoy considerable freedom in deciding things by themselves.

Nevertheless, chief sales executives should keep top management informed on important decisions made and on the department's plans and accomplishments. They should transmit all required ordinary reports promptly, and special reports when appropriate. They should exercise some restraint in reporting their own activities, but they should see to it that their superiors have all the information needed to evaluate their personal effectiveness. Their reports should ensure that top management knows in broad outline the problems encountered in selling the company's products, the ways they are handled, and the results accomplished.

Chief sales executives should pay careful attention to the manner in which they communicate with top management. They should not hesitate to give their superiors the benefit of their thinking, but, unless matters of high principle are involved, they should generally be willing to modify preconceived ideas. However, as the outstandingly successful executive David Ogilvy has written:

> In the modern world of business, it is useless to be a creative original thinker unless you can also sell what you create. Management cannot always recognize a great idea unless it is presented to them by a good salesman.[4]

When the sales executive has a great idea, is absolutely sure of it, and top management is unconvinced, the sales executive must play the role of a supersalesperson and "sell" to those with the authority to decide. When the facts do not speak for themselves—when those in authority fail to grasp their full significance—the sales executive, like any competent executive, should bring to bear his or her full powers of persuasion.

In all their dealings with top management, chief sales executives should make a special effort to listen and learn. They should keep a dated record of important conversations. They should refrain from voluntarily discussing the personal competence of fellow executives unless they can do so in a manner favorable to the executive involved. They should avoid relaying rumors. And they should exercise close control over their executive contacts, never missing scheduled engagements without justifiable reason. Sales executives following such commonsense rules of conduct experience little difficulty in winning top management's confidence and respect.

## RELATIONS WITH MANAGERS OF OTHER MARKETING ACTIVITIES

Although chief sales executives spend the greatest portion of their time on activities relating directly to management of the personal selling function, they also are concerned with other marketing activities. The degree of responsibility over these activities, and the amount of time allocated to them, vary with the particular job; but sales executives are almost always concerned to some extent with product, promotion, pricing, and distribution management. They may also have an important role in achieving control over these activities and coordination among them.

### Relations with Product Management

Executives responsible for product planning and the formulation of product policies make numerous decisions. Periodically, each product in the line needs appraising in terms of its profitability and its ability to fulfill buyers' wants. When products come up for review, decisions have to be made on whether each should be retained, changed or improved, or dropped from the line. Other decisions have to be made on adding new products and on changes in product design and other product features. Still other product decisions concern product quality, services rendered in connection with product sales, and packaging.

Product decisions are often a shared responsibility of marketing, production, research and development, and financial executives, operating as a product committee. Chief sales executives provide important inputs for such decisions. Their continuous con-

---

[4]David Ogilvy, "How to Lead a Creative Organization," *Advertising Age* (October 22, 1962), pp. 98-100.

tact with the market through subordinates and sales personnel provide them with feedback about product performance and acceptance generally not available from other sources.

## Relations with Promotion Management

While chief marketing executives are primarily responsible for setting promotional policies, chief sales executives participate importantly in their formulations. Their knowledge of the market and their direct control over personal-selling activity make chief sales executives a key source of information, and they occupy a highly strategic position in implementing promotional plans. Sales personnel, for instance, are responsible not only for transmitting sales messages directly to prospects but for securing the proper use of point-of-purchase displays and for coordinating dealer efforts with advertising programs. Clearly, then, chief sales executives, because of the key roles they play in making and implementing promotional policies, must coordinate very closely with other executives participating in the formulation and implementation of the promotional program.

Almost every product marketed relies on personal selling as a necessary promotional method at one or more points in the marketing channel. Personal selling's effectiveness traces to the use of personal contacts in conveying the sales message to prospective buyers. But, personal selling also is the most expensive promotional method in terms of cost per sales message transmitted. For this reason, the proportion of personal selling in the promotional mix generally must be limited, and it is the sales executive's responsibility to keep selling costs at a level regarded as reasonable by top management.

The chief sales executive is responsible for making certain that salespeople are kept abreast of important aspects of current advertising campaigns. Sales personnel need briefing, for example, on the specific advertising appeals being used, enabling them, perhaps, to adapt their own selling approaches in ways that enhance the total promotional impact. The sales force should also know which media are scheduled to carry advertisements for which products, and the timing of each ad's appearance. In addition, advertising personnel need ready access to the top sales executive, since this executive is such an important source of information about customers, their needs, behavior, and motives.

Chief sales executives play similar roles with respect to other promotional methods. Decisions regarding the usage of these methods in the promotional mix are normally made by the top marketing executive or by other specialists. Besides serving as an important source of information, the chief sales executive is responsible for securing needed coordinative efforts by the sales force to ensure that each promotional activity obtains optimum results.

## Relations with Pricing Management

When major decisions on pricing policy are required, both the top marketing executive and the chief sales executive occupy especially influential positions in top management councils. Relative to other high executives, they should have much clearer ideas of the prices final buyers are willing to pay, the sales executive because of close and continuing contacts with the market, and the marketing executive because of knowledge of pricing information gathered and interpreted by the marketing research staff.

In spite of the fact that these two executives are particularly well quaified to speak with authority on pricing matters, price policies should be formulated and prices should be set by a group of executives. Each department affected should have some representation on this group, for policymaking in the pricing area is, by nature, an interdepartmental activity. Included in the policymaking group should be representatives not only of the marketing department but of such departments as production, cost accounting, credit, advertising, legal, and public relations. The pricing policies finally drafted should result from the cooperative action of the group rather than from compromises among its individual members.

Once pricing policy is established, its implementation is ordinarily the responsibility of the chief sales executive. For example, the pricing committee might decide to adopt a policy of resale price maintenance, but the chief sales executive is responsible for informing distributors and dealers, obtaining their conformance, and initiating action against the nonconformers. Responsibility for administering prices should be assigned to a single line executive. Usually the chief sales executive receives this assignment, because the sales department has the closest relationship with the market.

### Relations with Distribution Management

The distribution policies chosen by a firm are major determinants of the breadth and complexity of the sales department's organization and its functions. Selection of a marketing channel, or channels, sets the pattern for sales-force operations, both geographically and with respect to the classes of customers from whom sales personnel are to solicit orders. But this is only one aspect of distribution policymaking. It is also necessary to determine the number of outlets that are to handle the product at each distribution level, and this also affects the size and nature of the manufacturer's sales organization and the scope of its activities. Furthermore, marketing management determines policies in regard to the amount and extent of cooperation it desires to maintain with members of the distributive network—also influencing importantly, for example, the size of the sales force, the nature of the salesperson's job, the need for sales supervision, and the like. Because of the significant impact, then, that distribution policy decisions have upon the sales organization and its activities, chief sales executives must play a key role in providing information needed for their formulation, since they also bear major responsibility for the success of the implementation of distribution policy.

## CONCLUSION

Although sales executives' jobs vary from company to company and from position to position within companies, all are responsible for making decisions and seeing to it that others carry out these decisions. All sales executives, from the chief sales executive down, spend most of their time on managing personal selling activities. Lower-ranking sales executives, such as branch managers, devote nearly all their time to direct supervision of the salespersons under them. Thus, while sales executives should possess qualifications similar to those of effective executives in other fields, they must be particularly adept at leading people. And the higher their positions are in the organizational hierarchy, the more sales executives must concern themselves in working closely with decision makers in other marketing areas, since all marketing decisions ultimately have an impact on the personal-selling situation.

# 6

# The Sales Organization

A sales organization, like any organization, is a group of individuals striving jointly to reach certain goals, and bearing informal as well as formal relations to one another. Implicit in the concept is the notion that individual members of the group cooperate to attain certain objectives. The organization is the vehicle by which the members hope to achieve these ends; it is not an end in itself. It provides the framework within which activities of the group are carried on; the fact that an organization exists implies that various patterns of relationships have been established to facilitate accomplishing the aims of the group. An organization, then, is both an orienting point for cooperative endeavor and a structure of human relationships.

Managers—those in sales, marketing, and all other fields—should appreciate the importance of sound organization. Unfortunately, some sales executives still seem content with inefficient organizations—at least, as long as sales continue to be made. This contrasts markedly to attitudes of managers in other operating areas. Production executives, for instance, have thoroughly explored the advantages of logically conceived and intelligently implemented organization, probably because they recognized the necessity for realizing manufacturing economies and controlling production costs. Far too often, sales executives, because of immediate concern with sales volume, overlook the importance of realizing economies in the selling operation and of controlling selling expenses. They naturally tend toward sales-mindedness rather than profit-mindedness. But even if the marketing situation of a firm requires main emphasis on obtaining orders, the sales department should consummate more sales with a sound organization than with a jerry-built one.

Organizational defects in sales departments often exist because of the lack of attention accorded marketing activities during the early life of many manufacturing enterprises. When a business is first getting under way, management tends to be concerned primarily with manufacturing and financing problems. Executives of new enterprises devote a great deal of time to questions of organization, but these usually are related to manufacturing rather than marketing. As products are improved, manufacturing quantities increased, new products added, and new production processes developed, the manufacturing organization is adapted to the changed situation. Strangely enough, similar indicated alterations in the sales organizational structure are frequently neglected.

Sales departments in many companies seem to evolve without regard for organizational planning. The basic setup designed when the business was new remains unchanged, despite an increase in staff size. Normally the sales organization should be adjusted to fit—ideally, to anticipate—changing needs. A good sales organization early in a company's history is not necessarily the best type later. The combined impact of shifts in the relative importance of marketing and other business problems, in competition, and in other factors affecting the business, sooner or later compels appropriate adjustments in the organizational plan and structure. Perhaps the most important point to note is the need for adaptability in organization with a responsive, fluid environment reacting to changing conditions.[1]

## PURPOSES OF SALES ORGANIZATION

### General Purpose of Organization

In the ideally organized sales department, waste motion and duplication of effort would be eliminated, friction minimized, and cooperation maximized. Unfortunately, dynamic characteristics inherent in marketing preclude the achievement of such perfection. Nevertheless, when sufficient attention is given to sales organization, the ideal is approached, if not attained, and managerial effort and action made more productive. Most problems of organization are really problems of reorganization. The organization is usually already in existence, and the objective is most often to make it more effective.

Executive effort expended on sales organizational problems need not, indeed should not, go exclusively to questions of design—that is, of the "formal" organization plan. Modern organizational theory recognizes that how an organization actually works is of far greater practical importance than the way it is supposed to function. Therefore, sales management often should direct its main organizational efforts toward the "informal" organization. Through exercise of intelligent leadership and related "human relations" talents, the skilled manager moves both individuals and informal groups along lines that facilitate achievement of the purposes of formal organization.

### To Permit the Development of Specialists

As a business expands, various marketing and selling activities multiply and become increasingly complex. It is often difficult to fix responsibility for performance of all activities, particularly when executives are reluctant to delegate authority. Reorganization of the sales department is initiated to facilitate assignment of responsibility and delegation of authority. This often requires reshaping the structure so that it is easier for specialists to develop. In fact, specialization, or "division of labor" as economists call it, is the chief means through which the processes of organization and reorganization are effected. As tasks grow in number and complexity, they should be broken down into manageable units and assigned to specialized personnel. This breaking down involves "fixing responsibility" for specific tasks with specific individuals (or, occasionally, with certain groups), and the assignments made are called "delegations of authority."

---

[1]G.H. Labovitz, "Organizing for Adaptation," *Business Horizons*, Vol. 14, No. 3 (June 1971), pp. 19-21.

## To Assure That All Necessary Activities Are Performed

As the sales organization grows and specialization increases, it becomes increasingly important that all necessary activities be performed. When jobs are greatly specialized, danger exists that the organizational plan will not provide for supervision of all activities. Essential tasks may not be performed, simply because they are not assigned to specific individuals. When a company is small, for example, its executives are normally in close contact with users of the product. As the company grows, as marketing channels lengthen, and as the marketing area expands geographically, top executives become further and further removed from the customers. As soon as executives begin to lose their informal contacts with customers, an individual probably should be charged with responsibility for maintaining such relationships. If these contacts are considered highly important, responsibility for maintaining them should be assigned to a specialized executive in charge of customer relations.

## To Achieve Coordination or Balance

Another purpose of organization is to achieve coordination or balance. Individuals vary in competence, potential, and effectiveness. Particularly forceful executives may prevent a basically good organization from functioning smoothly. Their personalities may be such that through assumption of authority, failure to delegate it, or both, their positions are magnified out of all proportion to the true importance. Worse yet, total accomplishments of the organization are less than they could have been if, so to speak, greater advantage had been taken of the synergistic effect—when the sum of a combination effort exceeds the efforts of the same individuals working alone. By getting people to pull together as a team rather than as an assortment of individuals, the organization accomplishes more collectively than its members could independently.

Motivating individuals to work willingly together toward common objectives is, then, a highly important element in achieving coordination. Individual goals must be subordinated to, or reconciled with, overall organizational goals. Some of the means for accomplishing this are: indoctrination and training programs, group meetings, supervision and guidance, and maintenance of two-way communications. Throughout the sales department, different activities must be kept in proper relation to one another in order to realize the greatest organizational effectiveness.

As various specialists emerge in a growing organization, management must guard against a tendency of each to search for ways to justify his or her own existence. One form of justification is to devise technical nomenclatures that nonspecialists or specialists in other areas have difficulty understanding. This, in turn, leads to increasing communications difficulties with other specialists and a reduction in overall organizational effectiveness. Jack Schiff of Pace College refers to such situations as "instances of uncoordinated proliferation" and suggests that top sales executives should concern themselves continually with "orchestration of effort." Modern organizational theory suggests, also, that sales departments should be divided into small, freely communicating, face-to-face groups to decrease the possibility of uncoordinated proliferation.

## To Define Authority

Sales executives should know whether the authority attaching to each aspect of their positions is line, staff, or functional. Line authority carries with it the general power to require execution of orders by those lower in the organizational hierarchy. Staff authority involves only the power to suggest to those holding line authority the method for implementation of an order. Functional authority enables specialists in particular areas, such as in technical product service, to enforce their directives within a specific and limited field. Executives acting in a line capacity make decisions on the need, place, and time of action over a wide range of matters. Staff executives advise line executives about method but have no formal power to require or enforce the execution of their recommendations. Executives holding functional authority are most often specialists—experts in some clearly defined aspect of the business—who assist executives holding general line authority. For example, such specialists might advise on new product introduction. They do this by issuing orders, mainly on routine technical problems, directly to lower organizational levels. All executives should understand the nature of their authority with respect to each aspect of the operation; otherwise, friction is bound to develop. When, for instance, executives with staff authority attempt to exercise line authority, they are headed for trouble with executives whose line authority is usurped.

Certain people, however, in an organization receive directions from several sources. This conflicts with traditional organizational theory, which, in general, has said: No person should have more than one boss. The supporting argument is that, if individuals receive instruction from multiple sources, they may get conflicting and confusing directions. The argument is a good one, but the "one-boss" rule does not necessarily follow. Modern organizational theory points out, and rightly so, we think, that the real problem is one not of avoiding the multiple-boss situation but of harmonizing orders and directives from different sources. A smoothly operating organization is generally one that has found effective ways of achieving such harmony. Two important ways are continuing coordination of the work of different executives and free-flowing communications systems.

### To Economize on Executive Time

As a sales department's operations and activities increase in complexity and number, additional subordinates are added. This permits higher-ranking executives to delegate more authority. It also allows the more effective use of specialization, while higher executives devote less time to operations and more to planning and other functions. One purpose, then, of organization—and one often overlooked—is achieving economies in the use of executive time. High-ranking executives should not concern themselves personally with all problems and activities, particularly routine or technical ones, when they have capable and well-trained subordinates.

However, as executives gain subordinates, they must devote more attention, and probably more time, to coordinating the efforts of subordinates. Unless the executive is an effective coordinator, his or her subordinates may not work in harmony or discharge their assignments in line with expectations. Under these conditions, the advantages of specialization cannot be fully realized.

In building the organization, then, the need for effective coordination limits the number of subordinates who should report directly to certain executives. In organizational theory, this limit is called the "span of control." It is not possible to give a definitive answer regarding the "proper" number of subordinates. In general, however, the greater the abilities of the coordinator and of those reporting to him or her, the larger the number that can be effectively coordinated. Lower-level sales executives, those with salespeople reporting directly to them, have a wider span of control than higher executives devoting much time to planning and policy formulation and little to administrative and operating details. One must consider, therefore, not only relative abilities of the coordinator and the subordinates, but the nature and importance of other duties attached to the coordinator's position. Obviously, in deciding optimum span of control for a particular position in a given sales organization, many other factors should be taken into account. The span of control is widened: (1) with improvements in the efficiency, speed, and reliability of the communications system; (2) when subordinates perform routine, similar, or repetitive tasks; and (3) when subordinates are concentrated at the same location as the executive.

## SETTING UP A SALES ORGANIZATION

It is rarely necessary to build a sales organization entirely from scratch, for usually some structure exists from which to start and on which to build. It is appropriate, nevertheless, for the executive to approach the problem, each time it arises, as though a completely new organization were forming. Five major steps are involved:

1. Defining the objectives.
2. Delineating the necessary activities.
3. Grouping activities into "jobs" or "positions."
4. Assigning personnel to positions.
5. Providing for coordination and control.

### Objectives

The initial step is to define the sales department's objectives. Top management, of course, defines the long-run objectives for the company, and from these the general, or long-run, objectives for the sales department are derived. Considered collectively, general objectives constitute top management's vision of the company at some future time. Top management, for instance, may want the firm not only to survive but to achieve industry leadership, develop a reputation for outstanding technical research, diversify its product lines, provide excellent service to customers, furnish investors with a generous return, establish an image of public responsibility, and so on. From such composites, sales management, working in consultation with top management, determines the implications for the sales department and articulates a set of general objectives for the department. Survival, for instance, is undoubtedly the most basic objective of any enterprise, and this requires, among other things, a continuing flow of sales revenue; so, securing sales volume is an important sales-department objective.

Survival also requires profits. Hence, a second important sales-department objective is to produce profits, not only by making profitable sales but by controlling departmental costs and expenses. Furthermore, survival generally requires eventual growth in both sales and profits; otherwise, in a growing economy the company is destined to fall behind competitors or even risk being forced out of business. It follows that a third important sales-department objective is to realize long-term growth in sales and profits. Therefore, three of the sales department's general objectives—all traceable to top management's desire for survival of the firm—may be summed up in three words: sales, profits, and growth. Other general objectives of the firm, of course, must be similarly analyzed, their implications determined, and additional general objectives for the sales department derived.

More precisely stated objectives are also needed. General objectives are indispensable for long-range planning and must be kept in mind in short-range planning, but objectives phrased in specific terms are required as operating guideposts. Such specific objectives, nevertheless, must be in harmony with the general objectives from which, in fact, they are derived. Thus, the general objective of producing profits may be translated into such specific objectives as "increasing our share of the domestic portable typewriter market to 25 percent by the end of the current year" and "securing at least four wholesalers in Australia to introduce our portables to that market next year." People in the sales department, like people elsewhere, work more effectively, with less waste of time, effort, and money, when assigned definite goals. Similarly, the sales department functions more smoothly, and its activities are more purposeful, if specific objectives are established for it.

The long-run objectives of the sales department form the basis for the general policies governing performance over extended periods. The specific objectives are the foundation from which day-by-day sales operating policies are developed. Objectives, whether general or specific, should be the starting points from which sales policies are built. A thorough examination—perhaps even a restatement—of the goals of the sales department is the logical place to begin the task of designing its organizational structure.

### Determination of Activities

Fundamental to sound organizational practice is recognition that activities are what is being organized. Only after a full compilation of all necessary activities is it possible to provide intelligent answers to such questions as: What executive positions are required? What should be their relationships to other positions? What should be the duties and responsibilities of persons who fill these positions?

Determining the necessary activities is a matter of analyzing the sales department's objectives. Thorough examination will disclose which activities must be performed if objectives are to be attained. The activities involved in modern sales management are fairly similar from firm to firm, and although individual sales executives may think that their operations are "different," most differences are more apparent than real. Almost every sales department carries on the same general activities; differences among departments are those of detail, and of relative emphasis placed upon individual activities. Even so, one needs to know the exact activities that must be performed. As the sales department's objectives are analyzed, specific activities necessary to achieve them are disclosed. These should be noted carefully and checked afterward for completeness and accuracy. It is helpful to have a checklist of specific sales management activities available for reference.

### Conversion of Activities into Positions

Duties and responsibilities involved in carrying out the work of the sales department should be allocated in a logical manner to different positions. Activities should be classified and grouped so that closely related tasks are assigned to the same position. Each position should contain not only a sufficient number of tasks but sufficient variation to provide for job challenge, interest, and involvement.[2] Only in very large organizations, where extreme specialization is practiced, should a position comprise only a single

---

[2] J. R. Galbraith, "Matrix Organization Designs," *Business Horizons*, Vol. 14, No. 1 (February 1971), p. 30.

activity, and even here the burden of proof should be on those proposing such a move. Fortunately, pressures of administrative economy are generally strong enough that most position holders find themselves responsible for a number of diversified, although related, activities.

It should be kept in mind that certain activities are of crucial importance to success of the department. For example, in a highly competitive field, product merchandising and pricing should be allocated to positions fairly high in the organizational structure. Activities of lesser importance can safely be assigned to lower-level jobs.

When a large number of positions is set up, groups of related jobs should be brought together to form subdivisions of the department. In such cases, a number of intermediate-level positions would, in turn, have to be coordinated by the top sales executive. However, the organizational planner should guard against building too many levels into the department. The smallest number of administrative levels that permits the department both to discharge its responsibilities and to operate smoothly is best.

### Assignment of Personnel to Positions

The question of whether to tailor positions to capabilities of available personnel or to recruit special individuals to fill the positions that evolve logically from analysis of the objectives and required activities has long been controversial. In practice, compromises are made. Some individuals possess such unique abilities that it is prudent and profitable to mold the job specifications to fit them. Some position requirements are general enough that many individuals already possess the necessary qualifications, or can acquire them through training. In all cases, the best possible should be done in matching capabilities of available personnel with position requirements. But organizational planners find it easier, whenever the situation permits, to have individuals "grow" into particular jobs rather than to have jobs grow up around individuals.

### Provision for Coordination and Control

A strong leader will produce a strong organization. Every person who has others reporting to him or her must be provided with the means to control his or her subordinates and coordinate their efforts.[3] Those in authority must not be so overburdened with detailed and undelegated responsibilities that they have insufficient time to devote to coordination. Nor should they have too many subordinates reporting directly; this weakens the quality of control and prevents the discharge of other assigned duties. Proper consideration must always be given the span of executive control, taking into account such factors as those discussed earlier.[4]

One important instrument of organizational control is the written job description, setting forth the job objectives, activities and responsibilities, authority limits, and formal relation to other jobs. A job description should emphasize job objectives, and, to the extent possible, the position holder should be allowed to determine how to achieve them. This not only encourages position holders to use their own initiative but makes it clear that they are to achieve stated job objectives even if that requires performing activities and assuming responsibilities beyond those contained in job descriptions. Providing job holders with clear pictures of the roles they are to play in the organization contributes to

[3]Labovitz, *op.cit.*, p. 25.
[4]See pp. 134-135

the building of morale. Written job descriptions are also used in employee selection, to match job specifications with applicants' qualifications; where recruits cannot be found with all desired qualifications, job specifications form the basis for training. In addition, position holders may use their job descriptions as yardsticks against which to appraise their own performance. In all these ways, the job description serves as an instrument of, and contributes to, organizational control.

The organizational chart, another widely used control instrument, is mainly useful for showing formal relations among different positions. A chart showing relationships between personnel and jobs can reduce the individual's confusion about his or her role. However, the organizational chart delineates formal rather than informal relations and, because of this, rarely provides a true picture of how the organization actually works. Nevertheless, all members of the sales department ought to have access to an organizational chart to learn the nature of their formal relations with others, to know with whom they are expected to cooperate, and to know their formal roles in the organization.

An instrument of organizational control used increasingly is the organizational manual. It is best described as an extension of the organizational chart. Typically, it contains charts for both the company and the departments, write-ups of job specifications, and summaries of major company and departmental objectives and policies. The organizational manual brings together a great deal of information on the organization, and helps its users to learn and understand the nature of their responsibilities, authorities, and relations with others.

## BASIC TYPES OF SALES ORGANIZATIONAL STRUCTURES

If sound organizational practices are followed in setting up the sales department, the resulting structure will resemble one or more of four basic types; line, line and staff, functional, and committee. The grouping of activities into positions and the charting of relationships of positions causes the organization to take on structural form. The first two types are by far the most common. Functional organizations and the pure form of committee organizations are only rarely used. Most sales departments have hybrid organizational structures, with variations to adjust for personalities and to fit specific operating conditions.

The sales department's organizational structure evolves from the needs of the business. No two companies have identical sales organizations, because no two have identical needs. The customers, the marketing channels, the company size, the product or product line, the practices of competitors, and the personalities and abilities of the personnel are but a few of the many factors affecting the organizational structure of the sales department. So numerous are the factors influencing the structure of the individual departments that it is impractical to draw generalizations concerning the unique advantages and disadvantages of the many possible "mixed" types; the discussion that follows is limited to an analysis of the four basic types. Organizational planners should be thoroughly acquainted with the chief features of each type, and its respective merits and limitations. If they have this background and understand the factors influencing the structure of the sales department in question, they are equipped to evaluate its appropriateness.

### Line Sales Organization

The line organization is the oldest and simplest organizational structure. It is widely used in smaller firms and in firms with small numbers of selling personnel—in, for instance, companies that cover a limited marketing area or sell a narrow product line. The chain of command runs from the sales manager down through various subordinates. All executives exercise line authority, and each subordinate is responsible only to one person on the next higher level. Responsibility is definitely fixed, and those charged with it also have the power to make decisions and to take action. Lines of authority run vertically through the structure, and all persons on any one organizational level are independent of all others on that same level.

The line sales organization sees its greatest use in companies where sales personnel report directly to the chief sales executive. In such companies this executive often is preoccupied with active supervision and seldom has much time to devote to planning or to work with other top executives. Occasionally, however, the line organization is used where more than two levels of authority are present.

Figure 6.1 shows a fairly large sales department organized on the line basis. The sales manager reports directly to the general manager, assistant sales managers report to the sales manager, and salespeople report to assistant managers. Theoretically, there is no cross-communication between persons on the same organizational level. Contacts between persons on the same level are indirect, and are effected through the next higher level of authority. For example, the assistant sales manager of Division 1 arranges to confer with the assistant sales manager of Division 2 through the sales manager. Similarly, contacts by sales personnel with the office staff flow up through the organization to the sales manager and back down through the assistant sales manager in charge of the office to the office staff.

The basic simplicity of line organization is the main reason for its use. Because each department member reports to only one superior, problems of discipline and control are small. Lines of authority and responsibility are clear and logical, and it is difficult for individuals to shift or evade responsibilities. Definite placement of authority and responsibility saves time in making policy changes, in deciding new plans, and in converting plans

FIGURE 6.1
Line Type of Sales Department Organization

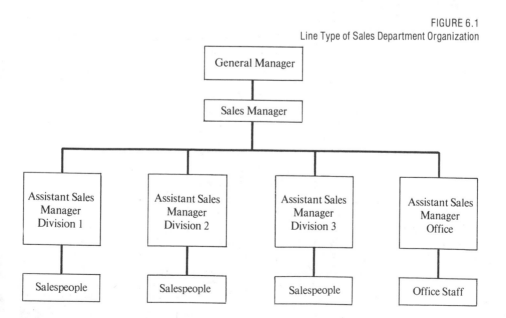

into action. The simplicity of the structure makes it easy for executives to develop close personal relations with salespersons. With this sort of working atmosphere, it is not surprising that executives who come up through a line organization are frequently very strong leaders. As the typical line sales department has few organizational levels, administrative expenses are low.

The most serious weakness of line sales organizations is that so much depends upon the individuals who head the department. They need outstanding ability and rare qualifications. They should be well versed in all phases of sales management, for they do not have the advice and assistance of subordinates with specialized skills and knowledge. Even if they are all-around experts, they may have insufficient time for policymaking and planning, since rigidity of the line structure requires them to devote most of their attention to direction of sales operations. Therefore, they often must make decisions and take action without benefit of planning and adequate forethought. Under such conditions, results are often disappointing, if not financially ruinous.

For rapidly growing concerns and for those with large sales staffs, the line organizational structure is usually inappropriate. As size of the department increases, new layers of executives must be added to retain the same degree of control. Orders and directions must be passed down through a growing series of administrative levels. Managerial effectiveness becomes impaired and results are less predictable, as directions tend to become more and more distorted and garbled at each succeeding organizational level. Moreover, as growth proceeds beyond a certain point, earlier advantages of close relations among executives and salespeople are sacrificed, and the problem of maintaining morale becomes greater. There is a scarcity of executives who possess all the talents needed to manage a large-scale line sales department effectively, and line organization offers little opportunity for subordinates to acquire these skills. Ordinarily, the stakes are too high, except perhaps in the smallest companies, for management to gamble on the availability of a replacement at the time needed. Sound organizational practice dictates that trained understudies be ready to step into the shoes of their superiors. But more often than not, chief sales executives in purely line types of sales organization fail to groom their own replacements.

### Line and Staff Sales Organization

The line and staff sales department is used most frequently by large and medium-sized firms, employing substantial numbers of sales personnel, and marketing diversified lines of products over wide geographic areas. In contrast to the line organization, the line and staff organization provides the chief sales executive with the assistance of a group of specialists—experts in dealer and distributor relations, sales analysis, sales organization, sales personnel, sales planning, sales promotion, sales training, service, traffic and warehousing, and similar fields. The staff helps conserve the time of the chief sales executive and free him or her from excessively detailed work. They make it possible for their chief to concentrate his or her efforts where he or she has the most skill. If the chief sales executive is not equipped, through prior training or experience, to handle certain problems, staff specialists can give considerable assistance in increasing overall effectiveness of the department. Similarly, by delegating to staff executives problems involving considerable study or detailed analysis, the chief sales executive has more time for planning and for dealing with matters of higher priority to the business.

Staff executives normally do not have the authority to issue orders or directives to other executives or to salespeople. Staff recommendations are submitted to the chief sales executive, who, if he or she approves, transmits necessary instructions to the line organization. Departures from this procedure are occasionally made. For example, staff members may be authorized to deal directly with line officials regarding execution of plans and implementation of policies developed by the staff and approved by management. Although staff members are acting on behalf of a line sales executive in such instances, they assume joint responsibility for results with the line officials involved. This departure from the normal procedure may be justified if it speeds the translation of staff plans into line action.

Figure 6.2 illustrates the line and staff type of sales organization. In this example, the general sales manager reports directly to the vice-president in charge of marketing, as does the advertising manager and the manager of marketing research. Six subordinates report to the general sales manager, but only one, the assistant general sales manager, is a member of the line organization. Four of the five staff officials have responsibilities in specialized fields; the fifth, the assistant to the general sales manager, is given assignments of a more general nature.

Note the difference between the "assistant to" and "assistant." The "assistant to" is purely and simply a staff officer who is given a broader operating area than those staff

FIGURE 6.2
Line and Staff Type of Sales Department Organization

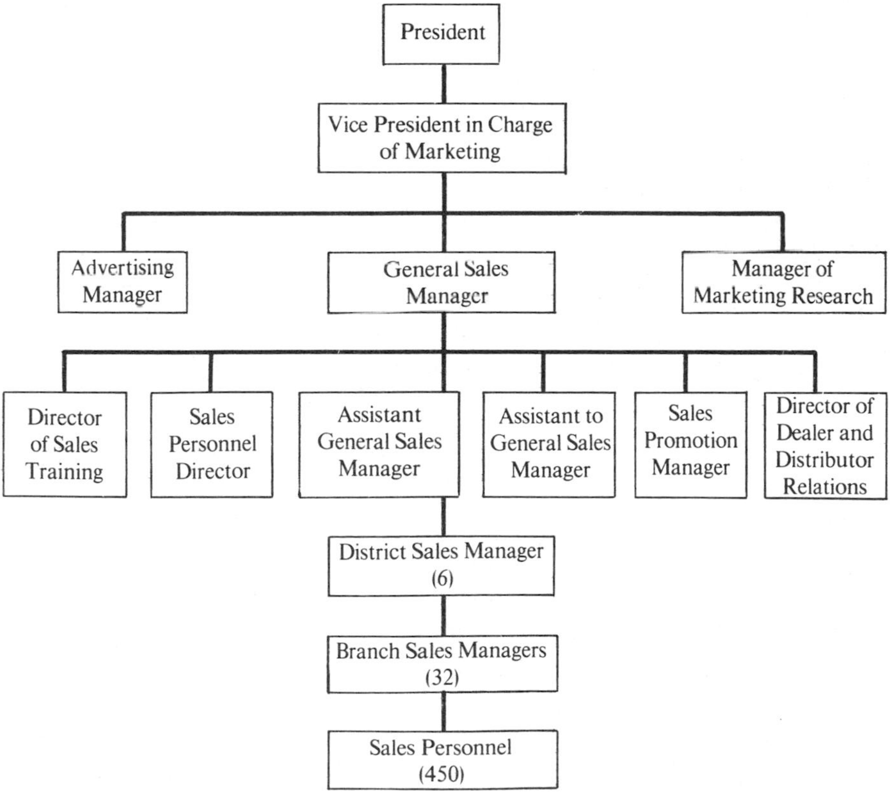

specialists with more descriptive titles. In contrast, the "assistant" is the recipient of general line authority delegated by his or her superior. The assistant general sales manager is an understudy of the general sales manager who performs assignments of a line nature in the name of his or her superior. The assistant to the general sales manager carries part of the general administrative load that would otherwise be borne by the general sales manager.

The advantages of the line and staff sales organization are mainly those of specialization. The chief sales executive, being relieved from much detail work, can take a broader view of the department. Problems now can be seen in proper perspecive, and connections between apparently unrelated problems are brought into focus. A pool of experts provides advice and assistance on questions that arise in specialized fields. Planning activities are subdivided and apportioned to the various staff members, and resulting decisions and policies should rest on a sounder base than in the line organization.

Meanwhile, the chief sales executive may concentrate on control and coordination of subordinates. Staff members assume much of the burden of solving problems in the areas they cover. Thus, the chief sales executive can devote more attention to the human aspects of administration, which should step up departmental effectiveness.

The specialization made possible by line and staff organization is also the source of its weaknesses. Work of the staff specialists must be coordinated, and such coordination is costly. Other administrative expenses may also increase, unless the number of staff executives is kept in line with departmental needs. The staff should be expanded only when it can be shown that the contributions of new staff members will equal or exceed the costs of maintaining them.

Close control over staff-line relations is essential. If staff officials issue instructions directly to line executives, it is difficult to prevent some persons from evading unwanted responsibilities. All areas in which line and staff executives share authority and responsibility should be duly noted in written job descriptions and in detail in the organizational manual. All other areas of responsibility and authority should be clearly delineated and assigned to specific individuals.

When the line and staff sales organization is used, the time interval between problem recognition and the taking of corrective action tends to widen. This results from the necessity for allowing staff executives time to study problems before making recommendations to the decision makers. This interval can be reduced by permitting staff planners to assist in expediting the implementation of the plan. But, as already indicated, this procedure may play into the hands of those wanting to evade responsibility. When time is an important consideration, though, it is wise to use staff people in this capacity.

### Functional Type of Sales Organization

Some few sales departments make use of the functional type of organization.[5] This type, derived from the management theory originally developed by Frederick W. Taylor, is based upon the premise that each individual in an organization, executive and employee, should have as few distinct duties as possible. The principle of specialization is utilized to the fullest extent. Duty assignments and delegations of authority are made according to function. No matter where a function appears in the organization, it is in

---

[5]Functional organization is seldom utilized for the enterprise as a whole. It is used principally in highly centralized departments, such as manufacturing. In departments that are by nature decentralized, such as the sales department, functional organization is little used.

the jurisdiction of the same executive. Thus, in the functional sales department, the sales-people receive instructions from several executives but on different aspects of their work. Provision for coordinating the work of the functional executives is made only at the top of the structure; executives at lower levels do not have coordinating responsibilities. In contrast to the line and staff organization, all specialists in a functional organization have line authority of a sort—or, more properly, they have what we referred to earlier as functional authority. Moreover, instructions, and even policies, can be put into effect with or without prior approval of the top-level coordinating executive.

A functional sales organizational structure is shown in Figure 6.3. The coordinating executive is the director of sales administration; all executives on the next level are specialists. As indicated, sales personnel receive instructions from six different executives.

The outstanding advantage claimed for the functional sales department is improved performance. Specialized activities are assigned to experts, whose guidance should help in increasing effectiveness of the sales force. However, this feature also has its drawbacks. When salespeople take instructions from several sources, confusion may result, especially if experts overstep the limits of their authority. Then, too, problems in maintaining contact with individual salespersons are multiplied.

The practicality of functional organization for the sales department is open to question. Small and medium-sized firms do not find it feasible, or financially possible, to utilize the high degree of division of labor. It is sometimes contended that functional organization is suitable for large firms with stable operations and with opportunity for considerable division of labor; however, certain characteristics of functional organization cause it to be rejected even by most large firms. Large companies with stable selling operations are the

FIGURE 6.3
Functional Type of Sales Organization

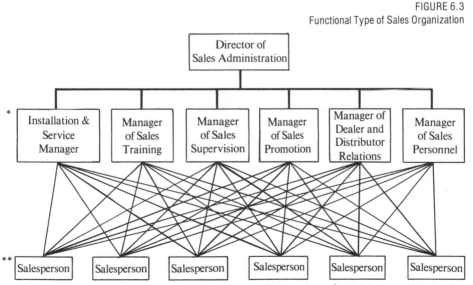

* In actual practice the number of executives on this level would be much larger, and their areas of functional responsibility would be broken down in much greater detail than is shown here.

**A sales department using the functional type of organization would undoubtedly employ more than six salespeople. Only six are shown in this example, because of the difficulties encountered in depicting lines of authority for larger numbers.

exception rather than the rule. Furthermore, the sheer size of the sales force in many large firms makes the highly centralized sales operations of a typical functional organization impractical. This limitation in the number of administrative levels may be traced to the requirement in the functional model for having a lone official to coordinate the work of the specialists. Most large firms find that more administrative levels are needed when the marketing area is extensive, when the product line is wide, or when large numbers of selling personnel are required. It is possible to use modified versions of the functional model—versions providing for a modicum of decentralization and for more administrative levels—but in its pure form, at least, functional organization for the sales department appears both inappropriate and unwise.

## Committee Type of Sales Organization

The committee is rarely, if ever, the sole basis for organizing a sales department. Rather, it is used as a method of organizing the executive group for planning and policy formulation while leaving actual operations, including implementation of plans and policies, to individual executives. Thus, many firms have a sales-training committee (comprised of such executives as the general sales manager, his or her assistants, the sales-training manager, and perhaps representative divisional or regional sales managers) that meets periodically to draft training plans and formulate policies on sales training. Implementation of these plans and policies, however, generally is the responsibility of the sales-training manager, if the company has one, or of the executives responsible for sales training in their own jurisdictions. Other committees frequently found in sales organizations include customer relations, operations, personnel, merchandising, and new products.

The use of committees in the sales department has certain advantages. Before policies are made and action is taken, important problems are subjected to deliberation by committee members and measured against their varied viewpoints. Committee meetings, where ideas are interchanged and a wide range of opinions are present, promote coordination among members of the executive team. When problems are aired thoroughly in committee meetings, cooperation is likely to be better than under any other plan of organization. However, unless decision making and policy formulation are left to specific individuals, it is impossible to fix responsibility definitely. Because committees render their most important service in providing focal points for discussion of problems and for the making of suggestions, many companies prohibit committees from making decisions or formulating policies. Certainly no committee should be allowed to develop into a vehicle for evasion of responsibility by an individual.

For committees to operate effectively, other precautions are necessary. The agenda must be planned and controlled to avoid wasting time of executives not directly interested in the topics considered. The tendency for committees to consume large amounts of time can be counteracted if the chairman keeps the discussion concentrated on the subject at hand. But committee meetings should not be dominated by chairmen. Although committee chairmen should guide discussions within specified bounds, they should not use their positions to force their opinions on others.

## FIELD ORGANIZATION OF THE SALES DEPARTMENT

Nearly every growing company faces, sooner or later, the necessity for establishing a field sales organization. The sales manager exercises adequate personal supervision over field selling operations when a company is young, when only a few salespeople are employed, when the sales force travels directly out of the home office, and when the marketing area is small. As more salespersons are added, it becomes increasingly difficult to supervise and control them. If growth in sales is to parallel additions to the sales force, either the same marketing area must be worked more intensively or new areas must be penetrated. Both alternatives call for closer supervision and control of personnel in the field. For a short while, letters, telegrams, telephone calls, and occasional visits by home office executives suffice. But difficulties of supervision by remote control multiply as the company expands; eventually, a field organization is needed.

The field organization, by definition, consists of all employees of the sales department who work away from the home office. Thus, all types of outside sales people are included, as are traveling sales supervisors, branch and district managers, and clerical employees in branch and district offices. Also included are service, repair, and sales-promotion personnel. Although not all are concerned directly with increasing the effectiveness of field selling operations, each makes contributions to that end. The two main purposes of a field organization are (1) to facilitate the selling task, and (2) to make more certain that salespeople achieve the goals set for them. Sales personnel should be able to count on the field organization for assistance and support; their jobs should be made easier, not harder, because of it.

Numerous factors influence the size of the field organization. The larger the firm, assuming similar marketing policies, the greater is the required number of salespeople, supervisors, and regional, branch, and district managers. The relative emphasis placed on personal selling in the marketing program directly affects the size of the field organization. For example, the firm selling directly to retailers, ultimate consumers, or industrial users commits itself to the performance of a sizable personal-selling task, and it requires a field organization of commensurate size. In contrast, companies using wholesalers find that their field organizations can be correspondingly smaller, since parts of the personal selling and other tasks are transferred to these middlemen. Other factors affecting the size of the field organization include desired frequency of sales calls, number of customers and prospects, and geographical spread of sales accounts.

The makeup of the field organization is influenced directly by the organizational philosophy of the management. Companies that consider centralization of authority desirable normally have complex supervisory organizations. Each salesperson is subjected to close supervision, hence the need for a considerable force of supervisors. Firms that believe in decentralization of authority, in contrast, usually permit individuals in the field to operate more on their own.

## CENTRALIZATION VS. DECENTRALIZATION IN
## SALES-FORCE MANAGEMENT

In examining the organizational practices and operations of individual companies, it is revealing to note the degree of centralization or decentralization evident in sales-force management. In the centralized organization, almost all activities, including sales-force management, are administered from a central headquarters. The central sales office has full responsibility for recruiting, selecting, training, compensating, supervising, motivating, controlling, and evaluating the sales force. In the decentralized organization, in theory at least, all these activities are handled in the field by field sales executives. In practice, however, a "decentralized organization" is one in which there is decentralization in management of various selling tasks and in performance of certain important personnel management activities. For example, branch or district sales offices may do the recruiting, selecting, motivating, and supervising; the central headquarters may handle training, compensating, and evaluating; and the branches and the central headquarters may share responsibility, in proportions varying with the marketing situation and management philosophy, for other aspects of sales-force management. It is rare, in other words, for sales-force management to be either 100 percent centralized or 100 percent decentralized. Management's appraisal of relative costs and effectiveness generally results in some aspects being centralized and others decentralized.

Centralization in sales-force management varies widely in different kinds of companies. Smaller companies that have few salespeople and confine their operations to a small geographical area, keeping the unit of sale high, the sales-call frequency low, and the caliber of salespersons relatively high, incline toward centralized sales-force management. Manufacturing firms relying almost entirely upon specialized wholesale middlemen for marketing of their products need only minimum sales forces and, therefore, tend toward centralization. Local wholesalers with restricted sales areas also have small sales forces and, by the very nature of their operations, are highly centralized. The principal factor determining centralization, then, is a small size of sales force; but other marketing factors, such as those illustrated, also move a company in this direction.

High decentralization in sales-force management is found mainly among companies with large sales forces. Likely to have considerable decentralization, for instance, is a manufacturing firm distributing a wide line of consumer products over a vast market area and selling direct to varied retailers—all conditions indicating the need for a large number of salespeople. Wherever marketing conditions require large sales forces, the economies and effectiveness of decentralization are likely to be found more attractive than those of centralization.

Other things being equal, there is a strong pull in the direction of sales-force decentralization as a company grows larger. This is true even though decentralization requires at least one more level of sales management, and the maintenance of branch or district offices (or both) causes additions to other fixed operating costs. With continuing growth, the advantages of decentralized sales-force management increasingly outweigh the higher costs. Among these advantages are:

1. More intensive cultivation of the market and, consequently, a higher sales volume to help absorb the higher fixed costs.
2. More effective control, improved supervision, and increased sales productivity resulting from the addition of at least one intermediate level of sales executives, and from reduction of geographical separation of executives and sales personnel.
3. Improved customer service stemming from more effective control of sales personnel.
4. Reduced need for and costs of territorial "break-in" time, since more salespersons are recruited from the areas to which they are later assigned.
5. Improved sales-force morale—there are more frequent contacts with executives, reductions in travel time, and fewer nights away from home.
6. Lower travel expenses—salespeople are dispatched from decentralized points, and fewer field trips by home office sales executives are required.
7. A "built-in" management development program—branch and district offices not only provide realistic training but serve as proving grounds for future high-level sales executives.

## PLANS FOR DIVIDING LINE AUTHORITY IN
## THE SALES ORGANIZATION

As marketing operations become larger, line authority and responsibility eventually become excessively burdensome for the chief sales executive, because of the increasing number of people to supervise. Ordinarily, the first remedial measure is the addition of a general line assistant, for example, an assistant general sales manager. As the burden of line administrative work continues to grow, it is necessary to provide additional assistants. These new subordinates, technically known as limited line assistants, are given line responsibilities narrower than those of the assistant general sales manager. Although they work with a variety of matters, their assignments cover a limited area of operations. Tasks of line administration are subdivided among these new assistants in one of three ways: (1) by geographic area, (2) by products, or (3) by customers or marketing channels.

### Geographic Division of Line Authority

The large firm with far-flung selling operations is likely to subdivide line authority geographically (see Figure 6.4). This is particularly so if the characteristics of large numbers of customers vary according to geographic location, if different selling problems are encountered in different areas, or if certain products are more strongly demanded in some regions than in others. However, a more compelling reason exists for dividing line authority geographically. As more customers are added and as a wider area is cultivated, the size of the sales task increases enormously. Setting up geographic divisions is simply a way of cutting the sales task down to manageable proportions. When centralized administration becomes too great a burden for the chief sales executive, secondary line executives are delegated authority to conduct sales operations within smaller areas. Geographic division is usually made first into rather large areas known as regions or divisions. These units may or may not be broken down further into districts or branches.

FIGURE 6.4
Sales Department Organized with Line Authority Subdivided Geographically

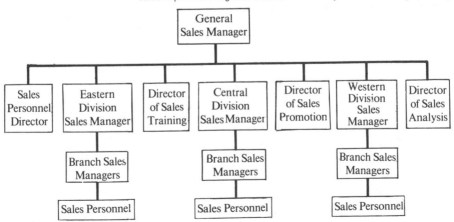

When line authority is divided geographically, local problems can be handled speedily and effectively. It is not necessary to wait for decisions from the home office; many questions of importance to customers can be answered by executives personally acquainted with local conditions. Shortening the lines of communication makes possible closer supervision of salespeople, which, in turn, helps in improving customer service. Local markets can be cultivated more intensively, and tactics of local competitors can be met and countered in the field. The net result should be a strengthening of the company's position in all sales regions. However, because this system calls for multiple offices, administrative expenses increase. Then, too, the chief sales executive faces the problem of coordinating several regional operations. Unless this coordination is effective, conflicting policies may develop in different regions.

### Product Division of Line Authority

A second scheme for dividing line authority is by products. The sales task is split among subordinate line executives, each of whom directs sales operations for part of the product line. When authority is so divided, more than one sales force may be required. For example, some companies' product lines are too wide to be distributed economically by a single sales force. Others sell both highly technical and nontechnical products; thus some salespeople need specialized training and some do not. In still others, economies of a single sales force are reduced or eliminated because different products are marketed to entirely different types of customers.

Figures 6.5 and 6.6 illustrate two schemes for dividing line authority by products. In Figure 6.5, the customary line and staff organization has been retained; in Figure 6.6, the primary division is on the basis of products, and each product sales manager has his own staff of specialists. The use of separate staffs, shown in Figure 6.6, is rather unusual. Often this is an intermediate stage resulting from a merger. Because of expenses involved in maintaining duplicate staffs, most companies, after mergers, gradually change the organization to the basic line and staff form shown in Figure 6.5. However, unless there are good reasons for retaining separate sales managers and sales forces, as will shortly be explained, line authority should be divided on some basis other than products.

FIGURE 6.5
Sales Department Organized with Line Authority Subdivided by Products,
but Retaining Basic Line and Staff Form

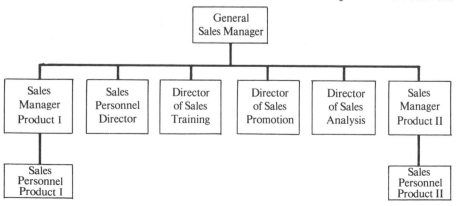

FIGURE 6.6
Sales Department Organized with Line Authority Subdivided by Products,
Utilizing Duplicate Staffs

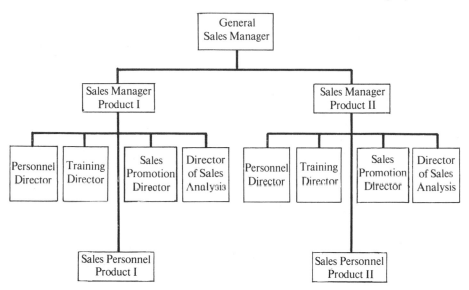

The decision to use the product type of sales organization should be based chiefly on whether the benefits of product specialization outweigh the additional expenses involved. Otherwise, it is generally wiser to organize the sales force on some other basis. Gains associated with the use of specialized salespersons, who concentrate on selling specific products, must be weighed against increased expenses. Maintaining more than one sales force normally results in higher administrative and travel expenses. There are almost certain to be times when two company sales personnel selling different products make calls on the same customers. Although specialized salespeople may give more "push" to individual products, many customers object to multiple calls from the same company. The benefits of specialized sales forces are greatest for companies selling broadly diversified lines, reaching different markets with different products, and encountering unique selling problems for the various products.

### Customer (or Marketing-Channel) Division of Line Authority

The third scheme for subdividing line authority is by type of customer (Figure 6.7) or marketing channel (Figure 6.8). This scheme is appropriate when nearly identical products are marketed to several types of customers and the problems of selling to each type are different. When the same, or similar, products are sold to a number of industries, they often find different applications in each industry. The company in Figure 6.7 sells its products to the lumber, construction, and mining industries. In each industry, the products are used for different purposes. Customers not only have different needs, they are influenced by different buying motives. Thus, special forces were organized to sell to each major type of customer.

Other companies, especially in the consumer-goods field, pattern their sales orga-

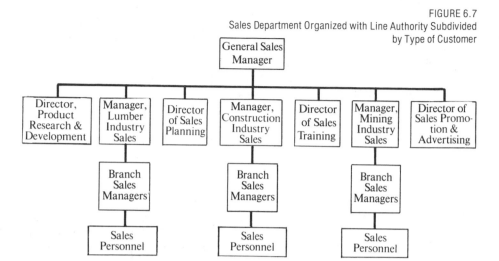

FIGURE 6.7
Sales Department Organized with Line Authority Subdivided
by Type of Customer

FIGURE 6.8
Sales Department Organized with Line Authority
Subdivided by Marketing Channel

nizations after the principal marketing channels. Although ultimate consumers may be substantially alike, they frequently must be reached in different ways (that is, they may buy the product in different types of outlets). Problems of distributing to chain stores are often unlike those of selling to independent wholesalers and retailers, and specialized sales training programs are often required. In cases of this kind, the problems of selling vary more with the marketing channel than they do with the product or geographical location; consequently, line authority is subdivided on the basis of marketing channels.

### Dividing Line Authority on More Than One Basis

Few companies use a single basis for subdividing line authority. Most use a combination, subdividing the selling task more than once, to permit greater specialization. Nearly every large sales department subdivides authority on the geographic basis at some level of organization, but this is done usually in combination with either the product or type-of-customer system. If geographical differences are more important than those of product or type of customer, the primary subdivision is one the geographic basis; the next, according to one of the other bases. If geographical differences are of lesser importance, the procedure is reversed. The factor most important to the marketing success of the company should form the basis for the first subdivision, and less important factors should determine subsequent breakdowns.

## CONCLUSION

Throughout American industry today, there is fast-spreading recognition of the necessity of applying sound principles of organization to the sales department. There is increasing awareness that organizational planning is a continuing activity, and that the sales-department structure must be adjusted to changing marketing needs. These modifications in management thinking have evolved, or are still evolving, as less emphasis has been placed on securing orders and more attention has been paid to control of costs and expenses and the realization of net profits. These are trends of great importance. As they continue, an increasing number of sales organizations will be structured more logically. Selling acitivities will be perfomed with less waste effort, and total effectivenss of the sales effort will be enhanced. Such advances should result in material benefits to the firms achieving them, and to their customers.

# 7

# Sales-Department Relations

The sales department occupies a strategic position relative to other departments and to the outside world. Functioning in cooperation with other departments, it spearheads the effort to supply customers with ever-increasing quantities of products at prices that return a profit to the company; to the extent that this is achieved, the company's reputation rests upon a sound foundation. Good products and competitive prices alone are not enough to ensure a company's success; company success is also affected by the dealings and associations of the sales department and its representatives with customers and with other important publics. Of course, the internal impact of sales-department relations with other departments also influences the company's reputation with many publics. Therefore, because all individual sales personnel, as well as the entire department, are in a position to add to or detract from the company reputation, it is important to assure that all are alert to their responsibilities for maintaining good relations.

There is a growing trend for firms to organize and staff separate public-relations departments, but in companies without such departments sales executives frequently have additional responsibility for public relations. The main reason for this is that they normally have close relations with the various external publics. Even sales executives who are not assigned the primary responsibility remain responsible for effective execution of the public-relations program as it pertains to the sales department. Under either arrangement, then, sales executives must consider the probable public-relations impact when planning and administering department programs, to ensure satisfactory relations with all those with whom they or their subordinates come into contact.

## INTERDEPARTMENTAL RELATIONS AND COORDINATION

Coordinating the activities of all departments so that maximum progress is made toward overall company objectives is one of top management's most important responsibilities. Department heads, in addition to implementing top management's directives, work to harmonize their activities so that the tasks of all departments are accomplished as effectively as possible. Each must know and understand the functions of other departments, and each is responsible for coordinating his or her department's activities to contribute significantly to company success.

Although the primary organizational responsibility of chief sales executives is to manage the sales department, they must be familiar with the operations of other departments and keep abreast of their problems. In particular, chief sales executives must have a good grasp of how other departments influence and are influenced by the sales department. These are dynamic relationships, inasmuch as a policy or procedural change in one department almost always has repercussions in others. Interdepartmental coordination and communication must be highly developed, and cooperation is essential if continuing progress toward company goals is to be registered.

### Formal Coordinating Methods

Formal coordination among departments is achieved by one or more of three methods. The first method is to build coordination into the organization through grouping closely allied activities under a single high-ranking executive. In most companies, chief marketing executives have reporting directly to them the heads of departments performing marketing activities, such as sales, advertising, marketing research, and service. Under this arrangement marketing executives are responsible for coordinating the operations of departments under them. The second method is to achieve coordination through the general administrative officers—the president, executive vice-president, or general manager. In such cases, the coordinating executive typically coordinates the operations of all company departments, not just those performing closely related tasks, such as marketing activities. This explains why the second method is most widely used in companies having only a minimum number of departments. The third method involves the use of policy, planning, and coordinating committees made up of representatives of concerned departments. On the surface, this appears to be the weakest method, inasmuch as no one executive clearly has responsibility for coordination. However, committees for obtaining interdepartmental coordination often work out quite satisfactorily in practice.

### Informal Coordination

Regardless of how much formal coordination is provided by the organizational plan, informal coordination is often more important. Department heads may solve an interdepartmental problem informally while it is being thrashed out through formal mechanisms. Indeed, informal coordination procedures are preferred in most companies, and solutions so developed may or may not be formally adopted later by action of a coordinating body. One thing is certain—unexpected problems with important interdepartmental implications should be handled with minimum delay, for to prolong their solution is to risk costly friction. Sometimes informal solutions are accepted as tentative and are subject to modification after review by the formal coordinating mechanism. To arrive informally at workable solutions to problems affecting the sales department, the chief sales executive must maintain satisfactory relations with heads of other departments; all should think of themselves as members of the same team, cooperating in the effort to reach company objectives.

Sales executives report that informal coordinating procedures are more important than formal methods, particularly where frequent communication is required for coordination. A study of four companies revealed that a large amount of communication took place informally among executives responsible for marketing-related activities. Basically, it was found that informal coordination was achieved partly through voluntary exchange of informational copies of correspondence, but largely through informal, nonperiodic exchanges of information occurring when executives met, by chance or arrangement, in their offices, or over coffee or meals.[1]

The same study revealed that one individual, or occasionally more than one, served as a communication center for exchanges of information relating to each important marketing decision area. These executives were involved, either as receivers or senders, in almost every exchange of information that took place with respect to their interest area. In fact, all executives, acting as "centers," assumed the responsibility for providing a continuous flow of information regarding their areas to everyone in the company who they felt might need or could use the information. It was also found that the top sales and advertising executives served jointly as communication centers for all activities that create demand, including personal selling, advertising, merchandising, sales promotion, and packaging.[2]

It seems clear, then, that the informal communication network is of major importance in coordinating the marketing activities of the firm; however, the existence of such a network poses several problems for the chief marketing executive:

1. Marketing personnel must be made aware of the need for the coordination of all marketing activities. The historical lack of close coordination and cooperation among many marketing-related activities makes this a particularly difficult challenge.

2. Marketing personnel must be given the opportunity to understand the role and responsibilities of other marketing jobs, and to know the people holding these jobs. This is especially important when personnel responsible for marketing-decision areas report to different superiors.

3. It is important for marketing management to establish a climate that encourages a continuous and free exchange of ideas and information.[3]

Sales-department operations influence and are influenced by the operations of departments performing closely related marketing activities, and of others, such as production, personnel, finance, and data processing, where interdepartmental influences are more indirect. In both situations, department heads must know the points where interdepartmental cooperation, coordination, and communication are necessary. The following discussion relates to instances where cooperation and coordination are essential and communications desirable for the chief sales executive. The main points of interdepartmental contact are covered; but it should be borne in mind that the dynamics and organizational peculiarities of an individual firm may require such cooperation and coordination in other situations.

---

[1]R. C. Andersen and E. W. Cundiff, "Patterns of Communication in Marketing Organizations," *Journal of Marketing,* Vol. 29, No. 3 (July 1965), p. 32.

[2]*Ibid.*

[3]*Ibid.,* p. 34.

## COORDINATION OF PERSONAL SELLING WITH
## OTHER MARKETING ACTIVITIES

### Sales and Advertising

The sales and advertising departments work toward the same objective—the stimulation of demand for the company's products through the communication of information to prospective buyers—but they use somewhat different approaches. In general, personal selling techniques are the province of the sales department and nonpersonal selling techniques that of the advertising department; but the two major types of selling effort need skillful blending to achieve an "optimum promotional mix." This requires careful coordination of the two departments' plans and efforts, since the activities of the sales force should be planned and directed along lines that increase advertising's impact, and advertising should be geared to help salespeople where and when they need it most. In addition, the sales department can assist the advertising department in selecting themes and media, in preparing advertising schedules, and in securing dealers' support for cooperative advertising programs. The advertising department can help the sales department in such ways as the furnishing of sales aids for the sales force and for dealers, and by providing sales personnel with leads. Furthermore, advertising, used effectively, conserves the sales force's time, for prospects presold through advertising should be easier to convert into customers. Proper timing and coordination of advertising and personal selling is essential, and promotional programs need skillful administration by executives who understand the functions and costs of both types of selling effort.

Because both departments work toward the same goals, formal coordination is usually best achieved by having both department heads report to the same high-ranking executive, for example, the marketing vice-president. However, because there are so many matters of joint interest and so many requiring frequent communication, coordination of most relations between these two departments must be conducted on an informal day-to-day basis, with frequent interactions of department heads and subordinates alike.

### Sales and Marketing Information

To obtain maximum returns per dollar spent for marketing information, the sales department must work in close harmony with the department or departments producing marketing information. In some instances such information is provided by marketing research, but in companies that have developed sophisticated marketing information systems, marketing research is only one of the subsystems providing information inputs. Such marketing information, whatever its source, assists the sales department by gathering data needed for analyzing sales problems, assisting in determining sales potentials and setting quotas, measuring the effectiveness of the sales effort, assisting with sales tests, and in other ways. The sales department provides the information system with many of the raw statistics and other information needed for sales and market analysis and forecasting. Sometimes, although the practice is controversial, salespeople are made available to marketing research to do field interviewing.

The marketing information system provides a pool of specialized knowledge and analytical skill that sales executives should utilize on a continuing basis. As marketing information systems and marketing research become increasingly sophisticated, and with the development of new techniques and experimental designs, it is probable that the sales department will work ever more closely with information personnel. One area in which surprisingly little systematic research has been done is that of evaluating the relative effectiveness of alternative personal-selling appeals and methods of making sales presentations. This lack exists in spite of the fact that considerable work has been done in the closely allied field of advertising content research.[4]

New opportunities are arising for sales executives to acquire data previously unavailable or uneconomic to obtain, and to attain a hitherto impossible level of sophistication in solving sales-management problems. Coordination of the sales department with the information system and its data-processing capacity is increasingly important. The sales department has to provide the marketing information system with definitions both of its information needs (desired "outputs") and the information it has available (the "inputs"). The data-processing unit may or may not combine the sales department's own information inputs with inputs from elsewhere. Thus, both in designing and operating a management information system, continuing formal and informal cooperation and communications are of the highest importance.

Improvements in the performance of traditional data-handling activities have been significant. From the sales department's standpoint, for example, it has always been important to bill customers correctly and promptly. But the automation of order processing has not only resulted in improvements in customer service, it has produced as by-products data that are needed for making rapid changes in sales and production plans, and for inventory control.[5] Traditionally, too, sales volume and profit reports have been prepared as a means of measuring the performance of the sales force. Computer installations are being used extensively to turn out these reports earlier than before, more frequently, and in greater detail.[6] In fact, the computer's capabilities for turning out reports are so great that sales executives are calling more and more for "exception reports" to avoid being buried in mountains of detail. Such reports highlight things requiring attention; details are available but are held in reserve until the executive requests them. Among the exception reports of interest to the sales executive are: sales personnel failing to achieve quotas; sales activities exceeding budgeted expenses; territories in which the company is losing competitive position; customers with declining purchases; and product lines having slow sales movement, declining profit margins, or both.[7]

In some companies, computer centers provide customers with automatic reordering procedures. Catalina swim suits, for instance, can now be reordered by department store buyers by punching out their orders on in-store console teleprocessing stations linked to a central computer at the Catalina data center that, in seconds: (1) scans the customer's account for a credit okay; (2) examines Catalina's inventories to see whether all the styles, sizes, and colors can be supplied; (3) discerns the age of the account; (4) types out a ship-

[4]On this point, see P. E. Green and D. S. Tull, *Research for Marketing Decisions,* 2nd ed. (Englewood Cliffs, N.J.: Prentice-Hall, Inc., 1970), p. 16. See also C. R. Wasson, *The Strategy of Marketing Research* (New York: Appleton-Century-Crofts, 1964), p. 501.

[5]D. F. Cox and R. E. Good, "How to Build a Marketing Information System," *Harvard Business Review,* Vol. 45, No. 3 (May-June 1967), p. 47.

[6]J. H. Meyers and R. R. Mead, *The Management of Marketing Research* (Scranton, Pa.: Intext International Publishers, 1969).

[7]M. A. Jolson and R. T. Hise, *Quantitative Techniques for Marketing Decisions* (New York: Macmillan Publishing Co. Inc., 1973), pp. 117-18.

ping order; and (5) stores the new inventory information in its memory.[8] This .
may appear to reduce the salesperson's role in servicing accounts; actually, howev.
net result has been simply to make it more convenient for customers to reorder and u
speed up order processing, both of which should result in improved relations with
customers. The continuing need for developmental selling and for keeping in close
personal touch with customers' problems means that the salesperson's role has been
changed, not eliminated. Automatic reordering procedures will probably spread and, as
they do, sales executives will have to work closely with data-processing specialists both in
setting them up and in monitoring their operations, adjusting them as required to meet
changing customer requirements.

The computer is also opening up new opportunities for sales executives to arrive at
much more sophisticated answers to problems than were previously attainable. In some
companies, routes and call schedules for sales personnel are already being planned by
computers. In another instance, a manufacturer has used computer-based techniques to
determine much more scientifically than before just how much of the time of sales
personnel should be devoted to sales development work to offset the attrition of business
from old, established customers.[9] Undoubtedly many additional applications of the
computer will be found that will help sales management in resolving such questions as:
How large should the sales force be? How should it be deployed geographically? How
should sales personnel spend their time? What relative selling efforts are appropriate to
different products and different customer classes? Thus, in their role as decision makers
and problem solvers, sales executives will have continuing need to maintain close relations
with information and computer specialists. There is much room for improved coordination and cooperation between the sales department and the information function, but
probably the greatest opportunity lies in the development of closer informal relationships
among personnel at all levels. Insofar as formal coordination is concerned, organizational planners generally recommend that both marketing-information and sales-department heads report to the same superior.

### Sales and Service

In companies manufacturing technical products or products requiring installation
and repair services by company personnel, maximum cooperation and close contact of the
sales and service departments are required. Availability of service, such as technical advice
in the installation of a new product, is a powerful selling argument, and there are important implications for the service department in a salesperson's promises to buyers. Moreover, in many industries (commercial refrigeration, for example), the recommendations
of service personnel often influence buyers' decisions; and in the case of consumer
products such as vacuum sweepers and other household appliances, service personnel are
active in a sales-making capacity. Where service plays an important role in sales strategy,
provisions for formal coordination should be built into the organizational structure. When
both the sales and service departments are decentralized, the organization should provide
for bridging the gap between the home office and the field. Sales and service should also

---

[8]E. B. Weiss, *The Communications Revolution and How it Will Affect All Business and All Marketing*
(Chicago: Advertising Publications, Inc., 1966), p. 23.

[9]R. F. Neuschel, "The Nature and Extent of Computer Usage in Marketing Operations and Decision
Making," in W. Alderson and S. J. Shapiro (eds.), *Marketing and the Computer* (Englewood Cliffs, N.J.: Prentice-
Hall, Inc., 1963), p. 416.

/ locating sales and service personnel in the same field offices, ~~p~~onsible for both activities.[10] Under both centralized and de- ~~p~~lans, sales and service functions should also be coordinated at ~~...~~l, probably by having those responsible for both report to the ~~...~~ve. Under all organizational arrangements, however, the critical ~~...~~operation between sales and service functions indicates that the gr~~...~~ ~~...~~iting should be informal, and between personnel on *lower* organiza- tional lev~~...~~

## Sales and Physical Distribution

The importance of achieving effective coordination of selling and physical distribution operations is being increasingly recognized. With the development of the marketing concept, more and more firms have accepted the notion that all operations of the business should be geared toward serving customers at a profit. Necessarily, achieving this objective requires the maintenance of favorable relations between volume and costs of various kinds, including physical distribution costs. Proper packing, accurate freight-rate quotations, and promptness in delivery—all physical distribution activities—are often important factors in securing sales volume; but unless the costs of performing these activities are kept under control, the resulting sales volume may yield less profit than it should. Clearly, then, there is a need for coordinating sales policies, such as those regarding delivery schedules, with the capabilities of the physical distribution operation and its costs. The benefits of effective coordination with physical distribution are significant for the sales department. These benefits, all of which can help to generate additional sales volume and profit, include the following:[11]

1. Minimize out-of-stock occurrences (helps reduce sales lost because of "outs" and helps raise the level of customer satisfaction).
2. Reduce customers' inventory requirements. (If a company can develop a more responsive distribution system than competitors, its customers can obtain an economic advantage by doing business with it. This should be a strong selling point.)
3. Solidify relations with customers (through integrating company delivery facilities with customers' receiving facilities, consignment of stocks to customers, and similar devices).
4. Allow greater concentration on demand creation. (Development of a well-organized physical distribution activity, in which a separate administrative group is set up to plan and operate the distribution system, can free marketing and sales personnel, allowing them to concentrate more on their basic responsibility—demand creation. In many companies this has led to an increased number of sales offices and a decreased number of warehouses, with a consequent reduction in total distribution costs.)

Probably the most effective formal coordination of sales and physical distribution results from having the heads of both operations report to a common superior, such as the marketing vice-president. Even more important is the informal coordination of sales and physical-distribution personnel, at all levels, on a day-to-day basis. Salespeople and their counterparts in the physical-distribution department, for example, should com-

[10]L. M. DeBoes and W. H. Ward, "Integration of the Computer into Salesman Reporting," *Journal of Marketing,* Vol. 35, No. 1 (January 1971), pp. 41-47.

[11]W. M. Stewart, "Physical Distribution: Key to Improved Volume and Profits," *Journal of Marketing,* Vol. 29, No. 1 (January 1965), p. 68.

municate directly and frequently, thus helping to ensure efficient processing of customers' orders.

## COORDINATION OF PERSONAL SELLING WITH OTHER DEPARTMENTS

### Sales and Production

Coordination of the activities of the sales and production departments is absolutely essential. Whereas at one time production was normally started only after orders were on hand, today most production is in anticipation of future sales. Similarly, although some products, such as defense materials for the armed forces, are manufactured to specifications established directly by buyers, most products today are manufactured according to specifications set within the company itself. These decisions, of course, reflect consideration of the preferences of potential customers. These changes have magnified the need for effective coordination of the two departments' activities.

Coordination is important both in planning and in actual operations. In the planning stages, joint consultation is required when deciding such matters as the products to manufacture, the quantities to produce, the production schedule, inventories, and packaging. But even the most carefully made plans rarely work out as originally visualized. On the sales side, the sales estimate (on which production schedules are based) may prove to be in error, or the sales department may accept rush orders, necessitating the reshuffling of production schedules, addition of extra shifts, or payment of overtime wages. On the production side, output may not conform to planned quantities because of labor difficulties, material shortages, adverse weather conditions, and the like. These are only some of the situations that require changes in plans that must be worked out jointly by sales and production personnel in the effort to meet customers' product requirements and the company's profit objectives.

A natural tendency exists for the two departments to work at cross-purposes, however, and this makes their coordination more difficult. Much has been said, and almost as much written, about the conflicting philosophies of "production-minded" and "sales-minded" executives, and there is little need here to restate these opposing views. It is sufficient to say that production executives are naturally concerned with such matters as product-line standardization and simplification, and achieving manufacturing economies through long and continuous production runs. Sales executives are just as naturally concerned over "having something for everybody." Thus, their inclination is to argue for wide selections of products and models, adapted as nearly as possible to the preferences of individual customers. Adoption of the marketing concept, however, signals a modern philosophy that rejects, or at least modifies, such extreme positions, and top management works to integrate both departments' interests into unified company policies.

The cooperation of the sales department can be most helpful to the production department. Sales estimates, prepared by or with the assistance of sales executives, are needed for efficient planning of production and purchase schedules. The sales department has a reservoir of market knowledge that is invaluable to production executives seeking more efficient utilization of plant facilities. If sales executives keep production executives informed of changes in market demand for different products, the chances of attaining optimum production levels are heightened. Being in constant touch with the market, sales executives are well placed to recommend elimination of slow sellers, addition of promising new products, and changes in product and model specifications. For all products, present and proposed, the sales department gives its appraisals from the standpoints of price and potential volume. Moreover, when inventories of raw materials, goods in process, or finished products are excessive, the sales department can assist by pushing sales of the products affected.

The production department can also be helpful to the sales department. It can provide selling ammunition in the form of detailed technical information on products, and assist in training salespersons in product information. When drafting promotional plans, sales executives should draw upon production executives' know-how on such matters as manufacturing costs at different output levels, limitations of production facilities, and the practicality of building given characteristics into products. By relaying information on unused plant capacity and work-in-process to the sales department, the production department can help in stimulating sales personnel to greater efforts. The same information is useful for detecting the need for changes in the sales emphasis given different products.

The methods used for achieving interdepartmental coordination vary from firm to firm but, because sales and production are both of critical importance, top management generally retains the primary responsibility. If the company has a separate merchandising department, top management delegates the authority to coordinate many sales and production activities through staff channels; in other companies, merchandising committees with representatives from both sales and production are used to obtain formal coordination. Problems involving addition of new products, or improvements of established products, are handled on a formal basis in various ways, as described earlier.[12] Formal coordinating mechanisms such as these are valuable, but close informal contacts between personnel at many levels in the two departments are also important. Only through such informal channels is it possible to solve many complex problems arising in the course of operations with minimum expenditure of executive time.

### Sales and Research and Development

In large firms and in most firms oriented toward product innovation, research and development is organized as a separate staff department at the same level as production and sales. In smaller or more conservative firms this responsibility may be placed in the marketing or production department. Research and development work, in general, consists of the scientific and engineering efforts required to develop new products and to improve established products. It is closely related to merchandising, that is, structuring the product line and adjusting product features to fit customers' wants, which matter is of prime concern to marketing and to the sales department, as well as to the production department. Because engineering and design characteristics strongly affect the salability of products, intelligent synchronization is required of research and development, sales, and production departments—all of which are involved in product innovation. Among these are:[13]

[12]M. C. Fox, "Hidden Investments in Marketing Decisions," *Journal of Marketing,* Vol. 32, No. 4 (October 1968), pp. 10-11.

[13]J. W. Lorsch and P. R. Lawrence, "Organizing for Product Innovation," *Harvard Business Review,* Vol. 43, No. 1 (January-February 1965), p. 115.

1.  Establishment of new-product departments with the primary function of coordinating the activities of research, sales, and production specialists in the development of new products.
2.  Appointment of liaison individuals (new product managers) responsible for linking two or more groups of functional specialists.
3.  Development of short-term project teams with representatives from the several functional departments to work on a new product.
4.  Reliance on permanent cross-functional coordinating teams to deal with the continuing problems of innovation relating to a given group of products.

Whether main reliance is placed upon formal or semiformal coordinating methods such as those just noted, or informal ones, the complexity and uncertainty of the factors involved indicates that coordination should take place at *lower* organizational levels. Department heads find it difficult to keep abreast of the multitude of rapidly changing factors that must be considered in the day-to-day process of developing new products. Only the specialists on the firing line have the detailed knowledge of markets and technologies that enables them to make the frequent decisions the innovation process requires.

### Sales and Personnel

Relations between the sales and personnel departments are discussed in detail in Part III, so only brief treatment is needed here. Because of the unique problems involved in managing employees located at a distance from home offices and facilities, most personnel departments are ill equipped to service sales personnel. For this reason sales departments ordinarily handle nearly all their own personnel problems. It is customary for the personnel department to act mainly in an advisory capacity to the sales department. Personnel-department specialists in such fields as job analysis, recruiting, selecting, training, and motivation often are consulted by sales executives. Much routine sales-personnel work, such as maintaining records or personal data on individuals in the sales department, is performed by the personnel department. There is considerable cooperation between the two departments in formulating policies on pensions, vacations, sick leaves, safety, health checks, and similar matters. Formal coordination is generally obtained through top management, but there is also significant informal coordination.

### Sales and Finance

The sales department cooperates with the finance department by furnishing sales estimates for the company budget, by developing the sales department's budget, and by assisting in control of selling cost. The finance department cooperates with the sales department by providing rapid credit checks on prospective accounts; keeping salespeople informed of customers' credit standings, to prevent waste of selling effort on poor credit risks; helping locate prospective accounts; and providing credit information on candidates for sales positions. In some firms, salespersons represent the financial department in making collections and securing credit information from accounts. These are important interdepartmental activities requiring good communications, consistent policies, and close working relationships. Most organizational plans provide for formal coordination through budget and executive committees on which both departments are represented.

The most effective coordination of the sales and finance departments takes place informally through personal contact, in a mutual effort to overcome the natural conflict of interest in the area of credit policy. Credit terms are frequently significant factors in obtaining orders. Length of the credit period, size and nature of discounts, relative liberality in granting credit—all can be instrumental in persuading prospects to buy. But good reasons exist for keeping control over credit policy and its implementation away from the sales department. Some sales executives, and far too many salespeople, are more interested in obtaining orders than in collecting amounts due, resulting in a tendency to grant credit to too many below-average risks. Furthermore, salespeople tend to shy away from making collections, especially from slow-paying accounts, for fear of antagonizing these customers.

In spite of these problems, however, it is desirable that credit terms be set to permit their use as selling points. And there is a need for tact in credit negotiations with prospects and customers, both by sales people and by credit personnel. Nowhere is this better illustrated than when a customer's credit must be shut off, a situation requiring not only tact but coordination to avoid buck-passing, and resultant loss of good will. Generally speaking, the sales department, in its desire to increase sales, favors liberalizing credit policies; whereas the credit department, in its desire to control credit losses, favors tightening them. Close coordination and communications, as well as mutual effort, are required to strike a balance between these opposing inclinations in order to serve the best interests of the whole company.

### Sales and Accounting

Traditionally the sales department has relied upon the accounting department to fulfill such supporting functions as billing customers, handling the department's payroll computation and disbursement problems, and providing data for sales analysis and marketing cost analysis. Today, with the increasingly widespread use of electronic computers and the development of managerial concern with the design and operation of company-wide "management information systems," actual performance of these functions has tended to shift away from the accounting department. That department, however, may retain primary responsibility or even, organizationally speaking, have the centralized data-processing unit under its jurisdiction. More and more companies have set up such units, sometimes called "computer centers," to handle data-processing and analysis functions for all, or nearly all, departments. With this change have come significant improvements in the performance of functions traditionally performed by accounting personnel.

### Sales and Purchasing

There are three main ways in which the sales and purchasing departments cooperate. First, the sales department provides purchasing with sales estimates so that adequate stocks of raw materials, fabricating parts, and other items can be procured in advance of scheduled production runs. Sometimes these data are furnished through an intermediary such as the production department or data-processing unit. Second, the purchasing department informs the sales department, again sometimes through an intermediary, of material surpluses and shortages, so sales emphasis can be changed with regard to products made from these materials. Third, data on sales-department needs (for example, office supplies and fixtures, and company cars) are furnished the purchasing department so that purchases can be made on advantageous terms.

A fourth point of cooperation exists in companies where reciprocity is approved policy, making interdepartmental coordination of sales and purchasing particularly important; in such cases the two departments coordinate their efforts, buying as much as possible from firms that are also customers, and selling as much as possible to firms that are also suppliers. Coordination of the two departments ordinarily is achieved formally through top management, and informally through personal contacts by executives and their subordinates.

### Sales and Public Relations

It was emphasized early in this chapter that the sales department should work closely with the public-relations department. Public relations should be consulted on any contemplated selling moves that might have public-relations repercussions; and the sales department can assist public-relations personnel by relaying information, secured through its contacts with various publics, that may have public-relations significance. Relations between the two departments are normally very informal and with frequent personal contacts, with formal coordination being the responsibility of top management.

### Sales and Legal

Legislation regulating and affecting marketing activities, so much in evidence since the early 1930s, has made effective coordination of the sales and legal departments imperative. Nearly every sales-department activity has, or can have, legal implications. Sales executives require frequent legal advice on contracts with sales personnel, pricing, relations with competitors and trade associations, sales people recruiting policy and practice, and disputes with customers. Sales executives and legal officers must be in continuing communication to avoid costly litigation and possible unfavorable publicity. Formal coordination of the sales and legal departments is achieved through top management, but interdepartmental coordination on legal matters is generally informal.

## SALES DEPARTMENT'S EXTERNAL RELATIONS

The sales department has important contacts with six main publics outside the company. In the remainder of this chapter, the department's relations with five of these publics are analyzed—relations with final buyers, the industry and trade associations, governmental agencies, educational institutions, and the press. Because of the unique and involved nature of the sales department's relations with middlemen handling company products, discussion of distributive network relations is deferred to Chapter 8.

### Final-Buyer Relations

Final buyers, whether ultimate consumers or industrial users, are the most important public that any marketer must strive to please. The competitive free-enterprise system is based on the premise that customers' wants must be satisfied; individual companies prosper only to the extent that their products contribute to this ideal. An analogous situation exists in politics. If candidates satisfy voters' requirements and win their confidence, they elect them to office; if such politicians fail to maintain this support, they meet defeat at the polls. Manufacturers and their products are on a trial with the final-buyer public; but in business, the trial goes on each and every day—not, as in politics, at regularly spaced intervals. Satisfaction, or the lack of it, is recorded daily in sales order books and at the nation's checkout counters and cash registers.

Prejudices play a role in marketing, just as they do in politics. Buyer attitudes and behavior patterns, formed over time and crystallized by experience, are not easily or quickly changed. Manufacturers gain a real competitive edge when they become aware of attitudes and prejudices attaching to their products and organization, and know the reason for them. Therefore, continuing research among final-buyer groups is necessary to gather the information required for planning ways of altering final-buyer attitudes and behavior patterns. Such research also is used for measuring progress toward overcoming prejudices, for determining prejudices against competitors and their products, for detecting the need for product improvement, and for evaluating middlemen's prestige.

The responsibility for maintaining good final-buyer relations is not the sales department's alone; it is shared with other departments and with middlemen. If the production department, for example, makes products that fail to meet final-buyers' expectations, unsatisfactory final-buyer relations result. In consumer-goods fields, personnel policies are part and parcel of the consumer relations program, since employees are often customers and have contact with other customers. Similarly, dividend and other financial policies affect consumer relations (but probably to a lesser degree), since stockholders and their friends may also be customers. When suppliers of industrial products are also customers, final-buyer relations are influenced directly by the seller's purchasing policies and procedures. Middlemen at all distribution levels help to mold final-buyer attitudes toward manufacturers and their products. The efforts of all departments need to be skillfully blended with those of middlemen; in this coordinating effort, the sales department plays a vital role.

Sales-department personnel play major roles in formulating basic product service policies and in implementing them. Skill in formulating and implementing such policies affects not only final-buyer attitudes but also the ease with which initial and repeat sales are made. For example, guarantees and service obligations should be honored promptly and cheerfully. If products fail to perform in the manner that final buyers have a right to expect, then adjustments, refunds, repairs, or replacements should follow. Instruction booklets should be clear and complete, not cluttered with technical jargon incomprehensible to final buyers. Final-buyers' requests for service or information should be answered fully and without needless delay. And, above everything else, all employees coming into contact with final buyers should be courteous, friendly, and competent in their jobs—everyone on the payroll should be a goodwill ambassador for the company and its products.

### Industry Relations

Perhaps the main point of contact of sales executives with their counterparts in competing companies is through their participation in industry-trade-association activities. Although trade associations have different objectives, most have two of special interest to sales executives: (1) to interpret the industry and its problems to outside publics, and (2) to encourage member companies to act in the public interest. Specific activities directed toward the first objective include trade association advertising, furnishing expert witnesses for legislative hearings, and disseminating industry information through news services. Activities directed toward the second objective include sponsoring and publishing studies of attitudes and opinions of final buyers toward the industry, and counseling member companies on public-relations problems.

Trade associations have other functions meriting the attention of sales executives.

Some serve as clearinghouses for the collection and interchange of industry production and sales statistics for use by individual companies in planning and controlling their activities. Others sponsor employee training programs; conduct management development programs; arrange for or conduct cooperative research; serve as vehicles for reaching the educational, governmental, and press publics; and provide management consulting services. Where products of different industries are in strong competition, it is not unusual for an association to coordinate advertising and other promotion to stimulate primary demand for its industry's products. Finally, some associations plan, organize, and direct industry-wide trade conventions attended by manufacturers, middlemen, and sometimes even final buyers. The sales executive makes additional contacts with competitors and other businessmen through membership in professional and service organizations. Sales and Marketing Executives—International, American Marketing Association, and American Management Association all furnish sales executives with excellent opportunities to exchange ideas. Participation in local businessmen's clubs and service groups is also often worthwhile. Although it is not absolutely essential to be a "joiner," most sales executives find it advantageous, professionally and personally, to maintain as many contacts as their available time permits.

Proper competitive conduct is difficult to describe, but the rules of common courtesy are good guides. Sales executives, as well as sales personnel, for example, should not ordinarily make disparaging remarks about competitors and their products. It is considered more ethical, and usually makes better sense, to play up the strengths of one's own company and its products. The border line between what is right or wrong, good or bad, moral or immoral, is not clear-cut in regard to other practices. In business, as elsewhere, ethical criteria are qualitative and relative, not quantitative and absolute. Many practices are controvresial, considered ethical by some and unethical by others. Among these are hiring sales personnel away from competitors, persuading suppliers not to sell to competitors, cutting prices in the hope of driving competitors out of business, and paying distributors' or dealers' employees to push the company brand at competitors' expense.

### Government Relations

Government lays down the rules and regulations under which business operations are directed along channels considered socially desirable. The rules and regulations affecting operations of the sales department have multiplied rapidly since the 1930s, and they are being continuously modified with shifts in judicial and administrative interpretations. Sales executives should be familiar with such basic pieces of legislation as the Robinson-Patman Act, the Miller-Tydings Act, the Wool Products Labeling Act, and the Food, Drug, and Cosmetic Act; and they should keep abreast of judicial and administrative interpretations of such laws. Proposed regulatory legislation is also of concern to sales executives. To protect company and industry interests, they should cooperate with, and appear as witnesses before, legislative committees investigating or holding hearings on industry problems and practices.

Although business executives tend to think of government primarily as a source of regulation, from the viewpoint of sales executives other aspects of governmental influence are more important. Federal and state governments, for instance, can affect the size of the market for many products by changing tax laws and rates. The effect of such legislation has been to change the shape of the income distribution curve—relatively speaking, lower economic groups have had their incomes raised, and higher groups have had theirs lowered. Most incomes have been rising, and fewer people are in the extremely high- and low-income groups. Thus, the average consumer has more disposable income, and this has made possible significant expansions in the markets for many products.

Government also exerts strong influences on operations of the sales department by virtue of its control over the volume of credit. Through the Federal Reserve System and the Treasury Department, the federal government has powers to expand or contract credit and thus to affect business conditions and the ease with which sales of many products are made. Changes in the relative availability of credit may expand or contract the market for such products as automobiles, consumer durables, and housing. Credit policy of the federal government, therefore, is a matter of considerable interest to sales executives in many fields.

Government affects the size of the market for many products in still other ways. Governmental units are themselves large buyers. During wars and other periods of national emergency, governmental purchases swell the sales of a long list of items; during peacetime, governmental purchases account for important shares of total sales for products such as paper, office equipment and furnishings, automotive equipment and supplies, laboratory equipment and supplies, and electronic computers and data-processing equipment. The armed forces are always important customers for foodstuffs, optical goods, photographic equipment and supplies, clothing, chemicals, arms and munitions, aircraft, aerospace items, communications equipment, and the like. Furthermore, government contracts often lie behind the purchases made by contractors working for federal, state, and local governmental units. Government business is so important to many companies that they have set up specialized staffs to negotiate and administer government contracts; and although these staffs may or may not be partially or wholly under the sales department's jurisdiction, sales executives certainly have a stake in their performance.

Sales executives should also keep in mind the fact that the government provides income for millions of individual consumers—government employees, of course, and other millions who receive income from governmental sources, including retired government employees, social security recipients, holders of government securities, disabled war veterans, and farmers participating in subsidy programs. The Medicare program has brought additional widespread benefits and has had a major impact on sales of drugs, pharmaceuticals, and other products in the health care field. The fact that large aggregations of purchasing power released from the public treasury eventually are used to buy the products of privately owned companies is of considerable significance in sales planning.

Many governmental agencies provide services or engage in activities that affect the sales executive. Both federal and state governments compile and distribute statistical and other information of considerable value for sales planning purposes. Federal agencies have helped in promoting standardization of product characteristics. The Federal Trade Commission has encouraged the development of voluntary trade and competitive practice regulations in many industries. For sales executives in large and small companies alike, it is of considerable importance that the government has taken up the cause of small companies, helping them through such agencies as the Small Business Administration and, at the same time, seeking to prevent large firms from gaining monopolistic control of many industries. Other governmental agencies seek to protect legitimate business enterprises from commercial shysters, and racketeers such as smugglers and bootleggers. From time to time, too, domestic firms have found relief and protection from overseas competitors through enactment and enforcement of tariff laws and other import regulations.

Sales executives assist in implementing government relations programs in ways other than those already discussed. They often can expedite the gathering of data needed by governmental statistical agencies. They should be certain that the communication lines from the sales department to governmental agencies are open and clear; and they should take full advantage of the vast amount of information government makes available. They should lend their support to governmental units seeking appropriations for purposes of gathering information of interest and use to business, such as the censuses of business made by the U.S. Census Bureau. Sales executives, in summary, should keep informed on developments within governmental agencies, just as they should keep abreast of changes in marketing legislation.

### Educational Relations

The sales department has a sizable stake in educational relations. Future members of significant publics, including the very important final-buyer public, receive their first, and usually most lasting, impressions of the business system and individual companies during their years in school. Similarly, schools at all levels serve as training grounds for future dealers, distributors, sales personnel, and sales executives. And the schools themselves are important customers for many products; as school enrollments expand, and the building of new schools goes forward, ever-increasing quantities of the products of many industries are being purchased by educational institutions. Thus, because there are both future and present payoffs in good relations with educational institutions, sales executives should be vitally interested and personally involved in establishing and maintaining them.

In addition to instructing present and future members of various publics, the educational world provides many services of value to sales executives. Collegiate schools of business, research bureaus and institutes, and individual instructors conduct studies on relevant problems and make the results available at little or no cost. Scholars and experts in numerous fields serve on the instructional staffs. Their expertise often can be brought to bear on problems of direct interest to sales executives, such as the application of computer techniques to determination of sales territories and analysis of sales performance. Some institutions maintain evening schools or extension divisions, whose services may be utilized to further develop sales department personnel. Moreover, many universities offer high-level management development programs for sales and other business executives, thus providing occasions for executives to blend their own experiential knowledge with the thinking of academic scholars in related fields.

Sales executives have many opportunities to further the educational relations program. They can assist in collecting and preparing teaching materials, and they can help educators and students doing research. They can recommend to top management that their companies award scholarships, fellowships, and grants-in-aid to educators seeking to advance the frontiers of knowledge. They can give freely of their time and knowledge by serving as guest speakers in such courses as marketing, sales management, and consumer behavior. Some companies provide summer internships for educators interested in making collegiate marketing and other instruction more realistic and practical; others work closely with educational specialists in developing case materials and new research techniques. Most teachers are interested in improving the quality of their instruction, and sales executives have the power to assist in this endeavor. Company publicity material generally is welcomed by members of the educational public, but the company preparing it should guard against making it overly commercial. Last, but by no means least important, sales executives should accept their responsibilities as public-spirited citizens. They should take an active interest in the welfare of the schools, especially in their local communities, and lend support to those seeking to improve the educational system.

One educational relations problem of special concern to sales executives involves the seemingly general lack of student interest in personal selling as an occupational goal. Numerous articles have highlighted this problem, but sales executives have not been particularly effective in selling personal selling as a career. One writer comments on these efforts as follows:

> The point about selling personal selling is especially interesting, in that it violates or ignores the major salesmanship principle that an objection should be completely understood before an attempt is made to overcome the objection. Indeed, the causes of the unsatisfactory occupational prestige of personal selling appear to be a void determinedly ignored.[14]

Sales executives concerned with building career interest in personal selling among students, in other words, should do their homework carefully and thoroughly. In their contacts with students and teachers, they should endeavor to determine the reasons underlying negative attitudes toward selling, decide what (if anything) can be done about them, and guide their actions accordingly.

### Press Relations

The press, itself an important public, is also a valuable medium for the sales department to use in communicating with other publics. The press public consists of writers and editors of newspapers, magazines, trade journals, news services, radio and television stations, and other communications media. Unfavorable comments in these media about a company, its policies, products, or personnel not only damage a company's reputation but impede the progress of its sales and other marketing efforts. Bad publicity makes it more difficult to make sales and increases the cost of those that are made; conversely, good publicity makes it possible to attain a comparable sales volume at less expense.

Good press relations help in obtaining good publicity but will not alone ensure it. For maximum effectiveness, press publicity should be planned as an integral part of the promotional program; planned press releases should complement or supplement other elements, such as personal selling and advertising. Skill in handling press relations, along with basic appropriateness of the publicity plan itself, are the factors that cause resulting publicity to be good, bad, or indifferent.

Sales executives should observe a few simple rules in managing the sales department's relations with the press. One such rule is that all stories given to the press should have news value—generally, a story has news value if it has "human interest," or concerns a subject of interest to the audience reached. Newsworthy stories originating in the sales department relate to such subjects as the introduction of new products and improvements, new models, promotional plans, additions to the sales staff, promotions of sales personnel, and retirements. A second rule is that press publicity should not be simply unpaid advertising. Presenting the press with copy that amounts to outright advertising, which the press refers to as "space grabbing," is one of the surest roads to poor relations.

Pressure, influence, or threats to discontinue advertising if publicity is not obtained

---

[14]J. L. Mason, "The Low Prestige of Personal Selling," *Journal of Marketing*, Vol. 29, No. 4 (October 1965), pp. 7-8.

should be scrupulously avoided; such actions generally lead to poor press relations and unfavorable publicity. Likewise, if a news story in the making is likely to present the company or its products in an unfavorable light, it is far wiser to provide reporters with all the pertinent details than to ask that the story be suppressed. If interviews are on controversial subjects, or involve material that might easily be misunderstood, reporters should be given typed statements covering the situation; in most other circumstances, prepared press releases, which reporters rarely use, should be avoided.

Sales executives should maintain an "open-door" policy with press representatives—all should be treated fairly and courteously. Any favorable publicity generated by according preferential treatment to some is offset by bad relations incurred with others. Finally, good press relations are more likely to be maintained if the sales executive compliments reporters and editors responsible for well-written stories. Building and maintaining good press relations, in other words, is largely a matter of the sales executive's exercise of good judgment.

## CONCLUSION

Good relations with other departments and with outside publics are of great importance to the sales department. Improvement of these relations necessarily begins inside the company. Internal frictions and inefficiencies inflate costs and are reflected in deteriorating relationships with external publics. Smooth internal functioning of an enterprise involves much more than adherence to formalized charted relationships—in the most basic way, it involves the ability of people on different levels and in different departments to work well together.

There are no simple rules for easily obtaining a favorable working climate. The unimaginative approach of simply avoiding frictions, interpersonal and interdepartmental, is not enough. Top management, along with the management of each department, must skillfully promote willing cooperation among executives and employees alike; and this cooperation must be directed toward achievement of the company's overall goals.

All executives must also be concerned with maintaining effective coordination. Formal coordination is secured through top management, which harmonizes the activities of the different departments, and through individual department managements, which coordinate the activities of their own personnel. However, informal coordination within and among departments and their personnel is of even greater importance to the smooth functioning of an organization.

Serving as an important point of contact with external publics, the sales department is in an especially strategic position. Of all company personnel, representatives of the sales department generally are in the closest touch with final buyers and middlemen. Sales-department personnel also work closely with such important publics as their industry, the government, the educational world, and the press. How these representatives conduct themselves in their relations with these publics directly affects the company's reputation. Good relations depend in large measure upon the skill with which personal selling and related programs are planned and executed. Sales management must make certain that personnel executing such programs constantly keep the public relations impact of their actions in mind.

# 8

# Distributive-Network Relations

For all practical purposes, the middlemen handling the product (or assisting in its sale) are extensions of the manufacturer's own sales organization. Often they are the final buyers' only points of contact with the manufacturer; and confidence in individual middlemen is frequently a crucial factor influencing decisions to buy or not to buy the manufacturer's product. Middlemen serve as the manufacturer's on-the-spot representatives; within their spheres of operation, their reputations are influenced by that of the manufacturer, its products, and its promotion. From the sales executive's standpoint, the importance of establishing and maintaining favorable relations with the distributive network can hardly be overstated, since they directly influence selling efficiency, costs, and profits.

No marketing program is complete if it lacks well-laid plans for securing and maintaining the cooperation of the distributive outlets. The fortunes of manufacturers rise or fall with the effectiveness of their respective middlemen. When a manufacturer determines its marketing channels and obtains middlemen to assist in the distributive process, it is in effect casting its lot with them. If they succeed in selling the product, the manufacturer also succeeds; if they fail, the manufacturer fails. Middlemen are vital links in the distribution chain, for they are charged with making the "payoff" sales. Unless the supply of product finally flows through to final buyers, the marketing channel becomes clogged, and all previous sales and marketing efforts are wasted. It is important, then, for the sales executive to bear in mind that middlemen are customers for the product, even though they may not be final buyers. At least as much attention should go toward securing and maintaining a harmonious working relationship with the distributive network as to building a good reputation among final buyers.

## SETTING UP COOPERATIVE PROGRAMS

The manufacturer must obtain the cooperation of its distributors if it is to achieve effective implementation of its marketing strategy. The dealers, for instance, must have adequate stocks of the product on hand prior to the launching of a national promotional advertising campaign. Similarly, they must be prepared to support national advertising through tie-in displays and local advertising. The initiative for establishing and maintaining cooperative programs on behalf of the product line almost always must come from the manufacturer rather than from the individual middlemen; and within the manufacturer's organization, the sales department is often the initiator of such programs and even more often the implementer. The product is, after all, the manufacturer's product; the manufacturer's interest in selling it is the most direct and, in most situations, also the strongest.

The manufacturer should clearly recognize its great dependence upon the middlemen for marketing success. Middlemen, however, commonly fail to recognize their parallel dependence upon any one manufacturer; and of course, they have contacts with (and in most cases represent) other manufacturers, sometimes even those with competitive lines. The manufacturer's organization normally is larger, more experienced, and better equipped to handle the planning and administer the details of cooperative programs. Therefore, middlemen usually look to the manufacturer to set up and manage any cooperative efforts established for mutual benefits.

It is sometimes possible for a manufacturer to achieve considerable marketing success without the willing cooperation of middlemen—even in spite of their hostility and resentment—but this is an option that few manufacturers can afford to implement. However, manufacturers of high-volume convenience goods occasionally achieve strong consumer preference through extraordinarily heavy expenditures for advertising, thus forcing the cooperation of dealers who recognize that they will miss an opportunity if they do not service the consumer demand. In such instances, although dealers tend to dislike the manufacturer and its products, they continue to serve its interests, mainly because this is profitable for them.

## ROLE OF MANUFACTURER'S SALES FORCE

Middlemen regard the manufacturer's salespeople not only as sales representatives for the product line, but also as agents through which the manufacturer's business philosophy is translated into action. Furthermore, their opinions of the company and its products are to some extent influenced by the way its sales personnel conduct themselves. Salespeople do not have to be public relations experts, but they do need to be well versed in interpersonal relations. Training, retraining, and experience all assist in making salespeople competent in applying the manufacturer's sales policies and practices; but only a thorough grasp of applied psychology makes them adept at getting along with people. Unless customers receive favorable impressions of the manufacturer from their contacts and dealings with its sales force, no program of cooperation with the distributive outlets is likely to be fully successful. The importance of selecting basically good people for the sales force, and of continuously developing their skills in interpersonal relations, is apparent.

Middlemen's attitudes toward manufacturers are particularly influenced when sales personnel apply undiplomatic sales tactics. In one study, dealers stated that they resented salespersons who: beg for business with personal hard-luck stories, become unpleasant when they do not receive orders, brag about big orders they have written for other dealers, act as though they are doing a favor for the dealer, carry gossip from dealer to dealer, hint at "great favors" in the future, and act as though they were entitled to business just for making calls. Such tactics are more common than many sales executives are willing to admit.

Since first-line communications with middlemen are usually initiated and maintained by the manufacturer's sales force, the utmost care should be observed in their selection, training, and supervision. Nothing damages the standing of a company or its products more than a salesperson who fails to win and hold the respect and confidence of middlemen. Management must place major reliance upon its salespeople to treat customers fairly and squarely. Sales personnel should never be allowed to make promises that cannot be kept, or that are later ignored or forgotten. Nor should they sell orders larger than customers can reasonably handle; overselling is a frequent cause of poor relations with middlemen. Making lasting friendships for the company is as much a part of the job as moving the merchandise itself. The sales executive should keep salespeople amply supplied with up-to-date information on the products, their applications, and any changes in sales and other marketing policies (or their manner of implementation) of possible significance to customers. With this information at their fingertips, sales personnel are equipped to handle most problems in customer relations promptly and effectively.

## OBJECTIVES AND METHODS OF MANUFACTURER-MIDDLEMEN COOPERATION

In all their cooperative efforts, the manufacturer and its middlemen share a common overall objective—to sell the manufacturer's products at a profit, which, in turn, generally requires both parties to emphasize service to their customers. To achieve the common overall objective, most manufacturers find it necessary to set more specific objectives for their programs of cooperation with their middlemen. These specific objectives, of course, differ with the particular set of marketing circumstances. Even though many variations exist, most of these specific objectives can be sorted into definite categories. Manufacturers undertake cooperative programs with middlemen in order (1) to build middleman loyalty, (2) to stimulate middlemen to greater selling effort, (3) to develop managerial efficiency in distributive organizations, or (4) to identify the source of supply for the product line at the final-buyer level.

Methods used to achieve these objectives differ from manufacturer to manufacturer and from time to time. Moreover, some methods are used in efforts to accomplish more than one objective. The selection of specific methods of cooperation depends upon the particular problem(s) that the manufacturer is trying to solve. The following discussion identifies various circumstances leading to the choice of specific objectives and analyzes the chief methods applied in attempting to achieve them.

### Building Middleman Loyalty to the Manufacturer

Whether middlemen actively promote, simply recommend, or "just handle" the product line depends importantly upon the nature of their relationships with the manufacturer and its sales force. If they value these associations, the manufacturer's chances of securing active promotion and satisfactory cooperation are very good. If they stock the product line merely for the convenience of their customers, it is considerably more difficult for the manufacturer to capitalize on market opportunities. Occasionally it is possible, through heavy advertising and promotion to final buyers, to "pull" a product through the marketing channel despite adverse attitudes of middlemen. But, if middlemen have to be forced to handle the product, marketing costs are often unnecessarily high.

In the long run, it is less costly and more effective to have the cooperation of middlemen than to have them operate under a state of passive acceptance, or even active resistance.

The most serious situations in the area of manufacturer-middlemen relations occur when middlemen are not merely apathetic but are outwardly hostile to the manufacturer and its product. Many manufacturers who experience this type of difficulty have little personal contact, such as through salespeople, with middlemen handling their products. Many manage to pull their products through marketing channels by liberal expenditures for advertising to final buyers. Such manufacturers evidently believe that a product is certain to sell successfully if a strong final-buyer preference or recognition is developed; but they underestimate the important contribution of middleman goodwill to overall selling and marketing efficiency. Middlemen who stock products only because the number of "calls" generated through advertising forces them to do so may provide the product with the least desirable shelf or counter positions, or even put it under the counter. If they handle competing products, they may give them better shelf positions and more space, and they may attempt to sell substitutions when final buyers ask for the manufacturer's brand. This particular type of situation is even more serious when the brand possesses few features that differentiate it from competitors.

In short, in many situations a manufacturer meets sales resistance not so much from final buyers as from middlemen. When this resistance evolves into the adoption of obstructive tactics by middlemen, the net result is all too likely to be a progressive deterioration in final-buyer respect for, and confidence in, the manufacturer and its product. The manufacturer's problem is to inspire in its middlemen a feeling of mutual interest and trust, and to convince them that it appreciates their contribution to the marketing success of the product. Generally, the sales department and the sales force play significant roles in solving such problems.

Any program designed to build or strengthen middleman loyalty, if it is to have a reasonable chance for success, necessarily includes two important components. First, there must be critical appraisals of the manufacturer's policies and their manner of implementation, with a view toward identifying the impacts on middlemen's attitudes. Second, there must be careful analysis of the communications system with the distributive network to assure that it is the best possible under the circumstances. In other words, most cases of middleman disloyalty have their roots in the manufacturer's policies, which may be inappropriate or misapplied, or in shortcomings of the communications system.

**Appraisal of the Manufacturer's Policies and Their Implementation.** The manufacturer seeking to establish and maintain mutually beneficial relations with middlemen should make critical appraisals of the product, the services rendered in connection with it, and the policies and practices followed in its distribution and promotion. The manufacturer should determine the degree to which the product matches the merchandising requirements of middlemen, and it should find out how well or how poorly the product conforms to middlemen's evaluations of final-buyers' wants. Manufacturer-performed services, such as installation and repair, should be offered in response to the recognized needs of middlemen and final buyers. All the manufacturer's distribution and promotion policies and practices must be intelligently conceived, uniformly and fairly applied, and fully understood by middlemen. If the manufacturer fails to take these precautions, no marketing and selling efforts can begin to approach full effectiveness.

Middlemen's interest in improving relations with manufacturers varies significantly from product to product. When the product is a mass-distributed convenience good, many manufacturers try to reach the ultimate consumer with essentially similar products. Each manufacturer competes for the attention of the same dealers, the majority of whom see little reason to cooperate with one supplier at the expense of others—unless a particular supplier can prove the benefits that it claims should accrue to the dealer. Since such products are generally distributed through multiple layers of middlemen, conditions are particularly unfavorable to the development of close relations between the manufacturer and those middlemen who sell to final buyers. Thus, the manufacturer, who sells through wholesalers, may find it very difficult to develop close relations with the retailers, who sell products to ultimate consumers.

With consumer products classified as shopping or specialty goods, some form of exclusive agency or selective distribution is generally used. In such instances, the manufacturer normally sells direct to the retail dealer. Dealers handling such products should have as much, or almost as much, interest as the manufacturer in the success of cooperative efforts in support of the product's movement through the marketing channel. Thus, as far as consumers' goods are concerned, programs for improving relations with middlemen are most appropriate, and stand the greatest chance of success, when the manufacturer markets a specialty or shopping good through a limited number of middlemen. In the industrial-goods field, most manufacturers distribute their products directly to industrial users; those who do utilize nondirect marketing channels usually have considerable opportunity to improve, and to benefit from, improving relations with their middlemen.

Dealers who pursue obstructive tactics often do so because of a manufacturer's unwise pricing practices. For example, when a manufacturer grants excessive discounts for large orders, the product may become a "price football" for large middlemen competing on a price basis. This frequently happens after a heavily advertised product becomes well known and is in strong demand. Under these circumstances, smaller dealers may not even try to meet their larger competitors' resale prices. Instead, they devote their efforts to promotion of substitutes for the manufacturer's brand. The underlying difficulty here, as in most cases of unwise pricing, is that some middlemen believe that they are receiving inadequate compensation for handling the product. The price and discount structure should allow all dealers, large and small, a reasonable and fair amount of gross margin. The solution to problems that are traceable to unwise pricing practices is often to overhaul policies on marketing channels and distribution intensity. For this reason, an appraisal of pricing policy should always be made in conjunction with a close examination of distribution policy.

The manufacturer should also regularly appraise the impact of its promotional policies on its relations with middlemen. These policies should be evaluated to determine how well the manufacturer's advertising program is coordinated with the sales force's efforts, for instance, and to assess the nature and relative effectiveness of programs to coordinate the company's total promotional program with middlemen's efforts. The manufacturer's salespersons can and should play an important role in implementing all programs to improve coordination of the company's promotional efforts with those of middlemen.

In appraising the manufacturer's policies, the manner in which each is administered should be given fully as much attention as the basic content. The manufacturer should have sound and appropriate policies, and these should be applied uniformly and fairly in all relations with dealers. The manufacturer, in other words, should abide by the rules that it itself has set up—it should refrain, for example, from such practices as allowing secret price concessions and furnishing special assistance to some dealers and not to others. But even though the manufacturer holds to its policies and refuses to make exceptions of any sort, dealer complaints still arise. Some are without merit, but each should be acknowledged, investigated, and adjusted before it evolves into permanent resentment.

Favoritism among middlemen should be scrupulously avoided, not just disapproved of officially. Sales personnel, and sometimes even sales executives, are especially tempted to play favorites when the product is in short supply. When final-user demand expands more rapidly than the available supply of product, or when total demand has been badly underestimated, salespeople and sales executives alike are bombarded with entreaties of important customers for greatly increased orders. Salespersons or executives who submit to such pleas, and who thereby neglect smaller accounts, should realize that they are setting a pattern that will affect future operations. When normal conditions return, customers whose business was ignored may prove unusually susceptible to competitors' selling arguments.

In attempting to avoid favoritism, some manufacturers go too far in the opposite direction. During periods of scarcity, they try to spread available supplies of their products over as many accounts as possible. Unless adequate controls are provided, large customers may receive allocations too small to be useful, and small customers much more than they have ordered in the past. If this happens, relations with the best accounts, the larger ones, may be affected adversely. Again, the likely consequence is a general weakening of the company's future competitive position. Allocation policies require careful formulation and should be based on the relative needs of all classes of accounts. Complaints of unfair treatment should be investigated and given hearings, and inequities should be adjusted. Under conditions of short supply it is impossible to keep every customer completely satisfied, but as many as possible should be convinced of the necessity for and essential fairness of the policies in effect.

**Analysis of Communications System with Distributive Network.** Lack of, or insufficient, personal contact of middlemen with the manufacturer often contributes to disloyalty. Particularly when the marketing channel includes several layers of middlemen, when personal selling plays an insignificant part (or no part) in the promotional program, or both, there are likely to be defects in the manufacturer's communications system with its distributive network. Although its product, distribution, promotion, and pricing policies may all appear fundamentally sound, a manufacturer's remoteness, institutionally if not geographically, from certain middlemen and their problems may cause certain policies to be inappropriate for them. When competitors have closer personal relationships, through their own salespeople, with these middlemen, they may regard the manufacturer as too distant to deserve their attention or cooperation. They may continue to handle its product, but mainly because of already established demand among their customers. Before the situation can be improved, steps must be taken to improve the communications system.

Improvements in communications with middlemen can be achieved in many ways. Sometimes drastic changes in distribution policy may be indicated—for example, a manufacturer may switch from the use of wholesalers to direct-to-retailer selling, and thereby obtain closer personal contact with retailers. Or it may be sufficient to supplement wholesalers' efforts with a force of missionary salespeople. A program involving occasional visits to middlemen by sales and other executives may do wonders in improving communications and in cementing relationships; similar benefits may accrue from company sponsorship of national or regional conventions for middlemen. Such relatively inexpensive methods as personal letters or telephone calls from sales executives, the circulation of specially edited dealer magazines, or advertising to the trade may sometimes prove effective not only in improving communications but in building and retaining dealer loyalty.

Strained relations with middlemen can result from ineffective handling of correspondence. When middlemen request information, or when sales personnel relay their queries, courteous and complete responses should be dispatched promptly. To procrastinate is to irritate the customer and to risk losing goodwill. All messages from middlemen should be promptly acknowledged; and if answers are not readily available, that fact should be communicated. Questions that cannot be answered at once usually relate to subjects that should command the attention of top-ranking executives, and it is the sales executive's responsibility to make certain that answers are found and forwarded at an early date.

Many methods are available to sales executives to keep track of middlemen's attitudes and opinions. In well-managed companies, salespeople are trained to report important changes which they observe or suspect are taking place. Internal analysis of sales records helps in detecting shifts in the source and size of orders received; often these are symptomatic of important changes in middlemen's attitudes. Studies by marketing-research personnel may be valuable for revealing specific criticisms of company policies and practices and suggestions for their improvement. Other companies may own and manage one or more outlets for their products so that they can obtain a better feel for middlemen's problems. Ownership of a few outlets also allows the firm to experiment with new merchandising and selling techniques that, if judged successful, are passed on to middlemen.

### Stimulating Middlemen to Greater Selling Effort

Dealer apathy, or indifference to the success of the manufacturer's promotional program, is common. Some manufacturers invest millions of dollars in advertising and other promotion but, for one reason or another, dealers, outwardly at least, are not only unimpressed but unmoved. Many dealers, especially the smaller ones, fail to see why it is important for them to tie in with the manufacturer's promotion or to provide extra push for the product. They feel, sometimes rightly, that the manufacturer wants more assistance from them than it is willing to extend—and all too frequently such feelings are traceable directly to inadequacies in salespeople's presentations. Under such circumstances, effective coordination of the promotional efforts of the manufacturer and its middlemen is difficult. The first step, then, in overcoming dealer apathy is to identify the reasons lying behind it. The second step is to take positive action to increase selling effort by middlemen.

**Changing Policies.**  The sales executive may conclude, after careful investigation, that the continued application of inappropriate or outmoded sales policies is the cause of dealer apathy. Alert competitors may have been more successful in adjusting their policies to the changing marketing situation, while the company, whose dealers are apathetic, may have lagged behind. Management may have clung to some policies for little more than sentimental reasons; other policies, once justified, may have long since become outdated. Bringing these offending policies into line with present marketing conditions is necessary to stimulate dealer effort.

For example, for many years, automobile manufacturers charged dealers for transportation expenses that were often partially fictitious—transportation charges were billed on the assumption that each car would be shipped from a central plant when actually it might be delivered from an assembly facility closer to the dealer. These fictitious charges, which were known as "phantom freight," were naturally the subject of much criticism by dealers. After World War II, such charges were also responsible for the "bootlegging" of new cars, where used-car and other unfranchised dealers purchased new cars from dealers close to the home factories and towed or hauled them to the Southwest or Far West, there to sell them in competition with franchised dealers. Several years later (in 1956), the automobile manufacturers, partly because of a congressional investigation of automobile marketing practices, and partly because they recognized the seriousness of growing dealer apathy, announced the abandonment of phantom freight charges. With much, or almost all, of the freight differential wiped out across the country, automobile bootlegging became less profitable, and the morale of authorized dealers greatly improved.

Companies utilizing multiple marketing channels to reach final buyers frequently encounter problems in obtaining the necessary support level from certain middlemen in some channels. A consumer-products company, for instance, may sell directly to large retailers such as corporate chains, and through wholesalers to smaller retailers. Company salespeople are in close and personal contact with large retailers, and one of their responsibilities is to gain the promotional support of these dealers. But to gain the support of smaller retailers, the sales personnel must work through the intervening wholesalers, earning their promotional support as well.[1] In analyzing this type of problem, M. R. Warshaw suggests that particular attention should be paid to the appropriateness of pricing policy. He writes:

> ... to gain promotional support from wholesalers, margins granted must be adequate in terms of the marketing job to be assumed by them. However, these margins must also take into consideration the rivalry faced from other suppliers for wholesaler cooperation, as well as the intensity of competition faced by the wholesalers in selling for resale or for final-use. Much of the latter rivalry may emanate from the manufacturer's own direct selling activities. Thus, the manufacturer himself may create competitive pressures which increase the price he must pay to buy wholesaler selling support.[2]

Reformulation of other policies also sometimes makes it possible to stimulate middlemen to greater selling effort. Policies regarding such matters as credit extension, service, advertising and selling allowances, and quantity and cash discounts should be scrutinized with a view toward determining the extent to which they may be responsible for dealer apathy. Furthermore, it may be discovered that even such high-level policies as those relating to marketing channels and distribution intensity are in need of revision.

Quite often, the chief reason for middlemen's indifference lies in the nature of their previous experiences with the manufacturer's and other companies' promotional programs. A. T. Kearney and Company, Chicago management consultants, in cooperation with the National Association of Wholesalers, made a study of 500 large wholesalers in twenty fields and seven major cities. Results showed that, on the average, only about

[1] J. Blood, "Despite Direct Selling, Jobbers Flourish," *Distribution Week,* Vol. 104 (September 4, 1973), p. 1.

[2] M. R. Warshaw, "Pricing to Gain Wholesalers' Selling Support," *Journal of Marketing,* Vol. 26, No. 3 (July 1962), p. 51.

one out of seven promotions offered to a wholesaler is accepted and pushed. The number of promotions offered to distributors each year ranges from more than 5,000 in the drug field to less than ten in the paper and lumber industries. The fewer promotions distributors are offered, the higher their rate of acceptance. Drug wholesalers, for instance, actively pushed only about 10 percent of the promotions offered them; wholesalers in the plumbing, heating, and cooling industry took on 22 percent. The study director reported: "In every industry there are companies doing very well in promotions. These are the ones that are geared to understand their channels of distribution." He also reported that the most important factor in motivating a wholesaler to support a proposed promotional program was the wholesaler's past relationship with the manufacturer. If the manufacturer has had good promotions in the past, then distributors have confidence in its current promotion; and to achieve such conditions, promotion should be easy for the wholesaler to administer and sell to its dealers.[3] Thus, a manufacturer should appraise its proposed promotional program from the standpoint of the middlemen, both wholesalers and retailers, whose cooperation it expects to obtain; and this appraisal should take into account past relations with these middlemen, as a measure of the manner in which the middlemen are likely to view the present proposal.

**Sharing Promotional Risks with Middlemen.**    On analyzing the attitudes of middlemen, the manufacturer is sometimes dismayed to find that these middlemen are not enthusiastic, because they are, or think they are, risking so little on the final outcome of its promotional program. Benefiting from the manufacturer's promotion over a long period, dealers come to depend upon the manufacturer to perform almost the entire selling task. In other words, they appear to feel that it is the manufacturer's job to bring customers into the store, and theirs to ring the cash register and total up the profits. Other dealers consider it "unfair" to show real enthusiasm for any one manufacturer's promotional program, since so many manufacturers' products are represented on their shelves.

To combat serious problems of this sort, manufacturers demonstrate considerable ingenuity and imagination in devising strategies to stimulate dealers to greater sales effort. In one widely used strategy designed to make dealers assume more of the promotional risk, the manufacturer, through its sales force, attempts to persuade dealers to invest time, effort, and money in certain aspects of promotional programs. Thus, in some cases, manufacturers who would be willing to provide free point-of-purchase display materials to retailers charge for these materials, theorizing that retailers who risk their own funds will exert greater efforts to make good use of the displays and, hence, justify their costs. Similarly, manufacturers who inaugurate dealer-cooperative advertising programs, in which advertising expenses are shared with dealers, commonly experience renewed dealer interest. Whenever dealers have a stake, even a limited one, in the final results of a promotional program, they are more inclined to work toward making it as successful as possible.

**Using Forcing Methods.**    In an effort to stimulate middlemen, the manufacturer may use techniques that compel them to provide extra push for the product. These techniques, known collectively as "forcing methods," seek to overcome middlemen's indifference by providing additional incentives. Such incentives are designed to appeal to middlemen, their salespeople, or final buyers.

[3] As reported in *Sales Management* (June 20, 1967), pp. 68-70.

**Incentives to the Middleman.** Dealers may be offered such enticements as special prices on larger-than-average orders, or a free case of the product for every so many purchased. These strategies are designed to persuade dealers to increase the size of their inventory investments, thus putting them under more pressure to promote the sale of the product. Other ways of accomplishing this result involve offering premiums to dealers who make purchases above a specified minimum size, or packing premium coupons, redeemable for merchandise of the dealer's choice, in each shipping case. Sometimes the manufacturer awards the premium only after resale of the product, thus shifting the emphasis from building up the dealer's inventory to making sales to the final buyer.[4]

A major liquor marketer devised an incentive program that kept its dealers actively promoting its products for six months. In November it made available to each dealer a $300 Sony color television set. To receive a set the dealer signed a conditional sales contract that was financed through a bank. Each month that the dealer made the assigned quota, the sponsoring firm made the payments. The dealers did well in November and December, but in January seventy dealers fell below quota and had to make their own payments. Nearly all dealers got back on quota in February and stayed there.[5]

Some manufacturers set sales quotas for their dealers and award prizes to those who succeed in reaching them. The Lincoln-Mercury Division of Ford Motor Company conducted a dealers' sales incentive contest that required dealers to meet their sales quotas between January 1 and June 30 to win one-week Caribbean cruises for themselves and their spouses. The cruises were planned near dealer introduction time for the new models, which were actually shown to the dealers both on-board ship and at a beach party held at St. Thomas, Virgin Islands. Thus, Lincoln-Mercury management sought not only to reward outstanding sales performance by its dealers, but to stimulate this important group to continued high performance by giving them an advance look at the new models.[6]

**Incentives to Middlemen's Sales Personnel.** Manufacturers attempting to stimulate the sales personnel of middlemen use a wide variety of incentives. Special premiums, and plans involving the award of trading stamps (redeemable in merchandise of the winner's own choosing), are used extensively. In some fields, as in cosmetics and women's accessories, it is common for the manufacturer to pay retailers' sales clerks a small sum (known as a "spiff" or "PM") for each unit of the product they sell. Even more common is the sales contest conducted for dealers' or distributors' sales personnel. The Ford Division of Ford Motor Company conducted an incentive program for its dealers' salespeople in 1966. Nearly 3,000 sales personnel and their spouses were awarded four-day incentive trips to Las Vegas; hundreds of others received "prize-point checks" redeemable in merchandise during the sixty-day contest period. Contests of such magnitude necessarily require skilled planning and administration. Unless well-qualified company personnel are available to handle the planning and details, the manufacturer is well advised to turn the planning, and sometimes the administration also, over to firms that specialize in this sort of operation. In the Ford incentive program for dealers' sales personnel, E. F. MacDonald Company planned and took care of most of the administrative details. During the contest period, MacDonald produced 185,360 promotion pieces, sorted and counted nearly 5,000

---

[4]"Join Suppliers in Promoting, Supers Told," *Advertising Age*, Vol. 43 (November 13, 1972), p. 17.

[5]S. Scanlon, "The Motivational Management of Premiums and Incentives," *Sales Management*, Vol. 108 (April 17, 1972), p. 26.

[6]*Sales Management* (Sales Meetings, Part II), (September 15, 1966), pp. 152-59.

pounds of this material, and shipped it to forty key locations. MacDonald also handled all hotel and plane reservations, arranged for entertainment and scenic tours, took care of local transportation and luggage-moving problems, and even had a Western orchestra at the airport to welcome the winners.[7] Planning and administrative services of sales-incentive agencies such as E. F. MacDonald are made available to clients at little or no cost; they make their profits from the markups on merchandise and travel used as contest awards, which, of course, are paid for by clients.

**Incentives to Ultimate Consumers.** Manufacturers of convenience goods often stimulate their dealers indirectly by using forcing methods to promote purchases by ultimate consumers. These forcing methods include couponing, sampling, consumer contests, premium plans, "cents-off" promotions, and special introductory offers. If such forcing methods work out as the manufacturer intends, the more rapid movement of the product helps in overcoming dealer lethargy. Numerous administrative details, however, must be handled effectively in successful implementation of most programs using forcing methods. The manufacturer must not only see to it that its own sales force exerts the needed effort, but obtain the required support from wholesalers and their sales personnel to assure successful implementation. Consequently, companies using numerous programs of this sort generally have a sales promotion manager (reporting either to the general sales manager or marketing vice-president), who is responsible for both planning and administration.

### Developing Managerial Efficiency in Distributive Organizations

In attempts to make its dealers more enthusiastic about its product, the manufacturer often loses sight of another opportunity for increasing the sale of its products—through increasing dealer efficiency. The dealer's primary concern is to continue to make, or better yet, to increase, profits. The manufacturer, who usually has access to superior managerial know-how, can search out better methods for its dealers to apply in their efforts to improve selling effectiveness. But it is not enough for the manufacturer to find better operating methods for the dealers to use; the manufacturer must see to it that they learn about these improved methods and how to put them into effect. The manufacturer should recognize, far more clearly than most of its middlemen, that a highly important key to success for both parties lies in the way middlemen operate their businesses. The more efficient middlemen move the manufacturer's products more rapidly through the marketing channel and produce larger sales and profits both for themselves and for the manufacturer.

Not all manufacturers can benefit from providing managerial training programs for their dealers; the importance of such programs varies with the product and its marketing characteristics. Generally management training programs for middlemen are most beneficial when the middlemen handle products requiring considerable personal-selling effort. Such programs tend to be less beneficial in those marketing situations where final buyers make purchases as a matter of habit or on impulse. Training programs are especially important, and require the most careful attention of sales and other marketing executives, when the product's unit price is high, when trade-ins are common, when the final buyer's purchase decision is postponable, when the product requires demonstrations, and when middlemen's recommendations play a major role in making sales. Under these conditions,

---

[7]*Sales Management* (Sales Meetings, Part II), (January 15, 1967), pp. 157-58.

the manufacturer has much to gain through sponsorship of management training programs for its middlemen.

**Assistance in Sales-Force Management.** In the manufacturer's efforts to develop its middlemen into more efficient outlets for the product, the key role of the sales executive often is to assist them in improving selling efficiency through more appropriate sales-force management policies and techniques. Middlemen are given advice on such matters as sources and methods of recruiting new sales personnel, sales compensation plans, and the supervision and control of sales personnel. Perhaps the most assistance is provided in the form of training the middlemen's sales force. This assistance might be nothing more than providing sales-training materials, including such items as films and slide presentations. More often, the manufacturer's sales force, specialized training personnel, or sales executives conduct, or at least participate in, the instructional program. The usual objective of such programs is to make certain that middlemen's salespeople know the product's "talking points" and how best to present them. Other objectives include improvement of sales techniques, improvement of prospecting effectiveness, dissemination of information on product uses and applications, and explanation of cooperative advertising and other promotional programs. Most manufacturers find that it is not usually advisable to standardize the training program for all dealer sales clinics; agendas should vary with dealers' problems in each area. With each clinic focusing on local problems, participants show great receptivity to ideas presented, and the immediate impact on sales of the manufacturer's product is impressive. Thus, it is important that the sales force report fully on dealers' problems in advance of planning the dealer clinic in each area.

Training of dealers' sales personnel generally is decentralized. Unless the manufacturer follows a policy of selective or exclusive agency distribution, dealers are reluctant to have their salespeople attend training sessions at the factory. However, if the product is an industrial good of high unit value, about which dealers' salespersons need to acquire considerable technical information, factory training schools are appropriate. When the training is at the factory, the cost to the manufacturer is high, because usually the only costs borne by dealers are trainees' travel charges. Dealers also object to having their sales force away from their territories for very long; and, if the persons involved are paid partially or wholly on a commission basis, they dislike making the financial sacrifice. For these reasons, as well as the fact that orientation to local problems is normally desirable, most training of dealers' sales personnel is decentralized; it may be conducted on the dealer's premises or, especially when each dealer has only a few salespeople, at hotel meeting rooms, convention halls, nearby resorts, or the manufacturer's branch sales offices.

**Assistance and Advice on General Management Problems.** The manufacturer's second main approach to improved efficiency of middlemen is to provide assistance and advice on general management problems. Dealers may be counseled on store location, store layout, arrangement of fixtures and stock, accounting methods and systems, control of inventories and costs, advertising, credit and collection policies, and other matters. The manufacturer furnishing management advice of this sort usually expects the dealer to pay, if at all, only for the actual cost of the service given. In some instances, the manufacturer regards the store advisory service as part of its own sales-promotional program and absorbs the entire cost. Some manufacturers go so far as to furnish dealers, or help them to obtain, usable data on their own markets, market characteristics, market potentials, and the like. United States Gypsum Company, for example, has its marketing research department predict its dealers' sales from the building permits issued in each area, and this information is passed along to dealers for use in their business planning. The performance of dealers, like that of sales personnel, is usually more satisfactory if they are provided with good information on market opportunities.

Many dealers simply do not manage their businesses soundly. As a consequence, they fail to reach sales volume and profit goals, even when the manufacturer provides them with well-planned promotion and selling support. Such failures have an adverse effect on the morale of both the manufacturer's sales force and the dealers themselves. To avoid dealer failure of this sort, the manufacturer must have a long-range program of evaluation and analysis of dealers, involving more discriminating dealer selection and a concentrated management training course emphasizing cost-control techniques. A program of this sort can be expected to pay off in reduced dealer turnover, dealer growth in profitability, and increases in sales of the company's products.[8]

The following account by a management consultant illustrates how a program for improving the general management efficiency of middlemen's organizations must sometimes be combined with other corrective measures:

> Over a three-year period, the southeastern areas sales manager for a large maker of commercial electrical equipment had watched his total sales decline from third to fifth place among the company's six sales areas. He decided to take a hard look at his distribution network. After talking with each of his thirty distributors and analyzing their sales performance over recent years, he sorted them into three categories:
>
> *Satisfactory*—Twelve distributors whose market shares of his brand stood at or above the national average.
>
> *Growth candidates*—Fifteen distributors who were short of the national average but capable of reaching it.
>
> *Replacement situations*—Three distributors for whom the national average seemed hopelessly out of reach.
>
> Next, this sales executive set up a vigorous program of sales support for the growth group. Most of them, he found, were not assigning enough sales personnel to the line because they were satisfied with their present volume and doubted that added efforts would bring them substantial added profits. Poor deployment of sales personnel and failure to analyze accounts effectively further weakened their sales effort.
>
> To induce them to build volume, the sales manager assigned five business management specialists to work full time with these fifteen distributors for a six-month period. He also arranged to subsidize the cost of six months' base salary for an additional person on each growth distributor's sales force. Finally, he sought out three strong replacements for the low-potential distributors, providing each with a full-time missionary salesperson and a direct subsidy for the first year. To avoid retaliation for loss of the franchise from the distributors who were replaced, he negotiated a payment to compensate each of them for most of his lost profits during the next year.
>
> The program was difficult and time-consuming, but ultimately it paid off. Sales dropped at first, largely because of the three replacements. Six months later the lost ground had been regained, however, and in a little more than two years the sales total had climbed by almost 35 percent, bringing the area from fifth to second place in the nation.[9]

[8]"Westinghouse Will Deploy Distribution Battle Plan," *Merchandising Week,* Vol. 104 (June 19, 1972), p. 36.

[9]A. L. McDonald, Jr., "Do Your Distribution Channels Need Reshaping?" *Business Horizons,* Vol. 7, No. 2 (Summer 1964), p. 33.

Manufacturers whose products are sold through self-service retail outlets have a special problem—that of securing proper allocation of shelf space for their brands. In attempting to deal with this problem, several major cereal companies have "shelf-allocation programs," which purport to outline for retailers an "ideal" shelf-space arrangement for their entire breakfast-cereal sections. Major grocery manufacturers also offer such merchandising aids as pamphlets describing inventory control methods and shelf-space allocation procedures for each grocery department. National Biscuit Company performs a great deal of shelf-allocation analysis for retailers on cracker and cookie displays, and its competitors offer similar services. The interest of manufacturers in receiving an important share of available shelf space stems from their desires to minimize out-of-stock conditions and to attract impulse buyers. They believe that retailers may tend to overallocate shelf space to private labels. They also feel that misallocation of space for their products may result because of the number of duplicate items stocked and because of the effect of store manager-competitor sales force relations.[10] The manufacturer's own sales force plays an important role in implementing shelf-allocation programs, especially in securing the cooperation of individual store managers.

**Use of Missionary Sales Personnel.** The manufacturer's third primary approach to the problem of making middlemen more efficient is to use missionary salespeople. In the marketing of consumer goods, missionary salespeople are employees of the manufacturer who work closely with wholesale distributive outlets and make calls on their customers and prospects—the retailers. Missionary salespersons check each wholesaler's inventory, make suggestions for increasing the effectiveness of wholesaler sales personnel, and sometimes assist in their training; they acquaint wholesalers with the manufacturer's advertising program and attempt generally to maintain close and friendly relations. In addition, they call on retailers in an effort to improve movement of the product at the retail level. Orders they obtain from retailers usually are turned over to wholesalers for filling. In the drug and certain other fields, missionary salespersons are known as "detail men," and they also make calls on persons who influence, but do not make, purchase decisions, such as doctors, dentists, hospital administrators, and school-board members.

In industrial-goods marketing, missionary salespeople perform functions similar to those just described; generally, however, they give more emphasis to training middlemen's sales personnel on product characteristics, new applications, and sales fundamentals. In selling highly technical products with numerous specialized applications, they are responsible for assisting the middlemen's sales force in analyzing customers' problems, and consummating sales. Furthermore, in industries served by outside professionals, such as in building and construction, missionary salespeople make special efforts to acquaint engineers, architects, and other professionals with the technical characteristics and applications of the manufacturer's product.

Missionary salespeople, then, perform services designed to improve relations with the distributive network. They perform an educational function in that they acquaint middlemen and their personnel with new products and applications, while they keep alive the trade's interest in established products. Their efforts supplement those of the middlemen's selling forces in translating this knowledge into greater sales volume and profits for the total distributive organization. The role of missionary salespersons is particularly signifi-

---

[10]National Commission on Food Marketing, *Studies of Organization and Competition in Grocery Manufacturing,* Technical Study No. 6 (Washington, DC.: Government Printing Office, June 1966), pp. 222-30.

cant when they call on persons influencing but not making buying decisions, or when the consummation of sales demands greater product knowledge than the middlemen's sales force possess.

Only rarely should missionary salespeople permanently assume functions that properly belong to the dealer. Generally, a manufacturer sets up a missionary sales force because its middlemen are not performing as satisfactorily as it would like. In effect, the manufacturer attempts to obtain quick improvement by substituting direct action for the much slower, indirect effort to upgrade the overall management efficiency of the middlemen's organizations. In such instances, it should be made clear that the missionary sales force is only a temporary way to fill the gap between the middlemen's present capabilities and the manufacturer's expectations. In some cases, however, the middlemen are not capable of attaining desired performance levels. For example, a middleman stocking competing brands may be unwilling to promote one at the expense of the others, and a permanent missionary sales force is necessary to achieve a satisfactory level of promotion. The manufacturer providing permanent missionary sales help should guard against continually increasing its range of services and allowing the middlemen to pass on the blame for their own inefficiency.

Missionary salespeople are often unpopular with the middlemen. They are accused of such practices as playing off one middleman against another, selling to poor credit risks and expecting middlemen not only to accept the resulting orders but to bear the likely losses, and interfering with the activities of middlemen's sales personnel. Therefore, it is advisable to restrict the activities of the missionary salespeople, as much as possible, to training middlemen and their sales force. The manufacturer should expect its middlemen, with rare exceptions, eventually to reassume the functions performed by the missionary sales force. The more effective missionary salespeople are as developers of managerial and selling skills, the sooner they can be reassigned to other duties.

### Identifying Source of Supply at Final-Buyer Level

Many manufacturers must make special efforts to ensure that final buyers can find the local outlets which handle their product and that, once in the right outlet, these buyers can locate the product with minimum difficulty. The significance of each aspect of this problem differs with the nature of the product, the manufacturer's policy on distribution intensity, and the middlemen's operating characteristics; thus, consumer-goods manufacturers, owing to the greater length and complexity of their marketing channels, generally have greater problems in this area than do industrial-goods producers.

For the manufacturer distributing its product through a limited number of middlemen, publicizing the identity of outlets stocking the product is important. Thus, for consumer-products manufacturers using selective or exclusive agency distribution, the identification of local retail outlets is an important objective. These manufacturers generally also invest heavily in consumer advertising. But it does little good to presell the product through advertising unless consumers can find the product when they want to buy it. In most cases, the consumer is not predisposed to spend a great amount of searching time in finding a store that stocks a particular item. If the manufacturer is to capitalize on the preconditioning of consumers through advertising to the fullest possible extent, steps must be taken to assure that consumers can readily and easily identify the proper retailers.

**Local Advertising by the Manufacturer.**     Manufacturers of consumer products in the specialty- and shopping-goods categories achieve this identification of their local outlets in different ways. Some buy space and time in local media and advertise over the names of local stores, occasionally with the stores paying part of the cost. Others list their dealers in national advertisements. Many list their dealers in local telephone classified directories, and a number provide their retailers with appropriate store signs. Some persuade their retailers to feature the manufacturer's product in their own local advertising and make available ready-made advertising layouts or matrices.

Local advertising of the manufacturer's product, whether paid for by the manufacturer or retailer or jointly, not only adds local flavor to a promotional program but also may increase its total effectiveness. In individual market areas, dealers frequently know better than the manufacturer which types of advertising are the most effective. In addition, because of regional variances, many manufacturers find it feasible to use prices only in local advertisements. The manufacturer desiring to advertise its product's price locally may find it advantageous to use the same advertising to identify its local dealers.

Manufacturers of industrial products using middlemen also use advertising to final buyers to identify the nearest sources of supply for their products. Direct mail, listings in trade directories and industrial catalogs such as *Sweet's,* and national advertising in trade publications are all used to identify middlemen as sources from which the product may be purchased. On the local level, especially in important industrial centers, listings of middlemen in the classified sections of telephone and business directories are also used.

**Point-of-Purchase Identification.**     Although the manufacturer of a consumer convenience good rarely attempts to identify all its dealers, it often takes steps to emphasize the presence of its product within stores where ultimate consumers customarily shop. When the item is one that consumers ordinarily buy on impulse, the manufacturer's sales force makes a special effort to secure point-of-purchase promotion. The only place in the entire marketing channel where the product and the ultimate consumer actually come into contact is in the retail outlet—at the point of purchase. The manufacturer has the best opportunity to make the "payoff" sale if the product is situated in the store where consumers can easily find it. Counter and floor merchandisers, shelf markers, preprints and reprints of national advertisements, mass interior displays (often erected by the manufacturer's salespeople), special display cases, and easeled display cards, to mention only a few of the many types of sales promotion pieces, are all used to identify the product inside the retail store. Where the manufacturer's sales personnel call upon the dealers frequently, it is common for them to ask for and receive preferred shelf or counter positions for the product display. When the outlets use self-service retailing methods, point-of-purchase pieces and preferred display positions (tied in with good packaging) are the only ways in which the manufacturer can significantly influence consumer buying behavior within the retailer's store. In such stores, point-of-purchase materials take the place of clerks in providing information to prospective buyers and even in persuading them to buy. As the trend to self-service continues to spread, and particularly as these methods are adopted by more stores specializing in specialty and shopping goods, point-of-purchase materials should become even more important as essential ingredients in the promotional programs of consumer-goods manufacturers.

Careful attention should be given to the distribution of point-of-purchase display materials, and special precautions may assure their use by retailers. Probably the most effective distribution method is to have the sales force (or a specialized display service company), both deliver and set up the displays in retail stores. When display pieces are distributed in shipping containers with the product, many, if not most, retailers (or their receiving clerks) promptly discard them. To avoid such waste of costly display pieces, some manufacturers seek to obtain distribution by publicizing their availability through direct-mail or trade-paper advertising; however, unless the display piece is most unusual or very effectively advertised, few dealers take the trouble to write in, or even to ask the salesperson, for it. This seeming lack of interest by retailers does not necessarily reflect disapproval of such promotional devices—more often it reflects lack of understanding or inspiration in their use, inability to cope with the volume of materials received, or simply inertia.

To maximize retailers' use of display pieces, they must be designed with retailers' problems in mind. A display piece should not be too complicated for the average retail employee to assemble, neither should it be too large nor too small for the space in which it will probably be erected in most retail stores. Above all, the design should make it perfectly obvious to retailers that the display piece will help them make more sales. In gathering the information needed for design purposes, the salespeople's knowledge of retailers' problems and operating circumstances should be fully utilized.

## DISTRIBUTIVE NETWORK CHANGES AND MAINTAINING RELATIONS

The evolution of new types of middlemen has been a recurring problem for many manufacturers. Within the past century or so, many new marketing institutions have appeared and grown in importance—department stores, mail-order houses, corporate chains, cooperative and voluntary chains, producers' and consumers' cooperatives, supermarkets, rack jobbers, discount houses, and discount department stores, to name but a few. Older, better-established types of middlemen have proclaimed loudly that each new institution was "illegitimate." They have pleaded with manufacturers for protection against such "unfair and unorthodox" competitors. Consequently, the newborn middlemen have had to fight all the harder to make sales and even to secure sources of supply—perhaps that is why new institutional forms almost always seem more virile than older ones. Whenever new types of middlemen have been successful, they have filled a market niche that went unfilled up to the time of their appearance. Manufacturers who do not allow their marketing channels to "freeze," those with truly dynamic marketing and sales policies, have less difficulty in maintaining adequate overall distribution. It may be appropriate occasionally for a manufacturer to assist its "conventional" outlets in coping with their new competitors, but the manufacturer must also ensure that its products are represented in the new outlets. It should recognize that marketing history is full of instances of manufacturers who have clung too long to losing causes. In this regard, two scholars comment as follows:

> More difficult to keep track of is the impact of economic, political, and social changes upon those we do business with. What was a sound relationship five years ago may no longer be so today. Routine control reports rarely reflect these kinds of changes directly, and the physical and legal separation of business associates may permit trouble to grow unnoticed. For example, one company found that being the major supplier of paper bags to independent grocery stores was of little value in (the) face of trends to packaged merchandise and supermarket selling.[11]

[11]W. H. Newman and T. L. Berg, "Managing External Relations," *California Management Review,* Vol. 5, No. 3 (Spring 1963), p. 85.

The best policy would appear to be neither to assist nor to throw roadblocks in the way of the newer institutions. If research of broad underlying economic, political, and social trends indicates that newer types of middlemen are capable of becoming important outlets for the product, changes in marketing channels and sales policies should be considered.

## CONCLUSION

Middlemen are important links in the chain of distribution for most manufacturers, and their wholehearted cooperation is needed to achieve high levels of marketing efficiency. Both parties have much to gain from such cooperation, and much to lose if it is lacking. Although cooperation is definitely a two-way street, generally the manufacturer must initiate it. This is especially so if the manufacturer contemplates using formal programs of cooperation. Those charged with the planning, administration, and implementation of formal or informal programs of cooperation with middlemen should give due consideration to the implications such programs hold for sales department operations.

# Cases for Part II

## II-1.  THE MODERNMODE COMPANY:

### Manufacturer of Electric Space Heaters— Problems of Chief Sales Executive

The ModernMode Company, located in a small town in upstate New York, manu-factured a complete line of popular-priced electric space heaters. With an annual sales volume of approximately $2.5 million, it was the world's largest exclusive manufacturer of electric space heaters. The first ModernMode heater was manufactured in 1929. In the beginning, production was limited to heaters designed for special applications. No attempt was made to offer ModernModes for all aspects of heating, since the size of the market was unknown and existing rate structures did not encourage the use of electric power for heating purposes.

During its early years, the company accumulated invaluable experience in the design and manufacture of heating units for special purposes. Chief among these were products manufactured to government order, including units for submarines, for control buildings at government-operated dams, and for airport control towers. Private industry also pur-chased ModernModes for such diversified applications as banana-ripening rooms, watch-men's buildings, and first-aid rooms, and for use in those atmospheres classified as hazardous by the National Bureau of Fire Underwriters.

Gradually, the company expanded its space-heater line until it included products designed for residential, farm, and commercial uses. The line included built-in wall units for residences, with automatic thermostats for individual room heating control; portable heaters for basement game rooms and sun porches; special heaters for farm milk and pump houses; and others designed especially for gasoline stations, dressing rooms, and restaurants.

The principal selling point of the ModernMode heater was a patented cast-aluminum heating element that did not have exposed glowing wires. Thus, use of the heater did not involve the danger of fire, shock, or burn. This feature, exclusive with the ModernMode design, also gave the unit a convection surface greater than that of the conventional heater. The heating-element design had been approved by the insurance underwriters and subsequently was guaranteed by the company for a five-year term. The unique safety features of the heating element, together with the trend toward generally lower electric rates throughout the country, indicated that there should be an expanding future potential market for a standard line of ModernMode heaters for complete residential and industrial heating.

To strengthen its competitive position, ModernMode had recently introduced electrical baseboard heating. Unlike the long-accepted hot-water method, this system entirely eliminated the need for a boiler, piping, chimney, and fuel-storage facilities. At the same time, the new system possessed all the advantages of the hot-water method. ModernMode anticipated that the addition of electrical baseboard heating to the line would make important contributions to sales volume in the future.

However, the largest domestic market was still for auxiliary or supplemental heating, and ModernMode had been extensively merchandised for this purpose—for places that were difficult to heat; where warmth was required only occasionally, or for short periods; or where changeable spring and fall weather made it extravagant to operate a central heating system. The company's promotion and advertising had been largely concentrated in this area, and it was thought that these applications had produced more than half the sales volume.

Since its organization, and while competitors were engaging in more diversified activities, ModernMode had devoted its research, engineering, and production facilities exclusively to the manufacture of electric space heaters. Because of this policy, ModernMode had gained a strong selling advantage in the field. This practice of concentrating entirely on one product was used as a promotional appeal to convince the consumer that a superior product was being marketed. The company had established itself strongly in the highly competitive market for electrical space-heating equipment.

The ModernMode line was sold through recognized wholesalers in the electrical appliance, building material and mill supply, and heating and plumbing fields. Selection of and continued contact with these wholesalers was the responsibility of twenty-seven manufacturer's agents, whose territories covered the United States and Canada. The choice of a wholesaler by an agent was subject to the approval of the home office, which had set up minimum requirements, such as the stipulation that the wholesaler had to agree to handle the ModernMode line exclusively.

The manufacturer's agent operated on the basis of 50 percent commissions computed on list prices. Manufacturer's agents sold to distributors at list prices less 35 percent. There were approximately 1,100 ModernMode distributors. These distributors sold to retail dealers and contractors.

Thirty authorized service stations were under the jurisdiction of the manufacturer's agents. Retailers sent requests for minor repairs to the distributors, who forwarded them to the service stations. If the requirements for service were covered by the terms of the guarantee, the service station relayed that information to the ModernMode Company. The home office decided, in all cases, whether repairs were to be made at the installation or whether the equipment should be returned to the factory. To reduce the amount of service that the company had to render, ModernMode expected its agents to contact their principal customers occasionally. The purpose of these customer contacts was not only to inspect equipment but also to advise users on the proper methods of care and maintenance.

ModernMode's advertising program was directed to both the consumer and dealer. Because the company did not employ a large sales force to promote the product, the promotional effort depended largely upon advertising. The administration of the advertising program was divided between the home-office advertising department and a national advertising agency. The media used included national trade and consumer magazines and direct mail. Direct-mail advertising was usually handled by the ModernMode distributors. Brochures and displays were provided to retail dealers, and their cost was split on a fifty-fifty basis by the ModernMode Company and wholesale distributors.

Currently, Charles Jolley, the vice-president in charge of sales, was faced with the four problems described below:

### Morgan Supply Company

In Denver, Colorado, the distribution of the ModernMode Line was handled by two wholesalers, Morgan Supply Company and Charles Jackson, Inc. Last March the Morgan Supply Company had been forced into bankruptcy, leaving ModernMode with inadequate coverage in that area. The failure of this distributor caused ModernMode to suffer a $5,000 loss, and this fact prompted the manufacturer's agent in Denver to refer the problem to the home office. Jolley turned the problem over to Clarence Cass, the assistant sales manager. He suggested that Cass go to Denver to investigate the situation personally. It was believed that the Morgan Supply Company had failed either because of unwarranted credit extension or because the firm had received inadequate advertising and promotional support. If it also turned out, as Jolley suspected, that the Morgan Supply Company had been using funds received from the sales of heaters (which were purchased on credit extended by ModernMode) to carry losses on slower-selling lines, the job of finding a new Denver distrbutor would be greatly simplified. Besides reporting on the reasons for the failure of the Morgan Supply Company, Cass was instructed to interview potential distributors and to make recommendations for action by Jolley.

### Wilson Distributors

In April, Jolley received a letter from Jack Wilson, president of Wilson Distributors of Fairmont, West Virginia. Wilson reported that prices on ModernMode heaters were being cut in his area and that he had traced the source of the trouble to the company's wholesale distributor in Allentown, Pennsylvania. Jolley wrote Wilson Distributors as follows:

Mr. Jack Wilson
President, Wilson Distributors
Fairmont, West Virginia

Dear Jack:

In reply to your letter of April 9th, this is to inform you that I am referring this entire problem to McConnell and Company, our agent in your area. We believe that it should be left to McConnell and Company to determine the extent of price cutting on our line. As you know, our policy is that prices must be maintained at fair-trade levels. However, unusual circumstances may, on occasion, necessitate lowering prices in certain areas. In such cases, it is the responsibility of our manufacturer's agents to investigate the circumstances and to straighten them out with the least possible amount of friction among the dealers. Naturally, any general reductions in prices should be uniform throughout the entire country. If price cutting is rampant in your area, you may rest assured that we will do everything possible to stamp it out.

Thank you again, Jack, for calling this matter to my attention.

Very truly yours,


Charles Jolley
Vice-President
(Sales)

### Summer-Cottage Market

Jolley was planning to conduct a market test to determine the possibilities of expanding the sale of the ModernMode line to owners of summer cottages. To clarify his thinking, Jolley had written the following memorandum:

The mounting number of people buying or renting summer cottages in recent years has prompted the management to promote a special campaign on cottage heating. Because of the light construction of summer cottages, there is a special need for some type of supplemental heating during the cooler evenings. Before attempting promotion on a nationwide scale, the company should test its campaign in a restricted area. Several problems must be considered before final preparations for the test campaign can be made:

1. What style of heater is best suited for summer cottages?
2. What area should be chosen for the test market?
3. What type of advertising will be most effective for contacting widely scattered cottage owners while they are still residing in their winter homes?
4. Which distributor should we select to cooperate in the test?

The type of heater most feasible for this purpose is the automatic portable, which requires no complicated installation or maintenance. The owner, if he so desires, may pack it up and take it back to the city with him at the end of the season

The logical region for the test is probably the shore area of Lake Ontario near Rochester. The company could contact the Cottage Owners Association office in this area for a list of names of summer residents. Direct mail is the best method for getting in touch with these people.

The electrical wholesaler or distributor chosen to cooperate in the market test should be one with a good working knowledge of the region and its inhabitants. He should be sent displays and a small amount of stock on a consignment basis; and once established, he could be signed up as a regular ModernMode distributor.

### Diversification of the Product Line

Because of the definite seasonality of heating-unit sales and the resulting necessity for curtailing production during part of the year (see Exhibit 1), Jolley had been investigating the possibilities of adding a new line to supplement the present product. The ideal new product, of course, would be one whose peak sales would occur during the off-season for heaters. The final decision on the addition of new products was the prerogative of the board of directors, and Jolley had been asked to present his suggestions at its next meeting. He had prepared the following notes:

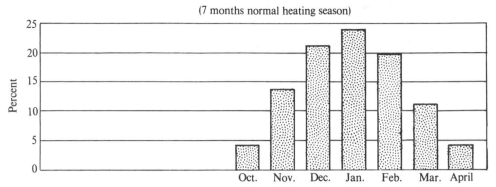

EXHIBIT 1
Comparative Monthly Heating Requirements
(7 months normal heating season)

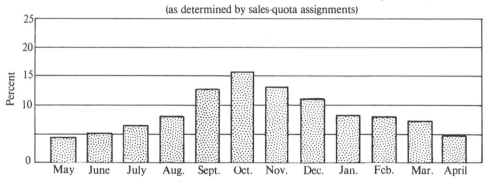

Comparative Monthly Sales of Space Heaters
(as determined by sales-quota assignments)

The addition of a supplemental product line should be considered very carefully. The manufacture of a product similar to the heater line would build up sufficient volume to eliminate seasonal layoffs in the factory, and the resulting high turnover in skilled labor personnel. The addition would, however, nullify the company's position as an exclusive manufacturer of electrical space heaters and equipment. This is a promotional loss that should not be ignored.

Two products might be considered. One—electric fans, which are highly competitive and already widely distributed—does not seem to have enough sales potential to warrant the expense incurred in development. It would seem that the ideal solution would be the manufacture of portable air-conditioning units. Although this would constitute a major product and require complete redesigning of our production facilities, it would be advantageous from a dealer standpoint, for heating and air conditioning are as complementary as one could desire. The products could be jointly promoted in ModernMode advertising, and the company could revise its promotion to claim exclusiveness in the field of electrical space heating *and* air conditioning.

Should the Board find this solution unacceptable, perhaps it should consider the possibilities of setting up a subsidiary, utilizing the same production facilities and the same sales organization as the heating line, but maintaining two separate sets of books and separate promotions.

*Evaluate the ways in which the four problems were handled by Jolley. How could these problems have been dealt with differently?*

# II-2.   DONALDSON MANUFACTURING COMPANY:
## Electrical Products Manufacturer—
## Selecting a Top Sales Executive

The president of the Donaldson Manufacturing Company of Chicago was faced with the problem of selecting a new general sales manager. The company had annual sales in excess of $75 million and more than forty years of experience in manufacturing electrical safety switches, circuit breakers, regulators, manual and magnetic starters, and related products. These products, which ultimately were used in industrial and institutional markets, were distributed through nearly 250 electrical supply wholesalers. Four divisional sales managers directed field operations from sales offices in Chicago, New York, Houston, and San Francisco. Each divisional manager supervised from three to eight salespeople and was responsible for recruiting, selecting, and training the personnel under his control. Sales potentials and quotas were determined by the general sales manager and an assistant, but these figures were often adjusted after consultations with the divisional sales managers.

The need for selecting a general sales manager was occasioned by the impending retirement of Mr. Preston, who had been with the company since its inception. For many years, Preston had been an advocate of increasing decentralization in sales-force operation and control. He felt that the central sales department should concern itself almost exclusively with planning, and that the sales divisions should have maximum freedom in deciding how goals should be reached. Sales personnel in the field, therefore, received little direction or control from the Chicago head office. Divisional sales managers administered their divisions like independent business people; they had grown accustomed to making decisions and to formulating policies for their own marketing areas. The result was that little standardization existed in the sales operating policies followed in the four divisions.

Price competition in the industry was of secondary importance, the main basis being that of product development and design. Donaldson sales personnel spent a high proportion of their time calling on industrial and institutional users with the representatives of electrical supply wholesalers. Their principal function was to analyze the problems of the wholesalers' customers and to prescribe Donaldson equipment as a solution. If standardized products were not adaptable to customers' problems, sales-force members often recommended that equipment be specially manufactured to meet users' requirements.

The twenty-five Donaldson salespersons all possessd degrees in electrical engineering or equivalent experience; and they had been trained under the personal direction of the divisional sales managers. Sales personnel were compensated on a straight-salary basis, partly because of the great amount of time spent working with wholesalers' salespeople, and partly because they were also required to assist in the installation of equipment and to make repairs in emergency situations.

Divisional sales managers were compensated on the basis of a minimum fixed salary plus a commission on the gross margin realized from sales originating within their respective divisions. The central office made decisions on changes in the salaries of divisional sales managers, but divisional sales managers had the power to make adjustments in the compensation of salespeople. Indeed, only recently had all divisions adopted the straight-salary plan for salespeople, a change that had been insisted upon and pushed through by the company president.

It had been impossible to assign the sales personnel to nonoverlapping territories—each person worked with several wholesalers and, in many instances, the same areas were cultivated by two or more wholesalers. However, it was unusual for more than one salesperson to make calls on the same industrial or institutional user.

Preston was responsible for setting sales quotas and determining sales potentials, planning promotional programs with the advertising agency, assisting in the setting of price ranges, developing the sales department budgets, and in formulating other basic marketing policies. He was also charged with the responsibility for conducting the public relations program.

The president of the company, who had the support of the board of directors, felt that the time had come to centralize more of the operations of the sales department. He realized that any changes would have to be made gradually, but he was certain that greater control over the salespeople in the field was essential. For example, the head office had very little information on the performance of individual salespersons. In fact, it was often several months before the head office learned of personnel changes made in the sales divisions.

The president had been authorized by the board of directors to screen all applicants for the position of general sales manager, and to submit his selection for final approval. Because he believed in the basic soundness of a "promotion from within" policy, he first considered the four divisional sales managers and the assistant general manager. He decided that two of the divisional managers were incapable of assuming the increased responsibilities; the third, although a competent individual, had previously expressed a desire to continue in his present capacity; the fourth was not only willing but frankly anxious to assume the added responsibility. The assistant general sales manager was also in the running, and four other applications had been accepted by the president. From his investigations of these six applicants, the following information was extracted:

1.   Thomas G. Gunning

*Personal information:* Age 48, German-French parentage, Lutheran, height: 6 feet 2 inches, weight: 225 pounds, brown eyes, ruddy complexion, fair health, divorced, 3 dependents by 2 ex-wives.

*Education:* Attended public schools in Denver, Colorado. Received B.S. degree in electrical engineering from the University of Colorado.

*Experience:* Past eight years Divisional Sales Manager, Southern Division (Houston). One year as salesperson, Southern Division. Outstanding sales record.

Three years in military service as infantry officer. Served overseas, principally in staff positions. Also assigned as an instructor at the Infantry Officers' Candidate School.

Three years as salesperson, Southern Division. Average record.

Three years as salesperson, Fort Worth Electrical Wholesale Supply Co.

Two years employed as engineer on various government projects, chiefly in the Mountain States.

Six years as partner in electrical contracting business, Denver. Business was liquidated as a result of financial reverses.

2.   Glen G. Parker

*Personal information:* Age 35, English parentage, Catholic, height: 5 feet 3 inches, weight: 150 pounds, blue eyes, fair complexion, good health, married, 5 dependents.

*Education:* Attended parochial schools in Syracuse, New York. Received B.S. degree in business administration from Syracuse University. Successfully completed three correspondence courses in electrical and mechanical engineering.

*Experience:* Past nine years Assistant General Sales Manager. Works directly under Preston, who was responsible for hiring him. His principal duties have been to gather economic and marketing statistics and to assist in sales forecasting.

Corporal, U.S. Marine Corps. Clerical duties, for three years.

Stock boy in department store, Utica, New York, for one year after college.

While in college, worked as a table waiter in a sorority house for three years.

3.   Joseph Q. Brunzell

*Personal information:* Age 38, Irish-German parentage, Protestant, height: 6 feet, weight: 175 pounds, green eyes, light complexion, excellent health, married, 2 dependents.

*Education:* Attended public schools, Oak Park, Illinois. Attended Indiana University, majoring in European history. Left college after three years because of lack of funds and death of father.

*Experience:* Past six years assistant sales manager of Logston Corporation, Chicago manufacturer of sound recording equipment. Is responsible for sales research work. Plans and conducts sales training programs and "training clinics" for company and distributors' salespeople.

Three years as salesperson, Chicago office supply firm. Work included the demonstration of various items of office equipment, and the making of suggestions to customers on methods of simplifying office procedures.

Three years U.S. Army, infantry private.

Two years as clerk in chain grocery store, Oak Park, Illinois.

4.   Sven A. Pelly

*Personal information:* Age 59, Swedish-English parentage, Episcopalian, height: 5 feet 9 inches, weight: 165 pounds, blue eyes, light complexion, good health, married, 1 dependent. Has son attending Princeton.

*Education:* Attended private elementary and secondary schools in Ohio. Received B.A. degree in political science from Princeton.

*Experience:* Past fifteen years account executive with New York advertising agency. Has participated in planning and executing promotional programs for several products, mostly in the consumers-goods field. Has had considerable experience in planning promotional budgets for large clients.

Ten years free-lance writer of promotional literature. Did work for a large mail-order house. Prepared some material, including sales portfolios, for companies manufacturing industrial goods.

Ten years employed by Cleveland stockbrokerage firm. At first was mainly a statistician, later became a customer contact man.

*Comment:* When interviewed, Pelly was extremely nervous.

5.   Richard E. Black

*Personal information:* Age 34, Scotch-Irish parentage, Presbyterian, height: 6 feet, weight: 180 pounds, good health, married, 2 dependents.

*Education:* Attended public schools in western Oregon. Received B.A. degree from University of Oregon. Received M.B.A. degree from Stanford University.

*Experience:* Past two years assistant sales manager of Morrow Electric Corporation. Has helped plan and execute marketing programs for several electrical products similar to those in Donaldson line.

Two years as market analyst, Morrow Electric Corporation.

One year as instructor in marketing, San Jose State College.

Two years as student, Stanford University.

One year as office manager, Chrysler automobile dealership, Portland, Oregon.

Five years U.S. Army. Discharged as First Lieutenant, field artillery. Served in Southeast Asia.

*Comment:* Applicant has been active in community service organizations.

6. John H. Curtin

*Personal information:* Age 40, Irish parentage, Catholic, height: 5 feet 9 inches, weight: 175 pounds, fair health, married, no dependents.

*Education:* Attended parochial schools in Boston. Completed two years at Boston College.

*Experience:* Past eight years—owns and manages wholesale electrical supply house in western Massachusetts. Donaldson distributor for past five years. Has completed preliminary negotiations for sale of his business.

Four years as production supervisor, Baltimore electronic plant.

Eight years as supervisor for a Boston electrical contractor.

*Comment:* Applicant appears to have substantial means. It is also rumored that his wife, the daughter of a wealthy New York banker, furnished the money that enabled him to go into business for himself eight years ago.

*Which, if any, of the six applicants should have been selected?*

# II-3.  FRITO-LAY, INC.:
# Manufacturer of Corn Chips—
# Reorganization of Executive Structure

Frito-Lay, Inc., had recently undergone an extensive reorganization of marketing-related activities in order to provide more effective control in regional and district offices. Arch C. West, the vice-president for marketing, found it necessary to reevaluate his role and his responsibilities under the new organizational structure, which had redefined his formal relationships with other executives.

Frito-Lay, Inc., with its home office in Dallas, Texas, was a national manufacturer of corn chips, potato chips, and related food products. Its sales accounted for about 75 percent of the national market for corn chips, and a much smaller share for potato chips. It also produced a line of canned processed foods, the most important of which was chili and beans, under the Austex brand. Owing to the perishability of the corn and potato chips, the company had a number of factories located throughout the United States close to major markets. Product perishability also made it necessary to maintain a sales force that could sell and deliver direct to retailers. To serve retail food stores directly on a national basis, it was necessary to maintain a sales force in excess of 3,000 persons.

To provide proper communication with and control over such a large sales force, Frito-Lay had developed a complex organizational structure, with three layers of geographical subdivisions of authority. The national market was divided into four zones, and these were subdivided into a total of fourteen divisions. The divisions were further divided into districts, each with a district sales manager and ten or twelve salespeople. The new organizational structure had placed the vice-president for sales under the line authority of the executive vice-president rather than under the vice-president for marketing. The position of vice-president for sales was a staff position, since the district and divisional sales managers were under the authority of their respective district and divisional managers. The relationships are shown in the organizational chart in Exhibit 1.

EXHIBIT 1
Organizational Chart of Frito-Lay, Inc.

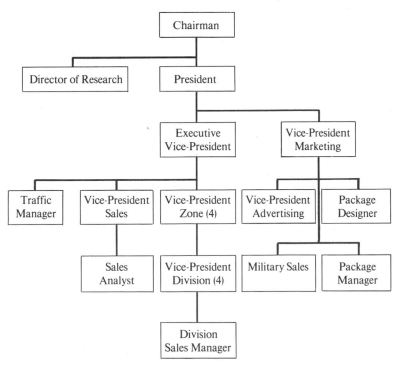

Under the formal organizational structure, the vice-president for marketing was assigned a staff position with respect to the sales organization. Yet, in actual practice, he exercised considerable control over activities of the sales organization. For example, the subdivision of each district into individual sales territories, and reshaping of territories, was handled by West's office. The availability of detailed computer-derived information about each territory made it possible for him to make such decisions at a distance.

*Explain how West can successfully deal with problems relating to the sales force when the formal organizational structure cuts him off from direct contact with them.*

*Under the Frito-Lay organization, what avenues are open to achieve coordination between various marketing-related activities?*

*What individuals in the Frito-Lay organization should be involved in new-product planning and development?*

## II-4.   MONROVIA OIL COMPANY:

### Petroleum Company—Decentralization of
### the National Account Department

The Monrovia Oil Company, with head offices in New York City, was one of the largest producers and distributors of petroleum products in the United States. Company executives were considering a change in the organization of the national account department. The purpose of the change was to achieve more coordination between the operations of the regional and division offices, which were engaged in direct marketing, and the national account department, which functioned as a sales-contact group in the handling of special accounts.

The national account department, functioning as a separate sales organization, was responsible for the distribution of gasoline, fuel oils, and industrial lubricants to approximately three hundred companies. These customers operated in industries where reciprocity was a major factor in the development of new business. This department came under the direction of the vice-president of sales. It was headed by a department manager who supervised the activities of six sales representatives. The purchasing department supplied the manager with a weekly report on all purchases made by the company amounting to $10,000 or more. The national account manager kept the sales staff informed of all such purchases made by Monrovia from accounts they were now selling, and from accounts to which sales had not yet been made. The sales personnel were responsible for the development of sales to each account assigned to them, and made weekly reports on their success. The regional and division offices were so notified when a salesperson sold an account, and it became their responsibility to service the account in question.

Regional and division offices were strategically located throughout the company's marketing area. Regional managers, who reported directly to the vice-president of sales, were assigned five specialists in a staff capacity. Each region was subdivided into three divisions. Under the division manager was a TBA manager, a retail sales manager, a wholesale sales manager, an industrial sales manager, and a superintendent of operations (see Exhibit 1). Each division manager supervised from five to eight salespeople who called on all classes of trade in their marketing territories, including national accounts after the initial contacts had been made.

The regional and division managers were highly critical of the activities of the national account department. They contended that the duplication of sales effort could be avoided by eliminating the department completely. On many occasions, salespeople from the division offices had quoted prices on fuel oil and gasoline that were different from those used by national account representatives. Since the division managers were responsible for the business developed by the national account department, they felt it should be their prerogative to quote prices advantageous to their own operations.

It was the opinion of the vice-president of sales that more business could be obtained through decentralization of the national account department rather than through its elimination. He made the following proposals to the board of directors at the spring meet-

EXHIBIT 1
Sales Organization of the Monrovia Oil Company

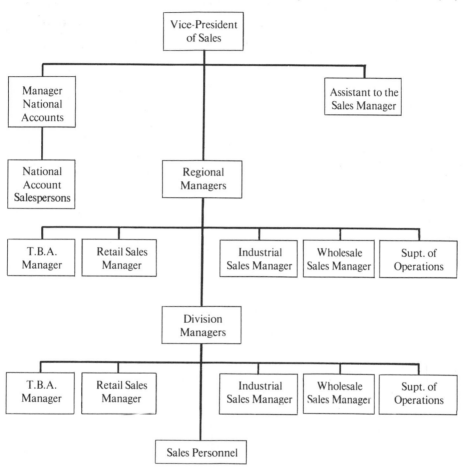

ing: (1) the national account department should be decentralized; (2) the national account manager should be made an assistant to the vice-president of sales in charge of special accounts; (3) a national-account salesperson should be assigned to each regional office to work with the division managers and their sales personnel; and (4) the activities of the national-account salespersons should be coordinated with those of the division sales personnel by the regional managers.

*What changes, if any, would you recommend in the organization of the national account department?*

## II-5.   LINDSAY SPORTSWEAR:
## Manufacturer of Sportswear—
## Sales-Department Reorganization

Lindsay Sportswear manufactured a wide line of men's and boys' sportswear, including sweaters, hunting coats, caps, gloves, sport coats, slacks, sport shirts, jackets, swimwear, walking shorts, and socks. Annual sales of $70,000,000 gave evidence of the wide consumer acceptance of the "Lindsay Sportswear" brand. The sportswear was distributed directly from the manufacturer to 8,000 men's and boys' shops and department stores. As Lindsay sales increased over the years, the company's sales organization evolved from a simple line type into a more complex organization, as shown in Exhibit 1.

EXHIBIT 1
Sales Organization of Lindsay Sportswear

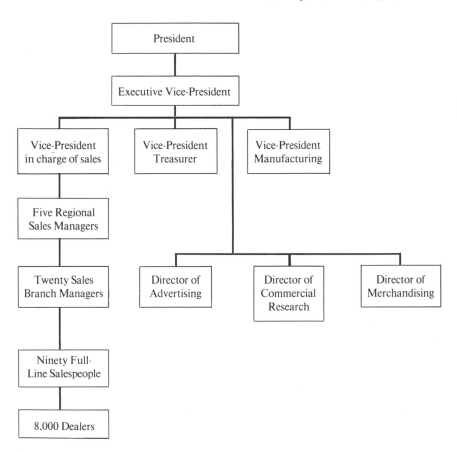

The vice-president of sales was responsible for the administration of the sales department and was concerned with the organizing, planning, directing, coordinating, and appraising of the total sales operation. The regional sales managers were responsible for sales in their territories, field supervision of the branch sales offices, and implementing the company's sales policies. The sales branch managers spent the great majority of their time in the field with the sales force. The ninety full-line salespersons operated out of the twenty sales branch offices.

The directors of advertising, commercial research, and merchandising reported to the executive vice-president of the company, as did the sales vice-president. The advertising director administered the $2,000,000 annual advertising appropriation and, in consultation with the sales vice-president, prepared the advertising budget and examined and approved all work done by the firm's advertising agency. The commercial research director planned and conducted surveys for the sales vice-president as well as for other department heads. Surveys measuring the market potential for sportswear, the preferences of buyers, the frequency of purchase, the attitudes of dealers, and the like were extremely useful for establishing sales policies and strategies, setting sales quotas, determining sales territories, selecting dealers, and evaluating salespeople's performances. The merchandising director was responsible for the coordination of the manufacturing and sales arms of the company, by taking demand preferences on the one hand and manufacturing costs on the other and working out a plan that balanced the two. His main function was to determine garment design and specifications and to make sure that dealers and consumers got what they wanted without building up excessive inventory.

Although the current sales organization of Lindsay Sportswear had been effective for a number of years, recent changes in the marketing and distribution of sportswear, as well as changes in Lindsay policies and practices, indicated that a revision of the present sales organization was required.

One of the developments which signaled a need for possible change in the sales organization was that company sales in boys' sportswear had more than doubled due to a number of factors such as an increase in the number of individual children's shops and the growing interest of men's-wear retailers in boys' wear. Thus, boys' sportswear became the largest seller in the Lindsay Sportswear line, a great change from just five years ago. The most significant effect of the boys'-wear sales increase was that Lindsay Sportswear sales personnel were devoting most of their efforts to the easier-to-sell boys'-wear line, to the neglect of the men's-wear line.

Greater dealer and consumer interest in the color, style, and fabrics of men's sportswear made it necessary to give closer consideration to buyers' tastes and preferences. The salespeople, by virtue of their being closest to the market, were in a good position from which to suggest garment-style preferences to the merchandising department. One Lindsay salesperson suggested to the merchandising director that a panel of famous personalities be established as style consultants from which would come sportswear the panel considered to be most fashionable. The initial panel consisted of several famous golfers noted for their apparel. The sales of the sportswear selected by the style consultants were good enough to warrant investigation of a possible change in the Lindsay Sportswear sales organization which would permit closer cooperation between the merchandising staff and the sales department.

As the Lindsay line expanded, it became apparent that the ninety full-line salespeople were spending so much time introducing new seasonal lines and promotions that they were unable to serve dealers properly. Much important service work by salespersons was being neglected, such as assistance in stock control, pricing, point-of-purchase display, and training retail salesclerks. This neglect of dealer service duties had resulted in the loss of some major accounts, who switched their business to competing lines of men's sportswear.

These developments prompted the vice-president in charge of sales to recommend to the executive vice-president that the Lindsay Sportswear sales department be reorganized to solve the following problems: (1) neglect of the full line of sportswear by salespeople who devote most of their sales attention to the fast-selling boys' wear; (2) the need to improve styling of the line by the merchandising department through closer cooperation with the sales department; and (3) neglect of dealer service by the sales force.

*How should Lindsay Sportswear have reorganized the structure of its sales department to eliminate the problems outlined in the case?*

# II-6.   ALLEN SPECIALTY COMPANY:
## Manufacturer of Writing Supplies—
## Coordination of Advertising, Sales Promotion, and Selling

The Allen Specialty Company manufactured and distributed a line of ballpoint pens, mechanical pencils, and, in the past five years, had added a line of stationery. Allen products were sold to stationery and office-supply wholesalers and retailers, as well as to department stores, discount houses, drugstores, variety stores, and supermarkets. A field sales force of eighty-two persons operated out of six district sales offices located throughout the United States. Allen management believed that a critical factor in the company's sales success was its sales-promotion program or the coordination between its national advertising and the activities of Allen salespeople and dealers.

The sales-promotion program was the main responsibility of the sales promotion manager and his staff, in conjunction with the sales planning committee at Allen headquarters in Detroit. The sales planning committee consisted of the managers of merchandising, advertising, and marketing research. The sales-promotion plan, for both new and existing products, described: objectives; roles of salespersons and dealers; anticipated sales; the national, local, and trade advertising to be used; and the point-of-purchase displays, deals, premiums, or contest offers involved in the promotion.

With approval of the sales-promotion plan by the sales planning committee and the general sales manager, the sales-promotion department prepared a sales-promotion kit for use by the Allen sales staff. The kit included: advertising proofs, product samples, illustrations of the point-of-purchase displays, samples of the premiums that were to be offered, and a description of the special deal or contest featured in the promotion.

The sales-promotion department prepared a timetable for each promotion plan, showing the date when each advertisement appeared in the various media involved in the promotion. The timetable was distributed to the sales force and dealers to enable dealers to time their sales and advertising to coincide with the national advertising, thereby achieving full impact from the advertising.

When the sales-promotion plan was approved by headquarters it was presented to Allen sales personnel at meetings held in each of the six district sales offices. The sales-promotion manager and the field sales-promotion manager, who reported to the former and whose job was to work directly with Allen salespeople and dealers on sales promotion projects, made the presentation to the sales staff. Following the meetings at each of the district offices, the field sales-promotion manager trained the salespeople in the proper presentation of the promotion and then called on key dealers to enlist their support.

The sales-promotion program used with a recent new product introduction was typical of Allen's efforts in this area. In addition to the objectives and timetables, the sales-promotion program for the new product included (1) selling tools for Allen sales-people—circular letters describing the promotion, a visual presentation portfolio for making promotion presentations, product samples, reprints of consumer advertisements; (2) selling tools for Allen dealers—presentation kits for use in selling the new product to consumers, mail circulars for dealers to send to consumers, mailing folders for use by dealers, sample folders, and a considerable amount of prize money for dealers' sales personnel; and (3) advertising support for Allen dealers—advertising in national media, and sample folders to be sent to people who responded to a coupon offer in consumer advertising.

*Evaluate the Allen Specialty Company's organization and plan for coordinating sales and advertising.*

# II-7.   SCRIPTO, INC. (B)[1]:
## Manufacturer of Writing Instruments—
## Relationship Between Sales and Marketing Research

For its marketing-research needs, until the mid-1960s, Scripto, Inc., utilized the services of Audits and Surveys, a national marketing-research firm. However, owing to budgetary restraints in the late 1960s, Scripto eliminated marketing research and channeled its financial resources in other directions. As a result, the writing-instrument company had extremely few of the data it required for important marketing decisions. For example, the company experienced great difficulty in securing comparative data for sales of its products in retail outlets and sales of competitive products.

Determined not to let the void of useful data affect the 19¢er, Scripto management decided again to consider using marketing research. While management was in general agreement that marketing research was an essential ingredient in its marketing orientation and sales strategy, there were two viewpoints as to the type of marketing research most needed for implementation and maintenance of the marketing program for the 19¢er. One group believed that market studies and data were most crucial to the success of the 19¢er; hence, they favored using the services of marketing-research companies, such as Audits and Surveys or A. C. Nielsen Company. Both Audits and Surveys and Nielsen

[1]For background information, see Scripto, Inc. (A), pp. 70-75

prepared bimonthly reports measuring sales and movements of products through stores (the former was used by Papermate). The major differences between the two research companies were (1) cost and (2) type of retail outlet sampled. It would cost Scripto $20,000 to use Audits and Surveys and $25,000 to use Nielsen. Audits and Surveys recorded sales and product movement primarily of mass merchandisers (variety stores) and a relatively small sample of drugstores and grocery stores, while Nielsen sampled more drugstores and grocery stores than A and S, but a smaller sample of variety stores.

Another management group, however, preferred a different course of action—the use of a marketing-research firm that specialized in consumer buying patterns rather than market studies per se. This group contended that consumer research was more instrumental in the future of the 19¢er. Such research was typified by the data generated by the National Consumer Panel of Market Research Corporation of America.

Decisions were required on (1) whether or not to again use marketing research; (2) if so, the type of marketing research most important for Scripto's 19¢er, market studies and/or consumer buying patterns; and (3) the relationship between sales and marketing research.

*What is your position on the three stated problems that had to be solved by Scripto? Defend your arguments.*

## II-8.   DEVONSHIRE BONE CHINA COMPANY:
### British China Manufacturer—
### Need to Improve Selling in United States

Anthony Pelham-Jones, newly appointed sales vice-president for United States and Canada of Devonshire Bone China Company, was concerned with his company's lack of communication with its American outlets. The Devonshire Company had been manufacturing fine chinaware for over two hundred years and twenty-five years ago had been one of the leaders in the American market. English bone china had enjoyed a peak of popularity at the turn of the century, when Devonshire had its period of greatest success in the American and Canadian markets. In those days, a bride did not think that her hope chest was complete unless she had a set of English bone china. Slowly, from that time until the late 1960s, Devonshire's sales fell off, until finally the American market was almost gone.

It was Pelham-Jones' responsibility as sales manager to rebuild the position of Devonshire in the American market for fine chinaware. When he assumed his new job, he believed that at least one of his company's problems had been corrected. Until recently, Devonshire had produced only English designs in its chinaware, failing to recognize a change in the tastes of the American and Canadian consumers. It was expected that several modern designs just introduced would restore the competitive balance from the standpoint of product characteristics.

Pelham-Jones believed that the primary problems left to solve were promotion and dealer relations; and since he hoped to achieve the greater part of the promotion through the cooperative efforts of dealers, the immediate task was to improve the dealer organization. Until 1939, U.S. sales had been handled by several independent importers, all of whom carried competing lines and had no interest in promoting one line over the others. At that date, an American sales subsidiary was formed to provide better promotional efforts, but the advent of World War II shut down British exports to the United States, almost eliminating Devonshire from the American market. For a number of years after the war, little effort was made to recapture a share of the market. Management seemed to feel that the Devonshire name was so strong that customers would beat a path to their door. Only three salespeople were provided to cover the 500 retail outlets in the United States and Canada.

When Pelham-Jones was appointed vice-president, he was given full responsibility for marketing in the United States and Canada. Within four months he had added five new salespeople, bringing the force up to eight. All staff members were required to live in their territories to increase their accessibility to customers. Efforts were concentrated on bringing in new retail outlets, and sales presentation kits were provided to aid in this task. Call schedules were set up, ensuring that large accounts were visited at least every six weeks. Salespeople were also given advice on how to select promising new prospects. Finally, the sales staff was for the first time given quotas, based on estimated sales potentials.

In conjunction with the steps taken to improve the sales force, Pelham-Jones introduced a program of product testing. Each new pattern was pretested in the American market to ensure acceptability. In the most recent test, seventeen of eighteen new designs were rejected for sale in the American market.

Despite gratifying increases in sales, the sales manager was still dissatisfied with the product's performance. So, in 1970, he invested in a survey of retail stores and retail salespeople, conducted by an independent research organization. According to the survey, retail salespeople offered little help or counseling to customers and cared hardly at all which brand of china they sold.

*Outline a program to help improve the selling of Devonshire china at the retail level.*

## II-9.   MORRIS MACHINE WORKS:
## Manufacturer of Centrifugal Pumps—
## Relations with Dealers

The Morris Machine Works of Baldwinsville, New York, was established in 1864 and was the first American company to manufacture centrifugal pumps. Morris pumps were sold to industrial users throughout the United States by thirty-two manufacturers' representatives, each of whom operated in an exclusive territory. Three representatives in Canada handled sales in that country, but all other foreign sales were made through various export houses. The majority of Morris products were manufactured to users' specifications, and the company required its representatives to be technically trained. Consequently, most representatives either were engineers or included engineers on their staffs. The turnover among representatives was very low, but the arrangement used for splitting commissions on interterritorial sales had been a continuing source of friction. Although the sales manager did not consider this problem of major importance, he had recently decided to review the entire situation.

Every Morris agent was required to sign an agreement governing his relations with the company (see Exhibit 1). This agreement included a general statement of company policy on the splitting of commissions among distributors. This statement did not provide specific rules for handling every situation that might arise. Consequently, this statement of written policy was not useful in handling many of the disputes among the manufacturer's agents.

EXHIBIT 1
Standard Form Used for Agreements with
Manufacturers' Agents

*Introduction:*

This Agreement has been adopted for governing the relations between the MORRIS MACHINE WORKS and its Agents, and between the different Agents of the MORRIS MACHINE WORKS in order to promote efficiency and cooperation.

It is realized that absolute and fast rules cannot be formulated to govern all conditions, but that fairness and justice must supplement all rules.

All questions as to interpretation of these rules or questions as to points not covered are to be passed upon by the Home Office, and its decisions are to be considered final.

In accepting the MORRIS MACHINE WORKS account, the Agent agrees to the provisions of these rules.

*Definition of Agent:*

The term AGENT (Representative or District Manager) as employed herein is used to designate such individuals, partnerships, or firms who are regularly accredited MORRIS MACHINE WORKS representatives, who have a definite exclusive territory, who have prices and discounts covering a full line of MORRIS MACHINE WORKS equipment, or in some cases one complete line only of MORRIS MACHINE WORKS manufacture, who do not handle any competing product, and who are active in promoting the sale of MORRIS MACHINE WORKS equipment.

*Definition of Territory:*

The term TERRITORY as used herein will designate only the area in which the Agent has exclusive rights to sell MORRIS MACHINE WORKS products, subject to such limitations and exceptions as are hereinafter specified. Only such an area will be assigned to an Agent as exclusive territory as he can actually cover; that is, in which the Agent can, and will, personally solicit business. Such territory as is not included in any Agent's exclusive territory will be open to all agents and to the Home Office; but to avoid complications, the Agents should communicate with the Home Office before quoting in the open territory.

Agents will not solicit in another Agent's territory except with that Agent's permission.

*Prices, Price Lists, and Data:*

MORRIS MACHINE WORKS will quote the Agents its best agent's prices and discounts in all cases, and will furnish price lists, data sheets, drawings, and catalogs as required, and will assist the Agent in every way with information and data.

Price lists, drawings, etc., are the property of MORRIS MACHINE WORKS and subject to return upon request.

Detailed drawings will not be furnished except in special cases, and when furnished must not be allowed to pass out of the Agent's hands, and must be returned to the Home Office when their purpose has been accomplished.

*Allocation of Inquiries and Orders:*

An Agent has exclusive rights to solicit and sell MORRIS equipment within his territory, and all inquiries and orders originating in that territory will be referred to, and credited to, that Agent except as provided hereinafter.

An inquiry received by an Agent from another Agent's territory is to be referred by him either to the Home Office or direct to the Agent for that territory.

Inquiries from dealers or from purchasing and engineering departments within an Agent's territory, for equipment destined to go into another Agent's territory, may be quoted on by that Agent, particularly if purchases are expected to be made in his territory; but a division must be made of the commission with the Agent into whose territory the equipment will go, as provided hereinafter.

*Direct Quotations by the Home Office:*

The right is reserved by MORRIS MACHINE WORKS to quote and to deal directly, without commission, for any Agent in the following cases:

1. On federal and state work that is publicly advertised and covered completely by the specifications.
2. To export houses, for shipment outside the United States or Canada.
3. To manufacturers, for resale as a component part of that manufacturer's equipment, to enable that manufacturer to quote competitive prices without the ultimate consumer having to pay two commissions.
4. On repair and replacement parts for equipment originally sold through other Agents or direct from the Home Office.

*Commission:*

The Agent's compensation will be entirely through commissions on sales. The Agent will be credited the difference between the sales price and the Agent's prices.

Commissions will be paid the Agent as payments are received from the customer except as may be agreed.

Acceptance of orders is subject to approval by the Home Office.

The Agent, knowing his trade, is given the privilege to fix his commission and add same to the Agent's price. The right is reserved, however, by the Home Office to fix the amount of an Agent's commission in special cases in accordance with the price lists and discounts.

1. The full amount of commission will be paid the Agent on all sales made by him for shipment within his territory.
2. If the sale is made by one Agent for shipment into another Agent's territory, two thirds of the commission will be paid to the Agent making the sale, and one third to the territorial Agent.
3. If inquiry originates and is preliminarily negotiated in the Agent's territory into which shipment will go, but must be further negotiated and sale closed in another Agent's territory, commission will be equally divided.
4. If necessary to make a sale by the Home Office for shipment into an Agent's territory, that Agent is to receive one half of the Agent's commission.
5. No credit or commission will be given an Agent on orders placed in his territory but destined for shipment elsewhere, and which did not originate or were not negotiated in his territory.

*Service and Cooperation:*

In accepting the MORRIS MACHINE WORKS account, the Agent is considered as having assumed an obligation to cooperate with other Agents and with the Home Office in promoting the sale of MORRIS equipment.

The Agent is to give assistance to prospective customers, regardless of what territory they may come from, in obtaining the required information, in making selections of equipment, in installing and operating MORRIS equipment, etc.

*Duration of Contract:*

The duration of the contract is for one year, and it is self-perpetuating unless three months' notice to terminate is given by either party.

MORRIS MACHINE WORKS

By:_____

Date:_____

Accepted by:_____

Date:_____

---

The initiation, negotiation, and final installation involved with one contract occurred in three separate territories, illustrating the difficulties of reaching an agreement on the division of commissions. A large aluminum producer, whose main office was located in Richmond, Virginia, was planning to build a plant in Corpus Christi, Texas, and a San Francisco firm was the contractor-engineer. Thus, three agents were involved: the Richmond agent who made the sale, the San Francisco agent who performed the required engineering, and the Corpus Christi agent who was responsible for proper installation and service. All three representatives incurred some costs in connection with this sale; therefore, each should have received some compensation. The out-of-pocket costs of the Richmond agent were the lowest, but his influence was the deciding factor in the sale. The agent in Corpus Christi stood to profit from this installation in the future, since he would receive commissions on all repair parts for the pumps. The commission split in this case could have posed a problem for the sales manager, had not the parties involved reached a mutual agreement independent of the home office.

Such problems were not always so easily solved, since disputing parties customarily looked to the Morris sales manager for a final decision. It was often difficult to work out compromises satisfactory to all parties. Because representatives were not employees but independent business people, it also was difficult to enforce such decisions.

Two solutions had been suggested to the sales manager. One was to pay the entire commission to the representative into whose territory shipment was made, regardless of who originated, negotiated, or closed the sale. The second suggestion called for establishment of a fixed schedule of payments for certain activities or conditions. The schedule was as follows:

10 percent for first quotation
10 percent for second quotation
15 percent to the territory in which equipment was installed
25 percent to the agent completing the purchase order
40 percent for influence on the sale

Thus far, the sales manager had rejected both proposals.

*Was the sales manager justified in rejecting both proposals? Why or why not?*

## II-10.   DELPHIC CORPORATION:
## Manufacturer of Appliances and Electronic Equipment—
### Distributor-Dealer Sales Training

The Delphic Corporation, located in St. Louis, Missouri, was one of the leaders in the electronics and appliance fields. The exclusive business of this corporation was the design, manufacture, sale, and, for large jobs, installation of this equipment. The Modern Kitchen Division manufactured a broad line of kitchen cabinets, dishwashers, and garbage disposals for residential use; these products were sold throughout the United States and Canada by a large distributor-dealer organization. This distributor-dealer network was expanding rapidly to meet the increasing desire for kitchen modernization. The sales-training department of the division, which in its two years of existence had become an important factor in Delphic's sales program, had developed a wide variety of training aids and was looking for additional ways to widen the scope and increase the effectiveness of its training activities. Refrigerators and ranges were manufactured and sold by the Major Appliance Division.

The Modern Kitchen Division had a sales volume of $38 million. No sales were made directly to ultimate consumers; all equipment was sold through franchised distributors and dealers by sixty salespeople who worked out of twenty-two branch offices. Delphic was one of the first to institute this type of distribution in the appliance industry, and executives were proud of the fact that many of the dealers originally franchised in the early 1930s still handled the line.

Franchises were written for a specific product with an assignment of a definite territory, within which the distributor or dealer was responsible for the sale of that product. The distributor-dealer organization consisted of eighty distributors and 2,000 dealers. Distributors were primarily merchandisers, promoting sales to their own organization of "associate" dealers, who were selected by the distributor, and controlled entirely by him. Dealers' territories were nonexclusive and were subject to change upon written notice. Technical and sales assistance were rendered by the distributor, aided when necessary by Delphic field personnel.

Associate dealers were primarily appliance stores, department stores, and hardware stores; but businesses such as plumbing and electrical contractors were also included. When selecting associate dealers, the distributor usually considered may factors. The distributor had to consider the prospective dealer's location, both in the area and in the city, his credit standing, and his personal integrity. Delphic distributors met with keen competition for dealers from other manufacturers and had to offer more than just a franchise and a convenient warehouse location. The distributor had the Delphic reputation to offer but, in many cases, he was expected to finance the initial stock of equipment. Training in kitchen-equipment sales and kitchen layout, and installation, were offered to dealers to enable them to become profitable producers.

Delphic's sales volume had more than doubled in the previous five years, and the number of retail outlets (associate dealers) increased in about the same proportion. Training of newer dealers became highly important to the success of the distributors' expanded operations. Each distributor looked to Delphic for assistance, and much of the task of dealer training was shifted to the manufacturer.

Before the sales-training department of the Modern Kitchen Division was organized, training was the responsibility of product managers. Under this arrangement, training was not given sufficient attention because of the pressing nature of other duties assigned to product managers—the design, development, manufacture, and sale of the various products, for instance. Although training was recognized as an important activity, a comprehensive study of dealers' needs was not made, and the overall training program lacked organization. After the sales-training department was formed, an analysis was made of all previous training methods and materials, and this department became the centralized source for all such aids. Sessions were held with distributors throughout the country to determine their requirements, and from the survey there evolved a variety of packaged training courses, films, and a monthly informational service. A booklet entitled *Dealer Training* was published as a guide for planning a dealer-training program.

It was decided that the sales-training department could best satisfy distributors' needs for materials and methods for training dealers with a program that covered three areas of interest: sales, installation, and management, that is, "business development." Accordingly, a series of packaged courses was made available under the name "Business Development Program." Training courses were prepared for each of the three product lines normally sold through associate dealers: kitchen cabinets, dishwashers, and garbage disposals. Student packets were made available for a nominal fee. Meeting guides were also prepared to aid the instructor in emphasizing the more important points and to indicate the normal amount of time and detail required for a particular phase of training.

One unit of the package training course on dishwashers was entitled "Selling Dishwashers." This unit dealt with problems encountered in selling home units and included some selling fundamentals applicable to automatic dishwashing. The material was printed in looseleaf form, and a complete packet was provided for each trainee. The course was built around nine selling steps:

1. Get set to sell.
2. Spark interest.
3. Dramatize the need.
4. Make the survey.
5. Prepare the proposal.
6. Present the proposal.
7. Capitalize on objections.
8. Get the order.
9. Follow through.

Each step was elaborated on and detailed to apply to actual situations encountered in the sale of dishwashers. For example, step 7, "capitalize on objections," listed objections that might be voiced by prospects, and each had a well-thought-out answer. A recommended procedure for handling competition and price objections was outlined, and sample letters effective for "getting back in" were exhibited. Also included were sales arguments and approaches to be used with the consumer, architect, builder, and real-estate agent. Sample proposal and submittal sheets were added as examples of recommended practice. Finally, the packet included a brochure that illustrated the available advertising and promotional aids, along with booklets that reproduced, in printed form, two sound-slide films used for selling dishwashers. One was for showing to the home owner, the other for showing to builders and realtors.

To introduce the new training material, sales-training-department personnel presented the courses at meetings of Delphic field representatives. The Delphic sales personnel presented the courses to distributor wholesale salespeople, who then held meetings with dealer personnel for whom the material was primarily prepared. The first sessions were for the purpose of "training the trainer" and were considered highly successful. The printed material was supported by films and/or sound-slide films, attractively prepared to appeal to dealers. The intention was to "sell" the dealer while training him to sell the retail customer. Training was considered a continuing activity, and many distributors recognized the usefulness of weekly training. Sales training was not overlooked, often constituting the bulk of the weekly training, and materials from St. Louis were frequently used to good advantage.

An important feature of Delphic's sales-training program was the "Sales Planning Series," which was made up of eleven separate units with companion films. The series was concerned with practical procedure and was a digest of successful selling practices followed by Delphic equipment salespersons. The eleven parts covered each of the nine previously cited steps in the sale, plus two preliminary steps, "Plan Your Time" and "Plan Your Sales." A student packet and meeting guide were available for each section. In the packet was a printed reproduction of the companion film, interspersed with self-improvement exercises that the student was to think out individually. The "Sales Planning Series" was the backbone of the Delphic training program, which provided basic selling instruction for the novice and for the experienced dealer's salesperson, and served as a means for evaluating and organizing one's sales practices.

Each month, a file folder of facts called the "Business Development Service" was distributed. Issues of this publication contained samples of new training materials, successful selling ideas, information on competitive activities, reports from other distributors, tips on getting and handling dealers, hints on improving personnel performance, advice on where to obtain training aids equipment such as projectors and flannel boards, and always a "Lost Sale" quiz, a cartoon-type lesson from *Sales Management* magazine.

One of the features of Delphic's "Business Development" program was a sales-control system developed especially for the retail salesperson. The system made it possible to organize and simplify record keeping of prospect activity and selling schedules, and it provided the sales manager with information on the salespeople's progress. Another development in the management-training field was being closely followed by the sales-training department; this was the recent formation of the Atlanta Corporation. This wholly owned subsidiary of Delphic Corporation, staffed with personnel from all parts of the Delphic organization, took over the distributorship in the Atlanta area and had an organization of associate dealers in operation. From Atlanta's experience, the home-office executives expected to learn more about the problems of distributors, so that better sales, engineering, and management assistance might be provided. This subsidiary also was to be used as a proving ground, especially with respect to new marketing techniques.

*Evaluate the methods used by the Delphic Corporation for training its distributors and dealers.*

# II-11.   HILLMAN PRODUCTS COMPANY:
## Manufacturer of Power Tools—
## Distributor-Dealer Problems

James Weston, Director of Sales and Marketing for Hillman Products Company, Springfield, Massachusetts, was faced with the problem of taking remedial action to improve the company's distributor and dealer relationships, which had steadily worsened. The effect of the worsening relationships was reflected in the latest company sales report, which recorded a 12 percent sales decline during the past year and a 17 percent decline over the past two years.

Hillman Products Company manufactured a wide line of power tools, such as saws, drills, and sanders, for use by the home handyman. Hillman products were distributed nationwide through ninety distributors, who, in turn, sold to more than 8,500 retail outlets. During the past two years, the number of distributors handling Hillman products had dropped from 115 to the present 90 and, while the number of retailers had remained about the same, the sales per dealer had substantially declined.

Several factors combined to cause a disturbingly high turnover rate among Hillman dealers, as well as to contribute to declining sales for Hillman products. The locations of many Hillman dealers were unfavorable. Dealer sales personnel were untrained and poorly informed about Hillman products. Few dealers did any advertising for the Hillman product line. Virtually all dealers carried competing lines and devoted little effort to selling the Hillman line. And, many retailers bought in such small quantities, often a single unit of each Hillman product, that sales were frequently lost to competitors because of stockouts.

The dealers showed little loyalty to Hillman products. Also, they knew little and understood less of the company's history, policies, performance, or capabilities. The sole contact the dealers had with Hillman was through the distributors and their salespeople, who themselves were often poorly informed. Many Hillman dealers expressed considerable dissatisfaction with the company and its distributors for actions such as overloading dealers with more products than they could ever hope to sell in a given period and, especially, for the total lack of company support in local newspaper advertising.

Hillman distributors criticized dealers for what they claimed was deceptive dealer advertising and because most dealers ignored the manufacturer's suggested retail prices. Some distributors had dropped the Hillman line and taken on competing lines.

Weston believed that immediate action was necessary to prevent further deterioration of the situation and to improve distributor-dealer relations. Consequently, he proposed a two-fold plan: (1) establishing a distributor-dealer relations staff at company headquarters, and (2) retaining a management consultant to investigate dealer operations.

The distributor-dealer relations staff would determine attitudes toward the Hillman company and its policies and make recommendations for the improvement of relations. Weston hoped that this would result in better understanding between Hillman and its various outlets and would serve to improve communications. To help distributors and dealers sell more Hillman products, the distributor-dealer relations staff would plan and implement a program of sales development, promotion, and mechanical service assistance for Hillman dealers.

Under Weston's plan, the management consultant would be asked to survey fifty of the most successful Hillman dealers to determine the best methods for merchandising Hillman products. Information from the survey would be used in designing and implementing the program of sales development, promotion, and mechanical service assistance.

Weston firmly believed that these two measures would reverse the alarming situation of poor distributor-dealer relations and would pave the way for more efficient marketing of Hillman products.

*Evaluate Weston's proposal for improving Hillman Products Company's distributor-dealer relations. Give the reasons for your position.*

# II-12.   SCRIPTO, INC. (C)[1]:

## Manufacturer of writing Instruments— Resistance in the Distributive Network

With its low retail price, the Scripto 19¢er yielded considerably less revenue per unit for the middlemen, and Scripto encounted resistance from some wholesalers and retailers who were reluctant to place the 19¢er on already overcrowded shelves. Consequently, Scripto management was searching for ways to break this resistance and gain trade acceptance of the 19¢er.

*What should Scripto have done to gain middlemen's acceptance of the 19¢er? Defend your solution.*

[1]For background information, see Scripto, Inc. (A), pp. 70-75.

# Part III

# SALES-FORCE MANAGEMENT

# 9

# Personnel Management
# in the Selling Field

Managing the sales department's human resources is an important concern of sales executives at all organizational levels. Since it is the salesperson who is responsible for achieving an important objective of the company, that of selling the product, every sales executive has an interest in the salesperson's success. For some sales executives successful performance by the sales personnel is the single most important responsibility. Sales supervisors, the level of administrators directly above the salespeople, commonly devote the bulk of their energies and time to managing the sales force. Others spend relatively less time on managing salespersons' activities but are concerned, nevertheless, with their effectiveness. Certain middle-level sales executives, such as regional sales managers, serve in line capacities managing lower-echelon sales executives who, in turn, manage the sales force. Other middle-level sales executives specialize either in some aspect of sales-force management (for example, sales training) or in a phase of marketing (for example, brand promotion) that affects the salesperson's job.

At the top of the organizational structure, the chief sales executive has general responsibility not only for managing subordinate sales executives and through them for managing the sales personnel, but also for the management of other important sales and marketing activities. Thus, as sales executives move to and through middle management levels and higher, they must retain their concern for management of the sales force. However, pressures of the responsibilities added as they move up causes them to ration their efforts among a growing and diverse set of responsibilities. They not only retain concern for sales-force management but participate increasingly in such important decision areas as long-range planning and forecasting, structuring the product line, setting prices, planning promotional programs, and managing marketing channels and physical distribution. Regardless of this, however, sales executives should never forget that one of the main reasons for their own job's existence is to contribute to the effectiveness of the sales force as it goes about obtaining sales, and implementing sales management's plans and decisions.

Management of a sales force involves several distinct and important activities. Promising new salespeople must be recruited and selected, as described in Chapter 10.

New sales personnel need introducing to their jobs and require orientation with respect to company policies and products to assure that they know how to discharge their primary job responsibility—selling; training makes up the subject matter of both Chapter 11 (Planning and Conducting Sales-Training Programs) and Chapter 12 (Instruction in Sales Techniques). Because salespeople are generally isolated from their fellow workers, it is particularly important to provide them with motivation, as analyzed in Chapter 13 (Motivating the Individual Salesperson). This same isolation feature of the salespeople's jobs also requires special communication, morale building, and motivational efforts, as discussed in Chapter 14 (Sales Meetings and Contests). Both the level and method of compensating sales personnel vary considerably from the compensation practices of most other employees, as described in Chapter 15 (Compensating Sales Personnel). The task of dividing a market among a group of salespersons to ensure optimum sales coverage by the sales staff is complex, as described in Chapter 16 (Assigning Sales Personnel to Territories). Finally, the sales manager has unique problems in evaluating and supervising the performance of the sales force, and these are analyzed in Chapter 17 (Evaluating and Supervising Sales Personnel). Part III, then, focuses on those activities that collectively make up sales-force management.

## SALES-FORCE MANAGEMENT

Sales-force management is a specialized version of personnel management. Yet, there are good reasons why the responsibility for sales-force management is assigned to sales executives rather than to personnel executives. While the same set of basic human problems must be dealt with in personnel management of sales, production, or office workers, each class of problem varies in nature and importance with the work field. In contrast to production and office workers, for example, sales personnel most often work independently; therefore, close and constant supervision is usually impractical. In further contrast, salespeople generally work at some distance from their immediate superiors and coworkers, so it is more difficult to develop a spirit of identity with and loyalty to the company and to weld them into a unified team.

Of necessity, then, sales personnel are given freer rein than most other workers at the comparable organizational level. To a considerable degree they must be relied upon as individuals to plan and control their own activities. Despite a growing trend for sales-people and executives to travel more by air, a salesperson's visits to the home office are still usually infrequent, and centralized direction of his or her activities continues to be mainly by letter, telegraph, or long-distance telephone. The nature of the salesperson's job provides only limited opportunity for face-to-face contact and supervision. Indeed, because of this necessary independence, sales personnel are often described as "account administrators."

Still other unique conditions surround the salesperson's job, often requiring that he or she be away from home and family for extended periods. It involves great dependence upon human actions and reactions. Disheartening order turndowns and dealings with rude customers frequently require the salesperson to repress natural responses and to suppress a natural tendency to become discouraged. The psychological effects of such conditions accentuate the need for sales management's continual attention to motivational factors.

## SIMILARITIES TO CONVENTIONAL
## PERSONNEL MANAGEMENT

Although there are distinctive features of sales-force management, there are similarities to conventional personnel management. People are still being managed, and substantially the same human relations concepts are applicable. Sales personnel share feelings resembling those of other employees with respect to job tenure, old-age security, guaranteed wages, and equality of opportunity.

The basic steps in general personnel management are equally basic to sales-force management. The starting point in all personnel work is job analysis, to determine the nature of each position in terms of its component tasks. Then, each job is evaluated to ascertain the necessary qualifications of employees. Next, there is the recruiting of qualified applicants, and the sales executive must be well informed with respect to prospective sources of employees. From the supply of applications, it is necessary to select those who meet the job specifications and, through interviewing and testing techniques, to evaluate qualifications of applicants. Once a person is hired, sales-force management focuses attention on training, which ranges from informal instruction to highly organized formal programs; training may consume a few hours or several years, depending upon the complexity of the selling job. An additional step is to develop compensation plans, and these range all the way from the straight salary to the straight commission.

Once a salesperson is assigned to the field, other personnel problems are encountered. The salesperson must be motivated and encouraged to plan and make productive use of working time. If a salesperson is to maximize the effectiveness of sales calls, counseling aimed at improving working habits and methods is required. The final step in sales-force management relates to control, which involves analysis of selling and other records with the objective of improving the planning and supervising of operations. For example, the salesperson's work week may be analyzed to determine the proportion of time spent in actual selling. Such information is used to plan territory coverage and to evaluate selling performance. Each of these aspects of sales-force management is discussed in greater detail in following chapters.

## INTERRELATIONS OF SALES-FORCE
## MANAGEMENT ACTIVITIES

The various activities performed in sales-force management mesh together and should be thought of as a system. Faulty execution of any part of the system results in complications for other parts. If a substandard job of recruiting and selecting is done, tasks involved in training are magnified, problems of supervision become greater, motivating and controlling salespersons is more difficult, and the sales-force turnover rate is accelerated. If training is inadequate or poorly administered, potentially good people fail to reach high productivity, the compensation system does not work as planned, supervision is ineffective, and there is high personnel turnover. Similar difficulties arise in cases of ineffective performance of other activities in the sales-force management system.

### Economies of Effective Sales-Force Management

Economies result from effective sales-force management. Assume that Company X has ten salespersons, each making five calls per day, a total of fifty per day for the company. If, through better management and control of workday activities, each sales-person increases the number of calls to six per day, the company's total calls per day become sixty. This is equivalent to adding two new salespeople at the old call rate. If sales personnel are paid wholly, or partially, on a commission basis, their incomes are now higher; and improved morale reduces turnover. Because some costs are related directly to the number of salespeople, the company's average cost per call is also reduced.

The expenses of maintaining sales people may be divided into fixed items identical for all sales personnel regardless of efficiency, and into variable items costing proportion-ately more for the least effective salespeople. Fixed expenses include those for transporta-tion and traveling, equipment (automobiles, sales folios, sales manuals, and so forth), and advertising used to assist the sales force. These expenses are essentially the same for every salesperson. Variable items are those for which the most efficient salespeople spend less than inefficient salespeople, and they include expenses for training, motivating, supervis-ing, controlling, and evaluating. For these items a company usually receives its highest return from its best salespeople.

Fixed and incentive pay are classified separately. From the fixed portion of compen-sation, the poor salesperson usually receives more than he or she deserves and the good salesperson is underpaid. Because the incentive portion of compensation varies with pro-ductivity, it is generally true that individuals are paid amounts proportionate to their efficiency. A useful generalization, which should be kept in mind by sales executives, is that expenses per unit of product sold tend to vary inversely with effectiveness of the salesperson.

### Reducing the Rate of Personnel Turnover

One measure of the quality of sales-force management is the rate of turnover of the sales personnel. This is calculated as the ratio of separations per 100 salespeople. For example, a company employing a sales force with an average strength of 250 persons and having twenty separations during the year has a rate of turnover of 8 percent.[1]

The sales executive should keep the turnover rate at a reasonable figure, because costs of sale-force management are strongly affected by the turnover rate. Costs of recruiting, advertising, fees to employment agencies, and so forth, often cost in excess of $250 per recruit. Interviewing costs are also high, because most companies interview several applicants for each selection. If an interview by an executive takes two hours, and executive time is worth $10 per hour, total interviewing costs amount to $600 per person hired if thirty people are considered for each vacancy. The costs of travel and time used for preparatory and follow-up training run as high as $2,500 per person.

Some costs are not so readily calculated. For example, new recruits do not usually produce as much as experienced sales personnel, and the ratio of selling expenses to sales for a new person is likely to be excessive for at least the first year. A conservative estimate of these excess costs is at least $3,500 per new salesperson during the first year, and in some companies this cost will be higher because it takes even longer for a sales-person to get fully into stride.

[1] A convenient formula for calculating the rate of sales personnel turnover is:

$$\text{Rate of personnel turnover (expressed as a percentage)} = \frac{\text{number of separations} \times 100}{\text{average total sales force}}$$

When costs of breaking in a new salesperson are totaled, a sizable sum is seen to be at stake. In a survey of member companies, the American Management Association several years ago found that the average cost for replacing a salesperson was $6,684. Almost one fourth of the respondents said their costs of turnover were $10,000 or more per salesperson. A few placed the cost at over $20,000.[2] No recent study is available, but a conservative estimate is that the current average cost of salesperson replacement exceeds $10,000.

The costs of personnel turnover can account for a significant drain on profits. For example, in a company with a sales force of 400 and an annual turnover rate of 25 percent, if the costs of replacing a single salesperson come to $10,000, the annual costs of turnover total $1 million—and this relates only to out-of-pocket costs. Other important costs are increased expenses for supervision and motivation, lost business, decline in customer goodwill from mistakes of inexperienced salespersons, and miscellaneous expenses associated with taking on people who do not succeed. Few companies have accounting systems that permit quantitative measurement of the impact on profit of excessive personnel turnover. But it cannot be denied that profits are lower because inexperienced salespeople are assigned where turnover has occurred. Profits are not realized from sales never consummated.

Little comparative information is available on average turnover rates for sales personnel in various industries. However, the annual turnover of sales personnel in companies selling staples and industrial products is usually less than 5 percent. Companies selling intangibles, such as insurance, securities, and specialty or luxury items have a higher rate, sometimes 50 percent per year. Sales forces of manufacturers generally show a lower rate than those of wholesalers; and firms whose salespeople call on middlemen and industrial users commonly experience less turnover than those engaged in door-to-door selling.

All turnover is not bad, even though it may seem expensive at the time. Many sales executives report that most salespeople who leave a company have less than three years of service. In other words, turnover is largely accounted for by relatively new personnel. If a person is proving unsuccessful, and it is likely that he or she will leave eventually, it is desirable that he or she do so immediately. The earlier the unsuccessful person leaves, the better for the salesperson and the company, both in terms of dollar costs and in terms of effect upon attitudes of other salespeople. Too low a rate of turnover may indicate that the sales force is overloaded with veterans who do not produce as much as new personnel might. Where this situation exists, it may be assumed that the entire system of sales-force management needs reexamining and possible overhauling. Some turnover is desirable. A sales force with no turnover may be growing stale; prospective new salespeople are not attracted, and older persons may linger on because of management laxity and the comparative security of established positions.

The age distribution among sales personnel should be analyzed for its impact on sales-force turnover. It is usually desirable to have salespersons' ages spread over a wide range. Otherwise, the productivity curves for all may rise together, with all reaching their peaks and decline together, and all reaching retirement at the same time. Under these circumstances, it is necessary eventually to recruit an entire sales force almost at once, at considerable loss in market coverage and customer relations. Companies should establish an average length of service, which management considers desirable for sales personnel,

[2]"It Costs $6,684 to Fire a Man," *Sales Management* (March 15, 1955), p. 29.

before evaluating the turnover rate. If management decides that the average length of service should be twenty years, then, assuming no errors in selection, the personnel turnover rate should be 5 percent—one twentieth of the sales force should be replaced each year. Because even the best selection procedure is far from perfect, the actual turnover rate would run higher than 5 percent. In addition, many people do not take sales jobs with the intention of keeping them forever. A sales job is often the springboard to higher positions, and a company using its sales force as a source of managerial talent should anticipate higher turnover.

Awareness of the current turnover rate is also necessary for planning the operation of service functions. The personnel turnover rate is an important factor in planning recruiting, selection, and training programs. For example, a company with a turnover rate of 25 percent is replacing its sales force every four years. It must organize its service functions to handle an annual volume of new recruits equivalent to one fourth of its sales force. The costs and extent of the recruitment selection and training programs largely depend upon the magnitude of turnover.

The personnel turnover rate should be analyzed periodically to determine the causes. Analysis often uncovers areas where improvement is needed. A useful information source is a terminal interview between the departing salesperson and either a line executive or a personnel consultant. This exit interview provides the sales executive with an opportunity to identify conditions contributing to personnel turnover. Identification enables management to modify or correct conditions that lie within its control.

Causes of personnel turnover can be separated into two main groupings, as shown in Figure 9.1. Management should take appropriate corrective action when the causes are largely concentrated on the conrollable list, particularly when turnover is caused by reasons 1 through 7. Turnover resulting from reason 8 sometimes is unavoidable, and that resulting from 9 and 10 is usually desirable. Managerial action may be called for, even in the cases of some reasons appearing on the "not controllable" list; in fact, only reasons 2, 3, and 6 may be regarded as completely unavoidable.

FIGURE 9.1
Causes of Turnover of Sales Personnel

| Caused by Actions Controllable by Company | Caused by Actions Not Controllable by Company |
| --- | --- |
| 1. Poor recruiting | 1. Retirement |
| 2. Improper selection and assignment | 2. Death |
| 3. Training deficiencies | 3. Illness or physical disability |
| 4. Inadequate supervision and motivation | 4. Personal and marital difficulties |
| 5. Breakdown in communications | 5. Dislike for the job—travel, type of work, working conditions, etc. |
| 6. Unsatisfactory performance—customer complaints, etc. | 6. Military duty |
| 7. Discharged for cause, e.g., alcoholism, conviction of a felony, dishonesty, etc. | 7. Better position elsewhere |
| 8. Cutbacks in personnel | |
| 9. Transfer to another department | |
| 10. Promotion to a higher position | |

## SALES EXECUTIVE AS LEADER

Competent sales executives are leaders, rather than drivers, of people. They earn and retain the voluntary cooperation of their followers, inspiring them to strive willingly toward mutual goals. They coordinate their followers' activities so that efficiency of the group is maintained at a high level; they find ways to overcome difficulties in the application of sales plans and policies; and they devise methods for dealing with other problems. Development of leadership ability is a matter of great importance.

Contrary to popular belief, leadership ability can be developed. Although some executives may be "born leaders," most acquire leadership ability through education, training, and experience. It is not possible, of course, for everyone to become a leader; not everyone possesses, or can acquire, the necessary qualifications. As to the exact nature of these qualifications, management writers are divided. Several have constructed lists of leadership traits.[3] Among the items included in such lists are:

1. The true leader possesses a high degree of self-control and has stable emotions. An executive who is moody and inconsistent misleads subordinates. If they are unable to judge their superior's reactions, they cease to function as a team.

2. A leader has a thorough understanding of how people think and react. By absorbing many points of view—those of superiors, associates, subordinates, competitors, and others—a leader can anticipate their reactions to particular situations.

3. A leader is decisive—both willing and able to make decisions. The poor administrator makes decisions by default, delaying and hoping that someone else will bring forth the solution or that the problem will solve itself. The effective leader decides and then acts. Because the decision is reached after a careful review of the facts, the leader acts with confidence.

4. The leader readily accepts responsibility. Although the capable executive delegates authority to subordinates according to their abilities, he or she willingly accepts final responsibility for their actions and never shirks responsibilities.

5. The leader's mental ability is superior to the majority of the followers, yet the leader is not surrounded exclusively with less able people. The leader secures capable subordinates to whom authority can be delegated, and develops the most capable of these as possible successors.

6. The leader is technically competent, skilled in the discharge of particular administrative tasks. The leader also has some competence in tasks assigned to subordinates; this is a prerequisite to effective training and supervision.

7. The leader possesses the ability to communicate ideas and thoughts clearly. Subordinates carry out the program more fully because they understand what is expected. Top management regards the leader more highly because the leader succeeds in communicating plans and needs effectively.

8. The leader has the ability to teach and to motivate others. The good leader knows peoples' motivations, desires, and ambitions, and uses this knowledge to lead them into the necessary activity—whether it is learning or performing.

9. The leader enjoys above-average health and energy, and sets the pace for the followers, and physical stamina enables the leader to do his or her own job alertly and enthusiastically.

[3]See, for example, James J. Cribbin, *Effective Managerial Leadership* (New York: American Management Association, Inc., 1972); Paul Hersey, *Management of Organizational Behavior* (Englewood Cliffs, N.J.: Prentice-Hall, Inc., 1972); Philip Selznick, *Leadership in Administration* (New York: Harper & Row, Inc., 1958); George T. Vardaman, *Dynamics of Managerial Leadership* (Philadelphia: Auerbach Publishers, Inc., 1973).

Beyond possessing leadership traits, the executive leader must use tested management procedures. First, as many problems as possible should be made subjects of group thinking. People cooperate more willingly in carrying out policies they have helped to make. Subordinates should feel that some plans are *their plans,* not directives imposed from above; but this does not mean that the administrator should abdicate executive responsibilities. The final decision is still the executive's. After problems have been discussed with subordinates, it is up to the executive to face the issues and decide.

Second, a leader is courteous to subordinates. Courtesy goes beyond mere politeness; it reflects sincere consideration for the ideas and feelings of others. Politeness is an outward manifestation of good manners. Courtesy and consideration arise from a genuine interest in others. Subordinates are quick to recognize the difference.

Third, a leader gives credit where it is due. When a subordinate's idea proves successful, recognition should be given. Some executives are too easily tempted to accept credit for subordinates' ideas in order to build personal prestige. In the long run, this discourages the submission of ideas and destroys the executive's effectiveness.

Finally, the leader sets a good example. The "do as I say, not as I do" approach is not effective in motivating people. The executive works with the same diligence he or she expects of the staff, and the executive leads his or her life as he or she expects them to lead theirs. It is natural for subordinates to emulate their superior. The superior is, or should be, a symbol of success.

## UNIONIZATION OF SALES PERSONNEL

The salesperson has been the target of organizing drives by various unions since the Great Depression of the 1930s. Despite such efforts, unions have made only slight inroads in organizing sales personnel as compared with their success elsewhere. There are several reasons. First, in most sales departments it is difficult to develop strong group identification because each person works alone and sees his or her peers on the sales force only infrequently. Little opportunity exists for mutual exchange of grievances, and organizing is difficult because salespeople are generally isolated from one another. Second, in contrast to most employee groups, salespersons usually think of themselves as independent operators rather than as cogs in a large industrial machine. Third, managements' working-hour problem is less significant with sales personnel than with other workers, because most people on the sales force have some control over their workday and work week. If they work excessive hours, it is often to add to their compensation; but they may occasionally take an afternoon off or start a working day later than usual. There are no time clocks to provide checks on their actions. And finally, higher wages have never served as a strong organizing incentive for sales personnel. Rightly or wrongly, sales personnel have been made to feel that low earnings are the result of personal ineffectiveness, not of the employer's niggardliness.

It is estimated that only one of ten salespersons belongs to a union. When unionization has occurred, it has usually been because of management failure. Some grievances of sales personnel are: too many reports, competition of house accounts, inadequate expense allowances, unequal territories, too many people on the sales force (which results in inadequate territories), and too many nonselling duties.

Unionization has made the most headway in industries where salespeople are paid largely on a straight-salary basis, where they work together on the same premises (retail selling), and where the selling job is combined with that of delivery, as in the distribution of beer and soft drinks. Unions have made little progress in organizing salespeople who sell directly to industrial users or those who make calls on middlemen. Sales personnel in these classifications, generally paid in whole or in part on the basis of productivity, almost all oppose union affiliation.

Many sales executives oppose unionization of their sales forces. Their opposition is based chiefly upon the effect that unionization may have on the control of individual salespersons and upon the limitations that union contracts place on aggressive management. Managerial action in important areas may be circumscribed by rules laid down in the collective-bargaining agreement, and uses of incentive systems of compensation are restricted. Commonly, unions object to sales contests and other devices for motivating the sales force; sometimes they insist that all additions to the sales force be recruited through the union; they discourage the use of quotas and other standards of performance; and a strict system of seniority is almost always among their demands. Furthermore, sales executives generally maintain that the organizational structure of existing unions does not harmonize well with the demands of the selling job, since selling and sales management require more flexibility than running a plant or an office. They argue that in the nature of things all salespeople are called upon at times for extra effort, this being the price a salesperson pays for comparative freedom from day-to-day supervision.

Federal law prohibits sales executives from active discouragement of unionization, and it is wise to take a positive approach. Progressive sales management has come more and more to recognize that the interests of the sales force are usually not in conflict with those of the company. Normally, sales personnel are reasonable people, and usually they regard themselves as members of the management team. The wise sales executive utilizes every opportunity to hammer home the mutuality of interests.

## SALES MANAGER'S CREED

Sales and Marketing Executives—International (SME-I), a professional association with members throughout the world, has long concerned itself with the improvement of relations among sales personnel and sales executives. In an effort to apply its members' knowledge of special conditions affecting the salesperson's job to the general problem of employer-employee relations, SME-I has published, and revised from time to time, a code of ethical conduct known as the Sales Manager's Creed. The most recent revision is reproduced in Figure 9.2. Although not every sales executive subscribes fully to this creed, all are well advised to study its provisions—most are directly or indirectly traceable to company practices and policies that have been frequent causes of unrest among sales personnel.

FIGURE 9.2

## A CREED

I SUBSCRIBE TO THIS SALES MANAGER'S CREED, PREPARED BY SALES AND MARKETING EXECUTIVES—INTERNATIONAL, WHICH I BELIEVE TO BE IN THE BEST INTERESTS OF AMERICAN BUSINESS:

All salesmen shall receive fair compensation during their initial or subsequent training periods.

Salesmen's expense reimbursement policies shall be uniform, after taking all variations of conditions into consideration.

FIGURE 9.2 (cont.)

While recognizing changes in compensation or territory to be functions of sales management, salesmen shall be consulted prior to establishing such changes and given reasonable notice of the effective date.

Earnings of commission of bonus salesmen shall be unlimited, unless otherwise specified at the time of their employment. Should basic changes in a business justify modifying this policy, all salesmen affected shall be advised of the fact a reasonable time prior to establishing such ceilings as become necessary.

When evaluating the ability of salesmen, conditions beyond their control, such as differences in the sales potentials of their territories, shall be given full consideration.

Salesmen shall be offered the same vacation, job or income security, and other employee benefits as are enjoyed by other employees in comparable positions in the same company.

The only "house" or "no commission" accounts shall be those clearly defined in advance of solicitation.

The paper work required of salesmen shall be held down to a minimum and its value clearly justified.

A sharp distinction shall be drawn between salesmen's earnings and expense allowance, and any system that affords salesmen either a substantial profit or loss on expense accounts shall be corrected.

Salesmen shall be given either a contract, agreement, or letter covering those conditions of his employment which might otherwise be the basis for later misunderstandings.

If quotas are used—
(a) Salesmen should know how their figures have been determined, and
(b) The quotas shall be based on reliable seasonal personal evaluation of accurate and adequate criteria.

A salesman whose health or well-being gives evidence of being prejudiced by the nervous tensions involved in his work, shall be given such relief as may be possible.

Pressure to achieve results shall be of a constructive nature, avoiding the use of "fear" psychology or threatened loss of employment.

No matter where a salesman may be located, he shall be provided with a simple means of stating his grievances, which shall be promptly considered and answered.

## CONTRACTS WITH SALES PERSONNEL

A sales employment contract is a formally executed agreement between the employer and the individual salesperson, outlining conditions of employment. Citing the possible avoidance of later misunderstandings as the justification, the Sales Manager's Creed suggests the use of written agreements ("contract, agreement, or letter") covering employment conditions. Proponents of salesperson's contracts argue also that some measure of legal protection is provided both parties—the sales personnel against arbitrary company action, such as cuts in commission rates, and the company against unauthorized action by the salesperson, such as selling outside the assigned territory. Figure 9.3 shows a salesperson's contract of the sort used by insurance companies for their "agents" (that

THE TRAVELERS INSURANCE COMPANY
THE TRAVELERS INDEMNITY COMPANY

_____

_____

of Hartford, Connecticut, hereinafter called the Company, and

of_____hereinafter called the

Agent, pursuant to request that the underwriting facilities and other services of the Company be made available to the undersigned as Agent and for the considerations hereinafter expressed, agree together as follows:

1. This contract shall become effective on the_____day of_____19____.

2. The Agent has full power and authority to solicit applications or proposals for insurance, and to bind the Company and issue policies, for such classes of risks as the Company from time to time may authorize; to countersign policies of insurance, renewal receipts, certificates, and endorsements pertaining to such classes of risks; and to collect, receive, and receipt for premiums on such insurance, except for premiums which the Company bills directly.

The Agent shall promptly forward applications, proposals or daily reports to the Company's Office at

_____

The Agent shall promptly pay over premiums to the Company's Office at_____

_____

3. Commissions shall be payable in accordance with the commission schedule adopted by the Company and supplied to the Agent. On business for which premiums are collected by the Agent, commissions may be retained by the Agent out of premiums collected, as full compensation for such business. The Company at any time, by written notice to the Agent, may change the commission schedule as to premiums due on and after the date specified in the notice, provided such notice shall be given 60 days in advance of the effective date whenever a material change in commission is involved.

4. It is a condition of this contract that the Agent shall refund ratably to the Company, on business heretofore or hereafter written, commissions on canceled insurance and on reductions in premiums at the same rate at which such commissions were paid to the Agent.

5. If the Agent notifies the Company within his customary accounting period that an additional premium is uncollectible which was developed by audit or report of values on any account where coverage is no longer in force and the Agent has exhausted his normal collection efforts, the Agent shall be relieved of the responsibility for collection and shall have no commission interest in such premium. This provision shall also apply to uncollectible anniversary premiums on court, probate, license, permit and other miscellaneous surety bonds.

6. Except as specifically authorized by the Company, the Agent has no authority to make, alter, vary, or discharge any policy contract, to extend the time for payment of premiums, to waive or extend any policy obligation or condition, to incur any liability in behalf of the Company, or to insert any advertisement respecting the Company in any publication.

7. The Company shall not be responsible for agency expenses such as rentals, transportation facilities, clerical help, solicitors' fees, postage, advertising, exchange, personal local license fees, or any other agency expenses whatsoever.

8. The Agent shall be responsible for all risks placed on the books of the Company through his agency by any sub-agents or brokers together with all premiums or moneys collected by them in connection with such risks the same as if they had been produced directly by the Agent.

9. Any Company supplies furnished to the Agent by the Company shall always remain the property of the Company and shall be returned to the Company or its representatives promptly upon demand.

C-9051   CF Edition   REV. 8-72   PRINTED IN U.S.A.          *(continued on reverse side)*

FIGURE 9.3 (cont.)

10. The Company shall indemnify and hold the Agent harmless from and against all sums, including costs and expenses of suit defense and settlement, which the Agent shall become legally obligated to pay by reason of liability imposed on him by law for damages sustained by policyholders, caused solely and directly by error or omission of the Company in the preparation and handling of policies, including timely premium notice.

11. All moneys collected or received by the Agent for or on behalf of the Company shall be held in a fiduciary capacity and shall not be used by the Agent for any purpose whatsoever except as specifically authorized by the Company and shall be paid over to the Company in accordance with the terms of this contract.

12. This contract cancels all previous contracts or agreements whether oral or written between any of The Travelers Companies and the Agent covering the classes of risks referred to herein. This contract may be terminated by either party at any time upon written notice to the other, provided any such notice by the Company shall be given 60 days in advance of the effective date if the Agent has paid all balances due the Company in accordance with the Company's customary arrangements with the Agent.

13. In the event of termination of this contract:

    a. The Agent's records, use and control of expirations, including direct billed business, shall remain his property and be left in his absolute possession.

    b. The Company shall furnish the Agent upon request a record of direct billed policyholders, expiration dates and details of the coverage provided, including the latest rating information recorded.

    c. Paragraphs 3 and 4 of this agreement shall continue to apply to additional or return premiums on policies written prior to the date of termination but expiring subsequent thereto.

The provisions of this paragraph shall apply so long as premiums are remitted in accordance with the Company's customary arrangements with the Agent. If at the time of termination the Agent has failed to pay balances due the Company, this paragraph shall apply only if the Agent shall thereafter pay all collected premiums to the Company immediately.

IN WITNESS WHEREOF, the Company has caused this contract to be signed at the Home Office and the Agent has subscribed his name hereto this_____day of_____19____.

_M. H. Beach_
President

_Stanley A. Gibson_
Second Vice President, Casualty-Property Dept.

_____
Agent

_____
Authorized Signature

is, independent salespersons) and by some firms manufacturing products sold on a straight-commission basis. The most extensive use of contracts is made by companies selling such "products" as insurance, securities, other intangibles, and real estate—in all of which sales compensation is primarily by commission. Some use of contracts is made by firms in other fields where salespeople are paid wholly or mostly by commissions. Otherwise, contracts are little used, the main reason being that many sales executives look upon written job descriptions (covering job objectives, duties and responsibilities, etc.) as a more effective means of avoiding later misunderstandings. Furthermore, unlike contracts, the written job description can be altered without necessarily obtaining the salesperson's consent.

Several other reasons can be cited for nonuse of contracts. One is that many employers consider them unenforceable, since it is often impractical, unwise, or both, to take sales personnel into court for nonperformance. When court action is taken and the judgment is favorable to the company, it may be difficult, often impossible, to collect it; yet the company is tied to the contract terms when the salesperson sues. It is seldom possible to foresee all contingencies at the time the contract is drafted, and changes in conditions may make certain stipulations unworkable. Still another reason for nonuse is that, since contracts generally set forth specific grounds on which salespersons can be discharged, the release of incompetents may be made more difficult. Although these problems do not destroy entirely the envisioned purpose of the sales contract, they do point up the importance of careful preparation and use. If the main role of the sales contract is that of reducing the seriousness of later misunderstandings on employment terms, its provisions must anticipate matters about which misunderstandings are most likely to arise, and on which it is especially critical to have a clear meeting of minds. The more common matters of this type are: work assignments, working hours, compensation arrangements, and requirements concerning reports and other written records.

## CONCLUSION

Sales-force management is an important part of the sales executive's job. In its essentials, it is personnel administration applied to the sales department. In its application, it requires adaptation to the special circumstances that surround the salesperson's job. Effective sales-force management requires leadership, plus administrative skills in planning, organizing, and controlling the personal-selling portion of the marketing program. Faulty sales-force management results in high personnel turnover and excessive selling expenses, which adversely affect company profits. The Sales Manager's Creed summarizes some of the duties and obligations of sales executives as they relate to sale-force management and sets forth recommended practices and policies. It suggests a program of positive action that must, of necessity, be modified to fit situations of individual companies and the philosophies of their sales executives.

# 10

# Recruiting and Selecting
# Sales Personnel

A prime concern of the sales manager is to field sufficient salespeople to service the needs of prospective customers for the company's products. Ultimately, sales managers must concern themselves with achieving efficient selling performance, but they must first find the potential performers. The effectiveness of selling performance depends both upon the caliber and the number of salespeople at the disposal of sales management. Spatial problems make the task of recruiting and selecting salespeople more difficult than for other employees. Since a sales force works over broad geographic areas rather than in restricted plant locations, it is often necessary to recruit sales personnel in the markets they are to serve, a factor that makes the recruiter's task much more difficult.

From management's standpoint, there are four important steps in recruiting and selecting a sales force. Step one is to determine sales personnel needs, and this requires job analysis and the establishment of job specifications. Step two is to identify the sources from which salespeople with good potential might be obtained. Step three is to locate and recruit prospective salespeople from the identified sources. Step four is to select from among these prospects the ones who have the highest probability of success.

## ORGANIZATION FOR RECRUITING AND SELECTION

Responsibility for recruitment and selection of sales personnel is assigned to the sales manager in some organizations, the personnel manager in others, and to the two executives jointly in still others. There is no one best place for assignment of this responsibility. Company size, executives' personalities, and departmental organization all affect this decision. Where the sales manager has a personnel staff assistant, recruiting and selection of a sales staff usually is handled entirely within the department. In companies with small sales forces, it sometimes is desirable to have these functions under the control of the personnel manager, but this is unusual. It is more common for the personnel department to handle recruiting and preliminary screening and for the sales department to make final selections. In all companies, whatever the formal organization, considerable exchange of information and consultation takes place between the two departments.

Location of responsibility for recruitment and selection of sales personnel in concerns with regional sales offices is another organizational factor that varies from one company to another. These functions tend to be centralized at the home office when the firm requires high-caliber sales personnel. Other factors, for example, size of regional organizations and location of training programs, make it difficult to draw further generalizations. However, decentralized recruitment and selection generally result in reduced interviewing costs and time and facilitates the hiring of local applicants for sales work.

### Need for the Proper Setting

For recruiting and selection programs to succeed, they must be installed in a favorable setting. Market exploration must have been carried to the point where management knows: the size of the potential business, identities and locations of customers and prospects, which individuals in customers' organizations influence buying decisions, and the best methods for reaching them. Product uses and applications must have been identified and the different selling appeals evaluated as to relative effectiveness. With this foundation of market and product knowledge, management is prepared to determine its sales-personnel requirements, draft appropriate recruiting and selection programs, and install them in an environment conducive to success.

### The Law and Recruitment and Selection of Sales Personnel

Since the passage of the Civil Rights Act of 1964, the personnel policies of U.S. companies have come under increasing scrutiny by agencies of the federal government. Two of these agencies, the Equal Employment Opportunity Commission (EEOC) and the Office of Federal Contract Compliance (OFCC), have issued guidelines to assist employers in implementing nondiscriminatory personnel policies (defined as policies that do not result in discrimination on the basis of race, color, religion, sex, or national origin).[1] The guidelines issued by the EEOC apply to all employers of twenty-five persons or more; those of the OFCC apply to firms with 100 or more employees that contract with the federal government.

Both the EEOC and the OFCC concern themselves with a broad range of personnel policies. Their regulations set down important limitations on the use of ability tests designed to measure eligibility for hiring, transferring, promotion, training, and referral or retention. They apply particularly to all formal, scored, quantified, or standardized techniques used to assess job suitability, including specific qualifying or disqualifying personal history or background requirements, specific educational- or work-history requirements, scored interviews, biographical information blanks, interviewers' rating scales, scored application forms, and the like. Both agencies require an employer using such techniques to have evidence of each technique's validity; this evidence must consist of empirical data demonstrating that the technique is predictive of or significantly correlated with important elements of work behavior which

---

[1]See *Guidelines on Employment Selection Procedures* (Equal Employment Opportunity Commission, August 1, 1970) and *Proposed Employment Testing and Other Selection Procedures* (Office of Federal Contract Compliance, April 15, 1971).

comprise or are relevant to the job or jobs for which candidates are being evaluated. Basically, then, federal regulations provide that employers using personnel administration techniques of this type for purposes of selecting from among candidates for a position must be prepared to prove that the techniques are being used in a manner which does not constitute discrimination on the basis of race, color, religion, sex, or national origin.

An important result of EEOC actions on alleged violations of the Civil Rights Act has been to make its significance in the recruiting and selection of employees more pronounced. Companies that have a serious imbalance in the number of minority-group members in their work force relative to the proportion who reside in the "employment area" are very likely to be found in noncompliance with the law. Although a company's hiring standards may be job-related, those reflecting the norms of the white community or involving preemployment inquiries as to race or national origin may also be considered as evidence of discrimination.[2]

Although most reported violations of the Civil Rights Act involve discrimination on the basis of race and color, an increasing number of cases relate to discrimination on the basis of sex. This trend is causing many companies to abandon certain long-standing employment practices. Today, for instance, it is rare for a company to specify sex in its help-wanted advertising. Similarly, an increasing number of companies are actively recruiting women for sales positions that were formerly regarded as being for men only. The EEOC recommends and some states require that help-wanted advertisements state that all applicants are welcome even though they may be labeled "Jobs of interest—male" or "Jobs of interest—female."[3]

Discrimination on the basis of age is prohibited by the Age Discrimination in Employment Act of 1967. This act applies to employers of twenty-five persons or more in industries affecting interstate commerce and protects individuals aged forty to sixty-five years against discrimination involving hiring, discharging, or compensation. This act, however, does not prohibit employers from asking job applicants to state their age or date of birth on application forms or in an interview. But companies should see to it that job applicants are informed that information about their ages will not be used to discriminate against them.

## SALES JOB ANALYSIS

No matter what position a company is seeking to fill—salesperson, file clerk, executive, factory hand, plant guard, or other—the task is approached, consciously or not, with some preliminary analysis of the job. Even though management may not have recognized this need for job analysis to the extent of making a formal evaluation, it recognizes instinctively the desire to fit the individual to the job. In companies where this need has been recognized, formal systems of job analysis have developed. Experience indicates that the formal, systematic approach to job analysis results in a much higher proportion of people being placed in the right job.

Analyzing a sales job is basically a matter of developing the information needed for a job description. It involves asking questions to determine the job's objectives

---

[2] H. J. Chruden and A. W. Sherman, Jr., *Personnel Management,* 4th ed. (Cincinnati: South-Western Publishing Company, 1972), p. 148.
[3] *Ibid.*

and to uncover what the salesperson does or should do in pursuit of them. The first question, for example, should be, What are the purposes of this job? What is the title of the job—salesperson, sales representative, sales counselor, or what? These questions might be followed by: To whom does this person report? What products does this individual sell? To whom does this person sell? What information should this person gather, and what reports should this person make? The answers might elicit details concerning special skills required, planning responsibilities, relations with customers, service duties, and the like. Such question asking, together with formal arrangement and systematic grouping of the answers, provides the means of analysis and results in a sales job description. Outlined below is a suggested nine-step procedure for sales job analysis:

1. Prepare a questionnaire for sales personnel, asking them to list the main objectives of their job, together with the major functions and subfunctions performed in doing the job effectively.
2. Prior to receipt of the completed questionnaires, have all executives interested in sales activities write down their conceptions of the salesperson's job objectives and the functions they feel *should* and *should not* be performed in achieving them.
3. Survey customers to find out what they believe should and should not be the functions of a company salesperson.
4. Tabulate the information received.
5. Reconcile differences revealed by the three viewpoints, write a concise statement of job objectives, and prepare a detailed list of activities that sales personnel are to perform.
6. Classify the activities into major functional groups, such as sales, service, territory management, sales promotion, executive, and goodwill duties.
7. Determine what a salesperson needs to know, the qualifications necessary to perform designated activities, and the reasons that necessitate performance of each activity. Assemble this information into a written job description.
8. Submit the written job description to salespersons for discussion and recommendations, and make alterations as required.
9. Periodically revise the job description, following the preceding eight steps, when changes in products, competition, the economic climate, or customers' demands require a review of job objectives and the activities involved in reaching them.

An alternative approach to sales job analysis is to use a checklist itemizing the functions and subfunctions generally accepted as comprising the salesperson's job. One such checklist, originally developed for the U.S. Small Business Administration, is shown in Figure 10.1. The checklist approach is less reliable than the suggested nine-step procedure, as it fails to provide for definition of job objectives; does not focus on the viewpoints of sales personnel, executives, or customers; and does not require "reasons" in support of activities eventually written into the job description. However, this approach can be helpful in preparing tentative descriptions of a new sales job when the time factor is important.

## JOB SPECIFICATIONS

The duties and responsibilities set forth in the job description should be converted into a set of qualifications that a person should possess in order to perform the

## Outline for Compiling a Sales Job Description

Sales:
  Make regular calls.
  Sell the line; demonstrate.
  Handle questions and objections.
  Check stock; discover possible product uses.
  Interpret sales points of the line to the customer.
  Estimate customer's potential needs.
  Emphasize quality.
  Explain company policy on price, delivery, and credit.
  Get the order.
Service:
  Install the product or display.
  Report product weaknesses, complaints.
  Handle adjustments, returns, and allowances.
  Handle requests for credit.
  Handle special orders.
  Establish priorities, if any.
  Analyze local conditions for customers.
Territory management:
  Arrange route for best coverage.
  Balance effort with customer against the potential volume.
  Maintain sales portfolios, samples, kits, etc.
Sales Promotion:
  Develop new prospects and accounts.
  Distribute home office literature, catalogs, etc.
  Make calls with customer's salespeople.
  Train personnel of wholesalers, jobbers, etc.
  Present survey reports, layouts, and proposals.
Executive:
  Each night make a daily work plan for the next day.
  Organize field activity for minimum travel and maximum calls.
  Prepare and submit special reports on trends, competition.
  Prepare and submit statistical data requested by home office.
  Investigate lost sales and reason for loss.
  Prepare reports on developments, trends, new objectives met, and new ideas on
    meeting objections.
  Attend sales meetings.
  Build a prospect list.
  Collect overdue accounts; report on faulty accounts.
  Collect credit information.
Goodwill:
  Counsel customers on their problems.
  Maintain loyalty and respect for the company.
  Attend local sales meetings held by customers.

job satisfactorily. This set of qualifications is called the "job specifications." If the job description states, for example, that the salesperson is to train dealers' sales personnel, then the salesperson must be qualified to conduct such training. What will the salesperson have to know about the products and the dealers' customers? About the dealers' operating methods and problems? About training methods? Will this duty require the salesperson to have a certain amount and kind of experience? Similar sets of questions must be answered with respect to each of the duties and responsibilities contained in the job description.

There are, of course, differences among the qualifications that a new addition to the sales force may be expected to bring to the job, those that an individual may acquire through training, and those that a person will gain through field selling experience. It is sales management's responsibility to decide which qualifications all new recruits should possess, and which should be provided through training. A company specifying somewhat higher entrance qualifications than another can expect, other things being equal, that its training program will have to accomplish less. But the first company is likely to encounter greater difficulty in finding as many possible recruits as the second company, with its lower entrance qualifications. A trade-off must be made between (1) recruiting persons with many qualifications, which reduces the need for training; and (2) recruiting persons with few qualifications, which increases the need for training.

Sales job specifications should set forth the personality characteristics required. These the salesperson must bring to the job, since sales-training programs are seldom effective instruments for personality development. All sales personnel should have certain traits: empathy and the ability to get along well with others; integrity and character; and maturity, in terms of a sensible self-perspective. Motivation is especially important—some sales jobs require their holders to be routine order takers only, but others serve as proving grounds for future managers. There is a kind of optimum level of motivation for each job. If new salespersons are too strongly motivated, they may not be content for long with a routine job or one lacking in advancement opportunities.

Job specifications may stipulate minimum requirements with respect to education and product or technical knowledge, but *legally so only if* the company can prove that such requirements are significantly related to successful job performance. The importance of such requirements, as one would expect, varies widely. Some selling jobs demand the detailed and highly technical training offered only by colleges of engineering; others require only average ability to read, write, and do simple arithmetic; and there are all gradations in between. Graduation from an educational institution is tangible evidence that the job candidate has a certain level of ability. If a specified amount of formal education is set as an absolute minimum requirement, however, a risk is taken that some otherwise highly qualified applicants will be eliminated from consideration. In addition, setting a specified amount of formal education as an absolute minimum requirement is dangerous on legal grounds—EEOC guidelines, for instance, specify that the employer must prove that this requirement is significantly related to successful job performance and does not result in discrimination on the basis of race, color, religion, sex, or national origin.

Flexibility in defining standards of age and physical appearance is usually desirable. A company that is putting new recruits through a long period of sales training and internship may well want to recruit younger persons than a company with only a brief training period. Except for this consideration, however, age should be a selection factor only to the extent that it helps or handicaps salespersons in their work. The same applies to physical appearance. Short, fat, or ugly salespersons may be handicapped in some selling situations, but they may have an advantage in situations where their appearance increases customer empathy.

Job specifications sometimes provide recruiters with an important device for the conservation of time and energy—the set of minimum requirements or standards to use in weeding out obviously unqualified applicants. This usually takes the form of a list of negative factors, the presence of any of which automatically disqualifies an applicant. Factors such as the following often were included in these lists prior to the passage of the Civil Rights Act of 1964: inability to express one's thoughts clearly; unusually poor language usage; sloppy or dirty clothing or grooming; job-hopping—more than a given number of previous jobs, or too frequent job changes; acne or other skin disease; or unusually unattractive teeth. Such a set of minimum requirements, or preliminary screening standards, should be prepared only after a company analyzes its dismissals and should reflect the main reasons why a company's sales personnel fail. Since 1964, companies have become increasingly careful in setting such minimum requirements or standards because they now must be prepared to prove that each is significantly related to successful job performance and does not result in discrimination on the basis of race, color, religion, sex, or national origin.

Analysis of the qualifications of a company's sales personnel helps recruiters determine what they should look for in job applicants and assists in planning the sales training program. Guidance to recruiters is provided by studying the qualifications which the company's successful sales personnel had when hired—for instance, education, marital status, previous experience, and size of savings. Guidance in planning sales training is furnished by answering such questions as: How specialized are the sales people? How long does it take to become familiar with the line? What were these people doing immediately before they came to the company? After analyzing company salespersons' backgrounds, one sales manager concluded that:

1. Sales personnel who previously sold competing or related lines learned more rapidly, but not significantly so.
2. The average salesperson knew the product line sufficiently well to sell productively in four weeks' time.
3. The new salesperson's awareness of specialized problems with respect to the product line equaled that of any veteran salesperson within four months' time.
4. All successful sales personnel had previous selling experience, although the range varied from house-to-house to industrial selling. This indicated that the ability to sell was transferable to the company's products.

Because no two companies have exactly the same situations, each must construct its own job specifications. Questionnaires are helpful in obtaining the necessary information. Salespersons, supervisors, and others of the sales staff can be asked to express their opinions of the qualifications for success. Customers, as well as others, can provide similar information. From the returns of wisely designed questionnaires it should be possible to write a description of physical, mental, and skill requirements.

## SOURCES OF SALES-FORCE RECRUITS

Thus far we have examined certain factors that sales management should consider in determining personnel requirements—job analysis comes first and results in job descriptions, from which are derived job specifications. These are necessary preliminaries to the next step—the identification of sources of promising recruits.

### Recruiting-Source Identification

One approach to the identification of the best source of recruits is to analyze those used in the past. Each source is analyzed to determine the total number of recruits produced, and "successes" and "failures." Each source, in other words, is analyzed quantitatively and qualitatively. One source may have provided numerous recruits but few successes; a second fewer recruits but a high proportion of successes. Consider the analysis given in Figure 10.2 of eighty salespeople recruited by one company over a period of five years:

FIGURE 10.2
Source Analysis of Sales Personnel Recruited by an Electrical-
Products Manufacturer, 1969-74

| Source | Number of Recruits | % of Total | Number of Successes | Ratio of Successes to Total |
|---|---|---|---|---|
| Recommendations by own salespeople | 22 | 27.50% | 10 | 0.455 |
| Educational institutions | 14 | 17.50 | 10 | 0.715 |
| Sales personnel for noncompeting firms | 12 | 15.00 | 2 | 0.167 |
| Employment agencies | 10 | 12.50 | 3 | 0.300 |
| Personal acquaintances of executives | 8 | 10.00 | 5 | 0.625 |
| Customers' employees | 6 | 7.50 | 1 | 0.167 |
| Unsolicited applications | 5 | 6.25 | 2 | 0.400 |
| Competitors' salespeople | 3 | 3.75 | 2 | 0.670 |
| | 80 | 100.00 | 35 | |
| Ratio of success to total from all sources | | | | 0.437 |

In the figure, the source accounting for the largest number of recruits showed a success ratio only slightly more favorable than the ratio for all sources—but it did account for ten of the thirty-five successes recruited and, for this reason, management might want to continue using it. Three sources had higher-than-average success ratios, and management should explore ways of increasing the number of recruits from them. Three other sources had very low success ratios, and management should use them sparingly in the future. A word of caution: These results indicate the experience of only one company, and should not be considered typical of industry in general. Furthermore, the definition of "success" adopted by a particular management affects this sort of analysis. In the example given, success was defined as "demonstrated ability to meet or exceed sales quotas in two years out of three." Other managements might well define success differently.

Another word of caution with regard to data of the above type: Its reliability depends upon the size of the group evaluated. More reliable conclusions could be drawn on the worth of a source producing twenty-two recruits than one producing only three recruits. However, even if only a small number of cases is available, the data may still serve as a helpful, although necessarily less reliable, guide in identifying promising sources of new salespeople.

Some frequently used sources of recruits are discussed below. The intent is to describe general source characteristics and to point up significant advantages, disadvantages, and other pertinent information concerning each source.

### Sources Within the Company

**Company Sales Personnel.** Many individuals apply for specific sales jobs because they know company sales personnel; and salespeople's recommendations may constitute an excellent source. Often such applicants already know something about the job and about company policies; and the fact that they apply is an indication of favorable disposition toward the company. Salespeople fairly typically have wide circles of acquaintances, since both on and off the job they continually meet new people and generally have many friends with similar interests. It is natural, then, that many of their contacts have good potential as sales personnel—indeed, many now sell for other firms. However, some salespeople are not discriminating in their recommendations, and for this reason such recommendations need careful appraisal. One special recruiting situation in which salespeople are a particularly useful source of recommendations is when jobs must be filled in remote territories; then sales personnel in the same or adjacent areas may know considerably more about unique territorial requirements and local sources of personnel than home-office executives.

**Company Executives.** Recommendations of the sales manager, the president, and other company executives are another internal source of recruits. Sales executives' personal contacts may yield top-caliber people because of their own involvement with the selling field and understanding of the needed qualifications. Other executives' recommendations, by way of contrast, more often are based mainly upon personal friendships and tend to represent less objective appraisals. Experience is almost the only way to evaluate each executive's worth as a source of new recruits, and the type of analysis shown in Figure 10.2 adapts easily to this purpose.

**Internal Transfers.** Two additional sources of personnel from within the company are other departments and the nonselling section of the sales department. Employees desiring transfers are already familiar with company policies, and the personnel department should have considerable detailed information about them. One factor that limits the recruitment of transfers is that the company usually knows little about their aptitude for selling work; an offsetting factor is that they often possess excellent product knowledge. Aptitude for selling, of course, can be tested formally or by "trial" assignment to the field. Transfers are especially good prospects for sales positions whenever product knowledge makes up a substantial portion of sales training, since their background makes it possible to accelerate field assignments.

**Sources Outside the Company**

**Educational Institutions.** This source includes colleges and universities, business colleges, high schools, and night schools. It is reasonable to expect that graduates have attained certain minimum educational levels, the amount depending upon the school. Moreover, many have had training in general business, marketing, and sales techniques. Schools are a particularly fruitful source of new sales personnel at graduation time, and some maintain year-round placement services for graduates seeking job changes. Most recent graduates represent net additions to the labor market and, consequently, need not be attracted away from other jobs.

Colleges and universities have become increasingly important sources of sales and management trainees, and competition is keen for their graduates. Often the graduating senior is in a position to choose from among several attractive job offers. Companies not maintaining close relations with the colleges are at a disadvantage, frequently being unable to obtain appointments on overcrowded campus recruiting schedules, and finding it difficult to attract students away from companies better known to the college. Even better-known companies face stiff competition with each other in hiring the cream of the graduates. A few companies offer sales-training programs to outstanding juniors during vacation periods. Thus, the trainee and the company have an opportunity to evaluate each other, and trainees who prove satisfactory are offered jobs upon graduating.

**Competitors' Organizations.** Sales personnel recruited from competitors' organizations generally require minimal training because of experience in selling similar products to similar markets. But this is often a costly source, because a premium must be paid to persuade salespersons to resign their present jobs. Some sales managers are reluctant to hire competitors' ex-salespersons because they suspect their loyalty. An individual hired away from one organization for higher pay may be similarly tempted at a future time. An important question to answer is: Why is this person leaving his or her present position? When the new job does not improve pay or status for the applicant, his or her desire to change may result from personality conflicts, or instability. Dissatisfaction with the present job is not necessarily the fault of the salesperson: If good reasons exist for making the change, it may be possible to obtain a first-class person who is ready at once for productive work.

**Salespeople for Noncompeting Companies.** Salespeople working for firms in related and nonrelated industries constitute a source of recruits. Such recruits may not be fully acquainted with the product line, but they do have selling experience. This source provides a channel of advancement for salespeople in "dead-end" jobs or those seeking to upgrade their employment.

**Salespeople Making Calls on the Company.** The purchasing agent is in daily contact with sales personnel from other companies and is in a strategic position to evaluate their on-the-job performances. It is not unusual for the purchasing agent to meet high-caliber salespeople for whom jobs with the company would be attractive financially or in other respects. The purchasing agent should be encouraged to make the appropriate recommendations.

**Employees of Customers.** Some companies regard their customers as a recruiting source. Customers are asked to recommend able persons in their own organizations who have reached the maximum potential of their existing jobs. Such transfers may have a favorable effect upon morale in the customer's organization. However, since customer goodwill is of prime importance, a customer's salespeople should normally be recruited only with the prior approval and recommendation of the customer.

**Sales Executives' Clubs.** Many sales executives' clubs operate placement services. Salespersons seeking new positions submit personal data sheets that are duplicated and forwarded to members. At regular club meetings, the sales executive has additional opportunity for informal discussion and exchange of placement information.

**Employment Agencies.** Many sales managers traditionally have regarded employment agencies as unpromising sources of recruits. Many use agencies only after other sources are exhausted. Many believe, usually with little evidence, that "good" salespeople neither need nor will use an agency's services. Experience, unfortunately, tends to reinforce such attitudes, because too often agency referrals fail to meet sales job specifications. Sometimes this is traceable to agency deficiencies (such as the overzealous desire to receive placement fees); but at least as often the fault is that of the prospective employer, who may be using unrealistically high job specifications, may not make the company's requirements clear, and so on. Unquestionably an employer would be unwise—as well as unjustified—in generalizing from unsatisfactory experiences with one or a few agencies, whether they be privately operated or local offices of state employment services. Experiences with individual agencies should be reviewed periodically, using the pattern of analysis illustrated in Figure 10.2.

Whenever an agency is used, it should receive a clear statement of the job's objectives and a complete rundown of job specifications. If possible, the recruiter should meet with the agency counselor to assure that pertinent information is furnished and fully understood. Also, agencies need time to learn about an employing firm and its unique requirements—thus, considerable gains accrue from continuing relationships with agencies that perform satisfactorily. Agencies have steadily improved and expanded their services (often they administer tests of various sorts, check references, and perform tasks otherwise done, if at all, by the employer). As the nature of these services becomes better understood by sales executives, this source should grow in importance. One development of interest to sales executives is the growing number of agencies that take the initiative in searching out promising job candidates, employed or not, instead of confining themselves to "volunteer" applicants. Unfortunately, most such agencies recruit only executives and are therefore of no use as a source of sales personnel.

**Direct Unsolicited Applications.** Most companies receive some unsolicited "walk-in" and "write-in" applications for sales positions. Some sales managers favor immediate hiring of applicants who take the initiative in seeking sales jobs, the reasoning being that this may indicate selling aggressiveness. Others reject direct applications automatically because they believe the proportion of qualified applicants from this source is low. Probably the most logical policy is to treat all volunteer applications the same as solicited applications—applicants not meeting minimum requirements as set forth in job specifications should be eliminated at once; those meeting these requirements should be processed together with other applicants. The selection system, if it works well, should result in hiring the best-qualified applicants regardless of the sources from which they come. It should be noted that direct unsolicited applications cannot be relied upon to provide a steady flow of applicants; the volume fluctuates markedly with changing business conditions.

**Older Persons.** In the past many companies, as a matter of policy, refrained from actively recruiting individuals over forty years of age. As noted earlier, the Age Discrimination in Employment Act prohibits discrimination in hiring decisions against persons forty to sixty-five years of age. In spite of the fact that discrimination against persons in this age group is outlawed, such individuals frequently have a difficult time obtaining jobs, so companies willing to consider them may select from a group for which there is little competitive bidding. Many people in this age group have years of selling experience and the maturity that is so valuable in most selling situations. It is important, of course, to ascertain why an apparently good person is unemployed, but the reasons are often beyond the control of the individual. When older persons are under consideration for sales jobs, assuming that their qualifications compare favorably with job specifications, hiring decisions may hinge upon the length of the training period needed to bring them up to full productivity.

## THE RECRUITING EFFORT

The sales-personnel recruiting effort differs in importance from firm to firm, the differences stemming in part from variations in the caliber of person desired. The higher the caliber desired, the more difficult it is to obtain. The caliber desired, of course, is influenced by the nature of the job, complexity of the product line, problems in servicing customers, and so forth. If job specifications call for a special talent, such as the ability to apply considerable imagination to the solution of customers' problems, then individuals of high caliber are needed. If job specifications require only order-taking ability, as in the case of many beer and soft drink sales personnel, then persons of lower caliber will suffice. Similarly, a higher caliber is generally indicated for a product that is technical, complex, or that sells at a high unit price.

The importance—and the scope—of the recruiting effort are also influenced by the number of recruits that must be obtained. Recruiting rises in importance with the number of persons needed, and this, in turn, is affected by such factors as forecasted sales, promotional and selling strategy, and the sales-force turnover rate. Normally, a large business with a large sales volume needs more salespeople than does a small business. But two firms of comparable size in the same industry may have significantly different-sized sales forces, often because one uses a different marketing channel or stresses advertising more in its promotional program. As might be expected, firms with high sales-force turnover rates must do much more recruiting than those with lower rates.

It is wise to precede actual recruiting with an analysis of methods currently in use, an evaluation similar to that used in identifying sources of promising recruits. Successes, failures, and terminations should be analyzed to determine if they are related to specific recruiting methods. Such analyses should aid in choosing the most appropriate methods. There are two basic methods of recruiting—personal recruiting and indirect recruiting.

### Personal Recruiting

Personal recruiting is chiefly used for recruiting graduates of schools and colleges. Campus interviewing is often planned as a company-wide affair, because this avoids much duplication of effort. Although representatives of different departments do the interviewing, the personnel department plans and coordinates the recruiting drive. In many efforts of this type, an assistant sales manager shares with the regional or district sales manager located nearest the campus responsibility for interviewing students. In other cases, home-office sales executives rotate campus interviewing responsibilities among themselves; sometimes each returns annually to the same campuses, thus building long-term relationships with individual schools.

College recruiting requires planning well in advance of the campus visit. Statements of trainee requirements should be mailed to college placement officers early, preferably no later than January. The list of colleges, based primarily upon past interviewing experience, is updated, and letters are sent out requesting interview dates. The best months for recruiting June graduates are February, March, and April; and March is in the most demand. If the visit comes too late in the spring, interviewers find that many of the best-qualified graduates have already taken jobs. After visiting dates have been confirmed, colleges are sent letters specifying such details as salary, desired marital status, and starting date of employment. Some recruiters also send copies of promotional materials, company histories, and application blanks.

College placement officers schedule a 20- to 30-minute interview for each student. All interested students are granted interviews—few companies prescreen college applicants. Generally, interviews are the only screening devices used. The most promising candidates are invited to company offices for follow-up interviews. However, many campus interviewers have authority to do actual hiring if it appears that promising candidates will be lost through delay.

### Indirect Recruiting

Advertisements in classified and other sections of newspapers and trade journals have long been used for recruiting sales personnel. Until recently, however, advertisements were considered useful only for hiring low-grade sales personnel for routine jobs. Even for this grade of personnel, the proportion of qualified to unqualified respondents to a given advertisement was often small; and it was time consuming and costly to screen all applicants. Furthermore, most sales executives believed that high-caliber people would not seek employment offered in such an impersonal way. Nevertheless, a change in thinking has occurred. Today, city newspapers carry many advertisements publicizing openings for sales personnel and even for sales executives.

So great is the number of prospective job candidates reached by a single advertisement that companies often must take steps to reduce the volume of applications. If the employer is willing to publish details about the compay and job, fewer persons who obviously are not qualified will answer the advertisement. Specific details vary with the company and its situation, and should be in the ad if it is to attract good applicants. Some ads mention the salary range of successful company sales personnel. Others explain that the person selected is to replace a regular salesperson in an established territory with active accounts. Still others specify that only professional salespeople need apply. Information of this sort helps convince promising applicants that the opening represents a legitimate established job.

Most sales managers favor "open" over "blind" advertisements, although mixed practice exists. The company name, especially if well known and respected, should be prominently featured so as to attract the best applicants. Location of the advertisement in the publication is also important. Newspaper advertisements on sports or financial pages are usually more productive but cost more per insertion than those in classified sections. Display ads on a sports page, for example, not only attract unemployed persons looking for work but employed individuals who are not in the job market but who can be attracted by the lure of better jobs.

Sometimes brochures outlining company sales-career opportunities are distributed to applicants answering advertisements as well as to those contacted by other methods. The most effective brochures are written from the viewpoint of the prospective sales recruit. Besides describing the company and its history, they make clear the qualifications required for sales jobs, and the salesperson's duties, responsibilities, and advancement opportunities. It is effective to include short case histories of those who are and have been successful salespeople with the company. Many brochures make liberal use of pictures, charts, diagrams, and other visual presentations.

Direct-to-consumer organizations have a particularly difficult time in recruiting sales personnel. The type of selling and the uncertainty of earnings result in high turnover rates among these salespeople. Fortunately, these companies can rely upon recruiting methods that are satisfactory in obtaining the lower-grade salespeople they require, although almost useless for recruiting high-grade sales personnel. Their best source of recruits is recommendations from their own salespeople, and they often offer bonuses for each new person recruited. When this method proves inadequate, direct-mail recruiting is used, the mailing list often consisting of the names of former sales people the company hopes to reemploy. In addition, "help wanted" ads are placed in local newspapers or in publications such as *Specialty Salesman*. As a last resort, direct-selling companies, especially those with field supervisors, use cold canvass recruiting in open territories.

## THE SELECTION SYSTEM

Selection systems range from simple one-step systems consisting of nothing more than a single informal personal interview, to complex multiple-step systems providing many devices and techniques designed to gather information. It is helpful to visualize a selection system as a set of successive "screens," at any of which the applicant may be removed from further consideration. Because some screens are more expensive to administer than others, the system should be designed to incorporate the most inexpensive screens early, thus eliminating unpromising candidates with minimum delay, and economizing on money and effort invested. Applicants who survive all screenings are offered positions.

No selection system is infallible; all eliminate some who would have succeeded as salespeople and recommend hiring some who fail. A selection system fulfills its main mission if it improves management's ability to estimate success-and-failure probabilities of individual applicants. Every company should design its selection system to fit its own requirements. Each step should be included for a purpose, and each should be eliminated when it no longer makes a worthwhile contribution. The selection system should be well integrated, with each step contributing needed information for hiring decisions.

## Pre-Interview Screening

Many companies use an initial screening before the first formal interview to eliminate obviously unqualified applicants and save the time of both interviewers and applicants. This screening may be in two steps: (1) providing the applicant with a job profile and basic data on the company, and (2) gaining initial information about the applicant from an interview application form and perhaps a screening test.[4] The interview application obtains information on the job candidate's basic qualifications. Before routine interviewing and testing are begun, predetermined minimum qualifications regarding such factors as education, health, and experience must be met. The interview application form, which is at most two pages long, is completed in a few minutes. It should not be confused with the longer, more detailed application form used later in the selection system.

## The Interview

The interview is the most widely used selection step, and in some companies it comprises the entire selection system. Some personnel experts criticize the interview as an unreliable selection tool, but it is an effective way to obtain certain needed information. No other method, for instance, is quite so satisfactory in judging an individual with respect to such matters as ability in oral communication, personal appearance and manners, attitude toward selling and life in general, reaction to obstacles presented face to face, and personal impact upon others.

Improvements over the years have operated to increase the reliability of interview results. Newer techniques, such as patterned and nondirective interviewing, are being used with apparent success. Many companies now provide training for all executives and staff members who interview, and scientifically designed rating scales and interview record forms help interviewers to guide discussions along orderly lines. The net effect is more reliable interview results that yield more easily to analysis.

Because of the time involved, interviewing is costly. Consequently, interviewers should avoid covering the same ground as other selection devices. The interviewer should review the completed application form before the interview in order to refrain from asking questions that have already been answered. Perusal of the completed application should indicate areas that require further questioning. Too often the interviewer spends far too much time in telling the applicant about the company and its policies. Although it is important to sell the individual on the organization, particularly when there is a scarcity of sales personnel, there are more efficient ways of accomplishing this. One is by providing the applicant with a brochure relating important facts about the company and asking that it be read before the interview. Another may be used when several applicants are to be interviewed consecutively, as in college recruiting: The interviewer holds meetings preliminarily with the whole group, and describes general company policies. But even after such orientation, it is necessary to answer additional questions during individual interviews. Nevertheless, most of the interview should be used for obtaining information about the applicant. A helpful rule is that, during an interview, the interviewer should do a minimum of the talking.

The job interview can be a trying experience for the applicant. Even for experienced salespersons accustomed to selling themselves and their products daily to

---

[4]"Not Wanted: 'Aggressive Industrial Salesmen,' " *Management Review* (May 1972), p. 47.

strangers, the great importance attached to a job change and the unfamiliarity of the situation may cause nervousness. The interviewer should put the applicant at ease. One way to relieve tension is for the interviewer to begin with questions on the person's family and educational background, subjects about which most people talk freely. The interviewer must remember that the applicant is not the only one selling himself. It is the interviewer's task to persuade the potential employee that the firm is a desirable employer. Far too often, the job interview impresses the applicant as an inquisition so that the applicant's nervousness makes the results less reliable. Throughout the interview, pleasant rapport between interviewer and job applicant should be maintained.

**How Many Interviews?**    A single interview seldom provides sufficient information to evaluate an individual as a potential salesperson. At the second interview, additional facts secured may cause a revision of the first impression. Many tensions present in the first interview are reduced, since the applicant no longer is a complete stranger in an unfamiliar situation. The applicant's behavior should be more nearly normal.

Commonly the first interview is short, perhaps no more than 20 minutes. Questions about the company and the job are answered while the interviewer determines whether the applicant meets minimum qualifications. If this hurdle is passed and the applicant expresses interest, he or she is asked to fill out a detailed application form, and an appointment is made for the second interview.

**Who Shall Interview?**    In filling most sales jobs, it is advisable to have several persons interview and evaluate all applicants considered worth hiring. In most large companies, first interviews are conducted by personnel department representatives. Next, promising applicants are invited to the home office or, in a decentralized company, to a regional office. These interviews vary in number and kind with the importance of the opening. One large steel company, which needs persons capable of highly specialized selling to important accounts, brings applicants to Pittsburgh for interviews by two assistant sales managers, and the general sales manager, and the marketing vice-president. All four executives must approve a decision to hire an applicant. A manufacturer of office machinery and supplies which requires sales personnel for more routine sales work hires applicants after two interviews, one by a branch sales manager and one by an assistant branch sales manager.

**Interviewing the Spouse.**    Because of the necessity for frequent overnight travel, the majority of outside salespeople are men. Some employers sound out the attitude of the male applicant's wife. If she objects, for instance, to having her husband out of town several days at a stretch, it is unlikely that he can succeed in a job requiring extended travel. This is the main reason that an interview with the wife is often part of the selection system. Frequently, however, the occasion amounts to nothing more than an impromptu dinner with the applicant and his wife, during which the wife's attitudes can be ascertained.

**Interviewing Techniques.**    The informal, unplanned interview has been giving way in many companies to newer techniques, some of which are described below:

1.  *Patterned interview.* Here the interviewer uses a prepared outline of questions designed to elicit a basic core of information. The interviewer may work directly from the outline, recording answers as they are given; but this tends to make the

conversation stilted and the applicant nervous. Greater spontaneity results when the outline is memorized and the answers recorded after the interview. Interviewers should avoid too many questions that can be answered with a simple "yes" or "no." It is better to use more penetrating questions that reveal the attitudes and thinking of the prospective employee.

2. *Nondirective interview.* Some personnel experts say that a nondirective technique yields maximum insight into an individual's attitudes and interests. In this technique the applicant is encouraged to speak freely about his or her experience, training, and future plans. The interviewer asks few direct questions and says only enough to keep the interviewee talking. The nondirective interview does not provide answers to standard questions, and much time is spent on outwardly irrelevant subjects. Expert interpretation, however, reveals much about the applicant—often including things of which the individual is not consciously aware. This technique's proponents claim that it is the best method for probing an individual's personality in depth. The main drawback to its use is that administering the interview and interpreting the results demand specialized instruction.

3. *Interaction interview.* The interaction interview simulates the stresses the applicant would meet in actual selling situations and provides the occasion for observing the applicant's reactions to them. This form of interview requires two interviewers. One uses psychological techniques to set up the simulated situations, and the other, who is present but not an active participant in the interview, observes and records the applicant's reactions. Because of their subtlety, the delicacy involved in application, and the need for expert interpretation, interaction interviews should be planned, administered, and interpreted by trained psycholgists.

4. *Rating scales.* One widely recognized defect of the personal interview is its tendency to lack objectivity, a defect that can be reduced through rating scales. These are so constructed that interviewer's ratings are channeled into a limited choice of responses. In evaluating an applicant's general appearance, for instance, one much-used form forces an interviewer to choose one of five descriptive phrases: very neat, nicely dressed, presentable, untidy, slovenly. Experience indicates that this results in more comparable ratings of the same individual by different interviewers. One drawback of the rating scale is that its very objectivity restricts precise description of many personal qualities. It is good practice, therefore, to encourage interviewers to explain ratings in writing whenever they feel comments are needed. Companies using rating scales as a technique for accessing job suitability must keep in mind—in accordance with the guidelines issued by the EEOC and OFCC—that they also need empirical data to demonstrate that the technique is predictive of or significantly correlated with successful job performance and does not result in discrimination on the basis of race, color, religion, sex, or national origin.

### Formal Application Form

The formal application form serves as a central record for all pertinent information collected during the selection process. When completed, it becomes part of the permanent personnel record of the new employee. As a general rule, a formal application is filled out only after a preliminary interview indicates that a job candidate has promise as a company salesperson. The application form may be filled out by the applicant personally or by an interviewer who records the applicant's responses. Practice varies in this respect, but in either case the completed formal application amounts to a standardized written interview, since most of the information that it contains could be obtained through one or more conventional and more personal interviews. Sometimes, sections are reserved for later recording of the results of such selection steps as psychological testing, reference checks, and physical examinations. Figure 10.3 shows a standardized application blank prepared by *Sales Management* magazine. Other standard forms are available, but ideally each company should prepare its own. No two companies have precisely the same requirements, and information significant for one may be useless for another. However, if a firm has only a small sales force, and recruits relatively few people, the time and cost of preparing its own application form may warrant the choice of a standard form. Firms using standard forms simply ignore inappropriate items and obtain needed additional information during interviews.

Certain items of information are almost always needed for selection decisions, and these can be conveniently assembled on the application form. Among these are: present job, dependents, education, employment status, debts, time with last employer, membership in organizations, previous positions, records of earnings, reasons for leaving last job, net worth, living expenses, and length of job-hunting period.

Final decisions as to the specific items to include on the form should be based upon analysis of the existing sales force. The names of sales personnel should be arranged along a continuum, the best perfomer at one end and the worst performer at the other. This list is then divided into three or more parts: for example, good, average, and poor; if the sales force is large, finer subdivisions are justified. In measuring current qualifications, data are collected from sales records, supervisors' evaluations, and similar sources. The next step is to compare good and poor performers according to qualifications possessed by each at time of hiring. This should reveal any factors that differentiate the two groups, and these are the items that should be included on the application form. The validity of this basis of evaluation depends upon the size of the several groups studied, and for reliable results no group should be smaller than thirty.

**Objective Scoring of Personal-History Items.** It is the total profile, rather than any single item, that determines the predictive value of personal-history items. Considered singly, few items have value as selection factors, but individuals with all the personal-history requirements are those most likely to succeed. However, many potentially successful salespeople do not possess all the requirements. One company, for instance, found that most of its best salespeople were hired between the ages of thirty and thirty-five years, yet there were some as young as nineteen and as old as fifty-two. The significance of each personal factor is relative, not absolute. Although thirty to thirty-five may be the preferred age range, applicants outside this age range should still receive consideration (since other factors in their backgrounds may more than offset the fact that they are outside the desired age range).

Some firms with large sales forces establish objective measures for personal-history items. A maximum possible score is assigned for each item, and the points given to a particular individual depend upon proximity to the ideal. In one firm fifteen personal-history items are used as selection factors, at a maximum value of ten points each. The maximum score is 150 points, and the cutoff score is 100. Successful salespersons in this company all scored over 100 when hired, and the company automatically disqualifies all applicants with scores under 100.

Objective personal-history scoring was pioneered by the life insurance companies. Their sales forces were sufficiently large to permit establishment of reliable standards. It is doubtful practice to set such scoring standards when the sales force is rather small (say, under 100 people), as the distortion of scores tends to increase in inverse

FIGURE 10.3

## APPLICATION FOR EMPLOYMENT

*(Please fill out this blank fully, in your own handwriting. The facts requested by this company will enable us to judge to the best of our ability whether we have a career opportunity for you. The Company will, on the other hand, supply you with all the information you care to have about our history and development, our products, our policies, and our personnel. An association that will be pleasant and profitable both to you and us rests, we believe, upon a complete mutual understanding. What you tell us below about yourself will be kept in strict confidence.)*

Office File _____

Name in full _____  Date _____
          (Last)            (First)            (Middle)

Home address _____  Phone No. _____
          (Street and number)        (City and State)

How long have you lived there? _____  Give below, with dates, all other addresses you may have had during the past 5 years:

_____

_____

_____

Business address _____  Phone No. _____
          (Company)      (Street and No.)      (City and State)

| Date of birth | | | (N.Y. Law Against Discrimination prohibits discrimination because of age) | | | | Social Security No. |
|---|---|---|---|---|---|---|---|
| Mo. | Day | Year | | | | | |
| | | | Are you a citizen of the United States? | | | | |
| Height | | Weight | | | | | |
| | | | | | | | |
| | | | Marriage Status | | | | |
| | Single | Engaged | Date Married | Date Separated | Date Divorced | Date Remarried | No. Children | No. Dependents Other Than Wife |

What brought you in contact with this company — how did you happen to apply for a position here?

_____

Have you ever applied here before? _____  Date? _____

Names of other employes of this company with whom you are acquainted; at the home office or elsewhere:

_____

## YOUR EDUCATIONAL ASSETS

| Type of School | Name and Address of School | Courses Specialized in | Yrs. in Attendance | Did you Graduate? | Year | Scholarship Rank: Designate as in Top 25%, Middle 50%, or Lowest 25% |
|---|---|---|---|---|---|---|
| Elementary | | | | | | |
| High School | | | | | | |
| College | | | | | | |
| Grad. School | | | | | | |
| Corres. School | | | | | | |
| Bus. College | | | | | | |
| Trade or Night School | | | | | | |

What languages do you speak other than English?

What periodicals do you read regularly?

(OMIT THOSE THAT HAVE A RELIGIOUS, RACIAL OR FOREIGN NATIONAL CHARACTER)

Source: Reproduced by permission of Sales Builders, 633 Third Avenue, New York, N.Y. 10017. Further reproduction not authorized.

FIGURE 10.3 (cont.)

## YOUR REFERENCES

Please list below:

*a. Personal References.* (Names, and addresses of 3 people other than relatives who have known you for at least five years, such as teachers, neighbors, public officials, etc.)

_____

_____

_____

*b. Business References.* (Names and addresses of executives of companies where you have been employed or with whom you have had frequent business dealings.)

_____

_____

_____

## YOUR SALES EXPERIENCE ASSETS

Please summarize your specific *sales* experience below:

House-to-house or office-to-office selling:
Years: _____ For Whom: _____ Product: _____

Selling to retail dealers:
Years: _____ For Whom: _____ Product: _____

Selling to jobbers:
Years: _____ For Whom: _____ Product: _____

Selling to the institutional market (Hotels, Hospitals, Etc.):
Years: _____ For Whom: _____ Product: _____

Selling non-technical products direct to business:
Years: _____ For Whom: _____ Product: _____

Selling technical products direct to industry:
Years: _____ For Whom: _____ Product: _____

List below the territories (give hdqr. city and indicate roughly territory areas) in which you have worked for a year or more:

_____

What territories do you feel you know *best?* Why? _____

Do you have any marked preference with respect to the territory you might, if employed by us, be assigned to cover? Specify and give reasons: _____

Which of all your assets (background, education, territory knowledge, etc.) do you feel would be most valuable in any association you might make with us? _____

Have you set a goal for yourself which you want to reach in the next five years? Summarize briefly:

_____

Is there anything in your family background or education or experience which makes an association with this company and type of business especially attractive to you? Specify: _____

Person to be notified in case of emergency: _____
                                            (Name)               (Address)           (Phone)

FOR COMPANY USE ONLY:

Interviewed by: _____ Date _____

Interviewed by: _____ Date _____

Interviewed by: _____ Date _____

FIGURE 10.3 (cont.)

**YOUR ASSETS IN**

| List below the names of all your former employers in the U. S. beginning with the most recent.<br>a) Employer's name.<br>b) Location of territory in which you worked. | City and State | Kind of Business | Time Employed (Record must be complete.)<br>From Mo. Yr. — To Mo. Yr. |
|---|---|---|---|
| 1a. | | | |
| b. | | | |
| 2a. | | | |
| b. | | | |
| 3a. | | | |
| b. | | | |
| 4a. | | | |
| b. | | | |
| 5a. | | | |
| b. | | | |
| 6a. | | | |
| b. | | | |
| 7a. | | | |
| b. | | | |
| 8a. | | | |
| b. | | | |

Why do you wish to leave your present employer? _____

## SPECIAL ACTIVITIES AND CONTACTS
(OTHER THAN THOSE HAVING A RELIGIOUS, RACIAL OR FOREIGN NATIONAL CHARACTER)

| | Did you actively participate? | Do you partici-pate currently? | Offices held during last 5 years | Average time given per week |
|---|---|---|---|---|
| Business Organization (s) (Identify) | | | | |
| | | | | |
| Clubs or Societies (Other than those whose names denote religion or nationality.) | | | | |
| | | | | |
| Athletic or Sports Activities (Describe) | | | | |
| Other | | | | |

## YOUR U. S. MILITARY SERVICE RECORD

If you have not served in our armed services, please explain why _____

If you did serve: Date you entered service _____ Date discharged _____ Honorable _____ Medical _____

Branch of service _____ Rank _____

Overseas service? (Give dates) _____ Where? _____

FIGURE 10.3 (cont.)

**BUSINESS EXPERIENCE**

| Position (s) you held | No. of people supervised | Amount of salary, monthly basis. If commission, estimate average monthly earnings and indicate with letter "C" after the amount | Why did you leave? | Give name of your immediate superior |
|---|---|---|---|---|
| | | | | |
| | | | | |
| | | | | |
| | | | | |
| | | | | |
| | | | | |
| | | | | |
| | | | | |
| | | | | |
| | | | | |
| | | | | |
| | | | | |
| | | | | |
| | | | | |
| | | | | |

Special training courses taken during period of service: _____

_____

_____

_____

_____

Do you have any physical disabilities or handicaps because of your military service? (Describe) _____

_____

_____

Citations or awards: _____

_____

_____

## YOUR PERSONAL BALANCE SHEET

Do you own your own home? _____ Amount of mortgage? _____ If you rent, what monthly rent do you pay? _____

Do you own your own furniture? _____ Do you own an automobile? _____ Give make and model: _____

How much life insurance do you carry? _____ What are your present monthly living expenses for yourself and your family?

_____ Do you have any source of income other than what you would receive from us if employed? _____ Amount of such

income yearly? _____ If your wife works, what is her occupation? _____ Amount of her income? _____

When did you last have a medical examination? _____ Have you any loans or debts past due? (Other than

encumbrance on home) _____ Total amount of such indebtedness _____

Do you carry American Express, Diners Club or other credit cards? If so, please name _____ proportion to the size of the sales force used for setting the standards. Furthermore, with the passage of the Civil Rights Act and the Age Discrimination in Employment Act, a company using objective personal-history scoring must be prepared to prove empirically that the technique does not result in discrimination against applicants on the basis of race, color, religion, sex, national origin, or age. Further, they must prove that the scores above the cutoff point are predictive of or significantly correlated with important elements of work behavior which comprise or are relevant to the sales position for which applicants are being evaluated. Therefore, sales executives should use objective scoring of personal-history items with great caution, although they may safely use "cutoff scores" to indicate the need for further investigation of an applicant's qualifications.

### References and Opinions of Acquaintances

References provided by friends and former employers of the applicant are used to secure information not available from other sources. The value of references is denied by some employers, who contend that writers of reference letters generally hesitate to criticize personal friends, or even ex-employees. But the experienced employer "reads between the lines" of letters of reference, where, for example, the weak candidate may be damned by faint praise. Personal contact is the best way to obtain information from references, since facial expressions and voice intonations can reveal a great deal, and most people are more frank orally than in writing. When a reference is located at a distance, a telephone call may substitute for personal contact. Solicitation of written recommendations is the weakest approach and should be a last resort.

Applicants tend to name as references only those on whom they can rely to speak in their favor. In addition, there is a natural tendency for references to be biased in favor of an applicant. These limitations can be partially offset by contacting persons not listed as references but who know the applicant. Individuals who know the applicant but who are not specifically listed as references often are excellent sources for candid appraisals of the candidate. These acquaintances fall into four classifications:

1. *Present or former employers.* These persons have observed the applicant under actual work conditions. As a matter of practice, however, many sales executives do not approach the present employer without the applicant's permission.
2. *Former customers.* If applicants have selling experience, their former customers are in a position to assess their sales ability. It is advisable to contact these individuals without the applicants' assistance. This helps avoid those who are personal friends of applicants.
3. *Reputable citizens.* If references suggested by the applicant are used, it is best first to contact those who are reputable, well-known citizens. Such people do not stake their personal reputations on those in whom they have little confidence.
4. *Mutual acquaintances.* Those who know both the applicant and the employer may give frank evaluations. What is even more important is that the employer is better able to judge the reliability of such evaluations.

## Physical Examinations

Since good health is important to a salesperson's success, most companies require physical examinations of all applicants seriously considered for sales positions. Because of the relatively high cost of the physical examination, it generally is one of the last steps in the selection system. Even in companies requiring entrance physical examinations, poor health often accounts for separations; but when the examinations are not compulsory, the number is higher. It is advantageous to the applicant as well as to the company to identify physical ailments that may later prevent the attainment of full productivity.

## Credit Information

Many companies run credit checks on applicants for sales positions. Credit files are compiled on most people by local credit bureaus, and special credit reports are obtainable through such organizations as Dun & Bradstreet. When a heavy burden of personal debt is found, it may be indicative of financial worries interfering with productivity, or of a motivating factor serving to spur productivity—to determine which one of these may be true requires, and should be given, further investigation. In analyzing the entire credit report the executive should look for the "danger signals"—chronic lateness in making payments, large debts outstanding for long periods, or a bankruptcy history—the presence of any of which should signal the need for additional probing of the underlying facts. Financial irresponsibility may or may not be indicative of irresponsibility in meeting job obligations; hence considerable data on all aspects of the applicant's behavior, nonfinancial as well as financial, must be on hand to warrant whichever conclusion is drawn.

## Psychological Tests

Psychological testing provides an objective way to measure many traits or characteristics of applicants for sales positions. Until the mid-1960s the trend was for more and more companies to make some use of psychological tests as one of the last steps in the selection system (the tests come toward the end because of their relatively high cost). Since the passage of the Civil Rights Act in 1964 and with the issuance of guidelines by the EEOC and OFCC, there has been a tendency for companies to either abandon or rely less upon psychological tests as an aid in making selection decisions from among job candidates. Roughly 20 percent of the complaints filed under Title VII of the Civil Rights Act charge that tests have been used in ways that result in unfair discrimination against members of minority groups.[5] One reason fewer companies use psychological tests today then previously is the difficulty in validating them and in securing the empirical data needed to prove that test results are predictive of or significantly related to successful job performance and—further— that test results are being used in ways that do not result in illegal discrimination.

The task of validating tests is complicated because many situations exist in which different sets of behaviors or attributes can lead to successful job performance. Because of this, separate validity studies should be performed for different ethnic

[5]W. C. Byham and M. E. Spitzer, "Personnel Testing: The Law and Its Implications," *Personnel* (September-October 1971), p. 9.

groups. The different cultural experience and exposure of each group may affect the relationship of test scores to job-performance criteria. Results of certain tests may underestimate the true ability of disadvantaged applicants and cause tests that are valid for the advantaged to be invalid for the disadvantaged. White sales personnel, for instance, may make effective use of certain selling techniques with white customers that are quite different from the techniques black sales personnel find effective with the same customers. Tests can predict aptitude for using these techniques; but such tests would be appropriate only for white applicants if the tests have not been validated for use with black applicants.[6] In some situations differential validity is found, in others not. Actual research is required in each situation to determine whether or not differential validity exists, and both the EEOC and OFCC emphasize the need to validate test results separately for minority-group members.

**Validation of Tests.**[7] Because of the increasingly important need for proof that a test is related to job-performance criteria and because of the possibility that differential validity exists (for different groups of applicants), it is important to discuss the validation of tests. The illustrations used relate to validity studies conducted on separate ethnic groups, but the same general approach is used for validity studies conducted on other types of groups, for example, for different age groups or for males and females.

Figure 10.4 is a scattergram illustrating a distribution of test scores and job-performance indices; each dot represents an individual's score on both the test and the job-performance criterion. The dots cluster in an elliptical shape, with more scores falling in quadrants 1 and 3 than in 2 and 4. This indicates a valid test, since people with high test scores tend to have higher performance scores, while those with lower test scores tend to have lower performance scores. However, the fact that dots are present in quadrants 2 and 4 indicates that the relationship is not perfect and that prediction errors will occur. If quadrants 2 and 4 contained fewer dots, the distribution would be more elliptical and the validity of the test would be higher.

Figure 10.5 also indicates a valid test because the dots are arranged in an elliptical shape. However, here there is an inverse relationship between test scores and job performance—persons with high test scores tend to have unacceptable job performance and those with low test scores tend to have acceptable job performance. In this case, it is the applicant with a low test score who should be selected. In the situations illustrated in Figures 10.4 and 10.5, knowledge of an applicant's test score can be used to predict job performance, but the direction of prediction is different.

If the cluster of dots is circular, as in Figure 10.6, the test has no validity. Regardless of how an individual scores on such a test, it is impossible to predict accurately whether job performance will be acceptable or unacceptable. Use of this test for selection purposes would lead to as many inaccurate as accurate predictions.

Next, consider some of the possible outcomes of studies of differential validity (that is, validity for different groups). Assume that a test has been given to a group of black and white applicants, with the results shown in Figure 10.7. The solid ellipse represents the test's validity for job performance using only data from the group of

---

[6]W. C. Byham and M. E. Spitzer, *The Law and Personnel Testing* (New York: American Management Association, Inc., 1971), pp. 128-29.

[7]Much of this discussion and the illustrations are adapted from Chapter 7 of Byham and Spitzer, *op. cit. The Law and Personnel Testing.* Byham and Spitzer credit Richard S. Barrett, City College of New York, for having provided the idea behind the types of illustrations.

FIGURE 10.5

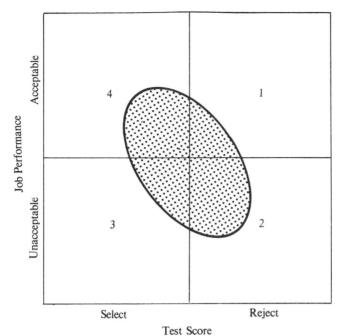

Test Score

Source: Reprinted by permission of the publisher from *The Law and Personnel Testing*, W.C. Byham and M.E. Spitzer. ©1971 by the American Management Association, Inc.

FIGURE 10.4

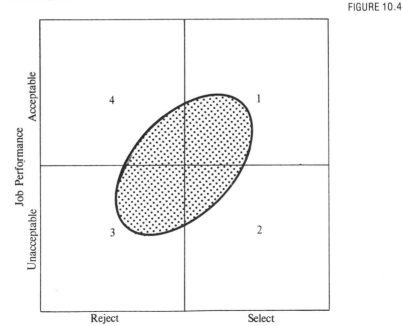

Test Score

Source: Reprinted by permission of the publisher from *The Law and Personnel Testing*, W. C. Byham and M.E. Spitzer. ©1971 by the American Management Association, Inc.

FIGURE 10.6

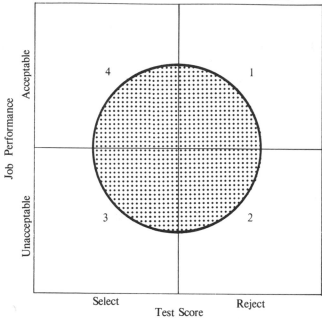

Source: Reprinted by permission of the publisher from *The Law and Personnel Testing,* W. C. Byham and M.E. Spitzer. © 1971 by the American Management Association, Inc.

FIGURE 10.7

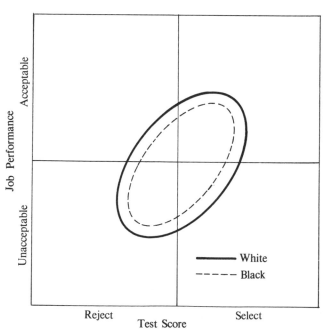

Source: Reprinted by permission of the publisher from *The Law and Personnel Testing,* W. C. Byham and M.E. Spitzer. ©1971 by the American Management Association, Inc.

white applicants, and the dashed ellipse represents this relationship for the group of black applicants. In this case, black and white applicants do equally well on the test and performance measure, and the test is equally accurate in predicting the job performance of both black and white applicants. Consequently, the same selection instruments and selection standards can be used for both groups.

But what if the relationship of the test and the job-performance criterion is as shown in Figure 10.8? Here the similarity of shapes indicates that the relationship between test scores and performance levels is about the same, but black applicants generally score lower on the test $(T_B)$ and perform more poorly on the criterion $(C_B)$. Evidently, in this situation the factors that depress test performance also depress job performance. Here a selection standard can be used that would have adverse affects against blacks, and it would not be considered unfair or illegal discrimination. Blacks do poorer on what the organization regards as an important measure of job performance, and this is sufficient justification to hire a disproportionate number of blacks. But management must recognize the legal requirement that in each individual case the hiring decision must be made on the basis of the lower test score, not whether the applicant is black or white. When, for instance, a white and a black applicant are being considered for a job and the black's test score is higher than the white's, as indicated by the letters B and W in Figure 10.8, the black should be hired. Furthermore, the EEOC and OFCC would probably want evidence that the measure of job performance is important to the organization and is itself not subject to racial bias. These two agencies also would probably demand proof that some other factor, such as length of service, is not a significant factor in producing the difference in job performance between black and white employees.

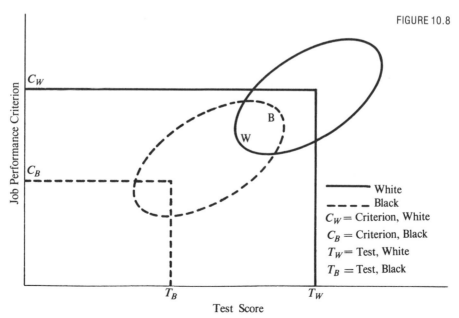

FIGURE 10.8

Source: Reprinted by permission of the publisher from *The Law and Personnel Testing,* W. C. Byham and M.E. Spitzer. © 1971 by the American Management Association, Inc.

Figure 10.9 shows still another possible relationship of test scores to a job-performance criterion. Here, too, the similarity of shapes indicates that the test is equally valid and predictive for both whites and blacks. But, in this case, blacks as a group attain lower average test scores than whites $(T_B)$ is less than $(T_W)$ but they achieve on the average the same level of performance $(C_B$ equals $C_W)$. If selection standards for all applicants are based on the test results obtained from the white group, or even from both groups combined, clearly there is unfair discrimination against blacks. The fact that blacks, as a group, score lower on the test does not mean that they would have lower performance scores; therefore, there is no reason to exclude a disproportionate number of black applicants.

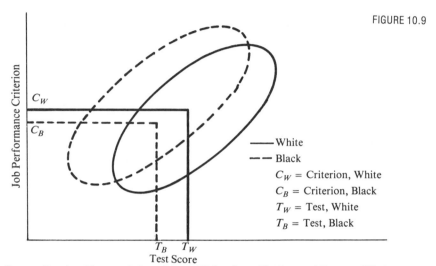

FIGURE 10.9

Source: Reprinted by permission of the publisher from *The Law and Personnel Testing,* W. C. Byham and M. E. Spitzer. © 1971 by the American Management Association, Inc.

If a differential-validity study were not made and both groups were combined, the statistical estimate of validity would be reduced. In addition, fewer black applicants would be hired even though they have equal probabilities of success as white applicants. That is precisely the kind of practice that the EEOC and OFCC seek to prevent, and both agencies require data on the validity of the test for each group and data on average differences between the groups on the test *and* the job-performance criterion. A company can still use a test in these circumstances, but it must use the test differently— the test scores used as the selection standard (that is, the cutoff score) would have to be lower for the black group than for the white group. Of course, too, in a similar situation where whites scored lower on the test than blacks, the whites would have to be subject to a lower selection standard than the blacks.

Now, consider a situation, as in Figure 10.10, in which a test is valid for one group but not the other. In this case both the black and the white groups do equally well on the test and in job performance, but the test if valid only for the white group (as the scores of the black group form a circle). Here the test should be used as a selection instrument only for white applicants, as there is no evidence that the test will predict

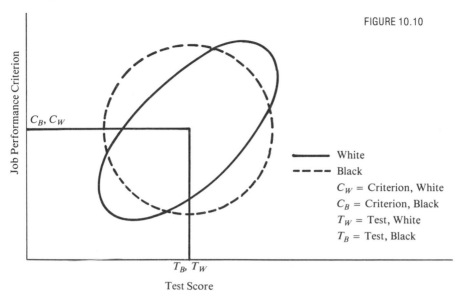

FIGURE 10.10

White
Black
$C_W$ = Criterion, White
$C_B$ = Criterion, Black
$T_W$ = Test, White
$T_B$ = Test, Black

Test Score

Source: Reprinted by permission of the publisher from *The Law and Personnel Testing,* W. C. Byham and M. E. Spitzer. © 1971 by the American Management Association, Inc.

accurately the job performance of blacks. If an organization used this test to select from among both black and white applicants, it would hire about the same proportion of applicants from both ethnic groups. But a larger proportion of whites than of blacks would succeed on the job; therefore, when this type of differential validity exists with a particular test, an employer should develop or seek other tests or selection procedures that are valid for black applicants.

Using psychological tests for selection purposes, then, requires considerable sophistication. Not only is there the possibility that certain tests possess differential validity, but the very objectivity of tests leads many users to expect more validity and reliability in predicting selling success than the tests can offer. Furthermore, it can be said in all fairness that some widely used tests are almost worthless for selection purposes, simply because they were designed for entirely different purposes; others are of questionable value even for measuring what they were intended to measure. Psychological testing is still an experimental field, and every experiment does not succeed. Yet more than a few testing "failures" are on the market, are even promoted and recommended by the producers, and are used by executives unaware of the limitations. In addition, tests tend to favor conformity rather than individual dynamics—they tend to rule out creative thinkers and imaginative, aggressive individuals who might be ideal for the job being filled.[8]

Nevertheless, there are some useful and reliable tests available, and certain basically weak tests can serve as screening devices as long as their limitations are recognized. But, as brought out earlier, it is increasingly important for test users to perform actual research to determine whether or not differential validity exists. The requirement for doing such research makes it even more critical that test users secure the services of trained specialists in psychological testing for purposes of selecting, administering, and interpreting the tests used for any particular company.

[8]M. Greenburg, "Judging the Job Applicant," *Office* (July 1971), pp. 41-42.

**Types of Tests.** Three types of psychological tests are used in selection systems for sales personnel: tests of ability, of habitual characteristics, and of achievement. Tests of ability attempt to measure how well a person can perform particular tasks with maximum motivation. They are tests of *best* performance, and they include tests of mental ability ("intelligence" tests) and tests of special abilities, or aptitude tests. Tests of habitual characteristics attempt to gauge how prospective employees would act in their daily work normally, i.e., not when they are on their best behavior. These are tests of typical performance, and they include attitude, personality, and interest tests. Achievement tests are designed to measure how much individuals have learned from their training or education.

**Basis for Evaluation of Tests.** Before examining the psychological tests used in salesperson selection, we need some criteria for evaluation. Earlier discussion emphasized the importance of a test having validity—that it measures what it purports to measure—and of detecting differential validity. But even in cases where statistical validity has been demonstrated, it is possible for a test not to be valid in a particular instance. For example, a written intelligence test in English is not a valid measure of the *mental ability* of a Spanish-speaking person with an English-language handicap. A low score does not necessarily indicate low intelligence; it may merely reflect poor understanding of the English language.

Test reliability is also important. Reliability refers to the consistency of test results. If a test has reliability, an individual should receive approximately the same score in subsequent retesting with the same or equivalent tests.

Test objectivity is important, too. If a test has objectivity, it is so administered that the scorer's opinion does not enter into the test results. Whenever a person giving or scoring the test can affect the test results, it is misleading to compare the results obtained by different testers.

Other factors to consider in selecting tests are cost, time, and ease of administration. Wide variation in cost exists, and even small differentials may be important if tests are given to large groups. Because there is little relationship between cost and quality, it is sometimes possible to obtain quality tests at low cost. There is, similarly, wide variation in the time required to administer and score tests. Because time frequently is cruical in selection of sales personnel, the employer must balance the time requirements of alternative tests against their relative effectiveness. If the best available test consumes more time than can be spared, a mediocre test that can be given quickly may provide more effective screening than no test at all. Some tests can be administered and scored only by experts; others can be given and scored by persons with little or no special training. Again, employers must balance the gains associated with more complex tests against their costs in time and money.

**Tests of Mental Ability.** Mental tests are used satisfactorily in a wide range of areas, and they have higher validity and reliability than most psychological tests. It must be understood, however, that they measure primarily the abilities that make for success in educational or training situations, namely, language usage and comprehension, and abstract reasoning, or problem-solving ability. They do not measure creativeness, originality, or insight. Therefore, they should be regarded more as measures of mental aptitude than of general intelligence. Because tests of mental ability are "timed tests," they provide an indication of an applicant's ability to learn quickly and to arrive at accurate answers under pressure.

Within these limitations, mental tests are helpful in the sales personnel selection process. Where there is no other evidence of ability, such as graduation from college, the mental aptitude test serves as a screen to eliminate applicants falling below a predetermined level. A wide variety of mental aptitude tests is available.

**Tests of Special Aptitudes.** Certain tests are designed to measure special aptitudes, such as: spatial and perceptual abilities, speed and reaction time, steadiness and controlled movement, mechanical comprehension, and artistic abilities. Aptitude tests used individually aid in making selections for some industrial jobs, as illustrated, for example, by the use of perception tests for selecting clerical personnel. But because selling requires diverse aptitudes, and sales job specifications differ even among competing companies, an especially designed battery of aptitude tests is more appropriate for sales personnel.

The procedure for developing a battery of sales aptitude tests for a particular company is fairly straightforward. The test expert begins with the job specifications (derived, as you will recall, from the job description), checking them to assure that the abilities required for job performance are correctly identified. Then the expert selects existing tests and/or constructs new tests to measure each aptitude. Finally, the test expert develops a scheme for weighting and combining the scores of individual tests. This work of preparing—and later validating—a test battery is time-consuming and costly, and calls for a psychologist's services. Thus, generally only those companies which process large numbers of sales job applicants annually feel they can afford specially developed test batteries to measure sales aptitude. Since, unfortunately, batteries not custom tailored for a particular sales job frequently have little validity, companies with small sales forces find it impractical to include sales-aptitude test batteries in their selection systems.

**Personality Tests.** Personality tests initially were used to identify people with psychotic tendencies—and certain tests have proved useful for this purpose. Subsequently, attempts have been made to use them for measuring personality traits in normal individuals, for which purpose they seem to have little or no validity or reliability. The basic limitation is the lack of uniform definitions for such traits as initiative or aggresiveness, which these tests purport to measure. To the extent that these tests are at all valid in measuring normal individuals, validity must be determined by the total score rather than by scores for individual traits. The chief use of the personality test is that of a screening device to identify persons with abnormal personalities.

Projective tests, of which the Rorschach is the best known, are a promising technique for personality measurement. However, they must be administered by skilled testers, and their results represent a subjective opinion rather than an objective measure. Further refinements of projective techniques eventually may provide useful personality measurements.

**Interest Tests.** In using interest tests as selection devices, a basic assumption is that a relationship exists between interest and motivation. Hence, if two persons have equal ability, the one with the greater interest in a particular job should be more successful in that job. A second inherent assumption is that interests are constant, that those of a person at age forty are essentially the same as they were at twenty-one.

The interest test is useful for vocational guidance, but it is not wholly satisfactory as a selection device. This is because of the opportunity for faking responses—individuals may select answers overstating their real interest in a particular field. Of the two most widely-used interest tests, the Strong and the Kuder, the Strong uses the more indirect and subtle approach and is harder to fake; but because of its greater complexity, it is more expensive to score. The U.S. Air Force, which has experimented with a technique to eliminate faking, uses an information test to measure interest on the theory that persons should be best informed about those fields in which they are most interested.

What proof is there of the value of interest tests in predicting selling success? Unfortunately, very little! Strong demonstrated that there is a positive but low correlation between interest scores and success in insurance selling. Significant variation has also been found in the interest test scores of successful and unsuccessful salespersons of accounting machines. Otherwise there is little tangible proof of the value of interest tests as devices for predicting selling success.

**Attitude Tests.** Attitude tests are more useful as morale-measuring techniques than as selection aids. They are used to ascertain employees' feelings toward working conditions, pay, advancement opportunities, and the like. Used as sales personnel selection devices, they may make limited contributions by identifying abnormal attitudes on such broad subjects as big business, labor unions, and government. Their validity is questionable, since people often profess socially acceptable attitudes they do not actually have. In addition, attitude tests do not measure the intensity with which particular attitudes are held.

**Achievement Tests.** Achievement tests seek to determine how much individuals know about a particular subject. Few standardized tests of this type are used by industry, because the special skills involved in each job require different types of knowledge. Tests of clerical and stenographic ability are one exception, and civil service examinations are another. For the employer who has decided that it is worthwhile to custom design an achievement test for sales applicants, such an instrument can provide an assessment of knowledge applicants possess in such areas as the product, marketing channels, and customer relations; however, as with other psychological tests, such test designing is a job for an expert, not an amateur.

Research has produced some evidence that the existence of two basic qualities, empathy and ego drive, are essential in good salespeople.[9] Empathy is the ability to feel as others do, to put oneself in another person's shoes. The empathic salesperson senses the reactions of his or her customers and is able to adjust to these reactions, achieving real interaction with customers. The second basic quality, ego drive, makes the salesperson want to make the sale in a personal way, not merely for the money to be gained. His feeling is that he has to make the sale. His self-picture improves by virtue of conquest and diminishes with failure. The good salesperson has a proper balance of these two qualities. The developers of this hypothesis have demonstrated in experiments that measurement of these two qualities alone (through the use of specially developed psychological tests) has greatly improved prediction of success or failure in a number of different selling jobs.

**Conclusions on Testing.** Besides the legal requirements that tests must not be used for making selection decisions in ways that discriminate unfairly against minor-

---

[9]D. Mayer and H.M. Greenberg, "What Makes a Good Salesman?" *Harvard Business Review,* Vol. 42, No. 4 (July-August 1964), pp. 119-25.

ity-group applicants, there are other important precautions to observe when incorporating psychological tests into a sales personnel selection system. It is essential to have accurate job specifications, derived from up-to-date and complete job descriptions, to make certain that the specific abilities required of a good salesperson are known. A qualified expert's services are required in the choice of tests (and in devising new ones when necessary), in determining test validity and in detecting differential validity, in administering the tests themselves, and in interpreting the significance of results. In addition, sales executives need to recognize the fact that psychological testing, although potentially capable of making a valuable contribution, is but one element in an effective sales personnel selection system.

## CONCLUSION

The specific sales people at sales management's disposal have a direct bearing upon the amount of success that a business experiences. Persons selected to fill sales positions should come to the company with some ability and education, acceptable physical appearance, good health, emotional maturity, and the desire to succeed. New employees should bring with them these minimum qualifications; additional ones are needed to fill positions requiring specialized knowledge or skills. The minimum standards for selection determine the scope and nature of the training and supervisory programs and set limits to the amount that such programs can accomplish.

Appropriate recruiting and selection policies and procedures, and their skillful execution, result in greater overall selling efficiency. A higher grade of salesperson is produced, and the advantages of having such employees make an impressive list—better work quality, improved market coverage, superior customer relations, and a lower ratio of selling expense to sales. Moreover, good selection fits the right person to the right job, thereby increasing job satisfaction and reducing the costs of personnel turnover. In addition, training costs are reduced, either because those hired are more capable of absorbing training or because they require less formal training.

The consequences of inappropriate recruitment and selection policies are generally higher selling expenses. The "misfit" salesperson has a higher expense ratio because of lower sales, higher traveling costs, more sales returns and adjustments, and inefficient distribution of working time. Because such salespersons rarely stay long with a company, the turnover rate rises along with hiring and training costs. Administrative costs also go up, since low-grade salespeople require more motivation and supervision. In short, the unsuccessful salesperson affects the profit picture adversely.

There are several hidden costs of poor selection, costs that cannot be expressed in terms of money. Customer relations deteriorate, for excessive turnover prevents establishment of close customer-salesperson relationships—and eventually customers grow weary of seeing so many new faces. Moreover, the effects of poor selection and resultant inadequate sales-force performance tend to spread to other departments. Costs rise throughout the business at work is disrupted in such departments as credit, accounting, advertising, and production.

# 11

# Planning and Conducting Sales-Training Programs

The modern sales executive's attitude toward sales training has changed markedly in recent years. Sales managers typically used to believe in "sink-or-swim" training—puting new salespeople into the field with scanty instructions and expecting them to do their best, learning what they could in the hard school of experience. For example, as recently as 1967, one of *Fortune* magazine's 500 largest corporations introduced its first formal sales-training program in one of its major industrial-products divisions. Prior to that time, this division gave product descriptions, a territory, and an order book to new sales-force recruits with instructions to "go out and sell."

The lack of recognition of the need to train salespeople reflected an attitude that many sales managers held toward selling. The older generation of sales managers operated on the comfortable—albeit superficial—assumption that good salespeople were "born," not "made." Admittedly, then as now, there are some "born" or "natural" sales people. But, given appropriate training, the majority of recruits can be "made" into sales persons; and both "born" and "made" sales personnel improve with continued sales training. Modern sales executives still consider experience the most valuable sales training but they believe strongly that formally planned and executed sales-training programs contribute significantly to the improvement of selling performance. They regard formalized sales-training programs as important supplements to, rather than substitutes for, field selling experience.

## ORGANIZATION FOR SALES TRAINING

### Placement of Training Responsibility

Organizational planners do not agree on the question of where to place primary responsibility for initial sales training. Some consider it a line function and assign the sales-training responsibility to the chief sales executive; others consider it a staff function and assign the responsibility to the personnel manager, reserving only an advisory role for sales management. In most situations, both executives should pay a role in initial sales training—the sales executive because he should be an expert on selling, and the personnel manager because he should be an expert on training. How a particular firm should decide the placement of responsibility for initial sales training depends upon comparative costs. If much of the initial training of new sales personnel parallels that given other employees, cost considerations often result in primary responsibility being assigned to the personnel manager. If very little of the initial sales training parallels other new employee training, then primary responsibility is assigned to the sales executive.

Once initial sales training is over, responsibility for continuing training definitely resides with the chief sales executive. Introduction of new products, adoption of revised sales policies, perfection of improved selling techniques, and similar developments call for training action—and logic dictates that top sales executives should be in the best position to recognize the need. In the well-managed business, sales training is a never-ending process and, regardless of who is responsible for the initial period of indoctrination, the chief sales executive has continuing responsibility.

### Sales-Training Staff

Even though chief sales executives may be ultimately responsible for both initial and continuing sales training, they usually delegate actual performance of the function to subordinates. Often large sales organizations have a full-time sales-training director, reporting directly to the chief sales executive. The director might personally conduct some training and coordinate that given on a decentralized (and usually part-time) basis by regional and district sales managers. In smaller organizations, some chief sales executives handle part of the training themselves, but, in most cases, they rely upon others, such as assistant sales managers or district managers, to do most of the training. Even companies without sales training directors often have full-time or part-time sales trainers, or both. The large sales organization generally can make efficient use of a full-time sales-training director and sometimes even a full-time staff, but the small organization ordinarily must rely on executives to do sales training "in addition to other duties." Because of specialized knowledge requirements, the tendency is for companies to train their own sales trainers rather than to recruit outsiders.

### Training the Sales Trainers

No sales-training program, however carefully designed, can be more effective than the people who conduct it. For this reason, a growing number of companies provide special training programs for sales trainers. The starting point is the identification of the subjects that trainers should know thoroughly, such as: the company and its policies, the products, the customers, and their problems, the salesperson's job, and sales techniques. If the potential trainers are not already experienced salespeople, they should be given field selling experience to provide a realistic feel for sales problems. Subjects presented formally should be handled by personnel already skilled as trainers, wherever possible using instructional techniques similar to those the trainers will use later.

Not only should sales trainers have expert and specialized knowledge, they must be effective teachers. Throughout their period of preparation, the theory and mechanics of teaching should be stressed. Trainers should be required to master these, learn how to apply them effectively, preferably through doing practice training themselves. They must also learn to plan and organize teaching material for clear and effective presentation.

Although formal training alone will not prepare an individual for effective teaching, a well-planned and executed program for sales trainers can certainly help. For the most part, however, sales trainers must develop their own teaching skills. To emphasize this point, management often reminds them that: "If the trainee hasn't learned, the trainer hasn't taught."

## BUILDING SALES-TRAINING PROGRAMS

Many companies conduct several types of sales-training programs. Generally, the most comprehensive and longest program is that for newly recruited personnel. More intensive and usually shorter programs on specialized topics are presented for experienced salespeople. In addition, periodic "refresher" sales-training programs are considered desirable in most companies. Some sales-training programs in certain firms are designed especially for the development of sales trainers or for persons whom management believes have potential as sales executives. Each type of program serves different purposes, and the scope and content of each should reflect its particular purpose.

There are several sequential steps in integrating sales training with the operating objectives of the business. First, these objectives should be clearly defined and phrased in terms of the sales force and its capability with respect to achieving these objectives. Then, it must be determined what sales training is necessary to close the gap between capabilities and objectives. At this point a minimal system of sales-training programs, procedures, and projects can be designed to close the gap.[1]

Building an effective sales-training program of any type requires a number of important planning decisions. The purposes to be served by the training must be clearly defined, program content must be decided, training methods selected, arrangements made for program execution, and procedures set up to evaluate the results. Some sales-training specialists refer to these planning decisions as the A-C-M-E decisions—aim, content, method, and execution and evaluation—each of which is considered in the following discussion.

### Defining Training Aims

The first step is to decide what the sales-training program should seek to accomplish. Of course, the general aim of all sales training is to improve selling performance— both of individual salespersons and of the entire sales force. Improved sales performance is achieved through measures taken to increase salespeople's productivity and to control selling costs. Without training, a salesperson's productivity tends to increase with experience; hence, if training can substitute for some portion of the needed experience or can usefully supplement it, higher productivity levels should be reached earlier. Selling costs per unit of product sold decline with rises in selling productivity, so they also tend to be related to experience. Furthermore, the sales-force turnover rate for new sales personnel nearly always is higher than for experienced people—often inexperienced staff members find themselves unprepared to do satisfactory jobs, become discouraged, and leave the company. If sales training can help salespersons to increase their productivity more quickly, the sales-force turnover rate will drop, hiring and training costs should fall, and

---

[1]"Ten Ways to Keep Sales Training on Track and on Time," *Sales Management,* Vol. 100 (April 10, 1971), pp. 17-26.

selling efficiency will rise. Selling performance is influenced also by the state of relations with customers and prospects, the sales force playing a crucial role in molding and maintaining these relations. Generally, experienced sales people make better impressions on prospects and maintain better continuing relations with established accounts. Here, again, sales training can contribute through accelerating the process of "learning through experience." In all these ways, then, sales training serves to improve selling performance by providing a mechanism through which the benefits from an "experienced" sales force can be realized much earlier and more surely than might otherwise be the case.

It is not sufficient, however, to define only general training aims—specific aims of particular programs also need to be identified. Although we may be interested, say, in increasing the sales force's productivity through training, we need to identify what must be done to achieve the general aim of increasing productivity. General aims need translating into more specific aims phrased in operational terms before the program can be planned in detail. The process of specific aim definition begins with a review of general aims and the means currently employed to attain them; however, the process cannot be completed until management actually perceives training needs from which specific training aims derive directly. In the next two sections, discussion focuses on factors that management should consider as it seeks to identify training needs for (1) initial sales-training programs, and (2) continuing sales-training programs.

### Determining Initial Training Needs

Determining the need for, and specific aims of, an initial sales-training program requires consideration of three main factors: requirements of the sales job, prior background and experience of individual trainees, and company marketing policies.

**Job Requirements.** Sales job analysis provides the information required for preparing the job description, which, as you recall, consists of a statement of job objectives and an explanation of essential tasks involved in its performance. Management should study the job description for clues about the points on which new personnel are most likely to need training. But it is at least as important to consider other information relative to sales job performance: How should sales people apportion their time? Which duties require the greatest proportion of sales time? Which tend to be neglected? Why? Which selling approaches are most effective? Answers to these and related questions help in formulating the qualifications that a salesperson should have to fill the job satisfactorily.

**Individual Trainees' Prior Background and Experience.** Each person in an initial sales-training program enters it with a somewhat unique educational background and a highly individualized record of achievement. Conceptually, then, the gap between required job qualifications for a particular trainee and those he or she already has represents the nature and amount of training needed. But in a large organization with a fully structured and formalized program, it is not always practical to adjust training precisely to individual differences in background and experience. Time and money may be saved by putting all recruits through identical programs. Nevertheless, in more flexible training situations, information about trainees' qualifications makes possible to some extent the tailoring of programs to individuals, increasing both trainee satisfaction and program efficiency. In all companies, large and small, determining recruits' real needs for training is essential to developing initial training programs of optimum benefit to company and trainee alike.

**Company Marketing Policies.** A company's particular marketing situation should be analyzed in determining the needs to be served by initial sales training. For instance, selling a line of machine tools requires emphasis on product information and customer applications, whereas selling simple, nontechnical products demands more emphasis on sales techniques. Thus, differences in products and markets make for differences in selling practices and policies, which, in turn, point to needed differences in initial sales training programs. The same applies to differences in promotion, price, marketing channel, and system of physical distribution—all have implications for the needs that the initial sales-training program should serve. In the case of promotion, for example, if advertising is not used or used relatively little, sales training should prepare sales personnel to handle considerable promotional work; but, if advertising is used extensively to supplement salespeople's efforts, there is a need to teach new sales personnel how to coordinate their efforts with advertising.

### Determining Continuing Training Needs

Training a sales force is a never-ending process. Even though the initial training program may be excellent, its graduates are soon in need of refresher courses as the company's product lines and markets change and as they become careless in their selling habits. Although the concept of continuing instruction for all sales personnel is still new in a great many companies, it is being rapidly accepted. The experience of the Armour-Dial division of Greyhound Corporation illustrates the value of such training. Armour-Dial ran a study on sales personnel who had attended a recent session at its Aurora (Illinois) sales training center. The result was a boost of 12 percent in case sales, 62 percent in displays sold, and 250 percent in sales to direct-buying or chain accounts.[2]

Determining the specific aims to be served by a continuing sales-training program also requires perception of specific training needs. Problems arising from forthcoming changes in company policy, procedure, or organization should be anticipated and studied—they may have implications for needed training. More basic changes in products and markets almost always gives rise to a need for additional training. It is also helpful to management, as it seeks to perceive needs for continuing training, to take such actions as: analyzing the sales job description relative to experienced persons' qualifications; surveying sales personnel for suggestions; scrutinizing salespersons' reports for symptoms of training needs; inspecting and analyzing sales records to uncover performance weaknesses; and personally observing salespeople in action to detect deficiencies. Sales management must know a great deal about how experienced sales personnel are doing their jobs in order to define specific aims for their continued training.

### Deciding the Content of Sales-Training Programs

The actual content of a sales-training program, whether initial or continuing, should be derived from the specific aims that management, after analyzing its training needs, has formulated. Initial sales-training programs generally are characterized by broader scope and coverage than continuing programs. Initial programs must provide instruction covering all important aspects of performing the salesperson's job; continuing pro-

[2] "The New Supersalesman: Wired for Success," *Business Week* (January 6, 1973), pp. 44-49.

grams may concentrate more on specific job aspects where management believes experienced persons to have more room for improvement. Therefore, the following discussion mainly relates to determining the content of initial sales-training programs.

For an initial sales-training program to contribute maximally toward preparing new recruits as sales personnel, it must cover all important aspects of the salesperson's job. Content varies considerably from company to company, because of differences in factors such as products, markets, company policies, trainees' ability and experience, organizational size, and executives' training philosophies. No two programs are, or should be, alike. Different companies tend to cover the same general topics despite the fact that variations always exist in the exact content and in the relative time devoted to each major topic. But it is possible to generalize to the point of saying that every initial sales-training program should devote some time to each of four main areas—product data, sales technique, markets for the product, and company information.

**Product Data.**  Some product training is basic to any initial sales-training program, even though all companies need not emphasize it. Companies with highly technical products commonly devote more than half of their programs to product training. But in many situations, especially with standardized products sold routinely, new sales personnel need receive only a small amount of formal product training. In all cases, however, management must make certain that new salespeople know enough about the products, their uses, and applications to serve customers' information needs adequately and promptly. Product knowledge is basic to a salesperson's self-confidence and enthusiastic job performance.

Understanding product uses and applications is especially important. Trainees should receive instruction on customers' problems and requirements and should learn how company products can help solve these problems and meet these requirements. Training should provide them with full appreciation for buyers' viewpoints, perhaps through role-playing instructional techniques. Through such training, new salespersons learn to relate company products to the fulfillment of customers' requirements, thus equipping themselves not only for effective selling but for effective handling of sales resistance met later in the field.

Creative selling is the name given a sales approach that places the emphasis upon buyers' needs. The National Cash Register Company pioneered the use of this technique around 1900. Progressive companies make extensive use of it today. In order to indoctrinate trainees in applying this approach, initial sales-training programs often provide a period during which trainees are in direct contact with ultimate users or consumers. Through personal experience, such as in retail selling or product servicing, trainees gain valuable insights on the ways different users react to company products.

More and more companies require a period of initial sales training at the factory. This provides trainees with opportunities to observe and study the products during the various manufacturing and testing phases. They have the chance, too, to talk with or even to work alongside factory personnel. The instructional benefits should be more thorough product knowledge and greater confidence in subsequently demonstrating or otherwise presenting products to customers. Inordinate amounts of time, however, should not be devoted to technical production detail—such detail is important only insofar as it helps the salesperson in actual selling situations.

Some training on competitors' products usually is desirable, particularly in highly competitive industries. Salespeople should not only know the important characteristics of competitors' products but be well posted on their uses and applications in solving customers' problems. They should be thoroughly familiar with how the strengths and weaknesses of competitive products compare with those of their own company's products. Thus informed, salespersons gain a decided advantage. They can structure their sales presentations to emphasize superior qualities or features of the company's product, and they are well equipped to answer customers' questions and to deal with their objections. Training on competitors' products must be continuous, the focus shifting as changes and improvements are made in both competitive and company products.

**Sales Technique.** Most new recruits need formal instruction in sales techniques, and an increasing number of firms provide such training. Some sales managers still believe, however, that careful selection of sales personnel and a heavy program of product training are sufficient to ensure effective selling. They believe, in other words, that if a person has an attractive personality, good appearance and voice, reasonable intelligence, and knows the product, he will be able to sell it easily. But the predominant view is that new sales personnel need basic instruction in how to sell. This is reflected in individual company sales training programs and in industry-wide programs offered by such groups as the National Association of Food Manufacturers and the National Association of Machine Tool Builders. In all sales-training programs the practical as well as the theoretical side of selling should be covered. In many companies, as an important adjunct to learning how to sell, new personnel receive training in the development of human-relations skills. In a few exceptional companies, training provides for practical analysis of the psychology of human behavior and motivation relative to company selling problems.

**Markets for the Product.** It is especially important for the new salesperson that training provides a comprehensive understanding of the market. The new salesperson must know who the customers are, the particular products in which they are interested, their buying habits and motives, their location, and their financial condition. In order to sell, in other words, the salesperson needs to know not only who buys what but, more important, why and how they buy. When trainees are not given adequate instruction on the market, they may take years to acquire the needed understanding independently. During this period of trial-and-error learning, through no fault of their own, their productivity is lower than it should be. In fact, left to their own devices, some trainees never gain important market information. For instance, a salesperson who is unaware of certain prospects' potentials as buyers may neglect completely to canvass them or even to canvass entire classifications of prospects. Because markets are always changing, training in this area should be continuous, the content changing as significant market changes occur.

**Company Information.** Certain items of company information are essential to the salesperson on the job; others, not absolutely essential, contribute to overall effectiveness. The training program should include coverage of all selling policies and, preferably, the reasoning that led to their formulation. The salesperson must know company pricing policy in order to answer customers' questions about it. The salesperson also needs to be fully informed on other policies, such as those relating to product services, spare parts and repairs, credit extension, and customer relations.

The initial training program must equip the salesperson to perform such tasks as recording and submitting customer's orders for processing and delivery, preparing expense and other required reports, handling inquiries, following up on customers' requests, and so forth. Each firm develops its own systems and procedures for handling these and similar tasks. If trainees are to perform them properly and efficiently from the very start of their field assignments, the initial sales-training program must provide the needed instruction. Otherwise, company systems and procedures are learned, if at all, through a costly and time-consuming process of trial and error.

Another aspect of company information that should be explained in initial sales-training programs relates to the sales department's personnel policies. Coverage includes selection procedures, training programs, compensation and incentive systems, advancement requirements and opportunities, savings and retirement plans, medical and insurance plans, and the like. Having such information improves employee morale and job effectiveness. Not having it shows up in employee uncertainty and needlessly excessive sales-force turnover rates.

Another ingredient that contributes to the building of morale among new employees might be described as "general company information." This concerns the company's history, its importance in the industry and economy, and its policies with regard to relations with stockholders, unions, competitors, government, and other groups. Having been briefed on these items, the new recruit's early and natural feelings of strangeness and uneasiness are replaced with some sense of belonging and company loyalty. Knowing something about the personality, or image, of the company also should bolster the confidence of recruits in its products, which they will shortly be trying to sell. It is worthwhile, then, to provide formal training covering selected items of general company information. But it also should be recognized that a common failing of initial sales-training programs is that too much time is spent on company background, history, and prestige building. The challenge is to provide sufficient general company information, but not to allocate instructional time disproportionate to its importance in the total program.

### Selecting Training Methods

Having defined specific training aims and determined program content, management must select appropriate instructional methods. There is a wide variety from which to choose. Professional educators and sales trainers have reevaluated and refined time-honored methods, such as lectures and discussions of different sorts, and, in addition, have developed new ones, such as the business game and role playing. Psychologists have influenced modern instructional methods through their studies of the learning process, motivation, retention, and so forth. From the many instructional methods available, the problem is to choose those that will most effectively and economically achieve program aims.

Instructional methods can be segregated into two major categories: those requiring group participation and those involving individual training.

**Group Instructional Methods.** These are used wherever trainees are grouped for instructional purposes. The group instructional methods most frequently used in sales training are: the lecture, the group discussion, role playing, and the simulation or game.

1. *The lecture.* Lecturing consists of primarily oral presentations, sometimes supplemented with visual aids, by an instructor in a formal classroom situation. This ancient teaching method, in use before the invention of printing, is still widely used in

sales training. Trainees participate mainly through watching and listening, although some versions of lecturing permit the asking of questions and allow for other interruptions. Generally, however, the lecture involves passive, rather than active, trainee participation, this feature constituting its main weakness—teaching is emphasized more than learning. But a lecture can be effective, provided the lecturer is an able and enthusiastic speaker and makes liberal use of examples, demonstrations, and visual aids. Compared with other group instructional methods, too, the lecture is economical in terms of time required to cover a given topic.

Many professional business teachers, perhaps most, regard lecturing as the least effective group instructional method. Professional sales trainers seem, by and large, to agree with this evaluation. Estimates are that the average trainee can immediately recall less than 10 percent of what he hears in a nonillustrated lecture, and no more than half of what he sees and hears in a lecture using visual aids. Furthermore, because of the absence of immediate participant feedback, no lecturer has any immediate or objective means for gauging the effectiveness of a lecture, but must rely on a personal appraisal of its reception, or on volunteered (and generally unreliable) comments by participants.

Even with its limitations, some lecturing in sales training is often a practical necessity. If formal training is brief, for instance, lecturing may be the only way to cover major portions of the desired content. It may also be the only practical way to handle instruction when the training group is too large to permit constructive audience participation. Given longer training periods and smaller training groups, however, lecturing is probably most appropriate for introductory and orientation sessions and for providing summaries of major topics taught mainly through methods such as case discussion and role playing. It also is used extensively, and in most instances appropriately, in continuing sales-training programs for providing new information about the company, its policies, products, markets, and selling programs. Recent research has indicated that, when it is necessary to use the lecture method, the learning process can be considerably improved by using a carefully planned multimedia approach.[3] In this approach the lecture room is equipped with two to six projectors and screens, and the entire lecture is projected visually on succeeding screens across the front of the room. Further lecture support is provided by projecting illustrations, charts, and graphs, and through the provision of sound effects, where appropriate. Tests have shown that this version of the lecture method significantly increases attention, comprehension, and retention.

√  2. *The group discussion.*  Group discussion differs from lecturing in several important respects. The instructor or discussion leader assumes a less dominant role, the trainees are active rather than passive participants, learning receives more emphasis than teaching, and the instructional atmosphere generally is much more informal and relaxed. Considerable flexibility is possible, too, in instructional format, the two main variations being the impromptu discussion and the case discussion. Because of these important advantages, and with the increasing sophistication of sales trainers, group discussion methods are not only being used more extensively, they are being incorporated into an ever-growing number of sales-training programs.

In the impromptu discussion, often called a sales seminar or conference, the instructor, group leader, or some group member makes a brief oral presentation on a

[3] W. H. Cunningham and E. W. Cundiff, "An Experiment in the Use of Multi-Media in Business Education," *AACSB Bulletin,* Vol. 10 (January 1974), pp. 41-45.

problem faced by sales-force members in their everyday work. This is followed by general give-and-take discussion. Group members gain a meaningful appreciation for and understanding of many problems that otherwise might be acquired, if at all, only through long personal experience. Many complexities and implications that might go undetected by individuals are revealed to all; and trainees may learn an even more valuable lesson—fixed selling rules and principles are often less important than careful analysis and handling of specific problem situations. Experience shows, in other words, that impromptu group discussion of problems improves the salesperson's ability in handling those problems, and others arising in connection with the job.

The case discussion involves individual and sometimes group study of write-ups of actual selling and other problems encountered on the job. Group analysis and discussion follows. This format, originated by professional business educators with a view toward providing a partial substitute for learning by experience, has been widely adapted for sales-training purposes. Each case should either describe a real selling or administrative problem, or be developed around a situation sufficiently real to stimulate emotional as well as objective involvement by trainees. Participants should be required to identify the issue(s), marshal the relevant facts, devise specific alternatives, and choose the one they consider most appropriate. Most users believe that securing a thorough grasp of the problem situation is more essential to learning than the rapid production of solutions. To derive maximum benefit from case discussion, each session should provide for the drawing of generalizations or "lessons learned."

Group-discussion methods are effective in training either new or experienced salespeople, but certain conditions must be met to achieve maximum benefits. Because discussion easily can drift into extraneous subjects or become sterile, an effective discussion leader or moderator is essential. The discussion leader must command the participants' respect, be skilled in dealing with people, and be extremely well informed not only on the subjects under discussion but on the salesperson's job and its problems. If advance assignments are made, as in case discussion, it is absolutely imperative that the participants be prepared—otherwise valuable instructional time is wasted. It is important, too, to realize that group discussion requires considerable instructional time to be effective. If the aim is to maximize trainee learning of specific points in depth, and not to provide a broad general survey, group discussion is an appropriate instructional method.

√ 3. *Role playing.* The role-playing method requires trainees to act out parts in contrived problem situations. As used in training on sales techniques, the role-playing session begins with the instructor describing the situation and the different personalities involved. The instructor provides all needed props, then designates trainees to play the roles of salesperson, prospect, and other characters. Each plays his or her assigned role and afterwards they, together with other group members and the instructor, appraise each role player's effectiveness and suggest how each might have improved his performance.

In another version of role playing, one of the group is given a bit of information on, for example, a buyer's objection to a particular product, and then is asked by the instructor to extemporize a solution. Sometimes called a "sweat session," this provides individual trainees a chance to apply what they have learned. "Postmortem" critiques afford opportunities to reinforce what has been learned through participating in, or viewing, the role playing.

Role playing, as an instructional method, presents comparatively few problems, but there are some. Those playing assigned roles must become not only actively but emotionally identified with the characters they portray; audience interest must be maintained throughout, even though spontaneous reactions should be suppressed. Achieving these conditions is not easy. It becomes even more difficult when role players "ham it up" or there is laughter or other involuntary audience reaction. Nonparticipants' comments should be saved for later, usually until the role playing is completed (although occasionally during "cuts" called by the instructor). If note taking is permitted as the play unfolds, some players tend to be distracted. This tendency, however, is overcome with repeated use of the method. These and similar problems can be minimized, provided that trainees are thoroughly briefed on what is and is not permissible, the group is limited in size (perhaps to no more than ten or twelve trainees), the instructor exercises discipline and control throughout, and role-playing assignments are realistic enough to make their learning potentials clear to all.

More than offsetting the few administrative problems are the many training benefits flowing from successful use of this instructional method. It provides realistic practice in applying what has been learned in other formal training or by experience. It is a highly flexible training method in that there is extreme diversity in role-playing situations. Experience shows, too, that role-playing instruction lends itself to easy adjustment for training new personnel, experienced salespeople, or even mixed groups. Among other benefits incidental to or derived from role-playing instruction are the following:

a. Most persons learn to accept criticism from others, and the group soon recognizes that sound suggestions benefit everyone.
b. When a person criticizes another's performance, that person has an incentive not to perform similarly later.
c. Role players practice introspection through participating in the appraisal of their own performances. The increasing use of tape-recording and playback equipment makes self-criticism even more beneficial and objective.
d. The "free-wheeling" nature of role playing is highly conducive to the generation of new ideas and approaches. Defects inherent in many stereotyped and "school" solutions soon become apparent.
e. In role-playing sessions for mixed groups, junior people have a chance to learn valuable "tricks of the trade," and experienced personnel are "kept on their toes" as a matter of personal pride.
f. Role players gain acting experience, which may be of great value to them later in handling difficult selling situations.

√ 4. *The simulation or game.* This instructional method, which somewhat resembles role playing, uses highly structured contrived situations, based on reality, in which players assume decision-making roles through successive rounds of play. A unique feature is that players have the benefit of information feedback. Trainees may play the roles of decision makers in customers' organizations, using data ordinarily available to make decisions on the timing and size of orders, managing selling forces and advertising efforts, and so on. The "results" of these decisions then are calculated by referees (sometimes using electronic computers) and fed back for the players to use in their next round of decisions.

Thus far, simulations or games used in sales-training programs have tended to be restricted to groups being prepared for management positions; but no insurmountable reason exists for not using them in other types of programs. Perhaps the main reason for not using games more extensively is the initial difficulty of preparing them. Preparation requires considerable research to dig out the needed facts, expert skill in incorporating these into a game model, development of detailed instructions for players and referees, and the writing of a computer program. Expertness and substantial investments in time and money, then, are required; but partially offsetting this is the fact that, once prepared, a game may see repeated use in many training programs.

The game or simulation has several attractive advantages as an instructional method. Among the more important are the following: (1) participants learn easily because they involve themselves enthusiastically in game play; (2) players develop skill in identifying key factors influencing decisions; (3) games readily lend themselves to demonstrations of the uses and values of such analytical techniques as inventory and other planning models; and (4) in contrast to other instructional methods, games, with their built-in information feedback features, are highly effective in emphasizing the dynamic nature of problem situations and their interrelationships.

Among the main instructional limitations of the game are the following: (1) some minimum time is required for playing, usually at least three or four hours, to generate sufficient decision "rounds" to provide the desired learning experience; (2) since game designs generally are based on ordinary decision-making processes, their rules often prevent payoffs on unusual or novel approaches; and (3) players may learn some things that aren't so," a limitation applying especially to carelessly prepared and/or poorly designed games. Most of these and other limitations may be partly or wholly overcome through careful game design and administration. Thus the game, or simulation instructional method, still in its infancy, possesses great potential for sales-training purposes.

√ **Individual Instructional Methods.**   Some methods are used for training salespeople on an individualized, one-person-at-a-time, basis. These techniques are used by large companies and are particularly appropriate for those with small sales forces, low personnel turnover, and small numbers of trainees. The more important individual methods are discussed below.

√1. *On-the-job training.*   This method, sometimes known as coach-and-pupil training, is a combination of telling, showing, practicing, and evaluating. The coach, who may be a professional sales trainer but is more often a seasoned salesperson, begins by describing to the trainee particular selling situations, explaining various techniques and approaches that might be used effectively. Next, accompanied by the pupil, the coach makes a number of actual sales calls, discussing each with the trainee afterward. Then, under the coach's supervision, the trainee makes sales calls, each one being followed by discussion and appraisal. Gradually, the trainee works more and more on his or her own, but with continuing, although increasingly less frequent, coaching sessions.

The instructional effectiveness of this method depends mainly upon the coach's qualifications. Given a qualified coach, the trainee starts off on the right foot, using selling techniques that the company wants used. Early deficiencies are corrected before they harden into habits difficult to change. If, however, the coach is not qualified, the trainee probably will learn the coach's bad habits as well as skills. Furthermore, many seasoned salespeople, otherwise well qualified for coaching, are unwilling to devote the necessary time and effort. This is especially true in companies whose sales personnel are paid commissions on sales. The problem of recruiting competent coaches, nevertheless, can be resolved through such means as paying bonuses for each person coached, or "overriding" commissions on pupils' sales for a certain period.

On-the-job training should form an important part of every initial sales-training program. There is no more effective way of learning about a job than by actually doing it. This method is uniquely appropriate for developing trainees' skills in making sales presentations, answering objectives, and closing sales. Training in these aspects of selling requires practice, and this method provides expertly supervised practice.

√ 2. *Personal conferences.* The potential of this instructional method commonly goes unrecognized, probably because many sales executives assume that learning occurs only in structured situations. Psychological research, however, has demonstrated repeatedly that learning may occur in structured *and* unstructured, formal and informal situations. In personal conference instruction, the trainer (often a sales executive) and trainee jointly analyze problems of mutual concern, such as effective use of selling time, route planning and call scheduling, and handling unusual selling problems. Because such training is expensive in terms of the trainer's time, idle chit-chat and purely personal conversation should be minimized. Maximum advantage should be taken of available time for instructional purposes.

√ 3. *Correspondence courses.* This instructional method is used both in initial and continuing sales-training programs. In the insurance field, for instance, it is used to acquaint new salespeople with industry fundamentals and for instruction in basic sales techniques. In companies with highly technical products and small but widely deployed sales forces, correspondence courses sometimes are used to acquaint experienced salespeople with new product developments and applications. Occasionally, too, this method is used for training noncompany sales personnel, such as distributors' salespersons, with a view toward improving their knowledge of the manufacturer's product line and selling techniques. But, despite these varied applications, effective sales training is difficult to achieve solely through correspondence, and few companies use the method exclusively.

For most companies, correspondence training is most appropriate as an interim method of instruction when trainees are scattered geographically, but groups are assembled periodically at central points for lectures, seminars, role playing, and other instruction. Initial sales training, for example, might be by correspondence courses begun at different times and places; continuing, or follow-up, training might come later through group instructional methods at a central location. Preparing a standardized correspondence course covering technical product data, general company information, selling techniques, and markets presents few difficulties other than those of choosing, organizing, and writing up the material.

Successful use of the correspondence method of instruction requires considerable administrative skill. The greatest problem is that of providing motivation for trainees to complete assignments on schedule. Not only are enrollees engaged in full-time work requiring that correspondence lessons be completed after hours, but few people have sufficient self-discipline to study without some direct supervision. Usually it is necessary to provide regularly scheduled examinations, prizes for completing work by given dates, or other incentives. Nor does this instructional method provide answers to individual enrollees' questions; hence, the most successful users arrange for periodic face-to-face discussions. Similar problems are met in processing trainees' completed assignments, in evaluating their work, and in correcting errors. If these and related administrative problems are solved, correspondence instruction serves as a useful supplement to other sales-training methods.

√ 4. *Programmed instruction.* This instructional method represents a considerable advance over the correspondence course. It involves breaking down subject matter into numbered instructional units called "frames," which are then incorporated into a book. Each frame contains an explanation of a specific point, plus a question or problem for the trainee to use in testing his or her understanding. Trainees check their answers by referring to another designated frame. If the answer is correct, the trainee is directed to new material; if it is incorrect, additional explanation is provided, and the trainee is re-tested on the point before going on to new material. Thus, trainees check their own progress as they work through the materials and may move through them at their own speed. Companies using programmed instruction, however, generally regard formal examinations as necessary incentives for the trainees.

To date, programmed instruction has not been widely adopted for sales training purposes. Most applications have been aimed at providing needed information. The Schering Corporation, for instance, provides programmed instruction on the clinical and pharmacological background of its drug products. This method is not used widely for training in sales techniques and market information because of difficulties in preparing appropriate programmed instructional materials. Preparation requires expert skills and thorough grounding in the psychology of learning. One ready-made programmed instructional course focusing on sales techniques, however, is available—prepared by Jack Schiff of Pace College, for Sales and Marketing Executives—International.

### Balancing Group vs. Individual Instruction

Generally group instruction is used in formal training programs, and individual instruction is given in the field. Both have contributions to make to the overall training program, so management must decide the role and the timing of each.

When there are large numbers of new personnel, group instruction is the most practical way to provide sales training at the least cost per person. In planning the curriculum content of the sales school, however, management must also determine the content that should and can be taught in the field—group instruction is often more effective when supplemented by individualized field training. To minimize needless overlap, and to maximize instructional results, careful attention must be paid to integration of what is taught by group methods in sales schools: product data, company information, market information, and the theoretical and practical fundamentals of selling. Advanced instruction in sales technique usually is best handled individually, in the field.

What is called "field training" is essentially on-the-job training, but it is conducted in the office as well as in the field. The trainee, under supervision, apportions his or her time between a branch, district, or regional office and a sales territory. Because field training is individualized instruction, it is quite informal. In the field, the trainee learns by watching an experienced salesperson in action and by practicing sales techniques under that individual's tutelage.

Opinion among sales executives is divided with respect to the best timing of group versus individual instruction. Most believe that the trainee should receive formal group instruction and indoctrination before meeting the customers and starting to sell. A sizable minority, however, believe in assigning trainees to selling jobs for individual instruction before sending them on to sales schools. In support of the minority view, three things can be said: (1) new personnel have a chance to prove that they have what it takes to sell before money is spent on their formal training; (2) new persons are not always, not even usually, hired in groups large enough to justify immediate formal training—people hired between programs can be put to work until the next school begins; and (3) there is considerable evidence to indicate that prior on-the-job experience not only furnishes needed learning motivation but makes formal instruction more meaningful. The minority position, nevertheless, clearly is inappropriate when highly technical products are sold to sophisticated buyers. In such cases, product training is not only highly important but best provided through formal group instruction at the outset of trainees' selling careers.

## EXECUTING SALES-TRAINING PROGRAMS

A great deal of planning work and attention to detail is prerequisite to successful execution of a sales-training program. Important decisions must be reached, as we have previously noted, on training aims, program content, and instructional methods. Organizationally, the executive must make certain that the trainers—whether full time or on special assignment—are themselves trained and fully understand their program responsibilities. Members of the group selected for training must be notified, necessary travel reservations made, and living accommodations arranged. Location of instructional facilities must be decided, instructional materials prepared, and training aids assembled. Once these things are done, the stage is set for actual execution of the program.

Effectiveness of program execution, of course, depends upon instructional skills as well as skillful coordination of different planning phases and "housekeeping" details. Successful program administration is very much an art, but, in essence, it involves doing everything that can be done to produce a training atmosphere as conducive as possible to learning. Discussion in the following sections centers on (1) the timing of training programs, (2) their location, and (3) instructional materials and training aids.

### Timing Initial Sales-Training Programs

The number of persons recruited annually directly affects the timing of initial sales-training programs. More precisely, timing depends upon the number of new persons who must be trained each year, and this, in turn, depends upon factors such as the size of the sales force, sales-personnel turnover, and management's plan for changing the size and composition of the sales force. When the number is large, comprehensive highly structured programs may be scheduled several times a year, the exact dates being set after consideration of recruiting quotas and deadlines. When the number is small, formal training programs, if held at all, necessarily are scheduled more infrequently, perhaps only once each year. Thus, for example, one company with a small sales force recruiting June college graduates schedules their training to begin in late June or early July.

There is an optimum number of trainees who may be effectively trained during a particular program. It depends upon such factors as training aims, subject-matter content, amount and availability of training talent, and instructional methods. Individualized training may be indicated in some situations; although it is expensive per individual trained, its timing can be highly flexible, depending only upon availability of trainees and trainers. In most situations, however, limitations of training funds and talent dictate that recruits be trained in groups, programs being scheduled whenever the backlog of untrained people approximates the optimum. No precise answer can be given to the question: How large is an optimum-sized training group? Experience indicates that, for most companies, groups smaller than twelve to fifteen involve inordinately high cost, while those larger than thirty to forty incur losses in training (that is, learning) effectiveness too great to be tolerated.

## Timing Continuing Sales-Training Programs

Modern sales management regards sales training as a never-ending process. This view recognizes that initial sales-training programs cannot prepare the salesperson for indefinitely effective job performance—the benefical effects of training gradually erode away. This view also stems from modern management's conviction that all training and all learning must be continuous—new information must be assimilated, and older concepts require modification in the light of new developments. New products, new refinements of selling techniques, new product applications and uses, new customer problems, new types of selling aids, new selling suggestions—all these and other developments require that each salesperson's training continue as long as he or she is on the job. In many situations, sales personnel may be kept abreast of new developments informally, perhaps through field distribution of information bulletins. But when new developments accumulate, are unusually important, or imply a need for significant changes in salespersons' attitudes and behavior patterns, a formal retraining program should be scheduled. Many companies integrate a short retraining program into a series of sales meetings or even into a single sales convention.

In some sales forces some but not all salespersons have deficiencies that may be correctable through training. If their weaknesses lie in different areas, the most practical and economical solution is to use on-the-job coaching. If several people are weak in the same general area(s), it is both practical and economical to use group instructional methods in an organized formal program (often scheduled for an off-peak selling period).

Even when sales management has no clear indication of the need, regular scheduling of retraining programs seems advisable. A survey of nearly 500 purchasing agents revealed that 60 percent felt that the majority of salespeople calling on them either had never learned or had forgotten how to sell. The same survey strongly implied that continuing training should provide sales personnel with more adequate product information and teach them how to present it in terms of user benefits.

Management's assumption should be that salespeople will welcome the opportunity for further training. Experience shows that most sales personnel are eager for help in improving selling techniques; most feel entitled to explanations of policy changes; most want to learn how to tie in their efforts more closely with advertising programs; and most are anxious to learn more about new products, model and design improvements, and shifts in market conditions. The majority of sales people, in other words, want to be kept abreast of current developments, and welcome efforts to interpret the significance of these developments in terms of their own job performance. If formal retraining programs are designed and "sold" as a means of helping salespeople do their jobs more effectively, they should not only be receptive to instruction but should derive benefits from it. Unless sales personnel are convinced of the future value of continuing training, its results will fall far short of what could be reasonably expected. If it can be demonstrated that training results in more take-home pay and increased job satisfaction, most salespeople will be motivated. And when salespeople believe that these benefits may be

obtained through a continuing sales-training program, the program's chances of successful execution are greatly enhanced.

## Location of Sales-Training Programs

Some companies hold formal initial sales-training programs at the central offices
and plant; others conduct separately executed programs at some or all branch offices.
Each plan has advantages and disadvantages. The centralized program held at a manufacturing plant generally provides better product training, but higher costs are incurred
in bringing trainees to the central point and housing them there. In many companies,
too, the small number of people to be trained does not justify decentralized formal
programs, and central location is a practical necessity. Many large companies, by way
of contrast, do have the option of using decentralized training programs. They can train
new salespeople in or near the territories to which they are later assigned, and thus can
acquaint them early with field selling problems. However, since decentralized product
training often requires the substitution of motion pictures, slides, and working models,
it may be less realistic, less interesting, and less effective than training given at a factory. But decentralized programs suffer from even more serious defects. Unless closely
supervised by higher management, their execution tends to be poor; and the trainers,
who commonly have other responsibilities and regard training as a diversionary sideline,
often turn in poor teaching performances. Generally, then, except in the very large
company, with its vast pool of administrative and instructional skills and other resources, formal initial sales-training programs should be held at central locations.

Retraining programs for seasoned salespeople also may be held either at centralized
or decentralized points. Because these programs often are short, the decision may hinge
almost entirely upon where the needed instructional talent is available and whether it is
more convenient and economical to transport and house the trainers or the trainees. If
retraining programs are timed to coincide with sales conventions, they may be held
nationally (either at the home office or convention headquarters elsewhere), or regionally, on a decentralized basis.

## ✓Instructional Materials and Training Aids

Critically important to successful execution of a sales-training program are the instructional materials and training aids. The exact nature of these will vary, of course,
not only for different companies but for programs with different aims and content.
Discussion in the following sections focuses on pertinent features and uses of the main
types of instructional materials and training aids.

✓**1. Manuals.** Often known as "workbooks," manuals are used in most formal
group-type sales-training programs. The best manuals generally contain: outlines or summaries of the main presentations, related reading materials, statements of learning
objectives for each session, orienting questions or "thought provokers," cases and
problems for discussion, plus directions for certain sessions, such as those involving role
playing or other simulations. Many manuals also include concise statements of selling,
pricing, sales personnel, and other policies, together with details on company systems and
procedures as they apply to the salesperson's work. A few contain detailed information on
the products and their applications. Discretion should be exercised in selecting items for
inclusion. It is all too easy to clutter up a manual with information of little or infrequent

value to the trainee. Manuals often are designed with a dual purpose in mind: to serve as study guides during formal training, and as references later; thus, many appear in loose-leaf form to facilitate subsequent additions and changes.

√ **2. Other Printed Materials.** Other printed matter includes regular company bulletins, sales and product handbooks, information bulletins, standard texts, technical and trade books, and industry and general business magazines and journals. Company publications are used chiefly to furnish field sales personnel with up-to-date and needed information. Keeping field sales personnel informed is also the main reason that many companies provide their salespeople with subscriptions to industry and general business magazines and journals. Texts and technical and trade books are used to supplement workbook materials, although trainees are rarely required to read them thoroughly during formal training. The usual practice is to assign or merely suggest selected readings, with the expectation that the books will be used later as references.

√ **3. Training Aids.** A training aid is an auxiliary device capable of contributing to instructional aims through transmission of sight and/or sound stimuli. Probably the most used and indispensable training aid is the blackboard—no training facility should be without one on which to illustrate points, summarize discussions, and the like, adding visual to vocal appeal. Modern substitutes for the blackboard (for example, the Vue-Graph projector, transparency roll, and screen) offer such improvements as making it possible for the instructor to face his class even while his or her writing appears on a screen, and conserving instructional time through using professionally prepared diagrams, charts, statistical tables, and so on. But no substitute is as fail-safe as a blackboard, none so free of possible mechanical or power failure. Even when main reliance is placed upon the Vue-Graph or other mechanically operated device, blackboard and chalk should be available for standby use, and to illustrate and explain points that arise in informal discussion. Although mechanical training aids supplement or support the blackboard as the basic training aid, none supplants it entirely.

The motion-picture projector and film form an appropriate training aid, especially when the instructional aim requires the depicting of motion or description and explanation of complex situations. In conveying technical information concerning installation and operation of new machine-tool models, for example, nothing short of actual demonstration is as effective as a movie. Substantial costs are incurred in producing special training film of high quality, since professional cameramen, actors, a director, and often specially constructed sets are needed. In deciding whether to produce tailor-made films then, management must seek to appraise their probable instructional effectiveness against the cost. Most sales-training films seek to convey information on products and their applications, but some aim at the refinement of sales techniques. One firm, for example, used an amateur-produced (hence, low-cost) "candid-camera" film of its sales personnel in action as an aid to improving their job performance. For the firm with limited funds, not wanting to resort to amateur-produced films, sales-training films of varying quality, most relating to selling fundamentals, are available commercially. It goes almost without saying that any training film, whether company-produced or commercially produced, should be previewed before it is used for instructional purposes.

Much of the motion picture's effectiveness can be achieved at lower cost with still pictures projected from slides or filmstrips. A sound disc may furnish a commentary together with "timed" changes in still pictures; or the instructor may make comments, varying the change interval between pictures by using a remote-control device. Many companies produce their own training slides and filmstrips, but a wide variety of commercially produced items also is available for purchase or rental.

Tape-recording and playback equipment is ideally suited for training aimed at improving sales techniques. Actual or simulated sales presentations may be taped and played back for individual or group appraisal. Recent advances in minature (and sometimes concealable) tape-recording devices even make it easy for salespersons to tape their own sales interviews and play them back later. Thus, they gain greater objectivity in appraising their own effectiveness, and in finding ways to improve their performance. Larger recorders are used in formal programs to tape group discussions and role-playing sessions, the tapes being played back later with appropriate commentaries and appraisals by participants and the trainer. Increasingly, too, instructors in sales-training programs tape their own sessions routinely. Later playbacks are helpful in improving teaching effectiveness and in conserving preparation time for repeat performances.

Closed-circuit television, not ordinarily classified as a training aid, is used in place of training films, especially where instructional timing is important. It is particularly appropriate in decentralized programs, such as those in which new product lines are being introduced to salespersons and/or dealer sales personnel. Other training applications of closed-circuit television include its use in short, decentralized retraining programs focusing on important policy changes, and as a substitute for national sales meetings devoted primarily to training.

## EVALUATING SALES-TRAINING EFFECTIVENESS

All sales training represents investments of time, money, and effort—and sales management should expect returns commensurate with the investment. Evaluating returns from sales training is not easy, however. Results, such as improved selling performance, may not show up until long after program completion. Despite such evaluation problems, it is possible to measure, somewhat roughly, training effectiveness. Management can make certain comparisons, such as the following: the length of time new sales personnel take to attain the productivity level of the average experienced person; sales results of trained vs. untrained personnel; and the respective training histories of the most and least effective salespeople. A few companies plot each salesperson's sales records on a "before and after" training basis, generally converting these records to share-of-the-market comparisons. It must be recognized, however, that any evaluation of training effectiveness based mainly on sales records can be, at best, only an approximation. Territorial sales volumes are influenced not only by salespeople's efforts but by such important factors as competitive activity, economic fluctuations, and advertising pressure. No method yet devised is fully satisfactory for precisely isolating the influence of any one of these factors. It should be noted, too, that any quantitative evaluation of sales-training effectiveness necessarily fails to take into account many intangible benefits from training (for example, improved sales-force morale). In spite of their technical deficiencies, however, comparative studies involving rough quantitative measures should provide management with a basis for evaluating training results.

Management should attempt to measure the effectiveness of individual sales training programs both while they are in progress and upon completion. The purpose should be to obtain needed insights for improving the effectiveness of future programs. Tests and examinations of various kinds are used for measuring trainee retention of materials presented. These are used most appropriately when trainees are expected to memorize information, as in the case of product specifications and applications. Most sales trainers see little value in using tests and examinations for evaluating the effectiveness of training in sales techniques. Trainees' performances in role-playing assignments may be a better means for appraising whether trainees have learned and, more important, are able to apply what they have learned. Trainers in some companies are required to rate each trainee's performance in sessions such as in role playing, panels, and other group discussion in which he or she takes an active part. Necessarily, such ratings are subjective, but they do provide trainees with learning incentives. It is interesting to note, too, that the practice of requiring trainees to rate each trainer's performance, either in each session or in the total program, is spreading. This may help in stimulating trainers to improve their instructional effectiveness. More than a few sales executives, however, argue that trainees are in no position to judge the trainers' effectiveness until they gain additional field experience. Nevertheless, "comment sheets" similar to that shown in Figure 11.1 are being used in an increasing number of sales-training programs. Many companies now also ask trainees to evaluate training programs after they return to their territories and have had a chance to put what they have learned into practice.

FIGURE 11.1
Form for Trainee Rating of Sales-Training Session

---

**Session Review**

A brief, candid review of this training session will help you evaluate what you have learned and help us in our efforts to improve the program. Please answer all questions. Do not sign your name; the results are anonymous.

Place an X where appropriate to describe your reactions to each of the following:

1. Material covered      Exciting ☐☐☐☐☐☐ Dull
2. Instruction      Excellent ☐☐☐☐☐☐ Poor
3. Worthwhileness of material      Great ☐☐☐☐☐☐ Little
4. Completeness of coverage    Very Complete ☐☐☐☐☐☐ Totally Inadequate
5. How might the session have been improved?

_____

_____

_____

---

## CONCLUSION

The entire production and marketing process culminates in the making of sales, and sales management's prime objective in training sales personnel is to strive for ever-improving sales performance. Effective sales training also assists sales management in discharging its social responsibility for reducing marketing costs. When salespeople perform assigned tasks efficiently and with minimum wasted effort, a real contribution is made toward cost reduction. With stepped-up marketing efficiency, cost savings eventually show up in benefits to consumers as well as in greater returns to the enterprise. At least in the long run, top management recognizes that the company's position in the industry is determined importantly by the performance of its sales and other personnel. Intelligently designed and well-executed sales-training programs have large potentials for helping sales personnel to achieve effective performance in their jobs.

# 12

# Instruction
# in Sales Techniques

The fully qualified sales executive has a thorough understanding of the various activities that make up the salesperson's job, is aware of the many problems that salespeople are likely to encounter, and is prepared to make practical suggestions for their solution. The sales executive must have a keen grasp of the theoretical aspects of sales techniques; and should have learned, preferably through field experience, how the theories relate to and work out in practice. Although many sales executives, some of them outstanding, have had little or no experience as salespersons, the normal progression to sales management is through selling. There are cases, however, of unusually good salespeople being utter failures as executives. The characteristics that make a person good at selling do not necessarily make him or her a good executive. Nevertheless, all other things being equal, usually the person who has had some selling experience is likely to prove successful as a sales executive.

Sales executives must be in close enough touch with actual selling situations to have a sympathetic understanding of the problems faced daily by the sales force. They realize that salespersons experience many frustrations. They know that salespeople must cope with obstacles to sales that often arise unexpectedly and require great ingenuity to surmount. Equipped with this understanding, sales executives have the background needed to train sales personnel for maximum productivity; they should also be able to direct the sales forces' efforts efficiently, and to evaluate individual's achievements realistically.

## WHAT IS "SALESMANSHIP"?

Although the terms "personal selling" and "salesmanship" are often used interchangeably, there is an important difference. Personal selling is the broader concept. Salesmanship may or may not be an important part of personal selling; it is never all of it. Along with other key marketing elements such as pricing, advertising, product development and research, marketing channels, and physical distribution, personal selling is a means through which marketing programs are implemented. Combined and integrated into a marketing program, these marketing elements become the strategy with which a firm seeks to achieve its marketing objectives. Whereas the broad purpose of marketing is to bring a firm's products into contact with markets and to effect profitable exchanges of products for money, the purpose of personal selling is to bring the *right products* into contact with the *right customers,* and to make certain that *ownership transfers* take place. Salesmanship is one of the skills used in personal selling; as defined by T. F. Stroh, it is *a direct, face-to-face, seller-to-buyer influence which can communicate the facts necessary for making a buying decision; or it can utilize the psychology of persuasion to encourage the formation of a buying decision.*[1] Salesmanship, then, is seller-initiated effort that provides prospective buyers with information, and motivates or persuades them to make favorable buying decisions concerning the seller's product or. service. The salesperson of today has to react and interact in many different ways to many different people. In addition to knowing the product thoroughly—regardless of how technical it may be—the salesperson has to be a psychologist with one prospect, a human computer with another, an adviser with another, and at the same time a friend with some buyers. Salespersons must adjust their personalities on every call, making sure that what they say and do is compatible with the personality of each prospect.[2]

Salesmanship may be implemented not only through personal selling but through advertising. In fact, advertising has been described as "salesmanship in print." The American Marketing Association defines advertising as any paid form of nonpersonal presentation and promotion of ideas, goods, or services by an identified sponsor.[3] Modern advertising is planned with motivation and/or persuasion as the objective.

Personal selling and advertising are simply two means that marketers use to inform and to motivate or persuade prospective buyers to buy; both means make use of salesmanship techniques. Salesmanship in advertising utilizes nonpersonal presentations. Nonpersonal, advertising-type presentations are necessarily less flexible than those made by sales personnel. An advantage unique to personal selling is that the salesperson can usually identify differences among buyers and pattern his or her presentation according to individual peculiarities.[4]

**Buyer-Seller Dyads.**   Fundamental to an understanding of salesmanship is recognition that it involves buyer-seller interactions. Sociologists use the term "dyad" to describe a situation in which two people interact with one another. The salesperson and the prospect, personally interacting with each other, constitute one example of what we will call a "buyer-seller dyad." Another example is provided by the interaction of a seller using advertising with a particular prospect in the reading, listening, or viewing audience. In both the advertising and personal-selling situations, the seller, generally speaking, is trying to motivate or persuade the prospective buyer to behave favorably toward the seller. Whether or not the buyer reacts as the seller desires depends upon the nature of the interaction. The opportunity for interaction is obviously less in the advertising case than in the personal-selling case, pointing up another advantage unique to personal selling. You should recognize, however, that in many situations, advertising and personal salesmanship supplement or support each other, and the buyer's reaction results from the combined impact of both.

In one interesting piece of research, Franklin Evans studied buyer-seller dyads in the life insurance business. This research revealed that prospects who bought insurance

---

[1] T. F. Stroh, *Techniques of Practical Selling* (Homewood Ill.: Dow Jones—Irwin, Inc., 1966) p. 7.

[2] P. J. Micali, *The Lacy Techniques of Salesmanship* (Homewood Ill.: Dow Jones—Irwin, Inc. 1972), p. xii.

[3] Committee on Definitions, American Marketing Association, *Marketing Definitions* (Chicago: American Marketing Association, 1960), p. 9.

[4] E. L. Brink and W. T. Kelley, *The Management of Promotion* (Englewood Cliffs, N.J.: Prentice-Hall, Inc., 1963), p. 7.

knew more about salespersons and their companies, and felt more positively toward them, than prospects who did not buy.[5] Furthermore, the more alike salespersons and their prospects were, the greater was the likelihood that a sale would result. This was true for physical characteristics (age, height), other objective factors (income, religion, education), and variables that could be related to personality factors (politics, smoking).[6] These findings have considerable significance for sales management. Wherever possible, sales personnel should be assigned to prospects whose characteristics are similar to their own, thus improving the chance that successful dyadic relationships will result. However, pairing of salespersons with customers of similar backgrounds is more easily accomplished in industrial selling, where there are fewer prospects about whom information is needed, than in consumer-goods selling, where the number of prospects and customers per salesperson is generally much larger.

In another interesting research project, Henry Tosi studied dyads made up of wholesale drug salespeople and retail pharmacists who made buying decisions. One apparent finding was that, when the buyer perceived the salesperson's performance to be similar to his or her concept of "ideal" performance, the number of sources from which purchases were made was low. Although this did not necessarily result in a larger percentage of purchases from the salesperson, customer satisfaction with the salesperson's behavior did at least allow the salesperson to get into the store. Tosi's suggested conclusion was that, in addition to the physical characteristics and objective factors cited by Evans, the customer's perception of how well the salesperson's behavior fits into the customer's conception of what that behavior should be is a necessary condition for the continuation of dyadic interaction.[7]

Another factor to be considered in these interactions among buyers and sellers is the buyer's initial conditioning with respect to selling. Salespeople have been maligned, and the butt of nasty stories for generations. People are taught from childhood to beware of the tricky salesperson.[8]

There are also definite indications that salespeople, not as stereotyped, but as they actually carry out their jobs, leave much to be desired in the impact they make on customers. Studies of the attitudes of buyers and purchasing agents reveal that they are heavily critical of the salesperson's lack of product knowledge, failure to follow up, general unreliability, slavish adherence to "canned" presentations, blatant use of flattery, bad manners, commercial dishonesty, and so forth.[9]

## SALES VARY IN DIFFICULTY

The relative degree of difficulty encountered in making sales varies considerably from one situation to another. In analyzing this problem, it is helpful to distinguish between two kinds of selling—service and developmental.[10] In service selling, the objec-

[5]F. B. Evans, "Selling as a Dyadic Relationship—A New Approach," *American Behavioral Scientist* (April 1963), p. 78.

[6]*Ibid.*, p. 79.

[7]H. L. Tosi, "The Effects of Expectation Levels and Role Consensus on the Buyer-Seller Dyad," *Journal of Business* (October 1966), pp. 516-29.

[8]A. Gross, "Psychological Blocks in Marketing," *MSU Business Topics,* Vol. 22, No. 1 (Winter 1974), p. 63.

[9]D. L. Thompson, "Stereotypes of the Salesman," *Harvard Business Review,* Vol. 50, No. 1 (January-February 1972), p. 160.

[10]G. N. Kahn and A. Shuckman, from whom we have borrowed this classification, actually refer to these two kinds of selling as sales maintenance and sales development. See "Specialize Your Salesmen," *Harvard Business Review,* Vol. 39, No. 1 (January-February 1961), p. 91.

tive is to obtain sales from people who are already customers and whose habits and patterns of thought are already conducive to such sales. The objective in developmental selling is not so much the creation of sales as the creation of customers out of people who do not at the moment view the salesperson's company favorably, and who are undoubtedly resistant to change.[11] McMurry points out that individual sales positions require different amounts of service and developmental selling, and he classifies sales positions according to their location on the spectrum involving degrees of developmental skill, from the very simple to the highly complex.[12] McMurry identifies seven main types of sales positions:

1. Positions where the salesperson's job is predominantly to deliver the product, for example, milk, bread, fuel oil.

2. Positions where the salesperson is predominantly an inside order taker, for example the sales clerk behind the counter in a dry-goods store.

3. Positions where the salesperson is also predominantly an order taker but works in the field, as the packing house, soap, or spice salesperson does.

4. Positions where the salesperson is not expected or permitted to take an order but is called on only to build goodwill or to educate the actual or potential user, e.g., the distiller's "missionary man," or the "detail man" representing an ethical pharmaceutical house.

5. Positions where the major emphasis is placed on technical knowledge, for example the engineering salesperson, who is primarily a consultant to the "client" companies.

6. Positions that demand the creative sale of tangible products, such as vacuum cleaners, refrigerators, siding, and encyclopedias.

7. Positions requiring the creative sale of intangibles, such as insurance, advertising services, or education.[13]

The more developmental selling required in a particular sales position, the more difficult it is to make sales. The amount of developmental selling required, in turn, depends upon the natures of the prospect (or customer) and the product. The easiest sales are self-service sales, which McMurry omits from his spectrum and rightly so; here the customers are aware of their needs, they know which products are capable of satisfying these needs, and they sell themselves. The most difficult sales are those that involve intangibles—the customers usually are not fully aware of their needs; someone must explain the existence of these needs and how the intangible can satisfy them. Such selling requires effective explanations of the benefits to be derived from the intangible and the consequences of not buying it. The level of difficulty of the majority of sales falls between these two extremes. The prospect has some awareness of the need; but, before the purchase is made, the salesperson must further define the nature of the need and explain the product and its benefits.

## THEORETICAL ASPECTS OF SELLING

There is considerable disagreement as to the extent to which selling can be described as a science with basic concepts that can be easily taught, or as an art that can be learned only through experience. In a survey of 173 marketing executives, 46 per-

[11] *Ibid.*

[12] R. N. McMurry, "The Mystique of Super-salesmanship," *Harvard Business Review,* Vol. 39, No. 2 (March-April 1961), pp. 113-22.

[13] *Ibid.,* p. 114.

cent perceived selling as an art, only 8 percent perceived it as a science, and 46 percent perceived it as an art that is evolving into a science.[14] The fact that some consider selling an art and others consider it a science has produced two theoretical approaches to explaining how sales are made.

The first source involved the distillation of selling theories from the experiences of successful salespeople and, to a lesser extent, advertising professionals. Many such persons, of course, have succeeded because of their grasp of practical, or learned-through-experience psychology and their almost intuitive ability to apply it in actual sales situations. Thus, it is not too surprising that such selling theories emphasize the "what to do" and "how to do" rather than explaining "why." It is important to recognize that these theories, based on an experiential kind of knowledge that is accumulated from years of "living in the market" rather than on a systematic, fundamental body of knowledge, are subject to Howard's dictum, "Experiential knowledge can be unreliable."[15]

The second source, which has been tapped only comparatively recently, includes the behavioral sciences, whose research findings a growing number of marketing scholars have been attempting to apply to the problems of buying and selling.[16] The late E. K. Strong, Jr., Professor of Psychology at the Stanford Graduate School of Business, was one of the pioneers in this effort, and his "buying formula" theory of selling is presented later in this section. John A. Howard of the Columbia Graduate School of Business has been in the forefront of the group of marketing scholars concerned with borrowing and adapting the findings of research in behavioral science to the analysis of buying behavior; his "behavioral equation" represents an attempt to develop a unified theory of buying and selling.[17] This behavioral equation is also discussed later in this section.

The purpose of this section, then, is to acquaint the reader with four attempts to identify and explain the nature of the process of influencing others to buy. The first two, the "AIDAS" theory and the "right set of circumstances" theory, are salesperson or seller oriented. The third, the "buying-formula" theory of selling, is buyer oriented. And the fourth, the behavioral equation, emphasizes the buyer's decision process but takes the salesperson's influence process into account. Our intention is not to provide the reader with a secret formula for successful selling; indeed, we are unaware of the existence of such a formula. Our belief is that readers will understand the selling process better if they understand these four "theories."

## √AIDAS Theory of Selling

The first theory—popularly known as the AIDAS theory, after the initials of the five words used to express it—forms the basis for many sales and advertising texts and

[14]J. L. Goldstucker, B. A. Greenberg, and D. N. Bellenger, "How Scientific Is Marketing? What Do Marketing Executives Think?" *MSU Business Topics*, Vol. 22, No. 2 (Spring 1974), p. 41.

[15]J. A. Howard, *Marketing Theory* (Boston: Allyn and Bacon, Inc., 1965), p. 71.

[16]For a discussion of the state of development of personal selling theory, see J. G. Hauk, "Research in Personal Selling," in G. W. Schwartz (ed.), *Science in Marketing* (New York: John Wiley & Sons, Inc., 1965), especially pp. 219-28.

[17]Considerably more in the way of borrowing and adapting from behavioral science research will have to be done if a "general theory" is to evolve. Establishment of a general theory in the social sciences themselves is more a goal than a reality. On this point, see T. Parsons and E. A. Shils (eds.), *Toward a General Theory of Action* (New York: Harper & Row, Inc., 1962), Torchbook Edition.

is the skeleton around which many training programs in selling are organized. Although some support for this theory is found in the psychological writings of William James,[18] there is little doubt that the construct is based mainly upon experiential knowledge and, in fact, was in existence as early as 1898.[19] During the successful selling interview, according to this theory, the prospect's mind passes through five successive mental states: attention, interest, desire, action, and satisfaction. Implicit in this theory is the notion that the prospect who buys goes through these five stages consciously; thus, the salesperson's presentation must lead the prospect through them in the right sequence if a sale is to result.

**Securing Attention.** In this phase the salesperson's goal is to put the prospect into a receptive state of mind so that the main body of the presentation may be started. The first few minutes of the interview are often crucial. The salesperson has to have a reason, or at least an excuse, for conducting the interview. If the salesperson has made a previous appointment with the prospect, this phase should present no great problem; but experienced sales personnel say that even with such an appointment a salesperson must possess considerable mental alertness, and be a skilled conversationalist, to survive the beginning of the interview. The prospect's guard is naturally up, since he or she realizes that the caller is bent on selling him or her something. So the salesperson must establish good rapport at once. The salesperson needs an ample supply of "conversation openers," and must strive to make a favorable first impression. Favorable first impressions are assured by, among other things, proper attire, neatness, friendliness, and a genuine smile. Skilled sales personnel often decide upon conversation openers just before the interview so that the gambits chosen will be as timely as possible. Generally it is considered advantageous if the opening remarks are about the prospect (people like to talk and hear about themselves), or if they are favorable comments about aspects of the prospect's business. A good conversation opener causes the prospect to relax his or her feeling of caution and sets the stage for succeeding phases of the salesperson's presentation. Conversation openers that cannot be readily tied in with the remainder of the presentation should be avoided, for once the conversation starts to wander, great skill is required to return to the main thrust of the presentation.

**Gaining Interest.** The salesperson's second goal is to intensify the prospect's attention so that it evolves into a state of strong interest. Many techniques are used for gaining interest. Some salespeople develop a contagious enthusiasm for their product, becoming so inspired that the prospect's interest is built up almost automatically. Another technique is to let the prospect handle the product or a sample. When the product is bulky or technical, sales portfolios, flipcharts, or other visual aids serve the same purpose.

Throughout the interest phase, one of the salesperson's main purposes is to search out the selling appeal that is most likely to be effective. If the salesperson is fortunate, the prospect drops hints, which the salesperson then uses in selecting the best approach. To encourage the prospect along this line, some salespeople devise stratagems to elicit revealing questions. Others draw out the prospect by asking questions designed to clarify attitudes and feelings toward the product. The more experienced the salesperson the

[18]See W. James, *Psychology* (New York: Henry Holt & Company, 1908).

[19]E. K. Strong, Jr., *Psychological Aspects of Business* (New York: McGraw-Hill Book Company, 1938), p. 24.

more he or she can rely for possible clues on what has been learned from other interviews with similar prospects. But even experienced sales personnel often must resort to considerable probing, usually of the question-and-answer variety, before identifying the strongest appeal. It should be mentioned, too, that prospects' interest is also affected by such factors as their basic motivations, the closeness of the interview subject to their current problems, the timeliness of the subject, and their mood—receptive, skeptical, or hostile—and the salesperson must take all these into account in selecting the selling appeal that he or she will emphasize.

**Kindling Desire.** The salesperson's third goal is to kindle the prospect's desire to the ready-to-buy point. The salesperson must remain in control of the situation and must keep the conversation running along the main line toward the sale. The development of sales obstacles, the prospect's objections, external interruptions, and digressive remarks are some of the factors tending to sidetrack the presentation during this phase. Obstacles have to be faced and ways found to get around them. Objections need answering to the prospect's satisfaction. Time frequently is saved, and the chance of making a sale improved, if objections are anticipated and answered before the prospect has a chance to raise them. External interruptions cause breaks in the presentation; and when conversation resumes, good salespeople normally summarize what has been said earlier before continuing. Digressive remarks should generally be disposed of tactfully, with finesse, but sometimes distracting digression is best handled bluntly: for example, "Well, that's all very interesting, but to get back to the subject. . . ."

**Inducing Action.** If the presentation has been perfect, the prospect is ready to order. However, this action is not usually automatic and, as a rule, must be induced. Experienced sales personnel rarely try for a close until they are positive that the prospect is fully convinced of the merits of the proposition. Thus, it is necessary for the salesperson to sense when the time is right to induce the prospect's buying action. Such devices as the trial close, the close on a minor point, and the trick close are used to test the prospect's reactions to the proposition. Some sales personnel never ask for a definite "yes" or "no" for fear of getting a "no," from which they think there is no retreat. But it is usually better to ask for the order straightforwardly. Most prospects find it easier to slide away from hints than from frank requests for an order.

**Building Satisfaction.** After the customer has given the order, the salesperson should reassure the customer that the decision was the correct one. The customer should be left with the impression that the salesperson merely helped in making the decision. Building satisfaction means thanking the customer for the order, which should always be done, and attending to such matters as making certain that the order is correct as written, and following up on any promises made. Because the order is the climax of the selling situation, the possibility of an anticlimax should be avoided—customers sometimes unsell themselves, and the salesperson should not linger too long.

### √ "Right Set of Circumstances" Theory of Selling

Often a salesperson comments: "Everything was right for the sale to take place"; and this sums up the popular version of the second theory. This theory, sometimes expressed by the term "situation-response," had its psychological origin in experiments with animals, and holds that the particular circumstances prevailing in a given selling situation cause the prospect to respond in a predictable way. More specifically stated: If the salesperson succeeds in securing the attention and gaining the interest of the prospect, and if the salesperson presents the proper stimuli or appeals, the desired response (that is, the sale) will result. Furthermore, according to the theory, the more highly skilled the salesperson is in handling the total set of circumstances, the more predictable will be the response.

The relevant set of circumstances, which the theory suggests that the salesperson should try to control, includes factors external and internal to the prospect. To use a simplified example, suppose that the salesperson says to the prospect, "Let's go out for a cup of coffee." The salesperson and the remark represent external factors. But at least four internal factors related to the prospect affect the response. These are the presence or absence of desires: (1) to have a cup of coffee, (2) to have a cup of coffee now, (3) to go out for a cup of coffee, and (4) to go out with the salesperson for a cup of coffee.

Proponents of this theory have been inclined to overstress the external factors and to neglect the importance of the internal factors. They have devoted their major efforts to seeking out selling appeals that generally can be depended upon to evoke desired responses. Sales personnel who try to apply the theory commonly experience difficulties traceable to prospects' ingrained habits and instinctive behavior. Although it is relatively easy to control the external factors in many selling situations, the internal factors do not readily lend themselves to manipulation by salespeople. Thus, this is a seller-oriented theory, and from that emphasis derives its chief drawbacks: it stresses the importance of the salesperson controlling the situation, does not adequately handle the problem of influencing factors internal to the prospect, and fails to assign appropriate weight to the significance of the response side of the situation-response interaction.

### √ "Buying-Formula" Theory of Selling

In marked contrast to the two theories just discussed, the third places emphasis on the buyer's side of the buyer-seller dyad. The buyer's needs or problems receive major attention, and the salesperson's role is conceived as being one of helping the buyer find solutions. This theory purports to answer the question: What thinking process goes on in the prospect's mind that causes the decision to buy or not to buy? The buying formula itself is a schematic representation of a group of responses, arranged in feasible psychological sequence. The buying-formula theory, in other words, emphasizes the prospect's responses (which, of course, are strongly influenced by internal factors) and deemphasizes the external factors, on the assumption that the salesperson, being naturally conscious of the external factors, will not overlook them. Since the salesperson's normal inclination is to neglect the internal factors, the formula is a convenient way to help the salesperson remember. The origin of this theory is somewhat obscure, but recognizable versions appear in a number of early books on advertising and selling by authors who evidently had experiential knowledge of salesmanship.[20] Several psychologists also advanced explanations substantially similar to that contained in the buying

---

[20]See, for example, H. Tipper, H. L. Hollingsworth, G. B. Hotchkiss, and F. A. Parsons, *Advertising, Its Principles and Practices* (New York: The Ronald Press Company, 1915), and W. W. Charters, *How to Sell at Retail* (Boston: Houghton Mifflin Company, 1922).

formula.[21] The name "buying formula" was given to this theory by the late E. K. Strong, Jr., and the following step-by-step explanation is adapted from his teaching and writings.[22]

Reduced to their simplest elements, the mental processes involved in a purchase are:

$$\text{need (or problem)} \longrightarrow \text{solution} \longrightarrow \text{purchase}$$

Because the outcome of a purchase affects the chance that a continuing relationship will develop between the buyer and the seller, and because nearly all sales organizations are interested in such continuing relationships, it is necessary to add a fourth element to our analysis of a purchase. The four elements, then, are:

$$\text{need (or problem)} \longrightarrow \text{solution} \longrightarrow \text{purchase} \longrightarrow \text{satisfaction}$$

Whenever a need is felt, or a problem recognized, it means that the individual is confronted with a difficulty or is conscious of a deficiency of satisfaction. In the world of selling and buying, the solution to such a difficulty will always be a product or service. And the product or service will belong to a potential seller.

In purchasing, then, the element "solution" involves two parts: (1) product (or service), and (2) trade name (name of manufacturer, company, or salesperson).

In buying anything, the purchaser proceeds mentally from need or problem to product or service, to trade name, to purchase; and, upon using the product or service, he or she experiences satisfaction or dissatisfaction. Thus, when a definite buying habit has been established, the buying formula covering the elements involved in buying can be diagrammed as follows:

$$\begin{matrix} \text{need or} \\ \text{problem} \end{matrix} \longrightarrow \begin{matrix} \text{product or} \\ \text{service} \end{matrix} \longrightarrow \text{trade name} \longrightarrow \text{purchase} \longrightarrow \begin{matrix} \text{satisfaction} \\ \text{dissatisfaction} \end{matrix}$$

To ensure purchase, the product or service and the trade name (that is, the source of supply) must be considered adequate, and the buyer must experience a (pleasant) feeling of anticipated satisfaction when thinking of the product or service and the trade name. In a great many cases, a commodity viewed as adequate is also liked, and vice versa; but this is not always the case. Some products and services that have been found quite adequate are not liked, and some things are liked and bought that are admittedly not as good as competing items. Similar reasoning applies in the cases of trade names— some sources of supply are considered both adequate and liked; others are adequate but not liked; still others are liked but patronized in spite of the fact that they are inadequate compared to competing sources.

When adequacy and pleasant feelings are included in the buying formula, the following diagram results:

[21]See, for example, A. T. Poffenberger, *Psychology in Advertising,* rev. ed. (New York: McGraw-Hill Book Company, 1938), pp. 16-39. The above explanation is patterned after Strong's, but some terminology has been changed in line with modern usage.

[22]Dr. Strong's own explanation can be found in his *Psychological Aspects of Business* (New York: McGraw-Hill Book Co., 1938), pp. 16-39. The explanation here is patterned after Dr. Strong's, but some terminology has been changed in line with modern usage.

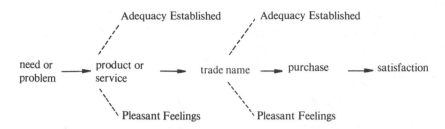

When a buying habit is being established, the buyer must be aware of the reason why the product or service is an adequate solution to the want or problem, and why the particular trade name is the best one to buy from. It is also necessary that the buyer have a pleasant feeling toward the product or service and the trade name.

Then, whenever the buyer's buying habit is challenged by a friend's remark, a salesperson's presentation of a competing article, or a statement in an advertisement, it is essential that the buyer have reasons with which to defend the action, and that, in addition, he or she have a pleasant feeling toward both the product or service and the trade name. All this is represented by the dashed lines in the formula.

The primary elements in a well-established buying habit are those connected by solid lines, on the central line of the formula. Probably the majority of purchases are made with scarcely a thought as to why, and with a minimum of feeling. And it should be the constant aim of the salesperson and advertiser to form such direct associations. Reasons, and pleasant feelings, are related to elements on the central line by dashed lines to indicate that they constitute the elements of defense in the buying habit. As long as they are present, buying will continue as in the past.

The solution to each selling problem is implied in the buying formula, and the differences among these various solutions are merely differences in the *emphasis* that is put upon the elements in the formula.

Where the emphasis should be placed depends upon a variety of circumstances. Without going into detail, it may be said that:

1.   If the prospect does not feel a need or recognize a problem that can be satisfied by the product or service, the need or problem must be emphasized.

2.   If the prospect does not think of the product or service when he or she feels the need or recognizes the problem, the association between need or problem and product or service must be emphasized.

3.   If the prospect does not think of the trade name when he or she thinks of the product or service, the association between product or service and trade name must be emphasized.

4.   If need or problem, product or service, and trade name are well associated, emphasis must be put upon facilitating purchase and use.

5.   If competition is felt, emphasis must be put upon establishing in the prospects' minds the adequacy of the trade-named product or service, and pleasant feelings toward it.

6.   If sales involving new prospects are desired, every element in the formula must be presented.

7.   If more sales to old customers are desired, the latter must be reminded. (Developing new uses is comparable to selling to new customers.)

## √ "Behavioral-Equation" Theory[23]

Using a stimulus-response model (which is a much refined and highly sophisticated version of the "right set of circumstances" theory discussed earlier), and incorporating numerous findings from behavioral science research, J. A. Howard explains buying behavior in terms of the purchasing decision process, viewed as phases of the learning process.

Four essential elements of the learning process included in the stimulus-response model are drive, cue, response, and reinforcement. These elements are described as follows:

1.  *Drives* are strong internal stimuli that impel the buyer's response. There are two kinds of drives:
    a.  Innate drives: The physiological needs, such as hunger, thirst, pain, cold, and sex.
    b.  Learned drives: Learned drives, such as striving for status or social approval, are acquired when paired with the satisfying of innate drives, and represent elaborations of the innate drives, serving as a façade behind which the functioning of the innate drives is hidden. Insofar as marketing is concerned, the learned drives are probably dominant in economically advanced societies.

2.  *Cues* are weak stimuli, as distinguished from the strong stimuli that underlie drives. Cues determine *when* the buyer will respond.
    a.  Triggering cues serve as activators of the decision process for any given purchase.
    b.  Nontriggering cues influence the decision process but do not activate it, and may operate at any time even though the buyer is not contemplating a purchase at the moment. There are two kinds:
        (1) Product cues are external stimuli received from the product directly, for example, color of the package, weight, or price.
        (2) Informational cues refer to external stimuli that provide the buyer with information of a symbolic nature about the product. Such stimuli may come from advertising, conversations with other people (including sales personnel), etc.
    c.  Specific product and information cues may sometimes also function as triggering cues. This may happen when price triggers the buyers decision.
3.  *Response* is what the buyer does.
4.  A *reinforcement* is any event that strengthens the tendency for a buyer to make a particular response.[24]

Howard incorporates these four essential elements into a behavioral equation, stated in its simplest form as follows:

$$B = P \times D \times K \times V$$

where

---

[23]This discussion is a greatly condensed version of the thorough explanation and analysis of the behavioral equation contained in J.A. Howard's book, *Marketing Management: Analysis and Planning,* rev. ed. (Homewood, Ill.: Richard D. Irwin, Inc., 1963). We are indebted to the author for permission to include this condensation.

[24]Howard, *Marketing Management,* pp. 41-43.

$B$ = response or the internal response tendency, that is, the act of purchasing a brand or patronizing a supplier

$P$ = predisposition or the inward response tendency, which is strength of habit.

$D$ = present drive level (amount of motivation)

$K$ = "incentive potential," that is, the value of the product to the buyer or its potential satisfaction to him or her

$V$ = intensity of all cues: triggering, informational, or product[25]

Notice that Howard believes the relation among the variables to be multiplicative rather than additive. Thus, if any independent variable has a zero value, $B$ will also be zero and there will be no response. No matter how much $P$ there may be, for example, if the individual at the moment is totally unmotivated ($D=0$), there will be no response.[26]

Furthermore, each time there is a response—a purchase—in which the satisfaction ($K$) received from the response is sufficient to yield a reward, predisposition ($P$) will increase in value as a result of the rewarded response. In other words, when the satisfaction received yields a reward, reinforcement occurs and, technically, what is reinforced is the tendency to make a response in the future to the cue that immediately preceded the rewarded response. After such reinforcement, the probability increases that the buyer will buy the product (or patronize the supplier) the next time the cue appears— in other words, the buyer has learned.[27]

**Buyer-Seller Dyad and Reinforcement.** To the extent that a salesperson and a buyer interact, each can display a type of behavior that is rewarding, that is, reinforcing, to the other. The salesperson provides the buyer with a product (and the necessary information about it and its uses) that the buyer needs; this satisfaction of the need is rewarding to the buyer, who, in turn, can reward the salesperson by buying the product. Each can also reward the other by another type of behavior, that of providing social approval. The salesperson gives social approval to a buyer by displaying high regard for the buyer with friendly greetings, warm conversation, praise, and the like.

In understanding the salesperson-client relation, it is helpful to separate the economic aspects from the strictly social features. The salesperson wishes to sell a product, and the buyer wishes to buy it—these are the economic features of the relationship. Each participant also places a value and cost upon the strictly social features. Behavior concerning these features of the relationship can be called sentiments, or expressions of different degrees of liking or social approval. Salespersons attempt to get more or less valuable reward (reinforcement) either in sentiment or economic activity, which they do by changing their own behavior or by getting buyers to change theirs.[28]

**Salesperson's Influence Process.** The process by which the salesperson influences the buyer can be explained in terms of the behavioral equation ($B = P \times D \times K \times V$). The salesperson can probably influence $P$ (predisposition) directly, for example, through

[25]*Ibid.*, pp. 43-45.

[26]*Ibid.*, p. 45.

[27]Howard states, however, that "additional reinforced purchases . . . increase $P$ at a negatively accelerated rate [as] illustrated in the shape of the learning curve. . . ." *Ibid.*, p. 45.

[28]*Ibid.*, pp. 427-28.

interacting with the buyer in ways that are rewarding to the buyer. The greatest effect on $P$, however, is thought to be the reinforcement that comes from using the brand. There is little doubt that the salesperson can exert influence through $D$ (amount of motivation), such influence being especially strong when the buyer seeks information primarily in terms of informational cues. If the ends to be served through satisfying a drive or a need are not clearly defined, by helping to clarify these, the buyer's goals, the salesperson again exerts influence through $D$. When the buyer has stopped learning— when the buyer's buying behavior consists solely of automatic responses—the salesperson influences $D$ by providing triggering cues. When the buyer has narrowed down the choices to a few sellers from whom to make purchases, the salesperson, by communicating the merits of the company brand, can cause it to appear relatively better, and thus affect $K$ (its potential satisfaction for the buyer). Finally, the salesperson can vary the intensity of his or her effort, so making the difference in $V$ (the intensity of all cues).[29]

**Salesperson's Role in Reducing Buyer Dissonance.** According to Festinger's theory of cognitive dissonance, when individuals choose between two or more alternatives, anxiety or dissonance will almost always occur because they know that the decision made has certain unattractive features in addition to its attractive features. After making decisions, people therefore tend, according to this theory, to expose themselves to information that they perceive as likely to support their choices, and to avoid information that is likely to favor rejected alternatives.[30] Although Festinger evidently meant his theory to apply only to situations involving postdecision anxiety, it seems reasonable that the theory should also hold for situations involving predecision anxiety. Hauk, for instance, writes that a buyer may panic on reaching the point of decision, and rush into the purchase as an escape from the problem, or put it off because of the difficulty of deciding among alternatives.[31] It would appear, then, that a buyer may experience either predecision or postdecision anxiety or dissonance, or both. Howard notes that the reduction of both pre- and postdecision anxiety or dissonance is an important function of the salesperson. Recognizing that the buyer's dissonance varies both according to whether the product is an established or a new one, and whether the salesperson-client relation is an ongoing one or new, Howard considers the following four main types of cases involving the nature of the salesperson's role in dissonance reduction:

1. An established product—an ongoing salesperson-client relation. Unless the market is unstable, the buyer tends toward automatic response behavior, in which no learning is involved, and thus experiences little, if any, dissonance; but insofar as this does occur, the salesperson would presumably be effective because the salesperson would be trusted by the buyer.
2. An established product—a new salesperson-client relation. The salesperson, being new, would presumably be less effective in reducing dissonance.
3. A new product—an ongoing salesperson-client relation. Unless the buyer generalizes heavily from personal experience with an established similar product, the buyer would experience dissonance, especially if it were an important product. Because of the established relationship with the buyer, the salesperson would be capable of reducing dissonance.

---

[29]*Ibid.*, pp. 429-30.
[30]L. Festinger, *A Theory of Cognitive Dissonance* (New York: Harper & Row, Inc., 1957).
[31]Hauk, *op. cit.*, p. 261.

4. A new product—a new salesperson-client relation. The buyer would need dissonance reduction, and the salesperson would be less capable of providing it.[32]

How can a salesperson facilitate the buyer's dissonance reduction? Zaltman, after analyzing a number of findings from behavioral science research, says that there are at least two ways: (1) by repeating and reemphasizing the advantages of the product purchased, and stressing the relative disadvantages of the foregone alternatives; and (2) in cases of dissonance traceable to buyers' feelings that they have purchased items not sanctioned by the relevant reference groups, the salesperson can try to show that many characteristics of the chosen item are similar to products the buyers have foregone, but which are approved by their particular reference groups.[33] In other words, the buyer experiencing cognitive dissonance should be reassured that the decision is or was a wise one; the salesperson can exert influence by providing information that will permit the buyer to rationalize the decision.

## √ PROSPECTING

Efficient organization of their time and thorough planning of their work are earmarks of above-average salespersons; only a small portion of their total time is devoted to actual selling but they are ever alert for ways to "stretch" this productive selling time. Above-average salespersons do many things to stretch out the time available for selling. They arrange their travel and call schedules to economize on time spent en route and distance traveled. They make advance appointments, to avoid prolonged waiting periods and unnecesary callbacks. Most important, they make certain that they do not waste time trying to sell to people who cannot buy or are not likely to do so. This planning work, which is essential in eliminating calls on nonbuyers from the itinerary, is called prospecting.

Improvement in prospecting is one of the most promising approaches toward more productive use of selling time. Unfortunately, many sales personnel devote too little time to prospecting and, as a consequence, too much to calling on nonprospects. Even though prospecting is one of the surest methods for salespersons to increase their own incomes and their worth to the company, many salespeople tend to neglect their prospecting duties. Salespersons who are proficient in prospecting are able to apply their selling efforts more productively; they waste less time in making calls on nonprospects, and devote more attention to those that are most likely to buy.

Some companies use specialized personnel for prospecting work, but most regard it as one of the salesperson's normal responsibilities. Regardless of who performs the task, the steps involved are similar. Even though salespersons may not personally do prospecting, they should understand the process. They are the ones in closest touch with the customers, and they often have access to sources of information on likely prospects not available to central office personnel.

### Steps in Prospecting

The steps involved in prospecting are implied in the statement of the purpose of personal selling given earlier. Personal selling brings the right products into contact with

---

[32]Howard, *Marketing Management,* p. 430.

[33]G. Zaltman, *Marketing: Contributions from the Behavioral Sciences* (New York: Harcourt Brace Jovanovich, 1965), p. 63.

the right customers and makes certain that ownership transfers take place. There are four steps: (1) formulating prospect definitions, (2) searching out potential accounts, (3) qualifying prospects and determining their probable requirements, and (4) relating company products to each prospect's requirements.[34]

✓ **Formulating Prospect Definitions.**  To be considered prospective customers, or prospects, potential buyers must fulfill certain requirements. They must have the willingness, the financial capacity, and the authority to buy, and they must be available to the salesperson. Salespersons waste valuable time when they attempt to sell individuals who have neither need for the product nor money to pay for it. Salespersons' efforts are similarly wasted if they try to sell to the wrong persons; so it is important to ascertain which individual in each firm has the authority to buy which of the salesperson's products. And although individuals may qualify as prospects in all the preceding respects, they may be completely inaccessible to the salesperson. The president of a large corporation, for example, may need insurance, and be willing and able to pay for it; but a particular salesperson may have no way to make the contact.

In addition to the above requirements, there are others unique to each company's customers and, before one can prospect effectively, these must be identified. Starting with data on the profitability of present accounts, any characteristics typical of profitable accounts but not shared by unprofitable accounts should be detected. These identifying characteristics ideally should be ones easily recognizable from information appearing in directories or lists. Prospects in many categories of businesses and professions, for instance, may be readily identified from the classified listings in telephone and city directories. Significant characteristics that identify profitable accounts are assembled into descriptions of the various classes of customers, and these serve as prospect definitions.

If the firm has a good sales-analysis system, the formulation of prospect definitions is comparatively easy. Most of the needed information on customer traits is already part of the system and requires only assembling. In the event that the sales-analysis system is inadequate, or fails to yield sufficient customer data, it is worthwhile spending the time and effort required for gathering, organizing, and processing the needed information. Once a company has a good sales-analysis system, it also has an information source for formulating definitions of the different categories of prospects.

✓ **Searching out Potential Accounts.**  Using the prospect definitions, the salesperson should comb all available information sources to search out the names of probable prospects, or "suspects," as they are called. Sources of prospect information include: directories of all kinds, news and notes in trade papers and business magazines, credit reports, membership lists for such groups as chambers of commerce and trade and manufacturers' associations, lists purchased from list brokers, and records of service requests. Other sources include: responses to company advertising, sales personnel of noncompeting firms calling on the same general classes of trade, conventions and meetings, bankers and other "centers of influence," and the salesperson's own observations. Salespeople selling services, such as insurance and mutual funds, find personal contacts an especially valuable source. They may uncover excellent prospects among their acquaintances; members of their professional, religious, and social organizations; and

[34]For an interesting discussion on the importance of knowing as much as possible about the account in advance of making the sales call, see B. P. Shapiro, "Manage the Customer, Not Just the Sales Force," *Harvard Business Review,* Vol. 52, No. 5 (September-October 1974), pp. 130-31.

from the referrals of friends. Another source of prospects for such salespeople is the "continuous chain-referral method"—satisfied customers often suggest, voluntarily or on request, other leads to the salesperson who served them.

√ **Qualifying Prospects and Determining Their Probable Requirements.** Names on the tentative prospect list are next subjected to more intensive investigation. With the assembling of more information, it becomes progressively easier to detect bona fide prospects and to eliminate those who are not. As the "picture" of each prospect develops, estimates are made concerning the extent to which each uses products similar to those of the company. Prospects with requirements too small to represent profitable business are removed from further consideration, unless their growth possibilities appear to show significant promise. Even after tapping all readily available information sources, additional information often is required before qualifying certain prospects. In cases of this sort, personal visits by salespersons may be the only way to obtain it. Although such visits may not result in sales, time is saved over the long run, since prospects are separated from nonprospects.

√ **Relating Company Products to Each Prospect's Requirements.** The final step is to plan the strategy to use in approaching each prospect. From the information assembled, it is usually possible to determine, more or less accurately, the nature of the likely needs of each. From what the salesperson knows about the company's products, their uses and applications, he or she selects those that seem most appropriate for the particular prospect. The salesperson has now finished most of the work preliminary to making the sales calls.

The salesperson's presentation should now be easy to construct, and it can be tailored rather precisely to exert strong influence upon the prospect. The salesperson should have rather clear ideas in advance of the specific objections the prospect may raise, and other obstacles to the sale that may be encountered. The salesperson is now ready to make actual contact with the prospect, the only tasks remaining being those of making an appointment, deciding how to open the presentation, and determining how best to influence the prospect to become a customer.

## SALES RESISTANCE

To succeed in converting prospects into customers, the salesperson needs skill in analyzing and overcoming sales resistance. Prospects show sales resistance by pointing out real or imagined obstacles to the sale, and by voicing objections, sincere or insincere. In analyzing sales resistance, skill in the accurate and rapid appraisal of people and their motivations is essential. A prospect's expressed sales resistance should be identified as either an obstacle or an objection. An obstacle must be classified as real or unreal; an objection, as sincere or insincere. After sizing up sales resistance in this manner, the salesperson is in good strategic position to select the next moves.

**Obstacles to Sales.** Obstacles are real or apparent reasons that the prospect has for not buying. If the obstacle is real, it precludes the consummation of the sale. But if it is only apparent, the salesperson can find a way of circumventing it. A prospect may say that he cannot buy because of a temporary shortage of cash—an obstacle, not an objection—and the salesperson may help the prospect circumvent it by explaining a method for financing the purchase. Some obstacles can be circumvented, others cannot. When salespersons perceive that an obstacle to a sale exists, they should determine at once whether or not there is a way to get around it. If they are sufficiently experienced to recognize the specific obstacle and know a way to circumvent it, the next move is to present their solution to the prospect's problem.

**Sales Objections.** Objections call for different treatment. They are almost never good reasons for failing to complete the sale, but they nearly always divert the salesperson's presentation from its main course. At best, an objection requires a short and satisfactory answer; at worst, it blocks the sale entirely. Adroitness in handling objections is an important difference between effective and ineffective salespeople.

Sincere objections often trace to incompleteness, inaccuracy, or vagueness in the salesperson's presentation. Prospects may not recognize the nature of their needs; or they may have real doubts about the appropriateness of the product to fulfill them, be confused in some respect, or may even react unfavorably to the salesperson's personality. Except when personality conflict is irresolvable (which case would be classified as a real obstacle, rather than as an objection), sincere objections ordinarily can be overcome by patient and thorough explanations.

Insincere objections are more difficult to handle, for prospects use them to discourage salespersons, to get rid of them, to test their competence, or to furnish false excuses for not buying. When salespersons sense that an objection is insincere, they should muster their persuasive powers and regain the offensive as soon as they can. Under no circumstances should they permit an insincere objection to provoke an argument—that is one of the surest ways to lose a sale.

Some sales executives feel that every objection, no matter how trivial or insincere, should be treated with the utmost courtesy and answered as well as possible. Others believe that insignificant objections should be ignored. One thing is clear—when the prospect raises an objection, the salesperson should try to use it to introduce additional reasons for buying. The best defensive strategy for a salesperson, as for a defending army, often is the strong counterattack, and the salesperson should seek to regain the initiative as soon as he or she can gracefully do so.

## CLOSING SALES

The tactics of selling followed during the presentation affect the ease of closing the sale. Generally, low-pressure sales are closed more easily than high-pressure ones. In low-pressure sales, to the extent that prospects are made to feel that they are reaching the buying decisions themselves, and primarily through rational processes of thought, there is less need for extra push by the salespersons just before the sales are consummated. By contrast, in high-pressure sales, the main thrust of the appeal is to prospects' emotions; salespersons attempt to propel prospects into buying decisions. Often the prospect suddenly regains normal perspective as the sale nears its climax and, if this happens, the salesperson needs truly unusual powers of persuasion to close the sale.

Nearly every salesperson approaches certain closings with considerable apprehension. At this point, either the salesperson sells the prospect an order, or the prospect sells the salesperson on a "no sale." But this point also provides the salesperson with an opportunity to register tangible proof of selling skill. Occasionally even the best salesperson has done inadequate prospecting, or made a below-par presentation; on these occasions, he or she must rely upon closing skills.

Prospecting, if well done, should put the salesperson in the proper frame of mind for the close. He or she should feel that a real service is being performed for the prospect, not that "a bill of goods is being sold." If the prospecting has been thorough, the salesperson should have little doubt that the product is the best solution to the prospect's problems.

When the sales presentation has been complete and clear, little difficulty should be met in closing the sale. All obstacles to the sale and all objections have been removed, to the prospect's entire satisfaction. Under these conditions, basic agreement has already been reached, and the prospect is ready to react favorably to the salesperson's proposal.

But even after an excellent presentation, and in spite of the thoroughness of the prospecting, some prospects refrain from positive commitments. The natural tendency of many people is to let inertia guide their reactions—many are perfectly happy to leave things as they are, and salespersons leave emptyhanded unless they somehow manage to jolt such prospects into buying. In some situations, the skilled closer gives the extra push that triggers a buying response. But it needs emphasizing again that failures to get an order are as much the result of poor prospecting and inept presentations as they are of ineffectiveness in closing.

When an attempt at a close fails, the salesperson should normally try again. The salesperson should not be too easily discouraged, because a refusal does not necessarily imply an unwillingness to buy; it may simply indicate the prospect's need for additional information, or for clarification of some point. Some sales executives recommend that their sales personnel attempt as many as five closes before abandoning a given effort. Early attempts at a close should be so expressed that the prospect's refusal will not cut off continuation of the presentation. A salesperson must learn to judge the sincerity of a prospect's refusal, surrendering gracefully when it becomes obvious that no sale will be made.

In most situations, the salesperson should first try an indirect close; that is, attempt to get the order without actually asking for it. The salesperson may ask the prospect to state his preference from among a limited number of choices (as to models, delivery dates, order size, or the like), so phrasing the question that all possible responses are in the salesperson's favor except for one—"None at all." Or the salesperson may proceed to summarize, emphasizing features that have visibly impressed the prospect, showing how the reasons for the purchase outweigh those opposed. Then the salesperson pauses for the prospect's response, which is expected to be, "Go ahead and write the order." Sometimes, the extra push may be a concession that makes the purchase appear sufficiently more attractive to effect completing the sale. Or the salesperson simply may assume that the sale has already been made, writing out the order and handing it to the prospect for approval—if the prospect balks, the issue becomes clearer. Perhaps one last objection is voiced; but after it is satisfactorily answered, the sale is made. Many other indirect closes are in common use, and books on selling contain numerous examples.

When one or more attempts at an indirect close fail, the above-average salesperson uses the direct approach. Surpri, ngly few genuine prospects respond negatively to a frank request for an order. In fact, many persons, especially those who are themselves engaged in selling, do not buy unless the order is asked for directly. Some evidence indicates that a high proportion of sales personnel fail to ask for the order directly, one study showing that more than 50 percent failed in this respect. But those who asked for the order averaged 300 percent more sales than those who did not.[35]

## CONCLUSION

In sales management, as in management work of all kinds, executives must know and understand the activities performed by those who report to them. Of the tasks assigned to salespeople, the most obvious, and certainly among the most important, are those involved in selling. To perform selling tasks effectively, selling skills are needed; and the techniques of selling, the "how to sell," are important parts of sales training for new and experienced sales personnel alike. New people must be brought to at least a minimum level of selling skill, and more experienced persons require refresher training. Only when sales executives thoroughly understand and have a realistic appreciation for the tasks assigned to the personnel under them, and only after they gain considerable insight into the ways in which the nature of these affects the thought processes and behavior patterns of the sales staff, are executives fully equipped to assume the responsibility for sales-force management.

[35]W. J. Tobin, "Do You Want to See Your Volume Grow and Grow?" *Printers' Ink* (February 16, 1951), p. 54.

# 13

# Motivating
# the Individual Salesperson

Many a "star" salesperson requires little external incentive "in climbing the ladder of sales success." To such people, selling is the world's most fascinating occupation, and they constantly challenge themselves to improve upon their selling performances. Unfortunately, however, such self-starters are all too scarce in selling. As a matter of fact, most sales personnel do not maintain consistently high levels of selling performance unless sales management provides additional stimulation. High productivity in a sales force comes about neither naturally nor accidentally; it develops through intelligent handling of relationships with salespeople and the timely use of appropriate incentives. Discussion in this chapter focuses on the motivation of salespersons as individuals.

## THE COMPANY AND ITS RELATIONS WITH SALES PERSONNEL

It is possible, although unusual, for a company to have rather poor relations with certain employee groups and still enjoy a good public reputation. But it is essential to have satisfactory relations with sales personnel. Insofar as customers are concerned, the sales staff is the company, and the image they project is strongly influenced by the nature of their relations with sales executives. Sales territories cover a wide area; and the opinions of the company's sales force are carried to, and affect the opinions of, distributors, dealers, and customers generally, as well as other groups. Hence, good public relations begin inside the company, and for the sales department, this means with the sales force. Moreover, the sales manager's main contribution to a marketing program's success generally is to get results through company sales personnel, further emphasizing the critical nature of this executive's relations with subordinates.[1] Whereas the salesperson's primary working relationship is with the customers, the sales manager's is with the sales force.[2]

---

[1] For a highly stimulating discussion regarding the importance of the sales manager's understanding what managing is and what it is not, see R. O. Loen, "Sales Managers Must Manage," *Harvard Business Review*, Vol. 42, No. 3 (May-June 1964), pp. 107-114.

[2] On the interconnections of these two sets of relationships, see R. T. Davis, *Performance and Development of Field Sales Managers* (Boston: Division of Research, Harvard Business School, 1957), p. 347.

It is generally easier to maintain good relations with salespeople if satisfactory relations exist with other employees; an important difference is that salesperson's interests are frequently more akin to those of executives than to those of other company personnel. Because sales personnel operate without personal supervision much of the time, more trust and confidence necessarily must be placed in them. Perhaps that is why the sales force so often serves as a proving ground for future executives and why some managements tend to develop paternalistic relationships with the sales staff. But paternalism should be avoided, and democratic administration should be more than just an ideal in the sales force: it should be customary practice. Close personal relations should exist among sales executives and sales personnel, and individuals in both groups should clearly understand the interests of the other. But favoring certain salespeople at the expense of others can have only adverse effects upon overall sales-force morale.

Job satisfaction and a feeling that what he or she is doing is worthwhile are key factors in motivating a salesperson to stay in a company's employ. Therefore, it is important for management not only to recognize each salesperson's contribution to company success but to let them know that management knows and appreciates the contributions they are making. All members of a sales force should be made keenly aware of their individual contributions to the overall good of the company.[3] Although it is impossible to prescribe all the other conditions necessary for building and maintaining satisfactory relations with salespeople, it is possible to tell when a company has achieved them. When sales personnel have pride, loyalty, and enthusiasm concerning the company, its products, its policies, and the executives who plan and direct their work, relations with salespeople are excellent.

## WHY SALES PERSONNEL REQUIRE ADDITIONAL STIMULATION

Why are some salespeople more successful than others? What, in other words, accounts for variations in selling success? The answer lies in the differing motivational patterns of individual salespersons and the resulting relative amounts and types of efforts they exert in performing their jobs. The analysis leading to this conclusion will be examined later; first we must review three aspects of the salesperson's job that affect the quality of its performance. Each aspect is also an important reason why most salespeople require additional stimulation to reach and maintain high productivity.

The first aspect concerns the nature of the salesperson's job itself. Generally, it is a succession of ups and downs, a series of experiences resulting in alternating feelings of exhilaration and depression. In the course of a day's work, salespersons call on many pleasant and courteous people; but they encounter some who are unpleasant and rude, with whom it is difficult to deal. They are frequently frustrated, particularly when aggressive competing salespeople are vying for the same business, and they meet numerous "turndowns." Furthermore, salespersons must spend not only working time but also considerable "after-hours" time away from home, causing them to miss many of the best parts of family life. These conditions can easily cause a person to become discouraged, to achieve performance levels lower than might otherwise be possible, or even to seek a nonselling position. The nature of the salesperson's job being what it is, then, additional stimulation often is required to assure effective job performance.[4]

[3]"Rewards, Recognition, and Job satisfaction," *Advanced Management Journal,* Vol. 33 (July 1968), pp. 20-25.

[4]"Behavior: Rejection Is a Part of the Selling Job; Train Your Salesmen to Cope with It," *Sales Management,* Vol. 108, No. 10 (May 1, 1972), pp. 45-55.

The second aspect concerns the natural tendency of some sales personnel to become apathetic, "to get into a rut." Salespersons who, year after year, cover the same territory and virtually the same customers, tend to lose enthusiasm. Gradually their sales calls degenerate into routine order taking. Because they feel they know the customers so well, they come to believe that good selling is no longer necessary. Their approach to a customer typically becomes: "Do you need anything today, Joe?" They fail to recognize that friendship with customers in no way obviates the necessity for creative selling, and that it is unusual for customers to sell themselves on new products and applications. The customer's response, as often as not, is: "Nothing today, Bill." Later a competing salesperson calls on the same account, uses good selling techniques, and gets an order. Many salespeople require additional stimulation to maintain continuing enthusiasm for their work or to generate renewed interest in it.[5]

The third aspect is related to the previous two. It concerns both the nature of the selling job and the natural tendency for job enthusiasm to decline. The salesperson, working alone for the most part, finds it difficult to maintain a feeling of group identity with other company salespeople. Team spirit, if present at all, tends to be weak. Thus, the contagious enthusiasm so necessary to improvement of the entire group's performance fails to develop. If sales management, by providing appropriate added stimulation, succeeds in developing and maintaining team spirit, individual salespeople strive very hard to meet group performance standards. Few people who consider themselves full-fledged members of the "sales team" want to appear as poor performers in the eyes of fellow salespersons. Providing a working atmosphere in which the entire sales force feels they are participating in a cooperative endeavor is not easy; nevertheless, sales management must strive continuously to achieve and maintain it.

Sales personnel, then, require additional stimulation both as individuals and as group members. Salespersons who become discouraged or apathetic are prime targets for personalized, informal efforts at motivation on the part of their superiors. Sales forces whose members have little feeling of group identity are ripe for more formal efforts by sales management directed toward welding them into effective selling teams.

## HANDLING RELATIONS WITH SALES PERSONNEL

Effective handling of relations with salespeople is a skill not easily attained. Experience, maturity, and common sense are necessary attributes and, although these cannot be gained through study alone, a few generalizations can be made. Sales executives should treat all salespersons fairly, particularly with regard to assignments, promotions, and changes in pay. They should commend salespeople for jobs well done; but if performances are not up to par, they should privately call that to their subordinates' attention. When sales executives find it necessary to discuss a salesperson's weaknesses, they should also make it clear that they are aware of the individuals' strong points. Before making changes, particularly ones affecting salespeople's jobs or their performance, sales executives should consult the sales personnel affected; this helps to prevent the damaging impact of rumors upon morale. The sales force should be convinced, individually and collectively, that when right is on their side, the sales executive can be depended upon, if the need arises, to carry their case to top management. And, above all else, sales executives must not lose sight of the fact that they are managing the sales staff.

[5]"Recharging a Sluggish Sales Force," *Business Management,* Vol. 35 (February 1969), pp. 41-44.

While encouraging the sales force's participation in decision-making, ultimately the sales executive must be certain that they are "sold" on plans, policy changes, and anything else that affects them. Real sales personnel are all the more sold on their jobs when sales executives habitually apply good sales techniques in their relations with them.

## COMMUNICATIONS AND MOTIVATING INDIVIDUAL SALESPEOPLE

Communications, simply defined, consists of the transmission and interchange of facts, ideas, feelings, and courses of action. In sales management, it is critically important that good communications exist between each salesperson and his or her superior—unless it does, there will be depressed morale and low productivity. The salesperson with pent-up grievances, real or imagined, is likely to display both low morale and unsatisfactory performance. Similarly, the salesperson, like everyone else, occasionally comes up against personal problems, such as sickness in the family, inability to pay overdue bills, or marital troubles, all of which can adversely affect morale and performance. Thus, the system of two-way communications between the salesperson and the superior should allow for free discussion of all business problems connected with the salesperson's job and, to the extent needed, of any personal problems that, left unsolved, may hurt job performance. For the salesperson, the existence of good communications represents freedom of self-expression—freedom to talk over problems, business and personal, with the superior in a friendly atmosphere. For the superior, it represents the responsibility for finding occasions and means for talking with the salesperson not only to determine what, if anything, is "bothering him," but also to provide assistance in solving any problems that come to light.

### Communication and Role Conflict

Nowhere else in the business organization are two-way channels of communication more important than in the sales department. The nature of the salesperson's job is that of a link between at least four different groups: (1) the sales-management group, (2) the balance of the organization who must be depended upon for fulfillment of orders, (3) the customers, and (4) other sales personnel, within the company and elsewhere. Each group imposes certain behavioral expectations on the salesperson and, in performing these different roles, the salesperson faces specific role conflicts.[6] J. A. Belasco describes three such conflicts:

1. *Conflict of identification* arises out of the multigroup membership of the salesperson. As the salesperson works with the customer, it is reasonable to expect identification with the customer rather than the company. However, on returning to the company, the salesperson must drop the identification with the customer and identify with the company.

2. *Advocacy conflict* arises when the salesperson has identified with the customer; it is logical to expect that he will seek to aid the customer by advocating the customer's position to the other groups with which is linked. Although this function may be very important and may be actually encouraged by the salesperson's superiors, it places the advocator in a very difficult position.

3. *Conflict inherent in the salesperson's dual role as an advocate* for both the customer and

---

[6]J. A. Belasco, "The Salesman's Role Revisited," *Journal of Marketing,* Vol. 30, No. 2 (April 1966), p. 7.

the company, and the salesperson's pecuniary interest as an entrepreneur. As an entrepreneur paid on the basis of sales volume, he has a decided interest in selling as much as possible in the shortest possible time. However, he may uncover facts overlooked or unknown to the customer, indicating that difficulties in the customer's organization will limit the product's usefulness. If the salesperson informs the customer of these observations and that, in all probability, the product will not fully meet the customer's needs, obviously the salesperson runs the risk of losing the sale and the income that goes with it.

Existence of potential or actual role conflicts traceable to the salesperson's linkage with groups that often have divergent interests explains why the roots of misunderstandings, grievances, poor morale, and even lack of productivity so often are found in communications breakdowns.

Compounding the communications problem is the fact that sales executives and salespersons usually work at a distance from each other, often not only throughout most of the workday but over extended periods; and most communications must be by mail and telephone. Despite this, however, sales executives should do some things to assure that communications are as effective as possible. They should make a point of meeting with their people as often as practicable, both at the office and in the field. To avoid faulty transmissions, they should speak and write in language that sales personnel understand—this does not mean that they should "talk down" to them but rather that they should gear their communications with them to their level. They should be certain that their sales forces understand them and that they understand their sales personnel. In all verbal communications, it is to the sales executive's advantage to be a good listener. By devoting close attention and analysis to salespeople's remarks, sales executives can learn a great deal about their subordinates. Similarly, the sales executive should look for hidden as well as apparent meanings in salesperson's written messages. Thus, the sales executive may gain insights that should go far in explaining why sales personnel act and react as they do. This knowledge is invaluable in directing salespeople's activities and in providing additional motivation.

### Interpersonal Contact

Interpersonal contact is the preferred way to communicate with and thereby to stimulate sales personnel. Through such contacts, management should make probing and comprehensive evaluations of individual salespeople's morale. Interpersonal contacts provide management's best opportunity for learning of financial, family, or other personal worries that can have important impacts upon salespeople's overall efficiency.

Sales executives at all levels, from immediate supervisor to chief sales executive, should have personal contacts with the sales staff. Particularly at the higher levels of sales management, however, face-to-face visits with salespeople tend to be confined to conventions and sales meetings. For the most part, then, most of the individual salesperson's interpersonal contact with management is with the immediate supervisor. Although supervisors have other important functions to perform, such as training, evaluation, and control, they should be made fully aware of their responsibilities for maintaining communications with the people under them. They should, in other words, use their visits with salespersons for detecting personal or business problems, and for inspiration and stimulation, in addition to discharging other supervisory responsibilities.

Even though the immediate supervisor is the administrator in closest contact with individual salespeople, sales executives at all levels should reserve some time for observing and conferring with sales personnel. District managers should allocate time in which to visit each salesperson on the job in the assigned sales territory. It may be impractical, especially in the large national sales organization, for the top sales executive to visit personally all territories or even all sales districts; however, there are other ways for him to maintain personal contact with sales personnel. One is to arrange individual conferences between salespeople and the top sales executive during regional or national meetings—the opportunity to visit with the "big boss" can provide strong stimulation for individual salespersons.

Although interpersonal contact generally is the best way to keep in touch with the sales staff, there are times when other communications media must be used. Not only is it physically impossible to be in close contact with all sales personnel all of the time, but, unfortunately, too often the least-valuable salespeople demand the lion's share of the personal attention. When this happens, executive contact with the better salespeople tends to be largely through written means. Confronted with this situation, many sales executives prefer to keep in touch with their better people, not through letters, but through regular telephone calls, this being particularly appropriate when the staff in the field are far from the home office and visit it only infrequently.

Several instances can be cited in which the executive should contact salespeople personally, or possibly telephone them, rather than communicate by letter. A drop in a salesperson's efficiency that the executive suspects was caused by family discord is not only difficult but awkward to discuss in writing. Similarly, when a reprimand is thought necessary, a face-to-face meeting with the salesperson unquestionably is better than dispatching a letter that could lead to further complications. Personal and disciplinary problems, then, are best handled by interpersonal contact and not through the mail. In exceptional cases, it may be possible through a clear and carefully phrased letter to avoid misinterpretations and misunderstandings, but the executive is still extremely well advised to follow up all such letters with personal contacts.

It is difficult for a sales executive, particularly for one who supervises sales personnel directly, to motivate a salesperson whom he or she knows only casually. The sales executive must make a special effort to know each salesperson well, and to learn what is important to each salesperson—he or she needs this knowledge if subsequent efforts to encourage improved performance are to be at all productive. Sales executives with direct supervisory responsibilities, then, must develop empathy with their subordinates and carefully plan the time they spend in individual communications with their sales personnel.[7]

**Motivational Interviews.** A recent trend, especially in more progressive companies, has been toward establishing planned "informational" goals for the executive to keep in mind during personal visits with individual sales personnel. A "motivation interview form," such as that prepared by Sales and Marketing Executives—International, is designed to assist sales executives in organizing their efforts to gather motivational data on individual salespeople.[8] Using such a plan, the executive attempts to find out as much as possible about salespeople's patterns of need fulfillment and the order of priority assigned to each category of need. Thus, insights are gained on individuals' motivational patterns, and guidance is furnished management in choosing appropriate incentives. Of course, it is unlikely that a single interview could be used to gather all

[7]*Ibid.*
[8]See Case III-3, Fenway Electric Company, pp. 402-5.

this information; but after many interviews, the executive should be able to assemble the information needed to put together a comprehensive picture. The motivational interview technique provides a way to gather information bit by bit according to some plan of which the sales personnel need not, probably should not, be aware.

## Written Communications

Supplementing personal contacts with salespeople, the sales executive attempts to keep them informed through letters, announcements, bulletins and other mailed pieces. Unfortunately, however, handling written communications tends to become routine and deadening—increases in volume and frequency of mailings often destroy their value. It is ironic, too, that some sales executives who think nothing of spending hours planning every detail to ensure the effectiveness of a sales meeting almost wholly neglect any attempt to appraise the probable motivational impact of their correspondence. It is true, of course, that no single letter or bulletin is likely to have as strong a motivational effect as a sales meeting; yet the total impact of written communication, effectively used, can be much greater than the occasional formal sales meeting.

The executive writing personal letters and bulletins to salespeople should avoid using generalities and concentrate upon specific helpful suggestions. A letter to Salesperson Brown, reporting that Salesperson Jones wrote a $20,000 order last week, and instructing Brown to go out and do the same provides little real motivation. Describing how Jones succeeded in promoting a new use for the product to a certain kind of customer furnishes much stronger motivation. Writing letters, especially those designed to cheer up and spur on salespeople in the field, is an art, and sales executives should do their best to master it.

One instance in which a letter is superior to interpersonal contact may be cited. It concerns the executive who wishes to compliment a salesperson for a piece of particularly good work. A letter provides the salesperson with lasting evidence that his or her performance has been recognized. Such letters can have a prolonged beneficial effect on the salesperson's morale, but, of course, they are poor substitutes for deserved promotions or compensation increases. Furthermore, a commendation letter should be supported, whenever possible, by a personal expression to the effect that management recognizes, and is pleased with, the salesperson's performance.

## CONCEPTS FROM THE BEHAVIORAL SCIENCES USEFUL IN UNDERSTANDING MOTIVATION

The concepts of need gratification and interdependence, developed by behavioral scientists, assist in understanding the nature of the problem involved in motivating salespersons as individuals. Sales executives can use these concepts to construct their own models for motivating the behavior of individual salespeople, and this should result in more effective motivational effort.

### Need Gratification

Psychological studies have shown that human activity—including the salesperson's behavior on the job—is directed toward satisfying certain needs. Patterns of individual behavior differ because individuals seek to fulfill these needs in different ways. How a particular individual behaves depends upon the nature of his or her unfulfilled needs modified by the environmental and social background. The motives lying behind any specific action derive from tensions built up to satisfy certain needs, some of which may be beneath the threshold of consciousness. Any action taken has the goal of reducing these tensions.

To understand motivation, then, we must first understand the nature of human needs. Needs may be grouped as either primary or secondary. Primary needs are the inborn or physiological needs for food, water, rest, sleep, air to breathe, and so forth, the fulfillment of which is basic to life itself. Until primary needs are satisfied, other needs have little motivational influence. Secondary needs, arising from an individual's interaction with the environment, are not inborn but develop with maturity. Secondary needs include those for safety and security, belongingness and social relations, esteem and self-respect, achievement, knowledge and understanding, and beauty.

A. H. Maslow, a distinguished psychologist, asserts that an individual seeks to fulfill personal needs according to some hierarchy of importance. He suggests the general priority of need fulfillment shown in Figure 13.1.[9] As this figure shows, Maslow suggests that after a person has gratified basic physiological needs, he or she generally proceeds to strive to fulfill safety and security needs, then belongingness and social relations needs, and so on—his or her level of aspiration rising as needs on higher levels are satisfied. Not every individual and certainly not every salesperson, of course, would establish the order of priority of need fulfillment suggested by Maslow. Some salespeople, for instance, definitely appear to assign earlier priority to filling the need for self-respect than they do to filling the need for social relations within a group.

After basic physiological needs have been met, it probably is impossible for most individuals to satisfy fully their needs on any higher level—needs seem to multiply along with efforts to satisfy them. As a particular need is satisfied, it loses its potency as a motivator of behavior; but other unfulfilled needs, some of them new, gain in potency. Individuals continually try to fulfill ever-larger portions of their need structures, and the unsatisfied portions exert the strongest motivational pull.

FIGURE 13.1
Hierarchy of Human Needs

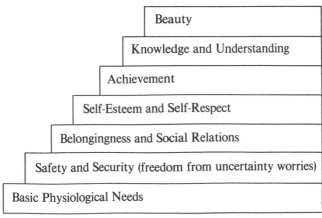

[9]A. H. Maslow, *Motivation and Personality* (New York: Harper & Row, Inc., 1954), pp. 80-85.

What, then, motivates salespeople in their work? Using the concept of need gratification, we can say that salespersons' motives for working vary according to the nature and potency of the unsatisfied portion of individual need structures. We must also recognize, however, that some of the salespeople's needs are filled off the job as well as on it. One salesperson works because of the need for money to feed a family; another because she views her job as a means for gaining esteem of others; still another because of a need to achieve to the maximum of his abilities, seeing his job performance as a means to that end.

If sales management knew the makeup of the unsatisfied portion of a salesperson's structure at a particular time, it would be able to determine the best incentives to use in motivating his or her performance along desired lines. The fact that an individual has needs causes him or her, consciously or not, to formulate goals in terms of them. If management can succeed in harmonizing the individual's goals with those of the organization, then individual behavior can be channeled along lines aimed at achieving both sets of goals. For a salesperson worried about providing for a child's education, an important individual goal becomes that of obtaining more money to remove the uncertainty. If management sees how furnishing the salesperson with an opportunity to earn more money will also further the attainment of organizational goals (perhaps that of increasing the size of orders), then offering the salesperson the chance to earn more money for obtaining larger orders would be a powerful incentive.

Money, however, rapidly loses its power as an incentive once an individual has gratified physiological needs and most of his or her safety and security needs. Other incentives (for example, a chance for promotion to a position of higher status, which is one way to fulfill esteem and self-respect needs) become increasingly effective. The promise of more money becomes progressively weaker as an incentive the further up in the hierarchy a particular individual's unfulfilled needs are pushed. Whatever power it retains probably is related most closely to the individual's unfulfilled esteem and achievement needs insofar as a larger income can gratify them. Of course, too, the threat or likelihood of receiving a lower income, a form of negative incentive, endangers the fulfilled part of an individual's need structure; and to the extent that this threat exists, money continues to have power as an incentive. Notice that whereas motives are internal to the individual, incentives are external. Sales management can influence the behavioral patterns of individual salespeople only indirectly through the incentives that it chooses to dangle before them.

### Interdependence

In the formal organizational plan, each salesperson reports to someone higher up in the structure, perhaps to a sales supervisor, a district sales manager, or, as in most small companies, directly to the chief sales executive. According to traditional organizational theory, the superior has the authority to require that the salesperson take action, and the salesperson is obligated to carry out the superior's orders and directions. The difficulty with this theory is that it assumes, tacitly if not explicitly, that authority ("the formal right to require action of others") can be equated with power ("the ability to get things done").[10] Practical sales managers long have recognized that issuing an order to a salesperson or suggesting how he or she should act (that is, change his

[10]D. R. Hampton, C. C. Summer, and R. Webber, in J. G. Hutchinson (ed.), *Readings in Management Strategy and Tactics* (New York: Holt, Rinehart and Winston, 1971), p. 30.

or her pattern of behavior) does not necessarily mean that henceforth the salesperson will be changed. On many occasions, of course, there is little problem in having orders and directions put into effect—as long as they are clearly stated and apply to simple tasks that can be done quickly. However, if orders and directions require significant modification in the salesperson's behavior over an extended period, perhaps permanently, then the salesperson's acceptance of the desired change becomes a great deal more unpredictable.

Whether or not orders and directions are accepted hinges upon the nature of the relations between the salesperson and the superior. In analyzing this relationship, the concept of interdependence, which seeks to explain how the appropriateness of authority varies as a function of dependence, is highly useful.[11] At one extreme, a salesperson may regard himself or herself as wholly dependent upon the superior, in which case he or she would consider that superior's exercise of authority as fully appropriate; this situation, amounting to blind obedience, is rarely found in business.[12] At the opposite extreme, the salesperson and the superior may be fully interdependent; that is, there is equal dependence both ways. Such a relationship is comparable to that between close friends, and authority is useless as a means of control. Although this situation is also rare, it seems highly desirable—in effect, the salesperson would be dependent on the superior for reaching his or her individual goals, and the superior would depend on the salesperson for help in reaching organizational goals. Thus, full integration of individual and organizational goals would be possible.

However, the usual situation in sales force-superior relationships is one of partial dependence. The salesperson feels partially dependent upon the superior and regards the latter's exercise of authority as appropriate in some circumstances and not in others; the superior feels partially dependent upon the salesperson for help in reaching the organizational goals for which he or she is held responsible by higher management. Each salesperson, then, has a "zone of acceptance," a range over which he or she will accept directions from the superior; and each superior has a similar zone over which he or she will honor requests from the salesperson. Within their respective zones of acceptance, too, both the salesperson and the superior exhibit a "degree of acceptance" that varies according to the exact circumstances from "grudging acquiescence" to "enthusiastic cooperation."

The sales manager should try to widen the zone and increase the degree of acceptance of each salesperson; but accomplishing this also means widening his or her own zone and increasing his or her own degree of acceptance. Actually this is only a very fancy way of saying that effective supervision is prerequisite to improved performance. Through effective supervision, the sales manager can satisfy many of the salespersons' needs and, at the same time, obtain fuller cooperation from them in striving for organizational goals By giving due credit for good work, by convincing each salesperson of his or her job's importance, by earning the sales personnel's confidence in his or her leadership, and by following other enlightened supervisory practices, the sales executive motivates his or her people to improved performance. Sales personnel under this sort of supervision work harder to earn praise and recognition and the resulting social ap-

[11]L. Gulick, "Structure and Coordination" in J. A. Litterer (ed.), *Organizations: Structure and Behavior* (New York: John Wiley & Sons, Inc., 1969), pp. 107-11.

[12]Probably the state of complete dependence is most closely approached, at least in the modern world, in the parent-child relationship found in highly authoritarian homes.

proval, esteem, and self-respect. Good supervision means, above all else, that sales-people are treated as human beings, as individuals in their own right, and not as mere cogs in an impersonal industrial machine.

## CONCLUSION

Sales executives are giving increasing recognition to the human relations aspects of sales-force management. Sales personnel are not only people but very essential people, and they should be treated as such. The uniqueness of salespeople's jobs and of the environment in which they work must be carefully appraised, and continually kept in mind, as management concerns itself with the motivation of the sales staff. Owing to the sometimes discouraging nature of the selling job and its loneliness, it is particularly important to provide continuing motivation for success to individual salespersons. Successful motivation is a matter of maintaining effective communication—both personal and written—with individual members of the sales force. The concept of need gratification and the notion of interdependence help sales executives to visualize the nature and extent of their problems in motivating individual salespeople.

# 14

# Sales Meetings
# and Sales Contests

The motivation of people as individuals only partially determines their total pattern of behavior. Many aspects of their total behavior are strongly influenced by individuals' interactions with others in groups with which they are identified. Particularly important in influencing many of an individual salesperson's job-related actions is the peer group made up of his or her fellows. For the newly recruited salesperson, for example, perhaps one of the strongest motives for learning how to perform the job is the desire to demonstrate to fellow workers that the recruit has attained an acceptable level of skill. Similarly, experienced salespersons find strong motivation to improve their performance in their desire to show other salespeople that they are star performers.

Discussion in Chapter 13 focused on motivating sales personnel as individuals, while discussion in this chapter is concerned with motivating salespersons as members of groups. The two main means for motivating salespeople as members of groups are through sales meetings and contests or incentive campaigns.

Sales meetings are necessary both for purposes of communication and motivation. When sales personnel work on the road away from their employer's premises without the day-to-day opportunity for employer communication and supervision, periodic group meetings provide important occasions for exchanging information and ideas. These meetings also provide appropriate occasions for motivating individual salespersons through the exertion of group pressures to achieve certain minimal levels of performance acceptable to the group.

Many sales executives regard contests as a highly effective means of motivating salespeople as members of groups, but some companies, as a matter of policy, do not use sales contests. Some executives are firm in their belief that sales personnel should not be rewarded a second time for doing what they are already being paid to do. Others contend that the beneficial effects of sales contests on sales performance are only temporary and do not result in lasting improvements of job performance. However, the experiences of most companies indicate that *when used properly* sales contests contribute significantly to the improvement of the performances of most salespeople participating in them.

## SALES MEETINGS

From time to time most companies assemble their entire sales force, or small regional or local groups of salespeople, for formal meetings. The ostensible purpose of such meetings is communication—to provide members of the sales force with needed information about new products, changes in sales policies, forthcoming promotional campaigns, and the like. In addition, an underlying, although sometimes well hidden, purpose of all such meetings is to provide occasion for motivating individual salespersons and for strengthening group identity.

### √ National Sales Meetings

The national sales meeting is one in which the entire sales force converges upon a central location. Although the costs of bringing all the salespeople to the convention site are substantial, national sales meetings are appropriate in certain situations. If, for example, comprehensive changes in marketing or sales policies are being made, a national meeting makes it possible to introduce these changes rapidly and uniformly, providing the occasion for standardized explanations and clarification of questions. Moreover, major executives whose time is limited may be able to attend a national meeting but not a series of decentralized meetings—and their actual attendance provides more stimulation than their written or recorded messages at decentralized meetings.

There are other advantages in holding a national sales meeting rather than a series of decentralized meetings. Each salesperson has the chance to meet informally with his or her counterparts from elsewhere, and there is much to be learned from the inevitable interchange of experience. On finding that others face and solve similar problems, the salesperson is encouraged to find his or her own solutions. Because of the opportunity provided for salespeople to meet home office personnel with whom they have been corresponding, better coordination between the office and the field should result. The very size of the national meeting, coupled with strengthening of team spirit, tends to generate contagious enthusiasm, which salespeople carry back to the field. Management spends much money and time in planning and staging the national meeting and brings in salespeople from great distances; and these obvious facts accentuate the meeting's importance to all who attend. If the meeting is held at or near a factory, there is opportunity to give sales personnel further product training, and to acquaint them with technical manufacturing details.

The national sales meeting also has its drawbacks. The expense of bringing in salespeople from all over the country is substantial. It is difficult to find a convenient time for all sales personnel to attend, unless the product line is seasonal. Often, too, company routine is disrupted and aggressive promotion by competitors may make inroads into company sales while salespeople are away from their territories. However, most national sales meetings are so brief that little chance exists of lasting adverse effects on a company's competitive position; and the meeting's stimulative effect upon salespeople constitutes a counterbalancing benefit. A temporary lapse in sales coverage should be more than compensated for by the more aggressive selling that results.

Some executives oppose national sales meetings on other grounds. A few object to the large amount of advance planning and organizing work required. This objection is of doubtful validity unless the only alternative is no meeting at all—the combined effort necessary to plan and organize a series of regional or local meetings is much greater than for one national meeting. Others object that the program for a national meeting must be general in nature, emphasizing problems faced on a nationwide basis. This objection, however, may be easily removed by breaking down a few sessions at the national meeting into smaller regional groups for purposes of discussing local problems.

### Regional Sales Meetings

There is a trend away from the national and toward the regional sales meeting system, under which a series of smaller meetings is staged at decentralized points. The reasons are several. Instead of the field force converging upon the central office, headquarters sales executives and personnel attend the decentralized meetings, thereby reducing total travel costs and lowering the loss of productive selling time. Headquarters executives are brought into direct contact with field personnel, learning about current problems at first hand; most such executives otherwise have a difficult time scheduling personal visits to the field. Although attending a regional meeting is not equivalent to a planned inspection trip, it is better than no visit at all. Each regional meeting may have a program designed to emphasize unique problems of that region. Because of the smaller attendance at regional meetings, participation time per person should be greater and the resulting discussions more meaningful. Then, too, in contrast to the attitude held by certain sales personnel toward national meetings, salesmen are inclined to regard district sales meetings as serious work sessions, not paid vacations.

The system of holding regional sales meetings also has its disadvantages. The demands on executive time may be excessive; executives may have to be away from the home office for several weeks at a stretch. Consequently, a tendency exists for the top sales executives to rotate attendance among themselves at regional meetings, rather than for all to attend each meeting. Thus, the smaller percentage of the "top brass" in attendance tends to depreciate the meeting's importance in the eyes of the sales staff and, because total attendance is also smaller, it is more difficult to develop a spirit of contagious enthusiasm. The stimulating effect is reduced further by the pressure to economize. The costs of conducting a series of district meetings, for example, preclude using the top-flight speakers and entertainers so often featured at national meetings. Furthermore, the total costs of holding several district meetings may well equal or exceed those of a single large national meeting because, in the final analysis, much planning and organizational expense is not fixed but is incurred separately for each meeting.

### National vs. Regional Sales Meetings

Both national and regional sales meetings, as the above discussion indicates, have important advantages and disadvantages. No generalization can be readily drawn as to which alternative, if either, is best for all companies. Each firm should select the type that best fits its own situation at the particular time. The regional meeting system is often the best where product demand is not seasonal and when strong competition exists. Where the sales force is small and widely dispersed and the sales personnel are of high caliber, the national meeting usually is the more appropriate choice.

## Executive Opposition to National
## and Regional Sales Meetings

Many sales executives are opposed to both national and regional sales meetings. Some say that the potential results do not justify the expected costs; but they admit that many of the benefits, such as the effect on the morale of the sales force, cannot readily be measured in monetary terms. Other executives, especially those whose companies operate in industries without slack selling seasons, contend that they can ill afford to have salespeople away from the field, even for a week. Still others base their opposition on the excessive demands on their own time; this objection is a particularly strong one against holding meetings at sites away from the home office; but even meetings held at the home office require much planning, organizing, and coordinating effort by major executives. In a few cases, sales executives are reluctant to hold national or regional sales meetings because of a low state of morale in their sales forces. They fear that sales personnel will use the meeting as an occasion to compare each other's complaints and to strengthen their convictions that the company is an unsatisfactory employer.

## Local Sales Meetings

Local, or branch, sales meetings should be an integral part of the program for motivating the sales force. The periodic national or regional meeting should supplement, not substitute for, frequent local sales meetings. Some sales executives, in fact, believe that larger meetings can be dispensed with if local meetings are held regularly and handled effectively. Local sales meetings generally are conducted every week or two by district sales managers or their assistants and, depending upon the frequency, last from fifteen minutes to several hours. Although such gatherings are considered formal meetings, the great strength of the effectively handled local sales meeting is its informality, each salesperson having ample opportunity to pose questions and to state personal views. Of course, the system also provides frequent occasions for sales personnel to get together, become better acquainted, and thus strengthen their feelings of group identity.

## Remote-Control and Traveling Sales Meetings

Certain forms of sales meetings seek to retain the national sales meeting's advantages while reducing its disadvantages in terms of cost and time expenditures. Among these forms are meetings conducted by closed-circuit television, sales meetings by telephone, sales meetings at home, and the traveling sales meeting.

**Closed-Circuit Television.** Closed-circuit television enables a company to hold a number of sales meetings simultaneously. The program is "live" at only one meeting site but is telecast to the others, thus retaining much of the inspirational value of the live show without incurring costs and losses of productive selling time comparable to those involved in a national meeting. Televised sales meetings are especially appropriate for companies with very large sales forces or large dealer organizations. Many companies use television sales meetings to introduce new products or to launch sales campaigns nationally. Large-screen projectors make it possible to gather a large group at each theater, under which condition the program can be seen and heard better than in the ordinary meeting room. Users report that their messages receive a high degree of attention.

**Sales Meetings by Telephone.** Open-circuit telephone conference calls are used effectively for small group meetings and discussions. For maximum impact, users say the group should be no larger than twenty. The meeting itself is conducted in a manner similar to other small group meetings. Usually the sales manager begins by welcoming the group and presenting the subject for discussion. The open discussion that follows is guided by two rules: only one individual may talk at a time, and all speakers must identify themselves and their cities. At the end of the conference call, the sales executive gives a brief summary. Companies using the telephone sales meeting report that sales personnel have a strong feeling of participation and are enthusiatic about such meetings. Compared to a centralized gathering of the same people, the telephone sales meeting affords significant savings in time and money; and, of course, salespeople lose little, if any, time from their selling activities. An obvious shortcoming, however, is the absence of visual stimulation, which is important, for example, in introducing a new product. But probably before long the "picture phone," which has been demonstrated by A.T.&T. but not yet commercially introduced, will overcome this handicap.

**Sales Meetings at Home.** Seeking to reduce the time and costs of sales meetings, some companies mail recordings or printed materials to salespeople at their homes. One format is to record a conference or meeting of executives and to provide sales personnel with copies of the tape. Another is to print an illustrated script of a home office meeting for distribution to salespeople. Sales executives using these unusual formats point to three advantages: (1) sales personnel receive the information in their homes, free from distractions; (2) they can review the information as many times as they please; and (3) there are substantial savings in time and money. Objectively, however, one must conclude that formats such as these, because of the absence of group dynamics, are most useful as supplementary motivational devices rather than as substitutes for periodic sales meetings except, of course, for companies where for one reason or another it is not feasible to hold formal meetings.

**Traveling Sales Meetings.** Certain meetings require numerous physical props. For instance, a manufacturer introducing a new product line may want to display and demonstrate each new product. It is difficult in such cases to stage regional meetings because the displays must be transported to, moved in, and set up at each of a succession of meeting sites. Some companies overcome this difficulty by outfitting one or more motorized vans and trailers with product displays and conference rooms. Thus, the sales meeting moves from city to city, and at each stop salespeople and/or dealers come aboard.

### Planning and Staging Sales Meetings

**Objectives.** In planning any sales meeting, well-defined objectives are important. The underlying goals are to motivate individual salespersons and to strengthen group identity. But more specific goals, sometimes jokingly called "excuses for holding a meeting," are required. When sales start to lag, for instance, a sales meeting may be held "to give sales volume a shot in the arm." Other specific goals served by sales meetings include: to provide refresher training; to correct selling faults; to introduce new products, models, and services; to explain changes in company policies and systems; to improve the quality of sales-force reports; to orient sales personnel regarding the advertising program and show how they can best tie in their efforts with it; and to increase the effectiveness with which sales people use their time. In setting a meeting's specific objectives, the executive should answer such questions as: Are these objectives clear and attainable? Are they realistic in terms of time, audience, and other conditions? Will the probable results justify the estimated costs?

Once specific objectives of the meeting are set, plans are made for achieving them. The means chosen should provide the maximum motivational impact upon the salespeople. With this in mind, training aids are assembled, speakers obtained, meeting materials (including a carefully thought-out agenda) prepared, and facilities secured. In addition, plans are made for whatever entertainment is thought necessary. If spouses are to attend, arrangements are made for dances, sightseeing tours, or similar events.

**Staging the Meeting.** For maximum motivational impact, a sales meeting should generate enthusiasm among the participants. To arouse their audience, speakers must make genuinely enthusiastic presentations. To maintain this pitch of interest, a rigid time schedule should be adhered to throughout the program. When a speaker runs overtime, participants frequently lose interest; this, in turn, may cause later speakers to fall behind schedule, whereupon any enthusiasm that has been built up tends to disappear.

Time should be set aside on the meeting schedule for group discussion. Sales personnel must be allowed time to criticize new programs, raise questions, put forth ideas, and air their complaints. Since the large sales meeting affords little time for widespread participation, the large group should be broken down, for a few sessions at least. This sets the stage for effective interpersonal reactions on such topics as the technical details of a new product, new applications, and new selling arguments. Precautions, however, should be taken to ensure that group leaders are capable of preventing overly talkative individuals from monopolizing the discussion.

The setting of the meeting and the nature of planned activities are controversial subjects among sales executives. Some argue that any sales meeting, particularly a national one, should be made up entirely of work sessions, covering as much as twelve hours per day. They contend that more is accomplished in such a working atmosphere. Others believe that participants learn more and are more highly motivated in a relaxed setting in which some time is reserved for recreation. They prefer attractive resort areas as meeting sites and provide organized entertainment as part of the program. The strength of each side of this argument appears to hinge upon the duration of the meeting and management's estimate of the state of salesperson morale. In many instances a compromise position is the most satisfactory. A 100 percent working atmosphere, for example, is more palatable for the participants if the surroundings are pleasant and comfortable. In almost every case, frequent breaks from working sessions are desirable—the saleperson's ability to concentrate tends to decline progressively as the length of the session increases.

## √SALES CONTESTS

Essentially, a sales contest is a special selling campaign offering sales personnel incentives in the form of prizes or awards above and beyond those regularly provided by the compensation plan. There are four main reasons for using sales contests: (1) they provide a mechanism for developing team spirit among salespeople or distributors who generally have little direct contact with each other; (2) they assist in boosting morale, counteracting the tendency of some salespeople to become apathetic, bored with their jobs, and depressed; (3) they are capable of stimulating salespeople to strive harder to better their usual performances; and (4) by pointing sales efforts toward accomplishment of important tasks, they assist in reaching predetermined sales and profit goals. These four reasons suggest the basic objective underlying sales contests—to so motivate the sales force that they are caused to produce increased and/or more profitable sales volume.

### Specific Objectives

The definition of specific objectives for each sales contest is necessary to concentrate sales efforts on the most promising areas. A study by Haring and Myers at the Indiana University School of Business uncovered the list of specific contest objectives in Fig 14.1. The first and third most frequently mentioned, finding new customers and getting better territory coverage, are aimed at motivating salespeople to tap more of the untouched market potential. The second, obtaining greater volume per call, is pointed toward upgrading selling performance with present customers. The fourth, promoting special items, is used to motivate sales personnel to exert greater effort in pushing slow-moving items, high-margin goods, or new products.

In formulating specific contest objectives, and later in designing the sales contest, the executive in charge of contest planning should keep in mind the underlying objective—to so motivate the sales staff that they will produce increased or more profitable sales volume. One formula for sales contest planning defines three prime requirements

FIGURE 14.1
Objectives of Sales Contests *

| Objective | Rank Order | Number of Mentions |
|---|---|---|
| Find new customers | 1 | 273 |
| Obtain greater volume per call | 2 | 208 |
| Get better territory coverage | 3 | 189 |
| Promote special items | 4 | 175 |
| Overcome seasonal sales slump | 5 | 165 |
| Get better balance of sales | 6 | 124 |
| Get renewal of business from former customers | 7 | 115 |
| Introduce a new product or line | 8 | 114 |
| Stop or slow a sales decline | 9 | 108 |
| Develop new sales skills | 10 | 95 |
| Ease an unfavorable inventory position | 11 | 91 |
| Lower selling costs | 12 | 67 |
| Sell higher-quality products | 13 | 62 |
| Improve sales service to customers | 14 | 61 |
| Build better product displays | 15 | 50 |
| Get better sales reports | 16 | 37 |
| Reduce selling time | 17 | 24 |
| Eliminate returns and mistakes | 18 | 13 |
| All other | — | 26 |

*Results of survey questionnaire of 542 members of National Sales Executives, Inc.

for a successful sales contest: (1) the contest must make greater sales effort pay off in terms of greater reward both for salespeople and the company; (2) it must motivate the sales force to expend greater effort; and (3) it must assist salespeople to pattern their efforts along the most productive lines. Notice that these requirements simply elaborate on what must be done to achieve underlying contest objectives.

### Contest Formats

Although the variety of sales contests is legion, each is built around a theme that provides the basis for the competition. The theme may be either a straightforward or a novelty type. In contests using straightforward themes, sales personnel sometimes compete with their own past records, and at other times with one another, in accomplishing certain tasks or goals. Some users believe that a sales contest is made not only more interesting but more effective if it is designed to tie in with a current event, sport, or similar novelty theme. They say that the theme should not only serve as a common denominator but be appealing to all participants. Other users contend that a theme describing the actual specific objectives, such as lower selling costs and promoting special items, should be used. They believe that novelty themes are insults to mature men and contend that it is not only possible, but less difficult, to motivate salespeople through the use of straightforward, or direct, themes.

Most successful novelty themes share certain common characteristics. Experience indicates that the theme should be timely, and its effectiveness is enhanced if it coin-

FIGURE 14.2
General Categories of Sales-Contest Themes

1. Games:
   a. Team type—football, baseball, basketball, hockey, bowling, tennis doubles, tug-of-war, soccer, etc.
   b. Individual type—tennis singles, golf, boxing, wrestling, archery, fencing, broad jump, high jump, pole vault, hammer throw, discus throw, shooting match, javelin throw, bull fight, climbing the greased pole, etc.
2. Races:
   a. Team type—crew, cross-country, relay, bobsled, yacht, etc.
   b. Individual type—horse race, dog race, air race, soap-box derby, auto race, hurdles, dashes, marathons, dog sled, trotting race, swimming races, speedboat races, etc.
3. Card games—poker, pinochle, bridge, black jack, etc.
4. Hunting or fishing—treasure hunt, big-game hunt, uranium rush, gold rush, land rush, fishing derby, trapping contest, etc.
5. Travel—trip around the world, to Miami, to New York, to Hollywood, to Waikiki, to the moon, to space, etc.
6. Climbing—ladders, stairs, mountains, cliff scaling, ascent to the stratosphere, etc.
7. The rising thermometer, pressure, gauge, etc.
8. Building contests—skyscraper, other new buildings, tower, smokestacks, etc.
9. Military—naval battles, artillery engagements, bombing runs, invasions, interplanetary wars, etc.
10. Clothing contests (in one contest of this type, the salesperson earns one item of clothing at a time and is required to appear at sales meetings clad only in those items that he or she has earned up to that point).

cides with an activity in the news. An analogous relation should exist between the theme and the product line or some other aspect of the company's marketing setup. The theme should be one that will intensify interest as the contest proceeds; in this regard, the best themes appear to be those in which the salespeople share a common interest. Finally, the theme should lend itself naturally to contest promotion both before and during the contest period. Many hundreds of themes have been used, but most fall into one or another of the ten general categories shown in Figure 14.2.

### Promoting the Contest

If a sales contest is to succeed, it must be effectively merchandised. To most salespersons there is nothing new about the idea of a contest. A clever new theme and attractive prizes may help arouse interest, but a planned barrage of promotional material develops the enthusiasm needed to make the contest a success. A teaser campaign sometimes precedes the formal contest announcement; at other times, the announcement itself comes as a complete and dramatic surprise to participants. As the contest progresses, other methods are used to hold and intensify interest. Results and standings are reported at sales meetings at frequent intervals or by daily or weekly bulletins. The sales manager may dispatch telegrams carrying news of important developments or changes in relative standings. At intervals, new or special prizes may be announced.

Management may encourage individual salespersons and various groups to compete against each other. Reports of relative standings may be addressed to the salesperson's spouse. If the prizes are so selected as to arouse the spouses' interest, continuing enthusiasm for the contest is generated in the home. The contest administrator should not wait for a lag in contest interest before injecting new life into it. From the start regular news flashes on comparative standings should be sent out and, if the initial incentives provided by the contest do not appear to be producing the desired results, the administrator should add the stimuli needed to make the contest a success.

The duration of the contest is an important factor in maintaining participants' interest. Sales executives' opinions differ as to the ideal length. Contests are run for periods as short as a week and as long as a year, but most last from one to four months. One executive claims that thirteen weeks is the ideal length; another states that no contest should last for more than a month; still another points to a successful contest lasting six months. There are no set guides. Each case is controlled by such factors as the length of time the salespersons' interest and enthusiasm can be maintained, the period over which the theme can be kept timely, and the interval needed to accomplish the contest objectives.

One effective way to promote continuing and widespread interest in the contest is to make it possible for every salesperson to win something. The basis for awards should take into account the sales people's present performance levels and, in order to motivate the average or inexperienced salesperson along with the star performer, the basis of award should be for improvement rather than for total performance. Hence, total sales volume is less effective as the basis for award than, for example, per cent of quota achieved or per cent of improvement in quota achievement. Many successful contests offer prizes for all persons showing improvement, but the worth of individual prizes varies with the amount of improvement. Offering only a few large prizes restricts the motivational force of such contests—because only a few people can win them, sooner or later, most salespeople become discouraged and stop trying.

## Contest Prizes

The majority of contest prizes may be classified under four general headings: cash awards, merchandise prizes, travel, and special honor or privilege awards. Surveys among sales executives show that cash and merchandise are the most widely used. A growing number of sales contests feature more than one type of award (for example, travel for the large awards and merchandise for lesser awards), and some give winners the option of accepting one type rather than another.

**Cash.**   One would think that a cash prize would be attractive to all sales personnel, but the potency of money as an incentive weakens the further up in an individual's need hierarchy his or her unfulfilled needs are pushed. Once basic physiological needs and most safety and security needs are satisfied, whatever potency money retains as an incentive is related most closely to unfulfilled esteem and achievement needs; and, of course, noncash prizes are capable of filling these needs at least as well, perhaps better, than cash.

Assuming that the regular compensation plan provides sales personnel with sufficient income to meet their basic physiological needs and most safety and security needs, an opportunity to win a cash prize is a weak incentive unless a substantial sum is involved; some sales executives say that this amount must represent from 10 to 25 percent of the salesperson's regular annual income. A cash prize of, say, $25 means very little to most salespeople and they exert only token efforts to win it. However, in many sales contests small cash prizes are awarded at frequent intervals, tending, users say, to keep interest at a higher pitch than might otherwise be possible. Another important objection, applicable even to large cash prizes, is that winners mix the money with other income, and thus are left without any permanent identifiable evidence of their achievement.

**Merchandise.**   The merchandise award is an incentive superior to the cash prize in several respects. Winners have more permanent evidence of their achievement and should continue to be motivated for a longer period. Because the merchandise prize normally is obtained at the wholesale cost, a value larger than the equivalent cash prize can be offered. For the same total outlay, too, more merchandise prizes than cash awards can be offered; hence, the contest rules can provide for more winners. Nevertheless, merchandise prizes must be selected carefully to assure that items offered are truly desired by salespersons and their families. One way to sidestep problems in this area is to allow winners to select their own prizes from a variety of offerings provided for each class of winner. This is effective from the psychological standpoint, too, since people generally are happier if they are permitted to assert their individuality and take their choice. A number of "merchandise incentive agencies," some of them providing a complete sales-contest planning service, specialize in furnishing prizes. Most of these agencies issue catalogs with "prices" generally stated in "points" rather than in money.

**Travel.**   Travel awards are growing in popularity as contest incentives. Few things can be glamorized quite as effectively as a trip to a luxury resort or an exotic land. The lure of a "trip of a lifetime" is a strong incentive, especially for the salesperson who longs for a chance to "escape" the job's routine, at least temporarily. Travel awards generally provide trips for both winners and their spouses, this being advisable both to obtain the entire family's motivational support and to avoid the family's opposition to encouraging solo vacation trips by the salesperson. The chief objection to the prize trip is that winners, frequently the better sales personnel, are taken away from their territories while collecting their awards; however, this objection is easily overcome by providing that prize trips will be taken during regularly scheduled vacation periods.

**Special Honors or Privileges.**   This type of award can take many forms. It may be a letter from a top executive formally recognizing the contest winner's superior performance; it may be a loving cup, a special trip to a home-office meeting attended by a restricted few, or membership in a special group or club that enjoys certain privileges. Winners, in addition, generally receive publicity through house organs and in their hometown newspapers. Such awards frequently appear to provide strong incentives, as, for example, in the cases of life insurance salespersons who push themselves to the limit to earn membership in "the million dollar club."

The special honor or privilege award is used mainly by firms employing sales personnel who are almost "independent entrepreneurs." Such awards, however, are appropriate incentives wherever management desires to strengthen group identity and build team spirit among the better salespeople. Note that this type of award appeals to the salesperson's belongingness and social-relations needs, which, according to Maslow, an individual generally strives to satisfy after he has taken care of basic physiological needs and most safety and security needs.

### Managerial Evaluation of Contests

It is sound practice to evaluate each sales contest both before it is launched and after it is concluded. By sizing up a proposed contest in advance, weaknesses are detected and corrected. Having an appraisal afterward provides insights helpful in improving future contests. In both pre- and postevaluations, questions similar to the following should be considered.

**Is the Contest Well-Designed?**   Overall, the prizes must provide sufficient motivation to cause the sales staff to exert the desired effort, yet the gross margin earned on sales volume must be increased at the very least by enough to pay contest costs. The theme, whether straightforward or novel, should not only tie in directly with specific objectives but also result in easy-to-understand and fair contest rules. The theme should also lend itself readily to contest promotion.

**Will Salespeople Consider the Contest Fair?**   At the time that the contest is announced, every salesperson should feel that the proposition is one that gives everyone a fair chance of winning the more attractive prizes. As long as the contest lasts, all members of the sales force should continue to feel that they have real chances to win something. To secure and maintain salespeople's cooperation in achieving contest objectives, all sales personnel must be convinced of the contest's basic fairness.

**What Is the Likely Long-run Effect?**   The contest should bring in new business; it is not a success if it merely borrows sales from preceding and succeeding months. Well-designed contests, too, help to inculcate desirable selling habits that salespeople retain long after the contest ends. The contest should boost salespeople's spirits while it is on, and provide a beneficial carryover effect upon sales-force morale.

**What Will Be the Effect on Team Spirit?**   A good sales contest should result in improved team spirit. If the contest is conducted in an overly competitive way (for example, if salespeople are encouraged to engage in personal rivalries to too great an extent), then it may have the counterproductive effect of creating jealousy and antagonism among the sales force. Even if salespeople are competing for individual awards, generally it is advisable to organize teams, and to place emphasis on competition among groups for recognition rather than among individuals for personal gain.

**Are There Better Alternatives to the Contest?** It may be that the contest will provide no more benefit than a temporary shot-in-the-arm type of improvement, especially if other aspects of sales-force management have serious defects. Deficiencies in selling performance caused by an inappropriate compensation plan, incompetent supervision, or ineffective training are not likely to be permanently overcome by a sales contest. Other avenues to improvement of selling efficiency should therefore be explored at the same time that a sales contest is being considered.

### Objections to Sales Contests

Sales contests are used by less than one fourth of all sales departments, so it is worthwhile to note the reasons for nonusage. Among the standard objections voiced by sales executives are the following:

1. Salespeople are paid for their work under the provisions of the basic compensation plan, and there is no reason to reward them further for performing regular duties.
2. Higher-caliber and more experienced sales personnel look upon sales contests as juvenile and silly.
3. Contests often lead to unanticipated and undesirable results, such as increased returns and adjustments, higher credit losses, and overstocking of dealers.
4. Contests cause salespeople to bunch their sales during the competition, and sales slumps occur both before and after the contest.
5. The disappointment suffered by contest losers causes a general decline in sales-force morale.
6. Contests are temporary motivating devices and, if used too frequently, have a narcotic effect. No greater results in the aggregate are obtained with contests than without them.
7. The competitive atmosphere generated by a sales contest weakens team spirit.

The first reason indicates a fundamental misunderstanding of both personnel motivation and contest design, and the second reason may or may not be true in individual situations. The reader should note, however, that all the other objections may be overcome through appropriate contest design, intelligent contest administration, and proper handling of other aspects of sales-force management. Assuming that sales management is competent in other respects, thorough planning and effective administration of a contest can produce lasting benefits for both the salespeople and the company. Only if a sales contest is used as a substitute for good management is it likely to have bad results.

Under some circumstances, nevertheless, sales contests are ill advised, at least for purposes of stimulating sales volume. If a firm's products are in short supply, for instance, it is ridiculous to use a sales contest to stimulate orders; but the same firm might find a contest appropriate to use as part of an effort to achieve such objectives as lowering selling expense or improving salespersons' reports. Nor do companies distributing industrial goods (that is, raw materials, fabricating materials and parts, installations, accessory equipment, and operating supplies) normally find sales contests appropriate for purposes of stimulating sales—except, of course, in cases where it is possible to take accounts and sales away from competitors. But, again, contests might be appropriately used along with other efforts directed toward reducing selling costs, improving sales-people's reports, and improving service to customers. Similarly, where the product is highly technical and is sold only after much spadework and long negotiation, as is the case with many industrial goods, sales contests conducted for purposes of stimulating sales volume are usually inappropriate.

## RELATIVE VALUE OF VARIOUS INCENTIVES

The relative value of various incentives varies not only for individual salespersons but for different groups and different companies, each with its own unique set of incentives. There is little doubt, however, that the most important incentive of all is the basic compensation plan. Without a sound basic compensation plan on which to build, other types of incentives are unlikely to produce desired results. Several years ago, the Indiana University School of Business surveyed sales executives about the relative values of different incentives in motivating the *average salesperson to do a better job than usual.* The survey results showed that, after the basic compensation plan itself, which ranked first, sales contests were most important, with a second-place ranking, sales-person-supervisor relations ranked third, honor awards and recognition fourth, and sales meetings fifth.[1]

## CONCLUSION

The basic compensation plan is the most important incentive but, if a company already has a good one, there is much to be gained from using other incentives. Sales meetings provide opportunities for motivating individual salespeople and for strengthening feelings of group identification. Sales contests offer a mechanism for providing sales personnel with incentives to stimulate effort toward increasing profitable sales volume and for achieving more specific objectives. The judicious use of both sales meetings and sales contests builds individual and sales-force morale and helps in the accomplishment of company goals.

[1]A. Haring and R. H. Myers, "Special Incentives for Salesmen," *Journal of Marketing,* Vol. 18, No. 2 (October 1953), p. 159.

# 15

# Compensating
# Sales Personnel

Good sales-compensation plans assist in channeling the efforts of sales personnel toward the most productive activities, and they help in attaining the objectives of the sales organization. Such plans are drafted to fit a company's special needs and problems, and from them greater returns should result for the company and for the salespeople. Sales and growth goals should be reached at less cost, and profits should be proportionately higher. Salespeople should be rewarded for greater productivity with commensurately higher pay. Improved *esprit de corps* among the sales force is the chief intangible benefit, since individual productivity and job satisfaction generally go hand in hand.

Compensation plans should be viewed as aids to, rather than substitutes for, good sales-force management. Unless the quality and skill of the management are of high order, even excellent compensation plans do not guarantee the significant benefits mentioned above. And many compensation plans are less then excellent. They may be based on a very simple and naive hypothesis that sales personnel are purely mercenary. Many compensation plans conflict with what may be important motives—to conform, to be like others, to belong, to be like by one's peers. A big earner may be branded as an apple polisher.[1] As important as the basic appropriateness of the compensation plans themselves are the ways in which they are implemented and administered. Indeed, fundamentally poor compensation plans often work satisfactorily enough when a skilled executive is charged with their administration.

In established companies it is rarely necessary to design completely new sales-compensation plans, and sales executives are concerned mainly with revising plans already in effect. Most changes are minor, usually instituted to bring the plan and marketing objectives into closer alignment. If, for example, additional sales effort is needed for the factory to operate at optimum capacity, an adjustment in the compensation plan may bring forth the extra effort required. This adjustment could involve paying bonuses on sales over the quota, paying additional compensation for larger orders or for securing new accounts, or simply revising commission rate schedules. Any such change, of course, could be either temporary or permanent.

---

[1] D. W. Belcher, "Employee and Executive Compensation," in H. G. Heneman et al., *Employment Relations Research* (New York: Harper & Row, Inc., 1960).

Because of possible adverse effects upon morale, it is wise to avoid drastic changes in the compensation scheme. Like most people, sales personnel tend to resist sweeping changes, particularly when they have to alter accustomed ways of doing things to adjust to a new plan. When a firm decides to switch from paying straight salaries to straight commissions, for instance, some people find it exceedingly difficult to adjust their living and spending habits accordingly. Opinions vary as to how far-reaching changes, when required, should be implemented. Some executives think that to introduce them gradually minimizes interference with established habits and elicits far less resistance from the personnel affected. Others claim that such changes should be made quickly, because continual changes often have a deteriorative effect upon salespeople's morale. Although explanation of impending changes is always important, a careful program of orientation should precede the introduction of sweeping changes. Whether a change should be made in one step or in many depends upon the specific circumstances surrounding the particular situation, and no easy generalization on this point is possible.

Two situations involving established companies in which complete overhaulings of compensation plans are in order should be mentioned. One involves the company whose sales force already has low morale, perhaps because of the compensation plan in effect. If the compensation plan is at the root of the morale problem, then drastic change is appropriate. Complete revamping of sales-compensation plans may also be appropriate in firms anticipating the cultivation of new and different markets. The problems resemble those of the newly organized company, which must build its sales-compensation plan from scratch—in both cases management must consider many factors, the nature and number of which vary with the company and the situation, but usually including: the types of customers, the marketing channels, characteristics of the products, intensity of competition, extent of the market, and complexity of the selling task.

### ✓ Requirements of a Good Sales-Compensation Plan

Although a sales-compensation plan should be tailored to fit a particular company's needs, any plan should meet six main requirements. First, it should be as simple as possible, so that sales personnel will easily understand it. Second, it should be fair—no plan should cause salespersons to be penalized because of factors beyond their control. Within limits of seniority and other special privileges, salespeople should receive equal pay for equal results. Third, the plan should provide a living wage, preferably in the form of a guaranteed income. The person who is worried about money matters cannot concentrate on doing a good selling job. Fourth, administration of the plan should provide for easy adjustments of pay to changes in performance. Fifth, the plan should be easy and economical to administer. Although highly complex plans may provide greater refinements in stimulation and reward, often their higher costs of administration are not offset by improvements in performance. Sixth, the plan should help in attaining the objectives of the sales organization. Not every compensation plan, of course, will meet all six requirements fully. In designing new plans or improving old ones. however, management should compare the prototypes under discussion with these requirements and make evaluations accordingly.

## DEVISING A SALES-COMPENSATION PLAN

Whether contemplating major or minor changes or drafting a completely new sales-compensation plan, the executive should approach the project systematically.

Good compensation plans are built on sound foundations, and a systematic approach is the best assurance that no essential step will be overlooked. The following discussion analyzes these steps in some detail.

### Define the Salesperson's Job

In designing a sales-compensation plan, the first step is to determine, or reexamine, the nature of the salesperson's job. Up-to-date written descriptions furnish the logical place to start. If the job descriptions are outdated, or if they do not constitute accurate and complete descriptions of the sales job objectives and work, revision is in order. The sales executive should ask: Does this description convey a realistic picture of what the salesperson is supposed to accomplish and to do? If there are no written sales job descriptions, they should be prepared.[2] Other aspects of company marketing operations should be considered in relation to their impact upon the salesperson's job. First, the objectives of the sales department should be analyzed for their effect on the salesperson's job. Sales volume objectives, for instance, whether in terms of dollars, units of product, or numbers of dealers and distributors, are translated ultimately into what is expected of the sales personnel, as a group and individually. Second, the impact on the salesperson's job of various company policies should be determined. The particular distribution policies that a firm chooses to follow, its credit policies, its price policies, and policies in many other areas all affect the salesperson's job. Third, the nature and extent of current and proposed advertising and sales promotional programs should be evaluated with respect to their significance for the salesperson and his duties. This review of company objectives, policies, and promotional programs should throw new light on the information contained in the job description. The precise nature of the salesperson's goals, duties, and activities should now be clear.

### Consider General Compensation Structure of the Company

The next step is to examine the general compensation structure of the company. Most large companies, and many smaller ones, have systems of job evaluation that are used for determining the relative value of individual jobs. Although job-evaluation techniques do not provide precise quantitative measurements, they do give an indication of the relative value of different jobs. The procedure is not scientific; it is an orderly approach based on judgment. It focuses only on the jobs themselves, without considering the ability or personality of the particular employees who do the work. The purpose of job evaluation is to arrive at fair compensation relationships among various company jobs. Therefore, the job-evaluation program should provide the data needed to fix equitable compensation differentials among jobs requiring varying degrees of: education and experience, mental and physical skills, responsibility, monotonous repetition of tasks, supervision given and received, exposure to unfavorable and hazardous working conditions, and similar job characteristics. There are three basic methods of job evaluation.

**Classification Method.** The classification method starts with the various job descriptions and ranks all jobs from top to bottom in order of estimated relative importance. The ranked list is then subdivided into several compensation classes, so that jobs

---

[2] See Chapter 10 for a discussion of the methods of sales job analysis and the preparation of job descriptions.

of similar comparable rank fall into the same class. This method is used by the U.S. Civil Service Commission and was widely adopted by American companies during and after World War II. It is easier to apply than other methods, but it gives less precise results and involves a greater element of judgment.

**Point System.** The point system is the most widely used job-evaluation method. It involves establishing and defining the several factors common to most jobs that represent the chief elements of value inherent in all jobs. The specific factors chosen differ from one company to another and should be selected with a firm's operating problems in mind. They usually include mental and physical skills, responsibility, supervision given and received, personality requirements, and minimum education required. Each factor is assigned a maximum number of points, different ranges being assigned in line with the relative importance of the factors. Next, each job is appraised for its requirements against the several factor scales, and individual factor scores are combined into a total point value for the job. Finally, bands of points are decided upon and become the different compensation classes. Less arbitrary judgment is required under the point system than under the classification method; but an even more attractive feature is that the use of point values makes it possible to determine the gap, or distance, between ranks.

**Factor-Comparison Method.** The factor-comparison method somewhat resembles the point system, but it is more complex than either the point system or the classification method. Except for its greater complexity, it has all the advantages of the first two methods; furthermore, it utilizes a scheme of ranking and cross-comparisons that tends to minimize error arising from faulty judgment. In a process similar to that used in the point system, this method employs certain selected factors and evaluation scales. However, the scale values are in dollars and cents rather than in points, and no upper limit exists to the valuation that can be assigned to any one factor. A selected number of "key" jobs, fairly typical of similar jobs throughout the company, are then evaluated, factor by factor. This is done by arranging them in rank order, from highest to lowest for each factor. As a check against this judgmental evaluation, the compensation dollars actually paid for each job are allocated to the various factors; the allocation automatically establishes the relationship among jobs for each factor. The judgment ranking and the ranking by allocation of compensation are compared and differences are reconciled, or the jobs are removed from the key list. On the basis of the dollar amounts assigned to the several factors making up key jobs, additional jobs are evaluated and their monetary values for each factor interpolated into the scale. This procedure is repeated until all jobs are evaluated.

**Job Evaluation and Sales Positions.** Considerable progress has been made in the field of job evaluation in recent years, but the evaluation of sales positions is still in the experimental stage. Many sales executives oppose the extension of job evaluation to sales positions on the grounds that compensation levels for sales personnel are more closely related to external supply-and-demand factors than to conditions within the company. Salespeople enjoy greater job mobility than most other employees, and they are often in everyday contact with potential employers. One thing is certain—if a job-evaluation program in which sales personnel are included is in operation, there should be sales department representation on the committee that arrives at quantitative evaluations for the various factors. If a company does not use job evaluation, or if it uses evaluation but does not apply the system to sales jobs, the sales executive should establish, as best he or she can, the relative value of the salesperson's job to jobs elsewhere in the organization. This precaution is needed to assure that the monetary attractiveness of sales positions is no less than it is for comparable jobs in other departments. Furthermore, if the sales executive keeps informed on the relative differences of sales jobs and other company jobs, he or she is preparing for the day, which is probably inevitable, when most sales positions will be regarded as proper subjects for job evaluation.

### Consider Compensation Picture in the Community and Industry

Because salespersons' compensation levels are often closely related to external supply and demand factors, attention should be directed toward the pattern of salespeople's compensation in the community and industry. Often the actual amounts of the employees' pay is not as significant as how much they believe they should be paid. This belief depends on whom they compare themselves with.[3] Management needs answers to several key questions: (1) What compensation systems are being used? (2) What is the average compensation for similar positions? (3) How do other companies seem to be doing with their plans? (4) Would it be wise to depart from industry or community practice? (5) Should industry or community practice be followed as a matter of policy? The answers to these and related questions, and the degree of significance of the responses, differ with the individual company and industry. But whenever a change in the sales personnel's compensation plan is under consideration, such matters should be discussed.

If there is a companywide job evaluation and salary administration program, it should take into account the going rates for similar positions in the community and industry. A salary administration program used for setting salespeople's compensation can be sound only if it considers the relation of external compensation practices to those of the company. Sales executives should maintain constant vigilance against the possibility that salespeople's pay will get out of line with what is being paid for similar jobs in the community or industry.

### Determine Compensation Level

One of the most fundamental steps is that of determining the amount of compensation a salesperson should receive on the average. Although this level might be set through bargaining between the salesperson and the sales manager, or on a more-or-less arbitrary-judgment basis, neither expedient is recommended. Before setting the compensation level, management should consider several pertinent factors. Management should ascertain whether the caliber of the present sales force measures up to what the company would like to have. If the present caliber is too low, or if it is decided that the company should have lower-grade people than those currently employed, research should be undertaken to determine the market value of salespeople of the desired grade. This requires further investigation of the compensation patterns of other companies. Management should also weigh the worth of individual persons to the company, but this assumes the availability of accurate productivity measures. Only a handful of firms have such measures, so, as a substitute, management should estimate the number of sales and profit dollars that the company would lose if particular salespeople resigned.

[3] B. M. Bass, *Organizational Psychology* (Boston: Allyn and Bacon, Inc., 1965), p. 76.

Still another consideration is the amount the company can afford to pay for the compensation of sales personnel; this depends, of course, upon a host of other matters. The result of examining these factors, as well as others pertinent to the situation of the individual firm, is a series of estimates for the total cost of salespeople's compensation. To shed additional light on this problems, it is excellent practice to plot each cost estimate on a break-even-style chart. When the several plots are compared with the company's cost goals, the sales volume needed to break even at each compensation level is revealed. Furthermore, the compensation level for individual salespeople under the proposed plan also should be plotted in break-even style. It is equally evident that similar analysis can be applied to the determination of individual sales quotas.

In some firms, company-wide job evaluation and salary administration programs are used to set the compensation levels for sales positions. In such instances, the procedure recommended above should be used as a check on the compensation levels prescribed through job evaluations. Any discrepancies found must be reconciled, or further studies must be made. When the salary administration program is sound, there should be few, if any, discrepancies.

Much confusion exists about the appropriate income levels for sales personnel. It is not unusual to find that two companies operate under similar selling conditions but with different levels. In other words, salespeople in one company earn more than salespeople who do essentially the same work in another company. Relatively speaking, the first group of salespeople is overcompensated. What explains such situations? Sometimes, management does not know, or is uncertain of the true worth of individual salespersons. In other cases, management is afraid that some salespeople are indispensable, or managerial inertia prevents the adjustment of the salespersons' compensation level in accord with changed selling conditions. In still other cases, sales managers are biased in favor of high compensation for selling jobs.[4]

### Provide for the Various Compensation Elements

A sales-compensation plan may contain as many as four basic elements: (1) a fixed element, either a salary or a drawing account, which is intended to provide some stability of income; (2) a variable element (for example, a commission, bonus, or profit-sharing arrangement), designed to serve as an incentive to productivity; (3) an element providing for reimbursement of expenses or payment of expense allowances; and (4) an element covering the fringe benefits or "plus factors," such as paid vacations, sickness and accident benefits, life insurance, pensions, and the like. Each of these elements is considered later in greater detail. Planners must decide which elements should be included and what proportion each should bear to the salesperson's total income. Not every company wants to, or should, include all four elements. Management should select the combination of elements that best fits the requirements of the firm's selling situation. The proportions of the total that different elements should comprise also varies with the particular selling situation. However, current practice indicates that most firms favor making about 80 percent of the salesperson's total income fixed and allocating the remaining 20 percent among other elements.[5]

---

[4] For a detailed and interesting analysis of overcompensation of salesmen, see K. R. Davis, *Are Your Salesmen Overpaid?* (Hanover, N. H.: The Amos Tuck School of Business Administration, Dartmouth College, 1956).

[5] *Sales Management,* Vol. 112, No. 1 (January 7, 1974), p. 66.

## Consider Special Company Needs and Problems

Special company needs and problems should be considered and the plan designed so that it will meet as many of these needs as possible, either eliminating or reducing the seriousness of the problems. Although a salesperson's compensation plan is no panacea for management's marketing ills, it is often practical to construct a plan that increases the effectiveness of other management policies. If a company's earnings are depressed because sales personnel overemphasize low-margin items and neglect more profitable products, it may be possible, despite the existence of other managerial alternatives, to adjust the compensation plan to cause salespeople to sell better-balanced orders. Specifically, provision might be made for variable commission rates on different products, with the higher rates applying to previously neglected products.

Or, to use another example, a firm might have a "small-order" problem. It is possible to design compensation plans that operate to encourage salespersons to write larger orders. Commission rates can be graduated so that higher rates apply to larger orders. However, in this instance, to realize maximum benefit, the revised compensation plan probably should be supplemented by a customer classification and call scheduling system, enabling management to vary the call frequency with the account size.

As still another illustration, a company may desire to obtain more displays or local advertising by retailers. With the rise of self-service merchandising, many manufacturers are well aware that the presence or absence of point-of-purchase displays can spell the difference between marketing success or failure. Under such conditions, securing retail displays of company products is highly important, and the task is often assigned to the salespeople. This is a task that sales personnel may neglect, especially if they are paid a commission based on sales volume. To overcome this tendency, an incentive payment for each retail display obtained is often incorporated in the compensation plan.

The three situations above by no means exhaust the possibilities for using the compensation plan as a vehicle to help solve special company problems. Plans may be designed to assist in securing new customers and new business, improving the quality of salespeople's reports, controlling expenses of handling complaints and adjustments, eliminating price shading by the sales staff, reducing traveling and other expenses, and making collections and gathering credit information. Management, however, should recognize that other means exist for dealing with such problems, the frequently transitory nature of which dictates that the company not resort to changes in the sales-compensation plan. Repeated tampering with the sales-compensation plan in an effort to solve many and varied management problems all too frequently results in overly complex and difficult-to-administer plans.

## Consult the Present Sales Force

To refine the plan further, management should consult the present sales personnel. Many grievances have their roots in the compensation plan. Salespeople should be asked what they like and dislike about the plan and what improvements they would suggest. Their criticisms and suggestions should be appraised relative to the plan or plans management is considering. But at this point again, management should compare the caliber of the present sales force with that of the people whom it would like to have. If the present salespeople are not of the grade that the company wishes to attract, their criticisms and suggestions may be of limited usefulness. Since, however, nearly every sales force has some people of the desired caliber, more weight can be attached to their opinions than to those of people falling outside the designated classification.

### Reduce Tentative Plan to Writing and Pretest It

If the preceding suggestions have been followed, the plan should be taking shape rapidly. For clarification, and to eliminate any inconsistencies that may have crept in, the tentative plan should be put in writing. Then it should be pretested. The amount of testing required depends upon the extent to which the new plan differs from the one in use. The greater the difference, the more thorough should be the testing.

Pretests of compensation plans are almost always mathematical and have become increasingly computerized. Past payrolls, for perhaps a year or two, are reworked to check the operation of the proposed plan against experience under the old system. Analysts compare what happened with what would have happened had the new plan been in effect. If the sales pattern has shown considerable fluctuation, calculations should be made for periods representative of average, good, and poor business. Then a look should be taken into the future. Utilizing data from the sales forecast, new and old plans can be applied to future periods. The plan should be tested for the sales force as a group and for individual salespeople faced with different selling conditions. Conclusions drawn from these tests should reveal whether the plan permits earnings in line with the desired compensation level. If deficiencies show up, management should recognize that the plan may not be at fault. Apparent weaknesses can be traced to the way in which territorial assignments have been made or to inaccuracies in sales forecasts, budgets, or quotas.

It is often advisable to conduct a pilot test. Several territories representative of different types of selling conditions are selected, and the proposed plan applied in each one sufficiently long to detect how it works under current operating conditions. Pilot tests are invaluable for spotting possible sources of trouble and in uncovering and correcting other apparent deficiencies before the plan is put into effect.

### Revise the Plan

After the test results have been thoroughly analyzed, the plan should be revised to eliminate trouble spots or deficiencies. If extensive alterations are made, it is wise to put the changed plan through further pretests and perhaps even another pilot test. But if there have been only minor changes, it is merely necessary to edit the revised plan.

### Install the Plan and Provide for Follow-up

At last the plan is ready for implementation. Opinion varies as to whether the plan should be submitted to sales personnel for approval before the actual installation; in any event, management should make a strong effort to convince them of its basic fairness and logic. Salespeople should be made to understand what management hopes to accomplish through the plan and just how this is to be done. Details of changes from the previous plan, and their significance, should be carefully explained. All salespersons should be given copies of the plan, and they should be taught to compute their own earnings. Written examples of the proper method for calculating earnings should be provided. Inadequate understanding of the compensation plan is a common cause of salespeople's dissatisfaction. Too often, management fails to realize that the sales compensation plan may require painstaking explanation. When salespersons do not fully understand the purposes of such features of a plan as quotas and variable commission bases, they are prone to think that unfair advantage is being taken of them. Provisions should be made for periodic checkups, to determine whether the plan is working out in practice. From such checkups, the need for further adjustments can be detected. Management has much to gain from an appropriate sales-force compensation plan and much to lose from a defective one. Periodic checks provide evidence of the plan's accomplishments, and they help detect areas of weakness if things are not working out as anticipated.[6]

## ✓ BASIC TYPES OF COMPENSATION PLANS

The four elements of compensation may be combined into literally hundreds of different sales-force pay plans, each of which is more or less unique. If the "expense reimbursement" and "fringe benefit" elements are excluded from consideration—as is entirely reasonable, since they are never used alone—there are three basic types of compensation plans: straight salary, straight commission, and a combination of salary and one or more variable elements.

### ✓ Straight-Salary Plan

The straight salary is the simplest compensation plan. Under it, salespersons receive fixed sums at regular intervals (usually each week or month but sometimes every two weeks), representing total payments for their services. In addition, they may receive an amount to defray all or part of the expenses incurred in performance of their duties. The straight salary was once the most popular sales-compensation plan, but it has been declining in importance since the early 1920s. A recent study by the American Management Association shows that just under 25 percent of all selling organizations operate exclusively on a straight-salary basis. Such plans are considerably more common in companies selling industrial goods than they are in ones marketing consumer products.[7] Firms that formerly used the straight salary have tended to combine a basic salary with an additional variable element—that is, they have switched to combination plans.

In spite of the trend away from its use, the straight-salary plan is still appropriate in certain situations. It is often the best way to compensate sales personnel when the selling job requires extensive missionary or educational work, when salespeople service the product or give technical and engineering advice to prospects or users, or when salespeople do considerable sales promotion work. Thus, if nonselling tasks bulk large in the salesperson's total time expenditure, the straight-salary plan is worthy of management's serious consideration.

Straight-salary plans are used for compensating salespeople engaged in more or less routine selling. These jobs, in which selling often is reduced to mere order taking, abound in the wholesale and manufacturing fields, where consumer necessities are dis-

---

[6] For a good discussion of the procedure used in the development of a compensation plan for a major industrial equipment manufacturer, see F. E. Webster, Jr., "Rationalizing Salesmen's Compensation Plans," *Journal of Marketing,* Vol. 30, No. 1 (January 1966), pp. 55-58.

[7] *Sales Management* (January 7, 1974), p. 67.

tributed directly to retailers. Quite frequently, too, the straight-salary method is used for paying driver-salespersons selling liquor and beverages, milk and bread, and similarly distributed products.

From management's standpoint, the straight-salary plan has important advantages. By its very nature it provides strong financial control over sales personnel, and management secures maximum power to direct their activities along lines that are potentially the most productive. Component tasks making up salespersons' jobs can be recast with minimum opposition from the people affected. Consequently, greater flexibility is obtained in adjusting field sales work to changes in the selling situation. If sales personnel are required to prepare detailed reports, follow up on large numbers of leads, or perform other time-consuming tasks, they tend to cooperate more fully if paid straight salaries rather than commissions. Straight-salary plans are also economical to administer, since their basic simplicity requires few mathematical manipulations and, as compared with straight-commission plans, accounting costs are significantly lower.

From the salesperson's standpoint, the chief attraction of the straight-salary plan is that the stability of income frees him or her from the financial uncertainty inherent in plans that contain variable elements. Additionally, because salaried salespersons expect to receive detailed instructions, they are relieved of much of the burden of planning their activities. Finally, because of the basic simplicity of the straight-salary plan, salespeople usually find it easy to understand.

The straight-salary plan has several marked weaknesses. Because there are no direct monetary incentives, many salespeople do only an *average* selling job rather than an outstanding one. They may be inclined to pass up promising opportunities for increased business, at least until management becomes aware of them and orders the taking of required actions. Unless the plan is skillfully administered, there is a tendency to undercompensate good salespeople and to overcompensate poor ones. If such inequities exist for long, the turnover rate rises; and it is often the most productive people who leave the company first. Situations of this type inevitably result in increased expenditures for recruiting, selecting, and training. Other problems are encountered in maintaining morale, inasmuch as arguments occur on such matters as pay adjustments for ability, rising living costs, and length of service. Because all the selling expense is fixed, the company finds it difficult to adjust to changing economic conditions—a particularly knotty problem during business downswings, when selling expenses can be reduced only by cutting salaries or releasing personnel. Moreover, during business upturns, the company may experience difficulty in securing its normal share of rising industry volume, because salespeople paid straight salaries commonly are not disposed to exceed previous sales records by any large amount. The reader should recognize, however, that many of these weaknesses of the straight-salary plan can be avoided or minimized through intelligent administration.

In administering a straight-salary plan, individual salespeople should be paid, insofar as possible, according to their relative performance. The difficulty in achieving this ideal is in validly measuring performance. Before performance can be measured, management needs to define what it means by "performance" and what constitutes good, average, and poor performances. When management has these definitions and develops methods for performance measurements, salaries of individual salespersons can be set fairly and intelligently. Users of the salary plan should define performance as total job performance, not merely success in securing sales volume or in performing some other aspect of the job—and this definition is theoretically correct, because the payers of salaries assume that they will be able to exercise maximum direction and control over the way salary receivers perform all aspects of the jobs. Some salary plan users, recognizing that it is illogical to use success in securing sales volume as the sole criterion, attempt instead to measure performance by relating total selling expense incurred by an individual salesperson (including his or her salary) to his or her total sales. Although it is desirable to hold total selling expenses within reasonable bounds, to use the expense-to-sales ratio as the sole criterion of performance is to overemphasize the importance of cost control.

In the absence of well-defined quantitative performance standards, and few companies have them, the sales job description, if up to date and complete, is the starting point from which to appraise sales performance.[8] All salespersons should be rated not only on their success in achieving sales and cost goals but on their performance of each assigned duty. The total evaluation of an individual is a composite of the several ratings, weighed according to relative importance. Persons rated as average should be paid average salaries. Salaries of below-average and above-average salespeople should be scaled to reflect the extent to which their performances vary from the average. Each salesperson's performance should be regularly reviewed and upward adjustments made for people who have registered improvements, and, to the extent possible, reductions should be made for those whose performances have deteriorated.

## Straight-Commission Plan

The theory supporting the straight-commission plan is that sales personnel should be paid strictly according to their individual productivity. The assumption underlying most straight-commission plans is that sales volume is the best measure of productivity and can, therefore, be used as its sole measure. This is a highly questionable assumption, as was brought out in the preceding discussion of the straight-salary plan.

Although the straight-commission plan, at least in its purest form, is almost as simple as the straight-salary plan, many commission systems develop into rather complex arrangements. Some provide for progressive or regressive changes in commission rates as sales volume rises to different levels. Others provide for differential commission rates for sales of different products, to different categories of customers, or during different selling seasons. Such refinements tend to make straight-commission plans more complex to operate than most straight-salary plans.

According to one source, the majority of straight-commission plans falls into one of two broad classifications:

1. Straight commission at a gross or inclusive rate with no defrayment of expenses by the employer. Salespeople therefore pay their own expenses. Advances may or may not be made against earnings.

2. Straight commission at a net rate in which the employer pays the travel expenses, again with or without advances against commission earnings.[9]

There has been a general trend away from the straight-commission plan, and today probably no more than 6 or 7 percent of all companies have such plans in use.[10]

[8] The use of quantitative performance standards as part of an integrated system for controlling sales personnel is discussed in Chapter 17. The present discussion relates to companies without such quantitative standards.

[9] H. R. Tosdal and W. Carson, Jr., *Salesmen's Compensation,* Vol. I (Boston: Harvard University Graduate School of Business Administration, Division of Research, 1953), p. 132.

[10] As reported in *Sales Management* (January 7, 1974), p. 67.

However, the plan is used in situations where the salesperson's nonselling duties are relatively unimportant and management wants to emphasize getting orders. Straight-commission plans are common in the clothing, textile, and shoe industries and in drug and hardware wholesaling. Firms selling intangibles, such as insurance and investment securities, often employ this method exclusively. It is also used extensively by manufacturers of furniture, office equipment, and business machines.

The straight-commission plan has several outstanding advantages. Probably the greatest is that it provides maximum direct monetary incentive for the salesperson to strive for high-level volume. The star salesperson is paid more than he or she would be under most salary plans, and low producers are not likely to be overcompensated. When a commission system is first installed, there is some tendency for the sales-force turnover rate to accelerate, but analysis usually reveals that the exodus has been mostly among the low producers. Ordinarily, the remaining salespeople work longer and harder and with more income to show for their efforts, perhaps because of the strong motivation provided such people by a feeling of "being in business for myself." Straight-commission plans also provide management with a means for cost control—all direct selling expenses, except for traveling and miscellaneous expenses (which may be reimbursable in plans of the second classification noted above), fluctuate directly with sales-volume changes and, in contrast to straight-salary plans, sales compensation becomes virtually all variable expense. The straight-commission plan also is characterized by great flexibility, making it readily adjustable to deal with particular company problems. By revising the commission rates applying to different products, for instance, it is often possible to stimulate sales personnel to give increased emphasis to selling the items with the highest gross margins.

However, the straight-commission method has certain weaknesses. The greatest is that it provides for little financial control over salespeople's activities, a weakness further compounded when they pay their own expenses. Salespersons on straight commission tend to feel that they are discharging their full responsibilities by continuing to send in customers' orders. They are careless about transmitting reports and other requested information, often neglect to follow up leads provided by the home office, resist proposed reductions in the size of sales territories, consider individual accounts their private property, are tempted to shade prices to make sales, and may resort to high-pressure tactics with consequent loss of customer goodwill. Moreover, unless differential commission rates are provided, some salespeople push the easiest-to-sell low-margin items and neglect the harder-to-sell high-margin items; if management seeks to correct this situation through using differential commission rates, increased record-keeping expenses are incurred. Under any straight-commission plan, in fact, the costs of checking and auditing salespeople's reports and of calculating payrolls are almost certain to be higher than under the straight-salary method. Finally, some salespersons' efficiency may decline because of worries caused by income uncertainties. If a sales force has many such worried salespeople, management may have to invest considerable time, effort, and money in the task of buoying up the spirits of downhearted persons. Since new salespeople, in particular, have difficulties in adjusting to fluctuating incomes, it is a wise policy to pay recruits straight salaries until they gain selling skill sufficient to enable them consistently to earn more on commission.

One comprehensive study of sales compensation concluded that certain of the following conditions are present in all successful applications of the straight-commission plan:

1. The need for strong incentive to secure the requisite intensive selling effort.

2. The desire to reduce fixed salary or other fixed selling expense to a minimum.

3. The need to make limited finances go further by reducing sales requirements for working capital.

4. The desire to fix definite cost ratios for personal selling so that accounting statements and price estimates can be made more accurate.

5. Inability or unwillingness, for financial or other reasons, to provide sufficient supervision to supplement lack of incentive of salary or other plans. Sometimes, the thinness of the market and the need for selling over large and widely scattered areas renders self-super - vision the only solution.

6. Straight commission is the accepted and desired method of compensation in the industry.

7. Personal selling is the primary and frequently the only means of selling. Advertising is secondary and supplementary. Consumer advertising is limited in amount.

8. Commission may be the only feasible plan of compensation when the salesperson works on a part-time basis or when he sells a number of products or lines for two or more employers or principals. Side-line salespeople, independent contractor salespeople, and others fall into this group.[11]

**Determining Commission Base.**   An important aspect of designing a straight-commission system is that of determining the base on which to pay commissions. Usually, selection of the base depends upon the individual company's particular selling policies and problems. If obtaining volume is the main concern, then total sales probably should be the base. If sales personnel are required to make collections on sales, it may be appropriate to base commissions on collections. If a firm is confronted with excessive order cancellations, it sometimes is wise to base commissions on shipments, billings, or payments. To control price cutting by sales personnel, some companies base commissions on gross margins. A sizable number of organizations use net profits as the commission base, thereby seeking simultaneously to control price cutting, selling expenses, and net profit.

**Drawing Accounts.**   An important modification of the straight-commission plan is known as the drawing-account method, under which the employer establishes separate accounts for each salesperson, to which commissions are credited regularly and against which they make periodic withdrawals. In practice, drawing accounts tend to resemble salaries, since salespeople commonly are allowed to overdraw against future earnings. If a salesperson becomes greatly overdrawn, he or she may lose incentive to produce, because some portion of the earned commission will be used to reduce the indebtedness. What is probably more important, the salesperson may become so discouraged with the prospects of paying back the overdrawn amount that he or she will quit the company.

To forestall the possibility that overdrawn salespeople may quit their jobs, some firms use "guaranteed" drawing-account plans that do not require the paying back of overdrawals. Sales executives in these firms must exercise considerable care and judgment in setting the size of drawing accounts for different people, for guaranteed drawing accounts are really combination salary and commission plans under a different name. However, the guaranteed drawing account provides a stronger incentive than combination salary and commission, because the rate of commission on each dollar of sales is higher. Commonly these plans include a provision in the person's contract that

[11] Tosdal and Carson, *op. cit.,* pp. 146-47.

covers the possibility of overdrafts. Legally, in most situations, an overdraft cannot be collected unless the salesperson specifically agrees that it will be repaid, unless it is really a personal loan or unless he or she has given a note acknowledging its receipt. Without a formal understanding of this sort, the court is likely to hold that the relationship between the salesperson and the company was really a partnership in which the company agreed to finance the salesperson, and that the resulting loss was only a normal risk incurred in doing business. Even if the company has an ironclad agreement with its sales personnel on this point, there remains the perplexing problem of collecting money that overdrawn salespeople do not have.

## ✓ Combination Salary-and-Incentive Plan

**Salary Plus Commission.** Most sales-compensation plans are combinations of the salary and commission methods. Most developed in an attempt to capture the advantages and offset the disadvantages of both the salary and commission systems. Where the straight-salary method is used, the sales executive often needs a means of stimulating the sales force to greater effort. Where the straight-commission system is used, the executive may be greatly handicapped because of weak financial control over sales activities. By a judicious blending of the two basic plans, management hopes to obtain both the required control and motivation. But it should not be inferred that these results are always forthcoming, as actual results depend mainly upon management's skills in designing and administering the plan. Unless there is an extremely fine adjustment of the salary and commission elements, weaknesses evident in the basic systems reappear.

**Use of Bonuses.** Many companies use bonuses as financial incentives. Technically, bonuses are different from commissions—a bonus is an amount paid for accomplishing specific sales tasks; a commission varies in amount with sales volume or other commission base. Bonuses may be paid for attaining a certain percentage of the sales quota, performing given promotional activities, obtaining a specified number of new accounts, following up on a certain number of leads, setting up an assigned quota of displays, or carrying out other assigned tasks. The bonus, in other words, is an additional financial reward paid to the salesperson for achieving results beyond a predetermined minimum.

Bonuses are never used alone—they always appear in conjunction with one of the three main sales compensation methods. If used with the straight salary, the resulting compensation plan resembles the combination plan. If used with the straight commission, the result is a commission plan to which has been added an element of managerial control and direction. When used with a combination salary and commission plan, the bonus simply becomes a portion of the incentive income which is calculated in a different way than the commission.

Companies have five principal reasons for adding the bonus feature to their basic compensation plans:

1. To increase the salesperson's income and give him or her a share of the profits of a favorable company year.
2. To provide special payments for reaching particular objectives in terms of sales volume, the volume of sales of particular products, the number of new customers, and the level of profits.
3. To provide recognition for special tasks or special attainments of value to the employer

which are not reflected in the usual measures of performance or which have not yet had time to demonstrate their value in sales or profit results; for instance, the acquisition of product knowledge, complaints or compliments from customers, cooperation in reducing surpluses or overstocks, and diligence and dependability in correspondence and reporting.

4. To develop team work and group action in selling, and in maintaining customers within a branch, district, or other territory.

5. To provide incentive payments without the unearned windfalls incident to salary and commission incentive plans or without adopting cutoff or other maximum earning features.[12]

Several administrative actions are crucial to success when a bonus feature is included in the compensation plan. At the outset, the bonus conditions should be thoroughly explained and, to minimize later misunderstandings, management must make certain that sales personnel understand them. Provision must be made for setting up and maintaining the necessary records. Procedures should be established to keep salespeople abreast of their current standings relative to the goals that qualify them for bonuses. In addition, any misunderstandings or grievances arising as a result of operation of the bonus feature should be dealt with fairly and with the utmost tact and diplomacy.

**Strengths and Weaknesses of Combination Plans.** If a combination plan is well designed and administered, significant benefits are gained. The salespeople have both the security of stable incomes and the stimulus of direct financial incentive. Management has both financial control over sales activities and the apparatus to motivate sales efforts in desired directions. Selling costs are composed of fixed and variable elements; thus, greater flexibility for adjustment to changing business conditions exists than under the straight-salary method but still less than under the commission method. Nevertheless, selling costs, to some extent at least, now fluctuate with the volume of business produced. There also may be beneficial effects upon personnel morale. Disagreements on such problems as salary increases and territorial changes should be much less violent than under a straight-commission plan. Further, if salespeople are made to realize that the company is sharing their financial risks, a more cooperative spirit should develop between them and the company.

The combination plan, however, is not without disadvantages. Clerical costs of operating a combination plan are likely to be higher than for either a salary or a commission system. More records have to be maintained, and these involve greater detail. Thus, there are risks that the plan will become too complicated and that the salespeople will not fully understand it. Sometimes a company seeking to provide adequate salaries and at the same time desiring to keep selling costs down must use such low commission rates that the incentive feature is insufficient to elicit greater effort by the salespeople. On the other hand, if the incentive portion is increased to a larger percentage of the total income, salespeople may neglect activities for which they are not directly paid. Therefore, the ratios that the base salary and the incentive portion bear to the total compensation are critical factors. As mentioned earlier, the most common distribution of payments in combination plans is 80 percent salary and 20 percent incentive and other elements.

[12]*Ibid.*, p. 200.

## REIMBURSEMENT OF SALES EXPENSES— POLICIES AND PRACTICES

With respect to reimbursement of sales expenses, the two general policy alternatives are: (1) to require sales personnel to pay their own expenses, or (2) to reimburse salespeople for all or part of the expenses incurred in performing their jobs. Although the first alternative is the simpler by far, few companies choose it. Those that do are organizations, by and large, that regard sales personnel as independent business people—an overwhelming majority of these organizations also use the straight-commission compensation method. The main advantage of this policy, from management's standpoint, is that no special expense records are necessary inasmuch as the sales personnel, rather than the company, are the ones whose desire to control expenses is stimulated. But in successful applications, the level of other compensation reflects the fact that they bear their own expenses. It is essential that their regular commission be sufficient to permit them to further the company's best interests. Even when the compensation level takes into account salespeople's probable expenses, some persons still skimp on expenses, to the company's detriment. To increase their earnings, they stay in second- and third-rate hotels, they economize on meals, dry cleaning, laundry, and other traveling expenses, and they avoid entertaining customers and prospects. Furthermore, they resist or ignore many of management's directions and instructions. Little management control can be exercised over their call and route schedules, especially in regard to accounts located in out-of-the-way places. Most salespeople who pay their own expenses refuse, or neglect, to perform non-sales-producing activities—they avoid missionary duties and follow up on sales leads only when no additional expenses are involved. They "high spot"; that is, they call only on large accounts that can be depended upon to give orders; and they feel justified in adding "side-lines," other manufacturers' products sold to the same general classes of trade. Taken all in all, except in the most unusual marketing circumstances, it is unwise to require salespeople to pay their own expenses.

Most firms choose the second policy alternative—full or partial reimbursement of sales expenses. When all or part of sales expenses are classified as reimbursable, sales management must be concerned directly with the amounts spent. After all, the funds used to defray sales expenses represent deductions from gross profits realized on sales. Although there is considerable variation among companies, the average costs of keeping sales personnel on the road are higher than commonly supposed. Many factors, of course, influence the amount of sales expenses. Some of these are: territorial size and characteristics, the caliber of the sales personnel, the nature and breadth of the product line, managerial efficiency, the intensity of competition, and the mode of travel.

Figures 15.1 and 15.2 show sales-force selling expenses as a percentage of company sales and daily expenses of field sales personnel, respectively. It may be seen in Figure 15.1 that of the twenty-two industries studied, total selling expenses as a percentage of sales declined in thirteen of them and remained constant in two others. Figure 15.2 clearly illustrates that in 1973 it was more costly to support an industrial-products salesman than it was a consumer-products salesman. Nearly three fourths (74.4 percent) of the industrial-products salesmen incurred daily expenses of $30 or more, whereas less than one half (47.3 percent) of the consumer-products salesmen had daily expenses of such magnitude.

To some extent at least, the excellence of sales management can be gauged from the way in which it handles salesmen's expenses. Liberality, on the one hand, is desirable—to ensure that salesmen have adequate funds to capitalize fully on market opportunities. The tendency to be too liberal, on the other hand, should be avoided, to avoid having a profit showing that is less favorable than it should be. In general, sales executives are inclined to be too liberal rather than too stringent, and, it must be admitted, overliberality is wiser than restricting salespeople's activities through insufficient expense reimbursement.

The degree of formal control exercised over sales expenses varies a good deal from company to company. Some firms establish close budgetary controls and try to hold

FIGURE 15.1
Sales Force Selling Expenses as a
Percentage of Company Sales*

| Industry | Compensation | | T&E Expenses | | Total | |
|---|---|---|---|---|---|---|
| | 1973 | 1972 | 1973 | 1972 | 1973 | 1972 |
| **Consumer products** | | | | | | |
| Apparel | 4.7 | 4.8 | 1.1 | 1.0 | 5.8 | 5.8 |
| Durable goods | 2.7 | 3.5 | 1.0 | 1.3 | 3.7 | 4.8 |
| Ethical pharmaceuticals, surgical supplies, and equipment | 3.5 | 4.4 | 3.0 | 2.3 | 6.5 | 6.7 |
| Food | 1.8 | 1.6 | 0.8 | 0.6 | 2.6 | 2.2 |
| Major household items | 4.0 | 2.1 | 1.4 | 1.0 | 5.4 | 3.1 |
| **Industrial products** | | | | | | |
| Auto parts and accessories | 2.4 | 3.2 | 1.1 | 1.2 | 3.5 | 4.4 |
| Building materials | 1.7 | 1.9 | 0.7 | 1.0 | 2.4 | 2.9 |
| Chemicals | 1.8 | 2.7 | 1.0 | 1.2 | 2.8 | 3.9 |
| Containers and packaging materials | 2.5 | 1.9 | 0.8 | 1.4 | 3.3 | 3.3 |
| Electrical materials | 1.3 | 3.1 | 1.0 | 0.9 | 2.3 | 4.0 |
| Electronics | 1.9 | 2.7 | 0.6 | 1.0 | 2.5 | 3.7 |
| Fabricated metals (heavy) | 1.7 | 1.7 | 0.7 | 0.9 | 2.4 | 2.6 |
| Fabricated metals (light) | 1.6 | 2.8 | 0.8 | 1.2 | 2.4 | 4.0 |
| Fabrics | 2.1 | 2.2 | 1.2 | 1.0 | 3.3 | 3.2 |
| Glass | 2.7 | 1.9 | 1.3 | 0.9 | 4.0 | 2.8 |
| Instruments | 4.4 | 3.1 | 1.4 | 1.3 | 5.8 | 4.4 |
| Iron and steel | 0.5 | 0.9 | 0.2 | 0.4 | 0.7 | 1.3 |
| Machinery (heavy) | 1.8 | 1.9 | 0.7 | 1.2 | 2.5 | 3.1 |
| Machinery (light) | 2.1 | 2.8 | 1.0 | 1.9 | 3.1 | 4.7 |
| Office supplies and equipment | 4.4 | 4.6 | 2.0 | 1.2 | 6.4 | 5.8 |
| Paper | 1.2 | 0.8 | 0.4 | 1.3 | 1.6 | 2.1 |
| Tools and hardware | 2.3 | 1.7 | 1.5 | 0.9 | 3.8 | 2.6 |

*Includes *only* total compensation plus expenses, that is, travel, lodging, meals, and entertainment. Note that some of the differences between years reflect changes in the organizations that reported data.

Source: American Management Association, *Executive Compensation Service.*

FIGURE 15.2
Daily Expenses of Field Salespersons

| | Percent of Companies | | | | | |
| | Consumer Products | | Industrial Products | | Other Commerce and Industry | |
| Cost per Day per Salesperson | 1973 | 1972 | 1973 | 1972 | | |
|---|---|---|---|---|---|---|
| Under $10 | 7.0 | 4.1 | 0.6 | 1.2 | 4.0 | — |
| $10-$19 | 15.8 | 22.4 | 9.5 | 7.1 | 8.0 | 19.0 |
| $20-$29 | 29.9 | 22.4 | 15.5 | 23.1 | 16.0 | 33.4 |
| $30-$39 | 7.0 | 14.3 | 28.6 | 22.5 | 12.0 | 9.5 |
| $40-$49 | 19.3 | 4.1 | 13.7 | 18.3 | 12.0 | 9.5 |
| $50-$59 | 10.5 | 16.3 | 16.7 | 14.2 | 20.0 | 4.8 |
| $60-$70 | 3.5 | 6.2 | 5.9 | 5.3 | 4.0 | 4.8 |
| Over $70 | 7.0 | 10.2 | 9.5 | 8.3 | 24.0 | 19.0 |
| Total | 100.0 | 100.0 | 100.0 | 100.0 | 100.0 | 100.0 |

*Includes food, lodging, travel, entertainment, and auto expenses. It should be noted that some of the differences between years reflect changes in the organizations that reported data.

Source: American Management Association, *Executive Compensation Service.*

sales expenses within a planned total amount, or to a certain percentage of sales volume or gross margin. Others control sales expenses only in the most general way, such as by careful scrutiny of expense reports or through written policy statements outlining the conditions under which expenses are reimbursable.

Several commonsense principles guide management in formulating expense-reimbursement policies. Reimbursable expenses should be large enough to permit the performance of assigned duties in the manner expected. Normally, all expenses incurred because sales personnel are away from their home bases of operation on company business should be reimbursable. Expense-reimbursement policies should take into account the customary standards of living of the salesperson and of the customers, but greater emphasis should be given the latter. The salesperson should eat in restaurants and stay at hotels of the class ordinarily patronized by the customers. In some instances, different salespeople in the same company should be allowed different amounts for expenses, reflecting deviation in customers' standards of living. Another reason for different-sized expense accounts is the fact that actual expenses vary a great deal from one territory to another. Reimbursement policies should operate to keep expenses within a reasonable range; they should not be allowed to cause bad feeling among the sales staff. It is desirable that these policies be economical to administer; that is, only minimum supervision and record keeping should be required of both the company and sales personnel, but the desire for economy in administration should not result in adoption of arbitrary or unfair procedures. Above all, both in formulating reimbursement policies and in defining procedures for implementation, management needs to guard against the natural tendency to overeconomize. Under no circumstances should salespeople be forced to economize to the point of impairing selling efficiency. Nor should salespeople have to dip into their own pockets to pay legitimate expenses. Reimbursement policies and procedures should be based upon the reasonable needs of the people incurring the expenses; for enforcement, they should rely largely upon each person's inherent honesty.[13]

## METHODS OF CONTROLLING AND REIMBURSING EXPENSES OF SALES PERSONNEL

### Flat-Expense-Account Plan

The flat-expense-account plan provides each salesperson with a stipulated sum to cover all expenses for a given period. Allocation of this sum among various expense items is left to the individual's discretion. Apparently, the chief reason for employing the flat expense account is to eliminate the necessity for keeping expense reports and the checking of expense accounts. One advantage of the plan is that, since individual expense accounts are determined in advance, the total amount of sales expenses can be included in the budget. Periodically, then, at budget-making time, management may appraise the reasonableness of total planned selling expenses relative to total planned sales. A second advantage is that sales personnel who are free to spend expense allowances as they see fit should have few grievances and arguments over expense accounts. A third advantage is that the plan's nature is such as to cause salespeople to control their own expenses and, if guided properly by management, they should do a better job planning route and call schedules in order that each expense dollar may be spent to the best advantage.

Successful operation of the flat-expense-account plan requires skilled administration. It works best either (1) when the exact amounts of expense accounts do not need changing often, as with companies whose salespeople have small territories in which to sell staple products, or (2) when an individual salesperson's expense allowances come up for frequent review and, possibly, revision. In other words, if the marketing situation is not relatively flexible, the amounts of the expense accounts should have flexibility built into them. If the plan is inflexible in a fluid marketing situation, salespeople may not capitalize on sales opportunities requiring expenditures in excess of the flat amounts. Even when marketing circumstances favor the use of this plan, management should regularly appraise each salesperson's allowance for adequacy and appropriateness.

The weakness of flat expense accounts results from the tendency of some sales personnel to overeconomize. These people come to think of the expense account as a regular addition to salary and are reluctant to spend the entire allowance, preferring to save a portion for personal use. Careful sales supervision is essential to avoid situations of this sort.

### Flexible-Expense-Account Method

The flexible-expense-account method, sometimes known as the "exact" plan, is the most common reimbursement method. The salient feature of this plan is that salesperson-nel receive reimbursements for all "allowable" expenses incurred and reported. If this method is to work successfully, management must (1) know the approximate total amount of sales personnel's probable expenses (otherwise there is inadequate informa-

---

[13] For an in-depth study of the practices and trends in controlling sales expenses, see *How 606 Companies Control Salesmen's Expenses* (Chicago: The Dartnell Corporation, 1966).

tion for planning and budgeting); (2) classify sales expenses into "allowable" and "non-allowable" categories, and furnish salespeople with clear descriptions of items included under each heading; (3) set up a system and forms for the sales staff to use in periodic expense reporting; (4) establish procedures for checking itemized expense reports and for expeditious handling of reimbursements.

The plan has much to recommend it. Inasmuch as expense accounts are flexible, sales opportunities may be capitalized on fully as they arise. There is a basic fairness about the plan, because, almost automatically, it takes into account and makes payments for differences in territories, marketing conditions, and other important factors. Therefore, management can exercise considerable control over sales routes and call schedules. Finally, salespersons are under obligation to perform all their assigned activities, nonselling as well as selling, with the degree of efficiency expected by management.

The flexible-expense-account plan's unattractive features come out in its administration. Administrative costs are sizable, because of the large amount of clerical and accounting work involved in checking expense reports and making reimbursements. Similarly, clerical and accounting work requires a great deal of the salespeople's time, and many executives contend that good sales personnel are often poor record keepers. Unless close control is maintained, some salespeople spend the company's money too generously, this situation being further aggravated by the existence of considerable opportunity for expense-account padding—and many disputes arise over various expense items. Hence sales-force morale and productivity may suffer unless highly competent people administer the plan.

### Honor System

Under this system, sales expenses are fully reimbursed. Sales personnel are not required to submit detailed, itemized lists of expenses but report only their total expenses for the period. The implication is that management has complete confidence in each salesperson's honesty, and this should affect sales-force morale favorably. The honor system is also easy to administer and, compared with alternative reimbursement plans, there are savings in both accounting expenses and time. Arguments over questionable expenditures do not arise, and salespeople do not envision management as parsimonious. Finally, at least in theory, the funds for territorial development should be adequate; however, both the amounts and the ways in which they are used are left to the salespeople's discretion.

With the honor system, management's control is characteristically weak, and this may cause certain problems to develop. Some salespersons evolve into free spenders, since detailed expense reports are not required. Others incur expenses from which the company has little chance of deriving benefit. Still others go so far as to appropriate company funds for their own use, for the system tends to encourage people to regard expense accounts as sources of additional income. Abuses such as these cause inequities in expense allowances, and this may have bad effects upon morale. To avoid such abuses, management, even though committed to the honor principle, should provide for some control over individual salespersons' total expenses. One way is to establish maximum ratios of selling expense to sales for each salesperson. It is advisable also to watch the trend of expenses; and sudden and sizable increases in a person's reported expenses, unless accompanied by parallel changes in sales, should be investigated. If dishonesty in expense reporting is detected, remedial action is definitely advisable. In spite of such problems the philosophy of the honor system lies behind the reimbursement policies and practices of many sales organizations.

### Expense-Quota Plan

The expense-quota plan is a compromise between the flat-expense-account plan and the honor system as well as the flexible-expense-account plan. This plan's objectives are to retain considerable control over salespersons' total expenses over long periods but to permit week-by-week variations in the amounts reimbursed. In setting up expense quotas, management first studies the size and characteristics of individual territories and estimates the sales volume each should provide, then establishes upper limits for each salesperson's total expenses likely to be incurred over a specified period. Under the expense-quota plan, sales personnel receive prompt and full reimbursements, regardless of how greatly "allowable" expenses vary from week to week. The budgeted figures are planned amounts only, and management does not hold rigidly to the upper limits. But because upper limits are established, salespeople have a strong moral obligation to keep their expenses under control. Thus, there are significant advantages to be gained. The principal drawback is that the burden for controlling expenses is placed, in effect, upon the salespeople rather than upon management. As is true of all expense-reimbursement plans, skillful administration is a necessary condition for successful operation of the expense-quota plan. Furthermore, unless sales and expense forecasts are accurate, and unless salespersons are convinced that the upper limits are estimates only, toward the end of budgetary periods salespeople may curtail their activities because of low balances left in their accounts.

### Handling Salespersons' Automobile Expenses

Companies using either the flexible-expense-account plan or the expense-quota plan, and whose salespeople operate their own automobiles (rather than company-owned or -leased vehicles), must adopt a system for determining the amounts that sales personnel should be reimbursed for using their automobiles on company business. Computation of "exact" automobile expenses is complicated by the fact that variable, semivariable, and fixed expenses are involved. Certain items, including costs of gasoline, lubricating oil and grease, and tires, vary with the miles traveled. Some items, such as insurance coverage, license fees, and inspection fees, are fixed. Other costs, such as charges for depreciation and obsolescence, vary with the automobile's age and its rate of use. Hence, total automobile expenses per mile do not vary at a constant rate—as mileage increases, total expenses per mile decline. Adding further to computation difficulties, expenses differ with the automobile make and model. Moreover, expenses of ownership and operation, even for comparable makes and models, vary substantially from one territory to another. And differences in road and traffic conditions also cause auto expenses to vary from territory to territory. These complications make precise computations of automobile expenses a highly involved and tedious process, and most companies have settled on less-exact procedures. Most studies of companies using salesperson-owned automobiles show that more than one half use flat mileage rates, about one fifth use graduated mileage rates, and the rest use standard allowances, combinations of standard allowances and mileage rates, the Runzheimer plan, or other systems. Each of the main systems is examined in the following discussion.

**Flat Mileage Rates.** Firms using the flat-mileage-rate system reimburse automobile expenses at a fixed rate per mile traveled. This is now the most widely used system, but there has been a trend away from it—probably because of management's increasing recognition that flat mileage rates are no better than rough approximations of true expenses. Users of this system must try to set the mileage rate high enough to cover all expenses of automobile ownership and operation, yet low enough to permit the company to buy transportation as cheaply as possible. Operating this system is simple. Sales personnel report mileages traveled on company business, the flat mileage rate is applied, and reimbursement checks are issued. The system appears to work satisfactorily when a company's sales force covers small territories (requiring little automobile travel) all in the same geographical area (incurring very similar expense amounts), and the mileage rate applied is on the generous side (eliminating arguments over actual and reimbursed expenses). Probably for these reasons, the majority of local and regional wholesalers, among other small companies, favor the flat-mileage-rate system.

For most companies, however, the flat-mileage-rate system has fundamental shortcomings. It is based on the erroneous assumption that automobile expenses per mile vary at a constant rate at all operating levels. It ignores cost differentials arising from the use of various makes and models. It similarly ignores very real territorial differences in expenses, for example in the prices of gasoline, oil, tires, insurance coverage, license and inspection fees, and even the automobiles themselves. Furthermore, in administering the flat-mileage-rate system, management all too often shows great hesitancy in adjusting the rate, upward as well as downward, in line with changing actual expenses.

**Graduated Mileage Rates.** Under this system, different mileage rates apply for mileages in different ranges—for example, 15 cents per mile up to 5,000 miles annually, 12.5 cents per mile for from 5,000 to 10,000 miles, and 10 cents per mile for over 10,000 miles. Thus, an important weakness of the flat-mileage-rate system is avoided, since mileage rates decline as mileage increases. It appears, then, that companies using this system recognize that the per mile costs of automobile operation are lower for long than for short distances; however, setting the cents-per-mile rates is difficult, since it is necessary to consider different operating levels in determining the mileages at which rates change. This system takes into account, almost mechanically, differences in sales territories, such as the length of route and frequency of calls. But, like the flat-mileage-rate system, it does not consider cost variations resulting from operation of different makes and models, and territorial expense differentials. Graduated-mileage-rate systems are most appropriate for use by companies whose sales personnel travel long distances annually but who serve fairly concentrated geographic areas (thus avoiding significant regional expense differences). The basic defect in all mileage-rate systems, whether flat or graduated, is that they consider nothing more than total costs that are assumed to vary only with the miles traveled, when, in fact, some costs are fixed, wholly or partially, regardless of the mileage or use.

**Standard Allowance.** Some companies simply grant salespersons a specified sum for each day, week, month, or other period during which they use their personal automobiles on company business. Taken all in all, the standard-allowance system has even less to recommended it than do mileage-rate systems. It assumes that total automobile expenses vary with duration of use rather than with mileage traveled. At best, the standard allowance can be but a rough estimate of actual costs of automobile ownership and operation. Companies using this system tend to penalize sales personnel whose territories are large and require extensive traveling for adequate coverage; and the standard allowance, unless amounts are varied for individual salespeople, fails to reimburse for these differences. If allowances, for all sales people are uniform, morale is bound to suffer, because the sales force will recognize the obvious inequities. Morale is affected adversely, too, by revisions in the standard allowance made as costs change, particularly when the revisions are downward. Only when the entire staff faces similar driving conditions, possess comparable makes and models of cars, and have nearly equal-sized territories, each requiring approximately the same sales coverage, is the standard allowance defensible. Needless to say, it is unusual for all these conditions to be present in the same situation.

**Combination Standard Allowance and Mileage Rate.** This system reflects recognition that both fixed and variable expenses are involved in automobile ownership and operation. A fixed periodic payment (intended to cover such fixed and semivariable costs as insurance premiums, license fees, and depreciation) is combined with a mileage allowance (for reimbursing all operating expenses, including the costs of gasoline, oil, and tires). This plan, then, is an improvement over both parent systems, because it allows for the fact that some expenses vary with automobile usage and some do not. In contrast to mileage-rate systems, it provides for the expenses that do not vary directly with the operating level; in contrast to the standard allowance system, it takes account of cost differentials arising from different operating levels. If all sales personnel are granted identical standard allowances, this system, like the others, fails to consider territorial expense differentials and cost variations resulting from operation and ownership of different makes and models of automobiles.

Some companies using the combination system accumulate reserves to cover depreciation charges on salespersons' automobiles and reimburse sales personnel when they buy new cars. This assures that the salesperson can buy a new car without resorting to outside financing. Furthermore, this practice makes it unnecessary for the sales force to request company financial help in buying new cars. It should be noted that these reserves represent, in effect, the withholding of some portion of automobile expense allowances that otherwise would be paid directly to the sales staff on a periodic basis. When the withholding, or reserve, feature is not used, salespeople often delay replacing old cars because of personal financial problems. The withholding feature assures that the sales staff will not have to drive dilapidated automobiles and hence risk embarrassing the company.

**Runzheimer Plan.** The Runzheimer plan, originated by the consulting firm of Runzheimer and Company, is basically a combination standard allowance and mileage-rate system. However, the plan is an improvement over most combination systems in that it takes account of geographical variations in expenses of automobile ownership and operation by dividing the United States into twenty-nine "auto-use basic cost areas." Standard allowances are expressed on a per diem basis and include provisions for insurance premiums, state licenses, title and driver's fees, and depreciation. Mileage rates are applied to cover expenses incurred for gasoline, oil, grease, washing, service maintenance, and tires. In addition, Runzheimer and Company recommends that certain expense items not provided for in the standard allowance be reimbursed as incurred and reported by sales personnel. Such expense items include local city license fees, property taxes, daytime parking, overnight parking away from the home city, and toll charges. A further refinement provides that automobile depreciation allowances for salespeople traveling more than 20,000 miles annually be adjusted, monthly or annually, at the rate of approximately $32 per 1,000 miles in excess of the 20,000. In other words, the standard allowances are computed for 20,000 miles of average annual travel within each of the twenty-nine cost areas. The purpose of the depreciation adjustment is to enable the high-mileage driver to trade in his car when it reaches the 60,000-total-mileage point. Standard allowances are also computed to allow for the operation of different makes and models of cars. Since the installation of the plan in 1933, the service has been greatly extended and refined; it is presently used by several hundred companies.

## FRINGE BENEFITS

Salesmen once were almost universally excluded from eligibility for the fringe benefits granted other employees; today, all but a tiny minority receive such benefits. Salespersons were regarded in the past either as independent contractors or as part of management, and the thinking was that salespeople and sales executives were supposed to arrange their financial affairs to provide for retirement, pay for their own vacations, buy their own insurance, pay their own medical and hospital bills, and so on. Changes in tax laws and rates, enactments of such laws as the Social Security and Medicare acts, and the increasing universality of the desire to fulfill security needs have drastically altered the picture.

Today's sales personnel normally share in all or most of the fringe benefits enjoyed by other company employees. More and more sales executives recognize that most salespeople regard such benefits as important, necessary, and attractive features of employment. They also recognize that appropriate choices of fringe benefits for sales personnel can have significant and beneficial influences not only upon sales-force morale, but upon productivity and the sales-force turnover rate.[14]

When a company provides fringe benefits for salespeople, essentially it pays them additional compensation. Fringe benefits represent additional, although sometimes deferred compensation (for example, social security and pension benefits), and, at least in theory, other forms of compensation (such as salaries and commissions) must be lower because of them. The costs of fringe benefits, of course, vary with their nature and number, but the proportion of salespersons' total compensation accounted for by fringe benefits has been steadily rising. Sales executives say that fringe benefits make up 20 to 25 percent of their total costs for sales-force compensation.

## CONCLUSION

Appropriately chosen and skillfully administered sales-force compensation policies facilitate the overall task of sales-force management. They directly affect the relative ease of building and maintaining a productive sales force. They attract promising recruits and encourage productive persons to remain in a company's service. This holds the sales-force turnover rate at a reasonable level, which, in turn, makes it possible to maximize returns from sales training. Similarly, for companies with such policies, the direction and control of sales activities become less-pressing problems and, at the same

---

[14]For an excellent discussion on the relationship between direct and indirect incentives, see H. R. Dodge, *Field Sales Management* (Dallas: Business Publications, Inc., 1973), pp. 256-90.

time, more effective. In short, effective implementation and administration of appropriate sales-compensation policies and practices reduce the relative amounts of time and effort that must be devoted to other phases of sales-force management. Nevertheless, the compensation plan, no matter how good, cannot substitute for good supervision.

# 16

# Assigning
# Sales Personnel
# to Territories

Establishment of sales territories facilitates management's task in matching selling efforts with sales opportunities. In effect, sales personnel are assigned the responsibility for serving particular groupings of customers and prospects, and thus they provide the contact points at which the line sales organization comes together with the markets. Territorial assignments lend important direction to management's efforts to gather and use information for the planning and control of sales operations.

Realistic sales planning must ultimately be done on a territory-by-territory basis rather than by the total market. Characteristics of customers and prospects vary significantly from one section of the country to another, and sometimes even from one county to the next; thus, analysis of market statistics should include breakdowns for individual sales territories. For sales planning, in other words, the territory is a more homogeneous unit than the market as a whole, which frequently obscures a great deal of underlying heterogeneity.

Furthermore, in establishing sales territories, management is also taking an important first step toward accumulating a fund of knowledge concerning the company's comparative strengths and weaknesses in serving different groupings of customers and prospects. Through taking these variations into account in planning sales operations, managerial efforts to improve the company's competitive position should be made more effective.

Similarly, control of sales operations should be made more effective by breaking the total market down into more manageable units. Assigning responsibility for achieving specific goals to subordinate line executives and individual salespersons should result in more appropriate alignments of selling efforts with sales opportunities. Direction can then be lent toward gathering and using information on individual performances for control purposes. Comparisons of actual performances with sales opportunities present in each territory provide a sound basis not only for appraisal of subordinate executives and sales personnel, but also for the further improvement of sales planning.

Although territorial assignments are usually made on a geographical basis, the emphasis in territorial design should be placed upon the customers and prospects rather than upon the areas in which salespeople are to work. In some companies, in fact, geographical considerations are ignored completely and selling responsibility is assigned to individual salespeople according to classes of customers, regardless of their locations. Operationally defined, then, *a sales territory is a particular grouping of customers and prospects assigned to an individual salesperson.* Despite the growing acceptance of this concept, sales executives customarily refer to sales territories as geographic areas—for example, the "Southern California territory" or the "Michigan territory." Realistically, however, even when designated geographically, a sales territory is basically a particular grouping of customers and prospects that can be called upon conveniently and economically by a salesperson.

In some companies, certain accounts are not assigned to individual salespeople but are dealt with directly by executives or home-office personnel. Frequently these "house accounts" are the most lucrative: this often has adverse effects upon the morale of salespeople, who may feel that they are deprived of the best customers. Generally, then, it is wise to minimize the number of house accounts; however, there are some large customers who refuse to do business in any other way. Companies in which sales personnel understand that their territories consist of particular groupings of customers and prospects, rather than of specific geographical areas, normally find that the existence of house accounts has little, or no, adverse effect on sales-force morale.

To emphasize further the point that designations of territories should not be made solely along geographical lines, consider the different circumstances under which such designations are generally the most inappropriate. When salespeople sell a product or service mainly to personal acquaintances, as is commonly the case in sales of property insurance, investment securities, and automobiles, little logical basis exists for dividing the market geographically. Similarly, in selling real estate, where the market is highly localized and where the customer usually seeks out the firm rather than the salesperson, geographically defined territories are not particularly useful. In these and related cases, salespeople are, for the most part, inside order takers; customers generally take the initiative in seeking out the supplier. But even, as in life insurance selling, where sales personnel are outside order getters and seek out prospects, the personal and localized nature of the market makes geographical assignments of territories generally inappropriate.

Still other situations exist in which companies do not designate sales territories geographically. Certain companies have highly specialized salespeople, each of whom is assigned responsibility for serving customers who need his or her special skills. For instance, one firm that makes and sells complicated machinery employs only five salespeople, each specializing either in part of the product line or in particular product applications; the geographical locations of customers are distinctly of secondary inportance. In other companies, it is common to have more than one salesperson assigned to work in the same city or metropolitan area; and it is difficult, if not impossible, to divide the area among them, not only because of the scattered locations of accounts but because "leads" furnished by established customers often require calls in different parts of the city. Small companies, and companies introducing new products requiring the use of different marketing channels, often do not use geographically defined territories at all or, if they do, make use of very rough divisions, such as states or census regions. In these instances, management evidently sees little reason to assign specific accounts and prospects to individual salespeople, since existing sales coverage capabilities are inadequate relative to sales potentials.

In most marketing situations, however, it is advantageous to "assign" sales personnel to "territories" in the sense that each person is given the responsibility for serving a particular grouping of customers and prospects. Usually, but not always, these assignments consist of geographical clusters of customers and prospects. Determining the nature of such assignments requires that both customers' service requirements and the company's costs of providing service be taken into account. Geography plays an important role, as it affects both a company's ability to meet customers' service requirements with respect to time and frequency and the costs involved in meeting them; therefore, territorial assignments are generally made on a geographical basis and are complemented by a routing and scheduling plan. However, even though territorial boundaries are set along geographical lines, management should not lose sight of the fact that each salesperson's assignment is first of all a particular grouping of customers and prospects, and only for reasons of convenience and economy a geographical cluster— the major emphasis should be on the customers, not on their locations.

## REASONS FOR ESTABLISHING OR REVISING SALES TERRITORIES

The principal reason for establishing or revising sales territories is to facilitate the planning and control of selling operations; but management ordinarily has more specific reasons for making this important move. Among these additional reasons, all of which incidentally contribute to improved planning and control of selling operations, are those discussed below.

### To Improve Market Coverage

Sometimes a company loses orders to competitors because it does not have proper market coverage. In such situations, technically speaking, sales management has failed to match company selling efforts with sales opportunities effectively, competitors have secured a better match, and they obtain the orders. To overcome problems of this type, generally management must establish sales territories, if the company does not already use them, or revise those which it already has. If sales territories are set up intelligently, *and* if individual salespersons' assignments to them are carefully made, it should be possible to obtain proper market coverage. Note that mere establishment or revision of the sales territories themselves is not the whole remedy; other managerial action is necessary also. The nature of the territories should permit salespeople to cover them conveniently and economically. They should represent reasonable workloads for the sales staff while assuring that all prospects who are potentially profitable can be contacted. Furthermore, because of variations in the profit potentials of different accounts, the coverage plan must provide for variations in the frequencies with which salespeople call upon different accounts. Therefore, in setting up or revising territories and in assigning sales staff to them, management must have considerable knowledge of the market and of the abilities of the salespeople.

### To Reduce Selling-Expense Ratios

Good territorial design combined with careful salesperson assignment should result not only in lower selling expenses but in higher sales volumes. Sales personnel spend fewer nights away from home, which reduces or eliminates many charges for lodging and food; at the same time, the necessary number of travel miles is reduced, with an accompanying decrease in transportation expenses. These savings, plus the higher sales volumes that should follow from the increased amount of productive selling time made available, should have a favorable effect upon the ratio of selling expenses to sales. In fact, even if dollar selling expenses remain unchanged, the sales increase made possible through improved market coverage should tend to reduce the selling-expense percentage.

Reduced selling-expense ratios do not, however, follow automatically from the establishment or revision of sales territories. In fact, if the territorial planning is unsound, or if it is not combined with appropriate plans for assigning sales personnel, selling-expense ratios may actually increase. If the planner, for instance, ignores normal travel routes and geographical barriers, salespeople may spend time in traveling when they could be calling on customers and prospects; such conditions result in higher selling expenses and probably in lower sales volumes.

Nor should management overlook the possibility that dollar selling expenses may have to be increased in order to obtain a lower selling-expense ratio. To secure larger sales volumes, it may be necessary to allow salespeople to incur additional expenses. Securing larger orders from customers, for instance, may require more frequent sales calls, which, of course, also involves increases in selling expenses. Well-designed sales territories and appropriate assignments of sales personnel to territories should increase the proportion of the salesperson's total time available for actual contact with customers and prospects, thus preparing the ground for improved sales volumes (although realizing these sales volumes may require increased dollar selling expenses). Sales management's problem in controlling selling expenses, in other words, is not to minimize them but to obtain the best possible relation between dollar selling expenses and dollar sales volumes. Furthermore, short-term reductions in the selling-expense ratio are not always desirable; it is the long-term result that is important. Rises in selling expenses may not be followed immediately by increased sales volumes, and higher current selling expenses may be needed to obtain higher sales volumes in the future. However, the intelligent setting up or revising of sales territories is one of the steps management can take in seeing to it that selling-expense dollars are spent to the best advantage.

### √ To Improve Customer Service

Good territorial design allows sales personnel to spend more time with customers and prospects and less time on the road. This permits them to become more conversant with customers' problems and requirements. Really successful selling is premised upon helping customers solve their problems, not just upon making sales or, even worse, upon taking orders. Well-designed sales territories, combined with appropriate sales-force assignments, should result in greater regularity of calls upon different classes of customers and prospects. Such regularity is especially important in selling products purchased on a repeat basis, and persistence turns many a prospect into a regular account.

### √ To Build Salespeople's Interest and Morale

Improved territorial designs help in stimulating salespeople's interest in their jobs and in improving their morale. Well-designed territories are convenient for sales personnel to cover; they represent reasonable-sized work loads, and salespersons should find that the efforts they exert are productive of results. All are responsible for achieving given levels of performance within their own territories, so all know specifically what

management expects of them and thus should guide their efforts accordingly. The results that come out of each salesperson's territory can be correlated more closely with
his or her efforts, and management should find it easier to appraise each salesperson's
performance. Furthermore, since good territorial design plus intelligent salesperson
assignment helps make each person more productive, this should provide the sales force
with higher earnings and increased self-confidence and job satisfaction. Morale should
be improved also because there ought to be fewer conflicting claims of salespeople to
the same accounts—when sales territories are not used, there are numerous conflicts.
Even with well-designed sales territories, some conflicts arise, because there are always
some customers who transact business in more than one territory; but well-designed territories serve to reduce the magnitude of the problem. Finally, salespeople's morale
should be improved because excellence in planning territories and making territorial
assignments should cause salespeople to spend less time on the road and more at home.

## To Coordinate Personal-Selling and Advertising Efforts More Effectively

Management may set up sales territories or revise existing territorial arrangements
with a view toward improving the coordination of personal-selling and advertising efforts. In most marketing situations, personal selling or advertising alone cannot accomplish the entire selling task as efficiently or as economically as these two major selling
efforts, skillfully harmonized, are capable of doing. By blending personal selling and advertising, management may take advantage of a synergistic effect (sometimes referred to
as the "$2 + 2 = 5$" effect), and obtain a performance greater than the sum of its parts.[1]

Sales personnel play key roles in management's attempts to capitalize on such an
opportunity. Prior to launching an advertising campaign for a new consumer product,
for example, salespeople may call upon dealers to outline the marketing plan and objectives, provide them with tie-in displays and other promotional materials, and make certain that adequate supplies of the product are on hand in the retail outlets. Establishing
territorial assignments makes every dealer the responsiblity of some salesperson; and
proper routing ensures that salespeople contact all dealers at appropriate times relative
to the breaking of the consumer advertising campaign. In some cases, the manufacturer's marketing plan calls for dealers to share in the costs of advertising the product;
here, again, salespeople "sell" such cooperative programs to dealers in their assigned
territories. Similarly, in other situations where salespeople perform work related to the
advertising effort, the results are usually more satisfactory if the work is delegated and
managed on a territory-by-territory basis rather than for the market as a whole.

## To Improve Sales-Force-Performance Evaluation

Well-designed sales territories should help management in securing meaningful
information to use in evaluating personnel performance. Selling and other problems encountered in marketing a company's product line tend to vary geographically, and the
impact of competition differs widely among regions. By subdividing the total market
into territories, analysis should reveal rather accurate pictures of the company's comparative strengths and weaknesses in different areas, and appropriate adjustments can then

---

[1]For a good discussion of this and numerous other opportunities involving synergy, see H. I. Ansoff, *Corporate Strategy* (New York: McGraw-Hill Book Company, 1965), pp. 75-102.

be made in selling strategies. Collection and analysis of sales and cost data are now done on a territorial basis. Accurate estimates of the sales potential that each salesperson should be held responsible for should result, as well as reliable estimates for the costs of realizing that potential. Thus, through analyzing the market on a territory-by-territory basis and pinpointing sales and cost responsibility to individual salespeople, management has meaningful information to use in setting quotas and in evaluating each salesperson's performance against them.

## PROCEDURES FOR USE IN SETTING UP OR REVISING SALES TERRITORIES

Whether management is setting up a company's sales territories for the first time, or revising boundaries already in existence, it should apply the same general procedures. Probably most companies are more concerned with revising existing territories than with establishing totally new plans for territorial division; the problem, however, should always be approached as though sales territories were being established for the first time. True, previous decisions may be left unchanged, but their basic soundness and continued appropriateness should be reevaluated whenever the problem of territorial determination comes up for consideration.

Why do problems in territorial determination arise? Probably most often because changes in a firm's marketing situation have served to outdate its existing scheme of territorial division—for example, changes in the product line, shifts in customer location and importance, and changes in competition all have significance for the appropriateness of continuing established territorial arrangements. Sometimes the problem is traceable to ineptness in setting up territories initially—perhaps they were established on the basis of inadequate research, or by unskilled executives. In some cases, territories were set up by simply copying the arrangements of competitors or distributors of related products, with little attention being paid to sales coverage and other company marketing needs. In other instances, territories have been built around population concentrations, transportation centers, or salespersons' home locations, although these factors might have had little or no relation to sales potentials, customer locations, or customer service requirements.

In setting up or in revising sales territories, there are four main procedural steps: (1) selecting a basic geographical control unit, (2) determining sales potential present in each control unit, (3) combining basic control units into tentative territories, and (4) adjusting for differences in coverage difficulty and redistricting tentative territories.

### Selecting a Basic Geographical Control Unit

The starting point in territorial planning is the selection of a basic geographical control unit. The most commonly used control units are states, counties, cities and metropolitan areas, and trading areas. Sales territories are put together as consolidations of the smaller basic geographical control units. There are two reasons for selecting a small control unit. One is to permit management to realize one of the basic values attaching to the use of territories, the precise geographical identification of sales potential. If the control unit is too large, areas having low sales potentials may be hidden by inclusion with areas having high sales potentials, and areas with high sales potentials may be obscured by inclusion with those having low sales potentials. The second reason is that, if carefully selected, these units in and of themselves remain relatively stable and unchanging, making it possible to redraw territorial boundaries simply and easily by redistributing control units among territories. If, for example, a company wants to add to Salesperson Jones's territory and reduce Salesperson Smith's adjoining territory, it is generally easier to transfer county-sized rather than state-sized control units.

**States.** States, when used as the basic geographical control unit, represent, at best, only a rough basis for subdividing the national market. Nevertheless, two situations exist in which the fixing of territorial boundary lines along the borders of states may be appropriate. One concerns the company using a small sales force to cover the market extensively rather than intensively; such a company typically has a fairly restricted number of customers and prospects, although they are located all across the nation. The other concerns the company first seeking national distribution, which assigns its salespeople to territories consisting of one or more states strictly as a temporary expedient pending the subdividing of the market along other and more appropriate lines. As soon as feasible, a change will be made to a smaller control unit, to achieve greater flexibility in making territorial realignments. If, for example, a firm has sales personnel of approximately equal ability and experience, it might desire to assign them territories containing roughly equal sales potentials. This is much more difficult, if not totally impossible, to accomplish with control units as large as states than it would be, say, with counties. Probably the main difficulty inherent in using states as basic control units is that they represent political rather than economic subdivisions of the national market. A Kentucky-Ohio boundary, for instance, ignores the fact that numerous consumers and middlemen in north central Kentucky do their buying in Cincinnati; and a Kansas-Missouri boundary similarly ignores the fact that many Kansas consumers and other buyers trade in Kansas City, Missouri.

**Counties and ZIP Code Numbers.** The county is the most widely used geographical control unit, and there are three basic reasons for this. One is that the county is small enough to prevent the obscuring of areas with high and low sales potentials, since statistical information broken down by the more than 3,000 counties in the United States is readily available from many sources. It is comparatively inexpensive and easy, then, to develop usable measures of market and sales potentials on a county-by-county basis. The second, closely related, reason is that the county typically is the smallest unit for which governmental sources make available statistical data; thus, companies wishing to develop market and sales-potential figures at a reasonable cost generally find the county an attractive control unit. The third reason concerns the relative permanence of the county as a control unit. Sales territories should be revised from time to time, and the control unit selected should facilitate the making of such changes. Since, for most firms, the county represents a considerably smaller market division than does the typical sales territory, a company using counties as control units usually can built up or revise sales territories without having to collect data on potentials on the basis of a different control unit.

The ZIP Code is another basic geographical unit that can be used. In this unique numbering system, the first three digits identify the Sectional Center (of which there are about 550 and each is larger than a county but smaller than a state), while the last two digits identify the associated post offices (which number about 33,000). ZIP Code has several advantages. First, the ZIP Code is readily available and inexpensive to obtain. Second, the ZIP Code tends to reflect the economic characteristics of the individual areas, in contrast to states, counties, and cities, which represent political subdivisions. Third, the ZIP Code/Sectional Center number system is very flexible. It permits a precise definition of markets according to economic and demographic characteristics and also serves as a control unit for the collection of data to analyze market potential. In this way, the ZIP Code system can lead to effective establishment of sales territories.[2]

**Cities and Standard Metropolitan Statistical Areas.** When the sales potential for a company's product line is located entirely, or almost entirely, in urbanized areas, the city may be used as the control unit, although, in some cases, such companies use both the city and the surrounding county (or counties outside the city) as "twin" control units. However, the city rarely is fully satisfactory as a control unit, inasmuch as most cities have grown beyond their political boundaries. For many products, suburbs adjacent to cities generally possess sales potentials at least as attractive as the cities themselves and, in addition, they often can be covered by the same sales personnel with little additional cost. For these reasons, the city is now rarely used as a control unit. Most firms formerly using the city for this purpose have shifted to either the county or the standard metropolitan statistical area.

Companies confronted by territorial problems traceable to the expansion of their markets beyond city lines and into suburbs and satellite cities have been helped materially by designation of 247 Standard Metropolitan Statistical Areas, as of mid-1971, by the Bureau of the Budget. As defined by this federal agency, each SMSA contains at least: (a) one central city with 50,000 inhabitants or more, or (b) two cities having contiguous boundaries and constituting, for general economic and social purposes, a single community with a combined population of at least 50,000, the smaller of which must have a population of at least 15,000. Each SMSA includes the county in which the central city is located, and adjacent counties that are found to be metropolitan in character and economically and socially integrated with the county of the central city; however, in New England the units comprising SMSAs are towns rather than counties. Thus, in constructing SMSAs, the Bureau of the Budget uses the county (or town in New England) as the basic statistical unit.

Because the definition is phrased in terms of counties, the tremendous amount of statistical data available for the counties themselves may also be tapped. If the planner is willing to accept the Budget Bureau's definition and the boundaries it has established for each standard metropolitan statistical area, he or she finds it comparatively easy to secure comparable data from governmental and other sources for use in estimating sales potentials for the product line. In fact, because the definition is in terms of whole counties, the planner is free to add to or subtract from the Bureau of the Budget's roster of standard metropolitan statistical areas. For example, *Sales Management,* which annually publishes its *Survey of Buying Power,* provides data useful for estimating sales potentials for 295 *Sales Management* metropolitan county areas, including most of the SMSAs plus areas that *Sales Management* considers as potential SMSAs. *Sales Management* also redefines the New England SMSAs along county lines, thereby reducing 26 SMSAs into 17 *Sales Management* metropolitan county areas. According to *Sales Management,* these 295 metropolitan county areas in 1972 accounted for 75.3 percent of the nation's population, 80.7 percent of the effective buying income, and 77.7 percent of total retail sales.[3] These statistics emphasize the highly urbanized nature of the

[2] C. Belen, "ZIP Code—Bonus for Business," *MSU Business Topics,* Vol. 15, No. 2 (Spring 1967), pp. 19-25.
[3] *1973 Survey of Buying Power, Sales Management* (July 23, 1973).

national market, and explain why an ever-growing number of companies assign territories consisting of one or more metropolitan areas to most of their sales personnel and either use "country salespeople" to cover nonmetropolitan areas or omit such areas entirely from their coverage plans.

Some companies find both the city and the standard metropolitan statistical area too large to serve their purposes as basic geographical control units. Most of these firms deal directly with large numbers of customers in urban areas, and it is not uncommon for them to assign two or more salespeople to the same city. In such cases, companies tend to use either minor political divisions of cities—precincts and wards, or clusters of contiguous census tracts—or city blocks as control units. The main problem in using such subcity units as control units lies in the relative difficulty encountered in obtaining market statistics, compared to the ease with which such data are obtained for cities, counties, and metropolitan areas.

**Trading Areas.** The trading area is, perhaps, the most logical geographical control unit, since it is based mainly upon the natural flow of trade and largely ignores political and other noneconomic boundaries. A trading area is defined as consisting of the geographical region surrounding a city that serves as the dominant retail and/or wholesale center of the region. Thus, the trading-area concept acknowledges the fact that consumers and middlemen pay little attention to political boundaries in deciding where to buy. In the case of consumers, for example, convenience and the selection available are the most significant factors affecting location of purchase. Although consumers may live in suburban Connecticut or New Jersey, they may reason that the best selection of the desired type of goods is available in New York City, conclude that New York is fairly convenient to get to, and subsequently shop and buy the desired item there. Similar situations exist elsewhere, particularly wherever population concentrations are located near state lines; at the county level, the crossing of political boundaries is even more common. Many products, including a long list of specialty and shopping goods, are available almost entirely in cities or in large planned regional shopping centers, so residents of small towns and rural areas must make such purchases at a distance. Even in sections where large cities are few and widely separated, as in the Rocky Mountain states, some towns, often the county seats, serve as trading centers for surrounding smaller towns and rural districts. Often it is difficult to define the exact limits of trading areas, and they vary from product to product; but the fact remains that, because trading areas are based mainly on natural trade flows, they should be taken into account in planning sales territories regardless of whether or not they are selected as geographical control units.

The main problems involved in using trading areas as control units, as implied above, are those of defining them and of obtaining statistics to use in estimating sales potentials for each trading area. Depending upon the product being distributed, both retail and wholesale trading areas vary in size and shape and change over time as competing trading areas encroach on each other. Rural consumers buy work clothes and routine supplies in the nearest small towns; but they go to larger cities to shop for dress clothing, and to even larger cities to buy expensive furniture or jewelry. Each such location is the focal point for a trading area, at least for products customarily purchased there. Trading areas for products purchased frequently and routinely are much smaller in size, and consequently, more numerous, than those for luxury products.

No standard set of trading areas applies to all products and all marketing situations, so each company must identify its own. Because the precise delineation of trading areas requires primary research into, and quantification of, customers' buying habits and preferences, considerable expense is involved. This is especially true when market and sales potentials for counties or other political subdivisions must be divided among two or more trading areas. For this reason, most firms using trading areas as control units take advantage of market data readily available on a county-by-county basis by arbitrarily adjusting their boundaries to county lines.

Other features of trading areas tend to limit their usefulness as control units for the designing of sales territories. Although every trading area has at least one city as a focal point, it may be far from the area's geographical center, thus complicating the planning of salespeople's route and call schedules. Because many contain both areas of high population density and vast sections of thinly settled forest, desert, or farmland, extra caution must be taken to prevent the obscuring of areas with high and low sales potentials. Some trading areas are circumscribed partially by impassable geographical barriers and partially by the relative trading importance of neighboring areas, both of which change with highway construction projects and development of new buying centers. Sizes and shapes of certain trading areas even fluctuate seasonally; climatic conditions, such as snowfall in intervening mountainous areas, cause some cities to have separate summer and winter trading areas.

Considerable work directed toward identifying trading areas has been done by governmental agencies, trade associations, business consultants, publishers, and many companies. The U.S. Department of Commerce has delineated wholesale trading areas for such product lines as groceries and dry goods. Figure 16.1 shows the map of wholesale-dry-goods trading areas as identified by the Department of Commerce. The National Wholesale Druggists' Association has published a map of wholesale drug trading areas. Both Curtis Publishing Company and Hearst Magazines, Inc., have published maps of retail trading areas. Rand McNally publishes a map of the United States showing 494 Basic Trading Areas and 50 Major Trading Areas. The Basic Trading Areas are based on their importance as centers of shopping-goods purchases, while the Major Trading Areas represent combinations of the Basic Trading Areas into larger groups. Unfortunately, the trading areas identified by all these publicly available maps represent rather rough approximations of the boundaries found for certain broad categories of products at a particular date; thus, their main interest for the territorial planner lies in the general picture they convey.

Some companies do research directed toward identifying trading areas for their own products and particular marketing situations. Blank maps are readily obtainable, and knowledgeable executives can rough out trading areas from sales statistics available in company files and from governmental sources, later refining them using data secured through interviews with customers and sales personnel. Perhaps the most difficult problem is that of allocating market and sales-potential data among the various trading areas. This problem causes some executives who are aware of the basic logic underlying the trading-area concept, nevertheless, to use other control units, such as counties or standard metropolitan statistical areas. Evidently, they feel that the greater realism obtainable through identifying and delineating trading areas for their company's products is not worth facing the added problem involved in allocating market and sales potential data.

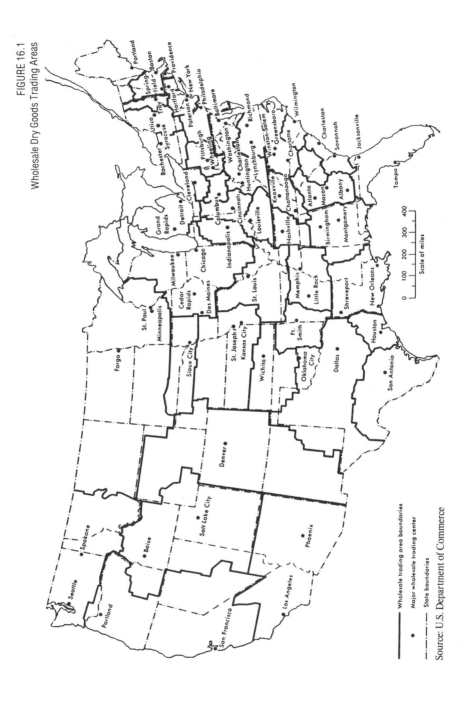

FIGURE 16.1
Wholesale Dry Goods Trading Areas

——— Wholesale trading area boundaries
• Major wholesale trading center
–·–·– State boundaries

Source: U.S. Department of Commerce

363

## ✓ Determining Sales Potential Present in Each Control Unit

Having selected the basic control unit, the next step is to determine the sales potential present in each such unit. Thus, the territorial planner must have some method for measuring sales potentials, each of which, you will recall, represents the maximum possible sales opportunities open to a specific company selling a good or service during a stated future period to a particular market segment.[4] For the present purpose, substitute "a particular control unit" for "a particular market segment"—in other words, each control unit is a particular *geographical* market segment. But geographical market segments, like all market segments, are made up of present and prospective customers, so the territorial planner must identify the buyers of the product as precisely as possible. A vague identification, such as "Our product is bought by women," is not sufficient. But if it can be determined that "Our product is bought almost entirely by middle-aged, lower-income women living in cities," a much better "fix" on the buyers comprising the market is obtained. Information concerning the identity of buyers may have to be obtained through formal market identification studies conducted by marketing research personnel.

Sometimes, company sales personnel, who generally have the closest contacts with buyers, may supply the needed information. But information supplied by salespeople is not necessarily usable; for example, a company's sales force may call only on wholesalers and have little contact with retailers or consumers who buy the product. Even when salespeople sell direct to final buyers, as in marketing many industrial goods, they may be neglecting certain classes of prospects completely and hence be able to provide only partial identification of the possible buyers. When sales personnel have no direct contact with final buyers, formal marketing research studies often are required in order to obtain precise identification of all possible classes of final buyers. Whether or not this process should be carried on down to actual personal identification of each possible buyer depends upon the product being marketed. In consumer goods, generally it is unnecessary and too expensive to go to this extreme; but in industrial goods, where often there are only a few possible buyers, exact identification is both desirable and feasible.

Having identified the potential buyers, the planner may next determine how much sales potential exists in each geographical control unit. The planner ascertains how many potential buyers in each class are contained within each geographical control unit, and what the total market potential in the unit is (that is, potential buyers' total requirements for the company's type of product). Then the planner estimates the portion of the total market potential that the company has an opportunity to obtain (that is, the sales potential accounted for by the particular geographical control unit under study).

Market potentials are generally converted into sales potentials by analyzing the company's historical market shares within each geographical control unit, altering them one way or the other to take account of recent or impending changes in company and competitors' selling strategies and practices and thus arriving at estimates. Having made these estimates, the territorial planner ascertains those control units with sufficient sales potential to justify allocating sales coverage to them. For the manufacturer following a policy of mass distribution, this is not a great problem. Generally such a manufacturer provides sales coverage in every control unit, regardless of how little sales potential it

---

[4]See Chapter 2.

represents, because management considers maximum sales exposure of the product crucial to marketing success. Many manufacturers, however, provide sales coverage only in those control units containing sufficient sales potential to assure profitable operations. Probably for most manufacturers there are at least a few control units where selling costs are bound to be excessive. Certainly this is the case for many industrial-goods producers, such as those, for example, selling machine tools and mining equipment. (Most studies of concentration in industrial-goods markets show that well over 90 percent of U.S. manufacturing is done in approximately 650 of the total of more than 3,000 counties.) It is probably also the case for most producers of consumer shopping and specialty goods. J. Walter Thompson Company, a large advertising agency, analyzed U.S. markets according to their population in 1960 and their retail sales in 1958, and reported, among other things, that just over 6 percent of U.S. markets (199 out of 2,944) accounted for 64 percent of the population and 69 percent of the retail sales.[5] In other words, more than two thirds of the potential for many consumer-goods lines may be reached by covering a bit more than 6 percent of the country's markets.

### ✓ Combining Control Units into Tentative Territories

Having measured the sales potential of each control unit and having decided which should receive sales coverage, the planner combines units into *tentative* sales territories. Completion of this step results in only a tentative arrangement because, as will be explained below, later adjustments must be made for differences in relative coverage difficulty. At this stage, the planner assumes, in other words, that no significant differences in the physical or other characteristics of individual control units exist to make some more difficult to cover than others. The planner's purpose now is simply to obtain a "first approximation" of how the total market should be arranged into sales territories and, given the assumptions just mentioned, it is logical to seek an arrangement through combining contiguous control units into tentative territories, each containing approximately the same amount of sales potential.

Immediately, however, the planner must decide how many territories there should be, and this, assuming that all sales personnel are of "average" ability, is the same as deciding the size of the sales force. Basically, the planner must estimate the percentage of the total sales potential that each average salesperson should be capable of realizing. Analysis of past sales experience should help in making this estimate, which, once made, can be used to determine the number of territories. In effect, the planner estimates the sales productivity per unit of sales personnel and divides this into the total estimated sales potential, thus arriving at the number of units of sales personnel—and territories—required. Consider a situation in which management estimates that an average salesperson should realize $2,500,000 of a total sales potential of $25 million—ten territories and ten units ($25,000,000/$2,500,000) of sales personnel would be required. When these estimates and this calculation have been made, contiguous control units are combined into tentative territories of roughly equal sales potential. To simplify this step, sales potentials for control units should be expressed as percentages of total sales potential. In the example just given, then, control units would be grouped into ten tentative territories, each containing, as nearly as possible, 10 percent of the total sales potential. Throughout this grouping process, the planner should combine only control units con-

[5]See J. Walter Thompson Company, *Population and Its Distribution: The United States Markets* (New York: McGraw-Hill Book Company, 1961).

tiguous to each other; individual control units should not be split into different territories, even if this results in tentative territories with different total sales potentials. Once again, then, an important advantage of selecting the smallest possible geographical control unit is emphasized.

## Adjusting for Differences in Coverage Difficulty, and Redistricting Tentative Territories

The final step involves redistricting the tentative territories through adjusting for differences in relative coverage difficulty. The territories have been tentatively set up so that each contains approximately the same sales potential, and the relative difficulty of obtaining sales coverage in each has been ignored, up to now. Almost certainly, however, territories with near-equal sales potentials will exhibit considerable differences in the selling effort required to realize that potential and, in turn, the amount of selling expense incurred. Earlier, the simplifying assumption was made that no significant differences in the physical or other characteristics of different geographical control units existed to make some more difficult to cover than others. Now the time has come to remove this rather unrealistic assumption, for the facts are that sales potential is almost never evenly distributed among control units. And this generally goes along with significant differences in physical and other characteristics that make providing sales coverage more difficult for some control units than for others. Certain large cities, for instance, almost always represent greater sales potentials for most products than some states; but the travel and other sales time required to contact all customers and prospects in cities is much less, and the same is true of the selling expenses incurred. Ideally, the optimum territorial arrangement is achieved by establishing territories so that the incremental sales per dollar of selling expenditures are equated among all territories.[6] In working toward this ideal, both sales potential and coverage difficulty must be taken into account. And, as J. G. Hauk writes: "It is only coincidental if equal potential territories achieve the optimum."[7] As the planner adjusts for differences in coverage difficulty, geographical control units will be taken away from some tentative territories and added to others. The final territorial arrangement almost certainly will be one in which different territories contain different amounts of sales potential.

The planner should recognize that differences in coverage difficulty really represent differences in the projected work loads that will be required of sales personnel. It is helpful, then, to ascertain how large the maximum work load—the largest work load to be assigned to any salesperson—should be. It is not necessary that all work loads be the same size, since salespeople vary in ability as well as in initiative, and some can safely be assigned larger work loads than others. However, there is an upper size limit to the "desirable work load," and this also limits the maximum geographical extent of any sales territory. When final adjustments for coverage difficulty have been made, sales territories will represent varying amounts of sales potential and different-sized work loads, but none should exceed the estimate for the maximum desirable work load. The work-load method was discussed in Chapter 4 as one approach to determining sales-force size. Here, the same concept, with minor modifications, can be used to help solve the redistricting problem.

[6]H. R. Wellman, "The Distribution of Selling Effort Among Geographic Areas," *Journal of Marketing,* Vol. 3, No. 3 (January 1939), pp. 225-41.

[7]J. G. Hauk, "Research in Personal Selling," in G. Schwartz (ed.), *Science in Marketing* (New York: John Wiley & Sons, Inc., 1965), p. 238.

Redistricting to adjust for differences in coverage difficulty (that is, in work loads represented) is done differently in different companies. The seven-step procedure outlined below illustrates how a typical company might go about its redistricting.

1. *Determine number, location, and size of customers and prospects in each tentative territory.* Existing customers are easily identified and located by examining sales records; prospects are identified and located through such sources as trade directories, subscription lists to trade publications, classified directories, and credit-reporting agencies. Size is measured in terms of the sales potential represented by each customer and prospect.

2. *Estimate the length of time required for each sales call.* The time required varies from account to account and from prospect to prospect, so it is helpful to classify customers and prospects into different groups, estimating an average time per call for each group. Time and duty analyses of sales personnel, if available, may be used to check these estimates.

3. *Determine the probable length of time between calls, that is, the amount of time it will probably take a salesperson to travel from one customer to the next.* This time varies considerably among regions, depending upon such factors as the density of customers and prospects and the condition of roads and transportation facilities. In this step, then, particular attention is paid to the physical characteristics of the various regions. Large rivers, lakes, mountains, and other barriers to travel often make natural and necessary territorial boundaries. The number of places where a large mountain range can be crossed by automobile are limited and often considerable time is consumed in the crossing. The same is true of large rivers, lakes, bays, and so forth. As important as physical characteristics are transportation facilities. If salespersons are to travel by automobile, their territories should be planned so that their driving can be mainly on primary, all-weather roads, with a minimum of cross-tracking. If they use public transportation facilities such as commercial airlines, territories must be planned with the locations of air terminals in mind. In this step the planner, in effect, inter-relates and balances differences in sales potential, physical geographical characteristics, and transportation facilities and routes. Thus, after sketching in on a map the tentative territorial division according to roughly equal sales potentials, the planner should make the adjustments indicated after scrutinizing and analyzing superimposed maps showing topographic and transportation features.

4. *Decide upon call frequencies.* Management must determine the frequency with which calls should be made on different classes of customers and propsects. Within certain control units, some or all customer and prospect classes will require frequencies of calls by sales personnel differing from those in other control units. Differences in the strength of competition may require variations in call frequency rates from one control unit to another. Similarly, call frequency rates are influenced by the relative market acceptance of the product line within different control units. Cost studies directed toward determining minimum profitable order sizes also should be made as a part of the analysis leading up to the decision on call frequencies.

5. *Calculate the number of calls it is possible to make within a given time period.* This calculation is a matter of simple arithmetic, and it must be made for each control unit. To determine the number of calls per day in a certain control unit, the average amount of time required for each call is added to the average time between calls and divided into the number of working hours in the day. Adjustments, of course, must be made when call lengths vary for different classes of customers and prospects.

6. *Adjust the number of calls salespeople can make during a given time period by the desired call frequencies for the different classes of customers and prospects.* This adjustment should result in an estimate for the total work load represented by the control units included in each tentative territory. Further adjustments then must be made to assure that the work load in any territory is not larger than the allowable maximum and that the budgeted estimates for selling expenses are not exceeded. To keep within these work-load and selling-

expense limitations, the planner probably will have to do considerable shifting of control units among the different tentative territories, adding units to some by taking them away from adjacent territories. Each such shift should bring the territorial arrangement closer to the optimum—that is, closer to a territorial plan in which the incremental sales per dollar of selling expenditures are equated among all territories. However, admittedly, how close is exceedingly difficult, if not wholly impossible, to determine.

7. *Finally, check out the adjusted tentative territories with salespeople who work or have worked in each area, and make further adjustments as required.* Personnel who are thoroughly familiar with customer service requirements, competitive conditions, and the topography, roads, and travel conditions often are able to point out basic weaknesses in proposed territories that were not obvious to the planner. Because salespeople's suggestions can result in territorial arrangements that come much closer to maximizing productive selling time, their suggestions should be solicited. Again, these suggestions may cause further shifting of control units from one territory to another, each shift hopefully bringing the final territorial arrangement a little closer to the ideal.

## DECIDING ASSIGNMENT OF SALES PERSONNEL TO TERRITORIES

When management is satisfied that the sales territorial arrangement is the best obtainable, it is ready to assign salespeople to territories. Up to this point in the territorial planning, an implicit assumption has been that all salespeople are "average," that is, that all represent interchangeable units of sales personnel, each capable of producing similar results at similar costs regardless of the territorial assignment made. Clearly, this is an unrealistic assumption, adopted only for territorial planning purposes, and one that management must discard when it decides which salespeople should be assigned to which territories. Few salespeople, if any, are exactly average—they vary in ability, initiative, and effectiveness as well as in physical condition and energy. What constitutes a reasonable and desirable work load for one salesperson may not be appropriate for the next. Furthermore, many a salesperson's effectiveness varies with the territory to which he or she is assigned. A person may be outstanding in one territory and a failure in a second, even though territorial sales potentials and coverage difficulty factors are identical; a person's relative performance, moreover, is conditioned by environmental factors such as customer characteristics, customs and traditions, ethnic influences, and the like. Dyadic interactions of an individual salesperson with customers and prospects, in other words, may vary in their outcomes from one territory to another depending on many factors, most of them outside the salesperson's control. As management goes about the task of assigning sales personnel to territories, then, it must be keenly aware not only that salespeople vary in individual effectiveness but that their effectiveness differs with the particular territories to which they may be assigned.

In assigning sales personnel to territories, management should seek to obtain the most profitable alignment of selling efforts with sales opportunities. The territories, containing varying sales potentials, represent different amounts of sales opportunity; the salespeople, differing in ability and potential effectiveness, represent the range of talent available for deployment in attempting to convert sales opportunities into actual sales and profits. Therefore, the manner of assigning salespeople to territories is highly important and deserving of management's most careful thought and attention. Sales territories must be intelligently designed, and salespeople must be measured and ranked according to relative ability and potential effectiveness. The general guide that management should follow in making sales assignments, as the following illustration will demonstrate, is: *Assign each salesperson to the particular territory where his relative contri-*

*bution to profit is the highest.*[8] Although, as a practical matter, this guide cannot be applied in all aspects of every problem involving assignment of salespeople to territories, this is nevertheless the "ideal" that the planner should work toward.

The general guide for assigning sales personnel to territories is not universally applicable for one very practical reason: the amount of discretion management has in making these decisions differs considerably from company to company. At one extreme, some companies display great reluctance to transfer presently assigned sales personnel to completely different territories, management evidently fearing not only sales-force resistance and resentment but the consequences of breaking established salesperson-customer relationships. These companies adhere generally to a "no transfer" or "infrequent transfer" policy and, in order to secure a proper alignment of selling talent and territorial sales opportunities, restrictions on shifting salespeople must be worked into territorial designs. The planner, accordingly, must expand and/or contract territorial boundaries, adding to or subtracting from individual territorial sales potentials, until the resulting territories contain sales potentials appropriate to the abilities of salespeople already assigned. These companies, in effect, design sales territories around, and to fit the ability of, sales personnel already assigned to the same general areas.

At the opposite extreme, management in a few companies appears to enjoy the maximum possible freedom in assigning any salesperson to any territory, designing territories (according to procedures similar to those discussed earlier), and closely aligning salespeople's ability levels with territorial sales opportunity levels. Management in these companies, in effect, is free to shift sales personnel to (predesigned) territories where their relative contributions to profit are maximized.

The situation in most companies is somewhere between the two extremes. For various reasons, some totally outside management's control, certain salespeople cannot be transferred, but others can be freely moved from one territory to another. This means that, in most cases, management must design some sales territories to fit the ability levels of certain nontransferable salespersonnel while identifying and reassigning other salespeople with ability levels appropriate to sales territories designed according to the suggested procedures.

**Illustration of Assigning Sales Personnel to Territories.**[9] Now let us work through several situations involving assignment of sales personnel to territories, our purpose being to demonstrate that, where practical, management should assign each salesperson to that particular territory where his or her relative contribution to profit is maximized. First, let us consider a highly unlikely situation in which the territories are of equal sales potential and coverage difficulty, but the sales personnel differ in ability. Figure 16.2 depicts a situation of this type. Predicted sales are obtained by multiplying each territory's dollar potential by the ability index of the salesperson assigned. Predicted profit contributions are assumed to amount to 25 percent of predicted sales. The total profit contribution is $312,500, the maximum attainable here regardless of how the sales personnel are assigned.

Now suppose that these territories are redesigned so that their sales potentials vary in direct proportion with the ability of the sales personnel assigned, with the same total dollar potential as before (that is, $1.5 million). The results obtained from this assignment pattern are shown in Figure 16.3.

[8] *Ibid.,* pp. 241-42.

[9] Much of this illustration is adapted from Hauk, *op. cit.*

FIGURE 16.2
Assignment of Sales Personnel to Territories of Equal Potential

| Territory | Dollar Potential | Salesperson Assigned | Ability Index | Predicted Sales | Predicted Profit Contribution (25% of sales) |
|---|---|---|---|---|---|
| A | $ 500,000 | 1 | 1.0 | $ 500,000 | $125,000 |
| B | 500,000 | 2 | 0.8 | 400,000 | 100,000 |
| C | 500,000 | 3 | 0.7 | 350,000 | 87,500 |
| Total | $1,500,000 | | | $1,250,000 | $312,500 |

Redesigning the territories so that their sales potentials are directly proportional to the abilities of the sales personnel assigned has increased the predicted profit contribution by $7,000 (from $312,500 to $319,500).

But what would be the predicted profit contribution if the total sales potential were divided some other way—after all, the number of possible ways of dividing it is very large. Consider Figure 16.4, which shows a different division of the $1.5 million sales potential; salespeople, however, are still assigned territories in rank order of their respective abilities.

FIGURE 16.3
Assignment of Sales Personnel to Territories
Containing Sales Potentials Proportionate to Salesperson's Abilities

| Territory | Dollar Potential | Salesperson Assigned | Ability Index | Predicted Sales | Predicted Profit Contribution (25% of sales) |
|---|---|---|---|---|---|
| A | $ 600,000 | 1 | 1.0 | $ 600,000 | $150,000 |
| B | 480,000 | 2 | 0.8 | 384,000 | 96,000 |
| C | 420,000 | 3 | 0.7 | 294,000 | 73,500 |
| Total | $1,500,000 | | | $1,278,000 | $319,500 |

Again there has been an increase in the predicted profit contribution, this one even more impressive than that in the preceding example. However, it is most unlikely that this territorial division and salesperson assignment plan would be feasible. The coverage difficulty and associated work load now involved in salesperson 1's attempt to cover territory A would probably exceed his capacity to perform; thus, his or her ability index should be lowered accordingly. Similarly, territories B and C now have such greatly reduced sales potentials (which also means that their coverage difficulty is less than before) that neither would likely represent large-enough work loads for salespeople 2 and 3.

There are, after all, both upper and lower limits to the amount of sales potential that should be incorporated in any one territory. These limits are set by the magnitude of coverage difficulty and the associated size of work load that it is reasonable to expect any salesperson, regardless of ability, to assume. Then, too, selling expenditures do not fluctuate directly with predicted sales volumes throughout all possible sales-volume ranges. They may rise more or less in proportion to sales-volume increases, but after a certain point is reached, the rate of rise accelerates greatly (that is, as the difficulty of

FIGURE 16.4
Assignment of Sales Personnel According to Ability to Territories
Containing Different Sales Potentials

| Territory | Dollar Potential | Salesperson Assigned | Ability Index | Predicted Sales | Predicted Profit Contribution (25% of sales) |
|-----------|-----------------|---------------------|---------------|-----------------|---------------------------------------------|
| A | $1,000,000 | 1 | 1.0 | $1,000,000 | $250,000 |
| B | 300,000 | 2 | 0.8 | 240,000 | 60,000 |
| C | 200,000 | 3 | 0.7 | 140,000 | 35,000 |
| Total | $1,500,000 | | | $1,380,000 | $345,000 |

making sales becomes increasingly greater); and they may decline proportionately to sales-volume decreases until a minimum level is reached (where potential sales are no longer large enough to support needed selling expenditures). Work-load restrictions, in other words, tend to confine the uniformity of variation of selling expenditures within fairly narrow limits.

As brought out earlier in this chapter, optimum territorial arrangement is reached when the *incremental* sales produced per dollar of selling expenditures are equated among all territories.[10] Clearly, after a sales territory reaches a certain size in terms of sales potential, adding successive increments of sales potential is feasible only up to the point at which the last dollar of selling expenditures just brings in sufficient sales to provide a dollar of profit contribution. Furthermore, a company seeking the optimum territorial arrangement probably would find that it should cut off additional selling expenditures before reaching this "point of feasibility." This is because the best condition requires the equating among all territories of the incremental sales produced by the last dollar of selling expenditures in each.

Thus far, the situations examined have included the implicit assumption that indexes of salespeople's ability do not change with the assignment of sales personnel to different territories. Earlier, however, we mentioned that a salesperson might demonstrate different degrees of effectiveness when transferred to other territories, since environmental forces might condition selling performance. It is not realistic, in other words, to assume that ability indexes for individual salespeople will remain fixed regardless of the territorial assignment. Let us consider, then, a situation where salespersons maintain their rank order according to ability indexes as they are switched among territories but where the magnitude of these indexes changes. With the assignment pattern 1A, 2B, 3C, the respective ability indexes might be 1.0, 0.8, and 0.7 (as in Figure 16.3, for example); but with the assignment 1B, 2A, 3C, the respective ability indexes could be 1.0, 0.9, and 0.7—salesperson 1 in this situation performs better than salesperson 2 regardless of the assignment. Using the basic data in Figure 16.3, the results of making the 1B-2A-3C assignment are shown in Figure 16.5. Clearly, this assignment pattern results in a higher total profit contribution than that secured by assigning sales personnel to territories strictly in accord with their abilities (that is, $328,500 vs. $319,500). Thus, in some territorial designs the best salesperson should not necessarily be assigned to the territory with the highest sales potential; and in some, a salesperson should not necessarily be assigned to the one territory where his or her profit contribution is higher

[10]See page 371.

than that of any other salesperson who might be assigned to the same territory. It should now be clear that each salesperson should be assigned to the territory where *his or her relative contribution* to profit is the highest. In Figure 16.5 it is easy to see that salesperson 1 could make a higher dollar profit contribution than salesperson 2 in territory A; but 1 contributed more, relative to 2, when assigned to territory B. Similarly, salesperson 2's inferiority relative to salesperson 1 is less when 2 has territory A, not territory B.[11]

FIGURE 16.5
Assignment of Sales Personnel to Territories
Where Ability Indexes Vary with the Assignment

| Territory | Dollar Potential | Salesperson Assigned | Ability Index | Predicted Sales | Predicted Profit Contribution (25% of sales) |
|---|---|---|---|---|---|
| A | $ 600,000 | 2 | 0.9 | $ 540,000 | $135,000 |
| B | 480,000 | 1 | 1.0 | 480,000 | 120,000 |
| C | 420,000 | 3 | 0.7 | 294,000 | 73,500 |
| Total | $1,500,000 | | | $1,314,000 | $328,500 |

Ability indexes can change with different assignment patterns; consequently, management ideally should estimate ability indexes for each possible assignment pattern. The large number of possible assignment patterns thus called into play makes the task of achieving an ideal assignment of personnel to territories rather complex. When twelve salespeople are to be assigned to twelve territories, for example, there are 12! (that is, 479,001,600) such patterns. It would be possible, although not very practical, for the planner to write down all 479,001,600 assignment patterns and select the one providing the maximum profit contribution; fortunately, however, the assignment technique of linear programming and the electronic computer afford a more rapid and less laborious way to find the solution.[12] But even such a solution technique requires data regarding, in this case, the probable results in terms of net profit contribution for each salesperson for each possible assignment pattern; and this requires not only considerable knowledge of the nature and peculiarities of the market in each territory, but a great deal of insight concerning how each salesperson might perform in each territorial environment.

## ROUTING AND SCHEDULING SALES PERSONNEL

One important aspect of the establishment of sales territories is the routing and scheduling plan. The specific purposes of such plans are: to maintain the lines of communication, to improve coverage of territories, and to minimize the amount of wasted

[11]Strictly speaking, of course, the planner might now reapportion the total sales potential among the three territories in direct proportion to the revised ability indexes of the salespeople assigned to each, thus obtaining a still further increase in the total profit contribution. The perceptive reader will readily see that this reapportionment would involve making territory B a higher-potential area than territory A. The resulting personnel assignment pattern, then, would be one in which the best salesperson (No. 1) would have the territory with the highest sales potential (now territory B); but note carefully that each salesperson still would be assigned to the territory where his or her relative contribution to profit is the highest.

[12]The assignment technique is explained in almost all books on operations research. A particularly clear explanation may be found in M. Sasieni, A. Yaspan, and L. Friedman, *Operations Research* (New York: John Wiley & Sons, Inc., 1959), pp. 185-92.

time. When management is informed at all times of all salespersons' whereabouts in the field—or at least knows where they should be—it is easier to contact them to provide needed information or last-minute instructions. Existence of a planned route and call schedule also improves the chances that salespeople will be where they are supposed to be at the appointed times; thus, management brings the movements of individual salespeople under closer scrutiny. The improvement in communications results in more effective control once the sales territories have been established.

Installation of routing and scheduling plans should also help to improve the coverage of sales territories, but accomplishing this means that management must have a considerable amount of detailed information about each territory. The actual mechanics of setting up a routing plan are fairly simple. In working out the plan, there must be detailed information on the numbers and locations of customers, the available means and methods of transportation connecting the various concentrations of customers, and the call frequency rates most appropriate for different sizes and classes of customers. Detailed maps must be available showing not only towns and cities and transportation routes but factors such as trading-area boundaries and such topographical features as mountain ranges, lakes, bridges, and ferry lines. If sales personnel are to travel by air, airport locations relative to cities on the route must be known. The route, or routes, finally laid out should permit the salesperson to return fairly frequently to his or her home base of operations. For purposes of maintaining morale, most sales executives feel that most salespeople should be able to return home at least on weekends. After the route plan is completed, the salesperson is given a copy for information and guidance.

If, as recommended above, the route planner considers the call frequency rate most appropriate for each customer on the route, the call schedule results as a by-product of setting up the route. In many cases, however, making up the call schedule is a more involved process than planning the route itself. Customers and prospects should be segregated into different groups according to the frequency with which calls should be made upon each group. Again using detailed maps, the planner must identify the locations of members of each customer and prospect group and reconcile the route with these locations. Hence, it often develops that the salesperson must be provided with a different route each time he or she travels the territory, in order to achieve the desired call frequency for each account in the territory and to incorporate new customers and prospects into the itinerary. Furthermore, because changes are bound to occur in account classifications, in the numbers of prospects, in the nature and intensity of competitive activity, as well as in such factors as road conditions, it is usually impractical to set up definite route and call schedules for long periods in the future.

Perhaps the greatest gain from using routing and scheduling plans comes from the opportunities to reduce salespeople's wasted time. If the salesperson's route is planned by management, much backtracking, travel time, and other "non-selling" time can be eliminated. If the salesperson's calls are scheduled, the call frequency can be adjusted to fit customers' needs and, incidentally, it may be possible to build up almost automatically the size of the average order.

In scheduling sales personnel, some firms not only designate the customers to be called upon each day but prescribe the hour at which each call is to be made. Generally, such detailed scheduling is coupled with a system for making appointments in advance of actual calls. Companies not using scheduling plans usually suggest that their salespeople make advance appointments, but probably more often than not this suggestion is ignored. For detailed scheduling to be effective, the planning agency must have current information on the exact time required to make each call, the probable waiting time at each stop, the travel time between calls, and the time needed to interview each customer. Such information is difficult to collect and keep up to date. Detailed scheduling is most feasible when management can count upon customers' full cooperation. Most firms find it necessary to allow their salespeople "time cushions" to take care of the many variations met on each selling trip.

Companies, almost without exception, benefit from systematic routing and scheduling of sales personnel, but not all find detailed scheduling feasible. However, the petroleum marketing companies, and other firms with combination driver-salespersons, use detailed routing and scheduling plans successfully, as does at least one large manufacturer of pharmaceuticals. Somewhat less detailed routing and scheduling plans are used to advantage by wholesalers of groceries, drugs, and hardware. Detailed scheduling plans are most useful and appropriate in trades typified by frequent calls, great homogeneity among customers, short travel time between calls, and highly standardized products that do not require large amounts of creative selling time.

**Routing, Scheduling, and Control.** The routing plan, the scheduling plan, or both can assist sales management in obtaining closer control over salespeople's movements and the way they spend their time. For this reason the routing and scheduling plan should be considered an integral part of the overall process of establishing sales territories and assigning sales personnel to those territories. If plans set up for individual salespeople are not followed, either the plans should be adjusted to fit the salesperson, or vice versa. An unrealistic plan, or one based upon inaccurate or incomplete data, almost always fails to produce the expected results. Any routing or scheduling plan should be subjected to frequent checkups to see how it is working and to detect needed adjustments or revisions. Call reports should be compared with predetermined route and call schedules to determine whether plans are being followed. Variations or discrepancies should be noted and salespeople asked for explanations. Adherence to the plans can also be enforced if supervisors or branch sales managers make frequent and unannounced visits to the field.

## CONCLUSION

The intelligent and logical design of sales territories facilitates the planning and control of sales operations. Territories so designed assist sales management in its attempts to improve market coverage and customer service, reduce selling-expense ratios, secure more effective coordination of personal-selling and advertising efforts, and improve the evaluation of personnel performance.

Good territorial design is based upon thorough knowledge of sales potentials and differences in coverage difficulty. The four main procedural steps in setting up or revising sales territories are (1) selection of a basic geographical control unit, (2) determination of sales potential present in each unit, (3) combination of basic control units into tentative territories, and (4) adjustment for differences in coverage difficulty and redistricting tentative territories. In assigning sales personnel to territories, management should seek the best possible alignment of selling efforts with sales opportunities, and to accomplish this a systematic plan for routing and scheduling salespeople is required. Since salespersons vary in individual effectiveness, which varies with the territories to which they are assigned, management ideally should construct ability indexes for each possible assignment pattern. This practice is necessary if each salesperson is to be assigned to the territory where his or her relative contribution to profit is maximized.

# 17

# Evaluating and Supervising
# Sales Personnel

This chapter focuses on evaluating and supervising sales personnel. A carefully planned program of evaluation and supervision can assure that sales-department objectives will be reached with a minimum of wasted effort. In fact, only through an intelligently constructed plan for evaluating and supervising sales personnel can effective sales-force control be achieved. This means that sales-force control (as opposed to controlling the sales effort, which is the subject of Part IV) is a most important phase of sales-force management, since it is the general purpose of control to monitor the balance between standards and actual performance. Planning, organizing, and coordinating activities involved in managing a sales force have been treated in earlier chapters, and two other subjects closely related to sales-force control, motivating and compensating sales personnel, were dealt with in Chapters 13 and 15, respectively. Discussion and analysis of evaluation and supervising sales personnel (that is, sales-force control) completes the coverage of the sales-force management process.

Let us examine how control fits into sales-force management. The management process starts when top management makes known the firm's goals, and department heads, including the head of the sales department, use these goals to derive appropriate objectives for their departments. For the sales department, the next step is to formulate departmental policies and plans that will facilitate achievement of these objectives. The sales-management group then maps out sales programs and campaigns, determines specific methods and procedures, and takes other needed actions, including the making of any needed changes in the sales organization to execute the policies and implement the plans. In performing the managerial activities thus far mentioned, as well as those described below, sales executives also coordinate the department's activities with each other and with related activities performed in other departments and by middlemen in the marketing channel. Up to this point in the management process, then, sales executives are concerned mainly with the managerial functions of planning, organizing, and coordinating.

Before the sales-force management process—some refer to it as the "management cycle"—is complete, four important steps remain: (1) establishing standards of performance; (2) recording actual performances; (3) making evaluations, or comparisons, of actual performances against the standards; and (4) taking the indicated action. These steps constitute what is known as control. The first three steps, all of which are static in nature, enable sales management to measure the progress made toward achieving departmental objectives. If the fourth step in control, action, is not forthcoming, the three static steps are not of as much help to sales management as they could be, despite the important information they contribute. Yet it is the "action" step, the dynamic feature of control, that is so frequently neglected. Only by taking the action suggested by the three preceding steps in control can sales management keep the department and its individual members "on course." Depending upon the circumstances surrounding particular situations, sales management may decide (1) to take "no action" at this time; (2) to take various actions that will result in an increased degree of attainment of objectives; (3) to revise the policy and/or plan, or the strategies used in their implementation, to facilitate achievement of objectives; or sometimes (4) to lower or raise the objectives, or the standards and/or criteria used to measure their degree of attainment, in order to make them more realistic.

These managerial functions—planning, organizing, coordinating, and controlling—are not performed in an unchanging straight-line sequence. More accurately, the order of performance can be described as circular; and nowhere is this better illustrated than in the controlling phase of sales-force management. The decision to set sales performance standards, that is, to take the first step in control, requires planning. Planning, in turn, involves analyzing and classifying internal records, forecasting market and marketing changes, setting objectives, formulating sales programs and campaigns, and selecting sales methods and procedures. Essentially, planning entails deciding where the sales department is going (that is, setting the objectives), and determining how the department is to get from where it is to where it wants to be. Furthermore, the initiation of control through standard setting can be done realistically only when the capabilities of the sales organization are taken into account. Because of deficiencies in organizational effectiveness and limitations in the number and quality of sales personnel, it does little good to set performance standards that are beyond its or their capabilities. In addition, before control can achieve maximum effectiveness, management must possess considerable skill in coordinating sales planning activities and sales efforts. Even after sales-force control is set in motion, further managerial actions are required in the functional areas of planning, organizing, and coordinating. Indeed, the benefits of dynamic control, the initiating of action based on analysis of comparisons of actual performances with the standards, cannot be fully realized unless sales management takes further planning, organizing, and coordinating steps.

## STANDARDS OF PERFORMANCE

Setting standards of performance for purposes of controlling the sales department's operations requires, first of all, keen recognition of the requirements of the selling job. Sales job analysis, in other words, is necessary in order to determine precisely what duties and activities the salesperson is expected to perform. As we saw earlier, these, in turn, depend upon the selling strategy the firm chooses to follow. In some companies, for example, the key problem is to obtain new customers. Selling to convince prospects that are not now using the firm's products to adopt them is known as developmental selling—the creation of customers rather than the creation of sales—and requires skills different from those needed in companies whose main problem is that of maintaining relations with and servicing established accounts.[1] Setting performance standards for sales personnel engaged mainly in developmental selling requires the use of measures unlike those used for sales personnel whose main task is to service existing accounts. In other situations, such as those of companies relying heavily upon dealer sales effort to push the product through the marketing channel to final buyers, selling strategy calls for the manufacturer's salespeople to devote major segments of their time to such activities as training dealers' sales personnel, assisting in the planning and preparation of dealer advertising, and securing "preferred" display space in dealers' showrooms. The performance standards chosen here should be designed to measure the quality of the salesperson's performance of activities that the company considers most important.

In still other situations, unique forms of sales jobs exist. The computer "salesperson," for example, must be both a management consultant and a systems analyst—often needing to know and understand the models or the programmed decision-making approach appropriate to the particular type of industry or establishment in which the computer is to be used.[2] Evaluating the job performance of a computer salesperson, then, requires standards that measure not only skill in developmental selling but, even more basically, effectiveness as a management consultant and skill as a systems analyst. Thus, the unique nature of the selling job must be recognized before deciding upon the standards to be used in appraising personnel performance.

Setting sales-performance standards also requires considerable knowledge of the market. The total sales potential and the portion that each salesperson's territory is capable of producing should be known. Boundaries of sales territories should have been so drawn that submarginal areas that have little chance of becoming profitable are eliminated. Evaluations of customers and prospects from the standpoint of potential profitability for each class and size of account should have been made. Marketing intelligence should have provided evaluations of competitors' strengths, weaknesses, practices, and policies. And management should be well informed concerning differences in selling expenses likely to be incurred in different territories. These are all items that bear significantly on the setting of performance standards, especially quantitative standards.

Sales management must take still other factors into account in setting performance standards. Management should reappraise the sales planning to assure that it is the best possible under the circumstances; and there should be a high degree of confidence in the appropriateness of the policies and procedures being used to carry the personal-selling portion of the marketing program into effect. Similarly, management should make adjustments reflecting consideration of the strengths and weaknesses of the individual sales personnel whose performances are to be evaluated and the many differences existing in the working environments of each person. In brief, sales management in each company must develop and put together its combination of sales performance standards to best fit the firm's needs, its marketing situation, its chosen selling strategy, and the caliber of its sales organization.[3]

[1] G. N. Kahn and A. Shuckman, "Specialize Your Salesman!" *Harvard Business Review,* Vol. 39, No. 1 (January-February 1961), p. 91.

[2] F. T. Malm, "Technology and Manpower Utilization in Distribution Agencies," *California Management Review,* Vol. 8, No. 2 (Winter 1965), p. 16.

[3] An excellent discussion of this and other matters pertaining to evaluating and supervising sales personnel appears in A. H. Dunn and E. M. Johnson, *Managing the Sales Force* (Morristown, N.J.: General Learning Press, 1973), Chapters 4 and 5.

## RELATION OF PERFORMANCE STANDARDS
## TO PERSONAL-SELLING OBJECTIVES

The standards of sales performance selected should facilitate the measurement of progress made toward departmental objectives, both general and specific. Although specific objectives vary from time to time with changes in the firm's marketing situation, they should always be reconcilable with the general objectives of volume, profit, and growth. For instance, a general objective might be to add $10 million to sales volume. This figure in itself is of little assistance for operating purposes. But using the sales-volume objective as a point of departure, management drafts the plans for use in the effort to expand sales volume from the present level to an amount higher by $10 million. In other words, management plans how the sales-volume objective is to be reached. Through analysis of various market factors, management may conclude that $10 million in additional sales can be made if two hundred new accounts are secured. Experience may indicate that 1,000 calls on prospects must be made in order to add 200 new accounts. Thus, in successive stages, the general sales-volume objective is broken down and translated into specific operating objectives. Performance standards are then established for the business as a whole and, ultimately, for each salesperson, which can be used to gauge the extent to which general and related specific objectives are being achieved.

The first quantitative standard that any firm should select should be one that permits comparisons of sales-volume performance with sales-volume potential. From the sales department's standpoint, the volume objective is the most crucial and should take precedence over the profit and growth objectives. Before profits can be earned and growth achieved, a certain sales-volume level needs to be reached. Thus, it is entirely logical for sales management to give its first attention to the development of a standard by which to gauge sales-volume performance.

Quantitative performance standards are required also to measure the sales department's success in achieving profit objectives. Profits are the end result of complex interactions of many factors, so the modicum of control over profits provided through the setting of a standard for sales volume is not enough. Standards designed specifically to bring some or all factors affecting profit under sales management's control should be set. Performance standards, then, should be adopted for such factors affecting profits as selling expense, the sales mixture, the call frequency rate, the cost per call, and the size of order.

Setting quantitative performance standards to gauge the progress made toward achieving growth objectives presents an even more complex problem. Growth objectives are met to some extent through the natural momentum picked up as a company approaches maturity; but the nature and effectiveness of the salespeople's performances do have direct implication for and impact upon a company's growth. In an expanding economy, where the gross national product each year is larger than the year before, it is probably reasonable for most companies to expect their individual salespeople to show annual sales increases; however, this assumes that marketing management possesses sufficient competence to keep its products, prices, promotion, and other marketing policies in tune with market demand and that sales management's efficiency is being continuously improved. If these assumptions can logically be made, then the standards that need to be set for individual salespeople (besides successively higher sales volume and profit quotas each year) relate to such factors as increased sales to old accounts, sales to new accounts, calls on new prospects, sales of new products, and improvements in sales-coverage effectiveness.

## Quantitative Performance Standards

Most firms desiring to improve the effectiveness of sales personnel through the installation and operation of control procedures use quantitative performance standards. The particular combination of such standards chosen varies both with the firm and its marketing situation. Quantitative standards, in effect, serve to define both the nature and desired levels of performance; hence, it is important that both be communicated to the sales personnel. Indeed, quantitative standards are used almost as much for stimulating good performance as for measuring it.

Quantitative standards should provide individual salespeople with clear descriptions of what management expects in terms of accomplishment. Each salesperson should have specific definitions of the various aspects of his or her performance that are to be measured and the units of measurement that are to be used. These definitions should assist the sales staff in making their activities more purposeful. Salespeople with well-defined objectives generally waste little time or effort in pursuing activities that do not contribute to reaching those objectives. Therefore, it is highly important that quantitative performance standards be selected and set with care.

Most progressive companies now recognize that a single quantitative standard, such as a figure for sales-volume attainment, rarely provides a reliable basis for appraising a salesperson's total performance. Too often in the past, and in some firms even today, the relative worth of individual salespeople has been measured solely in terms of sales volume. Today's progressive sales managers realize that it is possible to make sales without earning net profits, and that present sales may be made at the expense of future sales. In some fields—for example, the selling of industrial goods of high unit price—sales result only after extended periods of preliminary work, and in such cases it is not only unfair to the sales staff but misleading to management to appraise performance over short intervals solely on the basis of sales volume. Furthermore, salespersons have little or no control over many factors affecting sales volume. They should not be held accountable for "uncontrollables" such as differences in the strength of competition, the amount of promotional support given the sales force, the potential territorial sales volume, the relative importance of sales to national or "house" accounts, the amount of missionary and other nonselling work required and performed, and the amount of "windfall" business secured. Thus, ample reason exists for selecting and setting additional quantitative performance standards besides that for sales volume alone.

The following discussion considers various quantitative performance standards in common use. Each company should select that combination that best fits its own marketing situation and selling objectives; if necessary, developing its own unique standards designed to best serve those objectives. The standards discussed below constitute a small, but representative, sample of the many types in use.

**Quotas.**  A quota is a quantitative objective expressed in absolute terms and assigned to a specific marketing unit. The terms may be dollars, or units of product; the marketing unit may be a salesperson or a territory. As the most commonly used quantitative standards, quotas specify desired levels of accomplishment for sales volume, gross margin, net profit, expenses, performance of nonselling activities, or a combination of these and/or similar items.[4] When sales personnel are assigned quotas, management is, in essence, answering the important question: How much for what period? The assumption is that management knows which objectives, both general and specific, are realistic and attainable. The validity of this assumption depends upon the amount and accuracy of the market knowledge management has and utilizes in setting quotas. For instance, the first step in setting sales-volume quotas is to estimate probable future demand for the company's products in each sales territory—hence, sales-volume quotas can be no better than the sales forecasts underlying them.[5] When sales-volume quotas are based upon reasonably reliable sales forecasts, in which the probable strength of demand has been fully considered for the company's products, territory by territory, they are valuable standards to use in appraising sales performance. But when sales-volume quotas represent little more than guesses, or when they have been chosen chiefly for inspirational effect, much, if not all, of their value as control devices is dissipated.

**Selling-Expense Ratio.** Sales managers using this quantitative standard seek to control the relation between selling expenses and sales volume. Since many factors, some controllable by sales personnel and some not, cause selling expenses to vary with the territory, target selling-expense ratios should be set individually for each salesperson. The use of such ratios for control purposes, therefore, is defensible only when the ratios are determined after considerable study and analysis of expense conditions and sales-volume potentials in each territory. An attractive feature of the selling-expense ratio is that the salesperson can affect it both by controlling expenses and by making sales.

From the standpoint of its use for control purposes, the selling-expense ratio has several shortcomings. Such a ratio does not take into account variations in the profitability of different products—so a salesperson who has a favorable selling-expense ratio may be responsible for disproportionately low profits. Then, too, this performance standard may cause the salesperson to overeconomize on selling expenses to the point where sales volume suffers. Finally, in times of declining general business conditions, strict adherence to predetermined selling-expense ratios may prevent sales personnel from exerting the additional effort needed to bolster sales volume.

Sales executives differ with respect to the expenses that should be counted as "selling expenses" in computing the ratio. If such indirect expense items as national advertising, home-office sales department expense, and branch managers' and supervisors' salaries are included and allocated to each territory, it would seem that sales personnel are held accountable for expenses over which they have little or no control. But a small minority of sales executives argue that salespeople can influence the relation of such indirect expenses to sales simply by putting forth the appropriate level of selling effort. In most companies, however, only expenses incurred directly by the sales personnel, and controllable by them, are used for the computation. About one half of all companies using this type of standard include the salesperson's salary and/or incentive compensation in the computation; the rest tend to consider only selling expenses incurred directly by sales personnel in performing their jobs. In a few firms, mainly those in which salespeople pay their own traveling expenses, the selling-expense ratio is calculated by simply dividing sales volume into the salesperson's compensation.

Selling-expense-ratio standards are more extensively used by firms selling industrial

---

[4]Quotas are treated more fully in Chapter 19.
[5]For a discussion of sales forecasting, see Chapter 2.

products than by consumer-product companies. The explanation for this may be traceable to differences in the selling job in the two kinds of business. Industrial-product firms usually place the greater emphasis on personal selling and entertainment of customers; consequently, their sales personnel tend to incur higher costs for travel and subsistence. It is natural, then, that such companies should feel that expense control is for them a much more critical item than it is in firms selling consumer products.[6]

**Territorial Net-Profit or Gross-Margin Ratio.**   Target ratios of net profit or gross margin to sales for each territory are used to effect control by focusing salespeople's attention on the needs for selling a balanced line and for considering relative profitability (of different products, individual customers, etc.) in planning selling efforts. Managements using either ratio as a quantitative performance standard, in effect, regard each sales territory as a separate organizational unit that should make a contribution to total company profit. The sales personnel, whose performances are being judged, can influence the net-profit ratios they achieve by selling more volume and by accumulating lower selling expenses. They can also work toward this goal by emphasizing more profitable products and by devoting more time and effort to the accounts and prospects that are potentially the most profitable. Thus, the net-profit ratio provides a means that management can use in controlling sales volume and expenses as well as net profit. By contrast, the gross-margin ratio provides a way to control sales volume and the *relative* profitability of the sales mixture (that is, sales of different products and to different customers), but it does not serve to control the expenses of obtaining and filling orders.

Certain shortcomings of net-profit and gross-margin ratios, however, need recognizing. When either ratio is used as a performance standard, sales personnel may be tempted to "high-spot" their territories, to neglect the solicitation of new accounts, and to overemphasize sales of high-profit or high-margin products while underemphasizing new products that may be more profitable in the long run. Similarly, both ratios are influenced by factors largely beyond the individual salesperson's control. For instance, the pricing policy followed by management affects both net profit and gross margin; and delivery costs, which also affect both net profit and gross margin, not only vary in different territories but are almost entirely beyond the salesperson's control. Managements using either ratio standard need to use other quantitative standards to adjust for these shortcomings; they must also be especially careful that sales personnel will not be held accountable for factors outside their control. Neither ratio should be used without full recognition of its shortcomings.

Computation problems are also encountered when the net-profit ratio is used. Since allocations of indirect selling expenses to territories can only be made arbitrarily, the usual practice is to use contribution to profit, which takes into account only direct selling expenses clearly identifiable with particular territories. Similarly, questions arise concerning whether salespeople's salaries and commissions should be included in calculating territorial net profit, and the practice among companies varies on this point.

**Territorial Market Share.**   This standard provides management with a means for controlling its share of the market on a territory-by-territory basis. Through statistical analysis and projection of market-share trends, management establishes a target market-

---

[6]W. J. McBurney, Jr., *Goal Setting and Planning at the District Sales Level,* AMA Research Study 61 (New York: American Management Association, Inc., 1963), pp. 25-29.

share percentage for each territory, these serving as specific objectives for sales personnel. Management later compares company sales to industry sales in each territory and thus measures the effectiveness of the sales force in obtaining the market share for the company. Closer control over the individual salesperson's sales mixture may also be obtained by setting target market-share percentages for each product and each class of customer, even for individual customers, provided that management has the appropriate data with which to work. Such data might include statistics on industry and company sales broken down by individual products, by class of customer, or by individual customers. It should be noted, then, that target market-share percentages should be used only if the requisite market data are available.

**Sales-Coverage-Effectiveness Index.**    The sales-coverage-effectiveness quantitative standard is intended to control the thoroughness with which a salesperson works the assigned territory. The index consists of the ratio of the desired number of customers to the total prospects in a territory. To apportion the salesperson's efforts more profitably among various classifications of prospects, individual standards for sales-coverage effectiveness may be set up for each class and size of customer. Sales-coverage-effectiveness indexes, whether overall or individual, should be established only after a thorough study of the potential buyers in each territory.

**Call-Frequency Ratio.**    Through setting standards for call frequency, sales management seeks to control the interval between salesperson's calls upon each class of customers and/or prospects. A call-frequency ratio is calculated by dividing the number of a salesperson's calls on a particular class of customers by the number of customers in that class in the assigned territory. By establishing different call frequency ratios for different classes of customers, management has a way to direct salespeople's activities to those accounts most likely to produce profitable orders. In setting call-frequency-ratio standards, management should be especially careful to assure that the interval between calls upon each customer class is appropriate—neither so short that unprofitably small orders are secured nor so long that sales are lost to competitors. Detailed relevant information must therefore be available on the situation in each territory. Sales personnel who plan their own route and call schedules find target call frequencies especially helpful, inasmuch as these standards provide information essential to this type of planning.

**Calls per Day.**    Particularly in consumer-product fields, where manufacturers' sales personnel are in contact with large numbers of customers, it is often desirable to set a standard for the number of calls that a salesperson should make per day. Otherwise, some salespeople make too few calls per day and may need help in planning their routes, in setting up appointments before calls in order to reduce waiting time or the number of cases where buyers are found "unavailable," or simply in starting their calls early enough in the morning and staying on the job late enough in the day. Other sales personnel make too many calls per day and may require instruction in how to service their accounts properly. Standards for calls per day should be set individually for different territories, taking into account such territorial differences as customer density, road and traffic conditions, and competitors' practices.

**Order-Call Ratio.**    This ratio provides management with a way to measure the effectiveness of sales personnel in securing orders. This ratio, sometimes referred to as a "batting average," is calculated by dividing the number of orders that a salesperson secures in a given time period by the number of calls made. Since individual salespersons often vary in their ability to obtain orders from different classes of customers, order-call-ratio standards should be set for each class of account the salesperson has in the territory. When it is found that a salesperson's order-call ratio for a particular class of account varies from the standard, management knows that the salesperson needs help in improving his or her effectiveness in working with that class of account. It is not at all unusual for sales personnel to vary in their effectivenes in selling to different kinds of accounts—one person may be unusually effective in selling to small buyers and unusually poor in selling to large buyers, another may have just the opposite performance pattern.

**Average Cost per Call.**   When sales management wants to emphasize the importance of making profitable calls, it may set a target for average cost per call. When there is considerable variation in costs of calling on different sizes or classes of accounts, individual standards should be set for each category of account. Target average-cost-per-call standards may also be used to reduce the frequency of calls on accounts responsible for small orders.

**Average Order Size.**   The chief purpose of average-order-size standards being to control the frequency with which sales personnel call on different accounts, the usual practice is to set up different standards for the average size of order to be obtained from customers of different sizes and classes. By using average-order-size standards along with average-cost-per-call standards, management may control the salesperson's allocation of effort among different accounts in a way that will build up the size of order obtained on each call. Accomplishing this objective, of course, may require salespeople to reduce the frequency of calls on some accounts.

**Nonselling Activities.**   Some companies establish quantitative standards for salespeople's performance of such important nonselling activities as the obtaining of dealer displays and cooperative advertising contracts, training of distributors' personnel, and making goodwill calls on distributors' customers. Whenever such activities are considered critical features of the salesperson's job, appropriate standards should be set—both for the salesperson to use in planning his or her efforts and time allocation and for management to use in appraising his or her effectiveness. Since quantitative standards for nonselling activities are expressed in absolute terms, such standards are, in reality, quotas.

### Qualitative Performance Criteria

Because certain aspects of a salesperson's performance, such as personal effectiveness in handling customer-relations problems and the thoroughness of his or her product knowledge, do not lend themselves readily to precise measurement, the use of some qualitative criteria is unavoidable. Management uses qualitative criteria for appraising the performance characteristics displayed by a salesperson that affect sales results, especially over the long run, but whose degree of excellence can be evaluated only subjectively. Qualitative criteria defy exact definition and must be described generally. Many sales executives, perhaps most, do not attempt to define the desired qualitative characteristics with any exactitude; instead, they arrive at general and informal conclusions regarding the extent to which each salesperson possesses them. Other executives make some pretense of considering the qualitative factors more formally, one method being to rate sales personnel against a detailed checklist of subjective factors such as that shown in Figure 17.1. Note that the rating form shown in Figure 17.1

| | Date | Date | Date | Date |
|---|---|---|---|---|
| 5. Knowledge of Product and Company Policy | | | | |
| Knows his lines and all policies concerning them. | | | | |
| Has good overall knowledge of silverware business. | | | | |
| Has a good fund of and an interest in obtaining further trade lore. | | | | |
| AVERAGE. | | | | |
| SALESMANSHIP FACTORS: | | | | |
| 1. Likes Selling | | | | |
| Obviously happy with selling as way of making living. | | | | |
| Is a "good soldier" about territorial moving, etc. | | | | |
| AVERAGE. | | | | |
| 2. Ambitious and Aggressive | | | | |
| Works hard on own (good self-management). | | | | |
| Uses good judgment most of the time. | | | | |
| Accepts responsibility cheerfully. | | | | |
| Is enthusiastic in dealings with customers and management | | | | |
| AVERAGE. | | | | |
| 3. Plans Work and Time | | | | |
| Plans calls, route lists, presentations, etc. | | | | |
| Knows territory potential. | | | | |
| A good business analyst. | | | | |
| Alert to changes in business conditions, competition, etc. | | | | |
| Has good follow-through. | | | | |
| AVERAGE. | | | | |
| 4. Makes Good Contacts | | | | |
| Is respected by the trade. | | | | |
| Builds an Oneida territory. | | | | |
| AVERAGE. | | | | |

| | Date | Date | Date | Date |
|---|---|---|---|---|
| 5. Ingenious and Creative | | | | |
| Develops successful adaptations to plans. | | | | |
| Resourceful (has helpful ideas for dealers). | | | | |
| Presents Plans well. | | | | |
| Shows resale ability and works at it. | | | | |
| Persuasive. | | | | |
| Is good merchandiser. | | | | |
| AVERAGE. | | | | |
| | | | | |
| *6. WRITES BUSINESS | | | | |
| Is a closer. | | | | |
| AVERAGE. | | | | |

*YOU WILL NOTE THAT THIS FACTOR HAS BEEN GIVEN A WEIGHT OF 40% OF THE TOTAL FACTORS.

IT IS OBVIOUS THAT THERE ARE ALL SORTS OF COMBINATIONS OF FACTORS AND ABILITIES IN ANY HUMAN BEING, BUT IF THE OVERALL RATING FOR HIM IS NOT TOO GOOD IT DOES NOT ALWAYS MEAN THAT A PERSON IS NOT A SATISFACTORY SALESPERSON. SINCE SOME SALESPEOPLE PRODUCE QUITE A BIT OF CONTINUING BUSINESS, DESPITE WEAKNESSES IN MANY AREAS OF THEIR MAKE-UP, AND SINCE ANY COMPANY LIVES ON WHAT IT ACTUALLY SELLS, I.E. ORDERS WRITTEN AND CONFIRMED. IT IS THEREFORE BELIEVED THAT THE FINAL, AND VERY MUCH THE MOST IMPORTANT, FACTOR IN RATING A SALESPERSON IS: HOW MUCH BUSINESS DOES HE WRITE?

FROM TIME TO TIME, SPECIAL SITUATIONS WILL DEVELOP, SUCH AS A STEEL STRIKE IN THE PITTS-BURGH TERRITORY, AN AUTOMOBILE STRIKE IN THE DETROIT AREA, OR A FLOOD IN THE OHIO VALLEY, OR EVEN A DROUGHT IN THE MIDWEST. THESE SPECIAL SITUATIONS, OR EXTENUATING CIRCUM-STANCES, MUST BE TAKEN INTO ACCOUNT WHEN JUDGING THE AMOUNT OF BUSINESS A PERSON WRITES AT ANY GIVEN TIME. BECAUSE OF THIS FACT, THIS MERIT-RATING SHEET HAS TAKEN THIS INTO ACCOUNT BY REQUESTING THAT THE RATING MANAGER **INCLUDE IN HIS COMMENTS ON EACH INTERVIEW ANY SPECIAL SITUATIONS** OR CIRCUMSTANCES WHICH MAY EXPLAIN AN APPARENTLY POOR SALES-VOLUME PICTURE, AS SHOWN ON THE SUMMARY SHEET.

COMMENTS

Interview #1

Date

Interview #2

Date

Interview #3

Date

Interview #4

Date

requires raters to "quantify" their ratings of each factor, and this results in an overall numerical rating for the salesperson.

Companies with merit-rating systems for appraising personnel performance differ on the desirability of using numerical ratings. Most numerical scoring systems are found in companies that rate sales personnel primarily for such administrative purposes as detecting needed adjustments in compensation levels. Companies that use merit rating primarily to improve and develop individual salespersons usually do not try to assign numerical values.[7]

Executive judgment plays the major role in the qualitative appraisal of personnel performance. Regardless of whether a merit-rating plan or only an informal evaluation is used, written job descriptions, up-to-date and accurate, are the logical points of departure. Each firm should develop its own set of qualitative criteria, based upon the job descriptions; the manner in which these criteria are applied depends almost entirely upon the quality and experience of management. Thus, the validity of qualitative appraisals of personnel performance is a function of the maturity and soundness of judgment demonstrated by the executives doing the appraising.

## RECORDING ACTUAL PERFORMANCE

Once sales management has decided the performance standards for use in controlling and evaluating salespeople, it must determine and measure actual performance. Managerial emphasis in this phase of control, in other words, shifts to the gathering of information on performance. Sales management must define its information needs, determine the sources from which to obtain this information, and set methods in operation for actually obtaining the needed data.

Management's choice of performance standards, in effect, dictates the nature of the information needed for sales control. It should be kept in mind, however, that with the development of increasingly sophisticated companywide management information systems stimulated mainly by rapid strides in applying electronic data-processing equipment to company operations, sales management's choice of performance standards may actually be based as much on the availability of needed information as on the desire to use certain standards. In any event, sales management is well advised to review periodically the combination of sales performance standards currently in use and the availability of other types of information that might permit the use of different and/or additional standards.

There are two basic sources of the needed information on performance—sales and expense records maintained chiefly for accounting reasons, and reports of varous sorts obtained primarily for the use of sales management. Almost every company has a wealth of potentially pertinent data in its files of internal sales and expense records, but this information frequently requires reworking, or reprocessing, before it is useful for sales-control purposes. When sales and expense data are reclassified according to sales management's information needs, they should contribute significantly to the determination and measurement of actual performances.

Among the reports obtained primarily for sales management's use are those from the salespeople themselves and from the lower echelons of sales management; these are

---

[7]*Measuring Salesmen's Performance,* Studies in Business Policy No. 114 (New York: National Industrial Conference Board, Inc., 1965), p. 35. This source contains a number of case histories illustrating the use of merit-rating systems for sales personnel in various companies and industries.

discussed in the following section. In addition, companies using such quantitative performance standards as sales-volume quotas and target share-of-the-market percentages require the type of information contained in sales forecasts, which, of course, are prepared not only for sales management's use but for managerial planning throughout the enterprise.[8]

The methods that sales management uses for actually obtaining needed control information depend mainly upon the sources tapped. Internally generated information, such as that available from the company data-processing installation, may be provided on a routine basis, or in response to requests for special tabulations. Information that can be obtained only from sales personnel or sales-management personnel in the field is obtained principally through formal reports routinely submitted to and analyzed by home-office sales personnel; such information is also obtained, from time to time, through personal observation methods—by trips to the field by home-office sales executives or through field sales supervisors.

## System of Field Sales Reports

The fundamental purpose of field sales reports is to provide sales management with control information, and this information is obtained through communications. Good communications generally requires interaction between those preparing reports and those receiving them. Thus, a good field sales reporting system should provide both for communication from the salesperson and field sales management to headquarters and from the headquarters to the field.

Field sales reports provide headquarters' sales management with a basis for discussion with sales personnel and field sales management; they indicate the matters on which field sales people need assistance and they enable sales executives to make suggestions and offer encouragement. Assuming the availability of other requisite market knowledge, the sales executive may determine whether salespeople are calling on and selling the right people, and whether they are making too few or too many calls. Similarly, field sales reports assist sales management in determining, in general, what can be done to secure more and larger orders. Field sales reports provide the raw materials that sales management processes in order to gain insights preliminary to giving needed help and direction to field sales personnel.

A good field sales reporting system should also assist salespeople in their own self-improvement programs. Recording accomplishments in written form, for instance, forces salespeople to check their own work. They become, in effect, their own critics, and self-criticism often proves more valuable and more effective than criticism emanating from headquarters. To the extent that this motivates sales personnel to strive for improved coordination of their efforts with sales management's plans and directives, the managerial process functions more smoothly, and the administrator's task is lightened.

**Purposes of Field Sales Reports.**   The purpose a report is to serve determines the type of report, the nature of the information it contains, and the frequency of its transmittal. The general purpose of all field sales reports, of course, should be to provide information needed for measuring personnel performance; many reports, however, provide additional information. Consider the following list of purposes served by field sales reports in various companies:

---

[8]Sales forecasting is discussed in Chapter 2.

1.  To provide data for evaluating performance—for example, details concerning accounts and prospects called upon, number of calls made, number of orders obtained, days worked, miles traveled, selling expenses incurred, displays erected, cooperative advertising arrangements made, training of distributors' personnel accomplished, missionary work performed, and calls made with distributors' sales personnel.

2.  To help the salesperson plan his or her work—for example, planning itineraries, sales approaches to use with specific accounts and prospects.

3.  To record customers' suggestions and complaints and their reactions to new products, service policies, price changes, advertising campaigns, etc.

4.  To gather information on competitors' activities—for example, new products, market tests, changes in promotion, and changes in pricing and credit policy.

5.  To report changes in local business and economic conditions.

6.  To log important items of territorial information for possible later use in case sales personnel leave the company or are reassigned.

7.  To keep the mailing list for promotional and catalog materials current.

8.  To provide information requested by marketing research—for example, data on dealers' sales and inventories of company and competitive products.

**Types of Sales-Force Reports.**   The majority of reports from sales personnel can be classified into seven principal groups:

1.  *Progress or call report.* Most companies using reports at all use some form of progress or call report. It may be prepared individually for each call, or cumulatively covering all calls made daily or weekly. Progress reports keep management informed of the salesperson's activities, provide source data on the company's relative standing with individual accounts and in different territories, and record information that may assist the salesperson on revisits to customers and prospects. Usually the call-report form is designed to record not only the calls made and sales obtained, but more detailed data, such as the specific class of customer or prospect, competitive brands handled, the strength and activities of competitors, best time to call on the account, and "future promises" made by buyers.

2.  *Expense report.* Because most sales personnel are reimbursed for all or part of the expenses they incur in performing their jobs, and because itemized expense records are required for income-tax purposes, most companies use some form of expense report. From sales management's standpoint, the purpose is to control the nature and amount of salespersons' expenses. Some sales executives contend that this report also helps the salesperson exercise self-control over expenses. They say the fact that salespersons must record their expenses periodically forces them to be more aware of, hence, more careful in, the ways they spend company money. These executives say also that the expense report form helps remind salespersons that they are under moral obligation to keep their expenses in line with their reported sales volumes—some expense report forms require salespersons to "correlate" their expenses with the sales they make. The details of the report form, as might be expected, vary with the plan used for reimbursing sales expenses.

3.  *Salesperson's work plan.* The salesperson submits to sales management a work plan (giving such details as accounts and prospects to be called upon, products and other matters to be discussed, routes to be traveled, and hotels or motels) for a specified future period, usually a week or a month in advance. The main purposes of this report are to assist the salesperson in planning and scheduling activities and to keep management informed of his or her whereabouts. For management-control purposes, the report provides information needed for later comparison of the salesperson's plans with his or her accomplishments. Thus, the work plan gives management a basis for evaluating the salesperson's ability "to plan the work and to work the plan."

4. *New-business or potential-new-business report.* This report informs management of accounts recently obtained and prospects who may become sources of new business; it also provides data for evaluating the extent and effectiveness of development work by sales personnel. A subsidiary purpose is to remind salespeople that management expects them not to confine their calls solely to old, well-established accounts. By comparing the information secured with data in company files, management is able to evaluate the effectiveness of prospecting efforts. This report serves another subsidiary purpose in some companies—it provides the sort of information needed for keeping the mailing list for promotional and catalog materials current.

5. *Lost-sale report.* Information required for evaluating a salesperson's abilities to keep customers sold and to sell against competition is provided by this report. Lost-sale reports may point the way to needed sales training, changes in customer service policies, and product improvements. The salesperson should report the reasons, in his or her opinion, for the loss of the business; but receipt of a lost-sale report should also cause management to consider further investigation.

6. *Report of complaint and/or adjustment.* This report provides data for analyzing the nature and volume of complaints arising from an individual salesperson's work, the incidence of specific complaints by class of customer, and the cost of complaint adjustment. Information gleaned from such reports also assists management in detecting needed product improvements and changes in merchandising and service practices and policies. These data are especially helpful when making decisions on sales-training programs, selective selling, and product changes.

7. *Report on general business conditions.* This report serves three general purposes: (1) to orient management on the general business outlook in a territory; (2) to provide information needed for planning the overall sales programs and in designing sales aids for use in a territory; and (3) to furnish basic data for forecasting territorial sales and setting territorial sales quotas.

**Reports from Field Sales Management.** In decentralized sales organizations, field sales executives are playing an increasingly important role in setting sales-performance standards. Branch and district sales managers and, in some cases, sales supervisors are particularly active in establishing sales-volume quotas for individual salespeople who, in a growing number of companies, also are consulted on their own quotas. Branch and district sales managers, in addition, have important parts to play in breaking down branch and district sales-volume quotas to quotas for individual salespeople and to products or product lines and/or to types of customers—occasionally, even to individual accounts. At the district level, especially in larger companies, there is a trend toward profit planning with the district sales manager setting target net profit and/or expense quotas for individual salespersons and by product line.[9] More commonly, however, the district sales manager's planning report takes the form of a *district sales plan,* often prepared by compiling, with or without revisions, personnel work plans, and covering the work or results that each district salesperson expects to accomplish during the month, quarter, or year ahead. Besides breaking down dollar or unit sales-volume quotas by products or product lines for each salesperson, district sales plans generally include standards for such sales activities as the number of calls each is to make, the number of calls to be made on each type of account or on individual accounts, and the number of new dealers and/or distributors to be obtained. District sales plans also

dards. Qualitative performance criteria should also be taken into account, for salespeople with apparently poor performance records, as gauged by quantitative standards, may be making offsetting positive contributions. Sales personnel who may not reach their sales quotas or keep to prescribed call schedules, for instance, may be building for the future by improving relations with dealers and distributors. It should be clear, then, that considerable judgment, seasoned by experience and knowledge of market conditions, must be exercised in evaluating individual performances.

Trends in performance as well as the current record should be considered in evaluating sales personnel. A salesperson whose substandard performance shows improvement needs encouragement. And, of course, it is always possible that the standard is in error. In fact, when a salesperson continually fails to reach a standard, management should investigate the possibility that the standard is set unrealistically high, as well as the possibility that the salesperson may be at fault. Performance appraisal should be an ongoing process because both management and sales personnel must constantly be monitoring progress toward objectives and taking careful note of deviations from expected results.[12]

In comparing actual results with projected results, the general procedure is to set up tests that will measure the variable under observation while taking into account the effects of other variables influencing results. In the evaluation of sales personnel it is difficult to set up such tests. Each salesperson's performance is really the result of complex interactions of many variables, some of which are beyond the control of either the salesperson or of management. The time element changes and so do the sales personnel, the customers, general business conditions, competitors' activities, and other variables. However, some progressive companies have succeeded in measuring the impact of particular variables on personnel performance through careful design of experimental and control groups.[13]

## TAKING ACTION—THE DYNAMIC PHASE OF CONTROL

The evaluations, or comparisons of actual performances with standards, tempered and adjusted by executive judgment, point the way to decisions on needed action. If performance and standards are in alignment, then the decision may be: No action needed. Otherwise, the executive has three main alternatives from which to choose: (1) to adjust performance to the standards, thus increasing the degree of attainment of objectives; (2) to revise the policy and/or plan, or the various strategies used in their implementation, to better fit the achievement of objectives; or (3) to lower or raise the objectives or the standards and/or criteria used in measuring their degree of attainment to make them more realistic. The nature and effectiveness of the actions resulting from these decisions, in turn, are conditioned by the executive's judgment, his or her background and experience, knowledge of the situation, and skill as an administrator.[14]

[12]D. W. Jackson, Jr., and R. J. Aldag, "Managing the Sales Force by Objectives," *MSU Business Topics,* Vol. 22, No. 2 (Spring 1974), p. 56.

[13]For an illustration of the use of experimental and control groups in measuring the impact of particular variables on sales performance see J. G. Hauk, "Research in Personal Selling," G. Schwartz (ed.), *Science in Marketing* (New York: John Wiley & Sons, Inc., 1965), pp. 236-37.

[14]A good discussion of the tactics of corrective action may be found in H. R. Dodge, *Field Sales Management* (Dallas: Business Publications, Inc., 1973), pp. 338-43.

## CONTROLLING SALESPEOPLE THROUGH SUPERVISION

Sales management also exercises control over personnel activities through sales supervision. Regardless of who actually does the supervising, the overall purpose remains the same—to improve the efficiency and job performance of sales personnel in the field. The executive with supervisory responsibilities establishes working relations with sales personnel for such specific purposes as: observing, evaluating, and reporting on field sales performance; correcting deficiencies in job performance; clarifying job responsibilities and duties; providing on-the-spot motivation; keeping sales personnel informed of changes in company policy; helping salespeople solve business and personal problems; and continuing sales training in the field. This list of specific purposes makes it apparent that sales supervision is concerned mainly with the action phase of control—action directly aimed at enhancing personnel contributions to the achievement of company objectives. In short, there should be a conscious effort to assure allocation of sufficient resources and support for the sales staff, thereby allowing them every opportunity to achieve objectives.[15]

Sales executives have long debated the optimum amount of supervision. Some say that it is as bad to have too much as too little. It is difficult to prescribe just how much supervision is enough; however, certain conditions serve to indicate the possibility that more or different kinds of supervision are needed. One writer names the following as tell-tale signs that some sort of change in supervision is required:[16]

High turnover of sales personnel in an organizational unit.

High cost-to-sales ratio for direct selling costs—higher than in comparable organizational units.

High turnover of accounts.

Increase in complaints from customers.

Mail or phone orders increasing for no apparent reason.

Low morale, which may be signified by negative attitude toward company, failure of enthusiasm, signs of restlessness, and job hunting.

Low total number of calls.

Low order-call ratio.

It should be recognized that these conditions can be traced to too little supervision or to the wrong kind or too much supervision. A list such as this provides a useful guide for appraising the effectiveness of sales supervision; but those doing the appraising must also keep in mind that many of the signs may have their true roots in deficiencies in other phases of sales-force management. It sometimes happens, too, that a company upgrades the quality of its sales personnel and fails to make appropriate adjustments in the pattern of supervision. One writer contends that the selling task in many companies has changed so that all their selling has now become high-level, key-account selling; and this demands independent, self-reliant, highly educated salespeople who can and must make many of their own decisions. He argues that when management brings in highly trained and self-reliant people to meet the new selling challenge, the whole traditional pattern

---

[15]Jackson and Aldag, *op. cit.,* p. 57.

[16]C. L. Lapp, *Training and Supervising Salesmen* (Englewood Cliffs, N.J.: Prentice-Hall, Inc., 1960), p. 4.

of supervision—and the attitudes that typically underlie it—will stifle those whom management seeks to encourage. What worked for so long may be wrong for the more dynamic assignment of the newer type of person.[17] The type of supervision, in other words, should be adjusted to the type of person selected for the selling job—when the type of person changes, so should the type of supervision.

## Who Should Supervise?

Depending upon the company and its sales organizational structure, sales personnel may be supervised directly by home office personnel, by branch or district managers, or by field sales supervisors. Put another way, sales supervision may be effected either through executives who regard this as only one of their many responsibilities, or by specialists whose jobs are mainly concerned with supervising the sales staff. If the company sales force is small and chiefly composed of experienced personnel, sales supervision is generally the responsibility of the top sales executive or an assistant. Necessarily, the amount of control that can be exercised through such home-office supervision is minimal; but it may be enough, especially when the sales organization is sufficiently small to permit the development of close personal relations among salespeople and executives and when little or no field sales training is required.

Companies having decentralized sales organizations sometimes assign the responsibility for supervision to branch or district managers. Customarily promoted from the ranks, branch managers are presumed to be well prepared to supervise those directly engaged in field selling. However, even in companies with elaborate field sales organizations, there are definite limitations on the amount of supervision that branch managers can and should exercise. In practice, the branch manager is often a local general manager more than a specialized sales executive—in this capacity he or she is responsible for the local conduct of all the company's affairs, not only for managing salespeople but for warehousing, extending credit and making collections, providing service, and performing other routine work. Thus, the branch manager may have insufficient time to supervise personally all the activities of all the salespeople. Since branch managers must spend most of their time at the branch offices attending to details, it is unusual for them to devote much time to personal supervision of sales personnel. Most authorities agree, however, that branch managers should spend some time on that important activity. Especially when branch managers have relatively large numbers of salespeople under them, the time they can spend with each one is necessarily limited and, as is true of much sales supervision emanating from the home office in centralized sales organizations, they have to rely mainly upon the salespeople to supervise themselves.

To overcome the built-in inadequacies of top sales executives and branch managers as sales supervisors, many companies employ specialists as field sales supervisors. Such supervisors devote their full time and effort to the supervision of sales personnel. The results they obtain are usually expected to justify the costs—that is, the sales supervisors' work should result in enough increased productivity on the salespeople's part to pay for the costs of maintaining the supervisory organization. Therefore, when sales supervisors are used, total sales volume and gross margin must be higher than if salespeople supervise themselves.

[17]See W. C. Caswell, "Marketing Effectiveness and Sales Supervision," *California Management Review*, Vol. 7, No. 1 (Fall 1964), pp. 39-44.

## Qualifications of Sales Supervisors

Sales supervisors generally are selected from among the sales force; but besides possessing all the qualifications required for selling success, they need certain additional qualifications. They must be good teachers. They must be able to recognize training needs, know how to train, be patient with those who have less skill, and be able tactfully to point out better ways of doing things. As vital links in the chain of communications—go-betweens for higher sales management and the sales force alike—they must fully understand the needs and problems of both and attempt to reconcile them in the field. They must be skilled in the techniques of handling people and be equipped to deal with the many complex and difficult situations that arise. And because it is physically impossible for them to be with all the salespeople all the time, they must carry on interim correspondence with each salesperson. Beyond these supervisory duties, some companies expect sales supervisors to sell certain accounts personally, this being one way to motivate sales supervisors to keep up to date on the field selling techniques they are supposed to teach to the sales force. The field sales supervisor's job is difficult and, in most companies, it is also one with comparatively low pay. Nevertheless, many salespeople are eager for promotions to supervisory positions, since frequently they are steppingstones to higher positions.

## CONCLUSION—THE CONTROL FUNCTION IN SALES-FORCE MANAGEMENT

In this chapter we have analyzed the part that control plays in the sales-force-management process. The following outline summarizes the different phases in this process:

1. Company goals are defined, and appropriate objectives for the sales department are derived from them.

2. To facilitate achievement of these objectives, departmental policies are formulated and plans designed.

3. To execute the policies and implement the plans, promotional programs and campaigns are mapped out, specific methods and procedures are determined, and other needed actions, such as making indicated alterations in the sales organization, are taken.

4. Various sales-department activities are coordinated with each other and with related activities performed by other organizational units and middlemen.

5. Quantitative performance standards are set, and criteria for appraising qualitative aspects of performance are selected.

6. Actual performance is recorded.

7. Actual performance is compared with quantitative performance standards and qualitative performance criteria.

8. Indicated actions are taken after deciding:
   a. "To take no action" at this time.
   b. To increase the degree of attainment of objectives.
   c. To revise the policy and/or plan, or the various strategies used in their implementation, to better fit the achievement of objectives.
   d. To lower or raise objectives, or the standards and/or criteria used in measuring their degree of attainment, to make them more realistic.

In that they deal specifically with evaluating and supervising sales personnel, the last four steps above comprise "control," the first three being static, whereas the action called upon by new salespeople, were becoming more and more reluctant to place business with the company.

When new salespeople were recruited, Norton Brothers acquired them through the Men's Apparel Club, a national organization, or advertised in the "help wanted" columns of leading newspapers in the territories where the salespeople were to work. Occasionally, new sales personnel were hired from the ranks of customers' employees.

Because of the small size of the company, the training program was very brief. The new salesperson spent two weeks at the factory becoming acquainted with the stock and general factory and office procedures. To conclude this informal training, Norton or one of his assistants would go out on the road with the person, introducing him to the buyers and helping him to get started.

Norton recalled one case in which the expense of breaking in a new person was demonstrated. A new person out on the road with Norton finished making his calls at 4:00 P.M. and wanted to quit for the day, even though there was time to make one more call that afternoon and to travel to the next city on the route. Norton felt that a veteran salesperson would have made the call and moved on, saving time and obtaining more business.

A manufacturer of noncompeting but complementary lines had proposed recently to Norton a plan whereby a number of firms would jointly share a salesperson's services. Each business would pay a certain portion of the person's drawing account and each would pay regular commission rates on whatever goods were sold in each company's line. Norton was undecided as to whether or not to enter split-draw deals of this type. He felt in most cases that it would be well to accept offers of this sort, provided that the salespeople were reasonably certain to work out satisfactorily.

Norton saw no immediate solution to his greatest problem, that of keeping sales personnel who did not want to travel. A recent industry study had shown that the average neckwear salesperson was on the road forty weeks each year. The costs of traveling were high, and most people were dissatisfied when they were required to be away from home for long periods. In order to alleviate the situation, Norton Brothers was attempting to hire only single people and was considering the paying of different commission rates according to the type of territory of the salesperson. The company had tried in every way to satisfy its sales personnel, but it could not decrease the turnover.

*What should Norton Brothers have done to decrease the turnover of its salespeople? Should Norton have accepted the proposition involving split draws?*

# III-2.    TONAWANDA FOODS COMPANY:
## Manufacturer of Food Products—
## Filling a Sales Vacancy

The Tonawanda Foods Company was a large manufacturer of a wide line of food products sold directly to independent grocers, grocery chains, institutions, and industrial users. The United States was divided into six distribution divisions that contained fifty-nine branch offices. The branch office in Kansas City was staffed by a branch manager, a sales manager, and thirteen salespeople. Nine of the salespeople sold the Tonawanda line to independent grocers and to institutional and industrial accounts. Four experienced salespeople gave their full time to the solicitation of chain-store accounts. Early in 1972, one of the chain-store salespeople was promoted and, because of the importance of the chain-store business, the Kansas City sales manager felt that the vacancy should be filled immediately. Since the company attempted to adhere to a promotion-from-within policy, the vacancy represented a promotion opportunity for one of the more experienced and capable Kansas City branch salespeople then selling to independent grocers and institutions. The chain-store sales position was considered attractive because it offered advancement both in salary and in prestige.

The salespeople who sold to independent grocers and to institutions earned an average of $175 per week. They called on accounts specifically assigned to them by the branch sales manager. In fact, each salesperson was given ten route books that listed accounts and set forth the prescribed sequence in which calls were to be made. All such salespeople were subject to constant supervision by the branch sales manager.

By way of contrast, the chain-store sales position called for a weekly salary of $200, plus an end-of-the-year bonus based on the total volume of business written. Promotion to the position of chain-store salesperson was normally considered the beginning of a management career with Tonawanda. The candidate chosen in this case would serve as the sole representative to one large national chain headquartered in Kansas City. Sales to this chain averaged $300,000 per year, and this amount was approximately 20 percent of the sales of the Kansas City branch. Chain-store sales personnel wrote very large orders; it was not uncommon for them to sell merchandise in carload lots or even in trainload quantities. Each order ran into many thousands of dollars. Little direct supervision was exercised over chain-store salespeople, who were expected to be capable of making sound decisions and to be able to offer competent advice on merchandising and sales problems. Chain-store sales personnel called on the chain outlets more or less at their own discretion and gave instructions on merchandising matters to the store managers.

Three of the salespeople calling on independent and institutional accounts were under consideration for the chain-store sales position.

Salesperson A:    Age 25, married with one dependent, Protestant. Three years experience with Tonawanda, no previous experience, college graduate.
Energetic, loyal to company, pleasant personality, attractive appearance.
Honest, always gives the impression of having a sincere interest in customers, will go out of his way to offer them help.
Above-average intelligence.
Scandinavian ancestry.

| (my understanding of the person) | Incentives (my management action) |
| --- | --- |
| | |
| | |
| | |
| | |
| | |
| | |
| | |
| | |
| | |
| | |
| | |
| | |
| | |
| | |
| | |
| | |
| | |

ing and for certain aspects of training for the personnel in the district. Sales potentials and quotas were determined by the general sales manager and the assistant, but these figures were often adjusted after consultations with the district sales managers.

Price competition in the industry was of secondary importance, the main basis being that of product development and design. Fenway salespeople spent a high proportion of their time calling on industrial and institutional users. Their principal function was to analyze the problems of the customers and to prescribe Fenway equipment as a solution. If standardized products were not adaptable to customers' problems, salespeople often recommended that equipment be specially manufactured to meet users' requirements.

The twenty-five Fenway salespeople all possessed degrees in electrical engineering or equivalent experience; and they had been trained under the direction of the district sales managers, except for a one-week initial training program. Salespersons were compensated on a straight-salary basis, partly because of the amount of time spent working with wholesalers' salespeople and partly because they were also required to assist in the installation of equipment and to make repairs in emergency situations.

New salespeople were selected upon the basis of personal interviews with the district manager and personnel in the home office, personal-history information taken from application blanks, credit checks, and aptitude and interest tests. Although the results of personal interviews were by far the most important factor in selection, Harris recognized the weakness of interviews as selection devices because of interviewer bias, lack of objectivity, and lack of uniformity. It was for this reason that he proposed to adopt a uniform checklist for interviewing sales applicants. This patterned interview guide and record is shown in Exhibit 1.

When Richard Farraday, district manager of the San Francisco district, was shown a copy of the patterned interview guide, he protested vehemently against its adoption. He criticized it for being too detailed, awkward, unnatural, and unlikely to provide an improvement over informal interviewing methods.

*In your opinion, what action should Harris have taken?*

# III-4.   BELTON INDUSTRIES, INC.:
## Manufacturer of Toys and Bicycles— Selecting Sales Personnel

Albert Thompson, general sales manager for Belton Industries, Inc., was faced with a problem of high turnover of sales personnel in the sales force. He was led to believe that perhaps something was wrong with the company's selection process and felt that the selection procedure should be evaluated.

Belton manufactured a wide line of children's toys and bicycles. Its sales organization consisted of 110 salespeople operating out of seventeen branch sales offices. The branch sales managers reported directly to Thompson. Belton products were selectively cations, such as recruiting college juniors for summer employment more or less on a trial basis, concentrating on fewer schools, and getting on more friendly terms with placement directors and professors.

Holden's general sales manager clearly favored abandoning the college recruiting program and believed the company should adopt an active recruiting program utilizing other sources of sales personnel. He reasoned that, while engineering graduates had a fine technical background, their lack of maturity, inability to cope with business-type problems, and their general lack of experience precluded an effective contribution to the Holden selling operation.

The general sales manager felt that the 200 sales engineers currently working for Holden were an excellent source of new recruits, since they knew the requirements for successfully selling the Holden line and were in continual contact with other sales-people. By enlisting the support of the sales force, the general manager foresaw an end to Holden's difficulty in obtaining good sales engineers.

The president of the company preferred a program of internal recruiting from various nonselling divisions of the company, such as engineering, design, and manufacturing. He claimed that their familiarity with Holden and their proved abilities were important indicators of potential success as sales engineers.

It was certain that a complete analysis of Holden's entire personnel recruiting program was in order and, regardless of the approach finally decided upon, it was paramount that the company have a continuous program to attract satisfactory people to the sales organization.

*Evaluate the Holden Electrical Supplies Company's recruiting program, suggesting whether or not the company should have continued its college recruiting of sales engineers.*


# III-6.  AMERICAN MACHINE AND FOUNDRY COMPANY:

## Industrial Manufacturer—
## Proposed Establishment of Formal Training Program


Early in 1966, R. R. Woodruff, vice-president for marketing of the Bowling Products Division of American Machine and Foundry Company, was faced with a decision regarding a proposed new training program for bowling products salespeople. American Machine and Foundry Company, an old established manufacturer of several lines of industrial products, had gotten into the bowling market in 1951 through the acquisition and manufacture of the first commercially practical automatic pinspotter. The introduction of the automatic pinspotter resulted in a revolution in the bowling industry. Pin boys had always presented a managerial headache for bowling center operators. Unskilled and low-paid, they were unreliable and inefficient employees with a high rate of absenteeism and job turnover. Elimination of pin boys through the use of automatic pinspotters solved an enormous managerial problem and made it possible for bowling center management to expand the size of the typical establishment and devote more time to improving customer service.

During the period from 1951 to 1960, the bowling industry increased enormously in size, and bowling became a major American participation sport. By 1961 the expansion of the new centers reached a peak, and although expansion continued, it was at a much slower rate. As the bowling industry developed and changed, the role of AMF in the industry also grew and changed. AMF gradually broadened its bowling product line to include bowling lanes, seating and other bowling center furnishings, and a complete line of balls, pins, and other items of equipment for the bowler.

The only major competitor in the industry, the Brunswick Corporation, was three years behind AMF in getting an automatic pinspotter on the market; this delay allowed AMF to capture about half the market. As the market for new bowling installations moved toward saturation in 1960, and sales of basic equipment dropped to a somewhat lower level, competition became increasingly aggressive. Even so, in 1965 bowling products generated about one third of the company's $400 million annual sales and more then half the $20 million earnings.

Until 1966, bowling division products had been sold by two groups of sales personnel. Equipment, including pinsetters, bowling lanes, and furniture, was sold by bowling equipment salespeople. These people spent part of their time seeking new sources of capital that could be sold on the profitability of building new bowling centers, but they also called regularly on existing lanes to sell equipment for modernization. Supplies, including pins, balls, bowling shoes, lane finishes, etc., were sold by supply sales personnel who called on bowling centers. Both groups of sales personnel operated out of district sales offices under the direction of district managers. In turn, the fifteen district managers reported to five regional sales managers. Early in 1966, the two sales forces were reorganized into a single sales force of 100, with all salespeople responsible for selling both equipment and supplies.

At the time of the reorganization, it became necessary to provide a program of retraining for the new combination salespeople. Many of the former equipment salespeople had started as supply salespeople, so they needed only a brief review of the current supply line. Most of the ex-supply salespeople, however, were almost completely unfamiliar with the equipment line. Many items of equipment were complex, and their sale or lease required extensive negotiation. For these reasons it would not be easy for the salespeople to train themselves on the new line.

G. Lindsay Crump, vice-president of marketing development, arranged for the development of a two-week retraining program for all sales personnel. This was scheduled in several sessions at the training center in Fort Worth, Texas. This well-equipped training center had originally been established to provide training in bowling center operation for owners and managers of centers. It was located in the same building with a company-owned bowling center, which provided a laboratory for the training program.

Crump suggested to Woodruff that it was time, now, to develop a formal training program for new sales personnel. AMF had never provided formal training for newly hired people. When the company first moved into the bowling business, there was no time to develop salespeople; capable people, experienced ones when available, were hired and started almost immediately on the job. Informal training was provided by sales executives and other more experienced sales staff. By 1966, the sales force had grown so large that normal turnover required the annual indoctrination of enough new salespeople to jority of the time was spent in product training. An outline of the training program is presented in Exhibit 1.

New sales staff were selected in the spring from the graduating classes of colleges and universities. Although these people reported to work as early as June or July, they did not begin their formal training in Syracuse until late September. Normally, there were from six to ten new persons enrolled at each annual training session. All instruction was carried on in a specially designed classroom, the walls of which were covered with displays of Crouse-Hinds products. A series of six films on sales techniques was shown, and Aspley's nine books on *Strategy in Selling* were used to augment regular classroom instruction. Methods of instruction involved use of the role-playing technique and round-table discussions. Mixed in with the formal training were several planned social events, which provided a change of pace and allowed the new personnel to become better acquainted with each other and with company officials.

Upon completion of formal training, new sales staff were given a regular field assignment. Although there were no written job descriptions, the district manager described the new person's duties to him or her and provided a list of customers and prospects. Full orientation on district procedures was completed before the new salesperson was permitted to make sales calls. The district manager continued to provide supervision and assistance as required.

A one-week refresher course for all sales personnel and district managers was held once every two years at the home office. A session was held in April for the district managers and their assistants; two or more sessions for salespeople were held in June or July, with thirty persons attending each course. During these sessions one day was

EXHIBIT 1
Outline of the Six-Week Training Program

1. General policies and introduction to Crouse-Hinds
   a. Organization
   b. Plant tours
   c. Introduction to home-office personnel
   d. Luncheons
2. Condulet course
   a. Introduction to conduit and Condulet fittings
   b. Applications of Crouse-Hinds Condulets
   c. Sales training
3. Traffic-signals course
   a. Traffic problems and control
   b. Product indoctrination and training
   c. Sales training
4. Airport lighting course
   a. Airport lighting and lighting equipment
   b. Lighting problems
   c. Product knowledge and applications
   d. Sales training
5. Illumination course
   a. Illumination problems and products
   b. Product applications
   c. Sales training
6. Summary and examinations

spent on each of the four product lines to provide a general refresher and to bring the personnel up to date on product changes. The remaining two days were spent in emphasizing the importance of customer service and methods of providing it.

Every year, between the refresher courses, the sales manager and his assistants visited the various districts to provide field training on new products and services. These visits also gave management an opportunity to evaluate district operations. By means of weekly sales bulletins and "special product" letters, salespeople were kept informed on trends in the industry and new product developments.

*Evaluate the Crouse-Hinds sales-training program.*

*Suggest changes in the training program that might have been used to increase the effectiveness of distributors' sales personnel.*

# III-8.  HOLMES BUSINESS FORMS COMPANY:
## Distributor of Office Supplies—
## Centralized vs. Decentralized Training

Holmes Business Forms Company distributed an extensive line of business-office products such as various types and grades of papers, envelopes, forms, ribbons, pens, pencils, tapes, staplers, and numerous other products, including small office machinery such as transcribers, paper collators, and electronic stencil makers. Holmes products were sold to retail stores and business offices throughout the country by 150 salespersons operating out of thirty district sales offices. Although the sales training program had been considered generally effective, it had been many years since it had been evaluated.

The prospect of hiring about ten additional sales personnel to keep up with increasing sales volume led Holmes' general sales manager to suggest that this was an appropriate time to appraise the training program. Any changes indicated probably could be implemented in time for training the new recruits. Specifically, he wanted to determine whether Holmes should continue with decentralized sales training or switch to centralized sales training.

New sales staff received a twelve-week sales-training course at the Holmes district sales offices where they were employed. This training was under the direction of the district manager. The first six weeks were devoted to intensive training covering company history, organization, operations and policies, the salesperson's job, sales techniques and methods of making sales presentations including answering objections and demonstrating the product and, finally, personal development. Among the sales training techniques used were lectures, discussions, and role-playing sessions. Examinations were given at the end of each two weeks of training.

The last six weeks of the training program were spent in the field. Arrangements were made for the trainee to spend the six weeks with at least two retailers so that he or she might gain firsthand knowledge of the problems involved in retailing business-office products. The trainee worked as both a salesperson and a buyer at the retail level. Upon completion of the trainee's work in each store, the retailer forwarded to the district sales

EXHIBIT 1

| FROM | J. L. Chambers | DATE | December 18 |
|------|----------------|------|-------------|
| TO | S. H. Young | SUBJECT | Proposal: New and Senior |
| | | | District Manager Training |

*PROPOSAL: New and Senior District Manager Training*

   **I. Objective.** The implementation of this program will minimize the maturation time of the early appointed District Manager and maximize the managerial capabilities of Senior District Managers.

  **II. Procedure**

   A.  *Field Contact.* Rather than a formal introductory meeting, the District Manager will meet his personnel through scheduling himself into their respective territories. Since this contact will be made prior to a review of personnel records or Regional Manager counseling on this subject, the new District Manager will not have preconceived opinions of his sales-force's capabilities. The resultant atmosphere will be conducive to open, candid discussion allowing both parties to meet on common ground.

   B.  *Orientation with Regional Manager.* After completing the above step, a thorough personnel discussion will also be reviewed at this time. Selected confrontations will then be shown the new District Manager. Because he will view his knowledge inadequate to handle the situations depicted, he will be motivated to search out the necessary information. Based on his recognition of those areas that require primary effort, the District Manager will outline a course of study with the Regional Manager which will be encompassed by the seven categories enumerated below. Case histories from former seminars and tape-recorded discussions of those topics listed below the categories mentioned will provide a reservoir of applicable information.

     1.  Office Organization—Procedures
         a.  Value of basic organization
         b.  Preparation for field contact
         c.  Report evaluation
     2.  Field Supervision
         a.  Training new personnel
         b.  The hospital salesperson—hospital penetration
         c.  Personnel evaluation techniques
         d.  Capturing government business
         e.  Drug and wholesale working
         f.  The pediatric salesperson
     3.  Personnel Improvement
         a.  Understanding the salesperson—application of drive patterns and motivational interviews
         b.  Motivation of senior salespeople
         c.  Counseling techniques
     4.  District Progress
         a.  Gathering distribution data—territory construction procedures—pool allocations
     5.  Reporting
         a.  Written communication techniques
         b.  Field contact report construction
     6.  Personnel Selection
         a.  Applicant screening—sources of candidates—interviewing the applicant

7. Special Duties
   a. Organization of district meetings

The Regional Manager orientation session will require approximately two weeks. Upon completion, the Regional Manager will contact other District Managers of the region and arrange for a one-day introductory visit, with each manager, for the new District Manager.

C. *Personnel Central*

1. *New District Manager.* The new District Manager will participate in a two-week training period in Trenton. During his stay, he will occupy the District Office, which has been established at Personnel Central. Since this office has been organized to be representative of a typical district office, he will have an opportunity to become acquainted with systems and procedures applicable to his new position. Upon entering training, the District Manager will be requested to bring personnel files relative to his sales staff. These records will be valuable in conducting routine district business while in training, as well as providing search material for confrontation assignments. Training will proceed in accordance with the steps enumerated below.

   a. *Video Confrontations.* Two video confrontations will be completed on primary district problems. Through telephone contact with the Regional Manager, the District Manager counselor will explore specifics required for role-play setting On completion, the counselor will suggest search of similar case histories, confrontation, and a review of personnel records involved before rescheduling further tryouts.

   b. *Sensitivity Training.* The District Manager will participate in sensitivity training through being assigned two salespeople upon their entering the course. He will occupy the third chair, counsel the salespeople assigned, and, in turn, discuss his progress with the District Manager counselor.

   c. *Recruiting, Screening, Hiring.* The District Manager will be required to complete confrontations as well as select four candidates for hiring. Basis for selection of personnel will be discussed with District Manager counselor.

   d. Time remaining, the District Manager will complete selected confrontations as suggested by the Regional Manager during the phone call previously mentioned, or through selection by the District Manager counselor.

   e. The District Manager will complete the confrontations mentioned in (a) above and accept as his Back Home Commitment the completion of these confrontations with the personnel involved.

2. *Senior District Manager.* The senior District Manager will complete steps (a), (b), (d), and (e) as listed under New District Manager training. The exception will be that he need only bring those records pertaining to the personnel that form the basis for confrontations listed under (a). Since emphasis will be devoted to primary areas of weakness, the District Manager counselor should thoroughly discuss these with the Regional Manager prior to commencement of training. Concentration in these areas can then be implemented as outlined in (d). Senior District Manager training should require one week.

**III. Materials Required.** As stated in IIB., Confrontation Capsules, selected case histories from former seminars, and the seventeen taped topics listed under subheadings 1-7 will require duplication and distribution to the Regional Managers. As well, each Regional Manager will require one Fairchild projector. The majority of our Regional Managers currently have facilities to implement Regional Personnel; those that do not will be required to secure adequate additional office space.

**IV. Implementation.** Implementation of this program depends upon several factors. First, a District Manager counselor must be appointed to fulfill this new responsibility in Personnel

*Shattuck:*    I don't see how I could use your shovel throughout the whole operation.

40    *Rennert:*    In the early stages you can use the clam shell or trench hoe for digging ditches and sluiceways. These can also be used for building up shoulders. The crane, which is 25 feet long, can be used for laying forms, putting out reinforcements of steel, and many other jobs of loading and unloading that must be done. When the concrete is ready to be poured, you can use the shovel boom and bucket for feeding

45                the batch bins and loading the trucks with gravel.

*Shattuck:*    That does sound practical, but I didn't know you could use a trench hoe or a crane with your shovel.

*Rennert:*    Oh, I'm sorry! I should have made that clear. The clam shell and trench hoe can be mounted on the shovel the same as a shovel boom and bucket can. There is also a

50                25-foot crane boom that can be mounted the same way, as you can see by these photos.

*Shattuck:*    How long does it take to make a changeover to any one of these attachments?

*Rennert:*    It takes approximately two hours. However, the job is usually done at night when the machine is not in use.

55   *Shattuck:*    That sounds good, Mr. Rennert. Now, I have a lot of bridge building in my work. Will your machine be of any use on these projects?

*Rennert:*    Absolutely! You can use the clam shell or the trench hoe for the digging, and the crane boom for laying the steel girders. Does that answer your question, Mr. Shattuck?

60   *Shattuck:*    Yes, it does. I have heard that your type of shovel has a lot of competition from other road-building equipment. Is that true?

*Rennert:*    Yes, there are a lot of specific machines that we compete with. However, ours can compete with almost all of them. It is all four machines in one—the clam shell, trench hoe, crane boom, and shovel boom and bucket. You can see that this is a

65                great saving in capital investment. You have one machine that does four different jobs.

*Shattuck:*    Well, that certainly sounds economical.

*Rennert:*    It is economical, Mr. Shattuck. The "Quick-Way" shovel is operated generally by one man who can also drive the truck from job to job. The shovel has positive

70                hydraulic controls and a wide-vision cab that gives the operator clear vision at all times. It has a 55-horsepower International engine that operates at low speeds. Therefore, your maintenance costs drop. It is full-revolving, making 7½ turns per minute. The shovel boom and bucket can dig to 3½ feet below ground level and can lift to a height of 11 feet above the ground for dumping. The trench hoe can dig

75                to a maximum depth of 15 feet below ground level. The total height of the machine is 10 to 12 feet, depending, of course, upon the type of truck on which it is mounted. This passes all the requirements for highway bridges and trestles. It is also classed as a power shovel and, therefore, does not require license plates in New York State. One of the outstanding features of our shovel is that it has no dead weight to

80                counterbalance the loads. By this, I mean that it is balanced right. Its weight is distributed proportionately throughout. This, of course, as you know, saves on repair costs and increases the utility of the machine.

*Shattuck:*    We've had a lot of trouble with our large shovels because of this factor of counterbalancing. I have looked over your specification sheet and have noticed that there is

85                a bronze bushing on the main spur gear. I would say that a roller bearing would be better because of the high speed at which your shovel operates.

*Rennert:*    Yes, you're right. The roller bearing would be faster, but this is the very reason for using a bronze bearing. When a ball bearing or roller bearing breaks down, there is

|      | | |
|------|----|---|
| 90 | | likely to be damage to the shaft and the racer. On the other hand, when a bronze bearing wears, there's no damage to the shaft, and the machine doesn't have to be stopped immediately. This, I think, is a definite advantage in that the shovel can be kept in operation until time is available to get a new bearing and to get it installed. I would also like to point out to you that all our hydraulic clutches are interchangeable. If any one of them breaks down it may quickly be substituted for by the clutch on the main boom lift, which has a mechanical stop and can temporarily be used in this way. You can see that this also saves on the number of parts that must be kept on hand to service the shovel. |

95

*Shattuck:* Do you have any figures on the actual operating costs of your shovels over a period of years?

100 *Rennert:* We have. We figured average cost per machine-year on 25 machines, a total of 130 machine-years. It was $325 repair and maintenance costs. Mr. Oldine, of the Oldine Contracting Company, bought a "Quick-Way" shovel two years ago and has had excellent results on this score. His total service costs have been $125 a year.

*Shattuck:* From what I have seen and from what you have explained, I'm interested in your
105 shovel. Do you have the cost figures with you?

*Rennert:* I have them right here. The basic machine plus the shovel boom and bucket comes to $8,241. The clam shell is $1,393. The trench hoe, $1,350. And the crane boom, $569. The prices are F.O.B. your place of business.

*Shattuck:* Your cost figures seem rather high since they don't include the price of the truck
110 needed to mount the shovel.

*Rennert:* No, Mr. Shattuck, experience has shown that it is possible to amortize the cost of our shovel over a two-year period. This also brings up another point. Our shovel can be mounted on any type of five-ton truck. This is a distinct advantage over other truck-mounted shovels—they all require a specific type of truck on which to
115 mount the shovel equipment. I have noticed that you have a Mack truck out in the lot which would be suited for our shovel. I have already looked at it and measured it. It's just the one for mounting our shovel on. That is, of course, if you can spare it.

*Shattuck:* Why, yes, I do have a few extra trucks, and that one you are speaking about is
120 one of them.

*Rennert:* I believe you'll agree that this is an added saving for you, and the price I have quoted, including attachments with outriggers, is reasonable.

*Shattuck:* Yes, it does make it sound better, but let me look over those specifications again.... Yes, I see. Just what is the capacity of this shovel? You know I have a lot of heavy
125 work.

*Rennert:* Well, with outriggers, the capacity over end or over side is 13,000 pounds at 10 feet and drops to 8,000 pounds at 15 feet. There is a 15 percent safety factor built in which increases its capacity correspondingly. I believe these capacity ratings will handle any work that you will encounter.

130 *Shattuck:* That would seem plenty. What attachments do you suggest I use?

*Rennert:* I made a complete study of the attachments you will be using for this job. I would suggest the shovel boom and bucket, the crane, and the trench hoe or clam shell. The trench hoe would probably be more practical, but the final decision is up to you.

*Shattuck:* I think I agree with you. The trench hoe will handle my work. If I need it, you can
135 always get me a clam shell, can't you?

*Rennert:* Yes. I can have one for you within a few days' time. Now Mr. Shattuck, here's the contract. The basic machine, shovel boom and bucket, crane, and trench hoe total up to $10,160. This includes installation and mounting on your truck.

ads and displays over and over, year after year, and I'd like some new and different ideas on the operation of my silverware department.

*Melville:* It will be a pleasure, Mr. Crane, to be of assistance to such an alert businessman. First of all, here is a bridal and gift registry card. (Hands card to prospect.) It includes a space for name, address, married name and address, pattern name, and a complete list of all pieces of flatware, hollow ware, china, and crystal. This card also serves as a record of birthdays and anniversaries. You put down only those pieces purchased for the woman, and the record tells you which items are needed to complete her set. All that the customers need to know is the woman's name. You tell the customers the pattern, the items she has, and those she needs. A follow-up letter can be extremely successful if you send it to her family, reminding them of her birthday, anniversary, and so on. Here is a birthday follow-up letter and an anniversary letter. (Shows letter to prospect.) We have an engagement letter, which is an excellent way to build up your prospect list and to create goodwill. It should be mailed to all women whose engagements are announced in the local newspapers. And here is a friendly welcome letter to newcomers to the city who are prospects for your store. (Shows letter to prospect.)

*Crane:* I'd like a copy of each of the letters, and I think the silverware record cards are an excellent idea. If they're not overly expensive, I'd like to order a thousand.

*Melville:* They're only a cent a card, or $10 for one thousand. Would you like that many? (Gives letters to prospect and puts order pad on counter.)

*Crane:* By all means, they'll be very useful.

*Melville:* Here is another idea introduced by World-Wide Silver Company. (Pulls an ad out of briefcase and places it on the counter.) This is a most effective way to advertise. It is similar to the testimonial ads featuring movie stars and athletes, but this one has a photograph of one of your sterling customers, with a write-up about her and a picture of her pattern. The copy informs the public that she has selected her pattern at your store. Her friends then know where to buy her silver gifts. They also know where they can select their patterns—often with the hope that their pictures will get in future ads. Here are a few examples that some of my accounts have been using. (Shows additional examples.) If you like, you may keep these samples. (Hands samples to prospect.) They will give you an idea of the layout and copy of such an ad.

*Crane:* Now, that's a very good idea. I've never seen anything like it. I'm sure Mrs. Crane will want to use it in her ads right away.

*Melville:* I think it will be very attractive in the newspapers, and it should be an excellent way to keep your name in the public eye. We have a film in color, twenty minutes long, entitled "Beauty That Lives Forever," that you can borrow any time. It is a good movie to show at women's clubs, at high school sorority meetings, and at classes of home economics students. Perhaps Mrs. Crane can introduce the film and answer questions after it is shown to each group.

*Crane:* I'll mention it to her. If she is interested, I'll let you know.

*Melville:* Fine! Please give us a week's notice for delivery, if you decide to use it. (Looks at counter sign.) I see that you use a club payment plan. Here are a couple of well-planned combination sterling, china, and crystal club plan ads. You may keep them if you like. (Hands ads to prospect.)

*Crane:* Thanks. I will.

*Melville:* Now here are some very effective booklets by B. J. Valenti, part of a series entitled "How to Operate a Silverware Department." (Hands booklets to prospect.) One is on the policies and history of the World-Wide Silver Company; another is entitled "Planning Sales to Promote Silerware;" one is called "Displaying to Promote Silver," and one is a sales manual, "Modern Selling of Silverware." Those are my personal copies.

Unfortunately, these are all out of print. If you and your employees would like to read them, I'll be happy to lend them to you. I'll pick them up the next time I call.

115 *Crane:* Well, I doubt if I'll have time to read them, but I would like the rest of my people to look them over. I'll see that you get them back on your next trip.

*Melville:* Thank you. There is a very good graduation teaspoon promotion which you can probably use. I'll send you some literature on it in plenty of time for graduation. The female graduates of the local high schools are invited to select their patterns at your
120 store. You give them the first teaspoon in the pattern of their choice. This giveaway plan really helps you make a whale of a lot of sales. I suggest you give this careful consideration. It has been a real money-maker for many of our customers. With a good follow-up, I think it will bring in a lot of business.

*Crane:* It sounds interesting. I'll keep it in mind.

125 *Melville:* And now—last but not least—we have a truly wonderful plan, one that will establish your store permanently as Niagara's leading silverware dealer. It is a time-consuming, costly promotion, but it is one that will bring you immeasurable goodwill and future business. The plan I am referring to is a table-setting contest and exhibit. It is a contest in which you contact officers of all the local ladies' groups and clubs and
130 suggest that each group set a table at the show. The various clubs compete for cash prizes to be given for originality, beauty, and style. This showing takes place at a local auditorium or hotel ballroom. The public is invited to attend, and various door prizes are offered. You ask the sales representative of each of your sterling, china, and crystal lines to be present. They should be willing to cooperate and bring displays and
135 their samples. This will help decorate the room. These shows have been tremendously successful all over the country. When and if you are ready to plan one, just call on me to help you organize it. I helped run the contest by Thompson and Randolph. Here is the photograph; you can see what a large crowd there was at the exhibit. (Shows photograph to prospect.) Their trade has really gone up since that show. This booklet
140 will give you many of the details. (Hands booklet to prospect.) It also suggests that you write to some of the jewelers who have used the promotion for their advice and suggestions. Well, what do you think?

*Crane:* That's certainly an original idea. Right now I don't think I want to plan anything that expensive. But perhaps after Christmas, when business is slow, I can plan a
145 table-setting contest.

*Melville:* Surely. Just call on all your sales representatives for assistance. I know they'll all be glad to help make it the success it should be. Now, about that opening order?

*Crane:* I don't know exactly what I want. What do you recommend?

*Melville:* If it's O.K. with you, I'll write my own order. It will be a small one. I'm more
150 interested in repeat business than I am in loading you up with a large opening order. I can bring in a copy of the order I write the first thing tomorrow morning, and you can confirm it then. (Melville looks at clock on store wall.) I see it's closing time, and I don't want to take any more of your time today. Besides I want to decide carefully on the patterns that should be the best for you. I'll send you only sample place settings
155 in the other patterns. How do you feel about that?

*Crane:* That will be fine. I'll be seeing you in the morning, any time after 9:30.

*Melville:* Thank you very much, Mr. Crane. (Shakes hands.) It's been a pleasure talking to you, and I know you will always be pleased that you took on the World-Wide Sterling line. Goodbye, see you in the morning.

*Comment on the tactics used by Melville to overcome what appeared to be initial antagonism on the part of Crane.*

often so completely sold on the proposal service by this time that the contact assumed the greater share of the responsibility for the fifth step, that of selling top management. If the contact was not completely sold on the Hopkins service, it was virtually impossible to sell top management. Therefore, the Hopkins salesperson was particularly concerned with providing a total package that was attractive to the contact and would make him or her look good in the eyes of his or her bosses when he or she presented it to them as a cost- and time-saving service.

Completing the five-step process of selling the Hopkins, service took, on the average, one year; and often, a particular sales campaign ran into several years.

*Evaluate the sales methods used by Hopkins sales personnel. Do you agree that the entire sales process was too slow?*

# III-13.   UNITED CHEMICALS CORPORATION:
## Manufacturer of Packaging—Training in Selling

Frank Lambert, Product Manager for the Container Division of United Chemicals Corp., had just received a report from the company's general sales manager, outlining numerous complaints about the portion of the sales training program directed by Lambert. The report was the result of evaluations of sales training made by United sales personnel during the past two years.

United Chemicals Corporation was a major division of a leading petroleum com- pany. United Chemicals was organized into several departments, one of which was the Packaging Department, which, in turn, was divided into three divisions—Container Division, Food Service Division, and Film Division. The container product line con- sisted of package lids, reclosures, and containers for a variety of food and nonfood products. The food service product line consisted of paper cups, plates, and many other products used by institutions serving food. The film product line was made up of flexible plastic packaging such as polypropylene film for use in packaging food products. Unlike the food service and film product lines, which were sold "off the shelf," each product in the container product line was custom-made to fit the specific requirements of each individual packager's product. This made the container product line more difficult to sell.

United Chemicals was started six years ago as part of a diversification program by the parent oil company. Its products were distributed by a sales force of twenty- seven to users throughout the United States. The sales personnel were paid on a straight-salary basis and carried all three products in the packaging line.

The Packaging Department's sales training took place at the division offices in Portland, Oregon (Container Division), Minneapolis (Food Service Division), and Albany, New York (Film Division).

Since all salespeople carried the entire product line, management believed that each product manager should be responsible for conducting sales training in his or her particular product. Therefore, to undergo sales training, new sales staff had to travel to each separate location; however, preparations were being made to centralize the product managers of the three divisions at United's headquarters in Chicago, thereby eliminating this travel. It was originally believed that the product managers would be most effective at the production plant site for their products. However, difficulties in communications and coordination relating to a number of matters, including sales training, made it evident that a change was necessary.

In the sales-evaluation reports, the Container Division sales training, conducted by Lambert, was ranked a distant third in quality and effectiveness. The majority of the complaints were about the lack of time spent on sales techniques, during the two weeks of training in Portland. The entire time was spent on company knowledge and policies, container product knowledge, manufacturing aspects, packaging equipment employed by end users of containers, and competition. The evaluations indicated a good job by sales trainers in these areas.

Lambert believed that the unique selling circumstances surrounding containers made it impossible to develop "standard" sales techniques for that product. Since each product had to be specially designed and could not be sold "off the shelf" as the other packaging products, he believed that the sales personnel were better off developing their own sales techniques and adapting them to individual situations. For example, Lambert suggested, the container and lid for one brand of margarine was likely to be quite different from another brand of margarine because, among other reasons, the container and lid had to be made compatible with the individual margarine producer-packager's specific packaging machinery and other packaging line considerations. So, he contended, a number of factors combined to make it both impossible and useless to emphasize sales techniques in the sales-training program for containers. He felt that the time was better spent instructing new salespersons in the technical aspects of the endless variety of end-user packaging equipment, product knowledge, competition, and the like.

The general sales manager, located in Chicago, was disturbed about the salespeople's evaluation reports. He was unaware that no attention was being devoted to the techniques of selling containers. He agreed with Lambert about the importance of company policy, the product, packaging equipment, manufacturing aspects, and competition. However, he argued that instruction in sales techniques should form an essential part of the sales-training program. He further contended that a sales-training program that did not emphasize sales techniques was, in effect, not a sales-training program at all. Therefore, the general sales manager requested from the product manager a report showing (1) how the sales-techniques phase would fit in with the overall sales-training program for containers, and (2) the specific subject matter to be treated in the sales-techniques section of the training program.

*Evaluate Lambert's arguments opposing the inclusion of sales techniques in the United Chemicals Corp. sales-training program for containers. Describe in detail what should have appeared in the product manager's report to the general sales manager with reference to the place of sales techniques in the overall sales-training program and the specific subject matter to cover in the instruction in sales techniques.*

8. The opinion of other departments was low. Most of the sales staff felt that other department heads were uncooperative, failing to meet their requests and needs promptly.

9. Salespeople were not sold on company products. More than half saw no more customer benefits than those offered by the competition.

Results were also broken down into regions to further help management pinpoint the trouble areas and direct corrective action with the greatest efficiency. Another breakdown compared the opinions of salespeople with those of the field management staff. In presenting the report, the survey company noted that honest answers may not reflect reality. A salesperson who thinks his or her company pays lower salaries will act in certain ways; it doesn't matter what the truth of the matter is—his or her attitude is based on what he or she thinks.

One week after the survey results were in, Bruce held a meeting with the four division sales vice-presidents and the corporate industrial relations manager to determine what action might be indicated.

*What remedial action should have been taken as a result of the survey finding?*
*How could the survey results be used to improve personnel motivation?*

# III-15.  HAMMACHER COMPANY:
## Manufacturer—Use of Sales Incentives

Wallace Bain, sales manager of the Hammacher Company, was considering whether or not to make some basic changes in the company's annual end-of-the-year travel-incentive campaign. Many companies made use of travel incentives to motivate their sales personnel to extra effort; the Hammacher Company had been using this kind of incentive for almost twenty-five years. Over the years, the method of operation had been polished and perfected so that salespeople were motivated to greater and greater effort. Sales records were broken every year, and sales last year had been 12 percent better than the year before.

The main incentive for salespeople who met their quotas was an expense-paid "holiday" at a glamorous resort. The previous year's meeting had been at the Hotel Fontainebleau in Miami Beach, Florida in April. Although theoretically every salesperson had the opportunity to attend this convention, last year only 275 of the 500-person sales force had earned an invitation. Hammacher also awarded prize points to all sales-personnel in accordance with their sales records. These were subsequently redeemable for merchandise selected from a colorfully illustrated prize catalog. Despite the merchandise prizes, it was the opinion of Norton Dowdy, sales vice-president, that nothing made the sales staff sell quite so well as the chance at that free four-day vacation. He described it as a grand holiday, more in the nature of a reward than anything else. At the Florida convention the year before, business meetings had been scheduled on only two mornings, a total of six hours. These sessions were conducted primarily by home-office executives and were of an inspirational nature. The remainder of the time was set aside for recreation and pleasure. Among the activities available were boating and fishing, swimming, golf, sightseeing, entertainment, and fine dining.

The Hammacher sales-incentive program operated in the following manner. The campaign was scheduled from October 1 through December. Each salesperson was given a compaign quota derived by considering his or her sales volume during the year, his or her years of experience, and his or her market potential during the contest period. The sales staff was then divided into five groups with approximately equal quotas, to ensure that each person competed with others whose personal quotas were comparable. Branch managers formed a sixth group. All salespeople who sold their quota received invitations to the convention.

A still stronger incentive was provided by the opportunity to earn membership in the Hammacher sales leadership club, a very exclusive honor organization. To become members of the leadership club, salespeople had to sell a specified volume above their contest quotas, or a specified volume of business for the entire year. The highest honor of all, designation as an officer and board member of the leadership club, was given to the salespeople with the highest percentage of sales above their campaign quotas. These officers received an additional award—eligibility to attend a special two-day meeting just before the regular convention. Branch managers became eligible for the same honor by achieving their branch quotas during the campaign.

Wallace Bain, who was responsible for the incentive campaign, began the promotional program in August each year. The goal was to gradually build suspense and interest through the use of a barrage of notes and letters. He started by sending branch managers an August reminder to make preliminary preparations for the campaign. This was followed by detailed campaign instructions in September. Then, in late September, he provided a pep talk for managers to use for their group kickoff meetings with the sales personnel on October 1.

In July, when Bain met with Norton Dowdy to plan the campaign for the coming fall, he asked about the possibility of considering modifications in the plan. He pointed out that in any contest the average sales team is divided into three parts: one third who say confidently that they will win, and usually do; one third who think they can, and try hard to do so; and one third who give up before the start because they are sure they cannot win. The Hammacher Company had always tried to make the incentive good enough to motivate the top third to sell even more, to increase the number of winners in the second group, and to convince members of the third group that they at least have a chance to win if they try. Nevertheless, Bain believed that the annual campaigns were not really getting a satisfactory increase in effort upon the part of the third group.

In addition, Bain wondered whether the company was getting value for the money spent on its incentive campaigns. Did the chance to attend a convention where company business was discussed really motivate anyone, or were the salespeople actually working harder because of the honor and prestige attached to being invited? Would the same amount of money invested in travel or merchandise incentives that could be selected by the winners (and that allowed the salespeople's spouses to participate in the reward) provide stronger motivation? Should the prizes or rewards be forthcoming sooner than four months after the end of the campaign? Dowdy was of the opinion that they shouldn't rock the boat. Past campaigns had continued to increase sales performance.

*What changes, if any, do you think should be made in the Hammacher Company's annual sales-incentive campaign?*

*What action should have been taken to keep the sales personnel abreast of new product developments and applications?*

## III-17.  NATIONAL BISCUIT COMPANY:
## Manufacturer of Biscuits—
## Stimulation of Sales Personnel

The National Biscuit Company, incorporated in 1898, resulted from the merging of the American Biscuit and Manufacturing Company, New York Biscuit Company, United States Baking Company, and National Baking Company. Through the reinvestment of undistributed earnings, the acquisition of other companies (fifty-three mergers in the period 1898 to 1957), and the outright purchase of small firms, the company grew steadily. Over 250 food items were produced, chiefly bakery goods including biscuits, crackers, cake mixes, cereals, pretzels, pet food, and ice cream cones. These products were shipped from twenty-two bakeries for distribution by 248 sales branches. The National Biscuit Company accounted for approximately 40 percent of total industry sales; the next two largest companies accounted for approximately 25 percent of the total market. The company had used sales contests for many years, and it was decided to use shares of company common stock as contest prizes.

Previously, Nabisco had used a merchandise incentive plan for purposes of stimulating sales personnel. Salespersons were assigned quotas on certain products and awarded points for increases over each quota. The contest rules during this period were substantially as shown in Exhibit 1. The products used for these contests were known as "franchised varieties" and included such high-volume cracker varieties as Ritz and Premium and such cookie varieties as Fig Newtons, Oreo Creme Sandwiches, and Chocolate Chip Cookies. At the close of the period of special promotion, which usually lasted two months, salespeople were awarded certificates showing the actual number of points accumulated during the contest period. Sales personnel then applied their earned points toward merchandise prizes listed in catalogs issued by Cappel, MacDonald Company of Dayton, Ohio. The retail value of the available prizes ranged from a few dollars to several hundred dollars. Contest quotas were established that were equivalent to sales in the corresponding months of previous years. For instance, the contest on Oreo Creme Sandwich Cookies held during July and August was based upon total sales of this item during July and August of the previous year. Thus, the previous year's sales figures served as quotas for the sales staff during the current year's contest period. Since sales personnel worked in well-defined sales territories, this method of obtaining contest quotas was considered equitable.

In January of each year, in the old contest, Premium Crackers were the contest item; and during each successive year the average sales increase in each sales territory was considerable. The January Premium contest showed an average territorial sales increase of approximately 200 percent over January a year earlier. Since no significant price increases had been made during this period, the great increase in sales was attributed almost exlusively to the added incentive provided by the sales contest.

---

Important: Staple or paste this sheet on the inside front cover of your
present *Let's Cook Up Sales* Contest Prize Catalog.

## WIN A BIGGER AND BETTER PRIZE IN
## NABISCO'S OREO AND SWISS CREME SANDWICH
*Let's Cook Up Sales* Contest!
May-June 19--

Rules:

1.  This contest is open to all regular NABISCO Salespeople, Special Sales Personnel, Sales Representatives, Special Representatives, Branch Managers, Assistant Divisional Sales Managers, and Divisional Sales Managers.

2.  This Contest begins with deliveries on May 2, 19--, and ends with the deliveries of June 30, 19--.

3.  This contest is based only on the sales of #1 Cartons, Large and Small Cello Bags of OREO CREME SANDWICHES, and on Large and Small Cello Bags of SWISS CREME SANDWICHES.

4.  The basis of the contest for Salespeople is the total net dollar sales of the varieties in Salespeople's districts. The basis for supervisory personnel is the average sales per Salesperson in the spheres of influence assigned to them.

5.  Every contestant will be a winner, provided he or she shows a net dollar increase in sales of the contest varieties during the period of the contest.

6.  The base period for OREO CREME SANDWICHES will be May-June of last year. The base period for SWISS CREME SANDWICHES will be October-November of last year. Sales of both varieties will be combined in determining dollar and percent of dollar increases when figuring points earned.

7.  *11 points* will be awarded *for each dollar ($1.00) increase* and *38 points* will be awarded *for each percent of dollar increase* during the contest period over the base period sales.

8.  Points will be redeemable for the prizes listed in the prize catalog at the stated point value.

9.  Details concerning points earned and the correct procedure for ordering prizes will be forwarded in a special circular.

Sales Department, Marketing Division

---

The Nabisco sales-compensation plan was similar to that of other companies in the industry. Salespeople were paid a monthly salary, plus a 4 percent commission on sales over a given base. This base, which was set at the time a salesperson assumed responsibility for a specific sales territory, was never altered during the salesperson's assignment to that territory. Thus, Nabisco sales personnel were not penalized in future years for sales increases experienced in prior years.

Company-owned automobiles were supplied to all sales personnel who desired them. Salespeople desiring to use their own automobiles were permitted to do so and were paid a substantial monthly depreciation allowance. Regardless of whether salesperson's used company vehicles or their own automobiles, they were reimbursed for gasoline, oil, and other operating expenses. If salespeople desired to use company cars for personal use, a fixed amount was charged against their salaries each month.

## III-18.  UNIVERSAL AUTOMOTIVE, INC.:

## Manufacturer of Automotive Parts and Accessories—
## Motivating Sales Personnel with a Sales Contest

Joseph Mahoney, general sales manager of Universal Automotive, Inc., Chicago, recommended that the company conduct a sales contest to help improve a declining sales performance. This was his suggested response to first-quarter results that saw sales fall substantially below the established quota. Mahoney believed that a sales contest would, among other things, provide the incentive necessary to get sales up to or beyond territorial quotas.

Universal manufactured and distributed a complete line of automotive parts and accessories. Its sales force of sixty persons operated out of nine branch offices located throughout the United States. The sales-force's compensation plan consisted of a base salary and a bonus. The bonus was based upon the territorial quota, which was set by the general sales manager in consultation with the respective branch sales managers.

Mahoney proposed a sales contest that he believed would motivate the salespeople to achieve their quotas. He also felt that the salespeople's spouses should be involved in the sales contest. The proposed sales contest would run thirteen weeks and each of the sixty salespersons would be assigned a weekly sales volume quota for his or her territory, as determined by the general sales manager and the district manager. In addition, each of the nine sales districts would have a district sales-volume quota for purposes of competing with other districts.

Each week, a $100 cash bonus would be given to the sales personnel exceeding their quota by the greatest percentage, although Mahoney had seriously considered using total sales volume instead of a percentage. Also, each salesperson achieving quota for the thirteen-week period would earn a $200 bonus. The person exceeding the thirteen-week quota by the greatest percentage would receive an additional bonus of $200, with $150, $100, and $50 bonuses for salespeople in second, third, and fourth places, respectively.

Spouses of the salespeople would also participate in the sales contest proposed by Mahoney. For each $50 worth of bonus earned by a salesperson exceeding his or her weekly or quarterly bonus, the salesperson's spouse would receive five tickets or chances to win a merchandise prize.

All quota-making salespeople and their spouses would be invited to a three-day convention at the company's Chicago headquarters. The three days would be a mixture of business and pleasure, culminated by a gala dinner dance and drawing for the merchandise prize at the close of the convention.

In the competition among the nine sales districts, the district exceeding its quota by the greatest percentage would receive a $400 prize, with the money to be divided among that district's salespersons. Second, third, and fourth places for the districts would be worth $300, $200, and $100, respectively.

When Mahoney formally proposed his plan for a sales contest, several criticisms were voiced. Objections centered around the disappointments and frustrations of those people who did not win, the overaggressiveness that might result from ambitious salespeople striving to win at all costs, the disruption of normal activities caused by the convention, and the temporary nature of the stimulation provided by a sales contest. Several executives opposed the sales contest, arguing that the negative aspects outweighed the possible benefits.

Mahoney countered that a sales contest would help correct a poor sales performance, it would appeal to the sales-force's competitive spirit, it would enable salespeople to earn some recognition, and it would raise the morale of the entire sales force.

In spite of this apparent lack of agreement, Mahoney scheduled a meeting of his staff of eight people to discuss the advisability of conducting a sales contest.

*Should Universal Automotive, Inc., have held a sales contest to motivate its sales personnel to better sales performance? Why or why not?*

# III-19.  BRISTOL LABORATORIES:

## Pharmaceutical Company—Sales Contests

Bristol Laboratories, a division of Bristol-Myers, was one of the world's largest manufacturers of antibiotics and pharmaceuticals. It had 725 salespeople deployed throughout the United States. With a sales organization of this magnitude, Bristol faced managerial problems in motivation and in balancing the selling emphasis given its product lines. Sales-force management used sales contests to motivate and direct the sales staff. These ran continuously each month throughout the year.

Bristol's major brands included Tetrex, Saluron, Syncillin, Kantrax, Naldecon, Polycillin, Staphcillin, Prostaphlin, and Salutensin. Hospitals and drug wholesalers purchased direct from the company. Ultimate consumers bought Bristol's products from retail druggists on doctors' prescriptions.

Bristol's sales force was organized into ten regions containing sixty-five sales districts. Sales personnel were distributed within districts according to the sizes of individual territories and relative sales potentials. Their duties included calling on doctors, hospitals, and drug wholesalers, and making service calls on retail drugstores. Each salesperson visited an average of 120 doctors, ten hospitals, and two wholesalers per month.

The sales-force compensation plan consisted of a relatively small salary plus a relatively generous 5 percent commission on territorial sales volume. K. J. Ryan, sales manager, believed that his salespeople were among the highest paid in the drug field. They averaged over $13,000, the top man earning over $39,000.

Through its sales contests, Bristol sought to direct salespersons toward emphasizing all products in the line instead of only the high-commission, easy-to-sell items. While contests ran continuously, different products received emphasis each month. Ryan thought money to be less important as an incentive than merchandise and travel awards, especially to a highly paid sales force. Salespersons competed against predetermined territorial sales goals; management believed that using other bases for contests would have caused morale problems, as salespeople worked different territories and had grocery stores (independent supermarkets, drive-ins, and "mom and pop" stores), service stations, cafes and restaurants, drug and variety stores, and taverns.

The four-state area covered by Bravos was broken into eight regional divisions. Each of these divisions included from three to five warehouses, the number depending on the geographic size and sales potential of the division. Selling responsibility in each region was assigned to a regional sales manager who established selling and purchasing policies for the warehouse managers, hired and trained the sales personnel for each wholesale outlet, handled customer relations and complaints, and worked with manufacturers' representatives. For a number of years, these regional managers had been paid on a combination basis, with a base salary of $600 per month, plus a commission. Each region was expected to contribute a monthly profit of $2,200, and each manager received as a commission 25 percent of profits in excess of this amount for his or her region.

Rushmore had become dissatisfied with the method of compensation for regional managers because of the great disparity in income that it produced among these sales managers. Performance by the individual warehouses in different regions varied widely, affecting commissions accordingly. For example, one sales manager in the Roswell-Albuquerque area earned more than $600 per month in commissions, whereas the sales manager in the Midland-Odessa area rarely received a commission. Yet, this compensation disparity did not appear to result primarily from a difference in effort expended. In the opinion of Rushmore, the sales manager in the Midland-Odessa area worked just as hard as the one in Roswell-Albuquerque. He believed that the difference could be explained mostly in terms of the difference in sales potential and competitive activity in the two areas.

Because of the income disparity just described, and the dissatisfaction of the lower-paid managers, Rushmore came to the conclusion that the compensation plan should be changed. In an April 15 meeting with Henry Bravos, president of the company, he proposed a new compensation plan to become effective May 1. The new plan provided for a base salary of $750 per month, plus a bonus of 1 percent of total company net profit for all managers. He pointed out that all sales managers were essential to the financial well-being of the company, and in this way they would be rewarded equally. At the same time, the total dollar amount of compensation paid to sales managers would remain approximately the same. Bravos was very doubtful about the new plan. He could see that the lower-paid managers whose income would be raised would be pleased; but he was just as certain that the highest-paid persons would strongly resent any reduction in income. He also believed that salespeople and their bosses can be best motivated by relating their incomes directly to sales productivity.

*Which of these compensation plans would be more suitable for the Bravos Company? Would some other plan or modification of these plans provide a better alternative?*

## III-21.  ARCHER STATIONERS:

### Office-Supply Company—
### Sales-Compensation Problems

John Archer, owner of Archer Stationers, was troubled about the high rate of turnover among his outside sales personnel; he wondered if the compensation system for salespeople might be a contributing factor. Archer Stationers was started by John Archer in 1948 as a small stationery store in Oklahoma City, Oklahoma. The business had expanded continuously, adding lines such as office supplies and equipment. It grew from a small store to the largest office-supply company in central Oklahoma. By 1973 the company's product lines included office supplies, stationery, office machines and equipment, desks, files, engineering supplies, and accounting systems. The engineering supplies and the accounting-systems lines were the newest. John Archer added these lines because he felt there was a great potential for both in his market. An outside salesperson sold the engineering line by calling on various engineering firms in the market served by Archer. The accounting systems, ranging upward in price from $70, were sold similarly through an outside salesperson.

Archer employed a total of twenty-five people. Of these, four were outside sales-people who called on the various businesses in the area. The outside sales territories were divided according to product line. Al Caines, the company's number one person on the sales staff, and Cecil Grey sold exclusively items pertaining to the office. Jack Rubin was the engineering salesperson, and Otto Olsen sold the accounting systems. Al and Cecil had been with the company for many years, but Otto and Jack had been hired within the previous six months to replace two outside salespeople who had quit. With the exception of Al and Cecil, the company had experienced a very high turnover rate in its outside sales force. The rate was particularly high with new sales-people. Archer had found that if a salesperson remained for as much as a year, the chances were good that he might stay on the job several years.

The outside sales force was paid on a commission basis, with a $400 monthly drawing account. Thus, if in one month a salesperson did not earn commissions in the amount of $400, he would be paid that amount anyway. However, when a salesperson failed to earn $400 in any month, he was obligated to pay back the difference be-tween the amount earned and the amount paid; this was subtracted from earnings in excess of $400 in succeeding months.

The compensation system was initiated because Archer felt that commissions were the best way to get a person to put forth real effort. He thought the drawing account was good since it provided a steady salary in bad months yet kept the salesperson from depending completely on this guarantee by requiring repayment of such advances from future earnings. In his opinion, the commissions paid were good (10 percent of gross profit), and he felt that anyone who would work hard and stick with the company for several years could earn at least twice the drawing account. As examples, Archer pointed out the performances of the two senior salespeople. Al, who had worked with the company for twelve years, was making about $12,000 yearly. Cecil, who had been with the company for eight years, was still increasing his sales and, hence, his income from commissions.

Otto Olsen, the new systems salesperson, had yet to earn more than his drawing account in his five months on the job. He explained that the type of systems he sold

*Should the proposed sales-compensation plan have been adopted?*

*Appraise the plan from the standpoint of the individual salesperson.*

*What part should timing have played in the introduction of the new plan, assuming that the sales personnel approved it?*

## III-23.   CHRISTOPHER CANDY COMPANY:
## Producer of Candy Products—
## Controlling Expenses of Sales Personnel

The Christopher Candy Company produced and sold a wide line of candy products, including various kinds and sizes of candy bars, bag assortments, and box candies. The product line was distributed nationally through independent wholesalers, department stores, corporate chains, and mail-order houses. Salespeople's expenses had been increasing over the past few years, and the general sales manager regarded this as his most serious problem. He had addressed several memos to the sales personnel asking them to watch their expenses carefully, but their expenses had continued to climb.

A recent survey of sales expenses in the candy industry showed that Christopher sales personnel exceeded the industry norm by more than 30 percent. When the marketing vice-president saw the survey results, he asked the general sales manager to collect the needed information and develop a proposal recommending changes to bring Christopher's selling expenses into line with those of the industry.

After compiling and analyzing expense records over a six-month period, the sales manager decided to recommend that the company adopt a flat-expense-account plan. He was convinced that company sales personnel had abused the current system under which all sales expenses were reimbursed and which required them only to submit their total expenses for each period instead of a detailed itemization.

The sales manager proposed the following flat allowances for controllable expenses for all salespeople: room, $11-$13 per day; meals, $2 for breakfast, $3 for lunch, and $5 for dinner while the salesperson is on the road; entertainment, $10-$15 per week; communication, including telephone calls, $2 per day; and travel, 11 cents per mile while on business.

To permit a smooth transition from one expense plan to another, the sales manager suggested that district sales managers discuss the flat allowances with each of their sales personnel individually. This would give the sales staff opportunities to react to the new plan and to suggest modifications based upon unique territorial conditions. Minor revisions of the basic plan could be authorized by the district managers.

Under the sales manager's plan, each week salespeople would submit their daily expenses on itemized forms for approval by district managers and for payment by the headquarters office. For the first week under the new plan, the salespeople would receive an advance allowance of $75, and adjustments would be made weekly to account for the previous week's expenditures. Any salesperson spending more than the flat allowance would have the excess amount deducted from his or her annual bonus.

The marketing vice-president decided to discuss the proposed new expense plan with the district managers. There was no clear-cut majority opinion regarding the proposal. Some district managers felt that the flat-expense-account plan was equitable to all salespersons, since the district managers could modify the basic plan according to territorial differences. Other district managers opposed the proposal, arguing that it was essentially inflexible, would encourage salespeople to overeconomize, and would prevent them from capitalizing on sales opportunities requiring greater expense outlays. One district manager said that salespeople should pay their own expenses out of their salaries, thereby relieving management of the accounting and control problems.

The marketing vice-president recognized the validity of some of the objections raised by the district managers. However, he felt that the flat allowance was not only fair to all salespeople, but also the best way to cut selling expenses, which, in turn, would affect company profits favorably.

*Should the Christopher Candy Company have adopted the flat-expense-allowance plan proposed by the sales manager? State your reasons.*

# III-24.  UTICA DIVISION, LOVEJOY CORPORATION:
## Manufacturer of Restaurant Equipment— Reduction of Selling Expense

The Lovejoy Corporation, a large Cleveland-based manufacturer of commercial scales and related weighing equipment, had recently purchased a firm in Utica, New York, which manufactured commercial dishwashing machines, vegetable peelers, and silverware burnishers. The products of the Lovejoy Corporation were sold directly to institutional and industrial users throughout the United States by a sales force of 2,000 who worked out of 200 sales and service offices. The Utica concern had previously sold only through restaurant equipment dealers in the eastern half of the country and was almost totally unknown throughout the rest of the United States.

From the start it was realized that the products of the Utica Division could not be sold by the parent sales force; therefore, a second sales force was established to market the products of the Utica Division through restaurant-equipment dealers. To take advantage of the widely known name, national advertising, and service stations already maintained by the Lovejoy Corporation, it was decided to market the products of the Utica Division through approximately 400 selected restaurant equipment dealers located strategically throughout the country. No more than two dealers were selected in any one city, except for New York and Chicago, in each of which five dealers were authorized to stock and sell the Utica Division line. The country was divided into fifteen territories and one salesperson was assigned to each except for the New York territory, in which two people were situated (see Exhibit 1). Salespeople were paid on a straight-commission basis, but all expenses were reimbursed upon submission and approval of expense statements.

the Mississippi, or (2) to continue national distribution but restrict selling expenses to the maximum of 10 percent of sales in each territory.

After a good deal of thought, the dealer sales manager decided to continue national distribution of the Utica Division's products. He then faced the problem of controlling the sales-expense ratio. There were three courses of action open.

First, a concerted drive to increase sales in the West could have been attempted. However, this had been the company's strategy from the beginning, and it was felt that further effort might not produce greater results than those obtained thus far.

Second, selling expenses could have been cut by placing restrictions on traveling by the western salespeople. At the same time, the sales effort could have been concentrated in areas easily accessible from the home cities of the sales personnel. The balance of each territory could have been covered in long field trips once or twice a year. The salesperson would have been able to keep in touch with dealers in between calls by mail and occasional telephone calls. This alternative was ruled out because it was thought to be impractical. Although actual selling expenses would undoubtedly have been reduced, a smaller number of sales in outlying areas would have also resulted. Thus, commissions would have been smaller, and the salespersons involved would have been more likely to leave the service of the company.

The third plan was to release the company salespersons in the western territories and immediately sign them up as manufacturer's representatives. Under this plan sales personnel were to work on a 10 percent straight commission and were to assume all their own traveling expenses. The Lovejoy Corporation would encourage and assist them in acquiring the representation of related but noncompetitive lines of other companies calling upon similar prospects. Related lines would provide the representatives with additional sources of income; they would also assist in offsetting high traveling expenses. The dealer sales manager fully realized that the company would lose control over distribution of its products. The interests of the western representatives would be divided among the several products of a number of manufacturers, but even this was better than being without representation in that section of the country. The dealer sales manager believed that, in time, the company would find it profitable to reestablish its own sales force in these territories, and thus this arrangement was not to be thought of as a final solution.

The third alternative was finally adopted, and the sales personnel involved were converted into manufacturer's representatives without incident. The company agreed to pay them a 10 percent commission on all sales, and they agreed to assume all traveling expenses. The company assisted them in securing additional lines of noncompetitive products, which were sold to restaurant-equipment dealers. At the same time, the sales personnel in the eastern half of the country were given new sales contracts in which a base salary was established at approximately 70 percent of their estimated earnings, with the balance paid on the basis of a new commission rate. The company continued to pay all travel expenses incurred by the eastern sales force.

In the spring after the plan had been in effect approximately one year, it seemed, in general, to be working well. The Dallas and Denver territories were now well above their established quotas. The San Francisco representative was meeting quota regularly, and the representative in Los Angeles was short of quota by a very small amount. The Kansas City representative was the only failure. Sales in the Kansas City territory dropped steadily, and finally the representative there was replaced. However, the new person was unable to secure additional lines of other manufacturers, and, as a result, left the company in March. The company was still without representation in the Kansas City territory in May. The salespeople in the East were generally pleased with the steady salary month after month, and executives were convinced that the new plan of compensation was definitely paying off, both in terms of better morale and increased sales.

*Should national distribution of the products of the Utica Division have been continued? If so, what steps should have been taken to reduce the ratio of direct selling expense to sales volume?*

# III-25. McKAY CLOTHING COMPANY:
## Manufacturer of Work Clothes and Outerwear—
## Determination of Sales Territories

The McKay Clothing Company of Dallas, Texas, a regional manufacturer of work clothes and outerwear, had marketed its product line profitably since 1887 and had gradually obtained sales in the southwestern states of Oklahoma, Arkansas, Louisiana, and New Mexico. In 1972, Bryant A. Meeks, the sales manager, became concerned with the allocation of sales territories among the sales personnel; he asked Jim Carsdale, his assistant, to study the potential of the company's market and recommend an improved system.

McKay's work clothes accounted for approximately 65 percent of total sales volume. Dungarees, several styles of overalls, and items such as aprons were produced and sold under the McKay label. Both the company and its retailers considered the work-clothes line to be complete. The company offered its retailers more than thirty styles of dungarees, most of which had extremely good consumer acceptance, primarily because of the company's policy of producing a quality, full-cut product that would not bind or pinch the wearer. Attention to style was also considered to be a contributing factor in the company's success with work clothes. A portion of the line was restyled each year; and distinctive features, such as bib pockets and elastic straps on carpenter's overalls, were stressed on each garment. In spite of competition from four other regional and two national producers, many of the McKay lines were estimated to have between 30 and 40 percent of the market within their sales area.

Outerwear, lightweight jackets, ski clothes, and hunting attire constituted the remaining 35 percent of the company's sales volume. The lightweight jackets were suitable for casual wear and could easily be distinctively modified for club and group use. The line of hunting clothes, which included a complete selection of gunning apparel, was made in weights that would be comfortable in the generally warm Southwest. The outerwear line tended to be more highly styled than the work clothes, although primary attention was given to quality, comfort, and practicality. McKay had more national and regional competitors in the outerwear field, but some of the company's products held a sizable share of the market in its selling area.

*Should the Raleigh Furniture Company have continued to use disposable personal income as the basis for setting its sales territories or should it have switched to family income as the basis? Why?*

# III-27.  MARQUETTE FROZEN FOODS COMPANY:
## Manufacturer of Frozen Foods—
## Design of Sales Territories

The Marquette Frozen Foods Company manufactured a wide line of frozen foods sold directly to all types of food stores. The company's 100 salespeople worked out of thirty-five district sales offices located throughout the United States. Annual sales were nearly $40 million. Although the sales picture was quite favorable, certain recent developments indicated a possible need for redesign of sales territories.

Sales territories were established using population as the base and were composed of one or more counties, depending upon each county's population. The aim was to assign each salesperson to a territory containing about 1 percent of the county's total population. Since total population was approximately 205 million (exclusive of Alaska and Hawaii), an attempt was made to assign each person a territory consisting of about 2,050,000 people. Population statistics were obtained from the U.S. Bureau of the Census and were modified according to local area statistics.

The method of territory design was illustrated by the Northeast I sales territory, including Maine, New Hampshire, and part of Massachusetts. The Northeast I territory included the following Maine counties, along with their populations: Aroostook, 94,000; Piscataquis, 16,000; Penobscot, 125,000; Androscoggin, 91,000; Cumberland, 192,000; Franklin, 22,000; Hancock, 35,000; Kennebec, 95,000; Knox, 29,000; Lincoln, 21,000; Oxford, 43,000; Sagadahoc, 23,000; Somerset, 41,000; Waldo, 23,000; Washington, 30,000; and York, 112,000. Maine population: 992,000.

The following New Hampshire counties and their populations were included: Belknap, 32,000; Carroll, 19,000; Cheshire, 52,000; Coos, 34,000; Grafton, 55,000; Hillsborough, 224,000; Merrimack, 81,000; Rockingham, 139,000; Stratford, 70,000; and Sullivan, 31,000. New Hampshire population: 737,000.

Finally, the following Massachusetts towns were included to increase the sales territory population to the desired figure (the first six towns listed were in Essex County, while the last two were in Middlesex County); Amesbury, 12,000; Newburyport, 16,000; Haverhill, 46,000; Lawrence, 67,000; Salem, 41,000; Marblehead, 21,000; Tewksbury, 23,Q00; and Lowell, 95,000. Massachusetts population: 321,000. Total population in Maine, New Hampshire, and parts of Essex and Middlesex counties in Massachusetts: 2,050,000.

Analyses of population statistics were made every three years. When warranted by population changes, sales territories were redesigned; however, most changes were minor. The company supplied each salesperson with a detailed map showing the counties in his or her territory, the cities and towns, population, and the exact territorial boundaries.

This was done to prevent misunderstandings as to territorial assignments and to ensure a salesperson's exclusive rights to a given territory.

The Marquette sales manager had proposed and received acceptance of this method of determining sales territories several years ago. He favored this procedure because it guaranteed equal territories and similar sales opportunities for all company sales personnel and therefore eliminated an important cause of poor morale. With total population divided evenly, it was easy to compare relative performances of the sales force. Total population was an accurate estimate of potential demand, according to the sales manager, because everyone was a potential consumer of frozen foods. In addition, he said that the simplicity and economy of this approach made it even more desirable.

Careful analysis of a number of call reports, however, confirmed the sales manager's suspicions that many salespeople were "skimming the cream," or concentrating on the larger and easier-to-sell accounts, neglecting altogether a substantial number of prospects. Consequently, he concluded that territorial coverage was unsatisfactory. He believed that this situation could be remedied by reducing the size of the territories, permitting more intensive coverage.

The sales manager was aware that there were many reasons why a reduction in the size of the sales territories was difficult to implement. First, the sales personnel would feel that something was being taken away from them; in some cases they would lose accounts they had cultivated over a long period. The result was a possible morale problem. Second, high costs were involved in redesigning sales territories. Third, there would be a need to hire additional salespeople to cover the new sales territories. Fourth, someone would have to convince the sales force that the changes were in the best interests of the sales staff, the company, and the customers. It would be essential to secure the sales-force's acceptance of the new plan.

Since substantial problems were associated with reducing the sizes of the sales territories, the Marquette sales manager was still undecided whether to redesign the present sales territories.

*Should the Marquette Frozen Foods Company have redesigned and reduced the sizes of its sales territories? Justify your position.*

# III-28.  McBRIDE ELECTRIC CORPORATION:
## Manufacturer of Electric Equipment Accessories—
## Need for Revision of Sales Territories

McBride Electric Corporation, headquartered in Detroit, was a large producer of electrical equipment and accessories. Organized in 1910, McBride grew steadily and became one of the major U.S. suppliers of electrical products. McBride sold some of its products direct to a few large accounts, but most of the product line was sold through a nationwide network of distributors. The thirty-five-person field sales force, working out of eight district offices, was assigned territories which had been established along

EXHIBIT 1
Activities of Sales Supervisors[1]

*Selling:*

The typical sales supervisor apparently spends about 50 percent of the time in direct supervision. When a sales supervisor works with one of the sales staff, the major emphasis is on selling, which activity normally takes between three and one-half to five hours in a typical day. Selling appears to be important from another aspect; approximately three fourths of the sales supervisors in this study indicated that they handle personal accounts. These two factors suggest that selling activities are generally the major activities of first-line sales supervisors, on the basis of the amount of time spent in the activity.

*Discussing Salesmen's Problems:*

The most time-consuming nonselling supervisory activity is discussing problems with the sales staff. Typically, this activity takes somewhere between one and one-half to two hours of a supervisor's time when he or she spends a day working with a salesperson. The responses seem to indicate that, as a firm gets larger, the supervisor spends less time in this activity.

*Administrative Activities:*

The performance of administrative activities by first-line sales supervisors was almost universal among the companies of this study. There was some indication that, as a firm gets larger, the amount of administration performed at the first-line sales supervisory level tends to decrease.

*Recruiting and Hiring:*

Approximately 50 percent of the supervisors included in this study recruit sales personnel. Generally, their recruiting activities are centered around initial contact or screening of applicants, but first-line sales supervisors do not seem to have too much final authority in hiring the sales staff. There is some evidence that sales supervisors in firms selling industrial products have somewhat more recruiting responsibility than do those in firms selling consumer products.

*Training:*

Training sales personnel is an activity performed by almost all supervisors in this study, but very few supervisors indicated that they felt this to be one of their more important duties. The training given by the sales supervisor in most instances is predominately on-the-job training in which the supervisor and the salespeople actually make productive sales calls. The other major type of training at the supervisor's level occurs at the branch office, where emphasis is placed on acquiring product knowledge. Typically, supervisors give new sales personnel about three weeks of training.

*Reporting:*

The number of reports submitted by first-line sales supervisors and to first-line sales supervisors seems to indicate that supervisors in firms that sell industrial goods have somewhat more authority in approving sales expenses.

*Branch Meetings:*

Holding meetings seems to be considered important by the first-line supervisors of almost all companies. Ninety-six percent of the supervisors included in this study indicated that they hold sales meetings for the staff under their supervision. The average number of meetings held by supervisors is eighteen per year. Smaller firms hold meetings less often than large firms.

[1]Extracted from Z. W. Koby, *An Analysis of the Function of First-Line Sales Supervisors* (Austin: The University of Texas Press), pp. 128-35.

MISCELLANEOUS FACTORS OF SALES SUPERVISION

*Source of Sales Supervisors:*

The most usual route to the position of first-line sales supervisor seems to be by means of promotion from within the company. The responses in this study indicate that less than 10 percent of all first-line sales supervisors were hired from outside sources. Firms selling consumer products promoted 93 percent of their supervisors from the sales force.

*Training for Supervisors:*

This study revealed that only one of four first-line supervisors received specific training for their current positions. There is some evidence that this situation is changing, since almost half the top marketing executives indicated that they do train their sales supervisors. The most usual type of training offered is as assistant to another supervisor.

*Span of Control:*

The typical span of control for sales supervisors included in this study is somewhere between seven and eight salespeople. Firm size does not appear to be a significant factor when span of control is considered. The individual companies in the study varied from a span of five to sixteen salespeople.

*Supervisory Time and Salesperson Satisfaction:*

There is some indication that sales personnel are more content with the sales supervision they receive if their supervisor spends more than a token amount of time with them. The average time that supervisors spend with each salesperson in this study is slightly more than one day per month. The sales staff who would like their supervisors to do things that are not now being done are most numerous among the group whose supervisors spend the least time in direct supervision.

pated in the study. A year later, Graydon received a summary of the study results from Koby. These results were based upon detailed responses from top marketing executives, sales supervisors, and sales personnel. There were approximately 300 responses from supervisors and 1,500 from salespeople. Summarized extracts from this report are submitted as Exhibit 1. Fifteen of the firms were industrial-goods manufacturers; the remainder were consumer-goods manufacturers.

*Evaluate the role of first-line sales supervisors in the Dewey organization. Do you think that Graydon should have made any changes in light of the findings?*

## III-30.   MATTHEWS-MARTIN, INC.:

## Manufacturer of Packaging Materials—
## Supervision of Sales Personnel

Matthews-Martin, Inc., manufactured a broad line of paper products used for packaging. Its products were sold to packagers throughout the country by a field sales force of sixty-two salespeople operating out of eleven district sales offices. Each district office had a sales supervisor responsible for both group and individual supervision.

Group supervision for all sales personnel in each district office consisted of monthly half-day sales meetings. These meetings covered topics such as sales-force reports of their activities, special problems arising during the month, review of the district's sales performance, new business outlook, competitive and price conditions in the market, and advertising and sales-promotion comparisons (prepared by the headquarters staff). Some monthly sales meetings featured a film on a new product, or a new application. Each meeting closed with a statement by the district sales manager on sales progress and problems in the district.

Semiannually, a one-day group meeting was held at each district office. Various regional managers participated in these sessions by talking to the sales staff about new product introductions, new applications, maintenance problems, deliveries, production schedules, and credit problems. Salespeople were instructed in vital areas of sales techniques, communicating with customers about company policies, handling customer complaints, and assisting customers with their operating problems. Sales personnel were encouraged to express their views, to make suggestions, and to ask questions. Generally, these one-day meetings generated considerable enthusiasm among the sales staff.

Individual supervision of the sales force at each district office was the responsibility of the district sales supervisor. Normally, he or she talked on the phone with each salesperson at least twice weekly. Salespeople made weekly sales reports, credit reports on delinquent customers, and special reports as requested by the sales supervisor.

Every ninety days, the supervisor met with each salesperson at the district office for an appraisal of the salesperson's performance. The supervisor reviewed the salesperson's performance and sales and service activities. Customers were analyzed. A review was made of the salesperson's success in securing new customers. Sales of specific products were analyzed. Special customer problems were investigated. In short, the meeting was a comprehensive appraisal of the sales activities of the past three months.

The district sales supervisor also occasionally visited the salespersons in their homes to discuss individual selling problems. In addition, each salesperson was invited frequently to the supervisor's home for a strictly social get-together.

About 60 percent of the district sales supervisor's time was spent in the field observing sales personnel, giving them on-the-job training, and assisting them with sales problems. The supervisor rode with each member of the sales staff in their territories, listened as the salesperson made presentations to customers and, between calls, reviewed the previous call and previewed the next call.

*What is your opinion of the methods Matthews-Martin, Inc., used to supervise its sales force?*

# III-31.   CENTRAL CATV, INC.:
## Community Antennas Television (CATV) Service—
## High Turnover of Sales Personnel and
## Problems in Supervision

Thomas Wagner, Sales Manager for Central CATV, Inc., was concerned about what he regarded as an exceptionally high turnover of sales personnel, as well as certain other problems that had surfaced recently. The average Central CATV salesperson stayed with the company for less than seven months. Although actual sales stayed closely to projected levels, Wagner felt the need for immediate action to reduce the personnel turnover. He also believed that correction of the turnover problem would enable Central CATV to achieve higher sales.

Cable television was developed in the late 1940s to alleviate signal reception problems of rural areas, which, with the cable network, were usually offered three or four channels. Recognizing that people were willing to pay for variety in programming, CATV soon moved into cities that were receiving two or three channels and offered them between ten and twelve channels. Gaining acceptance in the medium-sized cities, cable television went into large metropolitan areas and offered up to twenty-five television channels. Approximately 2,800 CATV systems in the United States served nearly five million homes, or over 7 percent of the total homes with television sets.

The operational concept of CATV was simple. A large tower with antennas capable of bringing in broadcasts from various outlying centers was erected. The signals were then sent out via coaxial cables to subscribers' homes. Amplifiers were used to clarify and boost the signals along the cable network.[1]

Cable system start-up costs included construction of the master antennas, the cable network, and initial promotion. The initial outlay was relatively high and accounted for the fact that most cablevision companies did not earn a profit until the third year of operation. However, once the start-up costs were absorbed, generally there was excellent profit potential because of low operational costs.

For the past three years, Central CATV had served a southern market comprised of over 60,000 persons, nearly 40 percent of whom were students at a large university. The company bought the cablevision system from the "pioneering" operator and almost immediately expanded the cable network from 100 miles to 200 miles and from six stations to ten stations. Central CATV charged an installation fee of $25 and a monthly service fee of $4.95.

Central CATV serviced nearly 30 percent of the TV viewing market in its operating area. The company's goal was to have 50 percent of the market on the cable service by the end of the fifth year of operation. Wagner felt this was a realistic objective since, without the cable, it was possible to receive only two television channels.

The only advertising Central CATV had sponsored occurred shortly after its takeover of the operation. There had been a need to overcome a very poor service reputa-

---

[1]A more detailed description of the cable television system appears in the Scientific-Atlanta, Inc., case, pp. 99-101.

EXHIBIT 1
Salesperson Performance Appraisal

| Indicate achievement in the following areas of performance: | Comments |
|---|---|
| I. Obtaining Maximum Profitable Sales Volume<br><br>1. Calls on existing and prospective accounts with sufficient frequency.<br><br>Inadequate     Outstanding | |
| 2. Cultivates all purchasing agents, engineers, production personnel, and executives who influence the decision to buy.<br><br>Inadequate     Outstanding | |
| 3. Plans for each call in advance to be well informed and ready for an effective presentation.<br><br>Inadequate     Outstanding | |
| 4. Conducts sales interviews skillfully. Involves effective presentation, adept handling of objections, and ability to close.<br><br>Inadequate     Outstanding | |
| 5. Services customers and prospects by expeditiously handling complaints and claims; providing development and engineering assistance; expediting orders; providing information relative to company policies, products, delivery schedules, and prices.<br><br>Inadequate     Outstanding | |
| II. Managing Time and Activities to Ensure Maximum Productivity and Efficiency<br><br>1. Organizes time and effort for most effective coverage of territory.<br><br>Inadequate     Outstanding | |

EXHIBIT 1 (cont.)

2. *Develops sales plans based on an analysis of each account in terms of sales objectives and sales-call effectiveness.*

Inadequate                    Outstanding

3. *Submits required reports and keeps sales supervisor informed of conditions in territory.*

Inadequate                    Outstanding

4. *Corresponds effectively with customers and appropriate offices within the company.*

Inadequate                    Outstanding

III. *Knowledge of Company Products, Competitors, and Customers*

  1. *Knowledge of company organization and policies.*

  Inadequate                    Outstanding

  2. *Knowledge of company products and related technical information.*

  Inadequate                    Outstanding

  3. *Knowledge of competitor's policies, products, organization, and sales trends.*

  Inadequate                    Outstanding

  4. *Knowledge of each customer's operation, personnel, products, and market requirements.*

  Inadequate                    Outstanding

*Indicate overall evaluation of performance.*

Inadequate                                        Outstanding

COMMENTS OF REVIEWERS:

Date_____ Signed_____ (Salesperson)

Date_____ Signed_____ (Sales Manager)

Date_____ Signed_____ (Reviewing Manager)

# 18

# The Sales Budget

To the sales department, the budget is a blueprint for making sales. It involves money invested in distribution facilities, promotional efforts, and sales personnel. It is the foundation on which to plan sales objectives and the means of achieving them during the coming year. When properly prepared and administered, it is translated ultimately into dollar sales and profits.

The sales budget, like the sales forecast, provides management with information necessary to the setting of company objectives. Whereas the sales forecast results in the establishment of goals for company total sales volume, the sales budgetary procedure ultimately leads to the setting of goals for company net profits from selling operations. Defined in the simplest terms, a sales budget consists of estimates of the probable dollar and unit sales and the expenses of obtaining them. These two estimates are related to predict net profit on selling operations. The sales budget, then, is a projection of what a given marketing program should mean in terms of net profits and improvements in financial position.

The sales budget uses the sales forecast as a point of departure. The amount of involvement by the sales manager in this first step in budgeting depends on the degree to which buildup methods are used in forecasting. The preparation of the budget for sales expenses is primarily the responsibility of the sales manager, since he or she has personal control over many of these expenses. However, the actual preparation of the budget is a shared decision, involving everyone from the lowest level of sales management to the president.[1]

## PURPOSES OF THE SALES BUDGET

### Mechanism of Control

The main emphasis in sales budgeting is on the control function. The completed budget, which is essentially a statement of sales and profit goals for various sales units, serves as a yardstick against which the progress made toward business objectives is

[1] J. J. Breen, "The Marketing Budget," *Sales/Marketing Today* (January 1966), p. 11.

assist in forecasting sales, but have a voice in drafting plans to accomplish sales and profit goals.[3]

### "Selling" the Sales Budget to Top Management

The chief sales and marketing executives must recognize that every budget proposal they make to top management is in competition with many worthwhile proposals submitted by the heads of other divisions. At budget-making time, top management receives more proposals than it is financially able to carry out simultaneously. Therefore, in appraising proposals, top management looks not only at intrinsic merits but at the probable overall value or return to the organization as a whole. Too few marketing and sales executives realize that the sales budget has to be "sold" to top management. The budget should be presented to top management just as a salesperson would make a presentation to a new prospect. Since a competent company president or executive vice-president has too many varied responsibilities to be concerned with details of any one department, it is safe to assume that such high executives are wholly or partially ignorant of the problems faced by the department, and of many of the problems faced in putting together a good overall sales program.

As in any other selling task, the starting point should be a careful assessment of the wants and needs of the prospect. For the top executive, the major want is benefit to the company. How does the company, and incidentally the top executive, stand to gain from the proposed sales plan and budget? To top management, the budget is a proposal to spend money to bring in profit. It is the job of top management to divide the available money among the various departments of the firm; and the share received by each depends on the ability of the executive concerned to "sell" his or her boss on the benefits to accrue from the plan. Obviously, the sales-budgeting process does not proceed without consideration of the nature, mix, and cost of the marketing effort needed to achieve the sales goal. The selection of marketing methods and the right mix is part of the overall task of budgeting.[4]

### Handling Competition for Available Funds Within the Marketing Division

Similarly, the chief sales executive must be prepared to argue effectively for a maximum share of funds from the marketing division. The sales executive, like the advertising manager, marketing research manager, customer service manager, product managers, and any other staff executives in the marketing department, submits a budget proposal to the chief marketing executive. From the proposals received from subordinates, the chief marketing executive selects those which are of the greatest potential benefits and which the company can afford to implement. In discharging this function, the marketing executive checks to assure that the plans presented are the result of careful study, that the proposed expenditures will enable the subordinate to carry out the plans, and that the forecasted sales are attainable.

The sales executive should understand that the amount of money finally allocated to the sales department depends upon the value of the individual budgetary proposals

[3]For more detail, see J. C. Chambers, S. Mullick, and D. D. Smith, "How to Choose the Right Forecasting Technique" *Harvard Business Review,* Vol. 49, No. 4 (July-August 1971), p. 49.

[4]S. Schoeffler, R. D. Buzzell, and D. F. Heany, "Impact of Strategic Planning on Profit Performance," *Harvard Business Review,* Vol. 52, No. 2 (March-April 1974), p. 137.

to the company as a whole. The sales executive must also keep this in mind in dividing the sales department's budget among its subordinate divisions. If a buildup sales forecasting and budgeting procedure has been used, each subordinate has already prepared a forecast of his or her own sales and an estimate of the expenses that will be incurred in achieving these goals; thus the task of division is simplified. However, when the budgetary responsibility is subdivided in this way, each subordinate executive should be held responsible for budgeting only the expenses that are under his or her personal control.

### Actual Budgetary Procedure

The preparation of the budget normally starts at the lowest level in the organization and works upward. The lowest level involved in this budgetary process is sometimes called a financial performance center.[5] Thus, each district sales manager is asked to prepare an estimate of district sales and expenses for the coming period, plus an estimate of the district's contribution to overhead. This budget will include rent, heat, light, secretarial costs, and all other expenses of operating the district office. It will also include the salaries of the sales personnel and the district manager, and all selling expenses incurred by the district. These district budgets are submitted to the divisional or regional office, where they are added together and included with the divisional budget. In turn, these divisional budgets are submitted to the sales manager for the particular product or market group. At the end of this chain of subordinate budgets, the chief sales executive compiles a final selling budget for the company.

While the sales manager and his or her subordinates have been preparing budgets, the staff departments in the marketing department have been doing the same, showing credits for work they will be expected to perform for the sales department during the year. The office of the chief sales executive prepares its own budget, and this is then combined with the budgets of the sales department and the staff marketing department, to give a total of selling and other marketing expense for the company.

At each level in the budgetary process, each individual budget must be approved by the executive to whom it has been submitted before all can be combined. Each management level within the sales division approves the budgets for which it is responsible, incorporates them into its own budget, and submits this new budget to the next higher level for approval. In each instance, a detailed description of the units' plans for the coming period are submitted as support and justification for the budget. Without this information, there would be no satisfactory basis for evaluating and approving the budget submitted. When changes are made in the budget, corresponding changes must be made in the plans. For example, a cutback in funds requested for new sales personnel would necessitate a reduction in the planned number of salespeople to be hired.

Other divisions within the company use the same preparation period to compile their budgets, with the sales forecast as their point of departure. The production division goes through a similar process of building up an expense budget from each operating subdivision and combining these until a total budget is prepared for the division. The comptroller's division, research and development, personnel, and all other divisions have simultaneously been going through the process of budget preparation. These division budgets are all submitted to the president, who in turn submits a final total budget to the board of directors. Just as in the preparation of the sales budget, the process of

---

[5]J. B. Poe, *The American Business Enterprise* (Homewood, Ill.: Richard D. Irwin, Inc., 1960), p. 349.

costs to the adjusted volume figure. This system, known as "variable" budgeting, is the one used by most businesses today.

## CONCLUSION

The sales budget is a projected statement of income and expense built up from the sales forecast. It is used as a standard of performance for purposes of control and as an instrument of planning. The budget is best prepared on a buildup basis, with each echelon preparing preliminary estimates of income and expense. Each administrator must sell his or her own budget to higher levels of management if he or she wishes to secure its adoption. During the operating year, items in this final approved budget are compared with actual expenditures, and actions taken to bring the two into adjustment. The budget is a guide rather than an absolute standard and should be revised whenever necessary.

# 19

# Quotas

Quotas are quantitative objectives assigned to specific marketing units—individual salespersons, for instance—for use in the management of sales efforts. As the most important and most commonly used standards for appraising selling effectiveness, quotas specify desired performance levels for sales volume; for such budgeted items as expenses, gross margin, net profit, and return on investment; for accomplishing selling-related and non-selling-related activities; or for some combination of these and/or similar items. In most companies, sales management is most concerned with setting and administering quotas for organizational units of the sales department, such as for individual sales districts and salespeople. In some companies, however, sales management sets and uses quotas applying to middlemen, such as agents, wholesalers, and retailers. Quotas set for sales regions, or other marketing units on higher organizational levels, are customarily broken down and reassigned to lower-level units, such as sales districts or to individual salespersons. In all cases, quotas have a time dimension—they quantify what management expects in the way of accomplishment within a given period.

Fundamentally, then, sales management regards quotas as devices for directing and controlling sales operations. Their effectiveness depends upon the kind, amount, and accuracy of marketing information available and used in setting them, and upon management's skill in administering the quota system. In the most effective systems, management bases quotas on information derived from sales forecasts, studies of market and sales potentials, the sales budget, and cost estimates. Quantitative data from these and similar sources are important in assuring the effectiveness of a quota system but, in and of themselves, they are not sufficient; superior judgment and other administrative skills are required of those with quota-setting responsibilities. When soundly administered quotas are based on relevant and thorough market knowledge, they are effective devices for directing and controlling sales operations. But when quotas represent little more than guesses or wishful thinking, or when an unskilled executive is administering them, or both, much, if not all, of their value as control devices is dissipated.

ness is being appraised, in part, by their success in staying within assigned expense limits. Still others establish quotas for the dollar profit or profit percentage on sales on which salespeople are to be held accountable. Budget quotas serve to shift the emphasis away from making sales and toward keeping expenses within certain bounds, or increasing the profitability of sales. Such quotas are particularly appropriate when additional sales volume is obtainable only at greatly increased expense; thus profits can be increased only by improving selling efficiency (either by reducing selling expenses or by making sales more profitable).

### To Use in Connection with Sales Contests

Companies using sales contests frequently use "performance against quota" as the main basis for making awards. Management often believes that sales contests are more effective motivators if each participant feels that he or she has an equal chance of winning. By basing awards on percent of quota fulfillment, the desired "common denominator" feature is built into the contest. Assuming that quotas are set accurately, this adjusts for differences among territories (as in coverage difficulty and company competitive position) and for differences among sales personnel (as in experience with the company and in the territory). Generally, contest quotas are designed solely for use in the contest, the thinking being that "special quotas" are needed to stimulate extra-special effort, causing average salespeople to turn in above-average performances.

## TYPES OF QUOTAS AND QUOTA-SETTING PROCEDURES

Differences in forecasting and budgeting procedures, in management philosophy, in selling problems, and in executive judgment, as well as variations in quota-setting procedures, cause the quotas used by each firm to differ from those used by others. If small differences are ignored, however, almost all quotas fall into one of four categories: (1) sales volume, (2) budget, (3) activity, and (4) combination. Differences in quota-setting procedures, as will be evident shortly, show up mainly in the setting of sales-volume and budget quotas.

### Sales-Volume Quotas

The sales-volume quota is the oldest and most common type. Management regards it as an important standard for appraising the performance of individual salespersons, middlemen, or other components (both inside and outside the company) of the selling operation. By assigning sales-volume quotas, sales management communicates to each selling unit its expectations of "how much for what period." Sales-volume quotas may also be established for geographical areas, product lines, or marketing channels, or for one or more of these in combination with any selling unit, the exact design depending upon which facets of the selling operation management wants to appraise or motivate.

Generally, the smaller the selling unit for which a quota is set, the more effective it is as a device for directing and controlling sales operations. Setting a sales-volume quota for a sales region, for example, assists management in obtaining a certain amount of direction and control over sales operations; but by setting sales-volume quotas individually for each sales territory in the region, management is in position to obtain a much greater amount. Setting sales-volume quotas for smaller selling units, in other words, makes it much less likely that good or bad sales performance in one aspect of the selling operation will be obscured by offsetting performance in other aspects. The same line of reasoning holds when sales-volume quotas are set for products or time periods—generally, more direction and control are secured by setting quotas for individual products rather than for entire product lines, and for short periods rather than long.

Sales-volume quotas are used extensively, and it is easy to understand why. They are set by sales executives and, from the sales department's standpoint, achieving the sales-volume objective takes precedence over other objectives. Before any profits at all can be earned, a certain sales-volume level must be attained. Thus, it is not surprising, and entirely logical, to find that sales management gives its first attention to the development of standards for appraising sales-volume performance. Furthermore, sales personnel have little difficulty in grasping the significance of sales-volume quotas. This is not to say, of course, that sales management should sacrifice the earning of profits or the conservation of selling expense in order to obtain sales volume. Modern sales management recognizes that sales volume alone, although crucially important, is not sufficient—profits are necessary for survival of the firm itself.

Sales-volume quotas are most commonly set in terms of dollars, or of units of product. Most companies selling broad product lines prefer the dollar terminology, inasmuch as such firms frequently encounter numerous complications in setting unit quotas and in evaluating sales performance for individual products. One important advantage of the dollar terminology is that management is able to relate volume quotas to other performance data, such as selling expenses incurred, through computing ratios or percentages. In addition, when products have no firmly established prices, and salespeople have a certain amount of discretion in cutting prices to make sales, management tends to set either dollar-volume quotas or combined dollar-and-unit-volume quotas to assure that sales personnel do not too readily cut prices too deeply in order to build unit volume.

Sales-volume quotas in product units are used mainly in two types of situations. The first concerns companies selling products whose prices are expected to fluctuate significantly during the quota period; in this situation, if management desires to compare sales performance over different time periods, unit-sales-volume quotas are better yardsticks than dollar-sales-volume quotas. If a product is now priced at $80 a unit, 600 units must be sold to achieve $48,000 in sales; but if the price declines by 25 percent (to $60 a unit) 800 units must be sold to record the same dollar volume. The second type of situation obtains in companies with narrow product lines sold at prices that do not fluctuate significantly during quota periods. In these cases, dollar-volume and unit-volume quotas appear equally appropriate; but, especially if unit prices are relatively high, management often decides on unit quotas for psychological reasons—salespeople may look upon a $1 million volume quota as a greater psychological hurdle than a forty-unit volume quota made up of machines priced at $25,000 each.

Still another way of expressing a sales-volume quota is in "points," into which dollar or unit sales, or both, are converted. A company using point-volume quotas might consider each $100 sales as worth one point; it might value unit sales of product A at five points and of product B at one point; or a method might be developed for converting both dollar and unit sales into points. Most companies setting point-volume quotas have adopted them because of problems encountered in using dollar- or unit-volume quotas. Porter-Cable Machine Company, for instance, once used dollar-volume quotas exclusively. On analysis, however, management found that sales personnel often attained most of their quotas through selling only one or two easy-to-sell products.

FIGURE 19.1

Computation of Sales-Volume Quotas by Sales Regions

| (1) Sales Region | (2) Buying-Power Index | (3) Actual Sales (This Year) | (4) Sales Par (This Year) | (5) Surplus or or Deficit (4) − (3) | (6) Tentative Quota (Next Year) | (7) Quota (Next Year) |
|---|---|---|---|---|---|---|
| Total U.S. | 100.0000 | $20,727,743 | $20,727,743 | — | $21,487,000 | $21,487,000 |
| New England | 6.3513 | 1,711,314 | 1,316,481 | +394,833 | 1,364,704 | 1,760,000 |
| Middle Atlantic | 21.4685 | 4,214,437 | 4,449,936 | −235,499 | 4,612,937 | 4,325,000 |
| East North Central | 21.8393 | 3,318,956 | 4,526,794 | −1,207,838 | 4,692,610 | 3,500,000 |
| West North Central | 8.9802 | 2,110,412 | 1,861,393 | + 249,019 | 1,929,576 | 2,179,000 |
| South Atlantic | 12.0999 | 2,388,410 | 2,508,036 | −119,626 | 2,599,906 | 2,490,000 |
| East South Central | 5.3821 | 1,074,742 | 1,115,588 | −40,846 | 1,156,452 | 1,120,000 |
| West South Central | 8.8054 | 2,786,010 | 1,825,161 | +960,849 | 1,892,016 | 2,844,000 |
| Mountain | 3.5050 | 680,115 | 727,507 | −46,392 | 753,119 | 733,000 |
| Pacific | 11.5683 | 2,443,347 | 2,397,847 | + 45,500 | 2,485,681 | 2,536,000 |

U.S. Bureau of the Census. Column 1 lists each of these nine sales regions. Column 2, the buying-power index, indicates the percentage of total sales that should come out of each sales region under ideal marketing conditions and assuming, of course, perfect alignment of company sales efforts with sales opportunities. This illustration uses *Sales Management's* Buying Power Index, probably the most widely used market index; many companies use ready-made indexes obtained from outside sources, or especially prepared ones derived from such company data as historical share-of-the-market figures.

Column 3 gives "this year's" actual sales volume in each region. Column 4, sales "par," is obtained by multiplying column 2 (buying-power indexes) by the total of column 3, thus showing what sales in each region would have been had they been distributed according to the market indexes. Column 5, surplus of deficit, records the amount by which each region's actual sales exceeded or fell short of sales par. For example, New England sales show a $394,833 surplus, whereas South Atlantic sales show a $119,626 deficit. The total of column 6, tentative quota (next year), is the total company quota derived from the sales estimate after "first-level" adjustments have been made for projected company policy changes in prices, products, promotions, and the like.

The tentative quota for each sales region is obtained by multiplying column 2 (buying-power indexes) by the total of column 6. The figures in column 7, the final regional sales-volume quotas for next year, are arrived at after "second-level" adjustments have been made for regional, competitive, personnel, and other differences. Each region's tentative quota in column 6 is revised upward or downward in making the se second-level adjustments, and the previous year's surplus or deficit figures applying to each region provide convenient guides for converting these adjustments into quantitative terms. In this illustration, it is assumed that management does not expect below-par sales regions to make up their entire deficits in a single year—the usual practice is to adjust upward gradually the quotas of such regions over a period of several years.

The next quota-setting phase in this company would be the breakdown of regional quotas into territorial sales-volume quotas. In most companies, making this further breakdown is a responsibility of the regional sales managers, who may or may not follow procedures similar to that just illustrated. Most regional sales managers would want to make a third level of adjustments before setting territorial sales-volume quotas. In fact, most contend that territorial sales-volume quotas should not be set finally until the sales personnel assigned to the territories are consulted. The regional sales manager ordinarily calls in each salesperson to discuss the territorial outlook relative to the share of the regional sales-volume quota that the territory should produce; then the regional manager sets territorial sales-volume quotas. Quotas developed in this way should be more acceptable to the sales staff, because each person has participated in setting them, and each has had the opportunity to contribute special information that might have a bearing on the final quota.

**Sales-Volume Quotas Based on Past Sales Experience Alone.** One of the crudest procedures for setting sales-volume quotas is to base them solely on past sales experience. One company, for instance, simply takes last year's sales for each territory, increases them by an arbitrary percentage, and uses the results as sales-volume quotas. A second averages past sales for each territory over several years, adds arbitrary amounts, and thus sets quotas for sales volume. Probably the second company's method is the better of the two—by averaging sales figures, management recognizes that the personnel "expense bonuses" for incurring expenses less great than the quota estimates. Usually expense quotas are related, directly or indirectly, to estimates in territorial sales budgets. But, to reduce the administrative burden and the chances of misunderstandings, management commonly prefers to express expense quotas not in dollars but as percentages of sales volume, thus directing staff attention both to sales volume and the costs of achieving it.

Certain problems are met in setting expense quotas in the form of percentages of sales volume. For one thing, variations in coverage difficulty and other environmental factors, as well as in sales potentials, make it impractical to set identical expense percentages for all territories. For another, when different salespeople sell different mixes of products, some incur higher expenses than others, again making impractical the setting of identical expense percentages. But probably the most important problem is that selling expense does not necessarily vary in direct proportion to sales volume, as is implicitly assumed with the expense percentage quota. Requiring that absolute or relative expenses vary proportionately to changes in volume of sales may reduce a salesperson's incentive to obtain more sales. It may actually be true, for instance, that selling expenses amount to 3 percent of sales up to $700,000 in sales, but obtaining an additional $50,000 in sales requires increased expenses of $2,500, which amounts to 5 percent of the marginal sales increase.

Clearly, then, management should not arbitrarily set percentage expense quotas. Considerable analysis of territorial differences, the product mixes likely to be represented in individual sales, and variations in the expenses of securing sales at various volume levels should precede actual quota setting. Furthermore, because of difficulties in making precise adjustments for these and other factors, and because of possible changes during the operating period in territorial conditions, administering an expense quota system calls for great flexibility.

From sales management's standpoint, the chief attraction of the expense quota is that is tends to make sales personnel more cost conscious and aware of thier responsibilities for expense control. They are less apt to regard expense accounts as "swindle sheets" or convenient vehicles for padding take-home pay. Instead, they should view the expense quota as one standard that management uses in evaluating their performance. However, unless expense quotas are carefully set and intelligently administered, a danger exists that sales personnel may become overly cost conscious—they may stay at third-class hotels, patronize third-class restaurants, and avoid entertaining customers. Salespeople should understand that, although expense money is not to be wasted, management anticipates that they will make all reasonable expenditures. Most well-managed companies, in fact, expect as a matter of policy that their sales personnel will maintain standards of living in keeping with those of their customers.

**Gross-Margin or Net-Profit Quotas.** Companies not setting sales-volume quotas because of the fear of overemphasizing the importance of sales volume often use gross-margin or net-profit quotas instead, thereby hoping to shift the emphasis to the making of contributions to gross margin or profit. The general philosophy underlying these quotas is that sales personnel will operate more efficiently if they are made to recognize that sales increases, expense reductions, or both, are important only if increased margins and profits result. These quotas are particularly appropriate when the product line contains both high- and low-margin items. For example, an equal volume increase in each of two products may have widely different effects upon total margins and profits. Low-margin items are also normally the easiest to sell, thus sales personnel taking the path of least resistance often concentrate on them and, in the process, fail to give proper attention to more profitable products. One way to combat this and obtain better-balanced sales mixtures is to set gross-margin or net-profit quotas specifying the contributions management expects of each salesperson. Note, however, that essentially the same results are achieved by setting individual sales-volume quotas for different products, adjusting each quota to obtain the desired contributions.

Problems are met both in setting and administering gross-margin or net-profit quotas. If gross-margin quotas are used, management must face the fact that sales personnel generally do not set prices and have no control over manufacturing costs; therefore, they cannot be held fully responsible for gross margins. If net-profit quotas are used, management must recognize that certain selling expenses, such as those involved in operating a branch office, are beyond the salesperson's power to influence; this, coupled with their lack of control over prices and manufacturing costs, makes it very difficult to hold them wholly responsible for profits.

To overcome these complications, companies frequently set quotas in terms of "expected contribution" margins, thus avoiding arbitrary allocations of expenses not under the direct control of the sales staff. Arriving at expected contribution margins for each salesperson, however, is itself a complicated and involved process. Even if a company solves these accounting-type problems inherent in setting gross-margin or net-profit quotas, it faces further problems in administration. Sales personnel may have difficulties in grasping technical features of quota-setting procedures, and management may have to spend considerable time in ironing out resulting misunderstandings. In addition, special records must be set up and maintained to gather the needed information for evaluating sales performances. Finally, because some expense factors always are partially beyond certain salespeople's control, arguments and disputes are almost inevitable. Generally, then, the company using gross-margin or net-profit quotas must be prepared to assume increased clerical and administrative costs.[6]

## Activity Quotas

Management's desire to control how sales personnel allocate their time and efforts among different activities explains the use of activity quotas. A company using such quotas starts by defining the various important activities salespeople perform; then it specifies desired performance frequencies. Some of the activities for which quotas are set include: total sales calls. calls on particular classes of customers, visits on prospects, number of new accounts, missionary calls, product demonstrations, placement or erection of displays, and making of collections. Before setting activity quotas, management should have on hand reliable time-and-duty studies of how salespeople actually apportion their time among various activities, making whatever additional studies are necessary to determine how salespeople *should* allocate their efforts. Ideally, management should have available time-and-duty studies for *every* salesperson and sales territory, but, of course, this is seldom practical. Another desirable prerequisite is present if management is already planning the route and call schedules. Such a high proportion of most salespeople's time is spent in traveling and in making calls

---

[6]Michael Schiff of New York University has suggested that target return-on-investment percentages might be more appropriate than budget-type quotas in controlling field selling operations, particularly at the regional and district sales office levels. See his "The Use of ROI in Sales Management," *Journal of Marketing*, Vol. 27. No. 3 (July 1963), pp. 70-73.

that considerable opportunity to improve time-allocation patterns in performing these two important activities usually exist.

Activity quotas are most appropriate when the sales staff is responsible for performing important nonselling activities. For example, activity quotas are used a great deal in insurance selling, where salesmen must continually develop new contacts. They are also common in drug detail selling, where "detail men" spend most of their time calling on doctors and hospitals to explain new products and new applications of both old and new products. The unique advantage, then, of activity quotas is that they permit management not only to control but to give recognition to sales personnel for performing important nonselling activities and for maintaining contacts with customers who may buy infrequently, but in substantial amounts.

Together with the rather large amount of clerical and record-keeping work involved, the main problem in administering an activity-quota system is that of inspiring the sales force to perform the specified activities effectively. The danger is that salespeople will merely "go through the motions" and not perform activities effectively. Activity quotas used alone, as G. Risley says, "can reward salesmen for quantity of work, irrespective of quality, for a dangerously long time."[7] This problem is less likely to arise when activity quotas are used along with other performance measures, such as carefully designed sales-volume or expense quotas; still, in either case, adequate supervision and close personal contact with sales personnel are administrative necessities.

### Combination and Other Point-System Quotas

Combination quotas are used when management desires to control sales-force performance of both selling and nonselling activities through the medium of a single summary performance measure. Such quotas were developed to overcome the problem of using different measurement units to appraise different aspects of personnel performance (for example, dollars to measure sales volume, and number of calls on prospects to measure attention given to developing new business) and, consequently, of lacking a single quantitative measure of overall performance. Because performances against combination quotas are computed as percentages, such quotas are also known as point systems, the points being percentage points.

Figure 19.2 illustrates how performances, or point scores, are determined under a combination quota system incorporating both sales-volume and activity goals. In this system, each of four different aspects of the salesperson's job is weighted according to management's evaluation of its relative importance to overall performance. Column 1 shows the four quotas making up the combination for each salesperson, and column 2 records actual performance data. Column 3, indicating the percentage of quota attained, is then multiplied by the weighting factor in column 4 to yield the weighed performance in column 5. Finally, the column 5 total is divided by the column 4 total to determine each salesperson's overall performance rating. Thus, Snyder's rating is 87.145 percentage points (that is, 87.145 percent of his combination quota) and Thompson's is 85.143. Combination quotas may also be designed without attaching different weights to the various components (which, of course, is the same as equally weighting all components); but in most cases, different weights are justified because all components are rarely of equal importance. In the example, had different weights not been used, management would have appraised Thompson's performance as better than Snyder's—91 vs. 88 percentage points. This reversal emphasizes the importance of selecting weights with the greatest care.

---

[7]See G. Risley, "A Basic Guide to Setting Quotas," *Industrial Marketing* (July 1961), pp. 88-93.

FIGURE 19.2
Determination of Point Scores Under a Weighted Combination Quota System

*Salesperson:* T. Snyder

|  | *(1)* | *(2)* | *(3)* | *(4)* | *(5)* |
|---|---|---|---|---|---|
|  |  |  | *Percent* |  | *Quota* x |
|  | *Quota* | *Actual* | *Quota* | *Weight* | *Weight* |
| Sales volume | $75,000 | $67,500 | 90 | 3 | 270 |
| New accounts obtained | 20 | 15 | 75 | 2 | 150 |
| Calls on prospects | 50 | 50 | 100 | 1 | 100 |
| Displays erected | 150 | 135 | 90 | 1 | 90 |
|  |  |  |  | 7 | 610 |

$$\frac{610}{7} = 87.145 \text{ (Snyder's point score)}$$

*Salesperson:* J. Thompson

|  | *(1)* | *(2)* | *(3)* | *(4)* | *(5)* |
|---|---|---|---|---|---|
|  |  |  | *Percent* |  | *Quota* x |
|  | *Quota* | *Actual* | *Quota* | *Weight* | *Weight* |
| Sales volume | $90,000 | $63,000 | 70 | 3 | 210 |
| New accounts obtained | 30 | 27 | 90 | 2 | 180 |
| Calls on prospects | 90 | 100 | 111 | 1 | 111 |
| Displays erected | 200 | 190 | 95 | 1 | 95 |
|  |  |  |  | 7 | 596 |

$$\frac{596}{7} = 85.143 \text{ (Thompson's point score)}$$

Combination quotas make it possible to summarize overall performances of salespersons in a single measure, but they are not without disadvantages. Sales personnel may have difficulties in understanding them and in appraising their own achievements. Combination quotas also have a built-in weakness in that design imperfections may cause a person to place too much emphasis on one-component activity. Suppose that Snyder or Thompson, in the above illustration, decides to erect twice as many displays as the quota specifies and to do almost no prospecting. The possibility that some salespeople may try to "beat the system" in this or other ways indicates that, as with other complex quota systems, continual supervision and close contact with the sales force are essential.

Another widely used point system is the full-line quota, which is designed to stimulate sales personnel in securing a more proper balance of sales among various products. Figure 19.3 illustrates a point-system quota designed to obtain better-balanced selling. Two members of the sales staff, Ed O'Reilly and Dick Johnson, sell three products, A, B, and C. Products A and B are relatively low-margin items and easy to sell; product C is a high-margin item that takes extra effort to sell. Considering these important differences, sales management has to set a quota for each product and has established weights reflecting relative sales difficulty and profitability. By some coincidence, perhaps unrealistic but revealing, O'Reilly and Johnson were assigned identical quotas and, by an even greater coincidence, their performances resulted in equal sales volumes. However, Johnson receives the higher point score and therefore should be regarded as

*Salesperson:* Ed O'Reilly

| Product | Sales-Volume Quota | Actual Sales | Percent Attained | Weight | Percent Attained x Weight |
|---------|-----------|----------|---------|--------|----------|
| A | $20,000 | $20,000 | 100 | 1 | 100 |
| B | 20,000 | 20,000 | 100 | 1 | 100 |
| C | 10,000 | 4,000 | 40 | 2 | 80 |
| Total | $50,000 | $44,000 | | 4 | 280 |

$$\frac{280}{4} = 70.0 \text{ (O'Reilly's point score)}$$

*Salesperson:* Dick Johnson

| Product | Sales-Volume Quota | Actual Sales | Percent Attained | Weight | Percent Attained x Weight |
|---------|-----------|----------|---------|--------|----------|
| A | $20,000 | $16,000 | 80 | 1 | 80 |
| B | 20,000 | 18,000 | 90 | 1 | 90 |
| C | 10,000 | 10,000 | 100 | 2 | 200 |
| Total | $50,000 | $44,000 | | 4 | 370 |

$$\frac{370}{4} = 92.5 \text{ (Johnson's point score)}$$

the better salesperson. Why? He places more emphasis on selling product C and obtains a better balance in selling the three products.

## ADMINISTERING THE QUOTA SYSTEM

Skill in administering the quota system is basic not only to realizing the full benefit for control purposes, but to securing staff cooperation in making the system work. The most critical administrative aspect is that of securing and maintaining acceptance by those to whom quotas are assigned. Few people take kindly to having yardsticks applied in appraisals of their performance. Constitutionally, most salespeople oppose quotas; and anything that makes them doubt the accuracy, fairness, or attainability of quotas makes them even less willing to accept quotas, thus reducing the system's effectiveness for control purposes.

### Accurate, Fair, and Attainable Quotas

The quotas finally assigned to salespeople should be accurate, fair, and attainable. Obtaining accurate quotas is largely a function of the quota-setting method used; the more closely quotas are related to territorial potentials, the greater the chances for accuracy. But, in addition, regardless of the type of quota(s) being used—sales volume, budget, activity, or combination—sound managerial judgment is required in analyzing pertinent market data, adjusting for contemplated changes in selling and marketing policy (and for conditions peculiar to each territory), and appraising changes in personnel capabilities, as well as in setting the final quotas themselves. In general, then, accurate quotas result from the skillful blending of relevant planning and operating information with sound executive judgment. Setting a fair quota involves determining the proper blend of market potential and previous experience.[8]

Admittedly, whether a particular quota is both fair and attainable depends not only upon the quality of management's judgment but also upon the capabilities and motivations of the sales force. Sometimes, perhaps even usually, the extent to which a salesperson's quota is fair and attainable can only be ascertained after his or her performance has been recorded. Even then, management must exercise due care in appraising variations in performance from the quota—to what extent are they attributable to quota inaccuracies and to what extent to salesperson inadequacies? After all, quotas are not *absolute* performance standards, and errors can be made in setting them. If management believes that its quota-setting method produces accurate quotas and is confident individual sales people are being assigned fair quotas, then quotas should be attainable. Probably most quota-setting errors are ones of judgment, most commonly traceable to the practice of setting quotas slightly above each salesperson's expected performance to provide an incentive for improvement. Management must take care not to set wholly unattainable quotas; however, quotas that some salespersons fail to attain are not necessarily unfair—whether they are or not depends on which salespeople fail to attain them. One executive offers this general rule. "You have set equitable quotas for salesmen if your weaker salesmen fail to attain them, and if your better salesmen either reach or slightly exceed them."[9] Thus, in ascertaining the fairness of quotas, management faces a possible dilemma because the quotas themselves are the performance standards most used for appraising the quality of sales personnel. Clearly, subjective evaluations of salespeople according to qualitative performance criteria are required if management is to ascertain whether or not particular quotas are fair.

### Securing and Maintaining Salespeople's Acceptance of Quotas

Beyond making certain that quotas are accurate, fair, and attainable, management must direct its attention toward assuring that sales personnel understand their quotas and the method used in obtaining them. Conveying this understanding, in fact, is a critical step in securing staff acceptance of quotas. If salespersons do not understand the bases used in establishing their quotas, they may suspect, for example, that the quotas are merely a management technique designed to obtain extra effort from them at no cost to the company. Such an attitude, of course, destroys much of the quota's effectiveness as an incentive. It is equally important that salespersons understand the significance of quotas as communicators of management'a expectations of "how much for what period"; but, if they also understand the quota-setting methods, they are more likely to consider their quotas accurate, fair, and attainable. The quota-setting method, in other words, should be simple enough to be readily explainable to sales personnel, yet sufficiently sophisticated to permit

[8]K. R. Davis and F. E. Webster, Jr., *Sales Force Management* (New York: The Ronald Press Company, 1968), p. 294. Also see pp. 293-95 for a simplified but good example of determining a fair quota.

[9]E. P. Sheehan in *Incentives for Salesmen, op. cit.,* p. 67.

must continually appraise the operation of the system and make improvements and needed changes. One company president, in discussing this aspect of quota administration, said, "Constant review is needed to make absolutely sure that quotas and the method of setting them are as fair and accurate as possible."[10] Continuous managerial review and appraisal are required, since, for example, a quota that was accurate, fair, and attainable at the beginning of an operating period can easily prove totally unrealistic in view of rapidly changing selling conditions. Therefore, flexibility in administering the system is important—if a quota is proving unrealistic in light of changing conditions, it should be adjusted without undue hesitation. Administrative flexibility is desirable, but it is possible to have too much of it. Small changes can be ignored; important changes should call for appropriate adjustments. One company, for instance, adjusts dollar quotas in the event of a *significant* price change, or "any change of 5 percent or more in our industry forecasts."[11] What is needed, as Risley notes, is "a reasonable balance . . . between complete flexibility to every slight change and inflexibility regardless of changes."[12] Achieving this balance should not be difficult, once management recognizes the need.

## REASONS FOR NONUSE OF SALES QUOTAS

Some companies do not use quotas, particularly sales-volume quotas. In certain industrial-goods categories, it is difficult to obtain accurate sales estimates; thus, quotas, if used, would be based largely on subjective judgments. Executives commonly prefer not to use quotas, if it means basing them on "guesstimates." In other situations, it is possible to obtain accurate sales estimates, but executives, perhaps wrongly, contend that obtaining and analyzing other data necessary for quota determination would involve inordinate expenditures of time and money. Certainly, no quota should cost more than it is worth, but it is difficult indeed to visualize a situation in which accurate quotas coupled with intelligent administration would not produce a net gain in selling efficiency.

In a few companies, the fact that quota determination ordinarily requires the use of statistical techniques causes executives not to use quotas, not because they hesitate to use these techniques but because they fear that sales personnel will not wholeheartedly accept quotas prepared by hard-to-explain techniques that they do not understand. In other instances, although accurate sales forecasts are possible, management has difficulty in arriving at fair weights for such factors as territorial potential, competitive position, coverage difficulty, and salesperson ability, all of which affect the performance of individual salespeople. Thus, when quotas are tried, they may be set too high, which could cause high-pressure selling, or too low, which could provide insufficient incentive.

In other situations, executives oppose quotas on the ground that too much emphasis is placed upon making sales, to the detriment of other important activities. This may be a legitimate criticism of sales-volume quotas, but certainly not of all quotas. Finally, some executives simply object to the word "quota," which they say has negative conno-

---

[10]E. W. Rawlings, president, General Mills, Inc., in *Incentives for Salesmen, op. cit.,* p. 50.

[11]"Measuring Salesmen's Performance," *Business Policy Study No. 114* (New York: National Industrial Conference Board, Inc., 1965), p. 25.

[12]Risley, *loc. cit.*

tations, and prefer to assign "salesperson's objectives." These executives, in other words, really use quotas but under another name.

One situation where quotas, in the normal sense, are not appropriate needs mentioning. It occurs when a product is in short supply. In such cases, most managements believe that it is wise to encourage the sales force to divide the available supply equitably among customers. Therefore, each salesperson may be assigned an allocation for his or her accounts. In sellers' markets, the allocation serves as a substitute for the quota, which characteristically is appropriate for use only in buyers' markets.

## CONCLUSION

Quotas are quantitative objectives assigned to sales personnel and other units of the selling organization. They are intended both to stimulate performance and to evaluate it, through communicating management's expectations, and through serving as performance measures for detecting strong and weak points in the selling operation. In almost all successful quota systems, management has taken special pains to tie in quota-setting procedures with information on sales potentials and with planning data incorporated in the sales forecast and sales budget. Such systems are also characterized by the exercise of sound executive judgment in adjusting tentative quotas both for contemplated policy changes and for factors unique to each territorial environment. Furthermore, continuous managerial review and appraisal, and balanced flexibility in making changes in quotas and improvements in quota-setting procedures, characterize such systems: Each firm should select and use those types of quotas that best fit its selling situation. When based on relevant and accurate market information, and intelligently administered, quotas are effective devices for directing and controlling sales operations.

sales data, it has no way to evaluate the effectiveness of its own activities and those of the sales force. The fact that sales increased by 2 percent over last year but profit *decreased* by 1 percent would be a cause for concern upon the part of management but would be of little help in determining how the profit decline could be remedied. Sales analysis could provide management with additional information, for example, that the increased sales volume was achieved entirely in products earning a lower-than-average gross margin.

Through regular sales analyses, management seeks insights on such matters as: the sales territories where it is strong and where it is weak, the products responsible for the most and the least sales volume, and the types of customers who provide the most satisfactory and the least satisfactory sales volume. Sales analysis, then, is used to uncover significant details which otherwise lie hidden in the sales records. It provides information management needs in order to allocate future marketing efforts more effectively.

### Allocation of Marketing Effort

In most businesses, a large percentage of the customers, territories, orders, or products bring in only a small percentage of the sales. One sales executive, for example, discovered that 80 percent of the company's customers accounted for only 15 percent of its sales volume. Similar situations exist in most companies, a large percentage of the customers accounting for a small percentage of total sales and, conversely, a small percentage of customers accounting for a high percentage of total sales. And comparable situations are found where a large percentage of the sales territories, products, and orders bring in only a small percentage of total sales. Such situations are often referred to as instances where the "iceberg" principle applies.

Such sales patterns do not always result in unprofitable operations, but they are likely to reduce the profit that might potentially be earned. Why is this so? Simply because marketing efforts, and hence marketing costs, all too frequently are divided on the basis of customers, territories, products, orders, and so forth, rather than on a basis of actual or potential dollar sales. If usually costs, for example, just as much to maintain a salesperson in a bad territory as in a good one, almost as much to promote a product that sells slowly or not at all as one that sells in large volume, and as much to have a salesperson call on and service a customer who orders in small quantities as another who gives the company large orders. It is not uncommon for a large proportion of the total spending for marketing efforts to result in only a very small proportion of the total sales and profits. Detecting such situations is the important task of sales analysis.

### Sales-Analysis Methodology

Companies vary greatly in the type and form of information they have available on sales. At one extreme, some have none, other than that recorded by accountants as sales are made, and, of course, carbons of customers' sales invoices. At the opposite extreme, some maintain sales records in great detail and have information readily available and in usable form for making sales analyses by individual salespersons, by types of products, by classes of customers, by sizes of orders, and by other pertinent classification systems.

Generally, the most important source of data useful in sales analysis is the customer's sales invoice. If the company has a properly designed information system, the data from the invoices will be transferred to computer or data-processing cards in sufficient detail that it can be retrieved without ever going back to the original invoices. If it is necessary to go back to the original invoices to perform a sales analysis, the operation is very costly and time consuming and therefore can only be performed occasionally. The information stored on each transaction should identify and describe the customer (for example, name and geographical location), and it should contain data on the specific transaction (for example, the date of the order, the products sold and the quantities, the price per unit, total dollar sales per product, and total amount of the order). Information stored in this manner can be retrieved in the form of a sales analysis quickly and at low cost. Thus, it is possible to provide sales analysis as a regular tool of management instead of an occasional added source of information.

### Illustrative Problem—Sales Analysis

The general approach taken in sales analysis is indicated in the following illustrative example. Assume that a manufacturer's products reach final markets through different marketing channels. The output is used by both ultimate consumers and industrial users. Various types of middlemen account for most of the sales, but a few large retailers and large industrial users buy directly. The manufacturer wants to determine the relative importance of the different categories of customers. The resulting sales analysis by class of trade proceeds through three steps.

**Step 1—Establishment of Customer Classifications.** In some companies, this step is not required, since there may already be established customer classifications—for example, if the distribution policy specifies the types of accounts solicited. When no such policy is in effect, sales records must be examined to identify the various classes of customers from whom business is being obtained. We assume in this company that it is necessary to examine sales records. The examination shows that customers are: printers' suppliers, office-supply houses, industrial-supply houses, stationers, retailers, and direct accounts.

**Step 2—Tabulate Sales to Each Classification.** We assume, in our example, that the company maintains individual customer-account sales records and that these records are on punch cards. All that has to be done is to run a simple computer program which will tabulate the total sales for each group.

**Step 3—Present Results in Meaningful Terms.** Figure 20.1 shows the results obtained by the tabulation.

This information, although interesting, still is not very meaningful. There are two things we can do to bring out the data's significance more clearly: (1) present statistics on sales and classes of accounts in percentage terms, and (2) calculate average sales per outlet for each customer class. After these recastings, we have Figure 20.2.

Now, what has this sales analysis revealed? It shows that 49.7 percent of the customers (the stationers, retailers, and direct accounts) account for only about 5.4 percent of the sales, and their average orders are only about 1/15 the size of those submitted by the average wholesaler. It also shows that large orders come from just two classes of wholesalers, who together comprise 25.4 percent of the total customers, but who also account for 84.3 percent of total company sales.

5. A measurement is made of the share of the variable activity of each of these functional-cost groups which is utilized by the segment of sales whose cost is being measured. This indicates the share of the cost of that function allocated to a particular segment of sales.

6. The excess or deficit of dollar gross margin over the sum of the direct expenses and the shares of the various functional-cost groups allocated to a segment of sales indicates its relative profitability or unprofitability.[1]

### Illustrative Problem and Solution

Marketing cost analysis is essentially a matter of allocating expenses to various segments of marketing operations, separable expenses directly and common expenses according to logical bases of apportionment, and of determining relative profitability.[2] The following discussion, and Figures 20.3 through 20.6, illustrate the procedures used in solving a simplified marketing-cost-analysis problem.

Data for the illustrative problem are presented in Figure 20.3. Such information is assembled from basic accounting and other internal records and is necessary for the solution of any marketing-cost-analysis problem. If management desired analyses of marketing costs according to such breakdowns as territory, class of customer, marketing channel, or sales personnel, additional information would be required. The data in Figure 20.3 are sufficient to permit analyses of marketing costs according to size of account and by type of product.

Figure 20.4 shows the bases of allocation used in the illustrative problem. Separable expenses, of course, are assigned directly to the segment of sales for which cost is being measured. In this problem, sales commissions are a separable expense for analyses both by product and by size of account, but advertising expense is separable only for the analysis by product. The "common expenses" are the ones for which the selection of allocation bases is most troublesome. In contrast to the analysis of production costs, where frequently a single basis, such as the number of machine hours, is used for allocating all manufacturing expenses, marketing cost analysis requires the apportionment of marketing expenses on several bases. It is important to understand that allocation bases are factors that measure variability in the activities for which specific expense items are incurred. Allocation bases, therefore, should permit logical assignment of portions of common expense items to various segments of sales. The expense item should vary directly with the volume of activity measured by the factor; and, in most instances, the expense item should be caused by the volume of activity. Some marketing expense items, such as the costs of credit management, may be allocated according to a logical basis in any type of marketing cost analysis. But other marketing expenses, such as sales-force salaries, may be allocated to customers but not usually to products, unless studies are available showing the distribution of sales time among the various products.

[1]C. H. Sevin, *Marketing Productivity Analysis* (New York: McGraw-Hill Book Company, 1965), pp. 12-13.

[2]Common expenses are those that cannot, as a practical matter, be traced directly to specific customers, commodities, or other sales components. Separable expenses can readily be traced to customers, commodities, and so on.

Whether a given outlay is a common or separable cost may depend on the circumstances of the business and on the segment of sales for which cost is being measured. If sales personnel are paid on a salary basis, for example, the outlay for their wages is a common cost as far as individual commodities are concerned. On the other hand, if the sales force works on a commission basis, the commissions paid are a separable cost of selling individual commodities, and they also are separable in regard to the cost of selling to individual customers.

In general, the greater proportion of marketing expenses are common costs, either because the process of tracing such costs to specific units of sales may be too expensive, or, in some cases, because there may be no available method of making a practical and reasonably accurate separation.

FIGURE 20.3
Data for Illustrative Problem

| Size of Account (Annual Purchases) | Number of Accounts | Number of Orders | Total Sales | Sales by Product | | |
| --- | --- | --- | --- | --- | --- | --- |
| | | | | A | B | C |
| Under $100 | 830 | 2,100 | $ 74,000 | $ 19,000 | $ 35,000 | $ 20,000 |
| $101-$500 | 1,320 | 5,800 | 343,000 | 93,000 | 150,000 | 100,000 |
| $501-$1000 | 790 | 8,100 | 633,000 | 133,000 | 275,000 | 225,000 |
| Over $1000 | 260 | 4,100 | 780,000 | 190,000 | 350,000 | 240,000 |
| Total | 3,200 | 20,100 | $1,830,000 | $435,000 | $810,000 | $585,000 |

*Cost of sales:* product A, $232,000; product B, $440,000; product C, $290,000.
*Number of shipping units sold:* product A, 87,000; product B, 135,000; product C, 58,500.
*Weight per shipping unit:* product A, 10 pounds; product B, 15 pounds; product C, 20 pounds.
*Commission on sales:* 2.5 percent of sales.
*Advertising:* product A, $20,000; product B, $30,000; product C, $50,000.
*Selling and administrative expenses:*

| | |
| --- | --- |
| Sales salaries | $ 60,000 |
| Sales traveling expense | 35,000 |
| Sales-office variable expense | 17,000 |
| Sales commissions | 45,750 |
| Warehousing | 18,000 |
| Packing and shipping | 42,000 |
| Credit management | 20,000 |
| Advertising | 100,000 |
| Billing and misc. bookkeeping | 60,000 |
| General selling, administrative and other expenses | 300,000 |
| Total | $697,750 |

Figure 20.4
Bases of Allocation of Marketing Costs for Analyses by
Product and by Size of Accounts

| | Type of Analysis | |
|---|---|---|
| *Functional-Cost Group* | *By Product* | *By Size of Account* |
| Personal selling | | |
|   Sales salaries | Not allocated | Sales times number of customers in size class |
|   Sales travel expense | Not allocated | Number of customers in size class |
|   Sales-office variable expense | Not allocated | Number of customers in size class |
|   Sales commissions | Direct | Direct |
| Warehousing | Weight times no. of units | Weight times no. of units |
| Packing and shipping | Weight times no. of units | Weight times no. of units |
| Credit management | Volume of sales | Number of customers in size class |
| Advertising | Direct | Not allocated |
| Billing and misc. bookkeeping | Volume of sales | Number of orders |
| General selling, administrative, and other expenses | Not allocated | Not allocated |

For purposes of analyzing marketing costs by product, it is assumed in this problem that costs of credit management and of billing and miscellaneous bookkeeping tend to vary directly with sales volume. It is further assumed that costs of warehousing and of packing and shipping are functions of the weight of one unit of product multiplied by the number of units handled. The latter assumption also holds for the analysis by size of account. But, in analyzing by size of account, the basis for allocating credit management expenses is not sales volume but the number of customers in the size class. The same basis is used for allocating sales travel expense and sales-office variable expense. In the analysis by size of account, billing and miscellaneous bookkeeping expenses are allocated on the basis of the number of orders rather than the volume of sales. Advertising expense incurred for advertising specific products is assigned in the analysis by product but not in the analysis by size of account. Sales salaries, which cannot be allocated to products, are allocated to the groupings by size of account according to sales volume multiplied by the number of customers in each size class. It should be noted that in neither type of analysis called for in this problem is it possible to allocate all the items of expense. However, because the purpose of marketing cost analysis is to determine *relative* profitability rather than exact profitability, this is not a serious shortcoming.

Figure 20.5 shows the profit-and-loss statement that results from analyzing the given data to determine marketing costs by product. The bases shown in Figure 20.4 were used in allocating the various expense items to products A, B, and C. This analysis reveals that all three products are in the same range of profitability, but that product A (the product with the lowest sales) is relatively most profitable, whereas product B (the product with the greatest sales) is relatively the least profitable. On the basis of this analysis, management might consider instructing the sales force to give more emphasis to product A. However, management would want to look at other marketing factors, too. For instance, there might be reason to suspect the advertising program of being ineffective. Indeed, if the relative profitability of the three products is recalculated, and advertising costs are not allocated to products, C becomes relatively the most profitable

FIGURE 20.5
Statement of Profit and Loss with Analysis of Marketing Costs by Products

| | | Products | | |
| --- | --- | --- | --- | --- |
| | Total | A | B | C |
| Net sales | $1,830,000* | $435,000 | $810,000 | $585,000 |
| Cost of sales | 962,000 | 232,000 | 440,000 | 290,000 |
| Gross margin | $ 868,000 | $203,000 | $370,000 | $295,000 |
| *Allocated expenses* | | | | |
| Sales commissions | $ 46,000 | $ 11,000 | $ 20,000 | $ 15,000 |
| Warehousing | 18,000 | 4,000 | 9,000 | 5,000 |
| Packing and shipping | 42,000 | 9,000 | 21,000 | 12,000 |
| Credit management | 20,000 | 5,000 | 9,000 | 6,000 |
| Advertising | 100,000 | 20,000 | 30,000 | 50,000 |
| Billing and misc. bookkeeping | 60,000 | 14,000 | 27,000 | 19,000 |
| Total allocated expenses | $ 286,000 | $ 63,000 | $116,000 | $107,000 |
| Margin after allocated expenses | $ 582,000 | $140,000 | $254,000 | $188,000 |
| Margin as percent of sales | 31.8% | 32.2% | 31.4% | 32.1% |
| *Nonallocated expenses* | | | | |
| Sales salaries | $ 60,000 | | | |
| Sales travel expenses | 35,000 | | | |
| Sales-office variable expense | 17,000 | | | |
| General selling and administrative expenses | 300,000 | | | |
| Total nonallocated expenses | 412,000 | | | |
| Net operating profit | $ 170,000 | | | |

*All figures rounded to nearest $1,000.00.

product. Thus, the importance of not being bound by rigid methodology in analyzing marketing costs is illustrated.

Figure 20.6 shows the analysis of marketing costs by size of account. This analysis reveals that the 260 accounts in the over-$1,000 class (with a 38 percent margin after allocated expense) were nine and one-half times as profitable as the 830 accounts in the under-$100 class (with a 4.0 percent margin). Similarly, the 790 accounts in the $501-$1,000 class were about 50 percent more profitable per unit, and nearly three times as profitable in total, as the 1,320 accounts in the $101-$500 class. After such analysis, management might consider such actions as: setting a minimum size for the smallest account, selling smaller accounts through wholesalers or agent middlemen, or rearranging call and route schedules to reduce the expenses of selling to smaller accounts. Furthermore, management might decide that the $14,000 spent for salaries, commissions, and travel expenses to sell to accounts under $100 could be used more profitably to solicit additional large accounts, or to increase the purchases of existing large accounts.

### Cost Analysis—Summary

Estimates of the costs of marketing reflect both long-term and short-term goals, and there are two basic steps in preparing them. (1) An estimate is made of the volume

# Cases for Part IV

## IV-1.  STRYER CAP SALES CORPORATION:

### Manufacturer of Rubber Products—
### Establishment of a Sales Budgeting Program

For the past four years, Stryer Cap Sales Corporation had experienced a steady decline in net profits while there were small but regular increases in sales volume. As a result, management faced the task of improving profits through cutting expenses and increasing efficiency. Joseph Orlando, the sales manager, suggested the establishment of a sales budget to curb selling expenses, which he contended had gotten out of line. Currently, the company had no formal sales budgeting program, but Orlando firmly believed that one was absolutely necessary if the sales operation was to contribute to the overall improvement of the firm's net-profit picture.

Stryer Cap Sales Corp. was located in Miami and for 12 years had manufactured a wide line of products used in recapping tires, such as treadrubber (the new rubber for the recaps, referred to as "camelback"), inner tubes, curing tubes, bonding cements, and a variety of tire-repair accessories and equipment. The company had experienced an average annual sales growth rate of about 12 percent during its first eight years; however, sales had stabilized somewhat over the past four years, averaging about 2½ percent growth each year. During the same four years, net profits declined by more than 5 percent. The previous year's sales amounted to $9.2 million and yielded net profits of $239,200, or 2.6 percent of sales. This was down from a high of 7.8 percent net profit four years ago.

Stryer products were sold in thirty-two states by a sales force of twenty-four persons who operated out of five branch offices. The sales force was paid on a straight-commission basis. Earnings ranged from $15,000 to over $30,000, with the average just under $21,000. Stryer's sales force sold to over 1,000 of the approximately 9,000 tire retreaders in the United States. The company estimated that it had captured 10 percent of the retreading market.

Orlando's plan for establishing a sales budgeting program for the Stryer sales department consisted solely of forecasts of sales expenses. He planned to determine the expenses involved in selling Stryer rubber products by scrutinizing the records of the branch offices and headquarters. He proposed to ask each of the five branch managers to submit itemized records of salespersons' salaries, traveling expenses, overhead and maintenance, clerical costs, and the costs of branch management and supervision. Orlando suggested that the itemized records include expenses for the previous year, the average for the past five years, and a forecast of expenses for the coming year. Combined with the branch office sales operating expenses were to be the expenses of the headquarters sales staff and sales management salaries and expenses, and all other costs attributable to the sales effort. The forecasts of the branch office and headquarters expenses for the coming year were to be combined to form the sales expense budget.

Orlando proposed to limit the sales budget exclusively to forecasts of sales expenses for at least three years. At that time, he expected to develop forecasts of sales volume and combine them with expense forecasts into a complete sales budget, or projected statement of income and expense. It was Orlando's contention that the sales budgeting program must proceed slowly in order to gain acceptance and cooperation from everyone affected. Hence, he suggested a three-year interval between establishment of the sales expense budget and the sales budget complete with sales-volume forecast.

The general manager opposed having the company adopt any kind of sales budgeting procedure. He argued that sales budgets were nothing more than unreliable guesses and did not constitute a valid basis for executive action. He claimed that so many variables affected the forecasts of expenses and sales volume that the accuracy of any estimate was questionable. He also felt that any attempt to curb sales expenses through budgetary procedures would result in a reduction in the overall sales effort, harming both the company's sales and profits.

Orlando knew that it was a complicated matter to establish a sales budget program. However, he felt it should and could be done, despite the general manager's reluctance to accept the idea of a sales budget.

*Whose side of the argument do you favor? Why?*

*Evaluate critically Orlando's proposal for a sales budgeting program for Stryer Cap Sales Corp.*

# IV-2.   HANNA FILE CORPORATION:

## Manufacturer of Filing Equipment—
## Variance Between Actual and Budgeted Performance

Hanna File Corporation manufactured and distributed a line of filing equipment and systems. The product line consisted of mechanized filing equipment, storage files, lateral files, insulated files, document conveyors, visible record cabinets, rotaries, posting trays, record safes, and file folders. The company had been organized four years previously by Michael Hanna, who had fifteen years' experience in a management capacity older salespeople, who had been with the company longest. The other salespeople were paid on a salary-plus-commission basis. New sales recruits were started at a salary of $7,000 and received semiannual increases on a merit basis. The average salary was $9,500. Every salaried salesperson was given an annual quota and received a commission of 4 percent on all sales above the quota. In addition, Driskill paid all selling expenses incurred by the salaried sales personnel; expenses averaged $450 per month per salesperson.

Earnings of the sales staff on a salary-plus-commission basis averaged $10,000. For example, R. C. Andersen, who had been selling for Driskill for five years, had a quota of $220,000 in 1972 and received a salary of $9,000. Since his actual sales in 1972 were $250,000, he earned a commission of $1,200, or a total income of $10,200. R. A. Scott, who had been selling for Driskill for fifteen years, was paid on a straight-commission basis. His gross earnings in 1972 were slightly in excess of the average of $17,000 in gross income earned by the commission salespeople.

Since the commission sales personnel were generally more experienced, and since their incomes were directly related to their productivity, management had never felt it necessary to give them specific quotas or volume goals. Quotas for the salaried staff members were based on a running three-year average of each person's past sales. Arbitrary figures were selected for sales personnel who had not yet been three years on the job; these quotas represented a compromise between the experience of the salespeople formerly in the territory and the level of experience of the new person. Jack Dixon, the sales .manager, believed that the basis for determining quotas was a satisfactory one. During the past ten years, 85 percent of the salaried sales staff had managed to exceed their quotas and earn some commission. In Dixon's opinion, therefore, the motivation was satisfactory to achieve maximum selling effort on the part of the sales force.

Henry Granger, the newly appointed director of marketing research, was less satisfied with the existing quotas. He claimed that any good salesperson could have exceeded quota under conditions prevailing in recent years in the industry. He also believed that the existing system, based on past sales, merely tended to perpetuate past weaknesses. He suggested that future quotas be based upon a division of the annual forecast of sales among the individual territories and that the basis for division should be other than past sales.

Dixon supported the existing system, claiming that past sales had been an adequate basis for the establishment of quotas in the past. He held, furthermore, that if any new system of quota preparation were adopted, it should be based primarily on the buildup of sales estimates by the individual salespersons for the coming year.

*If you were acting as a consultant for the Driskill Company, what recommendations would you make with respect to the preparation of quotas for the sales force? How would you evaluate the arguments of the sales manager and the marketing research director?*

# IV-4.   ALLIED BOARD AND CARTON COMPANY:
## Manufacturers of Containers—
## Difficulties with Quotas

The Allied Board and Carton Company manufactured and distributed cardboard boxes, cartons, and other packaging materials. The sales force of twenty-five persons, assigned to territories throughout the United States, made calls directly on purchasing agents of manufacturers of industrial and consumer products. During the previous eighteen months, operating losses had been experienced, and a firm of management consultants had been retained to investigate the situation. The findings of the consulting firm indicated that the losses did not stem from manufacturing inefficiency, as previously believed, but rather from the fact that selling costs per order were significantly higher than for comparable companies in the industry. The problem, then, was to find ways to step up selling efficiency; management began its task by reviewing the methods used for compensating sales personnel, with a view toward uncovering a possible solution.

Salespeople were paid a base salary of $500 per month and a commission of 3 percent on sales over quota. The monthly quota was determined by adding the individual salesperson's expenses for the previous month to the $500 base salary and multiplying the result by 20. Since management was of the opinion that sales personnel would keep their expenses down in order to gain from the next month's lower quotas and increased expenses, this system of quota determination was designed to minimize selling expenses. Salespersons drove their own automobiles, but their expenses of operation were reimbursed at the rate of 11 cents per mile for the first 100 miles, 9 cents per mile for the next 100 miles, and 7 cents per mile for all miles over 200 traveled in any one month. Salespeople were not required to submit bills and receipts for expenditures made for rooms, meals, and incidentals. Reimbursements were made at the end of each month. Salespeople were allowed to draw monthly on anticipated commissions, and overdrawals were automatically wiped off the books at the close of the fiscal year.

At the close of each month, sales personnel submitted a report detailing the number of calls made, the number of presentations, and the number of orders written. At the same time, the monthly report of expenses was submitted. The credit department was responsible for approving all orders, but commissions were charged back against the salespersons when customers failed to pay their accounts.

Upon completing the review of the method of quota determination, management concluded that its effect was to increase, rather than decrease, selling expenses. As shown in Exhibit 1, a salesperson who managed to reduce his expenses by $100 in one month received an increase of only $40 in commissions the next month. Thus, sales personnel could make more money by increasing their expenses and quotas than they could by reducing expenses and working with lower quotas. Consequently, a new method of quota determination was adopted. The base for the new monthly quota was the previous year's sales for the corresponding month; this was adjusted to reflect changes in territorial potential, degree of competition relative to the previous year, and the salesperson's past performance.

At the same time, the expense-reimbursement procedure was changed. Now, before salespeople could receive reimbursements, they were required to substantiate their expenses by producing all bills and receipts. In addition, each salesperson was provided

The *new* bonus program will have a payoff of:

1.  80-100%  = $40.00 per percentage point.
2.  101-110%  = $50.00 per percentage point.
3.  111-120%  = $60.00 per percentage point.
4.  121-over%  = $70.00 per percentage point.

In addition to the higher rate of payoff, the bonus will be paid on a quarterly basis. This will be done on a quarterly averaging basis. An example of how this works is illustrated below.

*1st quarter:*

146% of quota =       80 — 100% = 20 x $40.00 = $   800.00
                            101 — 110% = 10 x $50.00 = $   500.00
                            111 — 120% = 10 x $60.00 = $   600.00
                            120 — 146% = 26 x $70.00 = $1,820.00
                                                                      $3,720.00

$3,720.00 yearly bonus ÷ 4 = $930.00 per quarter.
$930.00 bonus paid for 1st quarter.

*2nd quarter:*

114% of quota: to determine average rate, we add 146% + 114% = 260% ÷ 2 = 130% for two-quarter average.

130% of quota =       80 — 100% = 20 x $40.00 = $   800.00
                            101 — 110% = 10 x $50.00 = $   500.00
                            111 — 120% = 10 x $60.00 = $   600.00
                            121 — 130% = 10 x $70.00 = $   700.00
                                                                      $2,600.00

$2,600.00 yearly bonus ÷ 4 = $650 per quarter.
$650 x two quarters = bonus due for first two quarters of $1,300. Since payment of $930.00 was made in first quarter, we owe $1,300.00 — $930.00, or $370.00 in 2nd quarter.
$370.00 bonus paid in 2nd quarter.

*3rd quarter:*

143% of quota: to determine average rate, we add 146%  + 114%  + 143% = 403% ÷ 3 = 134% average for three quarters.

134% of quota =       80 — 100% = 20 x $40.00 = $   800.00
                            101 — 110% = 10 x $50.00 = $   500.00
                            111 — 120% = 10 x $60.00 = $   600.00
                            121 — 134% = 14 x $70.00 = $   980.00
                                                                      $2,880.00

$2,880.00 yearly bonus ÷ 4 = $720.00 per quarter. $720.00 x three quarters = $2,160.00
$2,160.00 — $1,300.00 paid = $860.00.
$860.00 bonus paid in 3rd quarter.

*4th quarter:*

138% of quota: to determine four-quarter average, we add 146% + 114% + 143% + 138% = 541% ÷ 4 = 135%. The yearly average is the same as it would have been under the old system.

135% of quota = 80 — 100% = 20 x $40.00 = $ 800.00
101 — 110% = 10 x $50.00 = $ 500.00
111 — 120% = 10 x $60.00 = $ 600.00
121 — 135% = 15 x $70.00 = $1,050.00
$2,950.00

$2,950.00 is the yearly bonus. 4th-quarter payment is $2,950.00 minus previous payments of $2,160.00, or $790.00.
4th-quarter bonus is $790.00.
As an additional incentive, we are making an extra bonus available to those who exceed 100 percent of their quota. The payoff for this extra bonus will be:

100 — 110% = $10 per percentage point
111 — 120% = $15 per percentage point
121 or over = $20 per percentage point

An example of this is as follows:

135% of yearly quota = 100 — 110% = 10 x $10.00 = $100.00
111 — 120% = 10 x $15.00 = $150.00
121 — 135% = 15 x $20.00 = $300.00
$550.00

This $550.00 will be paid in addition to the $2,950.00, for a grand total of $3,500.00. This shows an increase of $1,100.00 over the previous bonus program. It is roughly estimated that this new program will cost an additional $40.00 per $100.00 spent under the old system. Bonus payoffs under the new program are as follows:

| Percent of Quota | Regular Bonus | Extra Bonus | Total Bonus |
|---|---|---|---|
| 81 | $ 40.00 | — | $ 40.00 |
| 82 | 80.00 | — | 80.00 |
| 83 | 120.00 | — | 120.00 |
| 84 | 160.00 | — | 160.00 |
| 85 | 200.00 | — | 200.00 |
| 86 | 240.00 | — | 240.00 |
| 87 | 280.00 | — | 280.00 |
| 88 | 320.00 | — | 320.00 |
| 89 | 360.00 | — | 360.00 |
| 90 | 400.00 | — | 400.00 |
| 91 | 440.00 | — | 440.00 |
| 92 | 480.00 | — | 480.00 |
| 93 | 520.00 | — | 520.00 |
| 94 | 560.00 | — | 560.00 |

At the end of the fiscal year 1971, the company was faced with a regional problem. Region 40, the Kansas-Missouri area, was incurring high costs and disproportionately low sales. However, inventory turnover in the region was above average. Magcobar was servicing many accounts in the area but was not making a very good profit. In previous years the region had done well in inventory turnover, sales, and efficiency of operations. But in 1970 and 1971, sales declined to the point where operating costs in the region were not even covered. The marketing manager could not understand what was happening, because inventory turnover was still quite adequate. The company had important accounts in the region and did not want to abandon it; large capital investments were also tied up in the area. The personnel in charge of the region had been with the company for some time and were very upset about the recent trends.

In addition to the Magcobar warehouses, there were a number of independent dealers. These dealers were specialty firms, and they were supplied with mud products by Magcobar. They, in turn, sold these products to the drilling companies. These dealers made up a large part of the region volume.

Magcobar was faced with a major decision, since management did not want to continue serving a region that was showing an inadequate contribution to profit. The sales manager felt that there were three alternative solutions: (1) they could shut down the area and write off the loss; (2) they could supply the independent dealers but shut down the company warehouses; and (3) they could merge Region 40 with another adjoining region to reduce overhead expenses. The decision required a balancing, not only of monetary factors, but of human factors as well.

*In your opinion, what decision should Magcobar management have made concerning Region 40. Can you think of an alternative?*

# IV-7.  WORTHINGTON MILLS:

## Manufacturer of Baby Products—
## Decision to Discontinue Sales to Accounts with
## Unacceptable Profit Margins

John W. Ireland, Sales Manager for the Baby Products Division of Worthington Mills, manufacturer of baby diapers and other baby products, faced a decision on what to do with a number of baby-diaper accounts that had fallen below the "acceptable" profit margin. Since most of the accounts in question returned some profit, he was reluctant to write off these customers just because they did not reach the level of return desired by management. In the past, he had been willing to discontinue sales to those accounts that fell below the acceptable profit margin, but his position had changed during the past year because of the decline in demand for Worthington diapers. Ireland had strong opposition in this matter from Maurice Conte, Vice-President of

Sales, who had been the prime mover in establishing the return-on-profit criteria four years previously.

Worthington Mills, founded in the late 1800s, was located in Boiling Springs, Alabama. Over the years, Worthington had acquired three textile companies and grew to an annual overall sales volume of over $50 million. Originally, the company had produced only towels but, through acquisitions, it had expanded the product line to include a large array of textile items. The Baby Products Division, organized in the 1950s, manufactured and sold an extensive line of baby diapers, crib sheets, pillowcases, baby pants, bibs, and infant's wear. Baby diapers constituted the single biggest item in the Baby Products Division product line, accounting for $8 million of the division's total sales of $18 million.

Worthington made both gauze and birdseye cloth diapers on machines that had been developed and patented by the company. Gauze and birdseye were two different types of weave used in fabricating cloth diapers. The company was an industry leader in the development of special gauze fabrics for diapers.

Worthington cloth diapers were distributed nationwide by a sales force of twenty-four persons plus one selling agent. The twenty-four company salespeople sold directly to retail outlets, hospitals, and to diaper services such as Dandee and General Diaper Services. The company sales personnel were salaried and averaged about $17,000 in earnings, including bonuses. In addition to distributing its products to retailers, hospitals, and diaper services, Worthington also sold its diapers to Army and Air Force Exchanges and Navy Ship Stores. These sales were handled by a commission selling agent who sold exclusively to the military.

The major competition for Worthington's Baby Products Division came from Kendall Textile Division of The Kendall Company and from Riegel Textile Corp. Both companies marketed a complete line of baby products. In addition, there was heavy competition from numerous manufacturers making one or two items in the baby-products line. Worthington's prices were roughly the same as its competition. Selling prices to retailers and diaper services averaged 16 percent over production cost.

During the past year and a half, an investigation had been made of the profitability of baby-diaper accounts. This investigation was part of an overall revenue-cost analysis in the Baby Product Division, and its starting point had been the baby-diapers product line, which accounted for the largest sales volume in the division. The investigation revealed that over 18 percent of the company's 3,215 baby-diaper accounts (585) fell below the profit goal set by management. Of these 585 accounts, 68, or about 12 percent, were clearly unprofitable (this represented a fraction over 2 percent of the total 3,215 baby-diaper accounts). The remaining 517 accounts, although yielding a profit, were nevertheless below management's profit-return standards and therefore were considered accounts with unacceptable profit margins.

Although company policy dictated the dropping of all accounts with unacceptable profit margins, Ireland contended that certain factors made it logical either (1) to revise the acceptable-unacceptable profit-margin standards in view of changing market conditions, or (2) to make exceptions to the policy for a period of time to combat the decline in demand for cloth baby diapers. He pointed out that something had to be done soon, because overall demand for cloth baby diapers had declined and Worthington had lost nearly 200 accounts in the past two years.

The two major reasons for the drop in demand were, according to Ireland, the declining birth rate and the stiff competitive threat mounted by the disposable-paper-

## IV-9.  BURTON PEN COMPANY:
## Manufacturer of Ballpoint Pens—
## Marketing Cost Analysis

Burton Pen Company manufactured and distributed a line of ballpoint pens as well as other writing instruments and supplies. The company's marketing planning committee was scheduled to meet for its annual review of marketing operations as part of its responsibility to formulate the marketing plan for the coming year. The committee's first order of business was to conduct, for the ballpoint-pen line, marketing cost analyses according to size of account and by type of product. The ballpoint-pen line consisted of four models: the Economy, the Standard, the Custom, and the Deluxe. Burton management believed that marketing cost analysis was essential because it permitted determination of the relative profitability of various aspects of the company's marketing operations, and it also covered areas in which changes made in the new marketing plan could result in improved performance.

At the request of the marketing planning committee, the accounting department made available the data presented in Exhibits 1-4.

EXHIBIT 1

| Size of Account (Annual Purchases) | Number of Accounts | Number of Orders | Total Sales |
|---|---|---|---|
| Under $500 | 610 | 2,300 | $ 338,000 |
| $501-$1,000 | 1,540 | 6,500 | 595,000 |
| $1,001-$2,000 | 830 | 5,400 | 957,000 |
| Over $2,000 | 290 | 3,600 | 1,120,000 |
| Total | 3,270 | 17,800 | $3,010,000 |

EXHIBIT 2

| Size of Account (Annual Purchases) | Economy | Standard | Custom | Deluxe | Total Sales |
|---|---|---|---|---|---|
| | | Sales by Product | | | |
| Under $500 | $ 98,000 | $ 126,800 | $ 78,100 | $ 35,100 | $ 338,000 |
| $501-$1,000 | 170,000 | 206,200 | 131,200 | 87,500 | 595,000 |
| $1,001-$2,000 | 320,100 | 335,000 | 195,800 | 106,100 | 957,000 |
| Over $2,000 | 375,000 | 385,500 | 227,000 | 132,500 | 1,120,000 |
| Total | $963,200 | $1,053,500 | $332,100 | $361,200 | $3,010,000 |

EXHIBIT 3

| | Economy | Standard | Custom | Deluxe |
|---|---|---|---|---|
| Cost of sales | $491,232 | $558,355 | $303,408 | $266,152 |
| Advertising | $ 50,000 | $ 53,000 | $ 48,000 | $ 35,000 |
| Number of shipping units sold | 481,600 | 263,375 | 63,210 | 18,060 |
| Weight per shipping unit | 6 oz | 6 oz | 6 oz | 7 oz |

EXHIBIT 4
Selling and Administrative Expenses

| | |
|---|---:|
| Sales salaries | $ 135,129 |
| Sales traveling expenses | 45,078 |
| Sales-office variable expense | 20,777 |
| Sales commissions (3.2 per cent of sales) | 96,320 |
| Warehousing | 15,008 |
| Packing and shipping | 31,542 |
| Credit management | 35,871 |
| Advertising | 186,000 |
| Billing and miscellaneous bookkeeping | 70,665 |
| General selling, administrative, and other expenses | 450,000 |
| Total | $1,086,390 |

Develop a statement of profit and loss with analysis of marketing costs by size of account. Do the same by type of product. Analyze the data and develop a set of recommendations for Burton Pen Company management to improve its profit picture with respect to account size and product type.